fifth edition
Listening to Music

Jay D. Zorn

June August

PEARSON

Prentice
Hall

Upper Saddle River, New Jersey 07458

Library of Congress Cataloging-in-Publication Data

Zorn, Jay D.
    Listening to music / Jay D. Zorn with June August. — 5th ed.
        p.   cm.
    Includes index.
    ISBN 0-13-173339-7
    1. Music appreciation. I. August, June. II. Title.
    MT90.Z65 2006
    781.1'7—dc22   2006029314

Executive Editor: RICHARD CARLIN
Editor-in-Chief: SARAH TOUBORG
Editorial Assistant: JAMES RIZZOLO
Senior Managing Editor: LISA IARKOWSKI
Production Liaison: FRAN RUSSELLO
Manufacturing Buyer: BEN SMITH
Creative Design Director: LESLIE OSHER
Interior & Cover Design: LAURA GARDNER
Director, Image Resource Center: MELINDA PATELLI
Manager, Rights and Permissions: ZINA ARABIA
Manager, Visual Research: BETH BRENZEL
Manager, Cover Visual Research & Permissions: KAREN SANATAR
Image Permission Coordinator: ANNETTE LINDER
Photo Researcher: ELAINE SOARES
Composition/Full-Service Project Management: KAREN ETTINGER
Printer/Binder: LSC COMMUNICATIONS

Credits and acknowledgments borrowed from other sources and reproduced, with permission, in this textbook appear on appropriate page within text (or on page 478–480).

Pearson Education LTD.
Pearson Education Singapore, Pte. Ltd
Pearson Education, Canada, Ltd
Pearson Education–Japan
Pearson Education Australia PTY, Limited

Pearson Education North Asia Ltd
Pearson Educación de Mexico, S.A. de C.V.
Pearson Education Malaysia, Pte. Ltd
Pearson Education, Upper Saddle River, New Jersey

10
ISBN 0-13-173339-7

Contents

12 Beethoven: Bridge to Romanticism 146

13 The Romantic Style Period (1820–1900) 158

14 Early Romantic Music 164

27 Broadway Musical Theater   374

28 Music in the Movies   402

Authors' Note

Recently, we turned on the car radio in the middle of a performance of Leonard Bernstein's *Suite from West Side Story*—a piece we've heard many times. But something was different about this performance. We were so captured by it that we pulled over to listen to the music without the distraction of traffic.

As the music ended, the announcer said we had been listening to the New York Philharmonic, conducted by Leonard Bernstein. We had just experienced the music of a brilliant composer conducting his own orchestra, playing one of his most memorable works. Everything had come together perfectly, including the contributions of a recording engineer, who had used today's technology to digitally remaster an old recording for the enjoyment of today's audiences.

After you finish this book, you'll be prepared to experience all types of music. You'll be able to discuss great music with others and offer your special insights, and to choose recordings that keep it alive.

Tune your car radio to your local classical music station. Many television cable providers also offer music stations. In addition to pop, ethnic, and new age, you'll find such stations as Classical Masterpieces, Light Classical, Opera, Broadway Musicals, and Jazz. Then make an agreement with yourself: Choose those stations from time to time. If you don't like a particular piece being broadcast, you're free to choose another station. But come back; you're sure to hear something you'll enjoy. And perhaps you'll enjoy it enough to buy the recording or to look for it in live concert season programs offered in your area. You can keep great music alive.

Jay Zorn
June August

About the Authors

Dr. Jay Zorn was Professor Emeritus and former Chairman of the Music Education Department at the University of Southern California, Thornton School of Music, and a past president of the California Music Educators Association. Throughout his distinguished career, Dr. Zorn specialized in training music educators, teaching music appreciation and listening skills to thousands of students, and developing new courses designed for culturally diverse student populations. Dr. Zorn also served as an educational consultant for the recording, film, and television industries.

June August is the author of numerous educational programs and a playwright whose works have been produced internationally and throughout the United States, including California, Michigan, Washington, DC, Florida, and off-Broadway. She was Editorial Director of the Education Division of Walt Disney Productions; Director of Public Information for WPBT-Channel 2, Miami; and Director of Public Information for the University of Southern California, Thornton School of Music. June is a member of ASCAP and a writing consultant for Fortune 500 companies.

Preface

Preparing the fifth edition of a book is both an honor and a privilege. We are gratified by the response and enthusiasm of students and teachers who share our belief that the understanding and enjoyment of great music is an important element of a civilized society.

Listening to Music has been popularly described as *accessible* and *reader-friendly*. The information, explanations, and music are accessible; the language, style, and presentation are reader-friendly—appropriate for diverse student populations. According to one reader, "It's a book you can't get lost in."

The expanded **Fifth Edition** contains 100 biographies:

- 75 biographies of classical composers, complete with lists of principal works and their dates
- 25 life-and-career sketches of legendary pop and jazz artists

Challenge Your Expertise questions stimulate creative thinking and encourage thorough reading of the chapters. **Part 4** expands coverage of popular music and includes a new chapter devoted to jazz and the exponents of this art form. You'll find extensive coverage of key topics in a number of areas:

- becoming a musically aware concertgoer (audience development)
- exploring the contributions of music to film
- appreciating the cultural diversity that led to the creation and development of jazz and Broadway musicals
- understanding the impact of popular music over the decades

Part 1 The Musical Process presents strategies for listening to music, explanations of typical performing media, and guidelines for attending concerts:

- buying tickets
- preparing for the performance
- interpreting the printed program
- understanding what orchestra members, soloists, and conductors do
- knowing when to applaud

Part 2 The Materials of Music is a multimedia presentation of the elements of music and introduces basic concepts and terminology. Self-paced listening instruction frees valuable time for in-depth teaching and discussion.

Part 3 The Common Style Periods of Concert Music progresses chronologically from the Gregorian Chant to the present, with musical examples to illustrate the style periods. These examples were chosen because of their proven effectiveness for class use and because they are representative of today's concert programming. Detailed listening guides and listening insights reinforce instruction.

Part 4 Music of Cultural Diversity highlights popular music, jazz, Broadway musical theater, film music, and music of world cultures. Chapters have been updated to keep the information current and relevant.

Supplementary Materials

The **Fifth Edition** is coordinated with exciting supplements for the student: Prentice Hall's exclusive *Listening to Music* Companion Website™, http://www.prenhall.com/zorn, offers unique tools and support for students and teachers to integrate this online study guide with the text.

Recording Package

Four compact discs, containing the most important works discussed in the text, accompany the book. Appendix G is a complete list of music selections, including the location (track) of the recordings and running time. A complete Listening Guide for online listening is available if you take advantage of Prentice Hall's special arrangement with classical.com. For information, see www.prenhall.com/zorn.

Instructor's Manual with Tests is a complete teaching package that contains:

- a detailed outline for a typical 14- to 15-week course
- chapter-by-chapter teaching opportunities
- audio-visual and online resources
- forms for research reports and concert reports
- an extensive test bank, divided by chapter
- suggestions for optimizing use of the *Listening to Music* Companion Website™

Prentice Hall Custom Tests allow you to create your own personalized exams by using this computerized test item file, available for Windows or Macintosh.

Powerpoint Slides are available to instructors at www.prenhall.com/zorn.

Value Packages

The **Fifth Edition** of *Listening to Music* can be purchased in a package with any of the accompanying ancillary material at a reduced cost. Your campus bookstore can order the following shrink-wrapped packages directly from Prentice Hall.

Acknowledgments

The production of such a complex project as *Listening to Music* requires the contributions of many talents. We would like to thank the following: special thanks to distinguished announcer/musicologist Martin Bookspan whose musical expertise, dedication, and love of music permeates the project; Ken Bloom of the Zeisler Group and his staff for their assistance in locating and producing the superior recordings; Bud Therien, Prentice Hall publishers, whose vision guided the original edition of this project; Richard Carlin, Executive Editor for Music books at Prentice Hall; Lisa Iarkowski, production manager and Fran Russello, production editor, at PH and Karen Ettinger of TechBooks who managed the production; Elaine Soares at PH who did the photo research; and Laura Gardner, PH, who designed this beautiful book. We also wish to thank Leonard Stein, former Director of the Arnold Schoenberg Institute, for his judicious advice and editing of the chapter on Expressionism; and Frederick Lesermann of the University of Southern California, Flora L. Thornton School of Music, for his editing the chapter on Experimental and Technological music.

Special acknowledgment goes to my talented teaching assistants—more than 100 of them over the past thirty years. With their collaboration, I have had the pleasure of presenting the material in this text to thousands of music appreciation students—all of whom helped to shape the project.

Finally, we thank the following colleagues for their suggestions and input for the project over its four editions: Dr. Andrew Glendening, University of Redlands; Robin Connell, Grand Rapids Community College; John Brawand, South Dakota State University; Lisa McArthur, Campbellsville University; Eleanor Hammer, Los Angeles Valley College; Guilio Onagaro, University of Southern California; Raymond A. Barr, University of Miami; Thomas L. Riis, University of Georgia; Dan Schulz, Walla Walla College; Elaine Morgan, City College of San Francisco; Edward Szabo, East Michigan University; Marc Peretz, Ball State University; Dan Dunavan, Southeast Missouri State University; James Klein, California State University, Stanislaus; Diane Touliatos, University of Missouri, St. Louis; Christine Smith, Middlebury College; K. Marie Stolba, Indiana University, Purdue Campus; Nelson Tandoc, De Anza College; Leo Kreter, California State University, Fullerton; Earl L. Clemens, Northern Illinois University.

Jay Zorn
June August

fifth edition

Listening to Music

Prelude
Music Belongs to Everyone

Congratulations for accepting the challenge of sampling more than 400 years of music in a short time.

You have made yourself part of a powerful audience. Your choices will have a far-reaching effect on the music of tomorrow, just as yesterday's audiences have influenced the music of today.

The focus of this book is fivefold:

- to give you the tools and experience to build your knowledge of music
- to take that knowledge confidently into any concert hall, auditorium, theater, or opera house throughout the world

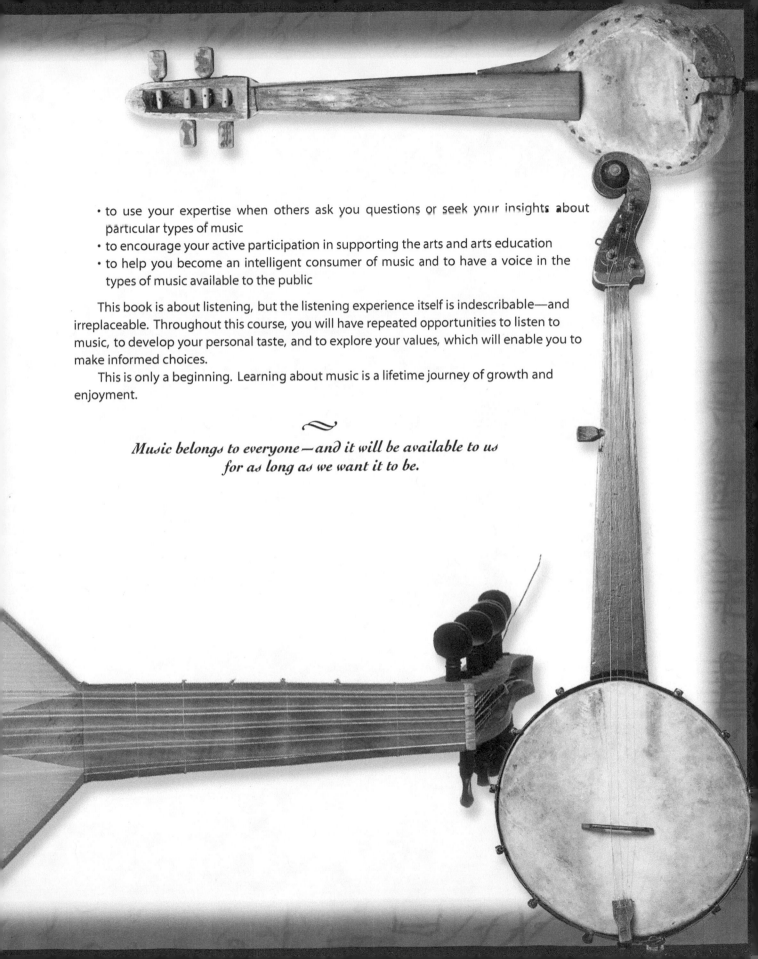

- to use your expertise when others ask you questions or seek your insights about particular types of music
- to encourage your active participation in supporting the arts and arts education
- to help you become an intelligent consumer of music and to have a voice in the types of music available to the public

This book is about listening, but the listening experience itself is indescribable—and irreplaceable. Throughout this course, you will have repeated opportunities to listen to music, to develop your personal taste, and to explore your values, which will enable you to make informed choices.

This is only a beginning. Learning about music is a lifetime journey of growth and enjoyment.

Music belongs to everyone—and it will be available to us
for as long as we want it to be.

Part I
The Musical Process

1

From the Creator
to the Listener

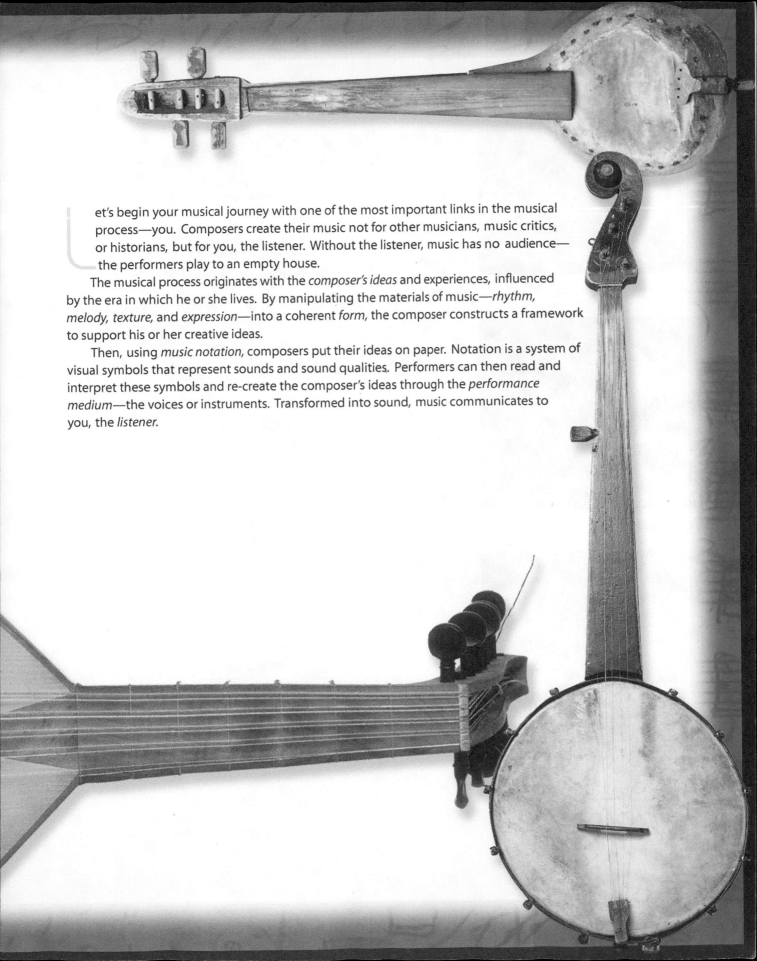

et's begin your musical journey with one of the most important links in the musical process—you. Composers create their music not for other musicians, music critics, or historians, but for you, the listener. Without the listener, music has no audience—the performers play to an empty house.

The musical process originates with the *composer's ideas* and experiences, influenced by the era in which he or she lives. By manipulating the materials of music—*rhythm, melody, texture,* and *expression*—into a coherent *form,* the composer constructs a framework to support his or her creative ideas.

Then, using *music notation,* composers put their ideas on paper. Notation is a system of visual symbols that represent sounds and sound qualities. Performers can then read and interpret these symbols and re-create the composer's ideas through the *performance medium*—the voices or instruments. Transformed into sound, music communicates to you, the *listener.*

CREATION
COMPOSER
(creator)

Ellen Zwilich

INTERPRETATION
PERFORMER
(interpretor)

Nigel Kennedy

RESPONSE
PERCEIVER
(listener)

THE MUSICAL PROCESS

CREATION

> musical ideas
> forms (framework)
> musical notation

INTERPRETATION

> medium

RESPONSE

> listener-audience

Part Title

CD Track

Time
(from beginning of selection)

Part Title

Key elements in the Listening Guides

2
What to Listen For in Music

Looking at a panoramic landscape from a mountain, you have many possible vistas: close, distant, left, right. What you see results from the way you focus your attention. Similarly, the way you listen to music depends on how you focus. As you take in more and more of what you hear, that focus keeps changing.

If you are tired—perhaps after a busy day—you may have less energy with which to follow an intricate piece of music. But during those times when you feel relaxed or adventurous, you may be more willing to accept this challenge.

Music, like all the arts, can accommodate all viewpoints. Each of us perceives music differently. Your listening experience is your private world. There are no restrictions, no "correct" approaches to listening.

Here are the ways in which many concertgoers listen to music:

The Sensory Approach

Some listeners prefer to let the music wash over them, without giving it much thought. This passive rather than active listening approach can be relaxing—like basking on a beach on a sunny day with the surf rushing back and forth over you. Because the *sensory level* is effortless and soothing, you can allow your brain to idle in neutral and your spine to tingle.

The Emotional Approach

Music can speak directly to your emotions. If you have ever listened to music and found yourself daydreaming or reminiscing, you were listening on an *emotional level*. On this level, your emotions become part of the listening experience. In your private world, that beautiful melody by Chopin stirs your deepest feelings—the ones that rarely rise to the surface, the ones seldom verbalized.

The Contextual Approach

Some music supplies a background for a familiar event, an activity, or an environment. When you hear it, you immediately associate it with some context—a football game, a circus, a graduation. Even "patriotic" music falls into this category. With *contextual listening,* the association may become more important than the music itself.

The Script Approach

Most music has no specific story for you to follow—although opera, ballet, and film music certainly do. But if you find yourself making up a story or unraveling a plot, you may be listening to music at the *script level*.

The Musically Aware Approach

Great music has layers of subtleties that include your involvement. Here at the *musically aware listening* level, the excitement begins. You may still enjoy using the sensory, emotional, and script approaches to listen to music, but as you become more aware, the music engages you at a heightened level of understanding.

Suggestions on Becoming a More Musically Aware Listener

You do not have to be a trained musician to reach this level of understanding. Without extra-musical guidance, pictures, or stories, you can develop the ability to focus on the music itself, understanding and experiencing the composer's creative choices.

This book is devoted to helping you achieving a greater enjoyment of music. Here are some suggestions:

- *Follow the listening guides together with the text.*
- *Use the materials in Appendix D as a checklist as you listen.*
- *Get to know the special suggestions "What to Listen For in The Music," highlighted throughout the text*
- *Listen! Listen! Listen!*

Marilyn Horne

Listening is a skill you can develop best by hearing a lot of music. To make this easier and more economical for you, you can get a discounted 6-month subscription to classical.com when you buy this book. This service offers over 90,000 performances. Visit the book's website, www.prenhall.com/zorn for more information. In addition, find the classical music radio and television stations in your area. Some record stores with classical music sections will allow you to preview new releases. Add to your record collection by acquiring recordings of those works in addition to the recorded musical examples coordinated with this text. If you're not sure what to look for, consult the 75 biographies in this book to find lists of the composers' major works.

Music Listening Checklist

Appendix D presents terms that will help you understand the music you are hearing. If you memorize the checklist, you'll be better prepared when you are sitting in a concert hall or listening to a recording.

Music Listening Boxes

Focusing on ways to listen to some 16 discrete musical genres, the Music Listening Boxes should help you gain insight into much of the music you are likely to hear, including the common traditional musical styles, jazz, and the scores of Broadway musicals and films.

Individual Listening Guides

More than 50 detailed music listening guides steer you through most of the recorded examples on the *Listening to Music* compact disc set.

Additional Listening Help

Become familiar with the text and recorded guides featured in Chapter 4: "How the Basic Elements Interact," and Chapter 5: "Performing Media."

3

Becoming a Musically Aware Concertgoer

What Are The Different Types of Concerts?

Symphony Orchestra

Symphony orchestra concerts are popular throughout the world. The rich variety of sounds emanating from a large orchestra is a marvel of civilized life and culture. With so many different instruments, the combinations of orchestral colors are vast. Talented and disciplined musicians, who have devoted a lifetime to perfecting their skills and intensely competing for positions, perform on instruments

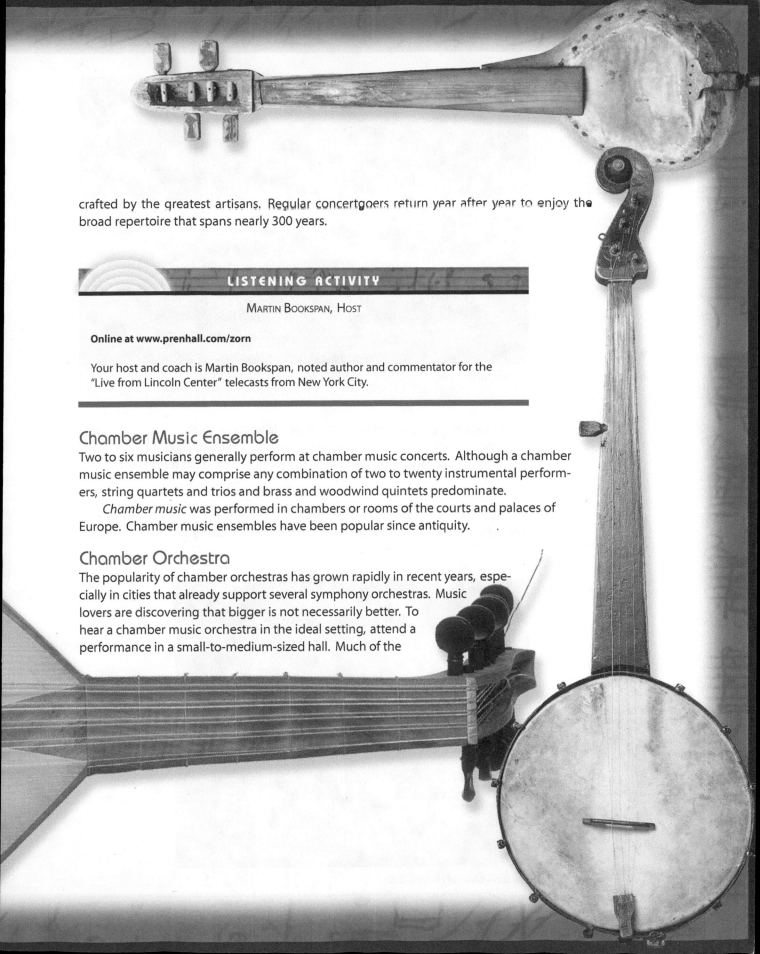

crafted by the greatest artisans. Regular concertgoers return year after year to enjoy the broad repertoire that spans nearly 300 years.

LISTENING ACTIVITY

MARTIN BOOKSPAN, HOST

Online at www.prenhall.com/zorn

Your host and coach is Martin Bookspan, noted author and commentator for the "Live from Lincoln Center" telecasts from New York City.

Chamber Music Ensemble

Two to six musicians generally perform at chamber music concerts. Although a chamber music ensemble may comprise any combination of two to twenty instrumental performers, string quartets and trios and brass and woodwind quintets predominate.

Chamber music was performed in chambers or rooms of the courts and palaces of Europe. Chamber music ensembles have been popular since antiquity.

Chamber Orchestra

The popularity of chamber orchestras has grown rapidly in recent years, especially in cities that already support several symphony orchestras. Music lovers are discovering that bigger is not necessarily better. To hear a chamber music orchestra in the ideal setting, attend a performance in a small-to-medium-sized hall. Much of the

A symphony orchestra

great music composed for chamber orchestra loses its original intimacy and clarity when performed by a large symphony orchestra in a hall with 3,000 or more seats. Like speech, musical ideas make more sense when you can hear them distinctly.

Recital

A recital features one or two musicians. Solo recitals are most commonly performed by singers, pianists, or violinists. The entire setting motivates artists to

The Boys Choir of Harlem, 2001

perform at their best, and they carefully choose music that displays their entire range of musicianship and vocal or instrumental mastery.

Vocal Ensemble

Concerts by vocal or choral ensembles are both vast and rich—a reflection of the long history of group singing. What follows is typical of the concerts you are likely to hear.

Secular Vocal Ensemble

Large Choirs   Varying in size and known by different names, large choirs include *chorales, choral societies, women's choruses, men's choruses, collegiate choirs,* and *gospel choirs.* These ensembles are accompanied by pianos or instrumental ensembles such as large orchestras, small orchestras, or various combinations of instruments.

Small Choirs   Small vocal ensembles include *a cappella choirs, chamber singers, madrigal choirs, jazz choirs,* or the smaller versions of the large choirs listed above.

Religious Choir

Hearing music in a great church or a cathedral is like traveling back in a time machine. Surrounded by stained-glass windows and elaborate, ornate architecture, you can imagine how it sounded when Johann Sebastian Bach played the organ and conducted the choir in Leipzig, Germany, 275 years ago. Churches and cathedrals have unique acoustics. The music resonates and reverberates in every nook.

Many performances of sacred music still take place in churches, presented as concerts to the general public rather than as religious services. Because an organ is often required as the main keyboard instrument, church settings facilitate its use to accompany the singers or instruments in an instrumental ensemble.

Opera

Giuseppe Verdi, composer of such enduring operas as *La Traviata, Rigoletto,* and *Tosca,* said, "Opera is passion before everything." Perhaps the reason for opera's lasting appeal is the integration of singing, instrumental music, drama, poetry, and dance with opulent sets and costumes. Opera is musical theater on a grand scale.

Over the past four centuries, thousands of operas in various languages have been staged around the world. Those works that have retained their timeless quality are still a part of the contemporary repertoire. In fact, some of the stories written for opera have been adapted for the Broadway stage, for example, *Aida, Miss Saigon (Madame Butterfly),* and *Rent (La Bohème).* The opera *La Bohème,* sung in Italian with English subtitles, opened on Broadway in 2002. If you enjoy Broadway musicals, opera would be a logical addition to your theater-going.

Thanks to accessible performances, such as those by The Three Tenors— Placido Domingo, José Carreras, and Luciano Pavarotti—opera is attracting new audiences and enjoying a resurgence in popularity. Recorded versions of their concerts have been televised and are available for purchase.

Among the rich traditions of opera are curtain calls. These occur not only at the end of performances, but also between acts and, often, between major scene changes. A curtain call can be a show in itself.

A scene from *Don Giovanni*

After the curtain closes, the leading and principal singers reenter to take bows. Sometimes they come from the wings. Often, an unseen hand holds back the center of the curtain, and the soloists sweep onto the apron (the area in front of the curtain). Then, the singers repeatedly bow and curtsey, which allows them to show their gratitude for the audience's adulation.

And opera-goers do love their stars. Devoted fans have been known to travel around the world to hear performances by their favorites. Some of today's stars include Cecilia Bartoli, Bryn Terfel, June Anderson, Dame Kiri Te Kanawa, Samuel Ramey, Thomas Hampson, Renee Fleming, Frederica von Stade, and Sumi Jo.

Broadway Musical Theater

Whether they're new or revivals, originals or adaptations, imported from London or developed in the United States, Broadway musicals continue to draw audiences of all ages. (See Chapter 27, Broadway Musical Theater.) Currently, Broadway theater is experiencing a rebirth as interest in and attendance at musical theater productions have soared. Recent productions such as *Rent, The Lion King, Aida, Wicked,* and *The Producers,* using the latest stagecraft and sound technology, have attracted younger audiences.

Ballet

Like opera, ballet creates its effects through a wonderful blending of the arts: drama, dance, sets, costumes, and especially music. The music inspires the choreography—specifically designed dance steps, movement, and combinations. Among the great masters who composed for ballet are Ludwig van Beethoven, Hector Berlioz, Peter Ilyich Tchaikovsky, Maurice Ravel, Igor Stravinsky, Sergei Prokofiev, Aaron Copland, and Leonard Bernstein.

Ballet orchestras perform in a pit in front of the stage. The number of players varies according to the music.

A scene from the London production of *Rent*

Pas de deux from *Romeo and Juliet,* danced by the Royal Ballet's Inaki Urlezanga (rear) and Tamara Rojo

How Can I Find Out About Concerts and Ticket Sales?

Newspapers

Most concerts are advertised in the entertainment or arts section of newspapers. Look for phone numbers, box-office location, dates and times, performers, and programs.

Online Sources

Today, theaters, opera and ballet companies, and ticket outlets throughout the world advertise concerts, schedules, and ticket prices on websites. You can use a search engine to obtain general or specific information. You will usually find the details you need, including a phone number if you have special needs or questions that aren't answered on the website.

For tickets to a particular concert, simply type in the name of the group, followed by the word "tickets," for example, Los Angeles Philharmonic tickets. Seating is not always guaranteed, but some venues provide seating diagrams and allow you to make a selection. If you rely solely on newspapers or the Internet, however, the seats you want might not be available.

Websites and Mailing Lists

Most concert venues, theaters, and ticket agencies have informative Websites about current and future programs, series, special events, and tickets prices and availabiity. For a local concert venue or theatre, click on the "contact us" box and have your name added to the regular mail or email list.

Season Subscriptions

Once you are on a mailing list, you'll receive an invitation to become a season subscriber. Many concert series offer reduced-price student subscriptions. After you determine the series of programs and seats you prefer, you can reserve them for the entire season. Subscribers enjoy several advantages: early notification about the upcoming concert season, access to the best seats, and ticket exchange privileges.

Box Office

If seats for a particular performance are available, you can always purchase tickets at the box office. Arrive as early as possible. The first time you go to a concert or

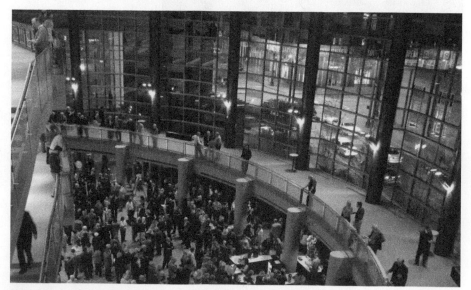

The lobby of Seattle's Benaroya Symphony Hall

concert hall you are not familiar with, ask box-office personnel to show you a detailed seating plan and advise you about the best seats.

Student-Rush Seats

Students often may have a considerable advantage over other concertgoers by arriving at the box office within an hour of the concert. Most orchestra concerts, operas, and ballets offer reduced-price, "student-rush" tickets. You must show current student identification, which usually entitles you to purchase only one ticket.

Attending Open Rehearsals

Many opera companies and symphony orchestras have regularly scheduled rehearsals that are open to the public for a small fee. Ask about this at the box office. Observing what goes on in preparation for a performance is fascinating. It is during the rehearsal that conductors and performers do their main work—unifying the interpretation and polishing the performance.

Special Needs

If you or a member of your party uses a wheelchair or other assistance device, be sure to ask for seats that will accommodate your needs.

How Can I Prepare for a Concert?

Become Acquainted with the Music

As often as possible, listen to recordings of the music that will be featured on the program so you will become familiar with the music. We tend to enjoy the music we know best. Besides preparing for a concert, purchasing the recordings is an excellent way to build your personal music collection.

Municipal and university libraries also can be excellent resources. You can listen to recordings at the library or check them out for a few days. Also, pre-set your radio to your classical music stations (usually FM stations), and you will become familiar with many styles of music. The Web has satellite radio stations and streaming audio sites dedicated to classical music.

Each musical style has its own characteristics. Knowing how to listen to the various styles makes it easier to follow and enjoy the music. To prepare for a concert, review the 16 "Listening Insights" boxes in this book.

Also, become familiar with the composer, the artists, and background of the music on the program. Sometimes this information is available on an insert accompanying a recording. Many of the greatest geniuses have been as fallible and vulnerable as any other human being. Their stories are very moving and can give you greater insight into their works.

How Can I Prepare For Opera?

If the original language of the *libretto* or story is not your native tongue or second language, read the translation before you go to the performance. Even if the opera is sung in English, it's a good idea to become familiar with the story in advance. That way, you'll be able to concentrate on the performance.

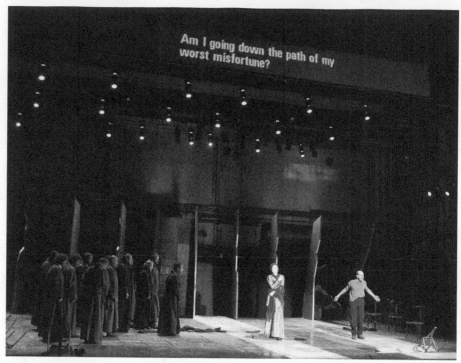

Am I going down the path of my worst misfortune?

Opera performance

More and more operas are available in various video formats. You can also find synopses of opera librettos online. One reliable website is sponsored by the Metropolitan Opera Company: *http://www.metopera.org/synopses/*

Supertitles   During a performance, many major opera companies in North America and elsewhere project translations of the libretto, which serve the same purpose as subtitles in a foreign film. Projections that appear above the stage area are called "supertitles." Some companies show the translated text on small television screens mounted on seat backs. In that case, each audience member has the option of turning off the screen, according to personal preference.

Why Aren't Operas Produced in North America Sung in English?   First of all, English is not the only language spoken in North America and other "English-speaking" countries. With rare exceptions, an opera sounds better when it is sung in the language used by the composer and librettist. For example, the Sydney (Australia) Opera Company and the Royal Opera Company (England) perform Puccini operas in Italian.

What Do I Neesd to Know Before the Concert Begins?

- Arrive at the concert hall early enough to pick up your program, find your seat, and read the printed information. Some programs are free; others are available for purchase.
- Turn off a phone, pager, watch, or anything else that makes noise. Unless you have specific permission from the concert management, you may not photograph, record, or videotape the performance.

What is in the Printed Program?

Program booklets or sheets contain useful information to help you follow along and enjoy the performance. You'll find the names of performers and soloists, the conductor, an overview of the music that will be played, and usually some interesting tidbits about the works and the composer. Both recital and concert programs featuring one or more soloists may include biographical information.

Concert Overview   You'll probably notice many people in the audience who keep the program open to the overview during the performance. If you look at the overview page shown below for the London Symphony Orchestra, you'll see why.

This overview lists the *composer* and *title* of each work and its *key* or *tonality*. For the four multi-movement works, each *movement* is designated by its *tempo*. On some programs, movements may also be numbered. Three of these works have a catalog designation. The date of composition is in parentheses. Two works include the name of the soloist.

LONDON SYMPHONY ORCHESTRA
MICHAEL TILSON THOMAS, Conductor

LUDWIG VAN BEETHOVEN

Symphony No. 5 in c minor, Op. 68 (1808)

    Allegro con brio
    Andante con moto
    Allegro, *leading into*
    Allegro

WOLFGANG AMADEUS MOZART

Concerto in A Major for Clarinet and Orchestra, K. 622 (1791)

    Allegro
    Adagio
    Rondo: Allegro

Franz Hoeprich, Clarinet Soloist

Intermission

PETER ILYICH TCHAIKOVSKY

Symphony No. 4 in f minor, Op. 36 (1877)
    Andante sostenuto; Moderato con anima
    Andantino in modo di canzona
    Scherzo: Pizzicato ostinato
    Allegro con fuoco

GEORGE GERSHWIN

Concerto in F Major for Piano and Orchestra (1925)

    Allegro
    Andante con moto
    Allegro con brio

Michael Tilson Thomas, Piano Soloist/Conductor

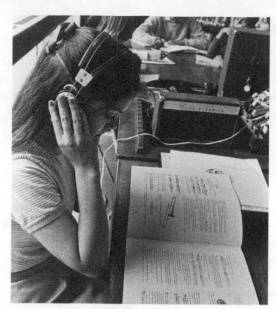

Music library
Laimute Druskis / Pearson Education / PH College

Key or Tonality   The first work on the London Symphony program is *Symphony No. 5 in c minor* by Ludwig van Beethoven. The term c minor is the key or tonality of the symphony. Knowing the key is interesting, but the information is important mainly to musicians.

Date of Composition   Knowing when a work was composed helps listeners place it in the context of history and within events in the composer's lifetime. Beethoven had lost most of his hearing by the time he wrote *Symphony No. 5*. Napoleon was Emperor of France, and his armies were victorious throughout Europe.

Cataloguing Systems   On the London Symphony program, notice numbers following the Op. and K. markings. These are catalog designations for composers' works, usually in chronological order. Op. stands for *Opus,* the Latin word for "work." Most composers kept track of their works and assigned opus numbers. Mozart, however, was too busy performing and composing. After he died, Ludwig von Köchel catalogued his works. *K.* is for Köchel.

Table 3.1 lists the most commonly used designations:

Table 3.1	Music Catalog Designations	
Composer	**Designation**	**Cataloguer**
Bach, J.S.	BWV (for "Bach-Werke Verzeichnis")	Wolfgang Schmieder: Thematischsystematisches Verzeichnis der musikalischen Werke von Johann Sebastian Bach
Haydn	H. or Hob.	A. von Hoboken
Mozart	K.	Ludwig von Köchel
Schubert	D.	O. E. Deutsch
Vivaldi	R. or P.	Peter Ryom

Tempo and Expression Terms Listed under each piece on the London Symphony program are some Italian terms that indicate the *tempo* for each movement or large section of a work. Once you understand tempo terms and descriptions, you'll be able to follow the music and understand the program. Between movements there is usually a short pause.

Gershwin's *Concerto in F,* has three terms:

Allegro
Andante con moto
Allegro con brio

Gershwin wanted the first movement of the concerto to be played *Allegro,* meaning "lively or fast." He indicated *Andante con moto* for the second movement. *Andante* means "slow to moderate walking tempo" and *con moto,* "with movement." *Allegro con brio* for the third movement means "fast, lively with spirit."

Table 3.2 lists Italian terms you will commonly find in concert programs:

Table 3.2	Common Terms for Tempo and Expression	
Tempo Indications (from slow to fast)		
grave	extremely slowly and solemnly	(*grah*-vay)
largo	very slowly, broadly	(*lar*-goh)
lento	slow	(*len*-toh)
adagio	slowly, leisurely	(ah-*dah*-gee-oh)
andante	slow to moderate walking pace	(ahn-*dahn*-tay)
moderato	moderate	(mah-der-*ah*-toh)
allegretto	moderately fast	(ah-leh-*greh*-toh)
allegro	fast, lively	(ah-*leh*-groh)
vivace	very fast	(vee-*vah*-chay)
presto	very fast	(*press*-toh)
prestissimo	as fast as possible	(press-*tee*-see-moh)

	Terms Often Used to Further Describe Tempos	
agitato	agitated	(ah-gee-*tah*-toh)
animato	animated	(ah-nee-*mah*-toh)
cantabile	singing style	(con-*tah*-bee-lay)
con brio	with spirit	(cohn-*bree*-oh)
con fuoco	with fire	(cohn-*fwoh*-coh)
con moto	with movement	(con-*moh*-toh)
e or ed.	and	(eh or ehd)
espressivo	expressively	(es-preh-*see*-voh)
grazioso	gracefully	(grah-tzee-*oh*-soh)
ma	but	(mah)
ma non troppo	but not too much	(mah-nohn-*troh*-poh)
maestoso	majestically	(my-*stoh*-soh)
meno	less	(*may*-noh)
molto	very, much	(*mohl*-toh)

Table 3.2		(Continued)
più	more	(pyoo)
poco	little	(*poh*-coh)
poco a poco	little by little, gradually	(poh-coh-ah-*poh*-coh)
sostenuto	sustained	(sohs-teh-*noo*-toh)

Terms Indicating Changes of Tempo

accelerando	quickening	(ah-cheh-lehr-*ahn*-doh)
ritardando	slowing	(ree-tar-*dahn*-doh)
rallentando	gradual slowing	(rahl-en-*tahn*-doh)
rubato	deliberate unsteady tempo	(roo-*bah*-toh)

Terms for Loudness Levels (from soft to loud)

Abbreviation	Italian Term	English Meaning	
pp or **ppp**	*pianissimo*	very soft	(pee-ah-*nee*-see-moh)
p	*piano*	soft	(pee-*ah*-noh)
mp	*mezzopiano*	moderately soft	(meh-tzo-pee-*ah*-noh)
mf	*mezzoforte*	moderately loud	(meh-tzo-*for*-tay)
f	*forte*	loud	(*for*-tay)
ff or **fff**	*fortissimo*	very loud	(for-*tee*-see-moh)

Terms for Changes in Loudness

crescendo	becoming louder	(creh-*shen*-doh)
decrescendo	becoming softer	(*deh*-creh-shen-doh)
or		
diminuendo	becoming softer	(dim-in-yoo-*ehn*-doh)

Other Commonly Used Performance Terms

a cappella	choir or voices without accompaniment	(ah-cah-*peh*-lah)
glissando	slide from pitch to pitch	(glee-*sahn*-doh)
legato	connected, smoothly	(leh-*gah*-toh)
pizzicato	plucked strings, usually done with player's finger	(pih-tzih-*cah*-toh)
staccato	detached, separated tones	(stuh-*kah*-toh)
tremolo	rapid repetitions of a tone or chord	(*treh*-moh-loh)
vibrato	pulsating tones for expressiveness	(vih-*brah*-toh)

What Concert Traditions Do I Need to Know About?

Like every activity that brings people together, music has developed formalities and traditions over hundreds of years. Similar traditions exist in other areas, such as sports. In golf and tennis, for example, the crowd is quiet while a player addresses the ball or prepares to serve. And in football, soccer, and boxing, the fans cheer whenever they feel like it.

Symphony and Chamber Orchestra Procedures

Warm Up   Before the concert, performers randomly enter and take their seats. Players warm up individually, checking the condition of their instruments and adjusting reeds, mouthpieces, bows, strings, and drumheads.

Concertmaster   The concertmaster usually is the last orchestra member to enter the stage. As the conductor's assistant, especially in musical matters, the concertmaster sits at the front of the violin section closest to the conductor.

Tuning   Before the conductor enters, the concertmaster signals the oboe to sound the traditional tuning pitch "A." The placement of the oboe in the center of the orchestra and its unique tone make it especially effective as a tuning instrument. If a work is a piano solo, the instrument is moved out to the center of the stage between the audience and the conductor, and the concertmaster sounds the tuning "A" on the piano.

Entrances and Exits of the Conductor and Soloists   Featured soloists usually enter and exit the stage just ahead of the conductor. If a piece of music does not call for a soloist, then the conductor enters the stage when the players are ready, greets the performers and the audience, mounts a podium, faces the orchestra, raises his or her arms (with or without a baton), and signals the down beat for the start of the music.

When Should I Applaud?

Here is the basic guideline:

When in doubt, wait until most of the audience applauds.

Unless you know the music well, avoid rushing to applaud, no matter how moved you are. You will find differences in when to applaud with each type of music.

An audience at an opera performance

During an opera, the audience usually applauds after an aria. However, during an instrumental performance a few people are likely to applaud at inappropriate times. For example, applauding during the pause between movements of a symphony breaks the continuity of the entire piece. Save yourself embarrassment by checking the printed program for the number of movements. A brief summary of appropriate times to applaud follows:

Symphony Orchestra, Chamber Orchestra, and Chamber Ensemble Concerts

- the concertmaster (first violinist) enters the stage from the wings
- the conductor enters from the wings
- a soloist or soloists enter from the wings
- the orchestra concludes an *entire* piece—symphony, concerto, overture, and so on
- the conductor acknowledges key players, who usually stand
- the conductor signals the orchestra to stand
- the conductor or soloist returns to the stage

Large, Mixed-Media Productions: Opera, Broadway Musicals, Ballets, Oratorios

- the conductor enters the stage or orchestra pit
- the curtain rises on the stage and set (except for very serious works—use previous guideline)
- the star or stars enter
- a powerful song, aria, or ballet display concludes (use previous guideline)
- the curtain comes down
- the soloist, conductor, or composer returns to the stage following a performance

What Is the Conductor's Role?

As you watch a conductor during a performance, you might get the impression that setting the tempo and beating time are the conductor's main functions. They are not. Almost any member of the orchestra can do those things. As important as beating time is, interpreting the music is more important.

Coordinating the ensemble's performance and *interpreting* the music are the conductor's most important responsibilities. The conductor's downbeat coordinates the start of the performance and sets the tempo, with the orchestra or chorus following and watching for changes.

To understand how conductors convey interpretation, you would have to attend a rehearsal or be on stage and watch how they use their hands, face, and body to urge musicians to play louder or softer, more forcefully or heroically, more smoothly or tenderly. Public television stations regularly broadcast symphony orchestra concerts. Camera close-ups of the conductor's face help reveal the interpretative process.

A soloist adds another dimension to the conductor's work, because the orchestra accompaniment must be coordinated with the

Sejii Ozawa

soloist's part. If, for instance, the soloist drags the tempo in a certain passage and speeds up in another, the conductor must inspire the entire orchestra to follow. Maintaining the balance between soloist and ensemble ensures that the soloist will be heard above the other instruments.

The Conductor As Music Scholar   It takes a lifetime of study for a conductor to learn the great body of music for symphony orchestra, chorus, ballet, or opera. Guiding an ensemble is demanding: A conductor must research various resources and examine writings about the music. Even a composer's note to a colleague can be informative.

Why Do Some Conductors Use a Baton or Stick?

If you think of the baton as an extension of the conductor's arm, you will understand why the conductor uses one. Players in all parts of the ensemble can see the conductor's beats more clearly. Using the baton to execute patterns maximizes visibility and reduces exertion.

In the past, conductors used other objects—rolled-up music, a violin bow, a cane—but none was as effective as the white baton. In the seventeenth century, the composer and conductor Jean-Baptiste Lully pounded beats on the floor with a wooden staff. During one performance, the story goes, he smashed the staff into his foot, which became infected. Lully died of complications, a victim of his own enthusiasm.

How Do Conductors Communicate?

Most conductors use standard conducting patterns that are universally recognized by classically trained musicians and even by many folk and popular music performers. This communication is one example of how music performance transcends geographic boundaries.

Getting Ready to Play

The conductor mounts the podium, waits until everyone in the orchestra is ready to perform, then raises his or her arms in the "ready" position.

Downbeat

The downbeat is the first beat of any pattern. The conductor moves the baton down from the ready position to somewhere near the front of the waist. When the baton reaches bottom and begins to move upward, the downbeat is complete, and the performers begin to play.

Standard Conducting Patterns

The standard conducting patterns are illustrated at right. The *meter*, or grouping of beats in the music, determines the pattern. Most music is grouped in recurring patterns—usually two, three, or four. Used less frequently are patterns of five or six beats.

Conducting Activity

Practice the standard conducting patterns for two, three, and four beats as shown. Then conduct the music on the recording accompanying this text.

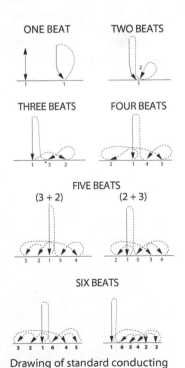

Drawing of standard conducting patterns

Here are some suggested selections:

The Two Pattern

CD Disc 1, Track 10	Bach, Brandenburg Concerto No. 2, Third Movement: moderately fast tempo
CD Disc 1, Track 13	Mozart, Horn Concerto No. 2, Third Movement: fast tempo
CD Disc 3, Track 2	Copland, "Hoe Down" from *Rodeo*: very fast

The Three Pattern

CD Disc 1, Track 15	Bach, Cantata No. 140, opening chorus: moderate tempo
CD Disc 1, Track 19	Haydn, Symphony No. 94, Third Movement: moderate tempo
CD Disc 1, Track 4	Handel, "For Unto Us a Child Is Born" from *Messiah*: moderate tempo

The Four Pattern

CD Disc 1, Track 9	Vivaldi, *The Four Seasons* Op. 8, No. 1, "Spring," first movement

Conductor's Left Hand Indications

Conductor John Williams

Expression   The conductor's left hand indicates expression. For example, if the trumpets enter too loudly, the conductor, often looking like a police officer halting traffic, motions them to play more softly. Urging the violins to play louder, the conductor might use another left-hand signal.

Cueing   The left hand also signals a performer or section to play. Imagine a cymbal player who has been following the music for fifteen minutes, waiting for his or her part. The conductor's cue increases the player's confidence that the crash of the cymbals will occur at the right moment—and will avoid an embarrassing situation!

CHALLENGE YOUR EXPERTISE

- During the performance of a symphony, what should you do if most of the audience begins to applaud at the "wrong" time?
- When is a piano instead of an oboe used to "tune" an orchestra?

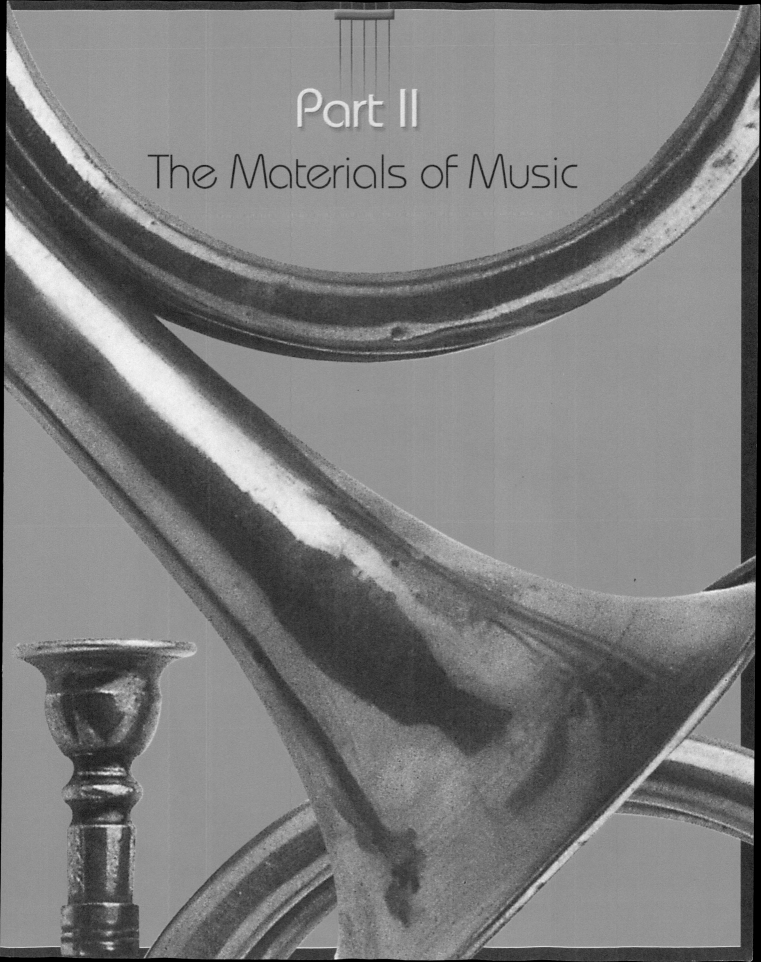

Part II

The Materials of Music

4

How the Basic Musical Elements Interact

Multimedia Presentation

The basic elements and the media through which they are performed make up the materials of music. To help you understand the basic elements, this chapter is coordinated with an online recording that introduces these key concepts. The printed part of this chapter is a summary of the materials to assist you after you have worked through the recording.

Suggested Sequence   First, navigate through the recording while looking at the text. When you are comfortable with that presentation, close your text and try to understand the presentation only through the audio. Your goal is to understand music through its sounds. Please follow the link on our website, www.prenhall.com/zorn to begin listening.

LISTENING GUIDE

Elements of Music
MARTIN BOOKSPAN, HOST

Online at www.prenhall.com/zorn

MUSIC
Leonard Bernstein

Composers use an assortment of sound materials—*the elements of music*—to organize their ideas. Just as painters use colors, shapes, light, and textures to create their works, composers use *rhythms, scales, melodies, harmonies,* and *textures* to create theirs.

Candide Overture

RHYTHM (Duration of Sound)

Music is a temporal art, existing in time. Sounds occur and continue for a certain duration, flowing at specific rates of speed, or tempos. You may have referred to this as *rhythm.* While listening, we flow along in time with the music, as though on a journey, for as long as it lasts.

Beat

MUSIC
Recurring drumbeat

Prominent Beat   When the beat is *prominent,* responding to it is easy. Even babies and animals react to a recurring, thumping beat. The beat motivates us to move—to snap our fingers, tap our feet, sway, dance, march, or exercise. An example of a prominent beat is Scott Joplin's rag, "The Entertainer."

MUSIC
Scott Joplin, "The Entertainer"

Weak Beat   Some music has a *weak beat,* creating a feeling of floating, drifting, or gliding, as in Claude Debussy's *Afternoon of a Faun.*

MUSIC
Claude Debussy,
Afternoon of a Faun

Tempo

The speed, or *tempo,* of the music also affects us. A slow tempo may evoke a mood of reflection or may help us relax. A brisk tempo can lift our spirits. You won't find soldiers marching or aerobics classes exercising to music with a slow tempo. Both activities depend on the uplift that a fast tempo creates.

Metronome

We can measure the speed or tempo of the beat with a device called a *metronome,* invented in 1816 by Johann Maelzel (1772–1838).

Metronome Markings

Composers usually indicate the tempos for playing their works by notating the metronome setting at the beginning of the music. A tempo indication of 84 in the music means that the basic beats should proceed at 84 beats per minute, which is a good tempo for a graduation march, for example, Edward Elgar's march *Pomp and Circumstance.*

MUSIC
Metronome ticking at 84 beats per minute

Measuring Tempos

Without a metronome, you can measure tempo the same way you measure your pulse. First, find your pulse on the inside of your wrist, below your thumb. Turn off the recording and count the number of pulse beats in 20 seconds, using a timer or the second hand of a watch. Then turn the tape on again. Do that now.

MUSIC
Edward Elgar, *Pomp and Circumstance,* March No. 1

In 20 seconds, you probably counted 22 to 30 beats. Multiply the *number* you counted by three, and you'll have your pulse rate.

MUSIC
Aaron Copland, "Hoe Down" from *Rodeo*

Now try to measure the tempo of "Hoe Down" from Aaron Copland's ballet *Rodeo.* Using a second hand or a stopwatch, count the number of beats you hear in 20 seconds.

MUSIC
George Gershwin, "Prelude II" (tempo: 84 beats per minute)

Perception of Tempo   Our perception of whether a tempo is fast or slow tends to correspond to our individual pulse rate. We perceive a tempo as moderate (*moderato* in Italian) when it is close to our own pulse, usually between 65 and 90 beats per minute.

Listen to George Gershwin's "Prelude II," which runs about 84 beats per minute. How did you react to a tempo close to your own pulse?

Steady Tempo   The tempo in most music usually remains steady—especially if dancers or marchers are trying to move with the music.

Flexible Tempo (Rubato)   Did you notice that the tempo of the Gershwin piece was not entirely steady? In highly personal and emotional music, the performer often uses a flexible approach to the beat. The musical term for this is *rubato*, meaning "robbed" in Italian. To execute rubato, performers vary the pace of the music slightly by increasing the speed for some beats and slowing it down for others.

Listen again to Gershwin's "Prelude II" and notice how the performer conveys the emotional quality of the music through rubato.

MUSIC
George Gershwin, "Prelude II,"
Andante con moto e poco rubato
(walking tempo with move-
ment and a little rubato)

Meter (Groupings of Beats)

Rhythmic groupings in most concert music are predictable. Created by stressed and unstressed beats, the recurring group is called a *meter*. Two, three, and four beats are the most common meters.

Triple Meter   Waltzes, for instance, use recurring rhythmic patterns of three beats, usually with the first beat of the pattern accented. A three-beat pattern is called a *triple meter*.

/		/		/		/		/		/
ONE	–	two	–	three	–	ONE	–	two	–	three
STRONG	–	weak	–	weak	–	STRONG	–	weak	–	weak
BEAT	–	beat	–	beat	–	BEAT	–	beat	–	beat

Listen to the triple meter in this waltz.

MUSIC
Johann Strauss (the Younger)
Blue Danube Waltz

Duple Meter   Because marches are intended for marchers with two feet, recurring groups of two, or duple meter, are standard:

/		/	/		/
ONE	–	two	ONE	–	two
STRONG	–	weak	STRONG	–	weak
BEAT	–	beat	BEAT	–	beat
Marchers: **LEFT**	–	right	**LEFT**	–	right

MUSIC
John Philip Sousa's march *The Stars and Stripes Forever*, trio section

Determining the Meter   Here is how to determine the meter of the music: Listen for the recurring pattern of strong, accented beats and weak, unaccented beats. Mark the beats on a piece of paper. Indicate an accented beat with a long line and an unaccented beat with a shorter line.

Examples:

Duple   /   /   /   /   /   /

                              2   2   2

Triple   /   /   /   /   /   /

                  3   3

Quadruple   /   /   /   /   /   /   /

                              4   4

MUSIC
Richard Wagner, Overture to
Die Meistersinger von Nürnberg,
opening section

You will now hear the opening section of the overture to the opera *Die Meistersinger* by Richard Wagner. Determine the meter by marking on your paper the accented and unaccented beats.

Did you hear the four pattern, or *quadruple meter*?

Listen to this next example and figure out the meter by marking the beats.

The music is a *minuet* by Joseph Haydn. The minuet was a popular *triple-meter* dance in the eighteenth century.

Minuet

MUSIC
Joseph Haydn, Symphony No.
94, third movement

Less Common Meters   If you cannot fit two, three, or four beats in a pattern, chances are you are listening to music with a less common meter, such as five, seven, or eleven.

Listen to "Take Five" by jazz composer Paul Desmond of the Dave Brubeck Quartet. Can you hear the five-beat meter?

MUSIC
Paul Desmond, "Take Five"

Multiple of Two (Duple Meter)   You may perceive meters such as four and eight as *duple meter*. Meters that are multiples of two tend to sound like a duple meter. Without looking at the printed notation, you will often not recognize the difference.

Multiples of Three (Triple Meter)   The same holds true for some multiples of three, such as six, nine, and twelve. A listener may hear them as *triple meter*.

Six Beats   Six is a multiple both of two and three. Depending on the tempo, you may hear six beats as either duple or triple meter.

Syncopation   Some music, especially jazz, uses rhythm patterns with unexpected accents. Or, there may be silence where you would anticipate an accent. This type of rhythm is called *syncopation*.

Listen again to Scott Joplin's ragtime piece "The Entertainer." Joplin used syncopated rhythms throughout.

Jazz drummer, Cindy Blackman

Jazz rhythms

MUSIC
Scott Joplin, "The Entertainer"

MUSIC
Igor Stravinsky, *The Rite of
Spring,* "Sacrificial Dance"

Rhythmic Ostinatom   Twentieth-century composers are especially fond of using a repetitive pattern called *rhythmic ostinato*. Jazz, rock, and dance music often depend on ostinato for the driving rhythm that motivates movement. Listen for the ostinato in the next piece by Igor Stravinsky.

MUSIC
Ludwig van Beethoven, Piano
Sonata No. 8, Op. 13, first
movement

Silence   Silence also is an important part of music. Listen to the opening of this piano sonata by Ludwig van Beethoven. Notice how the moments of silence create a dramatic effect.

PITCH (Melody and Harmony)

Pitches or tones are the materials of *melodies* and *harmonies*. Pitches appear on paper as *notes*. Performers read the notes and play or sing the corresponding pitches.

Melody

A melody is a succession of individual pitches that makes sense when you perceive them as a group. This is similar to perceiving a complete sentence from a group of individual words. Listen to this section from Felix Mendelssohn's Violin Concerto. Notice how the succession of pitches creates a coherent melody.

Describing Melodies

As listeners, we can describe melodies and pitches in a number of ways.

Prominent or Not Prominent   Is the melody *prominent* or *not prominent*? A prominent melody forms a coherent whole. You can often hum or remember a prominent melody after you've heard it a few times. You can even follow it the first time you hear it. A melody is *not prominent* if you have trouble following it. When a succession of pitches sounds fragmented or aimless, you can describe the melody as *not prominent*.

Listen to this twentieth-century piece by Arnold Schoenberg. Because the melody sounds fragmented, you may find it a challenge to remember or to hum it. For this reason, you probably would describe it as *not prominent*.

Length of Phrase   Another aspect of a melody is its length of *phrase*, or melodic idea. Is the melodic idea *short* or *long*?

Short Melodic Idea   What we notice immediately about Beethoven's Symphony No. 5 is the unusual shortness of the opening phrase. Beethoven uses this short statement as a structural element throughout the first movement. A melodic idea used in this manner is called a *melodic motive*.

Listen again as the orchestra plays this section of Beethoven's Symphony No. 5. Notice how the rhythmic idea (short, short, short, long) persists, even when the melody changes. Therefore, the opening motive is also a *rhythmic motive*.

Long Melodic Idea   Contrast Beethoven's short idea to the longer idea in Wagner's Overture to *Die Meistersinger*.

Cadences   Notice how the melody keeps moving forward until it seems to arrive at a resting place. In music, we call these arrivals *cadences*.

Ornamented Melodies   Some melodies are plain, for example, the opening of Beethoven's Symphony No. 5. Others are ornamented with trills and embellishments. The type of *ornamentation* used is often a matter of the prevailing taste and fashion of the composer's time.

Listen to this section of Wolfgang Amadeus Mozart's variations of the French folk song "Ah, vous dirai-je maman." We know it as "Twinkle, Twinkle, Little Star." First, the plain, unornamented melody:

Printed Notes

MUSIC
Felix Mendelssohn, Violin Concerto, first movement

MUSIC
Arnold Schoenberg, *Suite for Piano*, "Praeludium"

MUSIC
Ludwig van Beethoven, Symphony No. 5, first movement

MUSIC
Richard Wagner, Overture to *Die Meistersinger von Nürnberg*, opening section

MUSIC
Wolfgang Amadeus Mozart, main theme. Variations "Ah, vous dirai-je maman," K. 265.

MUSIC
Wolfgang Amadeus Mozart, K. 265, Variation No. 12

Trills   Now listen to the variations. Mozart ornaments the melody with *trills*—a rapid alternation of two pitches.

Repetition, Imitation, and Sequence

Composers want you to become familiar with their melodic ideas. To help you, they may use musical devices such as *repetition, imitation,* and *sequence.*

Repetition   Hearing a phrase or a melody again enables you to recognize it quickly. Repetition is like bringing a character from a play back on stage.

MUSIC
Wolfgang Amadeus Mozart, "Turkish March" from Sonata in A Major, K. 331

Listen to the catchy "Turkish March" by Mozart. You may be able to memorize it the first time you hear it, but Mozart eases the job by repeating it for you.

Imitation   *Imitation* is a form of repetition. We hear a motive or a melody. Shortly thereafter, we hear it played again, either by another voice or instrument or by the same voice or instrument in a higher or lower range. That restatement is called *imitation.*

MUSIC
Johann Sebastian Bach, *Brandenburg Concerto No. 2,* third movement.

Listen to this section from Johann Sebastian Bach's *Brandenburg Concerto No. 2.* Notice how the melody, stated first by the trumpet, is imitated by the oboe, then by the violin, and finally by the flute.

Canons and rounds. A *canon* is an imitation that continues throughout an entire work. Examples are "Row, Row, Row Your Boat" and "Frère Jacques." We sometimes refer to these songs as *rounds* or *circle canons:* different voices keep coming around to the same melody.

MUSIC
Ludwig van Beethoven, Piano Sonata No. 8, Op. 13, opening

Sequence   *Sequences* are another form of repetition: the same instrument repeats the melodic idea, using slightly different pitches.

Listen again to the opening of the Beethoven piano sonata. Beethoven takes the opening motive through a series of sequences.

MUSIC
Ludwig van Beethoven, Symphony No. 5, first movement

Listen for *repetition, imitation,* and *sequences* in the opening section of the first movement of Beethoven's Symphony No. 5. Notice how Beethoven manipulates the melodic motive using different pitches. This is called a *sequence.* Then the motive is passed around the orchestra. This is called *imitation.*

Notice which instruments imitate the motive until that section comes to a cadence. First you will hear the violins in a low range. Then the violas imitate the melody. Next the violins continue the imitation in a higher range. Then the full orchestra repeats the opening statement, followed by *imitation* and *sequences,* until the next cadence.

Scales

Scales consist of ascending or descending pitches arranged in specified patterns. Most melodies in Western concert music are based on one of two common scales: *major* and *minor.*

Major Scale   In general, the major scale has a bright, happy quality.

MUSIC
C major scale and chord

Minor Scale   The minor scale has a more plaintive quality.

MUSIC
c minor scale and chord

While you listen to concert music, try to discern the major or minor quality of the music you hear. The way the music makes you feel can sometimes be a clue.

Other Scales   To add freshness to their music, many twentieth-century composers have organized pitches in scale patterns other than major and minor. These innovations will be discussed in later chapters.

Harmony

Combinations of pitches sounded simultaneously create harmony. You will now hear three pitches. First they are sounded individually, as they would be in a melody. Then they are sounded together to form harmony.

A classical flutist

Chord   When those three pitches were sounded simultaneously, they become a *chord*—a major chord.

Consonant Chords   The chord you just heard evokes a feeling of stability and *balance*. This type of chord is *consonant*. Listen to it again.

MUSIC
Pitches C, E, and G individually, then together

MUSIC
C major chord

Dissonant Chords   In some chords, the pitches within the chord seem to clash with one another. They may even sound unpleasant or disagreeable to you. These types of chords are *dissonant*.

Listen to these three chords. You'll have no trouble picking out the one dissonant chord from the two consonant chords.

MUSIC
consonant and dissonant chords

Did you recognize the second chord as the dissonant one? If not, listen again.

Major and Minor Chords   We also describe chords by their quality, referring to them as *major chords* or *minor chords*.

Listen now to five chords that alternate between major and minor chords, starting and ending with major.

MUSIC
C major, f minor, E-flat major, a minor, and D-flat major

TEXTURES

With these musical threads—*rhythms, scales, melodies,* and *harmonies*—composers weave their ideas into *textures*. Using layers of sounds, they create a musical fabric. Most concert music employs three types of texture: *monophonic, homophonic,* and *polyphonic.*

Monophonic Texture   A *monophonic texture* is a melody without harmony, other melodic lines, or accompaniment.

Homophonic Texture   Seldom does music use monophonic texture. The most common texture is a melody with a harmonic accompaniment of some sort. This combination of melody and chordal accompaniment is called *homophonic texture.* An example of this texture would be produced by a singer with guitar accompaniment.

Here is the same Beethoven melody supported by a harmonic accompaniment. Notice the *homophonic texture.*

MUSIC
Ludwig van Beethoven, Piano Sonata No. 8, Op. 13, second movement (melody only)

MUSIC
Ludwig van Beethoven, Piano Sonata No. 8, Op. 13, second movement (original form)

MUSIC
George Frideric Handel, *Messiah,* Chorus: "For Unto Us a Child Is Born"

Polyphonic Texture   *Polyphonic texture* is more complicated. In polyphonic texture, you hear several independent, overlapping melodic lines.

Listen to this opening section of "For Unto Us a Child Is Born" from George Frideric Handel's *Messiah*. The constant overlapping of melodic lines is an example of *polyphonic texture.*

Conclusion   You have just heard some of the basic materials used in music—*rhythms, scales, melodies, harmonies,* and *textures.* As you listen to the remaining recorded music with this book, you will become more familiar with the works.

Cellist Yo Yo Ma

Table 4.1	Summary of Basic Musical Elements*

Rhythm (Duration of Sound)

beat prominence: strong, weak	rubato
tempo: slow, medium, fast	ostinato
meter: duple, triple, quadruple, other	rhythmic motive
less frequently used groupings	silence
	syncopation

Melody

prominent	imitation
not prominent	sequences
short phrase	repetition
long phrase	scales: major, minor
cadence	other scales: chromatic,
ornamented	pentatonic, whole-tone,
plain	gapped, tone-row

Harmony

mostly consonant	major and minor chords
mostly dissonant	

Texture

monophonic
polyphonic
homophonic

*See Appendix D for a more complete summary of the Basic Musical Elements.

CHALLENGE YOUR EXPERTISE

- What two things do a waltz and a minuet have in common?
- What term describes a melody or a section of the music that comes to a conclusion?

5

Performing Media: Instruments, Voices, and Ensembles

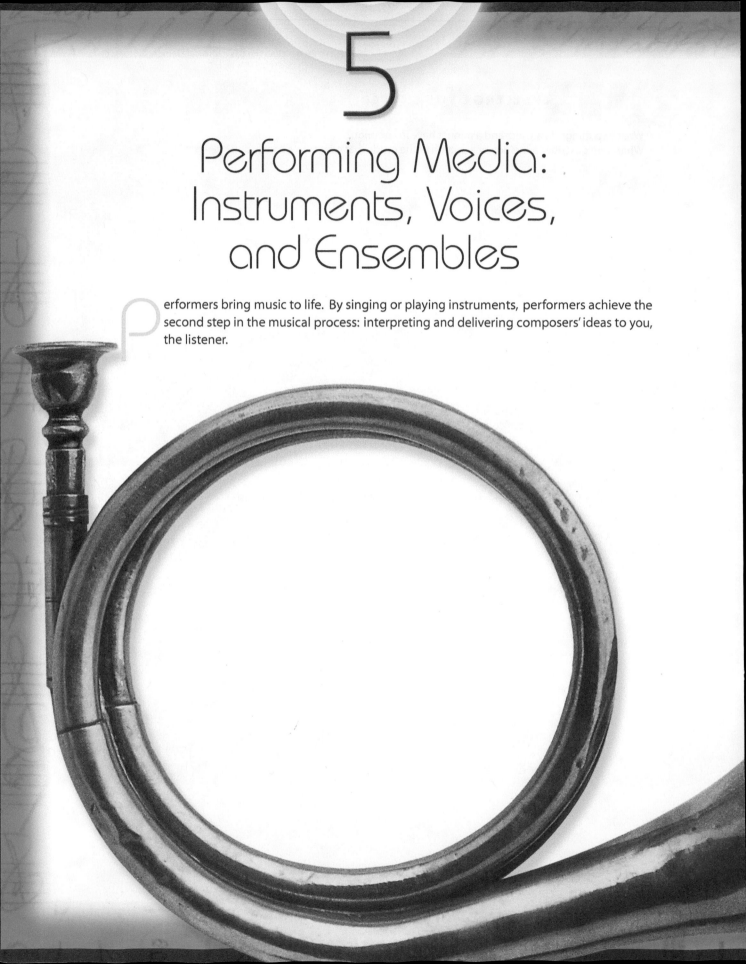

Performers bring music to life. By singing or playing instruments, performers achieve the second step in the musical process: interpreting and delivering composers' ideas to you, the listener.

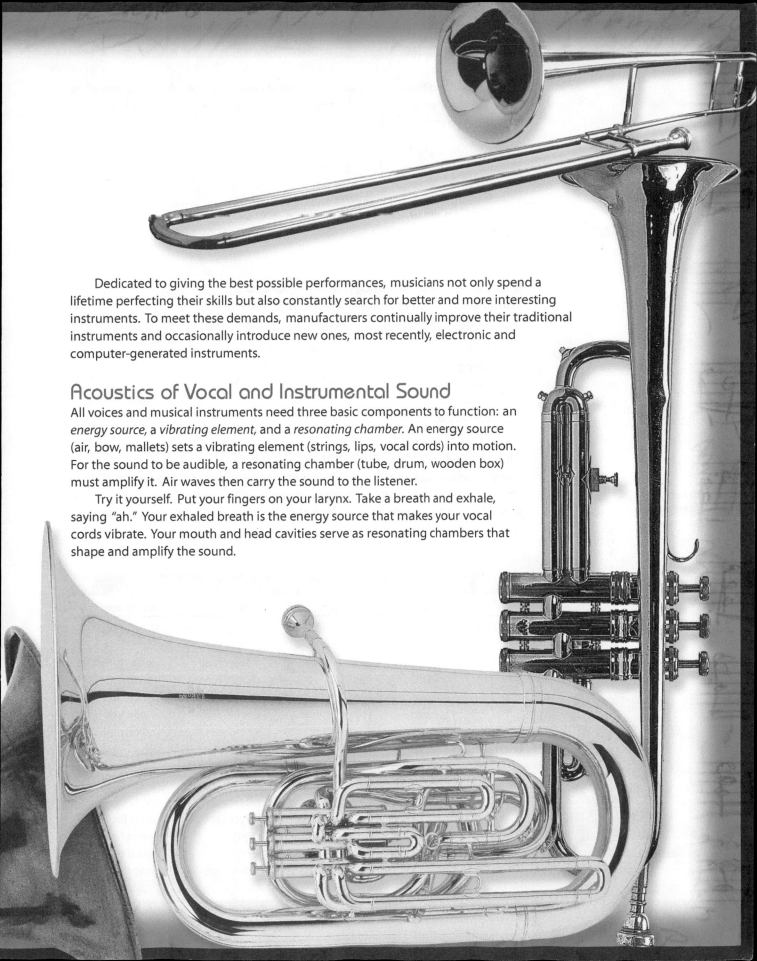

Dedicated to giving the best possible performances, musicians not only spend a lifetime perfecting their skills but also constantly search for better and more interesting instruments. To meet these demands, manufacturers continually improve their traditional instruments and occasionally introduce new ones, most recently, electronic and computer-generated instruments.

Acoustics of Vocal and Instrumental Sound

All voices and musical instruments need three basic components to function: an *energy source,* a *vibrating element,* and a *resonating chamber.* An energy source (air, bow, mallets) sets a vibrating element (strings, lips, vocal cords) into motion. For the sound to be audible, a resonating chamber (tube, drum, wooden box) must amplify it. Air waves then carry the sound to the listener.

Try it yourself. Put your fingers on your larynx. Take a breath and exhale, saying "ah." Your exhaled breath is the energy source that makes your vocal cords vibrate. Your mouth and head cavities serve as resonating chambers that shape and amplify the sound.

Notice the difference between the sounds you produce when your mouth is closed and when it is open. Also notice that the more energy you exert, the louder the sound you produce.

```
(air)        →    (vocal cords)   →    (oral cavity)   →    (waves)    →    (ear)
energy            vibrating            resonating           air              ear
source            element              chamber                               canals
```

Instrumental Performing Media

Instruments fall into at least one of six categories:

- woodwind
- brass
- string
- percussion
- keyboard
- electronic

How Instruments Produce Sound

Timbre
(*tam*-ber)

Many variables contribute to an instrument's tone and sound production. Differences in size, shape, and construction materials alter *timbre*—the quality of the tone. Table 5.1 presents an overview of the acoustical components of the most common musical instruments.

Table 5.1	Acoustics of Commonly Used Instruments			
	Instrument	**Energy**	**Vibrator**	**Resonator**
woodwind	flute/piccolo	air	air over mouth hole	metal tube
	oboe	air	double reed	wood tube
	English horn	air	double reed	wood tube
	clarinet	air	single reed	wood tube
	bassoon	air	double reed	wood tube
	saxophone	air	single reed	metal tube
brass	trumpet	air	player's lips	brass tube
	French horn	air	player's lips	brass tube
	trombone	air	player's lips	brass tube
	baritone horn	air	player's lips	brass tube
	tuba	air	player's lips	brass tube
string	violin	bow	string	wood box
	viola	bow	string	wood box
	cello	bow	string	wood box

The Kronos Quartet

Table 5.1		(Continued)		
	Instrument	**Energy**	**Vibrator**	**Resonator**
	string bass	bow	string	wood box
	harp	finger	string	wood box
	guitar	finger or pick	string	wood box
	mandolin	finger or pick	string	wood box
	banjo	finger or pick	string	wood box
percussion	cymbals	hands/arms	cymbals	metal disks
	snare drum	hands/arms w/sticks	drumhead (plastic or skin)	metal or wood cylinder
	bass drum	w/mallet	drumhead	wood cylinder
	timpani	w/mallets	timpani heads	metal bowls
keyboard	piano	fingers/hammers	strings	wood box
	harpsichord	fingers/plectrum	strings	wood box
	organ	fingers/air	air columns	metal and wood pipes
	celesta	fingers/hammers	steel bars	wood box
electronic	synthesizer	fingers/electricity	transistors	loudspeaker

Performing Media and Performances: Solo Instruments and Ensembles

Solo Recitals

A recital can feature almost any instrument. Except for keyboard performances, recitals typically present a soloist with an accompanist. For example, a violinist or cellist usually has a piano accompanist.

Ensembles

Although any combination of instrumentalists can play together in an *ensemble*, here are the most common:

Small Ensembles   Combinations of only a few instruments are called *chamber ensembles.*

> **String trio:** one violin, one viola, one cello
> **String quartet:** two violins, one viola, one cello
> **Woodwind quintet:** one flute, one oboe, one clarinet, one French horn, and one bassoon
> **Brass quintet:** two trumpets, one French horn, one trombone, and one tuba

Large Ensembles   The *symphony orchestra* and the *wind ensemble* are the most common large instrumental ensembles. Both ensembles may vary in size and instrumentation, according to the demands of the music. For special works, unusual instruments may be brought in. Our discussion of these ensembles begins with the symphony orchestra.

The Fine Arts Brass Ensemble

Chamber ensembles

Maelström Percussion Ensemble

The Orchestra and Its Instruments

Classical music concerts by symphony orchestras are by far the most popular and well attended. Concertgoers love the rich variety of tone colors emanating from the individual instruments as well as from the ensemble as a whole. Artistic directors of orchestras have an extensive body of works to choose from. Many of the large orchestral works have maintained a broad appeal from one generation to the next.

Typical Large Symphony Orchestra Seating Arrangement

Sections of the Orchestra

Modern orchestras use similar seating arrangements for the four main sections: *string, woodwind, brass,* and *percussion.* A conductor may vary the seating somewhat at his or her discretion. The figure shows the approximate placement of the instruments, and Table 5.2 shows the typical number of instruments used in today's major orchestras.

String Section   With more than half of the musicians playing *violins, violas, cellos* (short for *violoncellos*), and *string basses,* the string section is the foundation of the orchestra.

The violins, the smallest of the string family, have the highest pitch range. Divided into two subsections—first and second violins—all the violinists sit together next to the conductor (see figure). Much of the time, you will hear the

Members of an orchestra's string section

Table 5.2	Number of Performers in Typical Orchestra		
Section	**Instrument**	**Abbreviation**	**Number in Orchestra**
String	first violins	V-1	18
	second violins	V-2	16
	violas	Vla	12
	cellos	C	12
	double basses	Db	8
Woodwind	flutes (including piccolo)	Fl	4
	oboes (including English horn)	Ob	4
	clarinets	Cl	2–4
	bassoons (including contrabassoon)	Bn	2–4
Brass	trumpets	Tpt	4
	French horns	Hn	4–6
	trombones (including bass trombone)	Tbn	3–4
	tuba	Tba	1
Percussion	cymbals		1
	snare drum		1
	bass drum		1
	timpani		2–6
	chimes, marimba, bells, xylophone, triangle, miscellaneous		1
	harp		1–2

first violins carry the melody or theme in an orchestral piece. Sometimes the second violins play the same melody as the first violins; at other times, they play a harmony part.

Similar in appearance to a violin, the viola is slightly larger and plays in a lower range. Violas are usually placed next to the violins, as shown in the chart.

Although similar in shape to both the violin and the viola, the cello (or violoncello) is much larger. Cellists, who place their heavy instruments between their legs, often use a special forward-tilting chair for balance. A long pin supports the bottom of the instrument on the floor. Because of its larger size and longer strings, the cello produces pitches in a range lower than those of either the violin or the viola. You will most often find the cellos to the right of the conductor, toward the front of the stage.

The bass, the largest string instrument, is also known by several other names: double bass, contrabass, bass viol, standing bass, string bass. A bass player may perform standing up or partially sitting or leaning on a tall stool, usually behind the cellos on the outer edge of the orchestra.

String players produce sounds by drawing a *bow* across the strings. For a special effect, strings may be plucked (*pizzicato,* in Italian). To soften and change the timbre, string players can use a device called a *mute* on their instruments.

Violin
(vy-uh-*lin*)

Viola
(vee-*oh*-luh)

Cello
(*chel*-oh)

Violincello
(*vee*-uh-lun-*chel*-oh)

String bass
(bayse)

Bow
(bo)

Pizzicato
(pits-ih-*kah*-toh)

Mute

Flute

Piccolo
(*pik*-uh-loh)

Woodwind sections of an orchestra
Jim Four / Lebrecht Music & Arts Photo
Library

English horn

Oboe

Clarinet

Saxophone

Bassoon

Contrabassoon

Woodwind Section   Usually seated directly in front of the conductor behind the strings, the woodwinds make up the second most important section of the orchestra. The full section consists of *piccolo, flutes, oboes, English horn, clarinets, bassoons,* and *contrabassoon. Saxophones* may occasionally join the woodwind section for modern or jazz-influenced music.

Originally, all woodwind instruments were made of wood. Now, flutes and piccolos are nearly always metal. Whether wood or metal, all modern woodwinds have elaborate keying mechanisms that facilitate rapid playing.

Playing in the highest range of the flute section and the entire orchestra is the piccolo (Italian for "small"), the smallest woodwind. The flute is next in range and size. A flutist or piccolo player produces tones by blowing across a hole at the head of the instrument.

Placed next to each other, the oboe and the English horn both have a set of double reeds. The oboe has a highly audible, "reedy" sound. Its pitches are consistent and easily heard. For this reason, the first oboist usually sounds the "A" for the orchestra to tune by.

Slightly larger than the oboe, the English horn is distinguished by the curved pipe between its reeds and the body of the instrument. Neither English nor a horn, the instrument probably received its name because someone noticed that it resembled an angled hunting horn. In the early nineteenth century, when the instrument was introduced, "cor anglé" ("angled horn" in French) sounded similar to "cor anglais" ("English horn"). The name stuck.

Clarinets use a single reed. Capable of a wide range of pitches and timbres, these instruments vary in size from smaller, high-pitched soprano clarinets to large, deep-pitched bass clarinets. The instrument's upper register, higher than an oboe's, can be heard above the orchestra. The middle register can sound mellow, and the lower register, rich and "woody."

Saxophones also use a single reed. Although they have always been made of brass, saxophones are included in the woodwind category. The instruments range in size from the high soprano saxophones to the low baritones and basses.

With its double reeds, the bassoon is closely related to the oboe. Both the bassoon and its larger version, the contrabassoon, are made of large wooden tubes, with long pipes connecting their reeds to the body of the instrument.

Brass Section   The brass section, named for the construction material of its instruments, includes *trumpets, French horns, trombones,* and *tubas.* Because the brass instruments are powerful enough to produce the loudest sounds in the orchestra, they usually are placed behind the woodwinds, or in the outer ring of the orchestra.

All brass players produce sounds by forcing air through their lips, which creates a buzzing or vibration that is funneled into the instrument through a mouthpiece. Then, the unique construction of the individual instrument shapes and resonates these initial sounds differently.

Smallest of the section, the trumpets produce the highest tones. Depending on the requirements of a particular piece, players use trumpets of different sizes and pitches.

Distinguished from the other brasses by its mellower tones, the French horn can produce a wide range of pitches. This versatile instrument can easily blend

Trumpet

French Horn

with either the woodwinds or the brass section. Though not visible in the photo below, the horn player's right hand is partially inside the bell.

Playing in the middle and lower ranges of the brass section, the trombone is the only brass instrument without valves. Instead, the instrument has a telescoping slide that changes the length of its tubing, and therefore its pitch.

Trombone

Music often calls for the addition of a bass trombone. Its larger tubing and slightly larger bell make it capable of playing low and loudly.

Bass trombone

The tuba, easily recognized by its size, is the largest brass instrument and is capable of playing the lowest tones in the section. To prevent the tuba from overpowering other instruments in the orchestra, its bell is pointed toward the ceiling.

Tuba

The sousaphone, a popular marching band instrument (not an orchestra brass), is similar to a tuba. Named for "the March King," John Philip Sousa (1854–1932), the sousaphone is shaped so a player can carry it while marching.

Placing various mutes into the bell of a brass instrument will change its sound. The cone-shaped "straight" mute makes any of the brass instruments sound more like a woodwind instrument. The "cup" mute mellows sounds, and the "wa-wa" mute often is used in jazz pieces.

Brass mutes

Percussion Section Percussionists usually are placed at the outer perimeter of the ensemble. Members of this section strike, rub, shake, jiggle, pound, beat, or crash their instruments to produce a host of specialized sounds.

CHALLENGE YOUR EXPERTISE

- In terms of creating sound, what does a violin bow have in common with a pair of drumsticks?
- Which instrument is the smallest of the woodwinds?

Drums

Timpani
(*tim*-pa-nee)

Some percussion instruments—chimes, glockenspiel, celesta, bells, xylophone, and marimba—play defined pitches. Others do not, including drums of various sizes and shapes. Snare and field drums are played with sticks. Others, such as the bass drum, are played with padded mallets. Still others, such as the bongos and conga drums, are played with the hands.

The timpani, or kettledrums, deserve special mention for two reasons. First, they were the first percussion instruments to join the symphony orchestra. They made their debut in an opera orchestra around 1670. Later, Johann Sebastian Bach used them in some of his larger works. Two timpani were standard in Mozart's and Haydn's orchestras. In the nineteenth century, a third, fourth, and even more timpani joined the symphony orchestra when needed for particular works.

Members of an orchestra's brass section (front, left to right: French horn, trumpet; rear: trombones)

Orchestra percussion section (left to right): bass drum, tom tom, timbale, marimba, snare drums, conga drum, timpani, bass drum.

Non-Western Instruments

Second, they are the only drums tuned to specific pitches. Consisting of large, shiny copper bowls, timpani are impressive. Each bowl is topped with a stretched skin or a plastic head. The player uses an assortment of padded mallets to produce the desired effects. A pedal mechanism on today's timpani facilitates changing pitches and retuning during performances.

Various cultures have contributed to the percussion section:

Africa: drums, wood blocks, gourds, xylophone
Islamic North Africa and Turkey: various cymbals, triangle, bass drum
Asia: Korean temple blocks, Chinese gongs, Indonesian finger cymbals
South and Central America: maracas, timbales, bongos, conga drum,
    claves, cowbell
Europe: castanets, tambourine

For a more detailed discussion of the contributions of world cultures to concert music, see Chapter 29.

The Turkish cymbals in the orchestra are either crashed together or hit with a stick or a mallet. Because a player may have to wait through pages of music for a brief cymbal part, a percussionist often plays other instruments in the section.

Almost any sound can be included in the percussion section: whips, thunder, bird calls, breaking glass, crashing cars, blasting cannons, firing rifles, roaring aircraft, and an infinite variety of electronically produced effects. George Gershwin called for taxi horns to add realistic street sounds in his orchestral piece *An American in Paris*. Ottorino Respighi enhanced the atmosphere of *The Pines of Rome* by adding recordings of genuine bird calls.

Note: All the recordings in this chapter will be discussed in more detail later in the text. In most cases, the text also contains a detailed listening guide for each work.

Zubin Mehta conducting the Bavarian State Orchestra

How Do I Become Familiar With the Instruments?

Associating the sounds you hear with the instruments you see at concerts or on television is the best way to become familiar with them. Use the next listening activity to become acquainted with the instruments.

The Young Person's Guide to the Orchestra (1946), Opus 34, Benjamin Britten

Form: Theme, Variations, and Fugue
Performing Medium: Symphony Orchestra with Narrator

Online at www.prenhall.com/zorn

As you listen to *The Young Person's Guide to the Orchestra* by Benjamin Britten, follow along with the Listening Guide. Narrator Will Geer introduces the sections and individual instruments of the orchestra using a narration written by Benjamin Britten. As each instrument is introduced, notice its sound when it performs with its section and then later as a solo instrument.

Written to introduce concertgoers to orchestral instruments, *The Young Person's Guide to the Orchestra* is a set of variations and a fugue based on a theme by the seventeenth-century English composer Henry Purcell (*Pur*-sl, 1659–1695).

The work is in three sections, with a coda:

Main Theme	13 Variations	Fugue	Coda

Part one is a statement of Purcell's theme. The entire orchestra plays the theme. Next, each section plays it in turn—starting with the woodwinds, the brasses, the strings, and finally the percussion section.

Part two is a set of thirteen variations on Purcell's theme. Britten uses this part to introduce the individual instruments.

Part three is a fugue (see Glossary). The main melody or melody fragment is called a *subject*. Again, each of the main instruments of the orchestra plays the fugue subject.

The coda or conclusion of the piece starts with the percussion section and is answered by the full orchestra. The entire work ends with a loud, held chord.

Variations

Fugue
(fyoog)

How the Orchestra Developed

Toward the end of the eighteenth century, Joseph Haydn's thirty-piece court orchestra consisted of part-time musicians who had to double as servants, cooks, and stable hands to make a living. A generation later, Ludwig van Beethoven was limited to forty or fifty poorly trained instrumentalists, many of whom had difficulty reading his demanding music.

Today's symphony orchestra, with its highly skilled, professional performers playing the assortment of instruments we have come to know, developed during the latter part of the nineteenth century. Among the factors influencing this development were the emergence of both new and improved instruments, the growing popularity of public concerts in larger halls, and the establishment of funding sources to support expanded orchestras.

LISTENING GUIDE

The Young Person's Guide to the Orchestra (1946), Opus 34, Benjamin Britten

Form: Theme, Variations, and Fugue
Performing Medium: Symphony Orchestra with Narrator

Online at www.prenhall.com/zorn

THEME

| 0.00 | THEME | played by the entire orchestra; *f,* triple meter |

Moving and Majestic

0:28	THEME	played by the *woodwind* section
0:54	THEME	played by the *brass* section
1:17	THEME	played by the *string* section
1:38	THEME	played by the *percussion* section, featuring timpani
1:57	THEME	played again by the entire orchestra

VARIATIONS

2:20	VARIATION 1	*flutes* and *piccolo;* fast passages of music; duple meter; *p*
2:53	VARIATION 2	*oboes:* smooth, plaintive melody
3:50	VARIATION 3	*clarinets:* broken chords and fast scale passages
4:30	VARIATION 4	*bassoons:* marchlike melody
5:24	VARIATION 5	*violins:* dancelike melody
5:59	VARIATION 6	*violas:* songlike melody, covering a wide range
7:01	VARIATION 7	*cellos:* rich, flowing melody
8:14	VARIATION 8	*string basses:* melody based mainly on sequences
9:13	VARIATION 9	*harp:* an inversion (upside down) statement of the theme
10:00	VARIATION 10	*French horns:* variation, using chords
10:53	VARIATION 11	*trumpets:* marchlike passage
11:23	VARIATION 12	*trombones* and *tuba:* heavy and majestic
12:40	VARIATION 13	*percussion:* starts with *timpani;* followed by *bass drum* and *cymbals, tambourine, triangle, snare drum, Chinese wood blocks, xylophone, castanets, gong;* concludes with the *whip*

FUGUE

14:32	SUBJECT (melody)	played by piccolo; fast tempo; duple meter

Very Fast

14:38	SUBJECT	played by *flutes;* piccolo in counterpoint (counter melody)
14:47	SUBJECT	played by *oboes;* other woodwinds in counterpoint
14:52	SUBJECT	played by *clarinets;* other woodwinds in counterpoint
15:03	SUBJECT	played by *bassoons;* other woodwinds in counterpoint
15:13	SUBJECT	played by *first violins;* other instruments in counterpoint
15:15	SUBJECT	played by *second violins;* other instruments in counterpoint
15:23	SUBJECT	played by *violas;* other instruments in counterpoint
15:29	SUBJECT	played by *cellos;* other instruments in counterpoint
15:33	SUBJECT	played by *string basses;* other instruments in counterpoint
15:45	SUBJECT	played by *harp;* other instruments in counterpoint
15:57	SUBJECT	played by *French horns;* other instruments in counterpoint
16:03	SUBJECT	played by *trumpets;* other instruments in counterpoint
16:11	SUBJECT	played by *trombones* and *tuba;* other instruments in counterpoint
16:17	SUBJECT/	played by upper *strings* and *woodwinds;* counterpoint of MAIN THEME
	Main Theme	played in long tones by *brasses;* tempo slows

CODA

16:57	Percussion enters *f;* back to the fast tempo; full orchestra answers
17:16	Ending chord played by the entire orchestra

YOUNG PERSON'S GUIDE TO THE ORCHESTRA (Britten)
© Copyright 1947 by Hawkes & Son (London) Ltd. Copyright Renewed.
Reprinted by permission of Boosey & Hawkes, Inc.

Before the Seventeenth Century

Chamber Ensembles Chamber ensembles were the main instrumental groups before the seventeenth century. Two to eight musicians performed on an as-needed basis to entertain in the chambers or rooms of a palace or manor house. Composers did not specify the instruments because they did not know which ones would be available. So it was possible to hear a piece played on a different combination of instruments from one performance to the next.

The Roman Catholic Church, the leading employer of musicians before that time, was more interested in vocal music. Although an ensemble of instruments was occasionally featured in the church service, the instrumentalist's primary role was to accompany the singers.

The Beginnings of Instrumentation

In Venice, around 1600, Giovanni Gabrieli (c.1555–1612) surveyed the possibilities offered by the huge interior of St. Mark's Basilica, where he was first organist and composer. He realized that instruments playing in different locations of the church could produce very rich sound effects. So he experimented with different combinations of instruments until he was satisfied with the results.

To ensure the balance and quality of that sound, Gabrieli specified which instruments should play. Thus, we had the beginning of standardized *instrumentation*, which made it possible for a complex instrumental composition to be performed with the same instrumentation at each performance.

Another great Italian composer, Claudio Monteverdi, built on Gabrieli's ideas to set up the first orchestra with stable instrumentation. In 1607, he hired forty musicians to accompany his opera *Orfeo* (*or*-fay-oh).

2	flutes (one high and one low)
2	oboes
1	very high trumpet (clarino)
3	high trumpets
4	medium trumpets
2	cornets (looking and sounding different from the modern cornet, and made either of wood or ivory)
2	small violins
2	violins (regular size)
10	viole da braccia (similar to the modern violin)
3	viole da gamba (similar to the modern cello)
2	double-bass viols (string bass)
2	deep-tone lutes (a cross between a guitar and a mandolin)
5	assorted keyboard instruments, including harpsichords

The String Instruments Achieve Perfection

Between 1650 and 1700, a breakthrough occurred in the construction of string instruments. This breakthrough was the next important step in the development of the orchestra. In the northern Italian town of Cremona, a few generations of craftsmen achieved near-perfection in creating their string instruments. Nicolò Amati (1596–1684), Antonio Stradivari (1644–1737), and Giuseppe Bartolomeo Guarneri (1698–1744) crafted priceless instruments cherished and played today by such soloists as Itzhak Perlman, Midori, Nigel Kennedy, Nadja Salerno-Sonnenberg, Yo-Yo Ma, and Lynn Harrell.

Solo Performers   Around 1700, several composers, Antonio Vivaldi in particular, were inspired by the improved string instruments. A violinist himself, Vivaldi grew up in Venice, about 100 miles east of Cremona, and he later taught

Gabrieli
(gah-bree-*ay*-lee)

Monteverdi
(mohn-teh-*vehr*-dee)

Amati
(ah-*mah*-tee)

Stradivari
(strah-deh-*vahr*-ee)

Guarneri
(gwahr-*nayr*-ee)

at a girls' orphanage in Venice. Of his 500 concertos (music for one or several soloists with orchestra) featuring various instruments, he composed almost half for the violin.

Virtuoso Performers   Vivaldi's violin concertos were more technically demanding than earlier string music. With the availability of superior instruments, musicians aspired to become *virtuosos*—solo performers with exceptional technical ability.*

Highly proficient soloists could now earn more money—a fact that motivated other instrumentalists to attain virtuosity. After 1700, trumpeters, hornists, flutists, oboists, and bassoonists joined the ranks of virtuosos. A harpsichord or a chamber orchestra usually accompanied soloists.

Virtuosos
(vur-choo-*oh*-sohs)

Concertos
(con-*chayr*-tos)

Chamber Orchestra

A larger Baroque instrumental ensemble is now called a *chamber orchestra*. Not yet containing the variety of instruments associated with the modern symphony orchestra, the chamber orchestra consisted mainly of string instruments, a few winds, and harpsichord, often with the composer playing and conducting from the harpsichord, as illustrated in the figure below.

Concerto Grosso

With more instrumentalists becoming virtuosos, composers of the early eighteenth century began to write concertos featuring several soloists in the same piece of music. To distinguish this work from a concerto for one or two instruments, composers called it *concerto grosso,* or "large concerto."

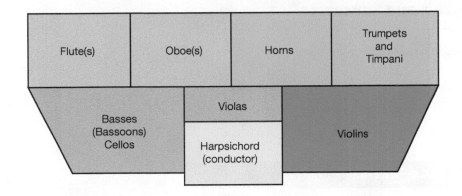

The Baroque Chamber Orchestra (10 to 20 players)

The Court Orchestra Evolves

By the latter part of the eighteenth century, almost every European court of the ruling nobility had its small resident orchestra. Fifteen to thirty part-time players were on call to provide familiar entertainment for their employers and guests.

The words "familiar entertainment" are significant: aristocrats resisted surprises. Catering to this desire for predictability, court composers wrote music with standardized instrumentation for these small resident orchestras. Thus, members of the leisure class could be assured of comparable entertainment, no matter where they traveled.

*In music, we use either the Italian plural ending of words (concerti, virtuosi) or the English ending (concertos, virtuosos).

HISTORICAL PERSPECTIVE

What Is the Secret of the Cremona Instruments?

Modern technology has not yet been able to replicate the quality of string instruments created by the Cremona craftsmen. What makes those instruments so great? Not only are their tones beautiful, but their sounds resonate over the symphony orchestra.

Theories abound about the secrets of these instruments, but all remain unproven: the secrets died with the craftsmen.

Some have conjectured that the varnish and the glue had special qualities. Perhaps. Some suggest that the instruments were crafted from wood soaked in the polluted waters in the canals of Venice. What "magical" powers this particular water may have transferred, no one knows. But recent analyses indicate that the soaking seems to have created a specially porous wood, which may indeed amplify sound.

The "Hellier" Stradivarius, made in 1679

CHALLENGE YOUR EXPERTISE

What do the tuba, contrabassoon, and bass viol have in common?

LISTENING ACTIVITY

The Four Seasons, Op. 8, Antonio Vivaldi

Concerto for Violin and Strings in E Major: "Spring"
First Movement: Allegro
Form: Violin Concerto
Performing Medium: Chamber Orchestra

Compact Disc: 1, Track 7
Running Time: 3:10

Listen to the first movement of this famous Vivaldi violin concerto, which features a violinist with a chamber orchestra. A more detailed discussion and Listening Guide appears in Chapter 9.

Franz Joseph Haydn (seated) portrayed by French painter Antoine Vestier with members of the Esterházy household.

Haydn's Contributions

Over a 30-year span of composing more than 100 symphonies for the classical orchestra, Joseph Haydn contributed significantly to the development of the orchestra. Adding a pair of timpani (kettledrums) to the standard orchestra and gradually phasing out the harpsichord, Haydn influenced Wolfgang Amadeus Mozart and other contemporaries to follow his lead. Haydn's refinements paved the way for the "modern" orchestra.

LISTENING ACTIVITY

Brandenburg Concerto No. 2 (1721),
Johann Sebastian Bach

Third Movement: Allegro Assai
Form: Concerto Grosso
Performing Medium: Violin, Flute, Oboe, Trumpet, and Chamber Orchestra

Compact Disc 1, Track 10
Running Time: 3:01

Bach's six Brandenburg concertos are among the most exciting examples of the concerto grosso. Concerto No. 2 features four virtuoso performers— *violin, flute, oboe,* and *trumpet*—with a small string chamber orchestra and harpsichord. Listen to the third movement. Notice how each of the four soloists contributes to the entire work. In Chapter 9, we will return to this work and discuss it in detail.

CHALLENGE YOUR EXPERTISE

Can you think of two reasons the brass section isn't in the front of the symphony orchestra?

Beethoven's Expanded Orchestra

Beethoven, who often expressed his reluctance to appear in palaces, took his music to larger halls where the middle class could gather. Consequently, a larger orchestra evolved to produce enough sound to fill the available space and to be heard by larger audiences. As orchestras moved into larger halls, composers were free to explore the expressive potential of the orchestral sound.

For his Symphony No. 1, Beethoven used an orchestra similar in size to the ones Haydn and Mozart used (see Table 5.3). A few years later, for his Symphony

The classical orchestra (18 to 30 players)

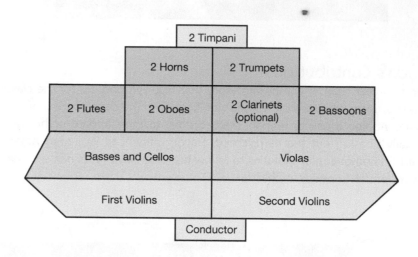

LISTENING ACTIVITY

Symphony No. 94 in G (*Surprise*), Joseph Haydn
Large Form: Symphony

Detailed Form: Minuet and Trio (Song Form and Trio)
Performing Medium: Chamber Orchestra

Compact Disc 1, Tracks 19–21
Running Time: 5:32

Listen to the third movement from Haydn's Symphony No. 94 (*Surprise*). It is derived from an eighteenth-century dance (the minuet) in a triple meter. Note the sound of this small, or chamber, orchestra.

No. 5, Beethoven added a piccolo, a contrabassoon, and three trombones, thus increasing the size and power of the orchestra.

By 1824, for his last symphony, the Ninth, Beethoven's orchestra had nearly doubled in size. Now it included new percussion instruments such as the triangle, bass drum, and cymbals (see Table 5.3). In the last movement of the Ninth Symphony, Beethoven calls for four soloist singers and a large chorus to perform with the orchestra.

Nineteenth-Century Expansion of the Orchestra

Inspired by Beethoven, other nineteenth-century composers continued to enlarge the orchestra. Berlioz added players in the wind and percussion sections. He also incorporated improved versions of existing instruments as well as newly invented instruments such as the tuba, English horn, saxophone, and contrabassoon. Berlioz was even adventurous enough to try several experimental instruments not usually found in orchestras (the ophicleide, basset horn, and Sax horn, for example). This last group of instruments was discontinued because of technical and tonal problems.

Brass Valves and Woodwind Keys   By the 1830s, many brass instruments had valves, enabling them to play in all keys. Formerly, brass instruments were largely limited to playing fanfares and bugle calls. Only a few early brass players could manage the instrument's extremely high register, where a few more pitches were

Table 5.3	Beethoven's Early, Middle, and Late Orchestras	
Symphony No. 1 (1800)	**Symphony No. 5 (1808)**	**Symphony No. 9 (1824)**
2 Flutes	1 Piccolo	1 Piccolo
2 Oboes	2 Flutes	2 Flutes
2 Clarinets	2 Oboes	2 Oboes
2 Bassoons	2 Clarinets	2 Clarinets
2 Horns	2 Bassoons	2 Bassoons
2 Trumpets	1 Contrabassoon	1 Contrabassoon
Timpani	2 Horns	4 Horns
First Violins	2 Trumpets	2 Trumpets
Second Violins	3 Trombones	3 Trombones
Violas	Timpani	Timpani
Cellos	First Violins	Triangle
Basses	Second Violins	Cymbals
	Violas	Bass Drum
	Cellos	First Violins
	Basses	Second Violins
		Violas
		Cellos
		Basses
		4 Vocal Soloists
		Large Chorus

LISTENING ACTIVITY

Symphony No. 5 in C minor (1808)
Ludwig van Beethoven
Op. 67, First Movement: Allegro con brio

Large Form: Symphony
Detailed Form: Sonata-allegro
Performing Medium: Medium-Sized Symphony Orchestra

Compact Disc 1, Tracks 28–32
Running Time: 7:18

Listen to the first movement of Beethoven's Symphony No. 5, one of the most popular symphonies in the orchestra literature. Compare the sound of the orchestra with the recording of the third movement of Haydn's Symphony No. 94. You will notice that although the instrumentation is similar, Beethoven calls for a slightly larger, more forceful orchestra. A more detailed Listening Guide appears in Chapter 12.

---

available. Bach had a specific, talented trumpet player in mind when he wrote that demanding trumpet part in his *Brandenburg Concerto No. 2*.

The trombone, which uses a telescoping slide to produce pitches, retains its basic mechanism to this day.

A new system of keying, invented in 1832 by flutist Theobald Boehm, eventually allowed flutes, clarinets, oboes, and bassoons to be played faster and with greater ease. The woodwind keys allowed the players to open holes in the body of the instrument that were formerly beyond the reach of the player's fingers.

With the capabilities of both woodwind and brass instruments, composers began creating more important musical roles for them in the orchestra, as well as for concerto performance. Though not employed as frequently as the string section in the orchestra during the nineteenth century, the woodwind and brass sections were significantly elevated in importance.

Rising Standards of Performance

Gewandhaus
(guh-*vahnd*-howse)

When composer Felix Mendelssohn accepted an appointment in 1835 as conductor of the Gewandhaus Orchestra in Leipzig, Germany, he began to transform the orchestra. He energetically recruited the best players in Europe, establishing the Gewandhaus Orchestra as the finest of its day. Living composers clamored to have the Gewandhaus Orchestra play their works, and audiences were able to hear superb performances of great masterpieces.

The Virtuoso Orchestra Emerges

Wagner
(*vahg*-ner)

Strauss
(shtrowss)

Rimsky-Korsakov
(*rim*-skee *kohr*-suh-koff)

Mahler
(*mah*-ler)

Sacre du printemps
(*sac*-ruh doo pran-*ton*)

To meet the performance demands of late-nineteenth-century composers—particularly Richard Wagner, Richard Strauss, Nikolai Rimsky-Korsakov, and Gustav Mahler—orchestras hired virtuoso performers for every section, giving us the orchestra we know today.

Then in 1913, Igor Stravinsky, for his ballet *The Rite of Spring* (*Le Sacre du printemps*), gave new prominence to the percussion section. Stravinsky calls for between 110 and 115 players for *The Rite of Spring*.

Symphonie Fantastique (Fantastic Symphony, 1830), Hector Berlioz
Fifth Movement: "Dream of a Witches' Sabbath"

Large Form: Symphony
Detailed Form: Sectional
Performing Medium: Large Symphony Orchestra

Compact Disc 1, Tracks 33–37
Running Time: 10:20

Listen to the fifth movement of Hector Berlioz's *Symphonie Fantastique* and focus on the variety of instrumental timbres in the orchestra. In addition to the woodwinds and brass used by Beethoven, you will hear chimes and a high-pitched clarinet (soprano, E-flat). To create the atmosphere of a graveyard, complete with rattling bones, Berlioz requests that the string players turn their bows around and strike the strings with the wood side. This special effect is called *col legno* (Italian, for "with wood").

A more detailed discussion and Listening Activity appear in Chapter 14.

Col legno
(cohl *leyn*-yo)

Strings (66 players)

18 first violins
16 second violins
12 violas
12 cellos
8 string basses

Woodwinds (23 players)

2 piccolos
3 flutes (third doubling as second piccolo)
1 alto flute in G
4 oboes (fourth doubling as second English horn)
2 English horns
1 clarinet in D
3 clarinets in A and B-flat
2 bass clarinets
3 bassoons
2 contrabassoons

Brass (19 players)

1 trumpet in D
4 trumpets in C (fourth doubling as bass trumpet)
1 bass trumpet in E-flat
8 horns
3 trombones
2 tubas

LISTENING ACTIVITY

The Rite of Spring, Igor Stravinsky
"Sacrificial Dance" from *Part II: The Sacrifice*

Large Form: Excerpt from a Ballet
Detailed Form: Complex Rondo or Sectional

Compact Disc 2, Track 14
Running Time: 4:33

Listen to the "Sacrificial Dance" from *The Rite of Spring* ballet by Stravinsky. Notice how the composer maintains a strong percussive drive throughout the entire piece. A more detailed discussion and Listening Guide appear in Chapter 20.

Percussion (4 to 7 players—some percussionists play more than one instrument)

   5 timpani (played by two performers)
   1 bass drum
   1 pair of symbals
   1 set of tam tam (Chinese gong)
   1 set of antique cymbals (tiny, 2$\frac{1}{2}$ to 3 inches)
   1 triangle
   1 guiro (a serrated African gourd, scraped with a stick)

The Wind Ensemble

During the twentieth century, concert bands, symphonic bands, wind orchestras, and wind bands became popular concert attractions. Consisting primarily of wind instruments and an occasional string bass, wind ensembles vary in their size and instrumentation.

John Philip Sousa (center) and the Marine Band, 1892

Since biblical times, outdoor music without string instruments has been associated with invading armies, powerful rulers, and successful conquests. Now wind ensembles are associated with pops concerts, summer outdoor concerts in park bandstands, and holiday celebrations. These ensembles bring music to masses of people who otherwise might never have the opportunity to enjoy a traditional symphony orchestra concert.

Around the turn of the twentieth century, the fine professional bands of John Philip Sousa, Arthur Pryor, and Patrick Conway spread the popularity of these ensembles throughout North America. During the world wars, bands marched in parades, provided inspiration at patriotic rallies and war bond drives, and performed concerts throughout the world.

Today, with the abundance of fine performing ensembles in high schools, colleges, and the military, contemporary composers have found a new, profitable outlet—writing music for wind bands. Wind ensembles now have a wide variety of music from which to choose their concert programs.

Keyboard Instruments

Keyboards of various sizes, sounds, and shapes have been popular since the Greeks invented a version of the organ, the water-powered *hydraulis,* sometime between 250 and 120 B.C. The *organ, harpsichord, piano,* and *electronic music synthesizer* now predominate at concert music performances.

Organ

Often called "the king of instruments," the organ is the largest and most powerful in the keyboard category. The sound from its hundreds of individual pipes fills churches such as St. Peter's in Rome, St. Mark's in Venice, St. Paul's in London, and the Washington Cathedral in Washington, D.C.

Organ performer

Early giant organs made great physical demands on the operators. For example, the organ installed in England's Winchester Cathedral in the tenth century required seventy energetic men to pump and jump and huff and puff to work the twenty-six bellows that provided air to its more than 400 pipes. The aerobics of these operators made it possible for the organist to produce music.

Today, most organs use electric energy to move the air through the pipes. Some pipes sound like woodwind instruments, others like brasses; still others produce sounds unique to the organ. The organist can select and combine any of the various pipes to create interesting timbres, similar to combining instruments in orchestration.

Most organs have at least two keyboards, and many have three or four, making it easier for the player to shift between the various combinations of pipes and timbres. Organists can produce additional tones on a pedal board, playing with their toes and heels of both feet.

Harpsichord

Until the advent of the pianoforte in the eighteenth century, European music patrons favored the harpsichord for both solo and chamber ensemble performance. Though similar in shape to a modern grand piano, the harpsichord produces its tone and sound quite differently.

Mozart at the harpsichord, with his father (violin) and his sister

LISTENING ACTIVITY

Fugue in g minor (*The Little*), BWV 578, Johann Sebastian Bach

Form: Fugue
Performing Medium: Organ

Compact Disc 1, Track 11
Running Time: 3:44

Listen to the Fugue in g minor (The Little) by Bach, composed in the early eighteenth century. Note the power and variety of sounds the organ produces. Try to imagine the famous organist Bach performing this work in one of the great cathedrals. A more detailed discussion and Listening Guide appear in Chapter 9.

When a harpsichordist strikes a key, a mechanism activates a plectrum, a picklike device made of bird quill or leather. This device plucks a string, resulting in a brittle twang. Hitting a piano key, in contrast, activates a felt-covered hammer that strikes the strings, producing full, more mellow tones.

An advantage of the harpsichord is that its lighter tone is useful for accompanying singers. A drawback to the harpsichord is that all tones have equal volume, no matter how hard the player hits the keys. To achieve a modest contrast in the volume, some harpsichordists have an additional keyboard that strikes louder-sounding strings.

Piano

Johann Sebastian Bach was not impressed by the piano collection of King Frederick the Great of Prussia. Although the monarch had specially invited Bach in 1747 to try out his array of newly invented instruments, the great master found them all in a rudimentary state of development.

LISTENING ACTIVITY

Variations, "Ah vous dirai-je, maman" K. 265, Wolfgang Amadeus Mozart ("Twinkle, Twinkle, Little Star")

Large Form: Keyboard Piece
Detailed Form: Theme and Variations
Performing Medium: Harpsichord

Compact Disc 1, Track 12
Running Time: 2:49

Listen to the sound quality of the harpsichord in this excerpt from Wolfgang Amadeus Mozart's variations on the French folk song, "Ah vous dirai-je, maman." A more detailed discussion and Listening Guide appear in Chapter 11.

LISTENING ACTIVITY

***Fantaisie Impromptu,* Frédéric Chopin**

Large Form: Short Recital Piece
Detailed Form: Three Part Form (A-B-A)
Performing Medium: Piano

Compact Disc 2, Track 3
Running Time: 4:42

Listen to the *Fantaisie Impromptu* by Frédéric Chopin. Chopin's music allows pianists to display their technical brilliance and the instrument's expressiveness.

Fortepiano
Royal Academy of Music / Lebrecht Music & Arts Photo Library

Fortepiano
(for-tay-pee-an-oh)

Starting in 1770, however, twenty years after Bach's death, piano makers began significantly improving their instruments. In a 1777 letter to his father, Wolfgang Amadeus Mozart expressed his enthusiasm about the new instruments. Having them available, Mozart later added to the growing repertoire for the piano by composing twenty-seven concertos and twenty sonatas.

By 1800, piano makers had produced an instrument very similar to the modern piano—short for *fortepiano* (meaning "loud-soft" in Italian). For the first time, a keyboard instrument had been named for its capabilities. Keyboard artists could control dynamic shadings—very soft to very loud—with the touch of their hands.

Championed by composer-performers such as Ludwig van Beethoven, Franz Schubert, Robert Schumann, Felix Mendelssohn, Frédéric Chopin, Johannes Brahms, and Franz Liszt, the piano enjoyed its golden era. With its greater expressive capabilities, it emerged as the preferred keyboard instrument of the nineteenth century, figuring prominently as a status symbol in the homes of prosperous and educated families.

Electronic Instruments

Electronic Keyboards and Synthesizers

Recently, electronic keyboards and electronic music synthesizers have paralleled the piano's popularity. However, the term *synthesizer* does not adequately describe these instruments. Early synthesizers were designed to imitate the timbre of harpsichords, organs, violins, flutes, and other instruments. They still are able to produce these sounds, but they are also capable of much more. When combined with computers, synthesizers can create virtually unlimited varieties of sounds.

Human Voice

Many people consider the human voice, with its tremendous range of sound and emotion, to be the most expressive musical instrument. Think of the differences between the jazz "scat" singer, the crooner, the rapper, the gospel singer, the pop vocalist, and the opera singer.

Computer music studio

Table 5.4	General Voice Classifications	
female voices	soprano	the highest voice
	mezzo-soprano (*met*-soh)	the next highest, usually with a slightly darker timbre (*mezzo* is "middle" in Italian)
	contralto (alto)	lowest female voice, heavier and darker timbre than soprano
male voices	tenor	the highest male voice
	baritone	lower, with darker timbre than tenor
	bass (*basso,* It.)	the lowest and darkest timbre

Classical music has several general voice classifications, as shown in Table 5.4.

Opera Singers

Additional subclassifications are used to describe the character, timbre, and type of roles, as shown in Table 5.5.

Table 5.5	Operatic Voice Classifications	
sopranos	coloratura	usually high range with great vocal agility (Olympia in Offenbach's *Tales of Hoffmann*)
	dramatic	powerful, dramatic roles (Aida in Verdi's *Aida*)
	lyric	lighter timbre; sweeter roles, ingenue— young leading lady (Mimi in Puccini's *La Bohème*)
tenors	robusto	full, powerful voice roles (the Duke in Verdi's *Rigoletto*)
	lyric	lighter timbre; smooth, lyrical singing roles (Rodolfo in Puccini's *La Bohème*)
	heldentenor (heroic tenor)	powerful, expressive, agile (Walther in Wagner's *Die Meistersinger*)
baritone-basses	profondo	deep range; powerful, solemn roles (Commendatore in Mozart's *Don Giovanni*)
	cantante	smooth, lyrical singing roles (Don Giovanni in Mozart's *Don Giovanni*)
	buffo	agile, comic roles (Leporello in Mozart's *Don Giovanni*)

LISTENING ACTIVITY

"Madamina" Aria from *Don Giovanni*, (1787)
Wolfgang Amadeus Mozart

Large Form: Opera
Detailed Form: Aria (Two-Part Song Form)
Performing Medium: Bass-Baritone
and Chamber Orchestra

Compact Disc 1, Tracks 26–27
Running Time: 5:53

Listen to the famous "Madamina." The aria from Mozart's opera *Don Giovanni* features a *basso buffo* ("comic bass" in Italian) singing the role of Leporello. Pay special attention to the quality of the singer's voice.

LISTENING ACTIVITY

La Bohème (The Bohemian Life, 1896), Giacomo Puccini

Act I (excerpt)
Form: Romantic Opera, Recitatives and Arias
Performing Medium: Soprano, Tenor, and Orchestra

Compact Disc 3, Tracks 7–10
Running Time: 12:40

This scene from Act I features two singers: a lyric soprano and a lyric tenor. Chapter 15 discusses this opera in greater detail.

Summary of Terms

Amati
bass trombone
bassoon
Boehm key system
bow
brass mutes
brass quintet
cello
chamber ensembles
clarinent
col legno
concerto
concerto grosso

contrabassoon
drums
electronic keyboards
energy source
English horn
ensembles; chamber
    ensembles
French horn
fugue
fortepiano
Gabrieli
Guarneri
Gewandhaus

instrumentation
keyboard instruments:
    electronic keyboards
    harpsichord
    organ
    pianoforte
    synthesizer
Le Sacre du printemps
Mahler
Monteverdi
mute
non-western instruments
oboe

orchestration
piccolo
pizzicato
resonating chamber
Rimsky-Korsakov
saxophone
sound effects
Stradivari
Strauss
string bass
string quartet
string trio
symphony orchestra
synthesizer
timbre
timpani

trombone
trumpet
tuba
variations
vibrating element
violin
viola
virtuoso
violincello
virtuoso orchestra
voices:
   female voices:
     coloratura
     contralto (alto)
     dramatic soprano
     lyric soprano

mezzo-soprano
soprano
male voices:
   baritone
   bass
   basso buffo
   basso cantante
   basso profondo
   heldentenor
   lyric tenor
   robusto tenor
   tenor
Wagner
Wind ensemble
Woodwind quintet

CHALLENGE YOUR EXPERTISE

- The term "movement" on a concert program refers to which of the following?

1. The orchestra enters and tunes.

2. The conductor's arms are raised.

3. A large section of a longer work is to be played.

4. The soloist enters.

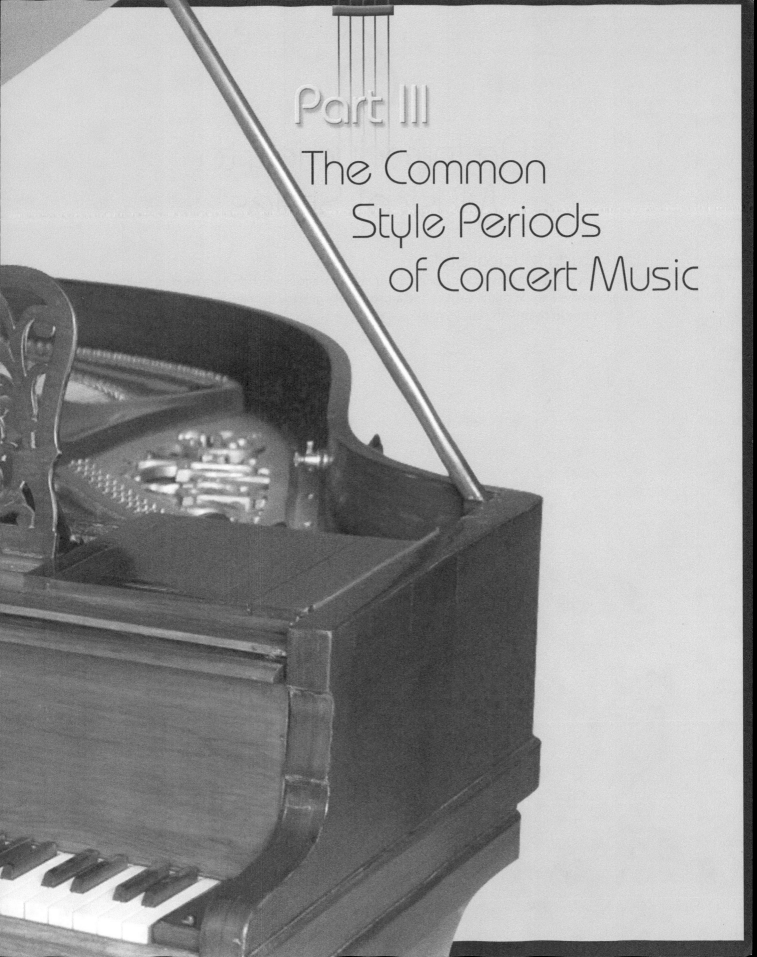

Part III
The Common Style Periods of Concert Music

6

An Introduction to Musical Styles

Why Study Musical Styles?

Musical styles reflect the tastes and cultural attitudes of the age in which they are created. People want their art to have certain characteristics, and artists usually give the people what they want—although this is less true in twentieth-century music.

Artists also influence one another and tend to use similar vocabulary in creating their works. In music, composers of the same style period tend to reflect that style. We cannot study all the works of any style period, but we can come to know the representative ones. With that foundation, we can understand music we have not yet heard.

For example, the music of Haydn and of Mozart sound similar. The more familiar you become with the compositions of these two masters, the more you'll recognize their similarities in *style*.

HISTORICAL PERSPECTIVE

Styles in the Arts

Stylistic similarities extend beyond music. Parallel trends have always existed among the other arts, philosophy, and even fashion. Artists and musicians seem to have an uncanny knack of anticipating these trends, often more accurately than business and governments do. Art not only reflects society and imitates life, but also *influences* society and changes life.

Rather than presenting all style periods since the beginning of time, we have focused our listening upon the musical styles you are most likely to hear at concerts—mainly music composed after A.D. 1600—although we will take a brief look at the music that preceded it.

Stylistic Exceptions   Not all composers of a particular age compose in a similar style. Some resist falling into the general style of their contemporaries. Others may adhere to an earlier style. Composers may express their creativity through innovation: They strive to produce new forms of expression. For instance, Finnish composer Jan Sibelius (1865–1957), though creating most of his works in the twentieth century, chose a musical style more characteristic of the preceding century. When listening to his music, you would place it in an earlier style period.

Stylistic Generalizations   Effectively describing the vast variety of composers and their music requires some generalization. As we encounter exceptions, we will point out how their music deviates from others of their time.

George Gershwin's *Porgy and Bess*

The style periods of Western art music are usually divided into eras, as follows:

THE COMMON STYLE PERIODS OF CONCERT MUSIC

Middle Ages
(Medieval)
(450–1450)

Renaissance
(1450–1600)

Today's Concert Music

Baroque
(1600–1750)

Classical
(1750–1820)

Romantic
(1820–1900)

Modernism
(1900–1970)

Post-modernism
(1970–today)

7

Music Before 1600

The Middle Ages (450–1450)

This 1,000-year span of European history begins with the decline of the Roman Empire and ends with the Renaissance. For centuries, the Roman legions had brought law, order, and stability to a vast region surrounding the Mediterranean Sea. With the gradual decline of the Roman Empire, Germanic nations captured these lands. The ensuing political and social chaos in many parts of Europe was relieved later by the growing influence of Christianity.

So dismal was the quality of life during the early Middle Ages that historians once labeled it the "Dark Ages." The late Medieval era, from A.D. 1000 onward, is sometimes called the "Age of Faith" because of the strength of the Church during those years.

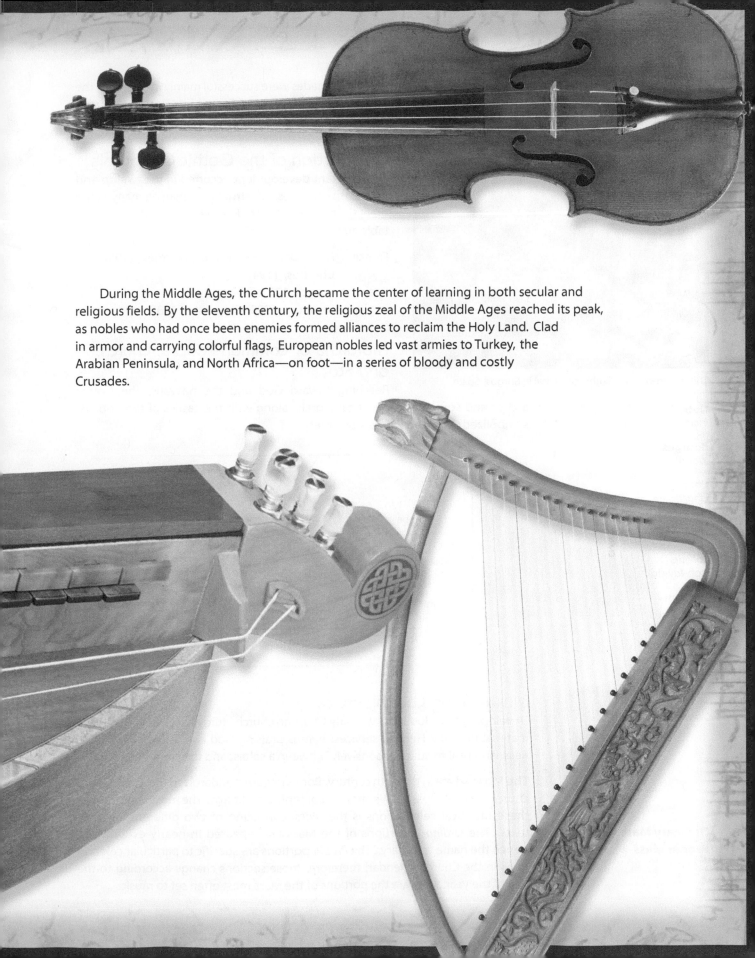

During the Middle Ages, the Church became the center of learning in both secular and religious fields. By the eleventh century, the religious zeal of the Middle Ages reached its peak, as nobles who had once been enemies formed alliances to reclaim the Holy Land. Clad in armor and carrying colorful flags, European nobles led vast armies to Turkey, the Arabian Peninsula, and North Africa—on foot—in a series of bloody and costly Crusades.

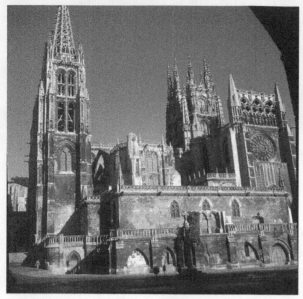

Thirteenth-century Gothic cathedral in Burgos, Spain

Notre Dame
(*noh*-truh *dahm*)

Bourges
(*boorj*)

Chartres
(*shart*)

Burgos
(*boor*-gos)

Toledo
(toh-*lay*-do)

Salisbury
(*sahlz*-burry)

Gloucester
(*glos*-tur)

The Crusades were successful mainly in changing the socioeconomic structure of Europe by weakening feudalism and expanding the cultural perspective of the people.

Construction of the Gothic Cathedrals
An important development occurred in the twelfth and thirteenth centuries: construction began on many of the great Gothic cathedrals of Europe. Among the most notable are:

France   Notre Dame (Paris), 1163; Bourges, 1195; Chartres, 1194
Spain   Burgos, 1221; Toledo, 1227
England   Salisbury, 1220; Gloucester, 1332

Hierarchy of Common People, Church, and State
Reaching toward God and the heavens, the Gothic arches and spires of the great cathedrals, along with the castles of the nobility, symbolized the medieval view of society.

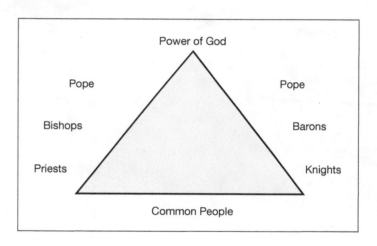

Music in the Church Service
Developing from Judaic roots, early Christian church liturgy borrowed much of its material from the Hebrew services: hymns praising God and asking for forgiveness, and psalms sung responsively between a soloist and the congregation.

Ordinary Mass
Proper Mass

The Mass   Late in the sixth century, Pope Gregory standardized the rituals of the church service as part of his efforts to organize the liturgy. The most important of these liturgical celebrations is the *Mass*, consisting of two different kinds of texts. The *Ordinary* portions of the Mass are repeated in nearly every Mass, hence the name "ordinary." The *Proper* portions are specific to particular celebrations in the Church calendar; therefore, those sections change according to the day of the year. Here are the portions of the Mass most often set to music:

Music of the Middle Ages

Gregorian Chants

The largest body of music that has survived from before the year 1000 is *Gregorian chant*, also known as *Catholic liturgical chant, plainsong, plainchant,* or simply *chant*. Its identifiable characteristic is its *monophonic texture*—a melody without harmony or accompaniment. All singers perform the same melody in unison. The texts of Gregorian chants are in Latin. Many incorporated Hebrew and Roman melodies.

Monophonic Texture

LISTENING ACTIVITY

Gregorian Chant: *Alleluia Pascha Nostrum*

Large Form: Mass Section
Performing Medium: Men's Choir

Compact Disc 1, Track 1
Running Time: 0:42

Listen to this Gregorian chant from an early Catholic Church Mass. Notice that all voices sing melody in unison—no harmony.

Since the chants used in the Catholic service were passed on mainly through oral tradition, many were lost. Gregory I (The Great), Pope from A.D. 590 to 604, charged his monks with the task of organizing the remaining monophonic chants so that they would be better preserved.

Some two centuries later, a notation system was devised to further assist in their preservation. Since Gregory's reforms saved that literature, we tend to call medieval monophonic chants "Gregorian chants," even though most of the chants used in Catholic Church services today were composed after Pope Gregory's time.

Gregorian Notation

Modern Notation (rhythm approximate)

The Beginnings of Polyphony

An important musical development began during the ninth century: a second musical line was performed with the monophonic chant. This created a texture called *polyphony*, meaning "many sounds."

One theory about the advent of polyphony is interesting, but unproven. The theory contends that men and boys were singing Gregorian chants together—the boys singing the same melody in a high range that the mature men were singing in a low range. When the soprano voices of some of the adolescent boys suddenly "cracked," this created an inner voice and a different pitch between the high part and the lower part. Church musicians called this early harmony *organum*.

organum
(*or*-guh-num)

Evidently, the monks liked the sound of organum. In addition to improvising this new line of music during performance, they began indicating it in the music written after about A.D. 1000.

Music in the Cathedral of Notre Dame

With the building of the great Gothic cathedrals in the Middle Ages came the need for larger choirs. This in turn created employment for resident cleric-composers, whose duties included composing and arranging music for church services.

Organum: Alleluia, Dies Sanctificatus, Leonin

Large Form: Mass Section
Performing Medium: Men's Choir

Compact Disc 1, Track 2
Running Time: 0:53

Leonin used polyphonic texture, assigning the original Gregorian chant to the lower voice. This excerpt is from the Proper portion of the Mass.

Notice the use of organum. The lower voice (chant) holds unusually long tones. The upper voice moves faster and more freely, creating two independent musical lines, or polyphony.

The School of Notre Dame

The School of Notre Dame   Until the construction of Notre Dame in Paris, composers had been mostly anonymous. Then, for the first time, two important music director-clerics of this new cathedral rose to prominence in the musical world—Leonin (1163–90) and Perotin (fl. 1200). Their works so influenced other church composers that they were referred to as the "School of Notre Dame."

Leonin
(lay-oh-*nan*)

Perotin
(pay-roh-*tan*)

trouvères
(tru-*vair*)

Secular Music of the Middle Ages

Examining the body of extant music before the eleventh century, you might suppose that church music was practically the only type of music that existed. We will never know. Unfortunately, most of the nonreligious, or *secular,* music for dancing, singing, and general entertainment has been lost because performers did not know how to preserve it through music notation. We know from paintings and illuminated manuscripts, however, that music formed a part of many medieval events.

Minstrels   Beginning in the tenth century, small groups of professional poet-musicians wandered the French countryside performing in castles, palaces, taverns, and town squares. These common folk, called *minstrels,* were the newscasters of their day. Their songs reported folk legends, recent events, and local gossip.

Minstrels were also the original vaudevillians—performing magic tricks, telling jokes, juggling, doing acrobatics, and exhibiting trained animals. But society treated these itinerant strangers as outcasts.

Notre Dame, Paris, side view

The Lute Player and the Harpist, engraved by Israhel van Meckenem

Dances in the Middle Ages

Interior, Notre Dame, Paris
© Michal Adamczyk/Fotolia

Perhaps minstrels did not take the time to document their songs because they were too busy struggling to make a living—and fleeing from officials.

Troubadours   Beginning in the twelfth century, some secular songs composed by troubadours were notated. Troubadours were knights in the courts of Provence in southern France. In this age of chivalry, they rhapsodized about love, the beauty of women, honor, and the Crusades.

Trouvères   Not to be outdone by their southern counterparts, noblemen in the courts of northern France composed songs in their own dialect. Known as *trouvères,* these musical poets of the twelfth and thirteenth centuries lyricized about the familiar topics of love and chivalry.

German Minnesingers   Modeled after the troubadours, German knights-of-the-court developed their own music. Love (minne, in Old German) was also the main subject for the *minnesingers'* songs. Among these are watcher's songs, which warn lovers of the approach of dawn. Many others celebrated the beauty of women and of nature.

German Meistersingers   Throughout the fourteenth, fifteenth, and sixteenth centuries, middle-class *Meistersingers* (mastersingers) built upon the minnesingers' tradition. Forming guilds, these Meistersingers established rigid rules for songwriting, just as the trade guilds had done. They even made aspiring songwriters take tests to demonstrate their adherence to "the rules."

Monophonic Notation   Although surviving medieval songs were notated in monophonic texture—melody only—literary descriptions and paintings suggest that the songs were accompanied by an instrument, usually a harp or a lute (a guitar-like instrument). Some harmony may have been used, but this is only conjecture.

Instrumental Music of the Middle Ages

Illustrations show medieval dancers accompanied by flutes, recorders, oboelike instruments (shawms), and early violins of various sizes. Some pictures show trumpets and drums, although royalty usually reserved these instruments for ceremonial purposes.

The Renaissance (1450–1600)

Rebounding from the cultural dormancy and devastation of the first wave of the Plague (Italy, 1348) and the Hundred Years' War (1337–1453) between England and France, the people turned away from the Church in favor of the secular world of art and science. Their quest for strength to cope with life led to a rebirth—the *Renaissance.*

Table 7.1	Important Composers of the Middle Ages
Troubadour Secular Songs	
Marcabru	(fl. 1128–50)
Bernart de Ventadorn	(died c. 1195)
Adam de la Halle	(c. 1250–c. 1290)
Church Music of Notre Dame	
Leonin	(c. 1163–90)
Perotin	(fl. 1200)
Church and Secular Music	
Philippe de Vitry	(1291–1361)
French prelate, composer, and theorist, known for his treatise *Ars nova* (new art), which explained early-fourteenth-century theory.	
Guillaume de Machaut	(c. 1300–77)
French court composer, cleric, and poet. Considered one of the greatest composers of the Middle Ages.	
Francesco Landini	(c. 1325–97)
One of the greatest Italian composers of the Middle Ages. Most of his compositions are *ballate,* a type of polyphonic song.	
Johannes Ciconia	(c. 1373–1412)
Born in France, Ciconia wrote church music and also secular madrigals, motets, and polyphonic vocal works.	
John Dunstable	(c. 1390–1443)
English composer who wrote mostly polyphonic music for the Mass and several secular songs.	

Statue of David by Michelangelo at the Galleria dell-Accademia, Florence, Italy

As the Middle Ages drew to a close, interest revived in ancient Greek and Roman arts and philosophy. The Renaissance inspired exploration, practical inventions, and discovery. Christopher Columbus, Vasco da Gama, and Ferdinand Magellan discovered and explored new lands; Nicolai Copernicus and Galileo Galilei expanded our knowledge of the universe through astronomy.

Humanism

In contrast to the focus on the sacred in medieval thought, the Renaissance was an age of *humanism.* As individual achievement took on a new importance, artists proudly signed their works. The humanistic spirit awakened an optimism that all things were possible and knowable.

Renaissance "Man"   Artists, philosophers, inventors, and scientists enthusiastically crossed disciplines. Niccolò Machiavelli (1469–1527), for instance, was not only a political official but a political philosopher, a historian, an essayist, and an author of the famous treatise *The Prince.*

CHALLENGE YOUR EXPERTISE

What group could be considered one of the first musicians' unions?

Leonardo da Vinci
(dah-*veen*-chee)

Perhaps the genius of Leonardo da Vinci (1452–1519) epitomizes the Renaissance. He is best remembered for his fresco *The Last Supper* and his painting *Mona Lisa*. He also provided the world with a legacy of inventions and knowledge in anatomy, architecture, hydraulics, hydrology, geology, meteorology, mechanics, machinery and gears, military weaponry and fortifications, human and avian flight, optics, mathematics, botany, and more.

Michelangelo
(mee-kehl-ahn-jeh-loh)

Leonardo's breadth of accomplishments is rivaled by that of Michelangelo Buonarroti (1475–1564), an Italian sculptor, painter, architect, and poet. His sculptures *David, Moses,* and the *Pietà*, and his paintings on the ceiling of the Sistine Chapel at the Vatican in Rome are among the greatest accomplishments in the history of Western art.

Music in the Renaissance

In contrast to the other arts, the music of the Renaissance had fewer significant innovations. As opportunities for performance increased, so did the number of composers, each contributing technical refinements.

Although religious music was still predominant, the demand for secular music increased. Court musicians were hired to entertain in the homes of the wealthy. Small instrumental groups performed in courtyards, on balconies, and in various rooms—thus, the term *chamber music.*

Sketch of helicopter by Leonardo da Vinci

Resident Court Composer With their own chapels and resident clergy, the courts of the aristocracy were self-contained. The resident court composer was responsible for supplying all music—religious music for chapel, chamber music for instrumentalists, dance music and songs for solo entertainers, and choral music for the court choir.

The Madrigal Madrigals, still performed today by small groups of singers, were composed expressly for court entertainment. Originating in the Italian courts, the first madrigals were sung in Italian. Important Italian madrigal composers were Carlo Gesualdo (1560–1613), Luca Marenzio (1553–99), and Claudio Monteverdi (1567–1643).

As madrigals spread to other countries, they were written in the language of the court. English madrigals became extremely popular during Shakespeare's time and are still performed in concerts of choral groups. Some of the leading English madrigal composers were Thomas Morley (1557–1602), Thomas Weelkes (1575–1623), and John Wilbye (1574–1638).

Romantic love, sometimes erotic love, was high on the list of favorite madrigal subjects. But many madrigals reflected on nature, and some were settings of sonnets or pious devotions.

A close-up of Michelangelo's painting of Jeremiah the Prophet at the Sistine Chapel in Rome, commissioned by the Vatican as part of the counter-Reformation.

LISTENING INSIGHTS

What to Listen For in Polyphonic Music

Polyphonic texture is sophisticated and somewhat complicated, often with four or five melodies sung or played simultaneously. During the Renaissance, one voice (or part) usually started the melody. Then a second voice picked up the melody, which was continually passed around through the several parts. As listeners, we tend to focus on the melody. In polyphonic music, that melody, or fragments of it, constantly shifts from part to part, requiring us to shift our attention with the music.

Counterpoint

In addition to the recognizable melody, composers use other connecting and supporting music—the glue that holds the work together—called *counterpoint*. Much of the beauty of Renaissance polyphony is its seamless interweaving of parts and the harmonies created both by the melody and the connecting material—like a group of independent dancers, performing separate steps yet interacting with each other.

This graphic representation of a section of four-part Renaissance polyphonic texture indicates both the imitative entrances of the melody and the connecting material:

Voice 1 MELODY —— (counterpoint) —— MELODIC IMITATION —— (counterpoint) —— **etc.**

Voice 2 MELODIC IMITATION —— (counterpoint) —— MELODIC IMITATION —— (counterpoint) —— **etc.**

Voice 3 MELODIC IMITATION —— (counterpoint) —— MELODIC IMITATION —— (counterpoint) —— **etc.**

Voice 4 MELODIC IMITATION —— (counterpoint) —— MELODIC IMITATION —— (counterpoint) —— **etc.**

GIOVANNI PIERLUIGI DA PALESTRINA (C. 1525–94)

Giovanni Pierluigi da Palestrina was born in 1525 or 1526 in Palestrina, a small town near Rome. After receiving his musical education in Rome, young Palestrina returned to his native town in 1544. There, the Bishop of Palestrina appointed him organist and choirmaster at Sant Agapito.

When his patron was elevated to Pope Julius III in 1550, Palestrina returned to Rome as the music director and choirmaster of the Cappella Giulia (Sistine Chapel) at St. Peter's. The appointment irked Vatican officials, who objected to the fact that Palestrina was married, among other issues. Therefore, after Julius's death five years later, Palestrina found it difficult to stay at St. Peter's, although he remained in Rome.

For the next six years, he was choirmaster at St. John Lateran, then moving on to a similar but more prestigious position at Santa Maria Maggiore, where he had once been a choirboy. In 1571, Palestrina returned to the Vatican, where he worked for the rest of his life.

Although Palestrina wrote secular madrigals, the great majority of his work is sacred. His compositions are considered perfectly representative of church style.

Of the many Renaissance composers, Giovanni da Palestrina stands out as one of the most respected by listeners and musicians. His seamless counterpoint is a mode of both the creativity and craftsmanship of the period.

PRINCIPAL WORKS

Sacred Vocal Music: Over 100 Masses, including *Missa Papae Marcelli* and *Missa brevis;* 375 motets; 35 Magnificat settings; 68 offertories; lamentations, litanies, sacred madrigals, and hymns.

Secular Vocal Music: Over 140 madrigals.

Palestrina
(pah-leh-*stree*-nuh)

LISTENING ACTIVITY

"Kyrie" from the Mass *De Beata Virgine,* Giovanni Pierluigi da Palestrina

Large Form: Ordinary Section of a Mass
Performing Medium: A Cappella Choir

Compact Disc 1, Track 3
Running Time: 3:37

Listen to the recording of Palestrina's late-sixteenth-century polyphonic treatment of the "Kyrie" section from the Ordinary portion of the Mass *De Beata Virgine (To The Blessed Virgin).* Four separate voice parts weave in counterpoint. The melody (*cantus,* in Latin) of this Kyrie is an old Gregorian chant, around which Palestrina added other voice parts.

Notice that the sopranos begin, and the altos enter with counterpoint. Then the tenors and basses imitate the sopranos and altos. What you hear in this style is almost constant imitation, prompting you to shift your focus to whichever voice enters with the melody.

Polyphony Continues   Characterized by many independent musical lines, polyphony continued throughout the Renaissance to dominate the musical texture of secular as well as sacred music. Creating as many as five and six parts, composers usually separated or staggered the entrances of voices. In contrast to Middle Ages polyphony, Renaissance polyphony is mostly *imitative;* that is, the voices all sing the same or a similar melody, starting at different times. This note-against-note or melody-against-melody technique is also referred to as *counterpoint.*

Important Composers of the Renaissance

Franco–Flemish Composers

Jacob Arcadelt (c. 1505–c. 1567)

   Wrote mainly *chansons* (songs) and madrigals.

Gilles Binchois (c. 1400–60)

   Composed *chansons* for the court of Philip the Good of Burgundy.

Jacobus Clemens (c. 1510–c. 1567)

   Composed mostly music for the church.

Guillaume Dufay (c. 1400–74)

   The leading composer of his day in Burgundy, Dufay wrote Masses and motets for church services and *chansons* for the courts.

Heinrich Isaac (c. 1450–1517)

   Composed both church and secular music.

Clement Jannequin (c. 1475–1560)

   Wrote mainly *chansons* for the French courts.

Claude Le Jeune (1528–1600)

   Composed motets and *chansons.*

Orlando di Lasso (1532–1594)

   Lasso, or Lassus, as he was known in Italy, was born in the Franco–Flemish north. One of the greatest composers of the period, Lasso worked in Milan, Naples, Rome, and Munich. He composed both sacred and secular vocal music.

Jacob Obrecht (c. 1452–1505)

   Composed church music and *chansons.*

Johannes Ockeghem (c. 1430–97)

   Known for his canons and intricate counterpoint, Ockeghem wrote both church and secular music.

Josquin des Prez (c. 1440–1521)

   One of the greatest composers of the Renaissance, Josquin was born in France but spent most of his productive life in Italy. He wrote both Masses and secular *chansons.*

Claudin de Sermisy (c. 1490–1562)

   Known mainly as a composer of *chansons.*

Jan Sweelinck (1562–1621)

   Mainly known for his keyboard music, Sweelinck also wrote *chansons.*

Adrian Willaert (c. 1480–1562)

   Born in the Franco–Flemish north, Willaert made his way to St. Mark's in Venice, where he was renowned as a church composer and teacher. He also composed *chansons.*

An early engraving of Orlando di Lasso

Italian Composers

Costanzo Festa (c. 1490–1545)

Composed church music at the Papal Chapel in Rome, though he is best known for his Italian madrigals.

Andrea Gabrieli (c. 1533–85)

Andrea Gabrieli preceded his nephew Giovanni as first organist at St. Mark's in Venice. He composed both church music and madrigals.

Giovanni Gabrieli (c. 1555–1612)

Composed church music, concertos, instrumental music, and madrigals. (More on Gabrieli in Chapter 9.)

Carlo Gesualdo (c. 1560–1613)

Mainly known for his innovative chromatic madrigals.

Luca Marenzio (c. 1553–99)

Known mainly for his madrigals, Marenzio also composed many sacred motets.

Claudio Monteverdi (1567–1643)

Besides his late opera works in the Baroque period, he wrote many madrigals as a young composer. (More on Monteverdi in Chapter 9.)

Giovanni da Palestrina (c. 1525–94)

Considered one of the greatest Renaissance church composers (see biography in Chapter 7).

Spanish Composers

Antonio de Cabezon (c. 1510–66)

Wrote mainly keyboard compositions.

Cristobal de Morales (c. 1500–53)

An important church composer.

Tomàs Luis de Victoria (c. 1549–1611)

The most important Spanish church composer of the period.

German Composers

Hans Leo Hassler (1564–1612)

Wrote German polyphonic *lieder* (songs) as well as church music.

English Composers

William Byrd (1543–1623)

One of the best English composers prior to the Baroque era, he composed church music, keyboard music, and songs.

John Dowland (1562–1626)

A prolific composer, Dowland wrote songs for several voices as well as music for the lute.

Thomas Morley (c. 1557–1602)

Morley is known mainly for his popular English madrigals.

Thomas Tallis (c. 1505–85)

Tallis wrote his most important works for the church.

John Taverner (c. 1490–1545)

One of England's finest church-music composers.

Thomas Weelkes (c. 1557–1623)

Weelkes wrote some of the most popular English madrigals.

William Byrd

Summary of Terms

cantus
chamber music
Chartres
counterpoint
Dark Ages
Gloucester
Gothic Cathedrals
Humanism
Leonin
liturgical chant

lute
madrigal
Mass
meistersingers
minnesingers
minstrels
Notre Dame
Old Roman chants
Ordinary Mass
organum

Palestrina
Perotin
plainchant
plainsong
Proper Mass
Salisbury Cathedral
troubadours
trouvères

Summary of Nonmusicians

Gregory I (Pope, called The Great) c. 540–604

Leonardo da Vinci (1452–1519)

Machiavelli (1469–1527)
Michelangelo (1475–1564)

8

The Baroque Style Period (1600–1750)

Protestant Reformation

When Martin Luther nailed a list of grievances on the door of Palast Church in Wittenburg, Germany, his protests included the widespread practice among Catholic clergy of selling indulgences to forgive sins and the lack of relevancy of the traditional church service. Thus, in 1517, during the Renaissance Period, the Protestant Reformation gradually challenged the omnipotence of the Church of Rome. By 1532, the Reformation had spread to Sweden, Scotland, and France, and soon after, across most of Europe.

Changing Church Service   Luther, a priest himself, doubted that his parishioners could derive full spiritual satisfaction by being merely passive observers of the traditional Latin service that the Roman

Catholic Church offered. In his own services, Luther instituted two important changes to make the liturgy more accessible to his congregation:

- *Language change* Luther translated his services from Latin into German, the language of his congregants.
- *Congregational singing* In his desire to involve the entire congregation, Luther wrote easily learned, easily sung hymns with a German text. Even those who could not read learned to sing them. (Today, most denominations throughout the world use books of hymns, or hymnals, for congregational singing.)

Portrait of Martin Luther, painted by Lukas Cranach

St. Peter's Basilica, Rome

Bernini
(bayr-*nee*-nee)

Bramante
(brah-*mahn*-tay)

The Cupola of St. Peter's in Rome

Counter-Reformation

Between 1545 and 1564, Roman Catholic church leaders met intermittently at the Council of Trent to devise strategies to deal with the Reformation. The result was the *Counter-Reformation,* which included a mandate for making the church more attractive—if not in substance, at least in image. Church leaders decided to implement this new image by enhancing eye appeal.

Baroque Façades   Highly ornate Baroque façades gave an architectural facelift to drab exteriors of older churches. Architects designed and built new, elaborate, Baroque-style churches.

One of the first projects became the showcase of the Vatican in Rome— St. Peter's Basilica (1546–1664). The exterior was completed in the early seventeenth century, with its rows of columns later designed by Gian-lorenzo Bernini (1598–1680). Michelangelo, who simplified an earlier plan by Donato Bramante (1444–1514), is largely responsible for the dome and the present appearance of the church. *Gold leaf* and colorful brocaded *tapestries* adorn the altar. Bernini and other sculptors created statues of the Trinity, Holy Family, and important saints for the interior and exterior.

Stained Glass   An important art form since the building of the great Gothic cathedrals in the Middle Ages, stained glass enjoyed a revival during this period. Baroque-style churches continued using stained-glass windows depicting scenes from the Bible. The colorful, cartoon-like scenes were useful instructional tools to help the mostly illiterate congregation understand church history and beliefs.

Counter-Reformation Succeeds

The mission of the Counter-Reformation was accomplished by 1600, and the initial impact of Protestantism had waned. Having experienced self-renewal, the Catholic Church was to play a new role in the arts from 1600 to 1750.

   CHALLENGE YOUR EXPERTISE

What were three purposes of stained-glass windows?

HISTORICAL PERSPECTIVE

Book and Music Printing

Books   Until 1453, few people had access to books or could even read. That year, Johannes Gutenberg [*goot*-en-berg] (c. 1390–1468) of Mainz, Germany, printed the first book using movable type—a bible. Printing remained a slowly developing art, so books were an expensive commodity for another 200 years. It is understandable that most people outside of the clergy or royalty had little access to the printed word.

Music   The first music was printed in 1501 by Ottaviano Petrucci (peh-*troo*-chee) of Venice. Petrucci used the Gutenberg's process of movable type.

Table 8.1	Overview of the Baroque Style Period (1600–1750)
Important Composers	Johann Sebastian Bach, Arcangelo Corelli, Giovanni Gabrieli, George Frideric Handel, Jean-Baptiste Lully, Claudio Monteverdi, Henry Purcell, Jean-Philippe Rameau, Alessandro Scarlatti, Domenico Scarlatti, Heinrich Schütz, Antonio Vivaldi
Artists	Gianlorenzo Bernini, Caravaggio, El Greco, Frans Hals, Rembrandt van Rijn, Peter Paul Rubens, Anthony Van Dyke
Writers	John Donne, John Milton, Jean-Baptiste Molière, Alexander Pope, William Shakespeare, Jonathan Swift
Philosophers	Francis Bacon, René Descartes, Thomas Hobbes, John Locke, Bernard Spinoza
Social, Political, and Cultural Events	First opera (c. 1600), Shakespeare's *Hamlet* (1600), King James version of the Bible (1611), Pilgrims land in America (1620), first opera house (1637), reign of Louis XIV (1643–1715), Newton's physical laws, beginning of Age of Enlightenment, expansion of colonialism

Sixteenth-century facade of the Gothic Duomo in Mantua, Italy

Characteristics of Baroque Style Music

General	Music often sounds heavy, grand, and expansive and often includes both singers and instruments
Performing Media	Chamber orchestras, chorus and chamber orchestra, soloist(s) and chamber orchestra, chamber ensembles, organ, harpsichord
Rhythm	Steady beats, running bass, complicated driving rhythms; meters: 2, 3, 4, 6; usually slowing of tempo at the end of the piece
Melody	Major and minor melodies; sequence, imitation, and elaborate ornamentation
Harmony	Strong harmonic movement; harmonic sequences and recurring cadences; major and minor tonalities
Expression	Contrasting layers of dynamics, echo imitation used; loud and soft juxtaposed—no crescendo or diminuendo
Texture	Mainly polyphonic, thick texture; one or more melodies in high parts with countermelodies; harmonic filler parts and continuous bass line; occasional homophony (sounding together)
Forms	Concerto, concerto grosso, suite, oratorio, cantata, opera; trio sonata and other sonatas for instruments, keyboard prelude, fugue, toccata

Summary of Nonmusicians

Bernini
Bramante
Gutenberg
Petrucci

9

Baroque Style Music
(1600–1750)

During the Renaissance, the motivation that generated cosmetic improvements in church buildings and paintings had not yet extended to church music. Even with the craftsmanship of Giovanni da Palestrina, its greatest master, Renaissance music, although beautiful, was still mostly austere, reserved, somewhat colorless, and usually performed *a cappella*—without accompaniment.

Changes Occur in the New Baroque Music

The Venice of 1600 was the commercial maritime center of the world, hosting visitors and merchants from many countries. It was also here that musical innovations in church services first appeared.

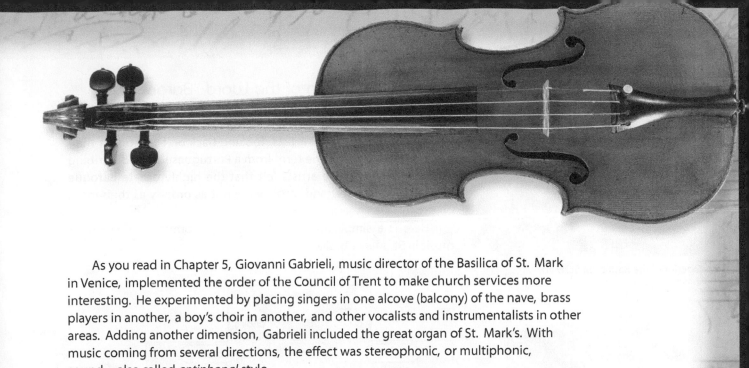

As you read in Chapter 5, Giovanni Gabrieli, music director of the Basilica of St. Mark in Venice, implemented the order of the Council of Trent to make church services more interesting. He experimented by placing singers in one alcove (balcony) of the nave, brass players in another, a boy's choir in another, and other vocalists and instrumentalists in other areas. Adding another dimension, Gabrieli included the great organ of St. Mark's. With music coming from several directions, the effect was stereophonic, or multiphonic, sound—also called *antiphonal* style.

Exterior of the Basilica of St. Mark in Venice

What Is the Origin of the Word "Baroque"?

Although we now refer to the style period between 1600 and 1750 as Baroque, the actual term *Baroque* appeared in the late eighteenth century. Classical artists, looking back on the work of their predecessors, derived the term from a Portuguese word describing irregular pearls. These artists felt that the highly ornate Baroque architecture, statues, and music were not as orderly as their more controlled art.

Here is a simplified floor plan for a performance of Gabrieli's music in St. Mark's Basilica:

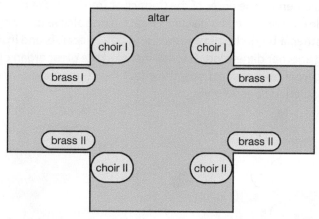

Simplified drawing of floor plan at the Basilica of St. Mark for the performance of *In ecclesiis*.

Interior of the Basilica of St. Mark in Venice

Baroque-Style Vocal Music

Concertato Style

Concertato

Concert

Concerto

Music combining vocal and instrumental ensembles was called *concertato style*. The words *concert* and *concerto* have the same root, and all three terms mean "bringing contrasting performing groups together." This type of music grew in popularity throughout the period in various genres: *opera, oratorio, cantata,* and the *Mass*. These genres are discussed later in this chapter, along with some of the great Baroque composers who championed them: Claudio Monteverdi, Heinrich Schütz, George Frideric Handel, Johann Sebastian Bach, and Antonio Vivaldi.

Baroque Opera

Opera was one of the most important innovations of the early Baroque era. The first full-length operas were staged around 1600 in northern Italy. Although drama with music existed in the Middle Ages and the Renaissance in the form of mystery plays and other liturgical dramas, nothing prepared audiences for the operas of the early 1600s. The spectacular combinations of dramatic solo singing, emotional choruses, orchestral music, scenery, and dance made opera attendance one of the most fashionable pastimes in Italy.

HISTORICAL PERSPECTIVE

The Sensory Appeal of the Catholic Church Service

During the Baroque period, sound (music) joined the other senses in appealing to the congregation. All five senses were now involved:

sound	rich blends of voices, keyboards, and instruments; bells during the service
sight	elaborate statues; gold-leafed altar; stained-glass windows; ceiling and wall frescoes; ornate, brocaded, jeweled vestments; huge candles; choreographed movement of the priests, altar boys, and congregation
taste	the flavor of the wine and the wafer during Holy Communion
touch	the handling of the rosary beads; contact with holy water; the feel of the benches, floor, wine, and wafers
smell	the aroma of burning candles and incense

Venice and Florence hosted some of the earliest opera performances. Claudio Monteverdi, after the success of his *Orfeo* (1607), moved opera from elite court performances to increasingly larger public audiences. The first opera house, open to the general public as well as to the aristocracy, was built in Venice in 1637.

Characteristics of Early Opera

Perhaps Monteverdi's operas have timeless appeal because they contain most of the same characteristics found in more contemporary operas.

Libretto   The *libretto* ("little book" in Italian) is the story or play upon which the opera is based. Some of the earliest opera stories were adaptations of classic Greek dramas, such as *Orfeo* (Orpheus) and *The Return of Ulysses to His Country*. Since then, composers have used stories from later times, including their own.

Libretto

Although opera quickly spread to England and France, the Italian language remained the favorite until the eighteenth century. Not only had the opera tradition developed in Italy, but for many years Italian was considered the most suitable language for singing. Today, an opera can be performed in any language. As a result of the unusual popularity of opera, some are translated from the original into the language of the country where the performance takes place.

Soloists   Rarely are lines spoken in opera; therefore, principal characters must be trained singers. The variety of voices—sopranos, altos, tenors, and basses—adds interest to the production.

Early opera, however, occasionally used male voices in female roles. Only in the more enlightened and principal operatic centers, such as Venice, were women allowed on stage. (In England, this was also the custom for plays by William Shakespeare [1564–1616], Monteverdi's contemporary.)

Several of the male protagonists' roles—heroes, generals, and so on—called for an extremely high range. Often, a *castrato* would sing this type of role. To ensure a supply of virtuoso singers, opera producers in the seventeenth and eighteenth centuries arranged for the castration of boys before their voices changed.

Castrato

CLAUDIO MONTEVERDI (1567–1643)

The birthplace of Claudio Monteverdi (mohn-teh-vehr-dee) was Cremona, Italy, the famous violin-making center. Monteverdi began his music career as a string player, later becoming *maestro di cappella* (music director) at the court of Mantua. *Orfeo* (1607), Monteverdi's earliest opera, premiered in Mantua, then played in Venice.

Soon after Giovanni Gabrieli's death in 1612, Monteverdi replaced him at St. Mark's in Venice, the most prestigious appointment in Italy at that time. There, Monteverdi quickly established a reputation for his operas as well as for his religious music. Unfortunately, many of his operas have been lost.

During 1630 and 1631, Venice suffered heavy losses from the Plague. To give thanks for its passing, Monteverdi wrote a stirring *Gloria* in concertato style. Soon after, he took holy orders in the Church and spent approximately ten years concentrating primarily on sacred music.

In his later years, Monteverdi returned to opera. His last opera, *L'incoronazione di Poppea* (The Coronation of Poppea), which premiered in Venice in 1642, is still in the repertoire of today's opera companies.

PRINCIPAL WORKS

Operas: *Orfeo* (1607), *Arianna* (1608), *Il ritorno d'Ulisse in patria* (The Return of Ulysses to His Country, 1640), *L'incoronazione di Poppea* (The Coronation of Poppea, 1642)

Secular Vocal Music: Nine books of madrigals for five to eight voices and instruments, twenty-five Scherzi Musicali for voices and instruments, canzonettas

Sacred Vocal Music: *Vespers* (1610), *Gloria* (1631) for voices and instruments, Masses, and psalms

---

Apparently, a boy who was a candidate for castrato had to have an unusual timbre: the upper range of a woman and the voice and power of a boy.

You may wonder why anyone would subject himself to castration, or how a boy's parents could consent to such an operation. To understand this practice, keep in mind that opera singers were major celebrities, with all the advantages that come with stardom. Therefore, many poor families, foreseeing a financially secure future for their children, agreed to the uncomfortable operation.

By the late eighteenth century, when women were permitted on stage to sing the female roles, the castrato gradually became a rarity. (Moreschi, the last of the castrati, died in 1922.)

Bel Canto

Bel Canto   Operatic *Bel Canto* ("beautiful singing" in Italian) represents the lilting flow of the melody, often containing elaborate embellishments improvised at the time of performance. To perform *bel canto,* a singer must be capable of a highly expressive delivery, which requires extensive training. Thus, when *bel canto* emerged in seventeenth-century Venice, so did employment opportunities for teachers of vocal technique. Venice became the European center for the training of singers.

Recitativo   To advance the story of the opera more quickly, opera composers used the technique of *recitativo* (recitative), a speechlike style of singing. Because singing takes more time than dialogue, the recitative offers an effective compromise between talking and singing. The accompanying orchestra or keyboard instruments usually are lighter than for arias because the text or story is most important in the recitative.

Aria   The solo song, or *aria*, began to dominate opera soon after its inception. In the aria, the vocal power, virtuosity, and expressiveness of the singer can be given free reign. Even today, the prospect of hearing a great performer deliver a magnificent solo draws enthusiastic audiences to opera productions. In some cases, a few good arias have made the difference between an opera's success or failure.

Aria Form   By the early thirteenth century, operas often contained a series of arias, connected by recitative. These arias usually have a three-part form:

A	B	A

A Section: Highly melodic, minimum of ornamentation.

B Section: Contrasts of mood, tonality, or change of tempo.

A Section: Repeat of the first section. Singer is free to improvise, ornament, or embellish the original melody.

Ensembles (Duets, Trios, Quartets)   *Duets, trios,* and *quartets* are songs for two, three, and four singers. Often using the same three-part form (A-B-A) as arias, these multivoice songs add dramatic interest and musical variety to the opera.

Choruses   Even in the earliest Greek plays, *choruses* of singers or choral speakers added depth to the drama by providing commentary on the action. In opera, the chorus adds realism and drama to the plot. Chorus members play the parts of soldiers, peasants, courtiers, onlookers, and others. The music provides balance and contrast to the solo singing.

Overture   Monteverdi pioneered the use of the orchestra to provide an overture or introduction to the opera and to play musical interludes during the performance. To establish a mood, he introduced evocative sounds in the orchestra, such as *tremolo* and *pizzicato* (see Glossary).

   As accompaniment for recitatives and arias, Monteverdi and his contemporaries preferred only a few instruments, or just a lute or a harpsichord. Because the earliest operas were performed in rooms without an orchestra pit, a full ensemble probably would have overpowered the singers, and the audience would have had difficulty understanding the text. By Handel's time, singers performed on elevated stages, making it possible for an orchestra and a harpsichord to accompany recitatives, arias, and choruses.

Recitativo
(reh-chee-tah-*tee*-voh)

Aria

Overture

Tremolo
(*treh*-mo-loh)

Oratorio

Baroque Oratorio

Another popular vocal form, the *oratorio*, developed during the late Renaissance. The name derives from the small prayer chapel, or oratorio, within the church where these works were first performed.

Two outstanding composers of oratorios were Heinrich Schütz and George Frideric Handel. They set bible stories to music in response to the Protestant movement's goal to reach parishioners.

HISTORICAL PERSPECTIVE

Use of Italian Terms in Music

You may wonder why music uses so many Italian terms, especially for expression and tempo indications. Some examples are *piano, allegro,* and *rallantando* (see Glossary). After Gabrieli introduced these terms, European composers who had come to Venice to study with him brought the new terms back to their native countries. Italian soon became the international language of music.

Since Gabrieli's time, the vocabulary has greatly expanded. In addition to Italian, composers occasionally use their native languages. This, of course, makes the description less universal than Italian and may pose interpretation problems to performers who are not conversant in a particular language.

HEINRICH SCHÜTZ (1585–1672)

From early childhood in his native Saxony, Germany, Heinrich Schütz (*shoots*) exhibited talent as a singer. When Prince Moritz, ruler of Hesse-Kassel, stayed overnight at the Schütz family inn, thirteen-year-old Heinrich sang for him. As a result, the prince invited the boy to live at the Kassel court and to sing in the choir.

Heinrich did well at court, and Prince Moritz, a composer himself, later subsidized Heinrich's traveling to Italy to study with Giovanni Gabrieli. Once in Venice, Schütz became one of Gabrieli's favorite pupils. After Gabrieli's death in 1612, Schütz returned to Germany to become

Kapellmeister, music director, at the Lutheran court of Dresden. There, Schütz carried on the polychoral work of his Venetian master, working Gabrieli's style into the Lutheran service.

Unfortunately for Schütz, the Dresden court was constantly overburdened with debts. He was poorly paid and miserable because he was never allowed to change positions. Finally, after fifty-five years of servitude, Schütz was released from his Dresden position. He continued composing until his death two years later at 70.

PRINCIPAL WORKS

Oratorios: *Christmas Oratorio* (1664), *The Seven Last Words of Christ on the Cross* (1657)

Passions: *St. Matthew* (1666), *St. Luke* (1666), *St. John* (1666)

Secular Vocal Music: *Italian madrigals* (1611)

GEORGE FRIDERIC HANDEL (1685–1759)

George Frideric Handel was born in Halle, Germany, near Berlin, into a family of clergy and doctors who concentrated their efforts on financial security rather than on the arts. His father, who died a week before George's twelfth birthday, encouraged his son to study law. But an event two years earlier influenced Handel profoundly.

Hearing that his father planned a short trip to visit his older son Karl, valet to Duke Johann Adolf, 10-year-old George asked to go along. When his father left without him, a disappointed but determined young Handel followed after his father's carriage on foot until he caught up with him. During the visit, George stayed in the palace chapel. Although he had studied music for only two years, Handel sat down at the organ and began to play. The duke heard his playing and was sufficiently impressed to present the boy with a gift of money. The elder Handel allowed his son to use the gift for music lessons.

At eighteen, Handel entered the University of Halle, and within a few weeks, he accepted a one-year contract to be church organist of the Domkirche—a position that provided a salary, lodging, and prestige. Money was not an issue for Handel: he had an income from his father's estate. So when his contract expired, he left Halle for Hamburg, a lively, sophisticated, wealthy commercial center. In addition to church-supported music, Hamburg had a magnificent opera house with 1,675 seats. Handel worked as a violinist in the opera orchestra. His first opera, *Almira,* was a success when it premiered there in January 1705.

In 1706, after his fourth opera, Handel left Hamburg to study composition with Italian opera composers. He arrived in Florence, but because it was not a center of music, Handel went on to Rome. There he met the violinist and conductor Arcangelo Corelli, whose techniques for bowing and managing an orchestra impressed Handel. Corelli insisted on the highest professional standards: An orchestra must behave and perform as an ensemble, with accuracy and consistency.

Venice, the opera center of the world, completely charmed Handel. He remained there until early 1708. Then he returned to Palazzo Bonelli in Rome, the home of Marchese Ruspoli, who became his patron. Ruspoli commissioned Handel to compose an oratorio for Easter, which was six weeks away. The two performances of *The Resurrection* were well received.

Handel returned to Germany with a pocketful of letters of recommendation. In June 1710, George the Elector of Hannover appointed him *Kapellmeister* (music director). But Handel needed more activity than Hannover could offer, so he obtained a one-year leave of absence to go to London. There, his music had its first local performance in early December at the famous Haymarket Theatre. In February 1711, his opera *Rinaldo* had its successful premiere at the Queen's Theatre.

Handel reluctantly returned to Hannover, using his time there to learn English. In the autumn of 1712, the Elector again granted Handel permission to return to London on the condition that he return promptly. Once back in London, Handel ignored his promise for two years.

Then, a coincidence caused an embarrassing predicament between 32-year-old Handel and his employer. Following the death of Queen Anne in 1714, King George I ascended to the throne—the same George who had been Elector of Hannover. Rather than create an unpleasant confrontation, George accepted Handel's apology and to show there were no hard feelings, doubled his salary.

In 1720, Handel became the director of the newly opened Royal Academy of Music. In addition to composing, his responsibilities took him all over Europe to audition opera singers. His operas, including *Giulio Cesare* and *Rodelinda,* premiered at the Academy.

After Handel's long career that brought wealth and fame, mainly as an opera and oratorio composer, his health declined. Although losing his eyesight, he continued to conduct and to perform at the keyboard but composed very few works during his last years. Handel remained in London until his death at 74.

PRINCIPAL WORKS

Operas: Over forty operas in Italian. *Rinaldo* (1711), *Giulio Cesare* (1724), *Rodelinda* (1725), *Alcina* (1735), and *Serse* (1738)

Oratorios: Over thirty oratorios. *Athalia* (1733), *Alexander's Feast* (1736), *Saul* (1739), *Israel in Egypt* (1739), *Messiah* (1742), *Samson* (1743), *Judas Maccabaeus* (1747), and *Solomon* (1749)

Secular Vocal Music: Over 100 Italian cantatas; trios, duets, and songs

Instrumental Music: *Water Music* (1717) and *Music for Royal Fireworks* (1749), six concerti grossos, Op. 3 (1734), twelve grand concertos, Op. 6 (1740), and organ concertos

Chamber Music: Trio sonatas for recorder, flute, oboe, and violin

Keyboard Music: Harpsichord suites, chaconnes, airs, preludes, and fugues

Handel's Oratorios

Handel earned his reputation as a German composer of Italian-style operas for English audiences, but he owed the success of his later career to the oratorio. In 1728, after John Gay's *The Beggar's Opera* in English, London audiences began to lose interest in Italian-language opera. Handel maintained his stature as the most popular composer in London by switching to composing oratorios with English text.

A financial consideration also motivated him. The Church of England banned all stage productions during the pre-Easter season of Lent. Oratorios, however, fit into a loophole. They had religious subject matter; they contained no acting, costumes, or staging; and they were usually performed in churches. Therefore, oratorios were permitted.

Immediately acclaimed, Handel's oratorios played throughout Lent, indulging London audiences in their desire to be entertained. Handel's appeal also extended to London's large Jewish population, which enjoyed his Old Testament oratorio subjects: *Solomon, Judas Macabbaeus, Israel in Egypt,* and others.

The English Baroque Soloists relaxing after a performance

LISTENING ACTIVITY

"For Unto Us a Child Is Born," George Frideric Handel Chorus from *Messiah* (1741)

Large Form: Oratorio
Detailed Form: Sectional
Performing Medium: Chorus and Chamber Orchestra

Compact Disc 1, Track 4
Running Time: 4:16

The sectional form can be charted as follows:

Orchestra Introduction	A B C	A B C	A B C	A B C	Orchestra Coda

Messiah, the oratorio Handel wrote more than 250 years ago, gives us a glimpse of his genius for writing exhilarating choral music. Note the extensive use of imitation and sequences in the vocal parts. Notice also how Handel's music reflects the text. For the opening text, "For unto us, . . ." the music is more aggressive.

The climax of the chorus comes with the musical fanfare, "And the government shall be called Wonderful, Counsellor, the mighty God, the everlasting Father, the Prince of Peace."

LISTENING GUIDE

"For Unto Us a Child Is Born," George Frideric Handel Chorus from Messiah (1741)

INSTRUMENTAL INTRODUCTION

4   0:00   MAIN MELODY   A   violin section of the orchestra; moderate tempo; 4 meter; *f*, major tonality; basso continuo

0:14   MAIN MELODY   A   sopranos enter, ***p***; accompanied by orchestra, moves with sequences, "For unto us . . ."

SOPRANOS

For un - to us a Child is   born,   un - to   us   a Son is giv - en,

| 0:28 | MAIN MELODY | A | imitated by tenors, *p*; "For unto us . . ." |

0:31	MAIN MELODY	A	imitated by sopranos, then running sixteenth-note counterpoint, "For unto us a Child is Born . . ."
0:44	MAIN MELODY	A	imitation by altos, *p*; imitated by basses, running sixteenth-note counterpoint in basses, "For unto us . . ."
1:04	SECOND MELODY	B	stated by tenors, *mf*; imitated by sopranos, then altos and basses together

1:21	FANFARE THEME	C	chorus and orchestra together, homophonic texture, *ff*; violins with steady sixteenth notes.
1:34	MAIN MELODY	A	stated by altos, *p*; imitated by altos and tenors *f*; then running sixteenth-note counterpoint in tenors, "For unto us . . ."
1:48	SECOND MELODY	B	stated by altos, *mf*; imitated by basses, "And the government . . ."
2:03	FANFARE THEME	C	all voices and orchestra homophonically, *ff*; violins steady sixteenth notes, "Wonderful, Counsellor . . ."

2:15	MAIN MELODY	A	sung by tenors, **p**; similar to beginning with imitations by the soprano, alto, and basses; "For unto us . . . "
2:33	SECOND MELODY	B	started by tenors; **mf**; imitated by sopranos, then altos and basses together; "And the government . . . "
2:51	FANFARE THEME	C	All voices and orchestra, homophonically, **ff**; violins steady sixteenth notes, "Wonderful, Counsellor . . . "
3:04	MAIN MELODY	A	sung by basses; **f**; imitated by sopranos, altos, and tenors together; followed by altos and tenors singing running sixteenth-note counterpoint together with strings; "For unto us . . . "
3:20	SECOND MELODY	B	stated by sopranos, quickly imitated by altos, imitated by tenors and basses together, then all voices together homophonically, "And the government . . . "
3:34	FANFARE THEME	C	all voices and orchestra together homophonically, **ff**; "Wonderful Counsellor . . ."
3:50			Chorus section ends with a cadence.

CODA

| 3:54 | MAIN MELODY | A | orchestral restatement, **ff**; cadence with ritardando (slowing down) |
| 4:11 | Final chord held. | | |

HISTORICAL PERSPECTIVE

Handel's Messiah

Handel composed *Messiah* in only twenty-four days—an amazing feat for a three-hour work containing some of the grandest music ever written. Waving off food and often sleep, Handel worked feverishly to complete the monumental work.

In April 1742, the public first heard the work in Ireland at Dublin's Music Hall. Handel staged a special preview there during an open rehearsal to build the public's anticipation for a formal premiere a few days later. His strategy worked. So great was the clamor for tickets after the preview that hundreds of people had to be turned away.

Dublin's Music Hall had no seats. Those attending *Messiah* had to stand for hours. In the interest of space, comfort, and additional sales, ticket holders were alerted in advance: women were not to wear their customary hoops; men had to forgo their swords. Despite these minor inconveniences, *Messiah* was a huge success. In fact, a special charity performance of the oratorio at the Dublin Cathedral raised enough money to free 142 people from debtors' prison.

Today, at concert performances of *Messiah*, audiences often stand during the "Hallelujah" chorus. This practice goes back to Handel's day when King George II, inspired by that section, rose to his feet. His subjects dutifully followed, thus inaugurating the tradition.

Messiah was first performed in New York in 1770. Since then, cities in North America have joined those throughout the world in presenting it during the holiday season. Fans of *Messiah* can participate in sing-along performances with professional choruses and orchestra. Watch your local newspapers for this opportunity.

Cantata
(can-*tah*-tuh)

Performance of a Lutheran
cantata

Baroque Cantata

The cantata, another popular vocal form during the Baroque period, features soloists, chorus, and orchestra. Although similar to the oratorio both in style and general format (see comparison, summarized in Table 9.1), the cantata is much shorter than the oratorio.

Secular Cantata   Cantatas performed as part of the Lutheran Church service usually glorified New Testament subjects. Secular cantatas, however, used popular themes. Bach's charming "Coffee Cantata" is an example of a secular cantata. He wrote this work for a Collegium Musicum student choir that assembled regularly at Zimmermann's Coffee House in Leipzig. The text, a comedy by the poet Picander, asserts women's desire to partake in the pleasure of drinking coffee and their objections to being excluded from the cafés.

Use of Chorales in the Baroque Lutheran Cantata   Simple hymns or chorales, an important part of the Lutheran Church service during the Baroque period, were usually incorporated into the cantata. Martin Luther himself was a lover of music, a singer, and a composer. He felt strongly that the congregation should take part in the musical portion of the service. To that end, Luther composed many chorales for his own services.

Luther's original chorales included only a text and melody—no harmony—and were intended for the congregation to sing in unison. Subsequent Lutheran Church composers harmonized the original chorales. Of all these, Bach's harmonizations are the most famous.

Table 9.1	Baroque Opera, Oratorio, and Cantata Compared		
	Opera	**Oratorio**	**Cantata**
text or plot	usually secular	religious, Old and New Testament	religious and secular
language	Italian	local language	local language
staging	yes	no	no
scenery	yes	no	no
costumes	yes	no	no
characters	yes	yes	yes
acting	yes	no	no
soloists	yes	yes	yes
overture	yes	yes	yes
recitatives	yes	yes	yes
arias	yes	yes	yes
duets, trios	yes	yes	yes
chorus	yes	yes	yes
orchestra	yes	yes	yes
keyboard	harpsichord	organ/ harpsichord	organ harpsichord

LISTENING INSIGHTS

What to Listen for in Baroque Music

To get the most out of listening to Baroque music, try to follow its use of basic elements and its grand sweep. Much of the music combines soloists, choirs, and instruments, producing a large, colorful sound. Like the highly ornamented palaces and churches of its time, Baroque music is busy—many things are going on at the same time. The characteristic overlapping lines of music—polyphonic texture—require the listener to follow the many entrances of ideas. It is similar to a play, with many actors on stage all speaking at once. Each comes forward with an idea, then steps out of the way to let the next one move forward, usually expressing the same idea.

The melodic movement relies heavily on three ingredients: repetition, imitation, and sequences. Try listening for these elements and you'll notice how frequently all three are used: long passages of sequences and imitations, and sections repeated exactly.

In addition to the polyphonic texture, the music often has an instrumental background support, consisting of a plodding or continuous bass line and harmonic fill lines in other parts.

Listen also for the rhythmic drive, which makes Baroque music lively and appealing.

JOHANN SEBASTIAN BACH (1685–1750)

Born in Eisenach, Germany, into a distinguished family of professional musicians, Johann Sebastian Bach (*bahk*) lived and worked throughout his life within a 100-mile radius of his birthplace. The Bach family took great pride in having been elevated to the middle class, a status that included the opportunity to attend university. They also took seriously the responsibility of preparing each new generation of the family for a career in music. Bach received most of his musical training from his oldest brother, Johann Christoph, an organist, with whom Bach lived after he was orphaned at age 10.

At 18, Bach secured his first appointment—violinist in the small, private orchestra of Duke Johann Ernst of Saxe-Weimar. But the assignment also relegated him to a variety of menial, subservient tasks unrelated to music. Realizing that quitting the post could damage his reputation, Bach instead resisted those tasks until, less than a year later, the court dismissed him. However, he was to return to Weimar five years later.

During the interval, Bach served four years as church organist in Arnstadt and one year at St. Blasius in Muhlhausen. It was in Arnstadt that Bach and a cousin

from his father's side, Maria Barbara, caused a stir. Maria Barbara, a singer, appeared as soloist for vocal pieces Bach had composed for the church service. Church officials objected: There had been no precedent in Arnstadt for a woman to be a soloist. Bach was able to withstand the criticism, and later, he and Maria Barbara were married.

Under Duke Wilhelm Ernst, the arts thrived in Weimar. The new duke appreciated and encouraged his organist, and Bach composed hundreds of organ works to play for him. The duke also acquired Italian musical works for his court orchestra, including compositions by Antonio Vivaldi, whose concerto structure greatly impressed Bach.

In 1717, when Bach did not receive a promotion to *Kapellmeister*, the top post for a musician at court, he indignantly requested his release. Angered by this request, the duke sent Bach to prison, where he remained for four weeks until the duke dismissed him.

Soon afterward, Prince Leopold of Cöthen hired Bach as his court *Kapellmeister*. Bach was very productive, composing *The Well-Tempered Clavier* for harpsichord, secular cantatas, orchestral music for chamber ensembles, concertos, and duo and trio sonatas. On a trip to Berlin to find a new harpsichord, Bach gave a command performance at the palace of Christian Ludwig of Brandenburg. Two years later (1721), Bach sent Ludwig six concertos for the court orchestra—the famous *Brandenburg* Concertos.

After the death of Maria Barbara, Bach remarried in 1721. He dedicated a book of clavier works to his new wife, Anna Magdalena. From these two marriages, Bach fathered many children, several of whom pursued a career in music.

In May 1723, Bach and his family arrived in Leipzig, where he assumed the prestigious post of Kantor of St. Thomas School. The post included music directorship for the city of Leipzig and its four principal churches. Bach also was director of the Collegium Musicum, which gave weekly performances throughout the year.

It was in Leipzig that Bach composed some of his greatest works, including *St. Matthew Passion* (1727). He began his *Mass in b minor* and, in 1733, submitted the "Kyrie" and "Gloria" as part of his application for the post of court composer for the King of Poland. Bach received that appointment, which he maintained in addition to his post in Leipzig. Under the patronage of Poland's Roman Catholic king, Bach was able to complete the *Mass* in 1749.

Bach remained in Leipzig until his death at age 65. Although blind (like Handel) in his last years, Bach remained an active composer and performer.

PRINCIPAL WORKS

Sacred Choral Music: *St. John Passion* (1724), *St. Matthew Passion* (1727), *Christmas Oratorio* (1734), *Mass in b minor* (1749), *Magnificat in D* (1723), nearly 300 church cantatas: No. 4 "Christ lag in Totesbanden" (Christ lay in the bonds of death, 1724), No. 80 "Ein feste Burg" (A mighty fortress, 1730), No. 140 "Wachet auf" (Sleepers, wake!, 1731), motets, chorales, sacred songs, arias

Secular Vocal Music: Over thirty cantatas: No. 211 "Coffee Cantata" (1732), No. 212 "Peasant Cantata" (1742)

Orchestral Music: *Brandenburg* Concertos 1–6 (1721), four orchestral suites (1725, 1731), harpsichord concertos, sinfonias

Chamber Music: six sonatas and partitas for solo violin (1720), six sonatas for violin and harpsichord (1723), six suites for solo cello (1720), *Musikalisches Opfer* (*Musical Offering*, 1747), flute sonatas, trio sonatas

Keyboard Music: Chromatic fantasia and fugue (1720), "The Well-Tempered Clavier" (1722, 1742), "Goldberg Variations" (1741), six English Suites (1724), six French Suites (1724), six partitas (1731), Italian Concerto (1734), French Overture (1735), *The Art of the Fugue* (1745), 600 chorale preludes, hundreds of preludes and fugues, inventions, suites, concertos, dances, toccatas, fantasias, and sonatas

LISTENING ACTIVITY

Cantata No. 140, "Wachet Auf" (1731, Wake Up!)
"Opening Chorus," Johann Sebastian Bach

Large Form: Cantata
Detailed Form: Sectional
Performing Medium: Chorus and Chamber Orchestra

Compact Disc 1, Tracks 5–6
Running Time: 6:06

In an elaborate, lively setting, Bach employs the Lutheran *chorale melody* written by Philip Nicolai in 1597. Notice the use of the animated polyphonic texture combined with instrumental accompaniment. After an instrumental introduction, the sopranos sing Nicolai's chorale melody. Then, different sections of the choir imitate the melody.

Notice how Bach's music emphasizes the action words employed in the text: *Wake up! Where? Cheer up! Stand up! Prepare yourselves! Go forth!*

Wachet auf, ruft uns die stimme	Wake up! Call to us the voices
Der Wächter sehr hoch auf der zinne,	Of watchmen high on the tower,
Wach' auf, du Stadt Jerusalem!	Wake up, thou town Jerusalem!
Mitternacht heisst diese Stunde;	It is now the hour of midnight;
Sie rufen uns mit hellem Munde:	They call us with shining faces;
Wo seid ihr klugen Jungfrauen?	Where are you now, clever maidens?
Wohl auf, der Bräut'gam kommt,	Cheer up! The Bridegroom [Jesus] comes,
Steht auf, die Lampen nehmt! Alleluja!	Stand up, and take your lamps! Hallelujah!
Macht eich tereit zu de Hochzeit,	Prepare yourselves, the wedding nears,
Ihr musset ihm ensprungen gehn.	You must go forth to welcome Him.

LISTENING GUIDE

Cantata No. 140, *"Wachet Auf"* (1731, Wake Up!)
"Opening Chorus," Johann Sebastian Bach

INTRODUCTION

5   0:00   INTRODUCTION THEME   orchestra; *mf*; triple meter; moderate tempo; dotted-rhythm ("long, short"); major tonality; alternating rhythms; polyphonic texture; basso continuo

0:07   INSTRUMENTAL COUNTERMELODY   alternating imitations between violin and oboe

Chorus

0:28   CHORALE MELODY   sung by sopranos; "Wachet auf" (Wake up!); polyphonic texture; counterpoint imitations by altos, then tenors, then basses

0:43	INTRODUCTION THEME	alternating imitations between oboe and strings
0:46	INSTRUMENTAL COUNTERMELODY	alternating imitations between violins and oboe
0:49	CHORALE MELODY	long note values; new text; "der Wachter" (the watchmen), sung by sopranos, other voices in counterpoint
1:05	INSTRUMENTAL COUNTERMELODY	instrumental interlude, alternating imitations between violin and oboe
1:15	CHORALE MELODY	sung by sopranos, "Wach'auf" (Wake up!), other voices in counterpoint
1:31	INTRODUCTION THEME	instrumental interlude, similar to opening
1:59	CHORALE MELODY	sung by sopranos, "Mitternacht" (Middle of the night), other voices in counterpoint
2:36	INSTRUMENTAL COUNTERMELODY	alternating imitations by violin and oboe
2:45	CHORALE MELODY	sung by sopranos, "wo, wo" (where? where?), other voices in counterpoint
3:04	INSTRUMENTAL COUNTERMELODY	alternating between violin and oboe
3:23	CHORALE MELODY	sung by sopranos, "Wohl auf" (Cheer up!), other voices in counterpoint
3:41	CHORALE MELODY	sung by sopranos, "Steht auf" (Stand up!)
6 3:57	ALLELUJA	sung by altos; imitated by tenors, then basses, then sopranos

Coda (A)

4:33	INTRODUCTION THEME AND ORCHESTRAL INTERLUDE	
4:41	CHORALE MELODY	sung by sopranos, "Macht euch" (Prepare yourselves!), other voices in counterpoint, chorus section, ends with cadence
5:33	INTRODUCTION THEME WITH INSTRUMENTAL COUNTERMELODY	exactly like opening, slowing tempo for the final cadence
6:02	FINAL CHORD	*f*; major tonality

HISTORICAL PERSPECTIVE

Evolution of Public Concerts: The Baroque Period

Today, we use the term *concert* for all kinds of public music performance: Anyone can buy a ticket and attend. However, before the Baroque period, attendance at concerts—presented in academic settings or private residences—was restricted to a privileged few. Public concert halls were virtually unheard of. Only in church could common people hear performances of fine music.

Venice: The First Opera House   Opera marked the first important breakthrough in offering music performances to the general public. The milestone was the opening of Teatro San Cassiano in 1637 in Venice. As a major commercial trading center, Venice attracted merchants from all over the world. Its lively economy helped create a thriving middle-class population, eager and able to pay for entertainment and exposure to the arts. By 1700, with its seventeen opera houses, Venice had become the opera capital of the world.

London Starting in 1672 and continuing for six years, the public could attend the first nonopera performances in London's Whitefriars. Building on the popularity of those afternoon concerts, a London coal merchant named Thomas Britton sponsored weekly performances in his storehouse loft. These "Coal-House Concerts" began in 1678 and continued for thirty-six years.

Other Early Opera Houses

1652	Vienna
1656	London
1671	Paris (Academie de Royale Musique)
1678	Hamburg Staatsoper—1,675 seats!
1705	Haymarket Theatre, London
1725	Prague
1731	Covent Garden, London

Dates of Interest

1725	First public concert in Paris
1731	First public concerts in Boston, Massachusetts, and Charleston, South Carolina
1735	First performance of ballade opera (*Flora*), Charleston

Baroque Instrumental Music

The Baroque Concerto

Developed during the Baroque period, the concerto quickly became the principal instrumental form. At that time, a harpsichord and a chamber orchestra of mostly string instruments accompanied the soloist. As a form, the concerto continued its popularity into the nineteenth and twentieth centuries, and today's audiences can hear renowned soloists perform concertos with symphony orchestras.

Concerto Form With few exceptions, the concerto has retained the same overall three-movement form that developed during the Baroque period:

The Concerto Plan

First Movement	*Fast* (Allegro)
Second Movement	*Slow* (Adagio, Andante, or similar tempo)
Third Movement	*Fast* (Allegro)

Concerto Grosso Composers realized that they could add even more interest to the already-popular concerto by featuring more than one or two soloists. They called this "large concerto" a *concerto grosso*.

While Bach was employed as music director at the court of Cöthen, one of his duties was to supply music for court entertainment. It was here that he composed his six famous *Brandenburg* Concertos. Numbers one, two, four, and five are concerto grossos.

ANTONIO VIVALDI (1678–1741)

A Venetian by birth, Vivaldi (vee-*vahl*-dee) began studying music at an early age with his father, a leading violinist at the Basilica of St. Mark. The young Vivaldi also became a violinist and performed in the same orchestra as his father.

Although music was his first love, Vivaldi studied for the priesthood and was ordained in 1703, when he was 25. That same year he was appointed teacher of violin and orchestra at Pio Ospedale della Pietà, a girls' orphanage in Venice. He was called *il prete rosso* (the red-headed priest) because of his bright red hair. Since the school specialized in music, Vivaldi discovered that he was working with an exceptional orchestra and outstanding students, many of whom were fine soloists.

With the immense popularity of the concerto at court and in public concerts, almost every eighteenth-century composer wrote in this genre. Vivaldi, however, had the distinction of being the most prolific. Some of his compositions have been lost. Of his more than 700 existing numbered works, he wrote approximately 450 concertos, 70 sonatas, 45 operas, 35 cantatas, numerous chamber pieces, and sacred vocal music.

Given the title maestro de' concerti in 1716, Vivaldi wrote many of his concertos for his students—works for violin, cello, oboe, flute, piccolo, bassoon, trumpet, guitar, mandolin, or whatever instruments the girls played. His most famous concerto is the programmatic work known as *The Four Seasons*—four violin concertos, each depicting a different season of the year, from a larger work titled *Il cemento dell'armonia e dell'inventione* (1725).

At age 49, Vivaldi left his homeland to accept the position of court composer to Emperor Charles VI of Vienna, where he remained until his death.

Today, many consider Antonio Vivaldi the most original, influential Italian composer of his day. He is recognized as an innovator in form, orchestration, and technique.

PRINCIPAL WORKS

Many of Vivaldi's nearly 800 works have been lost.

Concertos: About 500—including 344 solo concertos (about 230 violin concertos, 81 concertos for two or more soloists), *The Four Seasons*

Chamber Music: Over ninety sonatas and trios for instruments

Operas: Over forty-five operas: *Giustino* (1724), *Griselda* (1735)

Sacred Choral Music: Three oratorios, psalm settings, motets

Secular Cantatas: About forty cantatas

LISTENING ACTIVITY

The Four Seasons, Op. 8, Antonio Vivaldi
Concerto for Violin and Strings in E Major: "Spring"

First Movement: Allegro
Large Form: Violin Concerto
Detailed Form: Rondo or Ritornello
Performing Medium: Violin and Chamber Orchestra

Compact Disc 1, Tracks 7–9
Running Time: 3:10

You may recognize Vivaldi's popular *The Four Seasons* as background music in film and television productions. The entire work consists of four violin concertos, each based on a descriptive sonnet and focused on a different season of the year.

Previously, we discussed how other Baroque composers, specifically Handel and Bach, derived musical inspiration from the texts they used. Vivaldi chose to depict the seasons instrumentally. To assist with the interpretation, Vivaldi had sonnets printed in each player's musical score. Many scholars believe that Vivaldi also wrote the sonnets. The following is a translation of the sonnet for the first movement of the "Spring" concerto:

> Spring has arrived, and festively,
> The birds greet it with cheerful song
> And the brooks, caressed by soft breezes
> Murmur sweetly as they flow.
>
> The sky is covered with a black mantel
> Lightning and thunder announce a storm
> When the storm dies away to silence, the birds
> Return with their melodious songs.

LISTENING GUIDE

The Four Seasons, *Op. 8*, Antonio Vivaldi
CONCERTO FOR VIOLIN AND STRINGS IN E MAJOR: "SPRING"

7	0:00	INTRODUCTION THEME	"*Spring has arrived . . .*" violin soloist accompanied by a string orchestra; allegro; *f*; quadruple meter; E major; theme repeats *p*
	0:13	RITORNELLO THEME	violin solo and orchestra; *f*; syncopated melody, theme repeats *p*
8	0:28	BIRD CALLS	"*and festively, the birds greet it with cheerful song*" soloist and other violins answer each other with trills and scale runs
	1:00	RITORNELLO THEME	returns in violins, accompanied by other strings and continuo; *f*
	1:07	MURMURING BROOK	"*And the brooks . . .*" smoothly, alternating pitches; *p*
	1:29	RITORNELLO THEME	returns in violins, accompanied by other strings and continuo
9	1:36	STORM SECTION	"*The sky is covered with a black mantel . . .*" quick scale runs (lightning); arpeggios (fury of the storm)
	2:02	RITORNELLO THEME	solo violin; all strings and continuo; *f*
	2:09	BIRD CALLS	"*. . . and the birds return . . .*" violin trills and scales
	2:26	INTRODUCTION THEME	like introduction: violin soloist and full group
	2:51	RITORNELLO THEME	*f*; repeated *p*; cadence

Baroque Keyboard Music

The two most famous Baroque composers, Bach and Handel, were also virtuoso keyboard artists. Both played organ and harpsichord, the popular keyboards of the day. Other composers who wrote extensively for the keyboard include Dietrich Buxtehude (c. 1637–1707), François Couperin (1668–1733), Jean-Philippe

Buxtehude
(*books*-tih-*hoo*-duh)
Couperin
(koo-*pran*)

Rameau
(rah-*moh*)

Rameau (1683–1764), Alessandro Scarlatti (1660–1725), Domenico Scarlatti (Alessandro's son, 1685–1757), and Georg Philipp Telemann (1681–1767).

Scarlatti
(skahr-*lah*-tee)

Telemann
(*tay*-lih-mahn)

CHALLENGE YOUR EXPERTISE

- What was Antonio Vivaldi's distinctive physical feature?
- Which two Baroque-style period composers continued working after becoming blind?

The Fugue

A complex polyphonic instrumental composition, the fugue was brought to its highest level of perfection by Johann Sebastian Bach. Even though the fugue is basically an instrumental composition, usually for three or four instruments, the parts are called *voices*—reminiscent of voice parts from an earlier time of *a cappella* compositions. The composer's skill is displayed as the three or four voices interweave without stepping on each other—like three or four dancers moving on a small stage.

Subject

Subject (the Point)   As used by Baroque composers, the fugue is based on a short melody called a *subject,* the main point of the work, which is introduced at the beginning in a single voice, unaccompanied.

Counterpoint

Counterpoint (against the point)   A second voice enters with the same subject, while the first voice moves into the background (counterpoint). Each time a voice enters with the subject, the other parts move in counterpoint in the background.

LISTENING ACTIVITY

***Brandenburg Concerto No. 2* (1721),**
Johann Sebastian Bach

Third Movement: Allegro
Detailed Form: Concerto Grosso
Performing Medium: Violin, Flute, Oboe, Trumpet, and Chamber Orchestra

Compact Disc 1, Track 10
Running Time: 3:01

As discussed in Chapter 5, the *concerto grosso* (large concerto) features several soloists in the same piece of music. This concerto grosso example features four soloists with chamber orchestra: violin, flute, oboe, and trumpet. The tempo is marked *Allegro assai* (quite fast).

LISTENING GUIDE

Brandenburg Concerto No. 2 (1721),
Johann Sebastian Bach

10   0:00   MAIN MELODY   stated by the solo *trumpet*, **f**; with cello and harpsichord (basso continuo) accompaniment, allegro, duple meter (2), F major tonality

Allegro assai

0:08	MAIN MELODY	imitated by the *oboe, trumpet* in counterpoint
0:25	MAIN MELODY	imitated by the *violin, trumpet,* and *oboe* in counterpoint
0:33	MAIN MELODY	imitated by the *flute, oboe,* and *violin* in counterpoint
0:59		Orchestra *strings* enter with short accompaniment and counterpoint melodies in solo parts
1:11	MAIN MELODY	stated by *violin, flute* in counterpoint, with *cello* and *harpsichord* continuo
1:23	MAIN MELODY	imitated by *oboe, flute,* and *violin* in counterpoint
1:30	MAIN MELODY	imitated by both *cello* and *harpsichord* in orchestra, other instruments in counterpoint
1:40	MELODIC FRAGMENT	imitated by *trumpet* and *flute*
1:47	MELODIC FRAGMENT	stated by *oboe,* imitated by *violin,* later by *flute, violin,* then *trumpet,* back to *oboe,* then *flute* playing running sixteenth notes
2:16	MAIN MELODY	stated in *oboe,* imitations by *flute, cello,* and *harpsichord* in orchestra, *trumpet* then *flute* running sixteenth notes
2:52	MAIN MELODY	final statement by *trumpet,* accompanied by all soloists and orchestra, sudden slowing of tempo on last few beats
2:57	FINAL CHORD	F major tonality

Form of the Fugue (A B A)

[A] Exposition (Exposing the Subject)   When all the voices have entered with the subject, the exposition is completed. The following is a simplified graphic representation of the exposition:

Exposition

[B] Development (Episodes or Events)   The second section of the fugue tests the composer's inventiveness in manipulating fragments of the subject, mainly by using sequences, imitations, and changes of tonality.

Episodes

[A] Recapitulation (Restatement of the Subject)   Often, the main subject returns briefly just before the conclusion of the fugue.

GRAPHIC REPRESENTATION OF FUGUE EXPOSITION

cadence

Voice 1   SUBJECT ———— (counterpoint) ———— |

Voice 2   SUBJECT ———— (counterpoint) ———— |

Voice 3   SUBJECT ——— (counterpoint) ——— |

Voice 4   SUBJECT — (counterpoint) — |

Table 9.2	Overall Form of the Fugue
Exposition (A)	exposing of subject by all parts
Development (B)	free, fantasy section, containing imitation, sequences, and modulations of key
Recapitulation (A)	restatement of subject, similar to exposition
Coda	concluding section (may include a stretto)

Coda

Stretto

Coda   A short *coda* usually ends the fugue. *Coda,* the Italian word for "tail," means an ending section. The fugal coda occasionally contains a short section called a *stretto.* Here the subject is imitated by the voices in close succession.

Bach at keyboard with his family in a nineteenth-century etching

Performing Fugues   The challenge in performing a fugue on an organ is to keep each voice a distinctly independent melodic line. To sound all the parts, an organist must play more than one melody with each hand and use both feet on the pedal board.

LISTENING ACTIVITY

Fugue in g minor (little), BWV 578, Johann Sebastian Bach

Form: Organ Fugue
Detailed Form: Fugue
Performing Medium: Organ

Compact Disc 1, Track 11
Running Time: 3:52

This fugue is known also as "The Little" to distinguish it from other fugues Bach composed in the g-minor key. It is a four-voice fugue, meaning that it contains four different parts (voices). Because the main subject (melody) is stated at the beginning, try to remember and then follow it as it is imitated by other parts and as it goes through transformations.

LISTENING GUIDE

Fugue in g minor (little), BWV 578,
Johann Sebastian Bach

EXPOSITION (A)

| 11 | 0:00 | SUBJECT (VOICE 1) | played in the middle register of the organ; moderate tempo; quadruple meter (multiple of two); g-minor tonality |

	0:17	SUBJECT (VOICE 2)	played in lower-middle register, a fourth lower than original, voice 1 plays counterpoint, creating a polyphonic texture
	0:37	SUBJECT (VOICE 3)	played in low register in the original key of g minor, other voices in counterpoint
	0:53	SUBJECT (VOICE 4)	played in lowest voice in key of d minor, other voices in counterpoint

DEVELOPMENT (B)

| | 1:08 | SUBJECT FRAGMENTS | in middle register, imitated in high register, then other registers, sequences, changes of keys |

RECAPITULATION (A)

	2:06	SUBJECT (VOICE 4)	in bass, counterpoint in other parts, original key of B-flat major
	2:36	SUBJECT (VOICE 1)	in high register, counterpoint in other parts
	3:14	SUBJECT (VOICE 3)	in middle-low part, counterpoint in other parts

CODA

| | 3:28 | FINAL CHORD | short coda, sudden slowing, cadencing on a held chord of G major |

CHALLENGE YOUR EXPERTISE

- Why is Bach's Fugue in g minor known as the "Little"?
- What two developments resulted in the concerto grosso?

Summary of Terms

antiphonal

aria

aria form

baroque

Beggar's Opera

bel canto

Buxtehude

cantata

castrato

chorales

choruses

coda

concert

concertato

concerto

concerto grosso

Couperin

counterpoint

development

duet

episodes

exposition

expression indications

fugue

imitative counterpoint

instrumentation

kapellmeister

libretto

Lutheran cantata

maestro di cappella

Mass

motet

multiple soloists

opera

oratorio

overture

pizzicato

Rameau

recapitulation

recitativo

Scarlatti

secular cantata

stretto

subject

Telemann

tremolo

trio

10

The Classical Style Period (1750–1820)

Political and Social Background

Two contrasting moods characterized the Classical period. Inside the castles and palaces, the complacent aristocracy settled into a predictable life of manners, morals, and music. Outside the walls, the frenzied people began rising in revolt. The result was a tug-of-war between guardians of the status quo and insurgents who wanted control of their own destinies.

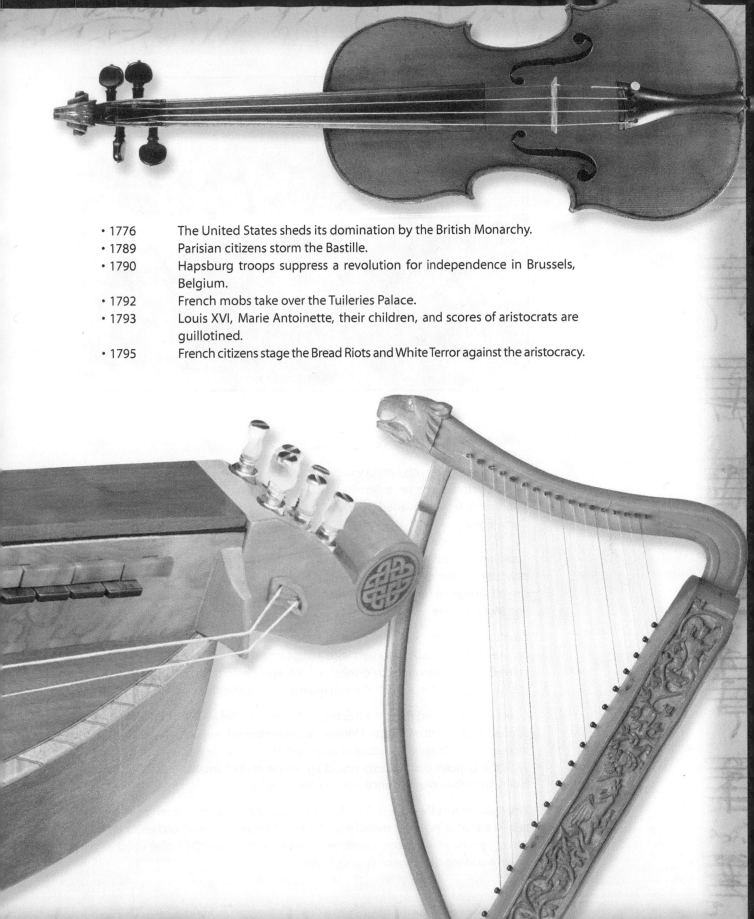

- 1776   The United States sheds its domination by the British Monarchy.
- 1789   Parisian citizens storm the Bastille.
- 1790   Hapsburg troops suppress a revolution for independence in Brussels, Belgium.
- 1792   French mobs take over the Tuileries Palace.
- 1793   Louis XVI, Marie Antoinette, their children, and scores of aristocrats are guillotined.
- 1795   French citizens stage the Bread Riots and White Terror against the aristocracy.

Dancing the popular minuet at court

As the eighteenth century drew to a close, Europe was a crazy quilt of wars. Spain declared war on a Britain weakened from its loss to the United States. Napoleon's armies invaded Germany, Italy, and Austria and defeated the Turks in Cairo, Egypt.

To drown out the cries of the mobs, the aristocracy demanded more music. Avoiding the reality of change, royalty retreated into greater self-indulgence, dependent for their comfort on the toil of the lower classes. Legions of servants served dinner on gold plates. Other hirelings, including musicians such as Haydn and Mozart, were meagerly paid to entertain their employers and guests.

Court Functions   Once a court function was scheduled, servants delivered ornate invitations and returned with acceptances. On the appointed day, guests arrived in the afternoon for drinks, snacks, and chit-chat. Later, they retired to the guest rooms for a nap before changing their clothes for dinner.

Court Concerts and Balls   After overindulging in food and drink, the entourage strolled into the music room. During the short concert, several guests would talk incessantly, others would doze noisily, and the rest would listen intermittently. With the concert over, guests would again nap and change their clothes for the ball, where they would dance into the morning hours.

The Musician's Life   Most French, German, and Austro-Hungarian courts maintained a staff of resident musicians who could become a small orchestra for concerts, operas, and dances. Considered servants, the musicians often had to put down a serving tray to pick up a violin bow.

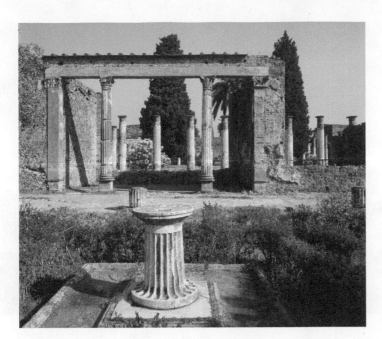

The discovery of Pompeii's ruins in 1748 renewed interest in Greek and Roman art.

Classical Origins

Buried since A.D. 79 in the volcanic ash from Mt. Vesuvius were the cities of Pompeii and Herculaneum. Archeologists excavated these ruins in 1748, uncovering Greek and Roman art, architecture, and artifacts. Their discoveries helped promote a renewed interest in classical art. Symmetry and simple, classical proportions became fashionable in the arts throughout the eighteenth century.

As applied to the music of this era, the concept of *classical* is appropriate because of its emphasis on clarity of sound and symmetry of form. This application certainly describes the music of the great classical composers—Haydn, Mozart, and early Beethoven.

Focus on Form and Symmetry   In court manners and daily life, as well as in the arts, form and symmetry were held in high regard. Notice in the photograph of the eighteenth-century mansion how the architectural design of the building consists of three parts.

As we discuss the music of the Classical period in the next chapter, you will discover how often the A B A form is used. Its balance and symmetry pervade classical forms.

A	B	A
First Section	Contrasting Section	Repetition of First Section

An eighteenth-century aristocratic mansion showing classic symmetrical design

Table 10.1	Overview of the Classical Period (1750–1820)
Composers	Joseph Haydn, Wolfgang Amadeus Mozart, young Ludwig van Beethoven
Writers	Robert Burns, Johann Wolfgang Goethe, Samuel Johnson, Alexander Pope, Johann Schiller
Artists	Jacques-Louis David, Jean-August Ingres
Philosophers	Denis Diderot, David Hume, Immanuel Kant, Jean-Jacques Rousseau, Voltaire (François-Marie Arouet)
Social, Political, and Cultural Events	Factory system spreads in England; James Watt invents steam engine; American and French Revolutions; Napoléon in power; Catherine the Great rules Russia; Hapsburgs rule Austria, Hungary, Italy, Spain, and the Netherlands; the American Constitution is written; the Age of Reason begins

Characteristics of Classical Music

General	Elegant, restrained, stable, balanced, mostly predictable, with clear musical ideas: you seem to know the music, even upon first hearing it
Performing Medium	Symphony orchestra, chamber orchestra and ensembles, soloists with orchestra, piano, opera companies
Rhythm	Simple, regular rhythms with steady beat; steady tempos with little change; meters mostly 2, 3, 4, 6
Melody	Lightly ornamented melodies; running scale patterns and broken chords; imitation and sequences; symmetrical phrases
Harmony	Chords by thirds, mostly built on scale tones; strong tonal center (key); major and minor tonalities
Expression	Moderate use of crescendo, diminuendo; neither very soft nor very loud (mostly *p, mf, f*)

Table 10.1	(Continued)
Texture	Basically homophonic—melody (usually on top) with chordal accompaniment; some less formal polyphony, mainly in development sections
Forms	Clear-cut, easy-to-follow sections set off by obvious cadences and stops; exact repetition of sections; detailed forms: two- and three-part forms; sonata, rondo, minuet and trio; theme and variations; large forms; symphony, concerto, sonata, string trio and quartet; opera; some oratorios and masses

11

Music of the Classical Period

Mozart

Why would some biographers characterize Wolfgang Amadeus Mozart as an intractable genius, quarrelsome and rebellious toward his patrons? What experiences had molded the young, undisciplined Wolfgang?

Raised in the luxury of the Hapsburg palaces, the infant prodigy was caressed and spoiled by Empress Maria Theresa. How surprising—even demeaning—it must have been to the adolescent Mozart when he realized that a composer was little more than a hired hand! No special station accompanied his employment in the court of the Prince-Bishop of Salzburg. His employer praised him extravagantly, but he paid him relatively poorly.

Haydn

Financially, as his spacious homes seem to attest, Joseph Haydn fared well. Employed by the Esterházy family for more than thirty years, Haydn led a considerably more stable life than Mozart.

Haydn also grumbled about his employer's treating him as a servant. Having to live in a tiny apartment over the kitchen at the Esterházy Palace was offensive to him. But Haydn was not as openly rebellious as Mozart, preferring instead to take little jabs at the aristocrats through his music.

Young Beethoven. Engraving by Johann Neidl after a drawing by Stainhauser.

Young Beethoven

About the same time Mozart was in Vienna writing some of his greatest works, Ludwig van Beethoven (*bay-toh-ven*, 1770–1827) was growing up in Bonn, Germany. Beethoven had always idolized Mozart, yearning for the day that he could study with him (see the boxed text in Chapter 12: "Beethoven Meets Mozart"). But when Beethoven finally settled in Vienna in 1792, Mozart was dead; thus, Beethoven studied with Haydn and other composers.

In 1778, Ludwig's father heard about the success Leopold Mozart had with young Wolfgang, so he dressed his eight-year-old son in short pants and tried to foist him off as an infant piano prodigy. Beethoven will be discussed in greater detail in the next chapter.

WOLFGANG AMADEUS MOZART (1756–1791)

One of music's greatest child prodigies was born in Salzburg, Austria. Wolfgang Amadeus Mozart displayed his extraordinary musical ability at the age of four by performing in public on both the violin and piano. At age five, Mozart started composing music, and by the time he was eight, he had composed his first symphony. Mozart completed his first oratorio at age eleven and his first opera at age twelve.

When he was six years old, Wolfgang toured the great courts of Europe with his sister Maria Anna (Nannerl), playing the violin and piano to the amazement of his aristocratic audiences. Their tours were supervised by their nurturing father, Leopold (1719–87). To promote his talented children, he had curtailed his own musical career as a violinist and court composer in Salzburg.

For all his prodigious beginnings and genius, Mozart never had the benefit of a stable patron, though recent evidence reveals that his financial situation was considerably better than previously thought (see Historical Perspective: "Mozart Myths Revealed," in this chapter). In 1781, after resigning from his position as concertmaster (principal violinist) in the court orchestra of the Archbishop of Salzburg, Mozart went to Vienna to make his way as a freelance musician.

Soon after his arrival in Vienna, he met and married Constanze Weber. They had six children, only two of whom survived into adulthood—the average survival rate in the eighteenth century.

It was in Vienna that both Mozart and his public realized his great talent in opera. His German singspiels (comic opera with spoken dialogue) *Die Entführung aus dem Serail* (The Abduction from the Harem, 1782) and *Die Zauberflöte* (The Magic Flute, 1791) were successes and major departures from the traditional Italian-language opera that had dominated opera since its inception.

Mozart's taste for expensive clothes, entertainment, and travel led him to outspend his income and prompted him to borrow heavily from his father and friends. After he died, some of his creditors went after his estate.

At 35, Mozart died prematurely (see Historical Perspective: "Mozart Myths Revealed"), leaving a legacy of more than 600 compositions in almost every form.

PRINCIPAL WORKS

Symphonies: fifty symphonies, including: No. 35 (*Haffner*, 1782); No. 36 (*Linz*, 1783); No. 38 (*Prague*, 1786); No. 39 (1788); No. 40 (g minor, 1788); No. 41 (*Jupiter*, 1788)

Concertos: twenty-three piano concertos, including: No. 15, *K. 450 (1784); No. 17 K. 453 (1784); No. 18, K. 456 (1784); No. 19, K. 459 (1784); No. 20, K. 466 (1785); No. 21, K. 467 (1785); No. 23, K. 488 (1786); No. 25, K. 503 (1786). Five violin concertos; concertos for flute, flute and harp, oboe, clarinet, bassoon, horn; Sinfonia Concertante for oboe, clarinet, bassoon, and horn, K. 279b

Other Orchestral Music: serenades: Serenata notturna, K. 239 (1776); *Eine kleine Nachtmusik*, K. 535 (1787); divertimentos; cassations; dances

Chamber Music: twenty-six quartets; six string quintets; clarinet quintet; flute quartets; piano quartets; piano trios, one string trio; violin sonatas (with piano)

Piano Music: seventeen sonatas; rondos; variations; fantasias; piano duets

Operas: twenty operas, including: *Idomeneo* (1781); *Die Entführung aus dem Serail* (the Abduction from the Harem, original in German, 1782); *Le nozze di Figaro* (The Marriage of Figaro, 1786); *Don Giovanni* (1787); *Così fan tutte* (Women Are Like That, 1789); *Die Zauberflöte* (The Magic Flute, original in German, 1791)

Choral Music: eighteen masses, including: No. 16 (Coronation, 1779); Requiem (1791, unfinished); Exultate jubilate (1773); oratorios; sacred music

*K. refers to Ludwig Köchel (*ker*-shul, 1800–77) an attorney and amateur musician who catalogued most of Mozart's works according to their composition dates. Because of Mozart's pressing need to make money with his compositions, he rarely had time to catalog his extensive output.

HISTORICAL PERSPECTIVE

Mozart Myths Revealed

Over the more than 200 years since Mozart's death, many myths have developed about his life. Recent investigations by physicians, economists, and historians seem to dispel some of these myths.

Lived in Poverty? The story that Mozart earned very little money, eked out a meager living, and died impoverished is not true. Mozart was too busy composing to keep accurate records of his finances, and his own accounting omitted major opera and other commissions, as well as many performances. A reasonable estimate of Mozart's earnings would certainly place him in an upper-middle-class category. How much did he earn? Responsible economists have given up on their efforts to convert the value of florins in the 1780s to that of today's dollars. The bottom line is that Mozart was no pauper, but rather a moderately affluent composer who chose to live beyond his means. As a young composer who was in demand, he apparently did not anticipate such an early death.

Murdered By a Rival? Mozart's premature death has stirred controversy over the years. Rumors have persisted that he was poisoned by the jealous Antonio Salieri (1750–1825), featured in the play and movie *Amadeus*. However, more recent theories suggest that the cause of his death was kidney failure.

Dumped into a Communal Grave? It is true that after his death Mozart was unceremoniously dumped into a common grave at the Central Cemetery of Vienna. However, according to historian Volkmar Braunbehrens (*Mozart in Vienna, 1781–1791*), Emperor Joseph II decreed in 1784 that all bodies were to be buried as follows:

• put in a communal grave far removed from the city
• covered in a linen sack without a coffin
• sprinkled with lime
• left unmarked with no headstones at the grave site

Sanitary and practical reasons governed the emperor's decree. He wanted to avoid the spread of disease and drinking-water contamination, and to help the bereaved conserve their financial resources. Mozart was treated the same as all other citizens of Vienna during this period.

Which is the higher number—Mozart's age at his death or the number of symphonies he composed?

JOSEPH HAYDN (1732–1809)

Born in Rohrau, a small town in eastern Austria near the Hungarian border, Joseph Haydn (*hy-dn*) began his music studies at an early age. At eight, he received a scholarship to study in Vienna, where he became a member of the Vienna Boy's Choir. Later, he held several court posts as a violinist, composer, and music director.

In 1761, Haydn was engaged as court composer and music director in the courts of the Esterházy family. Powerful and wealthy, this Hungarian family had palaces in both Hungary and Austria. During his thirty-year tenure there, Haydn traveled between the two palaces providing weekly operatic performances and orchestral concerts.

After the death of Haydn's Esterházy patron, the concert impresario Johann Peter Salomon made a special trip from London to offer Haydn a commission. Now in his sixties, Haydn found this period of his career fruitful. He wrote his twelve famous "London" symphonies—Nos. 93–104—for the concerts in that city.

Having become a famous and wealthy artist, Haydn spent his remaining years comfortably in Vienna. There he composed his last works, which included the two great oratorios inspired by his London visits—*The Creation* and *The Seasons*.

Among his great contributions, Haydn helped establish the symphony and the string quartet as major instrumental forms. He was a mentor and friend of Mozart and a teacher of young Beethoven.

PRINCIPAL WORKS

Symphonies: one-hundred-six symphonies, including: No. 45 (*Farewell*, 1772); Nos. 82–87, Paris Symphonies; No. 92 (*Oxford*, 1789); No. 94 (*Surprise*, 1791); No. 100 (*Military*, 1794); No. 101 (*Clock*, 1794); No. 103 (*Drum Roll*, 1795); No. 104 (*London*, 1795)

Concertos: numerous concertos for piano, harpsichord, organ, violin, cello, horn, oboe, trumpet

Chamber Music: More than seventy string quartets, thirty-two piano trios, string trios

Piano Music: fifty-four piano sonatas

Operas: Six German operas for marionettes, at least fifteen operas in Italian (many were lost)

Choral Musi: fourteen masses; oratorios: *The Seven Last Words of Christ* (1796), *The Creation* (1798), *The Seasons* (1801)

Classical Music Forms

Catering to their patrons' wishes for predictability, composers wrote their works in recognizable forms. So fond were audiences of these familiar forms that composers used them repeatedly. The challenge for composers was to create fresh, interesting works while using this symphonic plan.

Multimovement Plans (Large Form)   In addition to the symphony, most multimovement works, such as *string quartets, sonatas,* and *concertos,* used the same forms. That is why, if you have heard one symphony by Haydn, another might sound familiar to you the first time you hear it, and also why music by Haydn may sound similar to music by Mozart.

Esterházy Palace, called the "Hungarian Versailles"

HISTORICAL PERSPECTIVE

Haydn's Labor Protest: The "Farewell" Symphony

Haydn's Symphony No. 45 ("Farewell") is an example of his efforts on behalf of musicians. He composed it to protest the fact that members of his orchestra were not permitted to bring their wives and families to the Esterházy's palace in Eisenstadt, about thirty miles south of Vienna. Being away from their families for long periods and having to live in crowded and uncomfortable servant's quarters made life difficult for the musicians.

Haydn composed this clever symphony for one evening's court concert. The first three movements of the symphony were uneventful. In the middle of the fourth movement, according to Haydn's instructions, the second horn player and the first oboist packed up their instruments, blew out their reading candles, and walked out of the hall. Soon, others followed—the bassoonist, the second oboist, cellists and bassists, then the viola and violin players. All departing musicians blew out their candles and made a quiet exit. Finally, with only one candle burning, two violinists finished the symphony.

Haydn's labor protest produced the desired result: Prince Esterházy took the hint and declared an extended leave for the performers to visit their families.

HISTORICAL PERSPECTIVE

Evolution of Public Concerts: Classical Period

Court and Subscription Concerts   Orchestra and chamber music concerts took place mostly at court and at the stately homes of the aristocracy. However, with growing frequency during this time, subscription performances were offered in town to the general public. Because few public concert halls existed, many of the early sites were town meeting halls.

With their guarantee of prepaid ticket sales, composers began regarding subscription concerts as an important source of income. Mozart wrote many of his orchestral works for publi subscription concerts during his time in Vienna. In Haydn's later years, he traveled throughout Europe and England to perform his music at various subscription concerts.

Concert Programs   Eighteenth-century concerts consisted mainly of new music or music by living composers. The composer was usually present, often participating as a conductor, or soloist, or both. Motivated by the need to create their personal performing repertories, composers had little interest in performing music by other composers.

With music publishing still inefficient, composers such as Mozart and Haydn had to carry their original, handwritten copies to concerts. Printed music by other composers was hard to come by. By 1800, deceased composers, no longer around to promote their works, were gradually forgotten. Therefore, works by Bach, Handel, and others were rarely performed.

Typical Multimovement Instrumental Forms

- Concerto (three movements)
- Symphony (four movements)
- String trio and quartet (three or four movements)
- Sonata for solo instrument and piano (three or four movements)

The Concerto (Three Movements)   Since its development during the Baroque period, the concerto form continued to be an audience favorite in the Classical period. Featuring a soloist and an orchestra, the concerto allowed great pianists such as Mozart and Beethoven to display their virtuosity. The first and last movements typically included a *cadenza,* a highly virtuosic solo passage.

Cadenza

The Concerto Plan	
First Movement	*Fast* (allegro). Usually the most involved and serious movement. Often *sonata form* used as detailed form, with the orchestra playing the exposition and the soloist entering on the repeat of the exposition. One or two cadenzas for the soloist in the movement.
Second Movement	*Slow* (adagio, andante, or similar tempo). Usually a songlike movement, with prominent melody. Many detailed forms used such as sonata, rondo, and theme and variations.
Third Movement	*Fast* (allegro). Usually having the fastest tempo, with a light and witty style. Often, *rondo* form is used with another cadenza for the soloist.

The Classical-Period Symphony (Four Movements)   Most Classical-period symphonies contain *four* movements. The overall form is similar to the concerto, with the addition of a dance movement as the third movement. Occasionally, composers omitted the dance movement, producing a three-movement symphony with an overall form similar to the concerto—*fast–slow–fast.*

Typically, the tempo and mood of each movement of the four-movement symphony follow this plan:

The Symphony Plan

First Movement   *Fast* (allegro). This is usually the most involved and serious movement. Occasionally a slow introduction opens the work. Most often the *sonata* form is used.

Second Movement   *Slow* (adagio, andante, or similar tempo). Usually a songlike movement, with prominent melody. Using many forms: *sonata, theme and variations, rondo.*

Third Movement   *Moderately fast* (allegretto or menuetto). The popular dance of the period, the minuet, was used most often for this movement. The form is *minuet and trio* (song form and trio).

Fourth Movement   *Fast* (allegro). Usually having the fastest tempo, this movement ends the symphony with a light and happy mood. *Sonata* or *rondo* forms are the most common ones.

LISTENING INSIGHTS

What to Listen For in Classical Music

The key to enjoying Classical-period music is recognizing and following its *forms*. In no other style period is the understanding of form so important.

Mozart's and Haydn's audiences knew these forms well. Most of them played instruments and had studied music as part of their court education. Knowing the rules of the game, they followed the form with its themes (melody or melodic fragment). They enjoyed noticing the subtle deviations that composers used with a particular form.

You can easily follow the overall form (symphony, concerto, sonata) because there usually are pauses between movements. Once you understand the typical plan for these works, you know which movement you are hearing.

Within each movement, the detailed forms are often built around one or two clearly stated themes or melodies that are repeated several times. As you listen to them, try to remember the themes so you will recognize them when they return or are modified later in the work.

Detailed Forms

The four movements of the symphony or the three movements of the concerto are the overall plan or form. Movements are the outer structure, much like the structure of a building. Within each movement, composers organize their music in more specific forms. These forms, then, would be similar to the detailed infrastructure of a building.

Musical forms are guidelines; a composer may modify them to suit the needs of a particular work. Therefore, from work to work, slight differences may occur within the same form. The most commonly used classical forms used for movements in instrumental music follow:

- Theme and variations
- Rondo
- Minuet and trio (song form and trio)
- Sonata

Theme and Variations Form   A *theme and variations form* uses one main theme throughout the movement, usually stated at the beginning of the piece. Then

The young prodigy Mozart plays a duet with his sister Nannerl while their father watches.
Mozart House, Salzburg, Austria. Erich Lessing/Art Resource

each succeeding section presents a variation or modification. Because the theme is usually recognizable throughout its transformations, this form is easy to follow.

THEME AND VARIATIONS FORM

A main theme	A¹ variation 1	A² variation 2	A³ variation 3	A⁴ variation 4

LISTENING ACTIVITY

**Variations, "Ah, vous dirai-je, maman" K. 265
(also known as "Twinkle, Twinkle, Little Star"),
Wolfgang Amadeus Mozart**

Large Form: Keyboard Piece
Detailed Form: Theme and Variations
Performing Medium: Harpsichord

Compact Disc 1, Track 12
Running Time: 2:49

Listen to this abridged version of Mozart's set of variations on a popular French children's tune of his day, "Ah, vous dirai-je, maman" (Oh, what do you want me to tell you, mama?). You may know it in English as "Twinkle, Twinkle, Little Star." In 1778, while performing in Paris, Mozart heard the tune and wrote twelve variations to it. Two variations are performed here.

Because you probably know the theme, you will be able to recognize it throughout its variations. Mozart clearly states the main theme at the beginning with repetitions.

LISTENING GUIDE

**Variations, "Ah, vous dirai-je, maman" K. 265
(also known as "Twinkle, Twinkle, Little Star"),
Wolfgang Amadeus Mozart**

12 0:00 MAIN THEME moderately fast tempo, duple meter; C major tonality [MAIN THEME] and sections repeated exactly

0:56 VARIATION 1 same tempo, running sixteenth notes (four to a beat) in the upper register incorporate pitches of the main theme; all sections repeated; clear cadence

1:53 VARIATION 2 same tempo and key; modified main theme in the upper register while bass plays running sixteenth notes

Rondo Form *Rondo* was one of the favorite forms for the last movement of a concerto or sonata. Catchy, identifiable rondo themes also were used occasionally in symphonies and string quartets. As you listen to a rondo in a fast movement, you will immediately notice its light, humorous style. Though there are many plans for a rondo, its principal ingredients are a recurring main theme, contrasted with several shorter, less important themes. Here are the most typical plans:

Minuet

RONDO FORMS

THEME 1 (A)	THEME 2 (B)	THEME 1 (A)	THEME 3 (C)	THEME 1 (A)

Rondo Form 1

1 (A)	2 (B)	1 (A)	3 (C)	1 (A)	2 (B)	1 (A)

Rondo Form 2

1 (A)	2 (B)	1 (A)	3 (C)	1 (A)	4 (D)	1 (A)

Rondo Form 3

Minuet and Trio Mozart and Haydn realized the advantages of keeping the interest and attention of their audiences. Wisely catering to these audiences' fondness for dancing, especially the popular *minuet,* the composers included a minuet as the third movement of many of their symphonies, chamber music pieces, and even in some of their piano music. With its moderately fast tempo in triple meter, the minuet provides an effective contrast to the other movements in multimovement plans.

Mozart's apartment in a fashionable section of Vienna

CHALLENGE YOUR EXPERTISE

How long did Beethoven study with Mozart?

LISTENING ACTIVITY

Horn Concerto No. 2 in E-flat Major, K. 417, Wolfgang Amadeus Mozart

Third Movement: Allegro
Large Form: Concerto
Detailed Form: Rondo
Performing Medium: French Horn and Chamber Orchestra

Compact Disc 1, Tracks 13–16
Running Time: 3:24

This playful rondo movement is from one of Mozart's four concertos for horn soloist and chamber orchestra, written in his later years in Vienna. Mozart composed these concertos for his friend, hornist Joseph Leutgeb, with whom he had performed in the Salzburg court orchestra.

Because the rondo (theme 1 or A) is presented at the beginning, be prepared to become familiar with it so you can recognize it when it returns.

Here's the form of this rondo.

THEME 1 (A)	THEME 2 (B) with cadenza	THEME 1 (A)	THEME 3 (C)
THEME 1 (A)	THEME 4 (D)	THEME 1 (A)	CODA

LISTENING GUIDE

Horn Concerto No. 2 in E-flat Major, K. 417, Wolfgang Amadeus Mozart

13	0:00	THEME 1 (A)	horn solo with orchestra accompaniment, rondo theme; E-flat major key; homophonic texture; fast, duple-compound meter; orchestra imitates without soloist and repeats rondo theme, **f**
14	0:18	THEME 2 (B)	lighter; arpeggios in theme; same key; horn questions; strings answer
	0:33	TRANSITION	fanfare-like transition; horn imitated by strings; to cadence, B-flat major key
	0:42	CADENZA	solo horn featuring trills, arpeggios, and scales; transitions back to main theme
	1:00	THEME 1 (A)	exact repeat of opening main rondo theme, horn then orchestra without soloist; E-flat major key
	1:18	TRANSITION	fanfare-like transition; horn imitated by strings
15	1:25	THEME 3 (C)	legato (smooth) melody; c-minor key; horn solos; strings answer with playful ornaments
	1:51	TRANSITION	fanfare-like transition; horn imitated by strings
	1:55	THEME 1 (A)	similar to opening section; horn solo, then orchestra imitation; **f**; E-flat major
16	2:11	THEME 4 (D)	legato melody first in solo horn, then imitated by orchestra; **p**;
	2:28	TRANSITION	similar fanfare-like transition; trills in horn
	2:50	THEME 1 (A)	fragments of main theme, with pauses
	3:02	THEME 1 (A)	faster tempo; horn with main theme
		CODA	horn with fragments from transition fanfare; orchestra imitates; **f**; final cadence in original key of E-flat major

LISTENING ACTIVITY

Piano Sonata No. 8 in c minor, Opus 13 (Pathétique), Ludwig van Beethoven

Large Form: Piano Sonata
Detailed Form: Rondo
Performing Medium: Piano

Compact Disc 1, Tracks 17–18
Running Time: 4:16

Beethoven's rondo is in typical form, with three different themes and transition material between some of the themes:

THEME 1 (A) with transition	THEME 2 (B) with transition	THEME 1 (A)	THEME 3 (C) with transition
THEME 1 (A) with transition	THEME 2 (B)	THEME 1 (A)	CODA

Listen especially to the opening main theme because it returns throughout the work. After you hear it several times, you should be able to become familiar with the other themes as well; then you will grasp the entire form.

LISTENING GUIDE

Piano Sonata No. 8 in c minor, Opus 13 (Pathétique), Ludwig van Beethoven

17 0:00 THEME 1(A)   main rondo theme; *p;* fast duple meter; c-minor tonality

0:00 THEME 1   main rondo theme; *p;* fast duple meter; c-minor tonality
0:19 THEME 1   extension after cadence chords and silence
0:37 TRANSITION MUSIC   fast triplet patterns
18 0:48 THEME 2   *p* crescendo to *f*, cadence

0:57 TRANSITION MUSIC   returns, fast triplet patterns, *p* crescendo to *ff*, held chord
1:11 THEME 1   returns, *p*, similar opening section

1:30   THEME 3   new theme begins softly in new major key, imitations between high and low parts

2:03	TRANSITION MUSIC	returns, fast duple meter, triplet runs, **f** crescendo to **ff**, section ends with cadence on held chord
2:20	THEME 1	rondo theme returns, **p**, similar to opening, imitations and sequences
2:46	TRANSITION MUSIC	fast triplet patterns, ending with cadence
2:58	THEME 2	**p,** modulates through other keys, sequences
3:22	THEME 1	returns, **p**, original minor tonality, similar to opening, section cadences crescendo to **ff** chords
3:34	*Coda Section*	similar to TRANSITION SECTIONS, **p** crescendo to **f**, then **ff**, held chord
4:01	THEME 1	fragment returns slightly slower; **p** decrescendo to **pp**
4:11	ENDING	**ff**; burst of fast notes
		Final chord; **ff**; short, in the original c-minor key

CHALLENGE YOUR EXPERTISE

How did archeological discoveries in 1748 promote a renewed interest in classical art and music?

Trio

The basic minuet and trio form has three parts:

MINUET AND TRIO FORM

Minuet Section (A)–strongly rhythmic, triple meter, dance-style

| Theme 1 | Theme 1–modified | Theme 2 | Theme 2–modified |

each section repeats once

Trio Section (B)–lighter, smoother style

| Theme 3 | Theme 3–modified | Theme 4 | Theme 4–modified |

each section repeats once

Minuet Section (A)–(same as the first section)

| Theme 1 | Theme 1–modified | Theme 2 | Theme 2–modified |

usually no repeated sections

LISTENING ACTIVITY

Symphony No. 94 (*Surprise,* 1791), Joseph Haydn

Large Form: Symphony
Detailed Form: Minuet and Trio (Song Form and Trio)
Performing Medium: Chamber Orchestra

Compact Disc 1, Tracks 19–21
Running Time: 5:32

Listen to the third movement from Haydn's Symphony No. 94 (*Surprise*). Although tempo indications in minuets of Haydn's day are usually marked *allegro* or *allegretto*, this favorite dance could not be performed *too* fast because of the restrictive hoop skirts that women wore.

In this minuet as in most, the three-beat meter is obvious. The trio section offers a lighter, more lyrical contrast to the heavier and louder minuet section.

LISTENING GUIDE

Symphony No. 94 (*Surprise,* 1791), Joseph Haydn

MINUET

| 19 | 0:00 | THEME 1 | played by violins and bassoons, full orchestra, *f*; then contrasting quieter sections, fast, triple meter, strongly rhythmic dance style, major key (G major), homophonic texture, sequences |

	0:11	THEME 1—modified	flutes and violins, *p*; then *f*
	0:25		opening section repeats identically
	0:48	THEME 2	modification of Theme 1 played by violins, *f*

	1:00	THEME 2—modified	in violins, *f*; sequences, chords in winds, sudden *p*; imitation in woodwinds
	1:17	THEME 1	brief return, held chord
	1:30	THEME 1—modified	*p*, ending section, *f*

TRIO (B)

| 20 | 2:52 | THEME 3 | (trio theme) in violin and bassoons, same tempo and meter, *p*; softer and smoother than minuet, change of key to the dominant (D major) |

20	3:03	THEME 3	repeats exactly
	3:14	THEME 4	modification of Theme 3 in strings, still *p*

	3:40	THEME 4	repeats exactly

MINUET (A)

21	4:04	THEMES 1 & 2	loud, *f*; the minuet section with both themes returns, but without repeating shorter sections, *f*
	5:30		full orchestra, *f*; final chord in G major

HISTORICAL PERSPECTIVE

What Was Haydn's Surprise in the "Surprise" Symphony?

Haydn did not name his Symphony No. 94 "Surprise." Audiences named it because of one loud, unexpected chord (*ff*) in the second movement, following a simple, quiet *andante* theme. In 1791, during the symphony's first performance in London at one of the famous "Salomon" concerts, this surprising chord startled the audience. Haydn later denied having planned the effect "to make the ladies scream."

The Schönbrunn Palace in Vienna

Sonata Form Movements of symphonies, concertos, sonatas, string quartets, and many other works of the Classical period often use the sonata form. In a fast movement, this is called *sonata-allegro*. Typically you will hear this form in at least the first movement of a multimovement work.

Sonata-allegro

Haydn and Mozart often used a sonata form for two or three of the four movements in their symphonies. Mozart's Symphony No. 40, for instance, employs the sonata form in movements one, two, and four, with the minuet and trio form in the third movement.

Sonata-Allegro Form

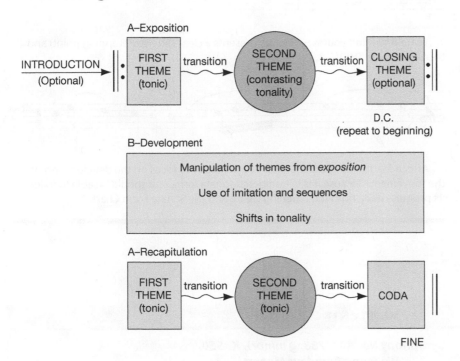

LISTENING ACTIVITY

Symphony No. 40 (1788, g minor), K. 550, Wolfgang Amadeus Mozart

First Movement: Molto Allegro
Large Form: Symphony
Detailed Form: Sonata-Allegro
Performing Medium: Chamber or Symphony Orchestra

Compact Disc 1, Tracks 22–25
Running Time: 8:02

Listen a few times to the first movement—Molto Allegro—of Mozart's Symphony No. 40 in g minor. First become acquainted with the overall progress of the work.

Subsequent hearings will increase your familiarity with the themes or melodies Mozart has used to take you on a symphonic journey through the form.

The entire movement is constructed from two main themes. THEME 1 is a rapid theme that uses sequences and running notes.

To help you find your way, Mozart presents a clear cadence (stopping point) and then introduces THEME 2.

After a few listening experiences, you are ready to focus on the detailed form of the movement. Because it is in traditional sonata form, you should be able to follow its progress using both the Listening Guide and the Sonata Form Chart.

LISTENING GUIDE

Symphony No. 40 *(1788, g minor), K. 550,*
Wolfgang Amadeus Mozart

EXPOSITION

22   0:00   THEME 1   played by violins, full orchestra, *p;* duple meter (4), g minor key, homophonic texture
     (2:01)

0:32   TRANSITION   in violins, *f;* complete cadence and pause
(2:33)   THEME

23   0:51   THEME 2   played by violin, then clarinet, *p*; major key
     (2:52)

    1:27   THEME 1   alternating soft and loud
   (3:27)   fragments
    1:41   THEME 1   used for cadence, violins, *f*; cadence, then pause exposition (complete) repeats
   (2:01)   fragments

Development (B)

24   4:00   THEME 1—   played by violins, *p*; fragments in sequence modulate through several keys
               fragments
    4:05   THEME 1—   *f*; alternating imitations of low strings and woodwinds and sequences
               fragments
    4:47   THEME 1—   in violins, *p*; imitations between strings and woodwinds, sequences
               fragments
    5:03   THEME 1—   in violins, *f*; imitated by low strings
               fragments
    5:12   THEME 1—   in flutes, imitations by clarinets, *p*; sequences, transition to recapitulation
               fragments

Recapitulation (A)

25   5:18   THEME 1   returns in violins, *p*; g-minor tonality, similar to opening section
    5:49   TRANSITION returns in violins, *f*; imitated by low strings and woodwinds, *f*;
               THEME   sequences modulate through several keys
    6:12   TRANSITION in violins; *f*; scale runs in strings to a cadence; pause
               THEME
    6:31   THEME 2   returns in strings, alternating with woodwinds, *p*; crescendo to *f*
    7:12   THEME 1—   alternating imitations by woodwinds, *p*
               fragments
    7:16   THEME 1—   alternating between violins *f* and woodwinds *p*
               fragments

Coda

    7:42   THEME 1—   in violins, *p*; imitated by viola and woodwinds, *p*; cadence of three strong g minor
               fragments   chords in full orchestra, *f*

Classical-Period Opera

Opera—the musical theater of the Classical period—was the favorite entertainment of both the middle class and the aristocracy. From its debut in Italy around 1600, opera grew in popularity throughout Europe.

Although most concertgoers today know Haydn and Mozart chiefly through their symphonic, piano, and chamber music, both composers depended heavily

Gilles Cachemaille and Juliane Banse singing a duet from Mozart's *Don Giovanni*

singspiel
(*zing*-shpeel)

on their operas for a living and reputation. Haydn composed more than twenty-five operas, some of which were lost. Of those that remain, six are in German, written for marionette theater, and nineteen are in Italian. Of Mozart's twelve major operas, nine are in Italian and three are in German.

Today, Haydn's operas are seldom produced, but several of Mozart's are part of the standard repertoire for most professional companies: *Don Giovanni, Così fan tutte, The Magic Flute, The Marriage of Figaro,* and *Abduction from the Harem.*

Opera Language

Why were most of Haydn's and Mozart's operas in Italian, even though they were written for German-speaking audiences? Because opera first appeared in Italy, the Italian language was considered traditional. Even the German-born Handel, composing operas for his English audiences, preferred an Italian libretto.

Mozart was the first important composer to break this tradition, in his *The Abduction from the Harem* and *The Magic Flute.* Written in German, both operas were first performed in the *singspiel,* or folk theater, rather than in the traditional opera house. The predominantly middle-class audiences spoke only German, and had no interest in Italian opera. To them, opera was a show, and they wanted the show in their native language.

Many have come to know Mozart best through his operas. They demonstrate his genius, wit, and uncanny sense of drama. No other composer of his day so keenly understood the qualities of good theater.

Mozart raised opera to new standards. Many of the plots for his operas were daring attacks on the decadence of the aristocracy. *The Marriage of Figaro,* for instance, exposes the aristocracy's frivolous court antics. His *Abduction from the Harem,* with its dancing, choruses of sailors, and lighthearted entertainment, directly influenced nineteenth-century operetta and modern Broadway musical theater.

LISTENING ACTIVITY

**"Madamina" Aria from *Don Giovanni* (1787),
Wolfgang Amadeus Mozart**

Large Form: Opera
Detailed Form: Aria (Two-Part Song Form)
Performing Medium: Bass-Baritone and Chamber Orchestra

Compact Disc 1, Tracks 26–27
Running Time: 5:53

Before you listen to "Madamina" ("dear lady"), also known as the "Catalog" aria, here is some information to help place this charming aria in context.

Background

Don Giovanni is the Italian name of Don Juan, the legendary Spanish philanderer. Completely disregarding the feelings and ethics of his victims, he seduced his way through Europe with ladies of every class, compulsively gratifying his own pleasures.

Convention-driven audiences of the late 1700s may not have sympathized with this unscrupulous cad, but they were fascinated by his ability to overthrow restrictions in order to follow his heart—or at least his hormones.

Mozart wrote this opera in 1787, eleven years after the American Revolution and two years before the French Revolution. Daringly, Mozart and his librettist, Lorenzo da Ponte (1749–1838), reworked the Don Juan legend to fit contemporary Seville—though any European court would have served as well—and poked fun at the excesses of court life.

Plot

As the curtain rises, Don Giovanni's servant Leporello is nervously guarding the courtyard, grumbling about having to work so late at night. His unappreciative master has sneaked into young Donna Anna's room to seduce her. With Donna Anna struggling to fight off her attacker, she and Don Giovanni noisily stumble down the palace stairs. Her father, the commandant, comes to her rescue with drawn sword, challenging Don Giovanni to a duel. In the skirmish, Don Giovanni kills the commandant and then flees.

In the second scene, Leporello mockingly consoles Donna Elvira after she complains that Don Giovanni had seduced and destroyed her. In one of the opera's comic moments, Leporello sings the "Madamina" aria. He pulls out a huge scroll, rolls it open across the stage, and summarizes his master's numerous affairs with women: 640 in Italy, 231 in Germany, 100 in France, 91 in Turkey, and 1,003 in Spain. Despite Don Giovanni's immorality and unscrupulous behavior, the opera has many comedic moments.

LISTENING GUIDE

"Madamina" Aria from Don Giovanni (1787), Wolfgang Amadeus Mozart

Compact Disc 2, Track 8
Running Time: 5:53

26	0:00	ORCHESTRAL INTRODUCTION	allegro; duple meter (4); p; major key (D Major)

0:02   ARIA *Leporello*

Madamina, il catalogo è questo	**Leporello**
Delle belle, che amo il padron mio,	My dear lady, this is a list
Un catalogo egli è, che ho fatt'io.	Of the beauties my master has loved,
Osservate, leggete con me.	A list which I have compiled.
	Observe, read along with me.

0:23   ORCHESTRAL INTERLUDE   *f*; continuous downward scales, staccato, like laughter

0:27   *softly*

In Italia seicento e quaranta,	In Italy, six hundred and forty,
In Alamagna dueccento e trentuna	In Germany, two hundred and thirty-one
Cento in Francia, in Turchia, novatuna,	One hundred in France, in Turkey, ninety-one.

0:42	*tempo slows and style becomes more lyrical*	
	Ma in Ispagna son già mille e tre!	But in Spain, already one thousand and three!
1:02	*gradual crescendo to* **f**	
	V'han fra queste contadine,	Among these are peasant girls,
	Cameriere, cittadine,	Servant girls, city girls
	V'han contesse, baronesse,	Countesses, baronesses
	Marchesane, principesse,	Marchionesses, princesses,
	E v'han donne d'ogni	And women of every rank,
	grado, d'ogni forma, d'ogni età!	every shape, every age!
1:22	*repetition of previous melodies,* **p**	
	In Italia seicento e quaranta,	In Italy, six hundred and forty
	In Alamagna duecento e trentuna,	In Germany, two hundred and thirty-one,
	Cento in Francia, in Turchia, novatuna.	One hundred in France, in Turkey, ninety-one.
	Ma in Ispagna son gia mille e tre!	But in Spain, already one thousand and three!
	V'han fra queste contadine,	Among these are peasant girls,
	Camerierei, Cittadine,	Servant girls, city girls.
	V'han contesse, baronesse,	Countesses, baronesses,
	Marchesine, principesse,	Marchionesses, princesses,
	E v'han donne d'ogni	And women of every rank,
	grado, d'ogni forma, d'ogni età!	every shape, every age!
	The entire opening section comes to a clear cadence.	

27   2:23   MINUET STYLE   slower tempo; triple meter; **p**

Nel - la   bion - da   e - gli ha l'u - san - za

	Nella bionda egli ha l'usanza	With a blonde it is his habit
	Di lodar la gentilezza;	to praise her kindness;
	Nella bruna, la costanza;	In a brunette, her faithfulness;
2:51	*music oozes sweetness*	
	Nella bianca la dolcezza.	In the light blond, her sweetness.
	Vuol d'inverno la grassotta,	In winter he likes fat ones
	Vuol d'estate la magrotta.	In summer he likes thin ones.
3:12	*crescendo, tempo slows to a held tone*	
	E la grande maestosa,	He calls the tall ones majestic.
3:35	*staccato tones, poking fun*	
	La piccina è ognor vezzosa;	The little ones are always charming.
	Delle vecchie fa conquista	He seduces the old ones
	Pel piacer di porle in lista.	For the pleasure of adding to the list.
3:57	*softly, almost spoken*	
	Sua passion predominante	His main passion
	è la giovin principiante.	Is the young beginner.
	Non si picca se sia ricca,	It doesn't matter if she's rich,
	Se sia brutta, se sia bella,	Ugly or beautiful
	Se sia ricca, brutta, se sia bella	If she is rich, ugly, or beautiful.
	Purchè porti la gonnella,	As long as she wears a skirt,

Coda

4:50	*slower and slower*	
	Voi sapete quel che fa	You know what happens.
	Purchè porti la gonnella, ecc.	As long as she wears a skirt, etc.

5:23	*vocalizing on fa and humming*	
	quel che fa!	You know what happens!
	quel che fa!	You know what happens!
5:38	*cadences and running tones in the orchestra*	
5:46	*final cadence in D major*	

CHALLENGE YOUR EXPERTISE

- Which Classical-period symphony ends with fewer players onstage than it begins with?
- Why did Haydn use mostly Italian librettos, even though his audiences spoke German?

Summary of Terms

cadence	opera	song form and trio
cadenza	recapitulation	string quartet
concerto	rondo form	subscription performances
development	singspiel	symphony
exposition	sonata-allegro	theme and variations form
minuet and trio form	sonata form	

12

Beethoven: Bridge to Romanticism

*The first association that springs to anyone's mind when serious music is mentioned is "Beethoven."
. . . What is the meat-and-potatoes of every piano recital? A Beethoven sonata. . . . What did we play
in our symphony concerts when we wanted to honor the fallen in war? The Eroica. . . . What is every
United Nations concert? The Ninth.*

—*Leonard Bernstein,* The Joy of Music

One of the most troubled yet greatest geniuses in music, Beethoven changed the course of music and influenced all composers who succeeded him. Not only did his music become the exemplar for the nineteenth century, his independence became an inspiration for all musicians.

Beethoven led the way for freelance composers to shed their dependence on noble patrons and to achieve financial security as freelance professionals.

Composing was a struggle for Beethoven because of his obsession with writing and rewriting his music. Several existing but discarded versions of many of his most famous themes attest to this, yet his output was considerable, and his influence on future composers and audiences was enormous.

LUDWIG VAN BEETHOVEN (1770–1827)

From his early years in his native Bonn, Germany, Ludwig van Beethoven (*bay*-toh-ven) showed extraordinary talent at the piano, performing his first public concert at age eight. His father, a musician at the court in Bonn, had Ludwig study composition, organ, and violin, as well as piano.

Beethoven was only eighteen years old on July 14, 1789, when Parisians stormed the Bastille and Napoleon Bonaparte was just beginning his military career. Having grown up in a highly formalistic society dominated by the aristocracy, Beethoven witnessed the social changes that ultimately resulted in new forms of government. Through his music, he articulated the transition from classicism to the freer forms of the Romantic period.

At age thirteen, Beethoven was hired as assistant organist at the court in Bonn. In 1790 and again in 1792, Haydn made special trips to see Beethoven on his way from Vienna to London. Haydn encouraged Beethoven's patrons to send young Ludwig to Vienna for more intensive studies. They were convinced, and later, in 1792, the twenty-one-year-old Beethoven was off to Vienna, the center of musical life. His music was well received there.

Despite his success, Beethoven was moody and withdrawn. At age twenty-six, he began to lose his hearing, and in 1802 he considered suicide, as documented in his *Heiligenstadt Testament* (see Historical Perspective, Beethoven's *Heiligenstadt Testament*).

Transcending his increasing deafness, Beethoven actively composed during his entire life. Within his lifetime, his music was performed extensively throughout continental Europe and the United Kingdom—although in his later years he was unable to hear it played. Beethoven was recognized by his contemporaries as the greatest living composer. He died a relatively wealthy man at age fifty-six.

PRINCIPAL WORKS

Symphonies: nine symphonies, including: No. 3 in E-flat Major (*Eroica*, 1803); No. 5 in c minor (1808); No. 6 in F Major (*Pastoral*, 1808); No. 7 in A Major (1812); No. 9 in d minor (*Choral*, 1824)

Concertos: five piano concertos, including: No. 5 (*Emperor*, 1809); Violin Concerto (1806); Triple Concerto for Piano, Violin, and Cello (1804)

Overtures and incidental music: *Leonore* overtures, Nos. 1, 2, and 3 (1805–06); *Coriolan* overture (1807); *Egmont* overture (1810)

Chamber Music: seventeen string quartets; five string trios; piano quintet; sonatas for piano and violin; octet for wind instruments (1793)

Piano Music: thirty-two sonatas, including: No. 8 (*Pathétique*), Op. 13; No. 14 (*Moonlight*); Op. 27; No. 2; No. 21 (*Waldstein*), Op. 53; No. 23 (*Appassionata*), Op. 57

Opera: *Fidelio* (1805)

Choral Music: Mass in D (*Missa solemnis*, 1819–23)

Songs: *An die ferne Geliebte* (*To the Distant Beloved*), song cycle for tenor and piano (1816)

HISTORICAL PERSPECTIVE

Beethoven's Deafness

Increasing deafness began plaguing Beethoven shortly after his arrival in Vienna in 1792. At thirty, he wrote to a boyhood friend, ". . . my ears continue to hum and buzz day and night. For almost two years I have stopped attending social functions, because I find it impossible to tell people: I am deaf!"

To find a cure, he went from one physician to another, each of whom subjected him to painful but useless treatments. One of his doctors suggested that he take thermal bath treatments in the small town of Heiligenstadt outside of Vienna. So during the summer of 1802, a desperate Beethoven rented rooms there and bathed at the local thermal baths.

When, by the end of the summer, he was no better, a deep depression overcame him. On October 6, contemplating suicide, Beethoven wrote a letter containing his will and testament to his brothers Carl and Johann. Written as a letter addressed to the world, to be opened only after his death, the Heiligenstadt Testament expresses his ambivalence about living or dying.

HISTORICAL PERSPECTIVE

Beethoven's Heiligenstadt Testament

For my brothers Carl and Johann Beethoven:

Oh my fellow men, who consider me or describe me as hostile, obstinate, or misanthropic, how greatly you do me wrong. You do not know the secret reason why I appear this way.

Since childhood I have been filled with love of humanity, and a desire to do good things. But for the last six years, I have been afflicted with an incurable complaint, made worse by incompetent doctors. From year to year my hopes for a cure have been gradually shattered. Finally, I must accept the prospect of *permanent deafness* (which may take years to cure, if at all possible).

Though born with a passionate and sociable temperament, I was soon obliged to seclude myself and live in solitude. When I tried to ignore my infirmity, it became worse. Yet I could not bring myself to say to people: Speak up, shout, for I am deaf! Alas! how could I possibly refer to the impairing of *a sense* which should be more perfectly developed in me than in others—a sense which once was perfect.

. . . Oh, I cannot do it: so forgive me, if I withdraw from you. My pain is double because it makes people misjudge me. But I cannot relax with others, nor even enjoy conversations or mutual confidences. I must live alone, coming out only when necessity demands. When I'm with others, I am filled with burning anxiety that they will notice my condition.

. . . How humiliating when someone standing beside me has heard a flute playing and *I heard nothing.*

. . . I have been considering suicide, but my *art* has held me back. For indeed how could I die before I have composed all the music I feel inside.

. . . Now I realize I must be patient.

. . . Oh my fellow men, when some day you read this, remember that you have done me wrong. Let me take comfort from the thought that there may be some other unfortunate person who has also risen above the obstacles imposed by nature, to be in the ranks of noble artists and human beings.

You, my brothers Carl and Johann, after my death, ask Professor Schmidt, if he is still living, to describe my disease and to attach this document to his record, so that the world and I may be reconciled as much as possible. I appoint you both heirs to my small property (if I may so describe it). Divide it honestly, live in harmony, and help one another. You know that you have long ago been forgiven for the harm you did me.

I again thank you, my brother Carl, in particular, for the affection you have shown me recently. I hope your life is better and more carefree than mine. Urge your children to be *virtuous,* for only virtue can make a person happy. Money can't. I speak from experience. Only my virtue and my art have kept me from killing myself until now.

Farewell and love one another. I thank all my friends, and especially *Prince Lichnowsky* and *Professor Schmidt.* I would like one of you to take care of Prince [Lichnowsky]'s instruments, provided you do not quarrel over them. If you ever need money, sell them. I shall be glad, in my grave, if I can still do something for you both.

Well, that is all. Joyfully I go to meet Death. If it comes before I have developed all my artistic gifts, then in spite of my hard fate, I would like to postpone it. Even if I do die, I'll be content, for death will free me from this continual suffering. Come, whenever you like, with courage I will go to meet you.

Farewell. When I am dead, I deserve to be remembered by you, because I have often thought of you and tried to make you happy. Be happy.

Ludwig van Beethoven

Heiligenstadt
October 6th
1802

Keyboard Music

Beethoven's Search for a More Suitable Instrument   As Beethoven's deafness intensified, so did his demand for more sound from his piano. The keyboards used by his contemporaries, Mozart and Haydn, did not satisfy him—they were not strongly built or versatile enough. Nor were they loud enough for the larger public concert halls that increasingly became the center of concert activity in the nineteenth century. So, in the early 1800s, Beethoven turned to John Broadwood, an Englishman who built both ships and pianos, and to Viennese piano builder Johann Streicher. He commissioned them to build larger, sturdier instruments similar to today's concert grands.

Beethoven's Broadwood piano

The new Broadwood and Streicher pianos were louder and more suitable for the large public concert halls than for the chambers at court or the rooms in Beethoven's own lodgings. His loud playing disturbed the neighbors, especially in the middle of the night. As a result, Beethoven was evicted from some eighty apartments in and around Vienna. Buildings throughout that city have plaques stating "Beethoven Lived Here."

LISTENING ACTIVITY

Piano Sonata No. 8 **in C minor, Opus 13 (***Pathétique***),**
Ludwig van Beethoven

Large Form: Piano Sonata
Detailed Form: Rondo

Compact Disc 1, Tracks 17–18
Running Time: 4:16

Listen again to the rondo from Beethoven's *Piano Sonata No. 8.* In the previous chapter, you followed the same work using the Listening Guide. For this hearing, try to follow the form and the musical events without the Listening Guide, as you normally would at a concert.

Beethoven composed this sonata in 1799 during his early years in Vienna. We are not sure why he titled the work *Pathétique.* We do know that he composed it during the onset of his hearing problems, only three years before writing his Heiligenstadt Testament.

The rondo in *Pathétique* shows a tinge of sadness. Classical rondos are usually extremely jolly, so this minor-keyed rondo tends toward the more melancholy moods of Romanticism. Following a basic rondo form, its main theme keeps returning, alternating with contrasting themes.

The form for this Beethoven rondo follows:

THEME 1 (A) with transition	THEME 2 (B) with transition	THEME 1 (A)	THEME 3 (C) with transition
THEME 1 (A) with transition	THEME 2 (B)	THEME 1 (A)	CODA

Beethoven's Orchestral Music

Because of the new avenues of emotional expression that Beethoven was exploring in his music, he began writing for more instruments and increasing the size of the orchestra. He also composed longer and structurally more complex symphonies than Haydn's and Mozart's twenty-minute works. Beethoven's Ninth Symphony, for example, takes about one hour and ten minutes to perform.

Beethoven used traditional Classical-period forms, expanding them to fit his Romantic-period viewpoint. Here are noticeable characteristics of Beethoven's symphonic works:

- The loudness of the orchestra increases along with the number of instruments.
- Developmental sections (free sections or side journeys) occur within almost all sections of the form (exposition, coda, etc.).
- Traditional forms are freer. He treated these forms with great originality in his later works.
- Music occasionally moves from one movement to the next without the usual breaks.
- Themes from one movement are occasionally restated in another.
- Changes in tempo within a movement are more frequent than in previous Classical-period works.
- Coda or finale sections are usually longer, more elaborate, and triumphant than those of Haydn and Mozart. They usually conclude with repeated, powerful chords.

Symphony No. 6 (Pastoral)   After the mighty Fifth Symphony, Beethoven began searching for new inspiration and direction for his music. Although not as

Concert Hall in the Streicher Piano Factory in Vienna. Beethoven performed on Streicher pianos in concerts in Vienna.

schooled in the traditional forms as court audiences, his new audiences at public concerts enjoyed the power and emotionalism in his music.

Music notebooks in hand, Beethoven roamed both the Vienna Woods and the Grinzing Woods near Heilingenstadt, seeking inspiration. Caught up in the beauty of the countryside, he worked quickly on his new work. Beethoven was touched by the romantic feeling of the woods, the delicate settings, the rustic life of the peasants, and the wonders of nature.

HISTORICAL PERSPECTIVE

Beethoven Meets Mozart

When Beethoven was a young child, his father pressured him to emulate Mozart, first as a keyboard *wunderkind,* and then as a composer. Beethoven might have grown up resenting Mozart, yet he idolized him. It was Beethoven's dream to study composition with the great master, only fourteen years his senior.

In 1787, at age seventeen, Beethoven journeyed from his native Bonn to the great cultural center of Vienna. Historical documentation is missing for much of this short trip; however, several accounts indicate that Beethoven actually met with Mozart briefly and performed for him at his studio.

According to these accounts, Beethoven's first selection was a piano piece he had been practicing. Apparently, Mozart was only mildly impressed with young Beethoven's keyboard ability—Vienna had many gifted young pianists. Sensing this, Beethoven asked Mozart to supply him with a melody upon which he could improvise. Mozart did so, and Beethoven proceeded to dazzle Mozart and his friends with a stirring improvisation. Turning to his friends Mozart declared, "Keep an eye on this man. Someday he will give the world something to talk about."

After only two weeks in Vienna, Beethoven had to rush to the bedside of his gravely ill mother in Bonn. She died a few days later. Not until 1792 did Beethoven return to Vienna. Mozart had died only months before his arrival.

Symphony No. 5 in C minor (1808), Ludwig van Beethoven Op. 67, First Movement: Allegro con brio

Large Form: Symphony
Detailed Form: Sonata-allegro
Performing Medium: Medium-Sized Symphony Orchestra

Compact Disc 1, Tracks 28–32
Running Time: 7:18

Following along with the Listening Guide, listen to the first movement of this popular symphony. Notice how Beethoven builds a monumental structure from a simple idea. The approach is similar to that of an architect who uses a geometric shape such as a rectangle or triangle as the fundamental building shape throughout a structure. Buckminster Fuller's geodesic domes of interlocking polygons are architectural examples.

Beethoven's building idea is the famous theme that he later uses both as a melodic motive and as a rhythmic motive.

The overall form of the first movement is traditional classical sonata form. Notice, however, that Beethoven extends the coda to last as long as each of the other sections.

EXPOSITION (124 measures)
THEME 1   THEME 2
              holds   horn strings   full orch. exposition
‖:―――――――――――――――――――――――――― ···· ―――――――――――――:‖ repeats
    ff p–   <f ff p   <f ff   p   < ff   ff

DEVELOPMENT (123 measures)
THEME 1 fragments
hns. hold   brass
ff p–   crescendo   ff ff ff diminuendo pp ff pp ff

RECAPITULATION (128 measures)
THEME 1   THEME 2
              oboe solo   bassoons   full orch   codetta
                                 ... strings   //////
―――――――――――――――――――――――――――――
ff p   < ff   p < ff   ff   p   crescendo ff   ff

CODA (127 measures)   THEME 1
THEME 1   THEME 2
full orch.   alternating
                        strings & woodwinds   :‖
―――――――――――――――――――――   ――――――――――――――――――――――
ff   f   ff   ff   ff   pp   ff

LISTENING GUIDE

Symphony No. 5 (1808), Ludwig van Beethoven
First Movement: Allegro con brio

EXPOSITION

| 28 | 0:00
(1:25) | THEME 1 | played by unison strings and clarinet; *ff*; duple meter, fourth tone held, same idea repeated as a sequence in the key of c minor |

	0:06 (1:31)	THEME 1	played softly by second violin, imitated by other strings; c minor; crescendo to *f* chords by full orchestra
	0:13 (1:39)	THEME 1	played by full orchestra; *ff*; fourth tone held
	0:21 (1:47)	THEME 1	transition section started by violins; *p*; imitations throughout the orchestra; crescendos to loud chords, then silence
	0:48 (2:09)	THEME 1 (*var*)	French horn introduces next theme; *ff*; major key

Horns

| 29 | 0:46
(2:14) | THEME 2 | played softly by violins, imitated by clarinets, then flutes; motive of Theme 1 played softly by cellos and basses every fourth measure |

Violins

| | 1:06
(2:32) | THEME 1 (*var*) | (closing section) played by violins, other instruments added, building to loud chords |
| | (1:26) | **Exposition** repeats | |

Development

30	2:51	THEME 1	played by French horns; *f*; then strings, with fourth tone held
	2:57	THEME 1	started in violins, then alternating imitations between woodwinds and strings; gradual crescendo
	3:21	THEME 1 (*var*)	full chords in winds, repeated tones of first theme, followed by silence
	3:40	THEME 1 (*fragments*)	two-tone motive (part of Theme 1); imitations throughout sections of the orchestra; reducing to one-tone imitations followed by alternating one-tone imitations

	3:51	THEME 1 (*fragments*)	
	4:09	THEME 1 (*fragments*)	stated suddenly and loudly

Recapitulation

31	4:14	THEME 1	played by full orchestra; *ff;* fourth tone held short oboe cadenza,
	4:32		ending on held tone
	4:44	THEME 1 (*var*)	acts as transition section, starting softly then getting louder as it is imitated by different instruments
	5:04	THEME 1 (*var*)	played by bassoons
	5:08	THEME 2	started by violins; *p;* then alternating imitations; gradual crescendo; C major

Coda

32	5:43	THEME 1	rhythmic pattern; alternating imitations between winds and strings containing many repeated tones
	5:52	THEME 1 (*var*)	imitations, then two-tone motive developed
	6:05	THEME 2 (*var*)	four-tone pattern; ascending sequences played by strings, then alternating imitations between woodwinds and strings, reducing to two-tone patterns
	6:55	THEME 1	full orchestra; *ff;* played twice with fourth tone held
	7:04	THEME 1	softly in strings, then suddenly loud by entire orchestra;
	7:10		series of loud chords
	7:17	FINAL CHORD	in c minor

var = variation

HISTORICAL PERSPECTIVE

Beethoven and the Changing Status of Composers

Before Beethoven, composers were almost totally dependent on either the church or the courts for employment. Mozart, for example, who lost his post with the Archbishop of Salzburg, struggled as a freelance musician. He was just beginning to achieve financial independence when his career ended with his untimely death.

Beethoven succeeded as a freelance musician. When he first arrived in the great musical city of Vienna, he accepted employment from the aristocracy. He tried to fit in, outfitting himself in the newest fashions and even taking dance lessons. But the clothes made him uncomfortable, and he claimed that he had difficulty moving in time to the music.

Beethoven felt out of place among some of his frivolous and snobbish patrons. First, he resented having to occasionally use the servants' entrance when he arrived to perform. Furthermore, when members of his audience talked during his playing, he became angry and often walked out in the middle of a piece.

So Beethoven searched for a new audience. Influenced by the social and political changes around him, he took control of his life by organizing and performing in concerts for the middle class at the public concert hall or in public buildings—and he usually turned a profit.

Toward the end of the eighteenth century, public concerts had grown rapidly in importance. The famous Salomon Concerts from 1791 to 1795 in London enabled the aging Haydn to amass more money than he ever could have from his wages at the Esterházy court. Beethoven studied briefly with Haydn during some of those years. He must have been encouraged by Haydn's financial successes with the London audiences because Beethoven began developing new public concerts in Vienna.

Music Publishing: A New Source of Income   Mozart had earned negligible royalties from his few published works—some of which were distributed without his knowledge. But Beethoven was a shrewder businessman and knew how to negotiate a profitable deal, often with a sizable advance. Stories have been told about his negotiating with two or more publishers at a time, playing them against each other until he won his price. Eventually, royalties were his main source of income. Beethoven's success in negotiating encouraged future composers to follow his example.

CHALLENGE YOUR EXPERTISE

Why did Beethoven earn more royalty income than Bach?

Beethoven's Symphony No. 6 (Pastoral), Opus 68		
Movement	**Tempo Indication**	**Beethoven's Movement Titles**
First Movement:	Allegro ma non troppo	"The awakening of joyful feelings upon arriving in the country"
Second Movement:	Andante molto mosso	"Scene by the brook"
Third Movement: *(into next movement without a break)*	Allegro	"Merry gathering of country folk"
Fourth Movement: *(into next movement without a break)*	Allegro	"Thunderstorm"
Fifth Movement:	Allegretto	"Happy, thankful feelings after the storm: shepherd's song"

Beethoven's Symphony No. 6 depicts the feelings that nature inspired in him. Evidence of that inspiration is in the title—"The Pastoral Symphony, more the expression of feeling than painting." Beethoven also affixed highly descriptive phrases to each of the five movements, with the intention of transporting the audience out of the concert hall and into the countryside.

The Great Ninth Symphony (Choral)

Beethoven composed his first eight symphonies over a twelve-year span, between 1800 and 1812, yet it would be another twelve years before he would release his tradition-shattering Ninth Symphony for its first performance. With the Ninth Symphony, Beethoven completely crossed the bridge into romanticism.

Beethoven attended the premiere performance of this work in Vienna on May 7, 1824, on a program featuring only his music. Word had spread of this premiere, and a large and distinguished audience streamed into the concert hall for the performance. Throughout the concert, they saw the composer himself standing at the podium, next to the conductor.

After the finale, the audience spontaneously rose for a standing ovation—cheering, applauding, and waving handkerchiefs. Beethoven heard none of this adulation. Finally, one of the soloists tugged on his sleeve to signal the composer to turn around and acknowledge the applause.

For the first time in a symphony, a chorus and vocal soloists performed with the orchestra. Beethoven set to music a poem that seemed to have meant a great deal to him throughout his life: Friedrich Schiller's "Ode to Joy." Its main idea embraced the spirit of emerging romanticism—the joy of the universal brotherhood: "Alle Menchen werden Brüder" (All men become brothers).

Schiller
(*shill*-er, 1759–1805)

Inspired by the grandeur of the Ninth Symphony, Romantic-period composers began writing larger, more emotional works, many containing choruses and soloists delivering texts and stories.

Summary of Terms

Appassionata Sonata	Heiligenstadt Testament	*Pastoral* Symphony
Choral Symphony	*Moonlight* Sonata	*Pathétique* Sonata
Emperor Concerto	Ninth Symphony	rondo form
Eroica Symphony	"Ode to Joy"	sonata form

13

The Romantic Style Period (1820–1900)

"The road of excess leads to the palace of wisdom."

—*William Blake,* Proverbs of Hell

After 1820 and throughout the nineteenth century, Romanticism became the predominant style, not only in music, but in all the arts—a style and an outlook that reflected a new concern with emotional expression.

Beholden to the Church and the aristocracy for financial support, artists had worked under tight constraints. Now, with other available sources of income, composers no longer had to defer to patrons. Thus liberated, artists could create art by their own standards and for art's sake. Throwing themselves into their work, many were victims of burnout, and many died young. Excess, exuberance, and optimism, often followed by pessimism and depression, characterized this creative mode.

Self-sustaining and self-reliant, the arts and artists gave impetus to the lively, great cultural centers—Paris, Vienna, Prague, Budapest, Leipzig, Dresden, Amsterdam, and London. Public concert associations, philharmonic orchestral societies, and opera and ballet companies were established throughout Europe and the United States.

At last, artists were celebrities—respected members of society. Suddenly they were invited to the homes of the wealthy, not just as entertainers but as honored guests.

Romantic Subjects

In art, literature, and music, the Romantic movement expressed intense introspection and a fascination with the supernatural and the exotic. Some of the more popular topics follow:

- nature
- beauty
- love
- death

Eugene Delacroix (1798–1860) "July 28th, 1830: Liberty Guides the People," oil on canvs, 260 × 325 cm. Louvre, Dept. des Peintures, Paris, France.
© Photograph by Erich Lessing, Art Resource, N.Y.

- the supernatural
- the mystical, magical, and mysterious
- travel, distant lands, and exotic cultures
- adventure
- drug-induced states
- the brotherhood of man
- the individual and the common man
- the superman and hero

Romanticism in Music

Evocative Titles for Musical Works   Romantic subjects inspired evocative titles: Beethoven's *Pastoral* Symphony, Mendelssohn's *Scottish* Symphony, Schumann's *Spring* Symphony, Brahms's *Tragic Overture*, and Dukas' *Sorceror's Apprentice*. When listening to these works, we can visualize the stories or images that the titles suggest.

Program Music   Public support was at a new peak, challenging composers to find ways of communicating with audiences who were unfamiliar with the classical forms. New ideas in the titles and stories seduced audiences into becoming involved with the passion of the music.

To carry these ideas further, some composers provided a detailed scenario, or *program*, to follow along with the music. Examples are Berlioz's *Symphonie fantastique*, Liszt's *Faust* and *Dante* symphonies, and Strauss's tone poems, *Don Juan*, *Death and Transfiguration*, and *A Hero's Life*.

Emotional Music   Romantic composers became fascinated with the possibilities of deep emotional expression offered by the expanded use of the musical elements and instrumental tone colors. Audiences were enthralled by these exotic, emotional works.

What about today's audiences? If you examine programs from any major orchestra or opera company, you will find that at least half the music is from the Romantic period. We still favor Romantic music. It gives us an opportunity to experience our feelings.

Table 13.1	Overview of the Romantic Style Period (1820–1900)
Important Composers	Ludwig van Beethoven, Hector Berlioz, Georges Bizet, Alexander Borodin, Johannes Brahms, Anton Bruckner, Frédéric Chopin, Claude Debussy, Henri Duparc, Antonín Dvořák, Edward Elgar, Gabriel Fauré, César Franck, Mikhail Glinka, Charles Gounod, Edvard Grieg, Franz Liszt, Gustav Mahler, Felix Mendelssohn, Modest Mussorgsky, Jacques Offenbach, Giacomo Puccini, Nicolai Rimsky-Korsakov, Camille Saint-Saëns, Franz Schubert, Robert Schumann, Jan Sibelius, Bedřich Smetana, Johann Strauss, Jr. and Sr., Richard Strauss, Peter Tchaikovsky, Giuseppe Verdi, Carl Maria von Weber, Richard Wagner
Visual Artists	William Blake, Paul Cézanne, Honoré Daumier, Edgar Degas, Eugene Delacroix, Paul Gauguin, Francisco Goya, Claude Monet, Pierre-Auguste Renoir, Auguste Rodin, Georges Seurat, Joseph Turner, Vincent van Gogh
Writers	Louisa May Alcott, Honoré de Balzac, Anne, Charlotte, and Emily Brontë, Elizabeth Browning, Robert Browning, George Gordon Lord Byron, Anton Chekhov, Samuel Coleridge, Charles Dickens, Emily Dickinson, Fyodor Dostoevski, Nathaniel Hawthorne, Heinrich Heine, Victor Hugo, Henrik Ibsen, Henry James, John Keats, Henry Wadsworth Longfellow, Edgar Allan Poe, Aleksandr Pushkin, George Sand, Percy Bysshe Shelley, Marie-Henri Stendhal, Robert Louis Stevenson, Harriet Beecher Stowe, Alfred Lord Tennyson, William Thackeray, Leo Tolstoy, Mark Twain, Walt Whitman, Oscar Wilde, William Wordsworth
Philosophers	Auguste Comte, Ralph Waldo Emerson, Friedrich Engels, Ernst Haeckel, Georg Hegel, Thomas Henry Huxley, Søren Kierkegaard, Karl Marx, John Stuart Mill, Friedrich Nietzsche, Arthur Schopenhauer, Herbert Spencer, Henry David Thoreau
Social, Political, and Cultural Events	Industrial revolution, steamboat, railroads, photography, telegraph, telephone, phonograph, Monroe Doctrine, California Gold Rush, unification of Germany and Italy, reign of Victoria, "Gay '90s," Darwin's *The Descent of Man*, American Civil War

Table 13.1	(Continued)

Characteristics of the Romantic Style Music

General	Music has an emotional, subjective quality with frequent mood changes; expansive sound with large ensembles; intimate music with small ensembles; literature or extra-musical ideas often serve as a basis for the music.
Performing Media	Large symphony orchestras, piano, chamber music ensembles, opera and ballet companies
Rhythm	Rubato used often; changing tempos within sections and movements; more complex rhythms than in previous periods
Melody	Long, flowing, emotion-laden melodies; also short themes representing ideas or people; major and minor melodies with chromatic alterations; instrumental melodies with wide leaps and range
Harmony	Tonal (key-centered), but with increasing use of modulations and chromatic tones; rich, complex harmonies
Expression	Full range of dynamics (extremely soft to extremely loud); extensive use of crescendo and diminuendo
Texture	Mainly homophonic (melody with accompaniment); occasional use of polyphony
Forms	Some continued use of Classical-period forms; symphony, often with titles; concerto; new, small piano forms (nocturne, ballade, étude, waltz, mazurka); opera, ballet, symphonic tone poem, concert overture; programmatic and descriptive works

14

Early Romantic Music

Orchestral Music

Hector Berlioz's (*behr*-ly-ohz) life typifies the spirit of the Romantic period. Although he placated his father, a respected physician, by attending one semester of medical school in Paris, Berlioz had other plans. According to his memoir, his first experience with a cadaver hastened his career change:

At the sight of that terrible charnel-house—the fragments of limbs, the grinning heads and gaping skulls, the bloody quagmire underfoot and the atrocious smell it gave off, the swarms of sparrows wrangling over scraps of lung, the rats in their corner gnawing the bleeding vertebrae—such a feeling of revulsion possessed me that I leapt through the window of the dissecting-room and fled for home . . . .

Now he could pursue his real interest—music. Though Berlioz had learned to read music, had composed a few small works while a youngster, and could perform a few pieces on flute and guitar, he was far from an accomplished musician. His father, fearing that his son's strong interest in music would interfere with his becoming a doctor, blocked his boyhood music studies. Specifically, his father prevented Hector from studying piano, the traditional instrument of composers. Yet at 19, Berlioz pursued his new career with enthusiasm. True to the Romantic spirit that *anything is possible if you really want to accomplish it,* Berlioz studied music in Paris, then in Italy, and eventually became one of the world's great composers.

(sam-fo-*nee* fahn-tah-*steek*)

Idée fixe
(ee-*day feex*)

Recurrent themes and melodies

Symphonie Fantastique   The events surrounding the creation of *Symphonie fantastique* exemplify Berlioz's Romantic spirit. In Paris, he attended an English-language performance of Shakespeare's *Hamlet* by a London company. Though he did not understand one word of English, Berlioz became instantly infatuated with the actress who played Ophelia, Harriet Constance Smithson (1800–54).

Vowing to marry her, he began writing letters to her. To further demonstrate his love, Berlioz dedicated his *Symphonie fantastique* to her. He even made Harriet the central character in the symphony by weaving a melody that represented her throughout the fabric of this five-movement, programmatic orchestral work. Berlioz called this type of central theme an *idée fixe*.

After Berlioz, many composers employed the technique of recurrent themes and melodies to represent characters, ideas, and locations. In the late nineteenth century, Richard Wagner, Franz Liszt, and Richard Strauss used the technique extensively in music dramas and tone poems. In today's films and Broadway musicals, a recurrent theme can serve as a unifying device to sustain suspense, heighten emotion, and define character.

Hector Berlioz and Harriet Smithson   Dedicating his *Symphonie fantastique* to Harriet Smithson was part of Berlioz's strategy. He invited her to a performance of the work, explaining that she had been the inspiration and was the central character. So impressed was Harriet that she consented to his courtship.

HECTOR BERLIOZ (1803–1869)

Born in a little town near Lyon, France, Hector Berlioz (*behr*-ly-ohz) began studying music seriously at nineteen, taking lessons in composition and orchestral instruments in Paris. Because of his late start, he was not accepted as a music student at the Paris Conservatory. Ironically, later in his career he was hired to teach orchestration and composition at the Conservatory.

Objecting to his choice of music for a career, his parents cut off his allowance. To support his studies, Berlioz gave music lessons and held odd jobs in the theater. He struggled until 1830, when he won the prestigious Prix de Rome.

Now with funds, he continued his studies in Rome. When he returned to Paris, he threw himself into composition and was accepted into the Parisian artistic community, which included musicians Frédéric Chopin and Franz Liszt, artist Eugene Delacroix, and writers Victor Hugo and George Sand.

Berlioz, fascinated with instrumental effects and new instruments, employed his latest discoveries in his orchestral works. He wrote the first important orchestration textbook, *Treatise on Instrumentation*. Because Berlioz was interested in the dramatic quality of music, his works often contained detailed stories.

PRINCIPAL WORKS

Orchestral: *Symphonie fantastique* (1830); *Harold in Italy* (viola concerto, 1834); *Roméo et Juliette* (Romeo and Juliet, 1839); *Le Carnaval romain* (The Roman Carnival, 1844)

Wind Band: *Grande symphonie funèbre et triomphale* (Grand Funeral and Triumphant Symphonie, 1840)

Operas: *Benvenuto Cellini* (1838); *Les Troyens* (The Trojans, 1858); *Béatrice et Bénédict* (1862)

Choral: *Requiem* (1837); *Te Deum* (1849); *L'enfance du Christ* (The Childhood of Christ, 1854)

Hector Berlioz at age twenty-nine. Oil portrait by Signol (1832).

Harriet Smithson at age twenty-eight, after a portrait by Dubufe (1828).

Berlioz learned some English. Harriet learned some tragic. A few years later, they married.

In spite of its romantic beginnings, the marriage came to a tragic ending. With Harriet out of his life, Berlioz was forced to seek other inspirations for his passionate creative genius.

HISTORICAL PERSPECTIVE

Berlioz's Innovative Orchestration

Most composers write at a keyboard because it enables them to work on a number of parts at once. Therefore, their notation of orchestral music usually resembles keyboard music, with occasional suggestions about which instruments might play which ideas. Later, they orchestrate the music—renotate it for full orchestra. The process is similar to that of many painters who first sketch their ideas on a piece of paper, and then transfer the idea to a large canvas and develop the painting in a full range of colors.

Since Berlioz could neither compose nor play his works at the piano, he started immediately to notate an entire orchestral score. What started as a handicap—his inability to play the piano—intensified his determination. Driven by his vision, he learned about each of the orchestral instruments until he was able not only to compose but to orchestrate brilliantly, setting a standard for those who followed.

Berlioz, the creative orchestrator, treats the listener to many interesting and unusual sounds, featuring unusual instruments and instrumental effects. In the "Witches' Sabbath," from the *Symphonie fantastique,* you will hear a high clarinet (E-flat clarinet) playing sounds that resemble squeaking laughter. Also featured are tubas and chimes, rare in orchestras at that time.

Occasionally Berlioz calls for the string performers to play with mutes attached to the bridges of their instruments—*con sordini* (con sor-*dee*-nee). He also calls for the players to run their bows very close to the bridges, producing eerie, glassy sounds—*sul ponticello* (sool pon-tee-*chell*-o). To simulate dancing skeletons—perhaps an image that remained from his disgust in the dissecting room—Berlioz requires the string players to turn their bows around and strike the strings with the wood portion to produce a sound like clattering bones—*col legno battuta* (cohl *len*-yoh bah-*too*-tah).

LISTENING ACTIVITY

Symphonie Fantastique (Fantastic Symphony, 1830), Hector Berlioz

Fifth Movement: "Dream of a Witches' Sabbath"
Large Form: Symphony
Detailed Form: Sectional
Performing Medium: Large Symphony Orchestra

Compact Disc 1, Tracks 33–37
Running Time: 10:20

Before you listen to the music, read the program that Berlioz wrote for the fifth and last movement of his *Symphonie fantastique*. Because he wanted his audience to know the story that Harriet had inspired, Berlioz wrote it out in detail. The entire story is usually printed in the concert program and accompanies the recording.

Introduction

A young musician of morbid sensitivity and ardent imagination poisons himself with opium in a moment of amorous despair. The narcotic dose, while too weak to kill him, plunges him into deep hallucinations. His strange visions, sensations, feelings, and memories are translated in his brain into musical ideas and images. Even his beloved becomes a melody for him and his fixation with her (idée fixe) haunts him.

Fifth Part "Dream of a Witches' Sabbath"

He sees himself at a Witches' Sabbath. Shadowy figures, sorcerers, and monsters of every kind have gathered for his burial. Strange noises, groans, bursts of laughter, and faraway cries seem to be answered by other cries. He hears the melody of his beloved again, but now lacking its noble and gentle quality, it is nothing more than a dance tune, mocking, trivial, and grotesque.

She (the beloved) arrives at the Sabbath, greeted by shouts of joy. She joins the diabolical orgy. . . . The funeral bell tolls, a burlesque parody of the Dies irae, dies illa *("Day of wrath, O judgment day"). While the day of wrath melody continues, the witches dance.*

The plan Berlioz uses for the last movement of his *Symphonie fantastique* is a *sectional form:*

Introduction

Theme 1—*idée fixe:* "Beloved Theme Modified"
Theme 2—*Dies irae, dies illa:* from the Gregorian chant, "Day of wrath, O judgment day"
Theme 3—"Witches' Round Dance," a loosely constructed fugue Coda

Here is the original *idée fixe,* the "beloved" melody, introduced in the first movement:

When this melody (*idée fixe*) reappears in the fifth movement, it is transformed into:

Symphonie Fantastique (1830),
Hector Berlioz Fifth Movement: "Dream of a Witches' Sabbath"

Introduction

33	0:00		violins and violas tremolo; **pp**; cellos and basses upward swoop; **p < mf**; three times capped off with soft thud on bass drum; duple meter (4), moderately slow

	0:11		woodwind-held chords, over rapidly repeated figures in upper strings into pizzicato strings, answered by winds
	0:32	FANFARE MOTIVE	playing staccato (short tones); **f** in piccolo, flutes, and "squeaky" E-flat clarinet ending with downward glissando (smear), imitated by muted horn over bass drum roll; **ppp**
	0:55		similar to opening with upward swoops
	1:20	FANFARE MOTIVE	returns in the same instruments, but louder; **pppp**; muted horn imitates still softer; **mf**; over quiet bass drum roll

Idée Fixe—"Beloved Melody"

| 34 | 1:37 | THEME 1 fragment "Beloved Melody" | clarinet plays mocking dance style; ***ppp***; over percussion; duple meter (2) compound, allegro; homophonic texture |

	1:45	TRANSITION SECTION	transition section, sudden full orchestra; ***ff***; faster, triplet patterns; section ends with clear cadence chord
	1:57	THEME 1 "Beloved Melody"	played by E-flat clarinet; ***f***; accompanied by woodwinds, later flute added to the melody with rapid arpeggio figures in bassoon and cellos; other instruments join in crescendo to ***ff***
	2:27	TRANSITION SECTION	transition section full orchestra chord; ***ff***; then descending and ascending chromatic scale triplet figures into string descending syncopated pattern, changing into descending long tones in bass instruments, quieter to held bass tone
35	3:10	TOLLING BELLS	ominous sounding bells/chimes, ***ff***; three sets of three notes C-C-G; each set interrupted by WITCHES' ROUND DANCE fragment

Dies Irae

| 36 | 3:39 | THEME 2 *Dies irae* Part 1 | played by tubas, ***f***; slow 2 meter, TOLLING BELLS continue; homophonic texture |

	4:01	THEME 2 *Dies irae* Part 1	imitated by ***f*** brass section, twice as fast; then imitated by ***f*** woodwinds and pizzicato strings, twice as fast as brass section; ending with upward swoop similar to the beginning
	4:17	THEME 2 *Dies irae* Part 2	tubas; ***ff***; imitated by pizzicato basses and cellos; then imitated by brass section twice as fast; then woodwinds and pizzicato strings twice as fast as brass section; ending with upward swoop
	4:43	THEME 2 *Dies irae* Part 1	returns in tubas and bassoons; ***f***; syncopated low strings; brass section imitates twice as fast; then woodwinds and pizzicato strings twice as fast as brass section, ending with upward swoop; TOLLING BELLS continue

| 5:20 | THEME 3 fragment Witches' Round Dance | transition section in strings, *mf*; several times, *crescendo* to cadence chord, *ff* |

violins and violas

Witches' Round Dance (loosely constructed fugue)

| 37 | 5:38 | THEME 3 Witches Round Dance | duple meter compound, slower tempo; fugue started in low strings, imitated in upper strings; then woodwinds, punctuated by loud, syncopated brass figures; later section quiets down; polyphonic texture |

7:28	THEMES 2 and 3 fragments	horns; *f*; DIES IRAE, strings; *p*; WITCHES' ROUND DANCE; long transition over bass drum roll, gradual *crescendo* to loud syncopated figures; section ends with a cadence
7:35	THEME 3 Witches' Round Dance	returns, *ff*; in strings, original tempo, continue through brass entrances
8:33	THEME 2 *Dies irae*	returns in winds, *ff*; continues together with THEME 3 in strings, *ff*
9:03	THEME 3 fragments	transition section (resembling dancing ghosts and skeletons), trill ornaments in upper strings, *f*; rattling wood part of their bows (*col legno battuta*) over the strings, staccato woodwinds (laughingly), then brass chords, full orchestra-held chord

Coda

9:41	THEME 2 returns *Dies irae*	in tubas, *f*; twice as fast, then woodwinds twice as fast
9:42	CODA MATERIAL	full orchestra, *ff*; triplet figures dominate, then loud chords, descending chromatic scale in trombones
10:25	FINAL CHORD	held, *ff*

What to Listen for in Early Romantic Music

To enjoy Romantic music more fully, look for extra musical clues that have possibly contributed to the composer's inspiration for the music. The most obvious clues come from the title of the work—*Spring* Symphony, *Faust* Symphony, *Italian* Symphony, *1812 Overture*. Before you listen to the music, anticipate how the composer might convey the title's meaning through the music. While you listen, decide whether the music confirms your images.

Read the printed concert program or notes accompanying the recording for the title and other clues. You may also find background information about the music and the composer in the library.

The Romantic Art Song

Lied (pl., Lieder)
(*leed, leed*-er)

The small, intimate *art song* (*Lied,* in German) epitomizes Romantic music. A composer of Romantic art songs would choose an existing poem—a work that stands on its own—and set it to music to heighten the drama of the text. Subjects include nature, beauty, love, death, and heroism.

Song Cycle

When a group of songs was designed to be performed together, often around a common subject or musical idea, composers placed them in a *song cycle*.

Art Song Performances

Performances of art songs became a favorite entertainment during the Romantic period. Originally held in the homes of the wealthy, these performances were part

FRANZ SCHUBERT (1797–1828)

Showing early musical talent, Franz Schubert (*shoo-bert*) studied violin with his father and piano with his brother. He became a choirboy in the Imperial Chapel of his native Vienna (Vienna Boy's Choir) and, as one of the benefits, was able to study music and other subjects at Vienna City School. At thirteen, Schubert studied composition with Salieri.

Schubert did well in school, and by eighteen, had become a schoolmaster, like his father. But he was unhappy teaching young students and resented the

rigidity of the teaching profession. Schubert's real interest was composing, which he was able to do full time when he left his teaching post at age twenty-one.

Schubert's meager income provided him a near-pauper's existence, occasionally alleviated by the help of his more fortunate friends.

His last five years were fraught with illness, but he kept composing until his death at age thirty-one. Like Mozart, he died young in Vienna, yet he left the world a wealth of beautiful music.

PRINCIPAL WORKS

Orchestral: nine symphonies, including: No. 5 in B-flat Major (1816), No. 8 (*Unfinished,* 1822), No. 9 (*Great,* 1825); Concert overtures; Incidental music: *Rosamunde* (1823)

Chamber Music: fifteen string quartets, including: *Death and the Maiden* (1824), String Quartet in C (1828); piano quintet: *The Trout* (1828)

Piano Music: twenty-one sonatas, six *Moments musicaux* (1828), impromptus, dances, fantasias, variations, marches

Songs: about 600: "An die Musik" (To Music), "Ave Maria," "Erlkönig" (The Erlking), "Der Wanderer" (The Wanderer), "Die Forelle" (The Trout); Song Cycles: *Die schöne Müllerin* (The Beautiful Maid of the Mill, 1823), *Winterreise* (Winter's Journey, 1827)

Operas: *Alfonso und Estrella* (1822), *Fierabras* (1823)

Choral Music: thirty choral works, including seven masses

A musical evening with Schubert at the piano and the singer Vogl (standing with score)

of an evening that typically included poetry readings and philosophical discussions. Guests included an assortment of poets, novelists, painters, musicians, philosophers, and patrons of the arts. As the popularity of the art song spread, performances often moved to small concert halls and were open to the general public.

Pianist's Role in Art Songs   In performing art songs, the singer and the pianist have an equal role. Accompanist and vocalist share the melodic ideas, providing a context for the poetry. The musical dialogue and constant interaction between soloist and accompanist elevate both the poetry and the music to a high artistic plane.

German Art Song Composers
The most notable composers of German art songs were Franz Schubert, Robert Schumann, Felix Mendelssohn, Johannes Brahms, Franz Liszt, Hugo Wolf (1860–1903), Richard Strauss, and Gustav Mahler.

French Art Song Composers
Gabriel Fauré (1845–1924) and Henri Duparc (1848–1933) used poems in their native French, as did the twentieth-century composers Claude Debussy, Maurice Ravel, Francis Poulenc, and many others.

Scandinavian Art Song Composers
Of the Scandinavian composers, Edvard Grieg (1865–1931) wrote many of the most beautiful songs in the genre.

Erlking (Erlkönig), **Franz Schubert**

Large Form: Art Song
Detailed Form: Through-Composed
Performing Medium: Baritone and Piano

Compact Disc 2, Track 1
Running Time: 4:14

Before following the Listening Guide and recording of Schubert's *Erlkönig* (Erlking), read the text. For this art song, Schubert chose a poem by one of the great German poets, Johann Wolfgang Goethe (1749–1832). Germanic legend describes the Erlking as a messenger of death who kills everyone he touches. The subjects, death and the supernatural, are typically Romantic.

Notice that there are four character roles in the poem, challenging the singer to distinguish among the characters by using distinctly different voice qualities for each portrayal:

- a narrator
- an ill child
- the child's father on horseback
- the beckoning Erlking

Through-composed

The form for the song is *through-composed*—the melodies keep changing with little or no return.

Notice how the piano, playing its repeated triplet patterns, adds to the agitated mood, and how the accompaniment enhances the ideas in the text.

Schnell (fast)

Erlking (Erlkönig), *Franz Schubert*

1	0:00	Ominous-sounding triplet patterns in piano accompaniment continue throughout, growing in intensity. Begins in key of g minor. With the entrance of each character and event, the key moves up.

0:23   ***Narrator***

Wer reitet so spät durch Nacht und Wind?	Who rides so late through the night and wind?
Es ist der Vater mit seinem Kind;	It is a father with his child.
Er hat den Knaben wohl in dem Arm,	He holds the young boy within his arm,
Er faßt ihn sicher, er hält ihn warm.	He clasps him tightly, he keeps him warm.

0:56   ***The Father***

"Mein Sohn, was birgst du so bang dein Gesicht?"	"My son, why do you hide your face in fear?"

1:05	***The Child*** (with fear)	
	"Siehst, Vater, du den Erlkönig nicht	"See, father, isn't that the Erlking?
	Den Erlkönig mit Kron' und Schweif?"	The Erlking with crown and cape?"
1:22	***The Father*** (calming his child)	
	"Mein Sohn, es ist ein Nebelstreif."	"My son, it's only a misty cloud."
1:32	***The Erlking*** (sweetly)	
	"Du liebes Kind, komm, geh' mit mir!	"You lovely child, come, go with me!
	Gar schöne Spiele spiel' ich mit dir;	Such pleasant games I'll play with thee!
	Manch' bunte Blumen sind an dem Strand,	The fields have bright flowers to behold,
	Meine Mutter hat manch' gülden Gewand."	My mother has many robes of gold."
1:54	***The Child***	
	"Mein Vater, mein Vater, und hörest du nicht,	"My father, my father, now don't you hear
	Was Erlkönig mir leise verspricht?"	What the Erlking whispers in my ear?"
2:07	***The Father***	
	"Sei ruhig, bleibe ruhig, mein Kind;	"Be calm, stay calm, my child;
	In dürren Blättern säuselt der Wind."	The dry leaves rustle when the wind blows wild."
2:18	***The Erlking*** (beckoning)	
	"Willst, feiner Knabe, du mit mir geh'n?	"My fine boy, won't you go with me?
	Meine Töchter sollen dich warten schon;	My daughters shall wait on thee,
	Meine Töchter führen den nächtlichen Reih'n	My daughters nightly revels keep,
	Und wiegen und tanzen und singen dich ein.	They'll sing and dance and rock you to sleep.
	Sie wiegen und tanzen und singen dich ein."	And sing and dance and rock you to sleep."
2:36	***The Child***	
	"Mein Vater, mein Vater, und siehst du nicht dort	"My father, my father, can't you see him there
	Erlkönigs Töchter am düstern Ort?"	The Erlking's daughters in that dark place?"
2:49	***The Father***	
	"Mein Sohn, mein Sohn, ich seh' es genau,	"My son, my son, all I can see,
	Es scheinen die alten Weiden so grau."	Is just the old gray willow trees."
3:00	triplet patterns in the piano	
3:07	***The Erlking***	
	"Ich liebe dich, mich reizt deine schöne Gestalt,	"I love you, your form enflames my sense;
	Und bist du nicht willig, so brauch' ich Gewalt."	Since you are not willing, I'll take you by force."
3:19	***The Child***	
	"Mein Vater, mein Vater, jetzt faßt er mich an!	"My father, my father, he's now grabbing my arm,
	Erlkönig hat mir ein Leid's getan!"	The Erlking wants to do me harm!"
3:34	***The Narrator***	
	Dem Vater grauset's, er reitet geschwind,	The father shudders, he speeds through the wind,
	Er hält in Armen das ächzende Kind,	He holds the moaning child in his arms,
4:00	***The Narrator*** (music slows)	
	Erreicht den Hof mit Müh und Not;	He reaches home with pain and dread:
	In seinen Armen das Kind war tot!	In his arms, the child lay dead!
4:13	final chord in g minor	

CHALLENGE YOUR EXPERTISE

What was Johann Maelzel's invention, and how did it affect music performance?

Romantic Piano Music

Nineteenth-Century Piano

The piano of the nineteenth century was greatly superior to the earliest versions in Frederick the Great's collection that Bach had found wanting. Enlarged, with an improved mechanism and more keys, the piano was now capable of producing a full range of expression and level of dynamics. It became the perfect medium with which to display the virtuosity of the Romantic keyboard performer in public concert halls.

Salon concerts

Salon concerts of piano music, art songs, or chamber music became the vogue among wealthy music enthusiasts. The hosts invited a select group of sophisticated guests to hear a recital by Chopin, Schubert, Mendelssohn, Liszt, Clara Schumann, and the influential piano teacher-composer Anton Rubinstein (1829–1894). Performances usually took place in a patron's home, or occasionally, for an audience larger than a residence could accommodate, in a public recital hall.

ROBERT SCHUMANN (1810–1856)

Robert Schumann (*shoo*-mahn) was born in Zwickau, Germany, near Leipzig. His father, a writer and publisher, sent Robert to Leipzig University to study law. But Robert's strong interests in music and literature distracted him, and he never attended classes.

At nineteen, he studied piano with Friedrich Wieck (*veek*). It was then that Robert met his teacher's nine-year-old daughter Clara, a piano prodigy. Robert moved into Wieck's home as a lodger the following year. In 1840, he married Clara Wieck, then age twenty-one. Clara became one of the nineteenth century's leading concert pianists and the greatest exponent of her husband's music. Their famous love affair was the subject of several Hollywood films.

As a result of syphilis, Schumann developed a lesion on his hand and began to have great difficulty with the flexibility of his fingers. Unsuccessful medical treatment probably aggravated the problem, which was devastating to his planned career as a performer.

Also contributing to Schumann's hand problems was his use of mechanical finger-strengthening devices, popular at that time, which may have damaged his flexibility. This, however, was a rumor.

Unable to perform in public, he followed his abiding interest in literature and journalism, founding the *Neue Zeitschrift für Musik* (The New Journal for Music), which is still in existence. As its editor and leading writer, Robert became one of the first and finest music critics, calling attention to such creative geniuses as Schubert, Berlioz, Mendelssohn, Chopin, and Brahms.

Toward the end of his life, Schumann was plagued by depression, hallucinations, and erratic behavior. He even attempted suicide by throwing himself into the icy winter waters of the Rhine River. In 1856, after being rescued from his suicide attempt, Schumann was taken to an asylum, where he died later that year at age forty-six.

PRINCIPAL WORKS

Orchestral Music: four symphonies, including: No. 1 (*Spring*, 1841), No. 3 (*Rhenish*, 1850); Piano Concerto in a minor (1845)

Chamber Music: twenty-three works for various chamber music groups

Piano Music: "Abegg" Variations, Op. 1 (1830); *Papillons* (Butterflies), Op. 2 (1831); *Carnaval,* Op. 9 (1835); and *Kinderszenen* (Scenes from Childhood)

Songs: Over 275 songs, including several song cycles: *Frauenliebe und Leben* (A Woman's Love and Life, 1840) and *Dichterliebe* (A Poet's Love, 1840)

Early daguerreotype photograph of Clara and Robert Schumann

CLARA [WIECK] SCHUMANN (1819–1896)

As early as age twenty-one, Clara Wieck Schumann had written in her diary, "I once thought that I possessed creative talent, but I have given up this idea; a woman must not desire to compose—not one has been able to do it, and why should I expect to?"

At age five, Clara began piano lessons with her father, Friedrich Wieck, a noted piano teacher in Leipzig, Germany. She progressed so rapidly that by age nine she performed a full piano recital in the famous Gewandhaus concert hall in Leipzig. The following year, her father organized a concert tour, and Clara performed throughout central Europe, traveling as far as Paris. Her fame quickly spread, and by sixteen, she was recognized as a highly talented child prodigy. Among her admirers were Felix Mendelssohn, Frédéric Chopin, and of course,

Robert Schumann, her future husband. After hearing Clara perform, the great virtuoso-pianist Franz Liszt declared that she had "complete technical mastery, depth, and sincerity of feeling."

While still in her teens, Clara had several of her piano compositions published. Because of her widespread fame, she had an easier time at this age getting her works published than most of her women contemporaries. This would change later in her life.

Clara continued concertizing through her teen years with great acclaim. Her successes on the stage were dampened by conflicts in her personal life. Clara and Robert Schumann had fallen in love, much to the chagrin of her father, who felt that marriage to Robert would threaten her brilliant career. Robert had moved into the

Wiecks' house as a twenty-year-old piano student and lodger when Clara was only ten years old. When Clara was eighteen, Robert asked Professor Wieck to give his permission for Clara to marry him. Friedrich refused, and a bitter legal as well as a personal battle began, which ended with the law court's ruling that the two lovers could marry. By then, the two were the talk of Europe's musical world.

Clara and Robert married in 1840. Much of her father's concern became a reality. Clara's performing and composing career waned for several years while she bore eight children, seven of whom lived beyond childhood. Clara tended to a very busy household, which later included a boarder and music student, Johannes Brahms.

After Robert's illnesses, attempted suicide, and eventual death in an asylum, Clara continued both composing and performing, though in a more limited way. She was no longer a child prodigy, and her composing was thwarted by nineteenth-century prejudice against women's asserting themselves in the arts and commerce.

Clara became a celebrated pianist, specializing in the music of both Schumann and Brahms. Clara and Brahms maintained a caring though mostly long-distance relationship that was rumored to have been quite serious. Mysteriously, they destroyed each other's correspondence. In addition to performing as she grew older, Clara became an influential teacher, working for some years at the Leipzig Conservatory of Music and later at the Hoch Conservatory in Frankfurt. She died at age seventy-six.

PRINCIPAL WORKS

Orchestral and Chamber Music: Concerto in a minor (1837); Three Romances for Violin and Piano (1853); Trio in g minor for Violin, Cello, Piano (1846)

Piano Music: Romance-Variations on a Theme of Robert Schumann (1853); Soirée musicales (1836); numerous works in many forms, such as variations, caprices, nocturnes, mazurkas, waltzes, and scherzos

Choral Music: Choral songs for a cappella mixed choir (1848)

Songs: numerous songs (*lieder*)

LISTENING ACTIVITY

Scherzo, **Opus 10, Clara Wieck Schumann**

Large Form: Short Piano Recital Piece
Detailed Form: Scherzo with Two Trios
Performing Medium: Piano

Compact Disc 2, Track 2
Running Time: 4:59

One of the most brilliant virtuoso pianists of her time, Clara Schumann composed many piano pieces like this scherzo (meaning *joke,* in Italian) to display her own abilities. It was Beethoven who made the form popular when he began using the scherzo to replace the traditional minuet in multimovement works such as the symphony and string quartet. Slower and more stately, the minuet had been a favorite dance of the leisure-class aristocrats at the courts of Europe. Revolutions and uprisings had brought down many of the courts; therefore, the late eighteenth and early nineteenth centuries were a time when composers began disassociating themselves with the courts to bring more music to the growing middle-class audiences.

Faster and more lively than the minuet, the Romantic-period scherzo developed into an entertaining vehicle for a variety of solo instruments to display the performer's technical prowess. With its extremely fast tempo (*presto*), Clara Schumann's Opus 10 scherzo makes great demands on the pianist to maintain the furious pace set in the beginning.

LISTENING GUIDE

Scherzo, Opus 10, Clara Wieck Schumann

| 2 | 0:00 | INTRODUCTION THEME | Solo piano; very fast tempo (presto); triple meter; alternating pitches and sequences in the upper register; **p**; d-minor tonality; homophonic texture; expression indication "with passion" |

Presto. Scherzo con passione.

| | 0:08 | SCHERZO THEME | Unison melody with accented chords, alternating with arpeggios; **p**; d-minor tonality |

	0:19	INTRODUCTION THEME	Introduction Theme restated; **g**-minor tonality; **p** to **f** then diminuendo to **p**
	0:36	SCHERZO THEME	Scherzo Theme returns in d-minor tonality
	1:04	SCHERZO THEME (modified)	alternating pitch figures
	1:30	TRIO 1 THEME	Slower tempo; smooth, expressive stepwise descending melody in upper voice with arpeggio chordal accompaniment creating a homophonic texture; followed by upward arpeggios and accents in lower part; crescendo, becoming more agitated

| | 1:57 | SCHERZO FRAGMENTS | in octaves in the bass, imitated in upper voice; **f**, A-Major tonality; original presto tempo; agitated; **ff**; gradually becoming smoother and calmer |

| 2:12 | SCHERZO THEME | restated *f* and rhythmically; gradually softer toward two pauses |
| 2:41 | TRIO 2 THEME | introduced; *p*; melody rising and falling, mostly stepwise; *p* bass chords on the second beat; E-flat Major tonality; section is repeated more accented; rubato; gradually slowing |

3:28		Original presto tempo; SCHERZO FRAGMENTS in lower part, upper part continues TRIO 2 THEME; then fragments of INTRODUCTION THEME in lower part; transitions to full INTRODUCTION THEME
4:04:	INTRODUCTION THEME	returns with the same tempo and tonality as in the beginning
4:12	SCHERZO THEME	returns in original d-minor tonality; then imitated in bass part; crescendo and more furious; fragments of INTRODUCTION THEME heard, followed by a loud lower-voiced chordal final cadence

FRÉDÉRIC CHOPIN (1810–1849)

Born near Warsaw, Poland, Frédéric Chopin (sho-*pan*) gave his first piano recital there when he was eight. Concentrating mainly on piano performance, he studied at the Warsaw Conservatory until he was nineteen.

Frédéric's father, a Frenchman, had left France to avoid serving in Napoleon's army. In Poland, the elder Chopin was a political activitist who vehemently opposed the czarist Russian occupation. Because the family lived in fear of reprisal, they thought Frédéric would be safer elsewhere so he could advance his career.

After Frédéric left Poland, he concertized first in Vienna, then throughout Germany. He finally settled in Paris, where the artistic community quickly accepted him.

Among his friends were painter Delacroix, musicians Liszt and Berlioz, and writers Victor Hugo, Honoré de Balzac, Alexandre Dumas (père), Heinrich Heine, and George Sand.

Sand was actually a woman, Aurore Dudevant. To become published, she was forced to use a man's name and circumvent the prejudice against women writers. She and Chopin lived together for years, and she nursed him through his bouts with tuberculosis. He finally died from the disease at thirty-nine. True to the romantic and nationalistic spirit, his body was buried in Paris, but his heart was returned to Poland for burial.

Chopin left a legacy of piano compositions that are among the greatest ever written.

PRINCIPAL WORKS

Orchestral Music: two concertos for piano and orchestra: No. 1 in e minor (1830), No. 2 in f minor (1830)

Piano Music: hundreds of pieces in a variety of short forms: ballades, preludes, fantasies, impromptus, nocturnes, polonaises, scherzos, études (studies), variations, and waltzes

Published Piano Music

The popularity of both public and salon performances encouraged composers to create and publish an unsurpassed variety of piano music. Learning to play the piano was considered an essential element of a nineteenth-century education, particularly among middle-class and wealthy families. The demand for published music increased, and composers now had a lucrative outlet for their works.

Intimate Piano Music

To take full advantage of the instrument's expressive potential and to hold the interest of their audiences, Chopin, Liszt, Mendelssohn, Brahms, and other composers generally wrote fewer of the longer, more formal piano pieces, such as the sonata. Instead, they developed a variety of simple, intimate forms, generally lasting from two to five minutes.

- ballades
- capriccios
- consolations
- études (studies)
- fantasies
- impromptus
- mazurkas

- nocturnes
- polonaises
- preludes
- rhapsodies
- scherzos
- songs without words
- waltzes

LISTENING ACTIVITY

***Fantaisie-Impromptu,* Frédéric Chopin**

Large Form: Short Piano Recital Piece
Detailed Form: Three Part Form (A-B-A)
Performing Medium: Piano

Compact Disc 2, Track 3
Running Time: 4:42

Listen to the *Fantaisie-Impromptu* by Chopin. Lasting less than five minutes, the piece covers a wide range of expression and allows the performer to dazzle the audience. Notice the slight deviations from steady tempo—*rubato*—which enhance the emotional mood of the piece.

The title, *Fantaisie-Impromptu,* gives two clues to the nature of the music. *Fantaisie,* or "fantasy," denotes whimsy, a fanciful vision, a pleasant daydream. *Impromptu* suggests extemporaneous or improvised music. Though Chopin notated the music on paper, he wanted the music to suggest a feeling of spontaneity.

Chopin's melody in the middle section (B) is so appealing that during the 1940s it was turned into a popular song called "I'm Always Chasing Rainbows."

The detailed form, A-B-A, which Chopin uses here, is one of the most popular in music. Often called a three-part song form because of its extensive use in songs, the first and last sections (A) are similar and bracket a contrasting middle section (B).

LISTENING GUIDE

Fantaisie Impromptu, Frédéric Chopin

Section A

3	0:00	THEME 1	Allegro, duple meter, rubato throughout, sixteen-note patterns in upper voice and triplet patterns in the bass, c-sharp minor tonality, *f* diminuendo to *p*, then brief swells crescendo and diminuendo
	0:48		chromatic runs from high to low, slowing and modulating to D-flat major tonality

Section B

	1:03	THEME 2	moderate tempo, softer, homophonic texture—melody with ornaments in high voice, rolling triplet arpeggios in bass accompaniment

Section A

	3:03	THEME 1	presto (very fast) like the beginning, c-sharp minor tonality, crescendos and diminuendos chromatic runs from high to low, still c-sharp minor tonality

Coda

	3:57	THEME 2	*ff* gradual diminuendo and slowing of tempo, brief restatement of melody from section B in bass, ending with two rolling chords, very soft

FRANZ LISZT (1811–1886)

Franz Liszt (*list*) was born near Sopron in the Austro-Hungarian empire. Because Sopron was once predominantly Austrian, Liszt's native language was German. The town is forty miles south of Vienna and only twelve miles from the Esterházy's Austrian palace in Eisenstadt, where Haydn worked. During Haydn's time, Liszt's father was one of the managers of the Esterházy's summer palace in Hungary, which Haydn frequently visited.

Liszt exhibited enormous talent as a pianist and was sent to Vienna to study with Antonio Salieri and Karl Czerny (*chair*-nee) (1791–1857). Following his piano debut in London at age eleven, Liszt began touring the musical capitals of Europe and was soon considered the greatest piano virtuoso of the nineteenth century.

Settling in Paris at age sixteen, Liszt was quickly welcomed into the inner circles of great artists: Berlioz, Heine,

Hugo, Sand, and later, Chopin. With Paris as his home base, Liszt toured extensively throughout central Europe, Russia, Turkey, the British Isles, Spain, and Portugal.

At age thirty-eight, he accepted the position of music director to the Grand Duke of Weimar (*vy*-mar), near Leipzig. There, Liszt devoted himself mainly to composing and conducting. He also introduced several works of his friend, Richard Wagner. That friendship became family when Liszt's daughter Cosima married Wagner.

At age fifty, Liszt moved to Rome and went through a religious stage there, taking minor orders in the Catholic Church. Later, he continued traveling and performing until his death at age seventy-four in Bayreuth (*by*-royt), Germany. Liszt's music is known for its extramusical associations, either through their titles, or from specific programs.

PRINCIPAL WORKS

Orchestral Music: *Faust Symphony* (1854); *Dante Symphony* (1856); Symphonic Poems: *Tasso* (1849); *Les Préludes* (1854); Piano Concertos No. 1 in E-flat (1849); No. 2 in A (1849); *Totentanz* for Piano and Orchestra (1849)

Piano Music: Transcendental Studies (1851); *Traveler's Album* (1836); *Six Consolations* (1850); Sonata in b minor (1853); Hungarian Rhapsodies, ballads, études (studies)

Mendelssohn's Concerts As the newly appointed conductor of the Leipzig Gewandhaus Orchestra, 26-year-old Felix Mendelssohn addressed his musicians, imploring them to make their orchestra the best in Europe. He was able to motivate them, and they worked harder than ever before. Finally, the orchestra did earn that distinction under Mendelssohn's direction.

To compensate them for their extra work, Felix used his own money to double the salaries of his players. He also established the first pension plan for orchestral musicians. Treated like professionals, they had greater feelings of self-esteem.

Mendelssohn created a new type of concert offering. Until his time, orchestras primarily played works by living composers, with rare performances of music by dead composers. Aware that a wealth of great orchestral music was being neglected, simply because the composer was no longer around to promote it, Mendelssohn assembled programs similar to what we find today—works by

FELIX MENDELSSOHN (1809–1847)

Felix Mendelssohn was born in Hamburg, Germany, into one of Europe's wealthiest and most interesting families. His grandfather, the noted writer and philosopher Moses Mendelssohn (*men*-dl-sun), was a political and financial advisor to King Friedrich the Great of Prussia. (Moses was largely responsible for the assimilation of Jews into German society.) Felix's father, Abraham, started the banking business that influenced European affairs until the Nazi era.

When Felix was an infant, his family moved to Berlin. He began receiving a thorough education through tutors when he was very young. Many people—including Felix's teachers and Goethe, a frequent visitor at the Mendelssohn home—described the boy as "an exceptionally attractive, agreeable, and talented child."

His musical talents were often compared to Mozart's. Performing brilliantly on the piano at an early age, Felix displayed his genius by writing six symphonies by age twelve, seven more by fourteen, and *A Midsummer Night's Dream* Overture at seventeen.

The Mendelssohns' Berlin home was a meeting place for some of the most influential artists and thinkers of the world. Felix's father added the name "Bartholdy" to the family name because of the pressures of anti-Semitism. Although he tried to pass this name on to his children, they secretly rejected its use. Felix often signed letters to his sister Fanny as "Felix 'not-Bartholdy' Mendelssohn."

Traveling extensively throughout Germany, England, Scotland, and Italy, Felix incorporated his impressions into musical compositions. At age twenty-six, he became conductor and musical director of the Gewandhaus (guh-*vahnd*-house, "Cloth Hall") Orchestra in Leipzig, a post he held for the rest of his life.

Also in Leipzig, he founded one of Europe's great schools of music, the Leipzig Conservatory. After the death of his beloved sister Fanny, his health began to fail. Mendelssohn died several months later at age thirty-seven.

PRINCIPAL WORKS

Orchestral Music: twelve string symphonies; five full orchestra symphonies: No. 3 (*Scottish,* 1842), No. 4 (*Italian,* 1833), No. 5 (*Reformation,* 1832); Overtures: *A Midsummer Night's Dream* Overture (1826), *Calm Sea and Prosperous Voyage* (1828), *The Hebrides* (*Fingal's Cave*) *Overture* (1830), *Ruy Blas Overture* (1839), Piano Concertos: No. 1 in g minor (1831), No. 2 in d minor (1837); Violin concerto in e minor (1844)

Chamber Music: six string quartets, two string quintets

Piano Music: forty-eight Lieder ohne Worte (Songs without Words)

Choral Music: oratorios in the Handel tradition: *St. Paul* (1836), *Elijah* (1846)

several composers, from several style periods. He staged concerts featuring Handel's oratorios, Bach's works for chorus and orchestra, and Mozart's and Beethoven's symphonies.

Mendelssohn showcased his contemporaries as well. Struggling composers could come to him for his generous financial help. By featuring their music in his Gewandhaus concerts, Mendelssohn enabled both audiences and publishers to become familiar with the works of Franz Schubert, Robert Schumann, Hector Berlioz, Luigi Cherubini, Franz Liszt, Giacomo Meyerbeer, Johannes Brahms, and Frédéric Chopin.

Hundreds of musicians and composers were indebted to Mendelssohn for his nurturing. During his short life, he served as a catalyst for promoting music as a desirable profession.

FANNY MENDELSSOHN (1805–1847)

Four years older than her brother Felix, Fanny Mendelssohn was described as being equally talented. Like her brother, Fanny began piano lessons with her mother. She made such excellent progress in her piano studies that by age thirteen she could play from memory Bach's entire *Well-Tempered Clavier*. Foregoing a performing career for a husband and a family, Fanny married painter Wilhelm Hensel. However, she and her family did travel extensively throughout Europe, with extended stays in Milan, Venice, Naples, and Genoa.

Fanny remained an excellent pianist as well as a composer, though most of her compositions were unpublished during her lifetime. Because of the discrimination against women composers, she had to publish six of her songs, which were well received, under Felix's name.

Fanny and her brother Felix remained close throughout their short lives, consulting each other on personal as well as musical matters.

Like her brother, Fanny nurtured new composers at the Elternhaus in Berlin, where she, like Felix, produced performances of their works. Fanny's death at age forty-one was a dramatic, tragic event. It happened on stage during a rehearsal of Felix's *Walpurgisnacht* cantata at the Elternhaus. Felix was devastated by Fanny's untimely death and went into a deep depression. He too died a few months later.

PRINCIPAL WORKS (OVER 200, SOME PUBLISHED WORKS FOLLOW)

Chamber Music: Trio in d minor for Violin, Cello, and Piano (Op. 11)

Piano Music: Romances without Words (7) (Op. 2, 6, 8); *Der Jahr* (The Year) a suite of thirteen pieces, various sonatas

CHALLENGE YOUR EXPERTISE

- Which composer courted his loved one in a language she did not understand?
- Which of the following composers could have been a guest at Chopin's thirtieth birthday party: Mendelssohn, Schubert, Liszt, Beethoven?

LISTENING ACTIVITY

Concerto for Violin and Orchestra (1844, Op. 64), Felix Mendelssohn

First Movement: Allegro Molto Appassionatto
Large Form: Violin Concerto
Detailed Form: Scherzo with Two Trios
Performing Medium: Piano

Compact Disc 3, Tracks 3–6
Running Time: 11:42

Mendelssohn's Violin Concerto in e minor is one of the most frequently played violin concertos today. He composed the work in 1844 for his friend Ferdinand David, a famous violinist. The concerto is in the typical concerto form of three movements: fast-slow-fast.

Traditionally, audiences would applaud the soloist after the first movement of a concerto, interrupting the mood of the music. Inspired by Beethoven's Piano Concerto No. 5 (*Emperor*), Mendelssohn indicates no stops between movements for the audience to applaud. Both composers wanted audiences to concentrate on the music rather than on the soloist.

Mendelssohn, like Beethoven, also wrote out the soloist's cadenzas, insisting that they be played as written. Thus Mendelssohn did not allow soloists to improvise or to insert their own cadenzas in his violin concerto.

The first movement is in classical sonata form. After only a three-beat, quiet orchestral introduction, the violin soloist enters with the main theme. This is a minor departure: Most Classical-period concertos contain two expositions, one by the orchestra and one by the soloist.

One of the outstanding features of this movement is its lyricism. All three melodies—Theme 1, Transition Theme, and Theme 2—are warmly melodic, allowing the soloist to display his or her rich violin tone quality and expressiveness.

LISTENING GUIDE

Concerto for Violin and Orchestra (1844, Op. 64), Felix Mendelssohn

Exposition

| 3 | 0:00 | THEME 1 | in solo violin, ***p***; after a three-beat orchestral introduction, song-like duple meter, e minor tonality; homophonic texture |

	0:29		solo violin passage, *f*; after short orchestral chords, *f*; repeated in sequence, violin continues with sequences accompanied by orchestra
	0:57	THEME 1	full orchestra without soloist, *ff*; original tempo and key, section moves into new theme
	1:29	TRANSITION THEME	introduced by the orchestra, *p*; then played by solo violin, same key (e minor)

Violins

p

	2:07	TRANSITION	transition section, *p*; solo violin sequences transition section, *p*; solo violin slowly, calmly, and expressively to held high tone; then descending line
4	2:46	THEME 2	introduced by woodwinds, *pp*; slower tempo, G-Major tonality

Clarinet

pp *tranquillo*

	2:58	THEME 2	played by solo violin, *pp*; calmly and expressively, imitations between soloist and orchestra move to held note and cadence
	3:48	THEME 1	returns in solo violin; *p*; original tempo and tonality (e minor); into brilliant solo passages, including sequences, with pizzicato string accompaniment
	4:37	THEME 1	solo violin and orchestra trills, *ff*; forcefully; section ends

Development

5	4:58	TRANSITION THEME fragments THEME 1 fragments	both used, rubato
	5:57	THEME 1 fragments	in solo violin, *pp*; descending sequences; orchestra crescendos to held loud dominant chord
	6:22	CADENZA	unaccompanied solo violin; arpeggios, trills, fragments of THEME 1, rapid arpeggios, diminuendo; transition back to orchestra

Recapitulation

6	7:51	THEME 1	played softly by the orchestra, original tempo and key
	8:07	TRANSITION THEME fragments	played first by orchestra, *ff*; then sequences, played by solo violin; becomes softer, slows down, modulates to new key
	8:37	THEME 2	returns first in woodwinds, then solo violin, E-major tonality; section ends with held high note, and cadence

9:48	THEME 1 fragments	played softly by orchestra, followed by solo violin passages accompanied by pizzicato strings; orchestra crescendo
10:28	TRANSITION	loud orchestra chords separate unaccompanied solo violin passage, similar to cadenza
10:31	THEME 1 fragments	solo violin, **ff**; separated by orchestra trills, **ff**; then diminuendo

Coda

| 10:54 | TRANSITION THEME fragments | played softly by solo violin; faster tempo, increasingly faster and louder until the end |
| 11:38 | | **ff**; e minor; orchestra stops, except solo bassoonist who holds one tone, softly as a transition to the second movement |

CHALLENGE YOUR EXPERTISE

- Can you think of two composers who published their works under someone else's name?
- How did Mendelssohn effectively use a combination of affluence and influence in his work with other musicians?

Summary of Terms

art song	lieder	rhapsodies
ballades	mazurkas	salon concerts
consolations	nocturnes	scherzos
études	orchestration	song cycle
fantasies	polonaises	songs without words
idée fixe	preludes	through-composed
impromptus	recurrent melody	tone poems
lied	recurrent theme	waltzes

15
Romantic Opera

Opera is dramatized music. With its sung dialogue, elaborate costumes and scenery, cast of characters, and dancing—all accompanied by an orchestra—opera naturally lends itself to romanticism.

Audiences have always been drawn to opera as a contrast to everyday realism. Though some operas are based on realistic plots, most operas transport you to another time and place, to idealized love, to magic and mystery. Operatic superheroes and superbeings can do what no mortal can. By its very nature, then, opera became a very popular medium for nineteenth-century Romantic composers and audiences.

Adding Dimension to Instrumental Music

With singers performing a text in his Ninth Symphony, Beethoven strove to say more than instrumental music alone could convey. With grand opera, all of the subjects, spirit, and extramusical ideas associated with romanticism materialized in the grandest manner—many within the same opera.

Here are a few examples:

- *Fidelio* (1805) by Ludwig van Beethoven
  heroism, love, death
- *Der Freischütz* (1821) by Carl Maria von Weber
  magic, mystery, the supernatural
- *La Traviata* (1853) by Giuseppe Verdi
  love, death, beauty
- *Die Walküre* (1870) by Richard Wagner
  hero, supernatural, love
- *Carmen* (1875) by Georges Bizet
  the common man, love, death, exotic cultures
- *Madama Butterfly* (1904) by Giacomo Puccini
  distant lands, travel, exotic cultures, love, death
- *Turandot* (posthumous, 1926) by Giacomo Puccini
  distant lands, travel, exotic cultures, love, death

Earlier Opera

Until the early nineteenth century, operas were primarily a series of songs (arias and duets). Adhering to tightly knit plots was of little importance to the early opera composers. Choruses and instrumental music served as introductions, interludes, or fillers between songs.

Often, when it was time for an aria, all action on stage stopped. The performers stood frozen in tableau, while the soloist crossed downstage and, with little regard for the dramatic situation, delivered his or her aria to the audience. Suddenly, the fair maiden, about to die in bed, would throw off her covers, stand up, and sing. Following the aria, the death scene continued. The hero, about to plunge his sword into the villain's chest, postponed the kill until after his aria.

HISTORICAL PERSPECTIVE

Opera in North America

Inaugurated in 1883, the Metropolitan Opera Company in New York City became the first major opera company in North America. Though many limited-season opera companies held occasional performances in various cities throughout North America after 1883, the next permanent opera company, the San Francisco Opera Company, did not start until fifty years later, in 1923.

Today, there are more than fifty major opera companies in North America, with productions rivaling those anywhere in the world.

Opera Stars

Since its beginning, opera has attracted loyal fans to hear their favorite singers. Just as they enjoy virtuoso concerto soloists, audiences marvel at a singer's range, special tone quality, and *bel canto* abilities.

Great opera stars are capable of far more than just the musical performance. They transform themselves into the characters they are playing: the resounding bass voice becomes a fierce villain; the ringing tenor with his high "C" becomes the handsome prince; the warm, lilting soprano becomes the fair young maiden.

Quality Plots

Romantic composers—Carl Maria von Weber, Richard Wagner, Giuseppe Verdi, Giacomo Puccini, Georges Bizet, Charles Gounod, and others—elevated the significance and quality of the stories and heightened the drama of their operas. Audiences began to come to the opera for its drama, not solely for the vocal abilities of the stars or for the grand spectacle of its production values.

Italian Romantic Opera

Italian Language

Italian composers and the Italian language had dominated opera from its inception. Even Mozart used the Italian language. To continue that dominance into the Romantic period, early-nineteenth-century Italian composers such as Gioacchino Rossini (roh-*see*-nee, 1792–1868), Gaetano Donizetti (don-ih-*tzeh*-tee, 1797–1848), and Vincenzo Bellini (beh-*lee*-nee, 1801–1835) created a new round of exciting Italian operas.

Bel Canto Style of Singing

Romantic-period Italian composers perpetuated the *bel canto* style that characterized early Italian opera. Their aria melodies became elaborate vocal gymnastics, designed to astound audiences with the soloist's virtuosity.

Verdi's Opera Innovations

Both Verdi and Wagner are credited with developing opera into a fully integrated art form. Verdi's characters continued to sing appealing arias, but their songs grew out of the plot more convincingly than ever before. Though audiences still applaud at the end of his arias, Verdi tried to manipulate the action on stage and the orchestration to sustain the mood of the drama throughout the scene without applause.

Scene from Verdi's opera *Falstaff*

Summary of Verdi's Opera Innovations

- His libretto (book or story) for each opera was of high quality—adapted from stories by Shakespeare, Hugo, Dumas, and Schiller.
- His characters were believable and human.
- His arias blended into the action.
- His orchestral interludes and accompaniment were highly expressive and contributed substantially to the mood of the entire work.

GAETANO DONIZETTI (1797–1848)

Born in the northern lake district of Bergamo, Italy, Gaetano Donizetti (dohn-ih-*tzeh*-tee) later studied opera composition with the German composer Johann Simon Mayr (1763–1845). Some of his early operas were produced in northern Italy, but the later productions in Rome and Naples greatly advanced his popularity throughout the Italian peninsula.

His popularity then spread to France. For most of his later years, Donizetti lived in Paris, writing operas with French texts.

Donizetti was one of the most prolific of all the opera composers. He became famous for his dazzling arias, such as the "Mad Scene" from *Lucia di Lammermoor* (1835), which requires great vocal flexibility and extraordinary range.

PRINCIPAL WORKS

Operas: 75 operas, including *Anna Bolena* (Anne Boleyn, 1830), *L'elisir d'amore* (The Elixir of Love, 1832), *Lucrezia Borgia* (1833), *Lucia di Lammermoor* (1835), *La Fille du régiment* (The Daughter of the Regiment, 1840), *La Favorite* (1840), and *Don Pasquale* (1843)

Other Works: About 100 songs, several symphonies, concertos, oratorios, cantatas, chamber music, and church music

VINCENZO BELLINI (1801–1835)

Vincenzo Bellini's (beh-*lee*-nee) ten operas brought him great success and fame before his death at age thirty-three. Like Donizetti, Bellini wrote in both Italian and French and was adored by opera audiences in both Italy and France. Most of his works are still produced regularly by opera companies around the world.

PRINCIPAL WORKS

Operas: *La Sonnambula* (The Sleepwalker, 1831); *Norma* (1831); *I Puritani e i Cavalieri* (The Puritans and the Cavaliers, 1835)

GIOACCHINO ROSSINI (1792–1868)

Gioacchino Rossini (roh-*see*-nee) was one of the last masters of opera buffa. He was born in the Italian town of Pesaro on the Adriatic coast and studied music in Bologna. Following the 1810 premiere in Venice of his comic opera *La cambiale di matrimonio* (The Bill of Exchange for Marriage), his reputation spread quickly. Commissions poured in from across Europe. Soon he was composing for the most important opera houses in Italy, including La Scala in Milan.

By age 21, only three years after his debut in the genre, Rossini had composed ten operas. By the time he was 30, he had produced 32 operas. Perhaps the most famous of that prolific period was *Il barbiere di Siviglia* (The Barber of Seville). His combination of appealing, flowing melodies and wit, comedy, and brilliant staging

made Rossini one of the most important opera composers of the early nineteenth century.

In 1823, Rossini settled in Paris where, for the next six years, he continued his considerable output. Then, at age 37, after a series of disappointing love affairs and bouts with ill health, Rossini suddenly turned away from opera. Using a libretto in French, he composed his 39th and last opera, *Guillaume Tell* (William Tell). In the twentieth century, the Overture to William Tell began to have a life of its own, attaining greater popularity than the original opera.

Although Rossini continued composing, he limited his works mostly to religious music and songs. Nevertheless, by his death at age 74, Rossini had achieved tremendous success and financial security. Many of his operas are regularly performed in the contemporary repertoire.

PRINCIPAL WORKS

Operas: *L'Italiana in Algeri* (The Italian Girl in Algiers, 1813), *Il barbiere di Siviglia* (The Barber of Seville, 1816), *La Cenerentola* (Cinderella, 1817), *Semiramide* (1823), *Guillaume Tell* (William Tell, 1829)

Sacred Choral Music: *Petite messe solennelle* (1864), *Stabat Mater* (1841), Masses

Secular Vocal Music: *Les Soirées musicales* (Musical Evenings, 1835), cantatas

GIUSEPPE VERDI (1813–1901)

Busseto, a small town in northern Italy, was Giuseppe Verdi's (*vehr*-dee) birthplace. And it was there that he studied music until age 18, when he applied for admission to the Milan Conservatory. But Verdi could not pass the entrance examinations because the administrators of the Conservatory claimed that his pianistic abilities were substandard. Instead, Verdi had to study with various private music teachers in Milan.

Between the ages of 26 and 80, Verdi composed more than twenty-five operas. His first, *Oberto*, premiered in 1839 at Milan's famous Teatro alla Scala (La Scala). What

should have been a year of joy and triumph for the young man was overshadowed by the tragic, mysterious deaths of his wife and two children. Fifty-four years later, La Scala staged Verdi's last opera, *Falstaff*. Today, many of his works, including some of the obscure ones, are consistently produced throughout the world during every opera season.

For a time, Verdi became involved in Italian politics and Italy's struggle for independence from the Austro-Hungarian Empire. His name was used as a rallying acronym—*Vittore Emanuele Ré D'Italia* (Victor Emanuel, King of Italy). When Victor Emanuel became the first king of a united Italy, Verdi was appointed to the new parliament and later elected to the senate. Among his accomplishments was the establishment of a home for retired opera singers and musicians. His death in Milan stirred Italy, and his funeral drew some of the largest crowds in that nation's history.

PRINCIPAL WORKS

Operas: *Nabucco* (1842), *Ernani* (1844), *Macbeth* (1847), *Rigoletto* (1851), *Il trovatore* (The Troubadour, 1853), *La traviata* (The Courtesan, 1853), *Un ballo in maschera* (A Masked Ball, 1859), *La forza del destino* (The Force of Destiny, 1862), *Don Carlos* (1867), *Aïda* (1871), *Otello* (1887), *Falstaff* (1893)

Sacred Music: *Requiem* (1874), *Quattro pezzi sacri* (Four Sacred Pieces, 1889–97)

LISTENING ACTIVITY

La Traviata (The Courtesan, 1853), Giuseppe Verdi

Act I: "É strano! É strano!" "Sempre libera"
Form: Romantic Opera, Recitatives and Arias
Performing Medium: Soprano and Orchestra

Compact Disc 2, Tracks 4–7
Running Time: 8:07

The text, or *libretto,* for the opera was based on Alexandre Dumas' (the younger) popular French novel *The Lady of the Camellias* (*La Dame aux camélias*). Verdi, along with his librettist, Francesco Piave, changed the name of the title role from Camellia to Violetta. Violetta is a Parisian courtesan, a French word literally meaning "a court woman." In nineteenth-century Paris, it meant that she was mistress to a series of wealthy patrons who supported her lavishly.

Act 1

Having temporarily recovered from a bout with incurable tuberculosis, Violetta throws a party at her opulent apartment. She is introduced to Alfredo, a young man from a wealthy, respectable family. Alfredo tells her that during her illness, he called on her many times to inquire about her health, and that he has fallen in love with her. She is touched by his passionate admiration, and she agrees to meet him the next day.

The guests leave. Alone in her apartment, Violetta contemplates the possibility that Alfredo is her true love. She sings about this in the next recorded example. By the end of Act 1, both Violetta and Alfredo are unable to resist their strong passion for each other.

Act 2

The couple decide to live together away from Paris in an elegant country home. Only Violetta's recurrent coughing spells interrupt their bliss. To maintain their lifestyle, Violetta has secretly sold most of her possessions. But their debts mount, and Alfredo goes off to Paris seeking funds.

While he is away, his father calls on Violetta. He pleads with her to give up her relationship with Alfredo because her reputation is jeopardizing his daughter's pending marriage. Violetta reluctantly agrees to end the love affair. When Alfredo returns, Violetta pretends to have fallen out of love with him and returns alone to Paris.

Act 3

Back in Paris, Alfredo is a party guest at the home of Violetta's friend. When Violetta arrives on the arm of another man, Alfredo publicly expresses his contempt for her lack of devotion to their relationship. Unaware of his father's role in the breakup, Alfredo leaves the party—and Paris.

Act 4

Violetta, alone in her apartment, is on the verge of death. Delirious, she dreams of her lost relationship with Alfredo, regretting the sadness of their parting. Having learned the true story of Violetta's decision to end their affair, Alfredo quickly returns to Paris and Violetta—a moment before she dies.

LISTENING GUIDE

La Traviata (*The Courtesan*, 1853), Giuseppe Verdi

After a night of partying and meeting her new love Alfredo, Violetta enters a quiet room. Alfredo and all the guests have left; she is alone. (See Act 1, paragraph 2 for the context of this recording.)

RECITATIVE

4   0:00   Soprano (Violetta) starts with a secco (dry) recitative without orchestra; allegro, rubato rhythm with pauses; then symphony orchestra enters filling in the pauses; *ff* then *pp*; homophonic texture

Violetta	*Violetta*
È strano! È strano! In core	*How strange! How strange! His words*
Scolpiti ho quegli accenti!	*Are burned upon my heart!*
Saria per me sventura un serio amore?;	*Would a real love be a tragedy for me?*
Che risolvi, o turbata anima mia?	*What decision are you taking,*
	O my soul?
Null'uomo ancora t'accendeva—	*No man has ever made me fall in*
O gioia!	*love—O joy!*
Ch'io non conobbi, esser amata amando!	*Which I have never known, loving and being loved!*
E sdegnaria poss'io	*Could I coldly reject it*
Per l'aride follie del viver mio?	*For the shallow folly of my existence?*

ARIA

5   1:06   Orchestral introduction; *p*, then *pp* when soprano enters; moderate tempo; steady rhythm in triple meter; homophonic texture; f-minor tonality; homophonic texture

Ah, for - s'è lui - che l'a - ni - ma
[Ah, per - haps he is the one whom my soul.]

Ah, fors' è lui che l'anima	*Ah, perhaps he is the one*
Solinga ne' tumulti	*Whom my soul*
Godea sovente pingere	*Lonely in the tumult, loved!*
Dè suoi colori occulti!	*To secretly imagine!*
Lui che modesto e vigile	*He who with modest vigilance;*
All' egre soglie accese,	*Came here while I lay ill,*
E nuova febbre accese,	*Awakening a new fever;*
Destandomi all' amor.	*The fever of love.*

Momentarily forgetting her long struggle with illness, Violetta is hopeful and in love. The melody of her aria is a reprise of Alfredo's aria in which he professes his love for her.

2:17   Change to F-major tonality; soft arpeggios in the orchestra; soprano is louder and highly expressive; homophonic texture

A quell' amor, ch'è palpito	*Of love which is the breath*
Dell' universo intero,	*Of the universe itself*
Misterioso, altero,	*Mysterious, noble,*
Croce e delizia al cor.	*Embracing the heart's sorrow and rapture.*

RECITATIVE

6   3:28   Soprano begins without accompaniment, then allegro; symphony orchestra enters with eighth-note and triplet figures accompanying the recitative; **p**; key of F major; homophonic texture

Violetta suddenly wakes from her day-dreaming.

Follie! follie! Delirio vano è questo!	*Folly! Folly! This is mad delirium!*
Povera donna sola,	*A poor woman, alone,*
Abbandonata in questo Popoloso deserto	*Lost in this crowded desert*
Che appellano Parigi,	*Which is known as Paris.*
Che spero or più? Che far	*What can I hope for?*
degg'op! Gloire,	*What should I do? Die,*
Di voluttà ne' vortici perir.	*In the whirl of earthly pleasures!*

ARIA "SEMPRE LIBERA"

7   0:00   Allegro; meter is duple-compound (fast 6/8); introduction played by full orchestra; **f**; melody in upper strings and woodwinds; A♭-major; after a short pause, soprano enters with same melody as the orchestral introduction.

Violetta   *assai brillante*

Sem - pre   li - be - ra   deg - g'i - o   fol - leg -
[For - ever   free.   I   must   pass   mad -

gia - re   di   gio - ia in   gio - ia
ly   from   joy   to   joy]

Sempre libera degg'io	*Forever free, I must pass*
Folleggiare di gioia.	*Madly from joy to joy.*
Vo' che scorra il viver mio	*My life's course shall be*
Pei sentieri del piacer.	*Forever in the paths of pleasure.*
Nasca il giorno, o il giorno muoia,	*Whether it be dawn or dusk,*
Sempre lieta ne' ritrovi.	*I must always live gaily*

0:35   After the orchestra stops, soprano holds high C, then repeats the aria's opening melody; homophonic texture. From the distant garden, we hear the voice of Alfredo professing his love.

A diletti sempre nuovi	*In the world's gay places*
Dee volare il mio pensier.	*Ever seeking newer joys.*

Last line of text is repeated several times; then aria cadences with a coloratura, cadenza-like sequence that moves up to a high D♭ above high C; aria ends in A♭ Major.

Born in Lucca, Italy, into a family of church composers and musicians, Giacomo Puccini (poo-*tchee*-nee) early in life planned a career as a church composer. But at age seventeen, when he saw a production of Verdi's *Aïda,* he became hooked on opera. Changing his plans, Puccini enrolled at the Milan Conservatory to study opera composition.

After his studies, Puccini began composing, finishing his first opera, *Le villi,* when he was twenty-five. The famous music publisher Giulio Ricordi was in the audi-

ence at that first production in Teatro alla Scala in Milan. He commissioned Puccini to write more operas, and their association lasted throughout Puccini's life.

Giacomo Puccini became one of the most important Italian opera composers of the late nineteenth and early twentieth centuries. Many of Puccini's operas are tragic love stories set far from Italy: Japan (*Madama Butterfly*), China (*Turandot*), and even California (*The Girl of the Golden West*).

PRINCIPAL WORKS

Operas: *Manon Lescaut* (1893), *La bohème* (The Bohemian Life, 1896), *Tosca* (1900), *Madama Butterfly* (1904), *La fanciulla del west* (The Girl of the Golden West, 1910), *Turandot* (posthumous, 1926)

Scene from La bohème, Act I,
Metropolitan Opera Production,
New York

LISTENING ACTIVITY

La Bohème (The Bohemian Life, 1896), Giacomo Puccini

Act 1 (excerpt)
Large Form: Romantic Opera, Recitatives and Arias
Performing Medium: Soprano, Tenor, and Orchestra

Compact Disc 3, Tracks 7–10
Running Time: 12:40

Few composers have had as great a gift as Puccini for composing operas with soaring, emotional melodies—one glorious aria after another. To the delight of singers, Puccini's arias display the singers' virtuosity without overtaxing their voices.

Based on a novel by H. Murger (1822–1861), *Scènes de la Vie de Bohème* (*Scenes from the Bohemian Life*), Puccini's *La bohème* (*The Bohemian Life*) uses the "realistic" *verismo* style of opera that became popular toward the end of the nineteenth century. Typical of this style, *La bohème* romantically depicts the borderline poverty of struggling Parisian artists and workers.

Although they were not necessarily connected with the country of Bohemia (the Czech Republic today), artists and artisans of the Left Bank were called *bohemians*—a term that was used to classify free-living artists who struggled to survive outside the establishment.

Rent: The Musical

Jonathan Larson's hit musical Rent *premiered on Broadway in 1996, exactly 100 years after the opening of Puccini's* La bohème. *Updated and set in New York City's East Village instead of Paris's Left Bank,* Rent *borrows heavily from* Bohème, *incorporating a story similar to the opera's libretto. For example, a song in the first act, sung at the Life Cafe, is called "La Vie de Bohème." In the* Rent *version, the heroine Mimi is dying from AIDS rather than tuberculosis. Rodolfo, the writer, becomes Roger, the ex-junkie songwriter, who is also HIV-positive.*

Larson's "candle" scene—the meeting of Roger and Mimi—is also similar to the Puccini opera. Alone in his loft apartment, Roger is composing what he hopes will be his one great song ("One Song Glory"), his last chance to redeem his empty, marginal life. Roger plays a short musical quote from La bohème—*several measures from "Musetta's Waltz." When the electricity goes out in the apartment building, Mimi knocks on Roger's door to ask whether he has a light for her candle ("Will You Light My Candle?"). The two are drawn to each other, but Roger, a recovering addict, resists when he realizes that Mimi is a junkie.*

Setting   Mid-nineteenth-century Paris. The curtain rises on a small, shabby loft apartment—the home of four young bohemian artists: the poet Rodolfo (tenor and leading man), the painter Marcello (baritone), the philosopher Colline (bass), and the musician Schaunard (baritone).

It is Christmas Eve. The apartment is cold because the impoverished artists cannot afford to buy wood for a fire. Rodolfo and Marcello are trying to work, but the cold distracts them, and their poverty depresses them. In disgust, Rodolfo tosses his manuscript into the fireplace for fuel.

The mood abruptly changes when Colline and Schaunard burst into the apartment, bringing money that Schaunard has earned. Their jubilance is interrupted by Benoit, their landlord, who has come to collect their past-due rent. Although they have a little money, they would rather use it to have fun. So the four young artists ply Benoit with wine, and when he is tipsy, they send him away without the rent. Marcello, Colline, and Schaunard want to celebrate at a local cafe, but Rodolfo chooses to stay in the apartment and work. He sends the others off, promising to join them as soon as he completes the article he has been writing.

After the others leave, Rodolfo tries in vain to write his article. There is a knock on the door. In the hall is Mimi—a frail, young seamstress—who explains that her candle blew out. She asks Rodolfo for a light so she can find her way back to her own apartment. The recorded excerpt enacts their first meeting and the blooming of their mutual love.

Noticing that Mimi is weak from climbing the stairs, Rodolfo offers her a chair and some wine. When her key falls to the floor, they both grope for it in the dark. Rodolfo finds it, but secretly slips it into his pocket. As they continue looking for it, their hands touch. Rodolfo is surprised that Mimi's hand is so cold and sings the famous aria, "Che gelida manina!" ("How cold your little hand is!"). Musically, we hear a mix of recitative and aria as Rodolfo and Mimi tell each other about their lives and begin falling in love.

JACQUES (JACOB) OFFENBACH (1819–1880)

Jacob Offenbach (later Jacques) was born in Cologne, Germany. He received his first music lessons from his father Isaac, who took the boy to Paris to audition for Luigi Cherubini. The crotchety, 73-year-old Director of the Conservatory was renowned for his reluctance to accept young students. Cherubini reportedly stopped 14-year-old Offenbach halfway through his audition to tell him he was accepted.

At that time, France welcomed Jews. Jacob easily assimilated and changed his name to Jacques. He began his performing and composing career by publishing a few symphonic waltzes using synagogue motifs or incorporating the Viennese-style waltz.

But Offenbach's passion was theater. He regularly attended performances at the Paris Opéra and the Opéra-Comique. He was soon hired as a cellist and attracted the attention of English concert manager John Mitchell, who arranged a concert tour of England. Jacques married Mitchell's French stepdaughter in the summer of 1844.

Offenbach's first commission as a composer was interrupted by France's July Revolution. Not yet a French citizen, Offenbach took his wife and daughter to the safety of Cologne. They returned to Paris in 1850. Jacques then became the conductor of the Comédie-Française and began to include his own compositions in the program.

Off the Champs Élysées was a 50-seat wooden building called Théâtre Lacaze. Offenbach rounded up some wealthy backers, leased and remodeled the building, and changed its name to Théâtre des Bouffes-Parisiens. When it opened its doors in July 1855, the theater guaranteed an outlet for Offenbach's works. However, he was limited to short productions because French licensing law restricted the number of speaking parts in a theater of that size. Offenbach composed three one-act operettas for that first season, all playing to full houses.

Although summer audiences were willing to sit in the drafty theater, winter audiences were not. By November, Offenbach moved Bouffes-Parisiens to warmer, appropriate quarters. The company went on tour during the spring and returned to Paris for the summer season. Their success encouraged Viennese and London composers and librettists to pursue the short operetta form.

France lifted licensing restrictions in 1858, allowing Offenbach to incorporate a chorus and as many characters as he wanted in his productions. The following year he created a sensation with his first full-scale, two-act operetta, *Orfée aux Enfers (Orpheus in the Underworld)*. Soon, Offenbach's music became as well known throughout Europe as it was in Paris.

At his death in 1880, Offenbach was still working on the last act of *The Tales of Hoffman*. Fortunately, Ernest

Guirand, who completed the work, maintained Offenbach's distinctive style.

Besides his countless songs and orchestral works, Offenbach's legacy includes more than 100 operettas, many satirizing issues of the era, social mores, life at the royal court, and works of other composers. To this day, he is one of the most-performed composers of his genre.

PRINCIPAL WORKS

Operas, Comic Operas, Operettas: *Orpheus in the Underworld* (1859), *Brigands* (1869), *Les contes d'Hoffmann* (Tales of Hoffman, 1881, posthumously)

Ballet: *Le papillon* (The Butterfly), *Gaité Parisienne* (includes the "Can, Can" dance)

CHALLENGE YOUR EXPERTISE

- Who composed the most operas: Puccini, Rossini, or Verdi?
- What is the difference between *castrato* and *concertato?*

French Romantic Opera

During the first half of the nineteenth century, the aftershocks of the French Revolution, the turbulent Napoleonic Empire, and the rising middle class all contributed to making Paris an important European political and cultural center. Its elaborate opera productions made it the opera capital of the continent.

Composers of all nations flocked to Paris to have their new works performed—Luigi Cherubini (1760–1842), Gasparo Spontini (1774–1851), Gioacchino Rossini, Gaetano Donizetti, Vincenzo Bellini, and Giacomo Meyerbeer (1791–1864).

Cherubini
(keh-roo-*bee*-nee)

Spontini
(spohn-*tee*-nee)

Meyerbeer
(*my*-er-beer)

French Grand Opera

Designed mainly to appeal to the relatively unsophisticated middle class, nineteenth-century French opera became known as *grand opera*. As important as the music was, it was the spectacle that drew audiences. Elaborately costumed crowd scenes, large choruses, plenty of ballet, and lavish sets are the hallmark of French grand opera.

French Comic Opera

Also popular was the less pretentious *opéra comique* (comic opera). With fewer singers and extras and less elaborate staging, *opéra comique* emphasized wit and satire, both in the libretto and in the music.

Offenbach

Gilbert and Sullivan

Strauss

Jacques Offenbach (1819–1880) was the first to write in the French comic-opera style. His operas *Orpheus in the Underworld* and *Tales of Hoffman* later influenced the operettas of the famous English team of William Gilbert (1836–1911) and Arthur Sullivan (1842–1900)—*The Mikado, H. M. S. Pinafore, Pirates of Penzance*—and those of Johann Strauss, Jr. (1825–1899) in Vienna (*Die Fledermaus* "The Bat," *Zigeunerbaron* "Gypsy Baron"), as well as the Broadway musical of the twentieth century.

GEORGES BIZET (1838–1875)

Georges Bizet was born in Paris, the son of professional musicians. His father was a singing teacher and composer; his mother was an excellent pianist. Georges was very young when he displayed his talents at the piano, and when he was nine, his parents enrolled him at the Paris Conservatory. There, at age fourteen, he won first prize in piano.

As part of his composition and orchestration studies at the Conservatory, Bizet wrote his now highly popular Symphony No. 1 in C. At age nineteen, he won the Offenbach Prize for a one-act opera, *Le Docteur miracle* (1857). That same year he won the coveted Grand Prix de Rome.

Now Bizet could study in Rome, but in exchange for tuition, the Grand Prix required the recipient to compose a Mass for the Church. The young Bizet accepted the prize money and fulfilled his obligation by writing his *Te Deum* (1858).

Returning to Paris, Bizet threw himself into opera composition. However, both audiences and critics received his operas coolly. Even his last and best-known opera, *Carmen*, performed thirty-seven times at the comic-opera theater during its first season, had mixed reviews.

At the end of that season, Bizet died. He was only 36 and had never experienced the acclaim his works would ultimately receive—especially *Carmen*, which has become a staple of the contemporary repertoire.

PRINCIPAL WORKS

Operas: *Le Docteur miracle* (1857), *Les pêcheurs de perles* (The Pearl Fishers, 1863), *La jolie fille de Perth* (1867), *Djamileh* (1872), *Carmen* (1875)

Orchestral Music: Symphony No. 1 in C (1855); *Vasco da Gama* (1859), a symphonic ode with chorus; Souvenirs de Rome (1869), a symphonic suite; *L'Arlésienne* Suites 1 and 2 (1872)

Choral Music: Cantatas: *David* (1856), *Clovis et Clothilde* (1857), *Te Deum* (1858)

Piano Music: More than 150 piano pieces, including *Jeux d'enfants* (1872) for four hands

Carmen Georges Bizet's opera *Carmen,* which premiered in Paris in 1875, was a landmark in French opera. Although classified as an *opéra comique* because of the spoken dialogue in the original version, *Carmen* was hardly comic. Rather, it is a realistic drama focusing on the passion and infidelity of two doomed lovers in Seville, Spain.

Bizet used melodic arias, brilliant orchestration, colorful dancing, exciting staging, and haunting rhythms to tell the story of a poignant, tragic romance. Despite these qualities, nineteenth-century audiences and critics were not as enthusiastic about the work as they are today. Perhaps it was too realistic for French audiences accustomed to more distant settings and otherworldly stories.

In contrast, *Carmen* draws us into the action until we are empathizing with the central characters: Carmen, the seductive cigar-factory girl, and Don Jose, the dashing bullfighter. What starts out as a playful flirtation quickly turns serious. Don Jose's immediate attraction for Carmen becomes almost an obsession. Tension mounts as he discovers that Carmen has been unfaithful. Don Jose cannot control

Sandrine Rouet dances seductively in the title role of Bizet's *Carmen*.

his jealousy. Carmen continues to taunt him. When he threatens to kill her, we can sense the danger. Then we witness the stark reality as he carries out his threat—not behind a curtain, but right there, in the Seville plaza.

Carmen began a trend of operatic realism (*verismo*) that inspired, among others, *Cavalleria rusticana* (1890) by Pietro Mascagni (1863–1945), *I Pagliacci* (1892) by Ruggiero Leoncavallo (1858–1919), and Puccini's *La bohème* (1896) and *Tosca* (1900).

German Romantic Opera

Nowhere in Europe was the bonding between music and literature as strong as in Germany. With Mozart's singspiel *Die Zauberflöte* (The Magic Flute) and Carl Maria von Weber's mystical opera *Der Freischütz* (The Freeshooter), German opera composers began using their native German instead of the traditional Italian language.

Der Freischütz
(der *fry*-shoots)

Imbued with the ideals of romanticism, German composers sought out librettos incorporating magic, mystery, the supernatural, the mystical, distant lands, exotic cultures, love, and heroes (see Chapter 13). Middle-class audiences were ready to embrace the new subjects and reject the typical court intrigues and farces that had been so popular with the mostly aristocratic audiences of the eighteenth century.

CARL MARIA VON WEBER (1786–1826)

Carl Maria von Weber (*vay*-ber) was born in the north of Germany into a family of musicians—Constanze, Mozart's wife, was one of Weber's cousins. Weber's early musical studies were with Michael Haydn (1737–1806), Joseph's brother, in Salzburg. He wrote his first opera at age twelve and two more before he was fifteen.

As a pianist and composer, Weber traveled extensively throughout central Europe, finally settling in Prague as music director for the Prague Opera Company. Weber's most influential opera, *Der Freischütz*, premiered in Berlin. It was a huge success. Audiences were stunned by its special stage effects and mysticism, especially in the Wolf's Glen scene. Weber composed other operas, but none achieved the success of *Der Freischütz*.

Weber never reached his fortieth birthday. He died in London during a production of his opera *Oberon*.

PRINCIPAL WORKS

Operas: *Der Freischütz* (The Freeshooter, 1821), *Euryanthe* (1823), *Oberon* (1826)

Orchestral Music: two piano concertos; two clarinet concertos; one bassoon concerto; Konzertstuck for piano and orchestra (1821); opera overtures: *Der Freischütz, Euryanthe, Oberon*

Choral Music: two Masses; six cantatas

Piano Music: Invitation to the Dance (1819) [modern transcription for orchestra], four sonatas; miscellaneous pieces

RICHARD WAGNER (1813–1883)

Richard Wagner grew up in Leipzig, Germany, his birthplace. Although Wagner (*vahg*-ner) claimed he was mostly self-taught in music, he did attend St. Thomas's School, where a century earlier Bach had been choirmaster. Later, Wagner continued his music studies at Leipzig University.

At age twenty, while employed as rehearsal director of the choir in a small opera house in Leipzig, he had a love affair with Minna, one of the sopranos in the chorus. Two years later they were married.

During the next ten years, Wagner and Minna lived in poverty while he was writing his first operas. Their restless, stormy marriage was plagued with infidelities on both sides. After *Rienzi* (1842) was produced, several other successes followed. Wagner's work caught the attention of the King of Saxony, who hired Wagner to be the Saxon State conductor.

In 1848, Wagner became a political activitist and published articles calling for revolution. To avoid arrest, he fled to Switzerland. His marriage to Minna ended, and he became involved with a succession of married women.

When Ludwig II, also known as "Mad King Ludwig," was crowned King of Bavaria, one of his first acts was to summon Wagner to Munich to produce operas. There, Wagner married Franz Liszt's daughter, Cosima, with whom he had been having an extended affair.

Cosima, a shrewd businesswoman, used her wiles to inveigle financial backing out of the "mad" king. The Wagners used the money to build Festspielhaus at Bayreuth, devoted entirely to staging Wagnerian operas.

Although artistically successful, the productions were far too costly, and the Bavarian treasury always had to subsidize Wagner heavily.

Exhausted after composing his last opera, *Parsifal*, Wagner went for a rest in Venice. He died there of heart failure at age seventy. Carried by gondola in an elaborate procession down the Grand Canal to the railway station, Wagner's body was transported to Bayreuth for burial.

PRINCIPAL WORKS

Operas: *Rienzi* (1842); *Der fliegende Holländer* (The Flying Dutchman, 1843); *Tannhäuser* (1845); *Lohengrin* (1850); *Tristan und Isolde* (1865); *Die Meistersinger von Nürnberg* (The Mastersingers of Nuremberg, 1868); *Der Ring des Nibelungen* (The Ring of the Nibelung); *Das Rheingold* (The Rhine Gold, 1869); *Die Walküre* (The Valkyrie, 1870); *Siegfried* (1876); *Götterdämmerung* (Twilight of the Gods, 1876); *Parsifal* (1882)

Orchestral Music: *Siegfried Idyll* (1870)

Songs: *Wesendonk-Lieder* (1858)

Wagner's Music Dramas

Gesamtkunstwerk
(guh-*zamt-koonst*-vehrk)

Richard Wagner carried Romantic opera to its extreme. His vision was to create a total art work (*Gesamtkunstwerk*), which he called *music drama*. Toward that goal, he exerted complete control: He wrote his own librettos; composed, orchestrated, and conducted the music; designed the sets; and directed the staging.

You might think all that involvement would have satisfied Wagner. Hardly. He persevered until he could design and build his own opera house—Bayreuth—a shrine to himself. Dedicated to performing only his music, exactly the way he envisioned it, the opera house continues that tradition today.

Leitmotif
(*lyt*-moh-*teef*)

Wagner delighted in composing long works, some lasting as long as five hours. As a way of unifying the music and drama throughout these works and sustaining the interest of his audiences, he used specific melodies and harmonies to represent particular characters or ideas. He called this pervasive theme a *leitmotif* (leading motive). You may recall that Berlioz used this idea (called the *idée fixe*) throughout his *Symphonie fantastique* to represent his beloved Harriet.

LISTENING ACTIVITY

Overture to Die Meistersinger von Nürnberg (1868), Richard Wagner

Large Form: Opera Overture
Detailed Form: Sectional
Performing Medium: Large Orchestra

Compact Disc 3, Tracks 11–14
Running Time: 8:39

Die Meistersinger

Die Meistersinger von Nürnberg (The Mastersingers of Nuremberg) concerns the relationship between the creative artist and his critics, the conflict between tradition and innovation. The opera is set in sixteenth-century Nuremberg, Germany, when the craft guilds (professional unions) were at their zenith. Older members of these guilds represent the Establishment—reluctant to upset the status quo. Membership as mastersinger had elevated them to the middle class.

Wagner opens the opera with a scene in the local church in Nuremberg, where Walther, a young stranger, spies Eva, the goldsmith's beautiful daughter, seated near him. They are instantly attracted to each other.

After the church service, the town begins preparations for its annual singing contest. We soon learn that it is the contest that has brought Walther to town.

Seemingly insurmountable bureaucratic hurdles are thrown into Walther's way to prevent him from competing. Even Hans Sachs, a respected member of the Mastersinger's Guild, cannot successfully intercede in Walther's behalf.

The goldsmith has offered his daughter Eva and her dowry as the prize to the winner of the singing contest. Adding further interest to the plot, Walther does not yet know that Eva is one of the prizes.

On the day of the singing festival, all masters and apprentices of Nuremberg's trade guilds parade onstage. Clad in robes, ribbons, and insignias, they carry their guilds' banners.

Just before the contest, Hans Sachs, favoring Walther, deliberately skews the rules, declaring that audience response will be one of the criteria. Beckmesser, a petty local clerk who also serves as one of the judges, starts the contest with a bungled rendition of Walther's song. When the audience laughs at him, he is furious. Beckmesser's philosophies closely paralleled those of a music critic named Hanslick, who consistently attacked Wagner's music for departing from tradition.

Hans Sachs seizes the opportunity. He tells everyone that the song is really lovely and suggests that the composer should sing it himself. The mastersingers accede to Sach's suggestion. Up steps Walther, the composer, who wins the contest with his "Prize Song," gets his membership in the Mastersinger's Guild, and the hand of Eva in marriage.

Listen to the Overture to Wagner's opera *Die Meistersinger von Nürnberg*. An overture, or a prelude to an opera, has the same purpose as in a musical show: to acquaint the audience with the main melodies and to set the mood for the story.

In this overture, Wagner introduces four of the main recurrent melodies—*leitmotifs:*

11 LEITMOTIF 1 represents the Mastersingers and all that was dependable and noble in the medieval German burgher.

12 LEITMOTIF 2 played first by the flute and then by the oboe, represents Walther's and Eva's love for each other.

13 LEITMOTIF 3 introduced by the brass represents the banner and heritage of the Mastersinger's Guild.

14 LEITMOTIF 4 is the Prize Song, a love song in which Walther imagines Eva in Paradise.

The overture climaxes with the full orchestra playing three of the four leitmotifs—the Prize Song, the Banner, and the Mastersingers—simultaneously.

LISTENING GUIDE

Overture to *Die Meistersinger von Nürnberg* (1868), Richard Wagner

Exposition

11	0:00	LEITMOTIF 1 Mastersingers	full orchestra, **ff**; moderate march tempo; 4 meter, key of C major
12	0:52	LEITMOTIF 2 Love of Walther and Eva	played by flute and clarinet, imitated by oboe, then flute, then clarinet; **f** with expression, **p** in the strings
	1:20	TRANSITION	transition section; crescendo to **f**; violins, starting high, descending in sequences
13	1:30	LEITMOTIF 3 Mastersinger's Heritage	played by brass section, marchlike; strings with upward swoops; **f**
	2:08	LEITMOTIF 1 Mastersingers	played by violins, then joined by winds; **ff**; sequences
	3:07	TRANSITION	transition; agitated fragments in violins; dynamic swells, **f** crescendo to **ff** and back to **f**
14	3:28	LEITMOTIF 4 Walther's Prize Song	played by violins, **p** and expressively, change of key to E major

Development Section

	4:39	LEITMOTIF 1 Mastersingers	fragments played first by oboe; **p**; melody is twice as fast as opening, though basic tempo is the same as the opening
	5:49	LEITMOTIF 1 Mastersingers	played by trombones, **f**, original style as opening

Polyphonic Section

(Leitmotifs 1, 3, and 4 together)

	6:05	LEITMOTIF 4 Walther's Prize Song	played by first clarinet, first horn, first violin, and cello; **p;** together
		LEITMOTIF 1 Mastersingers	played by bassoon, bass trombone, and string basses; **p**
		LEITMOTIF 3 Mastersinger's Heritage	twice as fast; played by flutes, oboes, horns, violins, and violas; **p**

Recapitulation Section

	8:08	LEITMOTIF 1 Mastersingers	full orchestra, **f**

Wagner and Hitler

Richard Wagner was and still is a highly controversial figure. He was an artistic genius and wrote great music; however, many feel that as a person, Wagner was despicable. To achieve his ends, he lied, cheated, walked out on debts, exploited people, and had affairs with some of his friends' wives.

Born six years after the composer's death, Adolph Hitler embraced Wagner's anti-Semitism. He adored Wagner's music and played it constantly, even during war-strategy meetings. How much was Hitler influenced by Wagner? We will never really know. But there is an ironic similarity between the ending of the Third Reich and the ending of Wagner's opera *Götterdämmerung* (Twilight of the Gods).

During the finale of that opera, the great warrior, Siegfried, is killed. His body is then burned on a funeral pyre. But the flames get out of control, and Walhalla, the home of the dead battle heroes, goes up in flames and collapses in the conflagration. To end the opera, the Rhine River overflows, flooding the land and drowning the flames.

Walhalla
(vahl-*hah*-luh)

Hitler, too, staged his own dramatic finale by deliberately ignoring several opportunities to end World War II, particularly in the last few days when Berlin was surrounded by the Allies. Instead of surrendering, Hitler locked himself in a Berlin bunker, leaving the city and thousands of its residents to die in the firestorm following the bombing and shelling of the city. He himself was consumed in flames in his bunker after committing suicide.

CHALLENGE YOUR EXPERTISE

What are at least three ways in which Wagner exerted total control?

LISTENING INSIGHTS

What to Listen for in Wagnerian Opera

One of the keys to following and understanding Wagner's operas is to associate the melodies, or leitmotif, with the characters or ideas they represent. For instance, when the hero Parsifal silently contemplates his quest for the Holy Grail, the orchestra plays the Holy Grail leitmotif. Although Parsifal is not singing, and the action onstage is static, we know that he is thinking about the quest because we recognize the theme.

Summary of Terms

Bayreuth
Cherubini
comic opera
Der Freischütz
French Grand opera
Gesamtkunstwerk

Gilbert and Sullivan
leitmotif
libretto
lyric opera
Meyerbeer

music drama
Offenbach
singspiel
Spontini
Strauss

16

Late Romantic Music

The State of Music in the Late Romantic Period

In the second half of the nineteenth century, Beethoven's vision for musicians became a reality. As professional composers became highly respected and revered, they also attained financial security. No longer did they have to devote the major portion of their energies promoting and staging concerts of their own works. Throughout Europe, public concert societies had assumed that task.

Advent of Philharmonic and Symphony Orchestra Societies   Throughout the nineteenth century, most major cities in Europe and the United States were beginning to establish philharmonic and symphony orchestra societies.

Demand for New Music   As concert audiences expanded throughout the nineteenth century, so did the number of performances. Solo recitals, chamber music, ballet, and opera flourished, creating a constant demand for new music.

HISTORICAL PERSPECTIVE

Evolution of Public Concerts: The Late Romantic Period

Early Orchestral Societies in Europe and North America   Founded in 1781, the Gewandhaus Orchestra of Leipzig was one of the earliest permanent orchestras. It was not until 1835, when Felix Mendelssohn took over as conductor, that it became a full-time professional orchestra. Mendelssohn's Gewandhaus Orchestra inspired other orchestras to attain professional status. A brief list of some of the most important orchestras and their founding dates follows:

1781	Gewandhaus Orchestra, Leipzig	1891	Chicago Symphony Orchestra
1792	Paris Conservatory Orchestra	1882	Berlin Philharmonic Orchestra
1842	New York Philharmonic Orchestra	1883	Concertgebouw Orchestra, Amsterdam
1842	Vienna Philharmonic Orchestra	1895	Cincinnati Symphony Orchestra
1874	Cologne Orchestra, Germany	1895	Pittsburgh Symphony Orchestra
1880	St. Louis Symphony Orchestra	1900	Philadelphia Orchestra
1881	Boston Symphony Orchestra	1906	Toronto Symphony Orchestra

Radical versus the Traditional

Mainstream concert music began to branch into two movements in the mid-nineteenth century. Richard Wagner championed the radical movement; Johannes Brahms, the traditionalist movement. Suddenly, European composers, artists, and audiences took sides. The Schumanns and others sided with Brahms. Liszt and later Richard Strauss were in Wagner's camp.

Wagnerians   With formal control now subordinate to emotion, music took new directions. Wagner and his followers embraced a wandering tonality, conveying the feeling of an extended journey. They expanded harmonic movement away from its traditional tonic or home key rooting. Using loose and often vague forms, composers began to rely increasingly on extra-musical associations (stories, ideas, poems) for continuity. They built their symphonic poems, overtures, symphonies, and chamber music around programs or descriptive titles.

Brahmsians   To those composers who aligned with Brahms, formal control still mattered. They adhered to the classical traditions of Haydn, Mozart, Schubert, and especially, Beethoven. Tonality and form, they believed, should remain recognizable, with minimal extramusical associations and overcharged emotionalism.

Continuing the classical tradition, both Schumann and Brahms focused their efforts on chamber music, three-movement concertos, and four-movement symphonies. Of the two, only Robert Schumann attempted to write an opera, though his *Genoveva* is rarely performed today.

Brahms's Orchestral Music

Brahms idolized Beethoven. He was so much in awe of Beethoven's nine symphonies that Brahms labored over his own First Symphony for twenty years, reworking it until he felt he had finally attained the Beethoven standard. He was right. Audiences hailed the first performance of Brahms's First Symphony as "Beethoven's Tenth."

Unlike Beethoven, Brahms was not an innovator. Proudly declaring himself a musical conservative, he avoided extreme changes in musical expression as proposed by the followers of Liszt and Wagner.

Brahms and Beethoven shared many characteristics. Both were born in Germany and composed their major works in Vienna. Both profited from freelance employment and publishing royalties. Both expressed their love of mankind, yet led reclusive lives, devoting their main creative energies to their art and never marrying.

Brahms's desire for personal freedom seems to have superseded his ability to develop close personal relationships. Although he had been in love with Clara Schumann for many years, he moved away from her after Robert Schumann's death. Possibly it was a conflict between his love for her and his devotion to his mentor that drove Brahms from Düsseldorf. Yet he remained close to Clara and loved her seven children throughout his life. Perhaps it was due to their age difference—Clara was fourteen years older than he. In Brahms's own family, though, his mother was seventeen years older than his father.

A mystery in Brahms's life was his deliberate avoidance of obligations that might restrict his freedom. A fine conductor, recognized as the foremost musician of his time, Brahms could have secured any post he wanted. Yet he accepted only minor positions—coaching women's choirs and directing minor orchestras. Throughout his life he remained a freelance musician, earning his living from private teaching, publishing royalties, occasional piano performances, and guest conducting appearances.

JOHANNES BRAHMS (1833–1897)

Johannes Brahms grew up in Hamburg, Germany. The family lived near the center of the city, not far from Alster Lake. Brahms's first piano teacher was his father, a bass player in a salon orchestra. As one story goes, Brahms's childhood was impoverished and, while still a teenager, he had to augment the family's income by playing piano in bars and brothels. Recent research, however, seems to contradict this long-accepted legend. Some agreement does exist that his early experiences indelibly marked his personality, making him seem aloof, misogynistic, and somewhat crude.

Nevertheless, Brahms's enormous talent brought him to the attention of prominent musicians, and by age 20, he was engaged in a concert tour with the Hungarian violinist Remenyi, considered one of the best European violinists of his time.

When Brahms decided to devote himself to composing serious music, he went to Düsseldorf to study with the highly respected Robert Schumann. Soon after their first meeting, Brahms was invited to remain in the Schumann home as a boarder. In an article in his influential publication *Neue Zeitschrift für Musik* (The New Magazine for Music), Robert described Brahms as the "new genius of music." But before long, Robert, who had grown progressively addled, entered an asylum for two years. During this period and after Schumann's death, a close and, some say, intimate relationship developed between Brahms and Clara Schumann.

Brahms eventually moved to Vienna where he maintained a permanent residence until his death at age 64. There, Brahms was employed as the director of a women's choir. He also performed regularly as a pianist and appeared as guest conductor of various orchestras throughout Europe. Although he was eventually celebrated as a leading composer, much of Brahms's life and work is surrounded by uncertainties and ambiguities because he deliberately covered his tracks. Not only did Brahms destroy what he considered to be his inferior compositions and early traces of his published works, but also many of his letters and other personal documents.

PRINCIPAL WORKS

Orchestral Music: four symphonies: No. 1 in c minor (1855–76), No. 2 in D Major (1877), No. 3 in F Major (1883), No. 4 in e minor (1885); two piano concertos: No. 1 in d minor (1858), No. 2 in B-flat Major (1881); other works: Violin Concerto (1878); *Academic Festival Overture* (1880); *Tragic Overture* (1881)

Chamber Music: two string sextets, two string quintets, three string quartets, Piano Quintet in f minor, three piano quartets, three piano trios, Clarinet Quintet, violin sonatas

Piano Music: sonatas, rhapsodies, intermezzos, ballades, capriccios, variations, *Liebeslieder Walzer, Hungarian Dances*

Choral Music: *A German Requiem* (1868), *Alto Rhapsody* (1869), and more than 180 songs

---

LISTENING ACTIVITY

Academic Festival Overture, Op. 80, Johannes Brahms

Large Form: Concert Overture
Detailed Form: Sectional, Medley of Songs
Performing Medium: Large Symphony Orchestra

Compact Disc 2, Tracks 8–12
Running Time: 10:22

The background of the *Academic Festival Overture* gives us a glimpse of Brahms's great prestige in the late nineteenth century. In 1880, the University of Breslau honored him with a Doctor of Philosophy degree for being "Germany's leading composer."

In appreciation, Brahms composed the *Academic Festival Overture.* Its form is that of a *concert overture*—an overture not associated with either a ballet or an opera. Nineteenth-century concert overtures are usually highly descriptive works.

Brahms described his overture as a "very boisterous *potpourri* of student songs." Most of them were actually drinking songs. The piece ends with the well-known "Gaudeamus igitur," a noble, anthem-like tune played by the full orchestra.

Hail to youth and hail to love! Hail to life so won-der-ful!

LISTENING GUIDE

Academic Festival Overture, Op. 80, **Johannes Brahms**

| 8 | 0:00 | THEME 1 | violins; ***pp;*** moderate tempo, duple meter; c minor tonality; homophonic texture |

| | 0:42 | THEME 2—interlude | in violas, imitated by horns and bassoons; ***pp;*** F-major tonality |

| 9 | 1:55 | THEME 3—"Stately House" | in trumpets, then horns added; ***p;*** same duple meter; C major tonality |

10   2:36   THEME 4   in violins, **ff;** duple meter (4); C major tonality; homophonic texture

         3:19   THEME 5   variant of themes 1 and 3 in violins, **f;** duple meter (4), C major tonality

         3:46   THEME 6—   in first and second violins, **f**, same meter and tempo, E-major tonality with shifts to
                    "The Fatherland"   G-major tonality

11   4:36   THEME 7—   in bassoons, imitations in oboe, violins, and violas; **p;** allegro tempo, duple
                    "Freshman Song"   meter; e-minor tonality

5:22	TRANSITION	
5:39	THEME 7— "Freshman Song"	
6:20	TRANSITION	horns; *p*
6:40	THEME 1	bassoons; *p*; similar to opening
7:16	THEME 4— fragments	
7:58	THEME 6— "The Fatherland"	strings, then woodwinds
8:49	TRANSITION	woodwinds; *p*
9:15	THEME 7— "Freshman Song"	returns briefly
12 9:27	THEME 8— "Gaudeamus igitur"	finale, in full orchestra, *ff*; triple meter, C-major tonality

| 10:32 | FINAL CHORD | *ff*; C major |

CHALLENGE YOUR EXPERTISE

- Can you name two symphonies that do not have four movements?
- How are Felix Mendelssohn's travels reflected in his works?

Romantic-Period Chamber Music

Increasingly during the nineteenth century, wealthy art patrons opened their homes for chamber music performances. Artists, writers, and friends gathered to hear the latest compositions of Mendelssohn, Schumann, Brahms, and others.

During the eighteenth century, string trios and quartets were the favorite chamber music groups. By the nineteenth century, string and wind chamber ensembles often added a piano. Works for these groups are *piano trios*, *piano quartets*, and *piano quintets*.

Though concertgoers know the Romantic composers mainly by their large orchestral works, Schubert, Mendelssohn, Schumann, Brahms, and others actually wrote more chamber music than orchestral pieces. Schumann and Brahms, for instance, each wrote four symphonies, yet each composed exactly twenty-three works for chamber music ensembles.

LISTENING INSIGHTS

What to Listen For in Romantic Chamber Music

The key to enjoying chamber music is to become involved in the intimacy of the performance. During a chamber music performance—usually in a small concert hall and close to the audience—chamber musicians communicate closely with one another. You'll notice that they sit close together, often in a semicircle facing the audience. As a member of the audience seated close to the stage, you can see as well as hear each player's performance.

Chamber music is usually woven like a conversation among friends. Players subtly pass musical ideas to one another and add gentle support when a background role is required. Since there is only one player on each part of music, all are equally important.

Because recordings cannot convey the intimacy of chamber music, you fully experience involvement only by attending a live performance.

GUSTAV MAHLER (1860–1911)

When Bohemia was part of the Austro-Hungarian Empire, Gustav Mahler (*mah*-ler) was born into a family living next to a military barracks. As a boy, Mahler was fascinated by two kinds of music. One was military music, with its strong emphasis on brass. The other was folk music that he heard in his village and in the surrounding towns. He later incorporated both types into his symphonies.

At age 15, Mahler's parents sent him to Vienna to study at the Conservatory. After three years, he was awarded a diploma in composition. Mahler's career as a conductor now began. He gradually secured increas-

ingly important conducting positions as he moved from Prague to Leipzig to Budapest to Hamburg and then to the Vienna State Opera. His last two conducting positions were in the United States with the Metropolitan Opera Company (1908) and the New York Philharmonic (1909–11). Ironically, although he spent most of his life conducting operas, Mahler never wrote one.

Mahler's demanding perfectionism earned him a reputation as a tyrant. Other problems plagued him too. Fighting against the tide of anti-Semitism developing in Austria, in 1897, at age 37, Mahler had to resort to trickery to secure his appointment at the Vienna State Opera. Because the management would not give the post to a Jew, Mahler promptly though reluctantly converted to Christianity. Unfortunately, once he was appointed, the anti-Semitic Viennese critics continued to hound him.

In 1902, he married Alma Schindler, a famous Viennese beauty. The death of their young daughter strongly affected Mahler.

Falling ill during his second season as conductor of the New York Philharmonic, Mahler returned to Vienna seeking medical help. He died there at age 50.

PRINCIPAL WORKS

Orchestral Music: 10 symphonies, including: No. 1 (*The Titan*, 1888); No. 2, with soprano (*Resurrection*, 1894); No. 4, with soprano (1900); No. 8, with soloists and choruses (*Symphony of a Thousand,* 1909)

Songs (with Orchestra): Song cycles: *Lieder eines fahrenden Gesellen* (Songs of a Wayfarer, 1885);

Kindertotenlieder (Songs on the Death of Children, 1904); *Des Knaben Wunderhorn* (Youth's Magic Horn, 1893–98); *Das Lied von der Erde* (The Song of the Earth, 1909)

Choral Music: *Das klagende Lied* (The Song of Sorrow, 1880)

LISTENING ACTIVITY

Songs of a Wayfarer (1885)
"Ging Heut Morgen über Feld"
("I Walked This Morning Over The Fields"),
GUSTAV MAHLER

Large Form: Song Cycle
Detailed Form: Modified Song Form
Performing Medium: Baritone and Large Symphony Orchestra

Compact Disc 2 Track 13
Running Time: 4:37

Mahler's songs are quite different from the art songs (*leider*) of Schubert and Schumann that you heard earlier. Those composers and others wrote piano accompaniment for a singer performing in an intimate setting—a small hall or a private home. The music more or less "whispered" their innermost romantic feelings. On the other hand, Mahler "proclaimed" his feelings, bearing his soul for large audiences. For his songs, a full symphony orchestra accompanied a singer on a stage in a large concert hall.

Mahler's emotionalism exemplifies the wonderful excesses of the Romantic period: "You never know what is enough until you know what is too much." Mahler's detractors see his self-indulgent displays of emotionalism as excessive. Others consider them glorious expressions of true feeling.

Keep Mahler's wide range of emotionalism in mind when you listen to the second song in his *Songs of a Wayfarer* cycle, "Ging Heut morgen übers Feld" ("I Walked This Morning Over the Fields"). Mahler's highly personal lyrics are mostly autobiographical, written between 1883 and 1885, after singer-actress Johanna Richter spurned his love. The first of the four songs of the cycle, "Wenn mein Schatz Hochzeit macht" ("When My Love Has Her Wedding Day"), conveys Mahler's sadness over his rejection.

However, by the second song, "Ging Heut' morgen übers Feld," Mahler seems to have recovered as a new day dawns. On this beautiful day, the wanderer (Mahler) walks through sunlit fields, with birds chirping greetings to him as he rediscovers the wonder of nature. His exuberance is short lived as he plunges into sadness, asking, "When will my luck begin?" ("Wenn sind mein glück voll an?"). He answers himself, "No! No! I don't think it ever will" ("Nein, nein, das ich mein . . .").

Born Jewish in Bohemia, a predominantly Protestant area, Mahler worked for most of his career in staunchly anti-Semitic Austria and Germany. Therefore, he considered himself an outsider and often commented that he thought of himself as a "wanderer," at home nowhere. His perfectionism and fiery temperament did not help his cause. Perhaps this inner turmoil contributed to his decision to move to the United States to conduct the Metropolitan Opera Orchestra and the New York Philharmonic.

LISTENING GUIDE

Songs of a Wayfarer (1885)
"Ging Heut Morgen über Feld"
("I Walked This Morning Over The Fields"),
GUSTAV MAHLER

13   0:00   WALKING THEME   flutes and piccolo staccato; duple meter; *p*; D major; baritone soloist enters with "Walking Theme"; homophonic texture

Ging heut' mor - gens ü - bers Feld, Tau noch auf den Grä - sern hing;

Ging heut' morgen übers Feld,	I walked this morning over the fields;
Tau noch auf den Gräsern hing;	Dew still hung on the grass;
Sprach zu mir der lust'ge Fink:	The merry finch spoke to me:
Ei du! Gelt?	Hey, you! Is that right?

0:19   WALKING THEME—SECOND PART   mostly strings accompany singer; *pp*

Gu - ten   Mor - gen! Ei gelt? Du!
So good   morn - ing! Good morn - ing!

Wird's nicht— ei - ne schö - ne Welt?   schö - ne Welt!?
Is— it— not a love - ly world?   love - ly world?

	Guten Morgan! Ei gelt?	Good morning! Isn't it?
	Du! Wird's nicht eine schöne Welt?	You there! Isn't it a lovely world?
0:33	*full orchestra, **ff**, then, **pp***	
	Zink! Zink! Schön und flink!	Sing! Sing! Pretty and quick!
	Wie mir doch die Welt gefällt"	How I love the world!"

0:45   *Short orchestral transition, loud diminishing to soft, "walking theme" returns*

WALKING THEME—FIRST PART

Auch die Gockenblum' am Feld	Also the bluebell in the meadow
Hat mir lustig, guter Ding'	—cheerful, kind creature—
Mit den Glöckchen, klinge, kling.	With its bells went ring-ring.
Klinge, kling.	Ring, ring.

1:08   **WALKING THEME—SECOND PART**

Ihren Morgengruss geschellt:	And rang a morning greeting for me:
Wird's nicht eine schöne Welt?	Isn't it a lovely world?
Kling, kling! Kling, kling!	Ring-ring! Ring-ring!
Schönes Ding!	Pretty thing!
Wie mir doch die Welt gefällt!	How I love the world!
Heia!"	Hey-ho!"

1:36   *orchestral interlude with soaring flutes and violins, modulating to key of B major; **pp***

1:55   **WALKING THEME—FIRST PART**

| Und da fing im Sonnenschein | Then in the sunshine |
| Gleich die Welt zu funklen an: | The world suddenly began to glitter; |

2:13   **WALKING THEME—SECOND PART**

Alles, alles Ton und Farbe gewann	All things took on sound and color
Im Sonnenschein!	in the sunshine.
Blum' und Vogel, gross and klein!	Flowers and birds, both large and small!
Guten Tag, guten Tag!	"Good day, good day!
Ist's nicht eine schöne Welt?"	Isn't it a lovely world?
Ei, du, gelt? Ei, du, gelt?	Hey you, Is that right?
Schöne Welt?	Lovely world?

2:56   **WALKING THEME—FIRST PART**   *tempo slows, orchestra very soft, tonality modulates to F-sharp major*

Nun fängt auch mein Glück wohl an?	When will my luck begin?
Nun fängt auch mein Glück wohl an?	When will my luck begin?
Nein, nein, das, ich mein,"	No, no, I don't think
Mir nimmer blühen kann!	it ever will!

4:15   *orchestra ends the song, fading softer and softer toward an F-sharp major chord*

The Virtuoso Orchestra

Economics had a favorable influence on music, just as it did on other professions. After Mendelssohn elevated the performance standards and professional prestige of his Gewandhaus Orchestra, higher-paying positions attracted players. Two outstanding composer/conductors continued the Mendelssohn tradition: Gustav Mahler and Richard Strauss.

Knowing that jobs usually went to the best players, musicians strove to improve their abilities. Beginning in the late nineteenth century, each player in the major symphony orchestras was a virtuoso, capable of performing as a soloist.

Mahler's Symphonies

Although Mahler's symphonies abound with extra-musical references, including poetry and philosophy, he considered them evolutions of the classical tradition. Awash with intermingled extramusical ideas, his long symphonies contain some of the most highly charged, emotional music of the Romantic period. The music reflects the composer's own emotional swings, for which he sought therapy from Vienna's leading psychiatrist, Sigmund Freud (1856–1939).

Freud
(froid)

Longest Symphony
Largest Symphony

Mahler established two records in music: one in length and one in number of players. His Third Symphony lasts 1 hour and 35 minutes, longer than any other. His Eighth Symphony, "Symphony of a Thousand," the largest work ever written for a symphony orchestra, used more than 1,000 performers at its premiere: an orchestra of 171, 8 vocal soloists, a children's choir of 350, and two choruses of 250 each.

Early in the twentieth century, his music was somewhat neglected. While Mahler was composing his last works—from 1900 to 1911—modern musical trends had begun. Yet he was rooted in the past and did not follow the changing times. Many listeners began to regard Romantic music as outmoded and overly sentimental in contrast to the cerebral, more concise twentieth-century music.

After Mahler's death, his music was still considered old-fashioned. In the 1930s and 1940s, Hitler banned Mahler's music throughout Germany and Austria, along with the music of other Jewish composers.

Then, in the 1950s, as many listeners began moving away from the harsh dissonances of modern music, seeking more consonant and emotional music, they rediscovered Mahler. Since the 1960s, his music has been enjoying a popularity greater than any he knew in his lifetime.

CHALLENGE YOUR EXPERTISE

- Which opera is associated with "tobacco and bulls"?
- Which opera contains elephants and pyramids?

Symphony No. 1 (*The Titan*), Gustav Mahler
First Movement

Large Form: Symphony
Detailed Form: Sectional

Compact Disc 3, Tracks 15–20
Running Time: 12:27

Mahler composed his First Symphony over a period of several years, mostly during summer breaks from his various conducting duties. After hearing Richard Strauss's tone poems, Mahler decided to write a symphonic poem as his first symphony, which he titled *The Titan*. His original plan was to produce a five-movement symphony with a program about nature—patterned after Beethoven's *Pastoral* Symphony. After reworking the music a number of times, he finally decided on four movements without a program.

Because Mahler had built his first movement on ideas of youth, flowers, early dawn, the forest, and endless spring. The Introduction may remind you of Beethoven's *Pastoral* Symphony, with its bird calls and the sounds of the forest and nature. This is no coincidence. Mahler even retraced Beethoven's steps through the Vienna Woods, trying to recapture the feeling and sounds that had inspired the *Pastoral*.

After the slow introduction, the first movement proceeds at a faster tempo into "Days of Youth." For its main theme, Mahler reuses a theme from his song cycle, *Songs of a Wayfarer*.

Note on following the Listening Guide: Melodies and their fragments enter and leave and are commented upon by various instruments of the orchestra. Mahler uses a highly flexible and complex form, mainly relying on melodic ideas for continuity. So varied is the form that a listening guide noting every sound event would distract you from following the mood and the broad sweep of the music. Therefore, only major events are included here.

Symphony No. 1 (The Titan), Gustav Mahler
First Movement

INTRODUCTION—marked: Langsam, schleppend wie ein Naturlaut (slowly and drawn out like a sound of nature)

15	0:00	FOREST SOUNDS	the pitch "A" high strings (harmonics); ***ppp***; slow tempo, duple (4) meter
	0:31	FANFARE	in clarinets, ***pp***
	1:07	FANFARE	played by distant (off-stage) trumpets, ***ppp***
16	1:33	FOREST MELODY	played by horns; ***pp***

	1:48	FANFARE	played by trumpets, slightly faster tempo
	1:58	FOREST MELODY	in horns, **pp**
	2:13	FANFARE	in trumpets
	2:20	TRANSITION SECTION	played by cellos and basses; **p**; faster tempo, horns and woodwinds in background
	2:58	BIRD CALL—cuckoo	played by clarinet, **p**

MAIN SECTION

| 17 | 3:02 | TRANSITION | played by cellos; **pp**; imitated by bassoon, then solo trumpet; BIRD CALL in clarinets; then violins enter, completing |
| | | WALKING THEME—Days of Youth | the melody; extensions of the melody in violins and woodwinds; rubato tempo; D-major tonality |

	4:36	WALKING THEME—Days of Youth	started again by horns, **ff**, continued by strings and woodwinds
	5:00	FOREST SOUNDS	slower; introduction music returns—forest sounds; BIRD CALLS played by woodwinds
	7:32	HUNTING HORNS	played by horns; **ppp**
	7:49	WALKING THEME—fragments	played by cellos; faster
18	9:09	WALKING THEME—Days of Youth	returns
Long developmental section, using new themes and hints of all themes already played; changing tempos and styles cymbals crash, full orchestra, fanfares, **ff**

FINALE SECTION

| 19 | 10:41 | HORN CALL | containing the interval of a fourth, similar to other melodies and earlier Forest Melody; **ff** |
| 20 | 11:21 | WALKING THEME—Days of Youth | returns in trumpet, **ff**; imitations by other instruments, tempo accelerates; pause; fast, agitated woodwinds; **ff**; pause; full orchestra cadence to final chord, **ff** |

CHALLENGE YOUR EXPERTISE

What sort of records did Mahler break?

RICHARD STRAUSS (1864–1949)

Richard Strauss (*shtrowss*—no relation to the waltz composers) was born in Munich, the son of the principal horn player in the Court Orchestra. (Notice how often Strauss favors the horn in his orchestral works; he also wrote two great concertos for that instrument.) Music was a large part of his family life, and Strauss began composing at age six. Soon he was studying composition and orchestration with members of his father's orchestra.

Strauss's earlier compositions were in the conservative tradition of Schumann and Brahms. After taking a series of conducting posts, he veered toward the more radical Wagner and Liszt camp.

In 1898, Strauss was appointed conductor of the Royal Court Opera in Berlin and soon after, devoted most of his remaining years to composing operas. In 1919, he was made director of the Vienna State Opera, a post formerly held by his longtime friend Gustav Mahler. During World War II, Strauss chose to remain in Nazi Germany, spending most of the war in retirement in Bavaria. At 85, he died in the Bavarian town of Garmisch.

PRINCIPAL WORKS

Orchestral Music: Symphonic poems: *Aus Italien* (1886), *Don Juan* (1889), *Death and Transfiguration* (1889), *Till Eulenspiegels lustige Streiche* (Till Eulenspiegel's Merry Pranks, 1895), *Also sprach Zarathustra* (Thus Spake Zarathustra, 1896), *Don Quixote* (1897), *Ein Heldenleben* (A Hero's Life, 1898), *Symphonie Domestica* (1903); Horn Concertos: No. 1 in E-flat (1883), No. 2 in E-flat (1942); Oboe Concerto (1945)

Operas: *Salome* (1905), *Elektra* (1909), *Der Rosenkavalier* (The Cavalier of the Rose, 1911), *Ariadne auf Naxos* (1912), *Die Frau ohne Schatten* (The Woman without a Shadow, 1919), *Arabella* (1933)

Songs: *Four Last Songs* (with orchestra, 1948), about 200 with piano

CHALLENGE YOUR EXPERTISE

What incentives encouraged musicians to improve their skills?

Late Romantic Period Program Music

Searching for new ways of expression, Romantic composers began to depict an entire "program," or story, through music. These stories are not the same as the "program" notes that provide background information about a composition, although the story or text may appear in the printed concert program.

Program

Music "programed" to follow a story or nonmusical ideas is not new. Songs, oratorios, cantatas, and operas usually translate textual ideas into musical ones. Handel's oratorios, such as *Messiah,* abound with such treatments. Other composers have written highly descriptive instrumental music. Based on a set of sonnets, Vivaldi created a musical description of each of *The Four Seasons:* bird calls in the *Spring,* thunderstorms in the *Summer,* harvesting in the *Fall,* shivering and ice in *Winter.*

In his *Pastoral* Symphony of 1808, Beethoven suggests the idea of program music by specifically titling each of the five movements. However, he cautioned that the titles suggest only "expression of feelings" (see Chapter 12). Later nineteenth-century composers carried these ideas further. Mendelssohn's *Hebrides* (*Fingal's Cave*) *Overture* describes his journey to the seascape and caves surrounding the islands off the western coast of Scotland.

Berlioz provides the listener with a blow-by-blow account of what is happening in his *Symphonie fantastique*. He specifically intended his story to be included in the printed concert program for the audience to follow. Franz Liszt used programs for several of his works. His *Dante* Symphony and *Faust* Symphony have particularly detailed programs.

Many pieces suggest that the composer did follow a detailed program, even though no story was written out. Several of Tchaikovsky's concert overtures and symphonic fantasies obviously follow a detailed story: *1812 Overture, Francesca da Rimini,* and *Romeo and Juliet.*

LISTENING INSIGHTS

What to Listen for in Programmatic and Highly Descriptive Music

You don't have to know its background in order to enjoy music. A fine orchestral work can stand on its own without associations to literature or any other art. Most music has no direct reference to a specific, extra-musical source.

When we encounter a work that openly calls attention to its source, we should look into that source—beyond the music alone—for greater understanding and enjoyment. A piece becomes more interesting after you have read the nonmusical ideas that inspired the composer.

If the story of a programmatic or descriptive work does not appear in your printed program or on the insert with a recording, a little detective work will pay off. Composers' biographies, histories of music, books, and magazine articles on specific composers or works can yield further insights into a composition. Often, the search for meanings and the concomitant pleasure provide some of the joys of music.

Tone Poems (Symphonic Poems)

Of all the programmatic music composers, Richard Strauss was the most successful in wedding a program with music. Calling his programmatic works *tone poems,* or *symphonic poems,* Strauss asks the listener to follow his orchestral accounts of detailed poems and stories.

In *Don Juan,* for instance, Strauss describes the infamous rake—the same character who inspired Mozart's *Don Giovanni.* Strauss's symphonic poem depicts Don Juan's searchings, seductions, flights from relationships, and emotional moods, ending in bitterness and despair.

Who wrote the words for a tone poem?

Summary of Terms

chamber music
descriptive music
Freud
longest symphony
largest symphony

philharmonic
 societies
program music
program notes
programmatic music

symphonic poem
symphony orchestra
 societies
tone poem
virtuoso orchestra

17
Nationalism

Political Influences

A spark of nationalism ignited Europe, Scandinavia, and Russia throughout the nineteenth century. Wars that followed, including the devastating World Wars I and II of the twentieth century, periodically rekindled the flames until the creation of the Common Market in 1957 (later becoming the European Economic Community).

As countries finally realized the value of pooling their resources, European nationalism subsided. Today, Eastern European countries, formerly cut off by political and economic differences, are rejoining the family of nations.

Historians are divided over the precise onset of nationalism, but it seems to have coincided with the American and French Revolutions toward the end of the eighteenth century. Weary of oppression, citizens began overthrowing monarchies and taking control of their own countries.

For centuries, without regard for the interests of citizens, rulers had been arranging marriages and royal successions in conquered lands intended to maintain family holdings. In fact, royalty often held their subjects in disdain. And because French or German was the language of the courts, most rulers in Russia, the Baltic states, Scandinavia, and the Slavic nations could not communicate with the people.

The Formation of New Republics   In response to the public outcry for a greater voice in their governments, clusters of independent cities and states consolidated into new republics:

- 1830   The Netherlands (Holland) and Belgium split off from the Grand Duchy of Luxembourg.
- 1861   The Italian Parliament created a unified kingdom from former city-states.
- 1871   Germany was unified into an empire.
- 1872   Portugal became a republic.
- 1917   The Russian people overthrew the Czar and began to establish the Soviet Union.

Industrial and Technological Influences   Contributing further to the growing nationalistic phenomenon was the industrialization of Europe. Farmers who flocked to the cities in search of a better life came into contact with people from all parts of their homeland. By discovering their shared values, these countrymen developed a sense of national pride and dared to become more politically active.

Wanderlust

Travel Influences   New, relatively inexpensive means of transportation encouraged *wanderlust*. More people could travel and become acquainted with other cultures. As early as 1828, tourists boarded France's new passenger trains. By accom- modating more people with greater efficiency and in relative comfort, railways soon replaced stagecoach lines as the primary means of mass transportation. The steamship replaced the sailing ship, reducing Transatlantic crossings from three difficult, uncertain weeks to a safer, nine-and-a-half-day passage.

Artists also explored the world, incorporating their discoveries into their works, such as Robert Browning's poem *Home Thoughts from Abroad,* Joseph Conrad's novel *Lord Jim,* Paul Gaugin's exotic paintings of Tahiti, and Felix Mendelssohn's *Scottish* Symphony and *Italian* Symphony.

Nationalism in Music

Since the time of Vivaldi and Bach, French, German, and Italian music and musicians had dominated almost every court, opera house, and concert hall from Moscow to Madrid. But as nationalism gained momentum, composers in Russia,

The Nutcracker Suite

Scandinavia, Spain, and other countries began examining their own cultures. Many realized that they could incorporate it into compositions indigenous to their countries. Thus, nationalistic music became the new fashion.

Russian Nationalism

The scene   St. Petersburg, Russia, on the Baltic Sea

The time   Latter half of the nineteenth century

The situation   Five Russian composers band together to create Russian nationalistic music.

Their training   Free from most of the Western European influences in music

Their goal   To promote purely Russian music

Their approach   Incorporating situations from history, folklore, legends, and native instruments and music

"The Mighty Five"

- Nikolai Rimsky-Korsakov (*rim*-skee *kor*-sa-kof, 1844–1908)
- Modest Mussorgsky (moo-*zorg*-skee, 1839–1881)
- Alexander Borodin (*bor*-uh-deen, 1833–1887)
- César Cui (*say*-zar *kwee*, 1835–1918)
- Mily Balakirev (*mee*-lee bah-*lah*-kih-ref, 1837–1910)

MODEST MUSSORGSKY (1839–1881)

A militant nationalist, Modest Mussorgsky was born in Pskof, Russia, into an aristocratic family. He studied at the Preobrazhensky Guard school in St. Petersburg and later spent three years on active duty with the Guard.

Although he was a fine pianist and had dabbled in composition, Mussorgsky had not considered music seriously until his later years. He resigned his commission in the Guard to earn his living as a clerk in the civil service—composing on the side.

His great difficulties with money and health were mainly due to his excessive drinking. Although his little formal musical training was primarily from Balakirev, he was one of the most original and influential Russian composers of his day. Searching for a new Russian musical language, Mussorgsky became fascinated with the Russian spoken language, incorporating its unique inflections into his songs and operas.

In spite of his older appearance in the 1881 portrait at left, Mussorgsky was only 42 years old when he died.

PRINCIPAL WORKS

Operas: *Boris Godunov* (1869), *Khovanshchina* (completed by Rimsky-Korsakov, 1886)

Songs: *The Nursery* (1870), *Sunless* (1874), *Songs and Dances of Death* (1877); more than fifty other songs

Orchestral Music: *A Night on Bald Mountain* (tone poem) (1867)

Piano Music: *Pictures at an Exhibition* (later orchestrated by Ravel); numerous songs and piano pieces

PETER ILYICH TCHAIKOVSKY (1840–1893)

A favorite composer of audiences around the world, Peter Ilyich Tchaikovsky was born in Votinsk, Russia. After studying law in St. Petersburg, he grudgingly worked as a clerk in the Ministry of Justice.

Returning to school at age twenty-three at the newly founded St. Petersburg Conservatory of Music, Tchaikovsky studied composition with Anton Rubinstein (1829–1894). Three years later, he was hired to teach music at the new Moscow Conservatory, where he remained until his retirement at age thirty-seven. He was then able to devote himself full time to composing and conducting music.

As guest conductor with various orchestras, he toured Russia, London, and Europe extensively. In 1891, the New York Philharmonic invited Tchaikovsky to the United States as guest conductor for the opening of Carnegie Hall.

Hounded by bigots and disgraced in court because of his homosexuality, Tchaikovsky fell into a severe depression. The cause of death was listed as cholera, but there is little doubt that he committed suicide at age 53.

PRINCIPAL WORKS

Operas: *Eugene Onegin* (1865), *Mazeppa* (1884), *The Queen of Spades* (1880)

Orchestral Music: 6 symphonies, including: No. 2 (*Little Russian*, 1872), No. 3 (*Polish*, 1875), No. 4 (1878), No. 5 (1888), No. 6 (*Pathétique* 1893); Concertos: Violin Concerto (1878); 3 piano concertos, No. 1 (1875);

Ballets: *Swan Lake* (1877), *Sleeping Beauty* (1889), *The Nutcracker* (1892); Fantasy Overtures: *Romeo and Juliet* (1869), *Francesca da Rimini* (1876), *Capriccio italien* (1880), *1812 Overture* (1882), *Marche slav*

Chamber Music: String sextet (1890), string quartets, piano trio

Kremlin Square in front of the Church of the Redeemer

Tchaikovsky as a Nationalist   Although he was their contemporary, the so-called "Russian Five" excluded Tchaikovsky from their group. They considered him an outsider—too cosmopolitan, too influenced by the music of other nations through his frequent travels, especially to Germany, France, and Italy.

Despite his exclusion by "The Five," their music inspired Tchaikovsky to compose nationalistic music. However, he did not limit his nationalistic sources to Russia. His ballets *Swan Lake* and *Nutcracker* (see Plate 11) include folk dances of other countries. His six symphonies, *March Slav*, operas, and numerous other works

What to Listen For in Nationalistic Music

Nationalist composers expected their listeners to focus on the native resources in their music. Listen for the folk and patriotic melodies and indigenous instruments, such as Russian balalaika and bells, and Spanish castanets, guitars, and tambourines.

The more rigid, intellectual forms that German composers favored held little interest for most nationalist composers. Their forms were loose, usually relying on forms suggested by descriptions, stories, and titles. You will generally hear many contrasting sections of music with only a smattering of repeated ideas and very little thematic development.

contain Russian songs. However, his orchestral work *Capriccio italien* is not Russian. It is a musical diary of his travels to Italy. (Rimsky-Korsakov, a member of "The Five," similarly memorialized his travels to Spain in his work *Capriccio espagnol*.)

Perhaps "The Five" were right. Tchaikovsky did not consistently display the nationalistic fervor that they did. But the *1812 Overture* epitomized his passion as a Russian nationalist.

A performance of Tchaikovsky's *1812 Overture* at Los Angeles' Hollywood Bowl featuring dramatic fireworks

HISTORICAL PERSPECTIVE

The 1812 Overture: Spectacular Performances

Tchaikovsky's *1812 Overture* is one of the most bombastic and nationalistic works ever written. It was originally commissioned by the czarist government to celebrate the seventieth anniversary of Napoleon's devastating defeat by the Russian army in Moscow and Napoleon's subsequent retreat to Paris with only about 400,000 of his original 550,000 troops. Moscow Square was the original setting. The piece includes army rifle and cannon firing, augmented by the great bells of the colorful Church of the Redeemer. (The firing of cannons and rifles is not random. Tchaikovsky treated them as orchestra members by indicating their exact entrances in the score.)

Today, this highly programmatic piece has become a favorite at outdoor concerts throughout the world. In addition to the large symphony orchestra, today's performances often are further enhanced by adding military-style bands to its concluding section. The work is often capped by spectacular fireworks display.

Indoors and on recordings, the sounds of the church bells, rifles, and cannons often are replicated by prerecorded tapes. During the reign of the Communists, who overthrew the Czar in 1917, the playing of the "Czars Hymn" that Tchaikovsky used was forbidden. The Soviets substituted a new, considerably less exciting melody. With the breakup of the Soviet regime, however, the original "Czar's Hymn" was back in the *1812 Overture,* even in Russia.

LISTENING ACTIVITY

The 1812 Overture (1882), Peter Ilyich Tchaikovsky

Large Form: Programmatic Concert Overture
Detailed Form: Sectional
Performing Medium: Large Symphony Orchestra with Additional Brass Band

Compact Disc 2, Tracks 15–18
Running Time: 14:34

Nationalistic Resources

With its rich setting and program focusing on a slice of Russian history, the *1812 Overture* exemplifies nationalism. It employs an abundance of resources associated with nationalities and cultures, including:

- Russian Orthodox Church hymns
- Russian folk songs and dances
- The French national anthem "La Marseillaise"
- Russian patriotic music: "Czar's Hymn"
- bells and chimes representing the great bells of the churches in Russia

The Program

The work opens with a Russian hymn, "God Preserve Thy People." In an agitated section, Napoleon's troops advance toward Moscow. The horns introduce a slow march as the Russian troops prepare for battle. The armies clash and fall back, as the orchestra plays fragments of the French national anthem, "La Marseillaise."

Freezing in the bitter winter's evening, the Russian troops think of their warm homes and families, as we hear a Russian lullaby and a playful Russian folk song.

Morning arrives, and the French troops advance with the "La Marseillaise." A minor battle ensues and both sides retreat to their camps for another cold night. We again hear the lullaby and the folk song.

Then a new, more furious battle begins—armies clash, cannons and rifles blast over the music. We hear the opening hymn again, this time with church bells and chimes signifying the Russian victory.

Triumphantly, the Russian troops march back to Moscow, greeted by the "Czar's Hymn." Bells toll. Rifle and cannon fire signal victory.

LISTENING GUIDE

The 1812 Overture (1882), Peter Ilyich Tchaikovsky

| 15 | 0:00 | THEME 1 Russian Orthodox Church hymn | Large orchestra, hymn begins in the strings; *p;* very slow (largo) tempo; triple meter; E-flat Major tonality; homophonic texture |

| | 1:20 | THEME 1 fragments | imitation and sequences between woodwinds and strings, crescendo to *fff* |

| 16 | 2:00 | THEME 2 Russian folk song | played by the oboe, *p;* imitations by flutes and cellos; c minor tonality |

	2:44	THEME 2 modified	imitation of short, rhythmic motive in minor tonality, *f* to *fff;* tempo gets faster, sixteenth notes
	2:54	THEME 2 fragments	full orchestra, sequences, two loud chords bring the music to a one-beat halt
	3:20	THEME 2 Russian folk song	played in strings, *fff;* slightly slower tempo, same c-minor tonality
	3:39	THEME 3 fanfare-type march	played by woodwinds and horns over snare drum; *mf;* slower tempo (andante), duple meter; E-flat major tonality
	4:08		Gradually slower and softer, to *p;* pause
	4:30	THEME 4	played by strings; *f;* agitated, quick tempo, duple (4) meter

| | 4:52 | THEME 4 | short, rhythmic motive moves in sequences; crescendo to *fff* |
| | 5:08 | THEME 5 La Marseillaise | played by horn over percussion, imitation and sequences of themes played by different instruments, shifting major and minor tonalities, trumpet completes the theme, *f* |

	5:47	THEME 4	heard briefly in the strings, *ff*
	6:20	TRANSITION	tempo slows, diminuendo to *p*
17	6:24	THEME 6 Russian folk lullaby	played by strings, *mf;* duple meter (4), b-flat minor tonality, then imitations between strings and horns

| | 7:49 | THEME 7 Russian folk dance | played by flutes over tambourine, *p;* same tempo, e-flat minor tonality |

8:31	THEME 5 La Marseillaise	held pitch in bass; *p;* change of key; agitated tempo; played by trumpets, fragments imitated by horns; crescendo to *f*
9:18	THEME 4 THEME 5	briefly returns in strings, *ff;* interspersed with fragments of fanfares in brasses; slowing of tempo
9:56	THEME 6 Russian folk lullaby	returns in high strings, *p;* imitated by low strings
10:37	THEME 7 Russian folk dance	returns played by violins over tambourine, *mf;* minor tonality
10:55	THEME 5 La Marseillaise	played by horns, fanfare fragments in a series of sequences; *mf;* shifting major and minor tonalities
11:27	THEME 5 La Marseillaise	played by trumpets, *ff;* rifles and cannons fire
11:39	TRANSITION	high strings play descending pattern of sequences, gradually slowing
12:17	THEME 1 Russian Orthodox Church hymn	in full orchestra, *fff;* church bells and chimes added
13:29	THEME 3 fanfare-type march fragments	faster tempo, *ffff;* continues to the end, major tonality
18 13:39	THEME 8 Czar's Hymn	in E-flat major tonality, cannons and rifles fire and bells ring

14:16	THEME 3 fragments	full orchestra and bells on one held E-flat pitch, *ffff;* final chord

NIKOLAI RIMSKY-KORSAKOV (1844–1908)

Born in Tikhvin, Russia, Nikolai Rimsky-Korsakov (*rim-skee-kors-a-cuff*) later served for eleven years as a naval officer with the title Inspector of Naval Bands. But Rimsky-Korsakov's interest was in music—not in the military. Thus, he joined the faculty of the St. Petersburg Conservatory of Music to teach composition and orchestration. Like his colleagues in the "Mighty Five," Rimsky-Korsakov used native folk melodies in his compositions. He also arranged and edited collections of Russian folk music.

A highly renowned orchestrator and composer, Rimsky-Korsakov edited many of Mussorgsky's and Borodin's works to facilitate their performance. His most famous students were Igor Stravinsky and Sergei Prokofiev (discussed in Chapters 20 and 22). Although his compositions include symphonies, chamber music, choruses, and songs, his most well-known works are his symphonic poems and operas.

PRINCIPAL WORKS

Orchestra Music: Concerto for Trombone and Brass Band (1877); Symphonic suite *Scheherazade* (1888); *Capriccio espagnol* (1887); and the *Russian Easter Overture* (1888)

Operas: sixteen operas: *Sadko* (1898); *Snegurochka* (Snow Maiden, 1882); *Mozart and Salieri* (1897); *Skzka o Tsare Saltane* (Tale of Czar Saltan, which includes "The Flight of the Bumble Bee," 1900); *Le Coq d'or* (The Golden Cockerel, 1909)

- To which professional association did Nikolai Rimsky-Korsakov, Alexander Borodin, Mily Balakirev, César Cui, and Modest Mussorgsky belong?
- Which popular Russian composer worked as a law clerk?

Twentieth-Century Russia

Many Communist-era composers retained a nationalistic approach in their music. The government not only encouraged them to do so but reprimanded them when their music became too "international."

Other Nationalist Composers

The Czech Republic Until 1919, the country we know today as the Czech Republic was part of the Austro-Hungarian (Hapsburg) Empire. It was home to several outstanding nationalist composers. *Antonín Dvořák (1841–1904)* and *Bedřich Smetana (1824–1884)* are the most widely known.

Dvořák
(d'-*vor*-zhahk)
Smetana
(*smeh*-tuh-nuh)

SERGEI RACHMANINOV (1873–1943)

Sergei Rachmaninov's (rahk-*mah*-nih-nof) early musical studies were at the St. Petersburg Conservatory. Later he studied at the Moscow Conservatory, graduating at age nineteen. A brilliant career as a pianist, conductor, and composer followed, affording him enough economic security to travel extensively.

When his First Symphony (1895) was not well received by the Moscow public, Rachmaninov withdrew from composing for a while. But with the completion and successful premiere of his Second Piano Concerto in 1901, Rachmaninov regained his stride and went on to compose some of his most popular works.

In 1917, fleeing the Russian Revolution, Rachmaninov and his family emigrated to the United States, where he was immediately acclaimed for his pianistic abilities. Subsequent concert tours and record contracts kept him extremely busy, yet he found time to compose, premiering several of his works with the Philadelphia Orchestra.

With his nineteenth-century Romantic style becoming increasingly anachronistic, Rachmaninov decided to abandon composition. He continued as a successful concert pianist until his death at his Beverly Hills home at the age of 69.

PRINCIPAL WORKS

Orchestral Works: Piano Concertos: No. 1 in f-sharp minor (1891); No. 2 in c minor (1901); No. 3 in a minor (1909); No. 4 in g minor (1926); Symphonies: No. 1 in d minor (1895); No. 2 in e minor (1907); No. 3 in a minor (1936); *The Isle of the Dead* (1909); *Rhapsody on a Theme by Paganini* for piano and orchestra (1934); *Symphonic Dances* (1940)

Piano Music: Preludes (23) (1904, 1910), sonatas, études, and variations

Choral Music: *Liturgy of St. John Chrysostom* (1910); *The Bells* (1913)

Opera: *Aleko* (1893)
    Miscellaneous songs and chamber music

BÉLA BARTÓK (1881–1945)

Béla Bartók (*bahr*-tok) was born in Hungary during the last years of the Hapsburgs' reign. After early piano training with his mother, he studied at the Budapest Royal Academy of Music.

Following graduation, Bartók embarked on a successful career as a concert pianist, composing in his spare time. Throughout most of his life, Bartók's main source of income was from piano teaching—thirty years at the Budapest Academy.

Bartók's studies had been mainly in the Austro-German tradition until 1904, when he began discovering the vast resource of folk music. Along with Hungarian composer Zoltán Kodály, Bartók compiled and analyzed the folk music not only of his native Hungary but of other countries. Both men used their findings in composing nationalistic music.

In 1940, when Hungary entered into a collaboration with the Nazis, Bartók fled with his family to the United States. In their haste, they had to leave most of their possessions in Hungary, settling in New York City with meager resources.

Unable to find work immediately, Bartók used what was left of his money to support his family. Financial difficulties were compounded by his bouts with leukemia.

Columbia University came to the family's rescue by appointing Bartók to a position as a folk music researcher at the university library. In addition, a few composing commissions helped ease Bartók's circumstances, especially the Boston Symphony's commission in 1943 for the *Concerto for Orchestra*. Bartók died at age 64 in a New York City hospital.

PRINCIPAL WORKS

Orchestral Music: *Kossuth* (1903); *Dance Suite* (1917); *Music for Strings, Percussion, and Celesta* (1936); *Concerto for Orchestra* (1943); three piano concertos; two violin concertos, Viola Concerto (1945)

Ballets: *The Wooden Prince* (1917); *The Miraculous Mandarin* (1926)

Opera: *Bluebeard's Castle* (1918)

Chamber Music: six string quartets; *Contrasts* for Violin, Clarinet and Piano (1938); Sonata for Solo Violin (1944); sonatas for violin and piano

Piano Music: *14 Bagatelles* (1908), *Allegro barbaro* (1911), *Suite* (1916), *Sonata* (1926), *Out of Doors* (1926), *Mikrokosmos* volumes 1–6 (1926–39)

Choral Music: *Cantata profana* (1930)

Miscellaneous choral works, songs, and folk song arrangements

Dvořák is particularly interesting to Americans. After having achieved fame as a composer in his native Bohemia, he moved to New York City to become director of the National Conservatory of Music (no longer in existence) from 1892 to 1895. During that time, he wrote his famous *New World Symphony* (Symphony No. 9).

Liszt
Kodály
(koh-*dye*)
Bartók
Grieg
(greeg)
Sibelius

Hungary   *Franz Liszt* (see biography in Chapter 14) and the twentieth-century composers *Zoltán Kodály* (*1882–1967*) and *Béla Bartók* (*1881–1945*) are the Hungarian composers whose music you are most likely to hear at concerts.

Scandinavia   *Edvard Grieg* (*1843–1907*) of Norway wrote many Norwegian songs and is well known for his nationalistic *Peer Gynt Suites*. *Jean Sibelius* (yan sib-*bayl*-yus) (*1865–1957*) of Finland is best known for his *Finlandia* Violin Concerto, tone poems, *Valse triste,* and his symphonies, especially Symphony No. 2.

Elgar

United Kingdom   *Edward Elgar* (*1857–1934*) was a distinctly English composer. His most famous works are the *Pomp and Circumstance* Marches and *Enigma* Variations.

Jean Sibelius at age twenty-three

Ralph (pronounced Rafe) Vaughan Williams (1872–1958), another English national-   **Vaughan Williams**
ist composer, once wrote:

> Art, like charity, should begin at home. If it is to be of any value, it must grow
> out of the very life of himself (the composer), the community in which he lives,
> the nation to which he belongs.

To accomplish this task, Vaughan Williams incorporated English folk songs into
many of his works, notably his *English Folk Song Suite* and *Fantasia on "Greensleeves."*
Percy Grainger (1882–1961) is less easy to classify. Born in Australia and edu-   **Grainger**
cated in London, he lived in the United States during the latter part of his life. For
many years, Grainger wandered through the English and Irish countrysides with
an Edison cylinder-recorder and music paper, recording and notating folk songs
that he heard. He abundantly incorporated these songs into his music. He is best
known for his many British folk song settings, such as *Irish Tune from County Derry,
Country Gardens,* and his wind band work *Lincolnshire Posy.*

Italy   Several famous opera composers are considered Italian nationalists. The
greatest were *Giuseppe Verdi* and *Giacomo Puccini,* both discussed in Chapter 15.
Ottorino Respighi (1879–1936) is best known for his orchestral works: *Roman*   **Respighi**
Festivals, The Pines of Rome, The Fountains of Rome, and *The Birds.*   (res-*pee*-ghee)

Spain   *Isaac Albéniz (1860–1909), Enrique Granados (1867–1916),* and *Manuel de*   **Albéniz**
Falla (1876–1947) incorporated lively flamenco and Andalusian dance rhythms into   (ahl-*bay*-neeth)
their colorful music. Also, because of the use of instruments indigenous to Spain,   **Granados**
such as castanets, tambourine, and guitars, their music sounds distinctly Spanish.   (grah-*nah*-dohs)
                                                                                        de Falla
North American   Chapter 24 through 27 discuss composers in the United States.   (*fah*-yah)

Summary of Terms

Andalusian rhythms	Czar's Hymn	La Marseillaise
balalaika	flamenco dance rhythms	Russian Five
bells	folk song	tambourine
castanets	guitar	wanderlust

18
Impressionism

Impressionistic Poetry and Painting

A Claude Monet painting, *Impression—Soleil Levant* (*Impression: Sunrise*), provided the inspiration for the name of a new movement in France. Alienated by German intellectualism and "oversentimentality," French artists of the late nineteenth century felt more spiritually attuned to quieter, more sensual expression. For example, the poet Mallarmé was more interested in beauty and in the sound of the French language than he was in the content.

French painters reflected their interest in the "impression" of a subject rather than in its detailed, specific content. The works of Monet, Manet, Renoir, and others epitomize the Impressionistic style—uncomplicated subject matter portrayed in the quiet of pastel colors, with vague definition.

New Inventions Influence Art

Two practical inventions boosted Impressionistic painting: the camera and the paint tube (similar to the toothpaste tube).

The Camera   Until the invention of the camera, a painter's primary role was that of a "photographer"—to capture the moment for posterity. Notice how Hans Holbein's sixteenth-century portrait of Henry VIII looks more like a snapshot than a painting.

In 1827, Joseph Niépce produced the earliest photographs on a metal plate, encouraging painters to look at a subject with a fresh eye. Painters gathered in Parisian cafés, intently discussing new options for capturing the feelings and impressions of the moment. Although the details of their paintings may seem veiled, as though you were looking at them through a slight haze, the mood is always clear (see Monet's *Les Meules*).

The Paint Tube   Before the invention of the lead tube of oil paint, artists rarely worked outdoors. When they did, they found it quite inconvenient. Oil paint thinned with alcohol dries in minutes in the open air. To avoid lugging containers of paints and alcohol everywhere, artists were limited to making pencil sketches of their outdoor subjects. Later, in their studios, they had to recreate the scene, mixing paint to match the colors that they could recall.

With the freedom of a tube, an artist could dab colors on a palette, cap the tube, and quickly paint a scene. And although artists still had to wait for sunlight and paint quickly, they could capture the spontaneity and mood of the moment. Impressionistic painting, with its sparse details, invites each perceiver to fill in the gaps with personal impressions.

Aided by the new paint tube, Claude Monet (1840–1926) painted the west façade of the Rouen Cathedral from the same location at various times of the day. Changes in light and shadow make each painting different. Monet was also fascinated by the effect of changing lights, shadows, and colors on the lily pads in the pond on his estate in Giverny, France. He thus created a series of masterpieces— his impressions of these lily pads as the sun progressed through the day.

Impressionism in Music

Toward the end of the nineteenth century, French composers rejected the Germanic mainstream in favor of their own music. Championed by Claude Debussy, the new French music reflected some of the new trends in poetry and painting. It came to be known by the same name: Impressionism.

Les Meules (Haystacks at Sunset, Frosty Weather, 1891), by Monet

CLAUDE DEBUSSY (1862–1918)

Claude Debussy (de-byoo-*see*) was born in Saint-Germain-en-Laye, a small town near Paris. At age eleven, he entered the Paris Conservatory, studying piano and composition. After winning the prestigious Prix de Rome, he went to study in that great city.

At age 25, returning to Paris to compose and perform as a pianist, Debussy became part of a wide circle of artists, writers, and musicians who met often to discuss new directions for the arts. He became the main developer of Impressionistic music.

Toward the end of his career, Debussy became associated with the Ballets Russes, composing his last work, *Jeux,* for that ensemble. World War I had its effect on Debussy: he produced only a few minor works until his death in 1918 at age 55.

PRINCIPAL WORKS

Orchestral Music: *Prélude à l'après-midi d'un faune* (Prelude to The Afternoon of a Faun, 1894); *Nocturnes* (1899); *Danses sacrée et profane* (1904); *La mer* (The Sea, 1905); *Première Rapsodie for Clarinet and Piano* (1910); *Images* (1912)

Ballet: *Jeux* (Games, 1913)

Incidental Music: *Le Martyre de St. Sébastien* (1911)

Chamber Music: *String Quartet* (1893); *Petite Pièce for Clarinet and Piano* (1910); *Sonata for Cello and Piano* (1915); *Sonata for Flute, Viola, and Harp* (1915); *Sonata for Violin and Piano* (1917)

Piano Music: *Suite, pour le piano* (1901); *Suite bergamasque* (1909); *Estampes* (1903); *Images* (1905); *Children's Corner* (1908); *Préludes,* two books (1910, 1913); *Études* (1915)

Opera: *Pelléas et Mélisande* (1902)

Songs: *Fêtes galantes* (1881, 1904); *Chansons de Bilitis* (1898); more than sixty others

Choral Music: *La Demoiselle élue* (The Chosen Maid, 1888)

Paris World Expositions

The Paris World Expositions of 1878 and 1889 profoundly influenced Debussy, who was searching for new material at the time. Hearing the Indonesian *gamelan* ensemble use delicate finger cymbals, Debussy decided to incorporate the instrument into his orchestral works. Groups from Japan and China also attracted his interest, and soon thereafter, Debussy incorporated Asian scales into his music.

Characteristics of Impressionism

Creating a new world of sound was Debussy's challenge. To accomplish this, he developed techniques that contrasted with those of the late Romantic composers.

Form: Avoiding Hard Outlines   Debussy avoided clear-cut cadences and resting points. Instead, his music has a feeling of wandering or floating. (Some have said that the undulating sounds of *La mer* [The Sea] make them feel "seasick.")

The painting *Rouen Cathedral, West Facade, Sunlight,* 1894 by Monet

Orchestral Colors: Using Delicate Tone Colors   Debussy's instrumental effects were delicate, subtle, and full of color, bearing a similarity to Impressionistic painters' choices of delicate colors. He preferred the following instruments (in order of importance):

flutes

oboes

clarinets

strings (often muted)

harp (sweeping arpeggios veil tonality)

brass (used sparingly, usually with mutes)

percussion (used sparingly, avoiding military instruments; employed antique cymbals and triangles)

Rhythms: De-Emphasizing Solid, Symmetrical Rhythms   To deviate from the predictability of typical rhythms (for example, those found in marches and waltzes), Debussy calls for vague beats and complex subdivisions (7, 11, 13). A run of seven tones to a beat may follow thirteen tones to a beat.

Scales: Incorporating the Nontraditional   Rather than use diatonic scales (do, re, mi), which give the feeling of a solid base, Debussy incorporated three other scale types: *pentatonic, chromatic,* and *whole-tone.*

Pentatonic Scales   Debussy had heard Asian performers use a variety of five-tone scales at the Paris Fair. The following is only one of the many pentatonic scales:

The Pentatonic scales that Debussy incorporated were not completely new to Western music. Many concert pieces and folk songs use them—European folk songs, cowboy songs, and Native American songs.

Chromatic Scales   The chromatic scale, though sparingly used, has appeared in Western concert music since the music of Bach. In music, "chromatic" refers to all the black and white keys on a keyboard. Moving in half steps, these scales incorporate all the tones used in Western music.

Because each interval in the chromatic scale is of equal size—a half step—the scale seems to avoid a home base or tonal center.

Photograph of Rouen Cathedral, West Facade

ASCENDING CHROMATIC SCALE

C   C#   D   D#   E   F   F#   G   G#   A   A#   B   C

half steps

Traditional diatonic scales are constructed with a mixture of whole and half steps, giving the feeling of key-based stability.

1   2   3   4   5   6   7   8

whole steps

half step   half step

Whole-Tone Scale In his search for music materials to convey the vagueness of Impressionism, Debussy used a *whole-tone scale*. A whole-tone scale consists of equal large steps (whole-step intervals). Similar to the chromatic scale, which consists of equal small steps (half-step intervals), the whole-tone scale seems to avoid a key centered on a specific pitch.

The Eiffel Tower

1   2   3   4   5   6

Harmony Because it provided a feeling of solidity based in a certain key base, traditional harmony did not easily fit into Debussy's style. So he extended the traditional chords of three and four tones built on any degree of the diatonic scale. (See Appendix A, Music Notation).

Extended chords

9th chord   11th chord   13th chord

Notice that the 13th chord contains all of the pitches of the scale. Because all pitches are equal, the 13th chord has only a remote reference to the root tone or key center.

LISTENING INSIGHTS

What to Listen For in Impressionistic Music

Debussy and the other Impressionist composers expected audiences to listen more sensually than intellectually, encouraging the listener to feel relaxed and unstressed. Imagine yourself at the seashore on a beautiful, sunny day watching the movement of the tide as sailboats glide by on the horizon and white, puffy clouds move lazily across a blue sky. Without following the music too intellectually, observe the interesting sound combinations and melodic movement.

LISTENING ACTIVITY

Prelude to the Afternoon of a Faun (1894), Claude Debussy

Large Form: Orchestral Tone Poem
Detailed Form: Modified Three-Part Form
Performing Medium: Large Symphony Orchestra

Compact Disc 3, Tracks 21–23
Running Time: 10:21

Stéphan Mallarmé inspired Debussy's tone poem *Prélude à L'aprés-midi d'un faune* (Prelude to The Afternoon of a Faun).

The poem concerns a mythical half-man, half-animal forest creature. Awakening from a dream of lovely nymphs, the creature is disoriented. Is he awake or still dreaming? Because the afternoon is warm and lazy, he decides to go back to sleep. Not much action, but the scenario is perfect for Impressionism.

A flute opens and closes the piece with a dreamy, chromatic melody. Fast runs in the orchestra make the middle section slightly more active. Notice that antique cymbals at the end, influenced by southeast Asian music that Debussy heard at the Paris World's Fair.

LISTENING GUIDE

Prelude to the Afternoon of a Faun (1894),
CLAUDE DEBUSSY

SECTION A

| 21 | 0:00 | CHROMATIC MELODY | flute solo, unaccompanied at beginning; *p;* slow tempo, changing meters, rubato; chromatic and pentatonic scales; extended chords; harp glissandos blur tonality |

	0:56	CHROMATIC MELODY	mainly in solo flute, tremolo strings; *pp*
	2:01	CHROMATIC MELODY	flute solo expressively with harp arpeggios
	2:42	CHROMATIC MELODY	flute solo with harp arpeggios
	3:16	TRANSITION	cadence; clarinet
	3:35	WHOLE-TONE MELODY	solos by clarinet, then flute; faster tempo, changing meters; whole-tone scales

| | 4:21 | TRANSITION | faster and animated; crescendo to *f;* gradual diminuendo and slowing; modulating and cadencing to A-flat tonality |

SECTION B

| 22 | 4:49 | TRANSITION | clarinet; descending string chords |
| | 5:05 | PENTATONIC MELODY | woodwinds; slower tempo, mostly triple meter; *p;* pentatonic scale used part of the section |

| | 5:38 | PENTATONIC MELODY | strings with pentatonic melody; harp arpeggios; full orchestra crescendo to *ff* |
| | 6:26 | PENTATONIC MELODY | violin solo accompanied by woodwinds; *p* |

SECTION A

| 23 | 6:46 | | slower tempo; similar to the opening section; flute solo with harp arpeggios and long chords in strings |

7:21	CHROMATIC MELODY	flute solo with harp arpeggios and long chords in strings
7:59	CHROMATIC MELODY	flute section; *p*; antique cymbals, shimmering strings with tremolos
8:39	CHROMATIC MELODY	flute and viola; *pp*; antique cymbals; harp arpeggios
9:43	CHROMATIC MELODY	muted horns; slow tempo, gradually slowing and diminuendo until the end; antique cymbals; *ppp*

Debussy was the most prominent of the Impressionist composers, but others, such as Maurice Ravel, used the same techniques. Although Ravel composed in many styles, including jazz, several of his pieces were influenced by Impressionism, for example, *Pavane pour une infante défunte* (Pavane for a Dead Princess) and the *Daphnis et Chloé* ballet.

CHALLENGE YOUR EXPERTISE

In addition to music, which creative art forms reflect Impressionism?

MAURICE RAVEL (1875–1937)

Maurice Ravel (rah-*vel*) was born in the Pyrenees in the south of France. Like Debussy, Ravel studied at the Paris Conservatory of Music. Though clearly the most outstanding student composer, Ravel was denied the prestigious Prix de Rome four times. So outraged were Ravel's teachers, friends, and the public about his not receiving the award that they forced the resignation of the conservatory director.

During World War I, Ravel drove an ambulance on the front lines. With the war over, Ravel resumed composing and was soon recognized as France's leading composer.

Early in 1928 when George Gershwin visited Paris, the two composers became friends. Gershwin had wanted to study European styles with Ravel. Instead, Ravel advised him to continue his unique style of incorporating jazz into his concert music. As a result of their discussions, Gershwin went home to compose the tone poem *An American in Paris,* and Ravel wrote his Piano Concerto in G, in which he used Gershwin-style jazz.

Ravel developed into a master of orchestration, as displayed in works such as *La valse, Daphnis et Chloé,* and his orchestration of Mussorgsky's *Pictures at an Exhibition* (1922). At age 60, Ravel contracted a brain disease and died two years later.

PRINCIPAL WORKS

Orchestral Music: *Alborada del gracioso* (1905); *Rapsodie espagnole* (1908); *La valse* (1920); *Bolero* (1928); *Piano Concerto in D Major for Left Hand* (1930); *Piano Concerto in G Major* (1931)

Chamber Music: *String Quartet* (1903); *Trio for Violin, Cello and Piano* (1914); violin sonatas

Ballets: *Ma Mère l'Oye* (Mother Goose, 1912); *Daphnis et Chloé* (1912)

Operas: *L'Enfant et les sortilèges* (The Child and the Spells, 1925); *L'Heure espagnole* (1909)

Piano Music: *Pavane pour une infante défunte* (Pavane for a Dead Princess, 1899, later orchestrated); *Jeux d'eau* (1901); *Sonatine* (1905); *Miroirs* (1905); *Valses nobles et sentimentales* (1911); *Le tombeau de Couperin* (1917)

Songs: *Shéhérazade* with orchestra (1903); *Histoires naturelles* (1906); *Chants populaires* (1910)

Summary of Terms

antique cymbals	gamelan	Prix de Rome
Ballets Russes	Paris World Exposition	13th chord
chromatic scale	pentatonic scales	whole-tone scale
extended chords		

19

Modernism and Post-Modernism

Influence of the World Wars

The fever of nationalism in Europe, so charmingly conveyed in the nineteenth century, veered out of control in 1914. As country after country entered the hostilities, Europe was swept into a world war.

When the war ended in 1918, many of Europe's prized libraries, theaters, concert halls, and museums were in ruins. Throughout the continent, economies were in shambles. The toll of World War I was staggering: 8.5 million killed, 21 million wounded, and 7.5 million prisoners and missing in action.

World War I also had a devastating effect on the European artistic community. Drafted into service to fight the war, many artists were killed. Some fled to the United States. Others sought refuge in neutral countries where they could continue working. The November 1918 armistice finally halted "the war to end all wars."

After only a brief period of recovery in the late 1920s, the Great Depression paralyzed Europe and North America. Playing on the panic of the people, the fascist governments of Adolf Hitler, Benito Mussolini, and Hideki Tojo laid the groundwork for World War II (1939–1945).

When peace finally returned in 1945, fifty-seven countries of the world were scarred by the greatest trauma in human history: an estimated

Guernica, by Pablo Picasso
© 2004 Estate of Pablo Picasso/Artists Rights Society (ARS), New York. John Bigelow Taylor/Art Resource, NY

54.8 million people killed, most of them civilians. Millions more were left crippled and homeless. The extent of the war's cruelty brought civilization to its knees. Nazi genocide killed at least 14 million Jews, Poles, Slavs, gypsies, homosexuals, and political dissidents.

Devastated, the artistic community revived slowly. With the cost of war, and post–war rebuilding, resources allocated toward the funding of the arts were strained. For approximately fifty years (1914–1964), the arts in Europe struggled. Aided partly by the United States' Marshall Plan, most European nations gradually regained financial and artistic stability in the 1960s.

Art Redefined

Before the twentieth century, most art was defined by the adjective "beautiful." Music was beautiful, harmonious sound; painting was beautiful pictures; dance was beautiful movement, and so on.

Igor Stravinsky (right) and Pablo Picasso, in a caricature by Jean Cocteau
© 2002 Artists Rights Society (ARS), New York/ADAGP, Paris/Estate of Pablo Picasso

Ram's Head, White Hollyhock-Hills, by Georgia O'Keeffe shows how modern artists explored perspective.
© 2000 The Georgia O. Keeffe Foundation/Artists Rights Society (ARS), New York

Could music, painting, poetry, dance, and the theater seem "ugly," and still be "art"? Picasso's *Guernica* (see painting above) depicts a hideous scene: the result of Hitler's *Luftwaffe* testing their new weapons by bombing the peaceful Spanish town of Guernica in 1937. Twisted, wrenching victims expose the horror of this despicable act.

Igor Stravinsky and Pablo Picasso were friends and shared views on art. Adhering to an outlook similar to Picasso's, Stravinsky composed his ballet *Rite of Spring* (discussed in the next chapter). Subtitled "Scenes from Pagan Russia," the ballet is characterized by angular dancing, stark scenery, and dissonant music. Its infamous 1913 debut changed the direction of music for the rest of the twentieth century.

Overview of the Modernist/Post-Modernist Period (1900–Today)

Composers

Samuel Barber, Béla Bartók, Alban Berg, Leonard Bernstein, Ernest Bloch, Nadia Boulanger, Pierre Boulez, Benjamin Britten, Carlos Chávez, Aaron Copland, Edward Elgar, Edward Kennedy "Duke" Ellington, Manuel de Falla, Gabriel Fauré, George Gershwin, Edvard Grieg, Paul Hindemith, Gustav Holst, Arthur Honegger, Charles Ives, Leos Janácek, Jerome Kern, Zoltán Kodály, Franz Lehár, Witold Lutoslawski, Oliver Messiaen, Gian Carlo Menotti, Darius Milhaud,

Francis Poulenc, Sergei Prokofiev, Sergei Rachmaninoff, Maurice Ravel, Ottorino Respighi, Richard Rodgers, Sigmund Romberg, Erik Satie, Arnold Schoenberg, William Schuman, Alexander Scriabin, Dmitri Shostakovich, Jean Sibelius, Karlheinz Stockhausen, Richard Strauss, Igor Stravinsky, Edgard Varèse, William Walton, Kurt Weill, Ralph Vaughan Williams, Anton Webern, Ellen Taaffe Zwilich

Visual Artists

Mateo Alonso, Max Beckmann, Georges Braque, Alexander Calder, Marc Chagall, Jean Cocteau, Salvador Dali, Willem De Kooning, Walt Disney, Marcel Duchamp, Max Ernst, Erte, Buckminster Fuller, Juan Gris, Freda Kahlo, Wassily Kandinsky, Paul Klee, Le Corbusier, Henri Matisse, Mies van der Rohe, Joan Miró, Amedeo Modigliani, Piet Mondrian, Claude Monet, Henry Moore, Georgia O'Keeffe, Pablo Picasso, Jackson Pollock, Auguste Renoir, Diego Rivera, Auguste Rodin, Georges Rouault, Henri Rousseau, Eero Saarinen, Maurice Utrillo, Andy Warhol, Frank Lloyd Wright, Andrew Wyeth

Writers

Edward Albee, Bertold Brecht, Truman Capote, Paddy Chayefsky, Joseph Conrad, e. e. cummings, T. S. Eliot, William Faulkner, F. Scott Fitzgerald, Robert Frost, Gregorio López Fuentes, Ellen Glasgow, Lillian Hellman, Ernest Hemingway, Aldous Huxley, A. E. Housman, Henrik Ibsen, Henry James, James Joyce, Franz Kafka, Federico Garcia Lorca, Norman Mailer, Thomas Mann, Arthur Miller, O. Henry, Eugene O'Neill, Dorothy Parker, Carl Sandburg, George Bernard Shaw, Neil Simon, Gertrude Stein, John Steinbeck, August Strindberg, Leo Tolstoi, Mark Twain, H. G. Wells, Tennessee Williams, Thomas Wolfe

Philosophers

Alfred Adler, Martin Buber, Teilhard de Chardin, John Dewey, Sigmund Freud, Eric Fromm, Mohandas K. (Mahatma) Gandhi, Carl Jung, Martin Luther King, Jr., Mao Tse-tung, Bertrand Russell, George Santayana, Jean-Paul Sartre

Social, Political, and Cultural Events

Freud's psychoanalytic theories, jazz, Einstein's relativity theories, United Nations, World Wars I and II, Russian Revolution, communism, Great Depression (United States and Europe), Korean War, Vietnam War, European Economic Community, pop art, Malcolm X, chance music and painting, dadaism, nonviolence (Gandhi), Civil Rights Movement (Martin Luther King), racial integration

Science, Technology

Ford's production-line automobile, telephone, airplane, computer, the Internet, electric automobiles, films, television, phonograph, microchip, semiconductor, laser technology, penicillin, smallpox vaccine, polio vaccine, *Sputnik*, organ transplantation, DNA research, gene splicing, cloning, computer animation

Characteristics of Modernist/Post-Modernist Music

General

Music often sounds dissonant, complex, asymmetrical, nonemotional, objective, satirical; often experimental, eclectic resources

Performing Media

Chamber orchestra and ensembles used more often than symphony orchestra; all previous media still used; electronic synthesizers and keyboards; mixed media: pre-recorded electronic sounds combined with traditional instruments; computer-generated sounds

Rhythm

Polyrhythms (layers of different rhythms), polymeters, irregular rhythmic patterns, ostinato (recurring patterns)

Melody

Wide ranges, both for voices and for instruments; fragmented, disjunct, exotic intervals and scales (Asian, chromatic, pentatonic, whole-tone, twelve-tone, quarter-tone)

Harmony

Extensive use of dissonance; polychords (two or more different chords together), clusters (chords by seconds), quartal harmony (chords by fourths); exotic, experimental sounds

Expression

All previous techniques still used; extreme effects, including silence

Texture

Polyphonic texture often used; mixes of polyphonic and homophonic; layers of ideas and sounds

Forms

All forms of the previous periods used, but highly modified; experimental forms; forms incorporate new sound sources and compositional techniques:

Musique Concrète: traditional and environmental sounds pre-recorded and manipulated on the tape recorder

Chance Music: also called aleatory—improvised, unpredictable, vague or non-specific notation, leaving much to the performer to decide

Electronic Music: electronically produced sounds, also called synthesizer music

Computer Music: sampling of voices and instruments organized and manipulated by the computer

Table 19.1	The Evolution of Musical Resources		
	Innovations	**Forms/Styles**	**Composers**
1600	tonal music, major-minor tonality	opera, oratorio, motet, sonata	Monteverdi
1700	traditional major and minor chords, scales, tonality perfection of the violin (craftsmen: Stradivarius)	concerto, concerto grosso sonata, cantata, oratorio	Bach, Handel Vivaldi
1750	standardized orchestra	symphony, string quartet	Haydn, Mozart
1800	orchestra expands brass valves, keyed woodwinds perfection of the piano chromatic harmony	loosening of forms descriptive/program music small piano forms, art songs realistic (verismo) opera	Beethoven, Schubert Berlioz, Mendelssohn Schumann, Chopin Puccini
1850	expanding harmony chromaticism	concert overture, symphony, tone poem, music drama, opera	Brahms, Wagner, Verdi Strauss, Mahler, Bruckner
1880	folk songs and instruments	nationalism, sectional forms, search for new materials descriptive pieces and tone poems	Tchaikovsky, Mussorgsky, Dvořák, Smetana, Kodály Liszt,
1900	whole-tone, pentatonic, chromatic scales, expanded chords by thirds large virtuoso orchestras	Impressionism expansive symphonies and tone poems	Debussy, Ravel, Griffes, Respighi Strauss, Mahler, Bruckner
1910	African-American influences polychords, polytonality, polyrhythms, dissonance atonality, 12-tone serial music	ragtime, blues, jazz, popular music ballet sectional forms symphony, songs short pieces and forms	Joplin, Irving Berlin Stravinsky Ives Schönberg, Berg, Webern
1920	back to tonality jazz elements	neoclassicism Broadway musical, popular music	Stravinsky, Prokofiev Gershwin, Kern
1930	mix of elements jazz, environmental sounds	eclecticism process oriented, free forms	Copland, Feldman, Gershwin
1950	graphic notation natural sounds manipulated by tape recorder	chance-aleatory music *musique concrète* composer control	Cage, Stockhausen Varèse, Cage, Stockhausen
1960	multitrack recording, amplified, electronic synthesizer fusion chance-electronic athematic tonal	pop, rock, eclectic, folk, blues electronic music composer control eclectic mix of forms	Beatles, Rolling Stones Luening, Ussachevsky Subotnick, Carlos Boulez
1970	mix of resources, tonality electronic sounds, MIDI	eclecticism, fusion new romanticism	Bernstein, Barber Babbitt, Davidovsky
1980	computer-generated sounds sampling, eclectic mix or elements multicultural elements	eclectic, traditional and free forms minimalism	Penderecki Steve Reich, Philip Glass Hovhaness, Wen-Chung

Table 19.1		(Continued)	
1990	computer-synthesizer non-Western scales	new romanticism multicultural	Del Tredici, Musgrave Corigliano, Zwilich
2000	digital computer technologies, eclectic approaches, non-Western instrument sampling	free and traditional forms fusion with world music	Machover, Lutoslawski Takahashi, Takemitsu

20

Stravinsky: Into the Twentieth Century

J ust as audiences were starting to grow comfortable with the soothing "new" music of Debussy and the Impressionists, Igor Stravinsky burst onto the scene with music to jar the senses: his 1913 masterpiece *The Rite of Spring*.

Stravinsky's Pivotal Position

As we reflect on musical giants and assess their respective influence, Stravinsky looms as one of the dominant musical forces of the twentieth century. The impact of *The Rite of Spring* on composers of the twentieth century was similar to the impact of Beethoven's Ninth Symphony on nineteenth-century composers.

During Beethoven's time, the pendulum of change had begun to swing from the objectivism of the Classical period toward the subjectivism of the Romantic period. A century later, the pendulum began to swing back to objectivism.

IGOR STRAVINSKY (1882–1971)

When Igor Stravinsky was born, his father was a leading basso at the Imperial opera in St. Petersburg, Russia. As a boy, Igor showed little interest in music, which pleased the elder Stravinsky. Despite his own success in music, he urged his son to pursue a more practical career. However, soon after enrolling in St. Petersburg University, Stravinsky revealed his real interests. He eagerly dropped his studies in civil law and began studying composition with Rimsky-Korsakov at the St. Petersburg Conservatory.

In the audience at the 1908 debut of Stravinsky's first major work, *Fireworks* (*Feu d'artifice*), was his distant cousin Diaghilev, a prominent avant-garde thinker. He was so impressed by Stravinsky's music that he commissioned him to compose music for the Ballets Russes, the Paris-based dance company of Russian expatriates that Diaghilev had founded two years earlier.

Thus began a 10-year association between the great impresario and one of the most enduring composers of the twentieth century. During those years, Stravinsky composed *Firebird* (1910), *Petrushka* (1911), the monumental *The Rite of Spring* (*La Sacre du printemps*, in 1913), and other notable works.

Both Russia and France were under siege in 1914: World War I had begun. The disorder of war and his wife's illness convinced Stravinsky to escape to neutral Switzerland where he lived and worked until after the war. In 1920 France became his homeland. That was also the year Stravinsky abandoned his earlier style of composition and adopted a neoclassical idiom (see Chapter 22) for his new orchestral, instrumental, and vocal works. He served as conductor for the Ballets Russes during the company's 1925 tour of the United States.

The 1939 outbreak of World War II in Europe coincided with the deaths of his daughter, wife, and mother. So Stravinsky accepted an invitation to lecture at Harvard and moved to the United States. After a year at Harvard, the newly remarried Stravinsky settled in Los Angeles where he composed most of his remaining works. He became a naturalized American citizen in 1945.

Stravinsky began to experiment with serial music in 1955, and he did compose several fully serial works during his later years. As part of the celebration of his 75th birthday, Igor Stravinsky toured the United States, conducting his works at concerts and music festivals from coast to coast.

In his eighties, Stravinsky's health began to fail. In 1969, after several illnesses, he and his wife Vera moved into the Essex House Hotel in New York City. It was to be his final residence. Stravinsky died two years later at age 88. Following his funeral in New York, his body was taken to Stravinsky's favorite city, Venice, for a gondola procession down the Grand Canal, followed by his burial.

PRINCIPAL WORKS

Operas: *Oedipus Rex* (1927); *The Rake's Progress* (1951)

Ballets: *The Firebird* (1910); *Petrushka* (1911); *The Rite of Spring* (1913); *Pulcinella* (1920); *Les Noces* (The Wedding, 1923); *Apollo Musagetes* (1928); *The Fairy's Kiss* (1928); *Jeu de Cartes* (The Card Party, 1937); *Orpheus* (1947); *Agon* (1957)

Music-theater: *L'histoire du soldat* (The Soldier's Tale, 1918)

Orchestral Music: *Symphonies of Wind Instruments* (1920); *Violin Concerto* (1931); *Dumbarton Oaks* Concerto (1938); *Symphony in C* (1940); *Symphony in Three Movements* (1945); *Ebony Concerto for Clarinet* (1945); *Concerto for Strings* (1946)

Chamber Music: *Duo Concertante for Violin and Piano*

Choral Music: *Symphony of Psalms* (1930); *Mass* (1948); *Cantata* (1952); *Threni* (1958); *A Sermon, a Narrative, and a Prayer* (1961); *Requiem Canticles* (1966)

Vocal Music: *Pribaoutki* (1914); *Abraham and Isaac* (1963)

Piano Music: *Sonata* (1924); *Concerto* (1925); *Sonata for Two Pianos* (1944)

HISTORICAL PERSPECTIVE

The Rite of Spring: Its Infamous Debut in 1913

Paris, 1912   Audiences enjoyed two new Impressionist-style ballets premiered by Diaghilev's Ballets Russes—Ravel's *Daphnis et Chloé* and Debussy's *The Afternoon of a Faun,* both choreographed by Nijinsky.

Paris, 1913   The Téâtre des Champs-Elysées—the Ballets Russes opened its season with the premiere of Debussy's *Jeux.* But Paris audiences were totally unprepared for the unleashing of the next work, *The Rite of Spring:* "Scenes from Pagan Russia."

Audience Reaction: At first, not knowing what to make of these new sounds, many in the audience began laughing. Soon, others began heckling and protesting, trying to stop the performance. A few slaps across the faces of the protesters— some from women—and a full-fledged riot broke out. Demonstrators tore out seats. Spilling out into the Paris streets, the melée continued until the Paris police brought it under control by arresting more than forty of the rioters.

To be fair to Stravinsky's music, the audience's disapproving reaction was compounded both by the shocking pagan rituals (see Listening Guide) and by Nijinsky's avant-garde choreography.

Cubism in Painting

Just as music departed from the predictable lines and harmonies of the nineteenth century, so did the visual arts.

Employing similar techniques around 1910, painters such as Picasso, Braque, and other artists created a style called "cubism." To grasp the essence of three musicians in costumes and masks on stage, Picasso breaks images into geometric shapes in his *Three Musicians* (see below).

The painting *Three Musicians* (1921), by Pablo Picasso

Debussy (standing) and Stravinsky

Polyrhythms

Polymeters

What Was New in Stravinsky's Music?

Unprepared for what they heard, the audience was disturbed. What was this music that reached out and assaulted them? Unfamiliar with Stravinsky's new musical language, many listeners felt lost and alienated.

Even today, some people are unable to accept *The Rite*'s dissonance and "modern" techniques. Curiously, audiences seem to not mind similar dissonances and modern techniques that effectively establish a mood in films or television. Hollywood film and television composers owe a great deal to Stravinsky.

Musical Double Exposure In *The Rite of Spring* and many of his other works, Stravinsky often superimposes two or more coherent ideas on each other, resulting in an entirely new idea. A double exposure in photography is the closest illustration. For instance, suppose you take a front-view snapshot of your friend. Without your knowing it, the film does not advance. Then, you snap a side-view picture. In the developed film, you see a novel effect. Although you can still recognize your friend, he or she looks different—because front and side views have been superimposed.

Stravinsky used musical double exposure through many elements:

Polyrhythms Two or more contrasting rhythms sounded simultaneously produce polyrhythms. Even if you cannot read music, you can still see that in the duration of each beat there are several different rhythmic patterns. On the first beat: 2-note pattern, 6-note pattern, 4-note pattern, and 7-note pattern. On the second beat: 4-note pattern, 6-note pattern, and 5-note pattern.

Polymeters These occur when two or more contrasting meters are sounded simultaneously. In the following example, the upper part is in four meter plus five meter, while the lower part is in nine meter with three groups of three eighth notes.

The Rite of Spring

Piccolo and Flute

2nd Flute and
Flute in G

THE RITE OF SPRING (Stravinsky)
© Copyright 1912, 1921 by Hawkes & Son (London) Ltd. Copyright Renewed.
Reprinted by permission of Boosey & Hawkes, Inc.

Polychords Two or more triads performed simultaneously, producing a novel harmony.   **Polychords**

This is a polychord.

Polytonality A section of music with parts simultaneously residing in different keys produces polytonality.   **Polytonality**

Here is the opening of Mozart's Sonata in C Major in its original form. Both upper and lower parts are in C major:

C major

C major

A twentieth-century treatment of the same section of the Mozart Sonata follows. This time, the upper part is in C major and the lower is in F-sharp major, producing polytonality:

C major

The Rite of Spring

Other Stravinsky Innovations   For centuries, music had predictable, recurring rhythm patterns—meters: for example, the three pattern of the waltz, minuet, and mazurka and the two and four patterns of the march. But does music need predictable rhythmic patterns? Stravinsky and other twentieth-century composers began employing irregular metrical patterns in their music.

Changing metrical patterns

Changing Metrical Patterns   A section from *The Rite of Spring*, "Dances of Youth and Maidens," which uses constantly changing metrical patterns, follows. The patterns are difficult to predict. Imagine how difficult they are to dance to.

Ostinato

Ostinato   Inspired by the complex rhythms of African music, Stravinsky uses recurring patterns of rhythmic and melodic ideas—an *ostinato*. Fascinated by the rhythmic energy and drive of the ostinato rhythms, he used them in his ballet music.

LISTENING ACTIVITY

The Rite of Spring, Igor Stravinsky
"Sacrificial Dance" from *Part II: The Sacrifice*

Large Form: Dance Movement from a Ballet
Detailed Form: Complex Rondo or Sectional Form
Performing Medium: Large Symphony Orchestra

Compact Disc 2, Track 14
Running Time: 4:33

Subtitled "Scenes from Pagan Russia," the ballet presents a series of primitive scenes built around the spring fertility rites of ancient Russia. Listen to this recording of the final section, "The Sacrificial Dance," to gain a greater understanding of this important work. Later, listen to a complete recording.

PART I: THE ADORATION OF THE EARTH

1. *Introduction: The Birth of Spring.* A group of girls is seated before the sacred mound. Each is holding a long garland. The tribal Sage appears and leads them toward the mound.

2. *Omens of Spring: Dances of the Youths and Maidens.* Youths and maidens dance around the mound in celebration of spring.

3. *Dance of Abduction.* In this frenzied ritual, one of the maidens is abducted and carried off.

4. *Spring Rounds.* Four couples remain. Each man lifts a girl on his back and, in a solemn procession, they begin making the Rounds of Spring.

5. *Games of the Rival Tribes.* Young warriors from the rival tribes display their prowess. The Sage pushes his way through the crowd.

6. *Entrance of the Sage.* The village Sage enters and assumes direction of the proceedings.

7. *Adoration of the Earth.* The dancers prostrate themselves in adoration of the mystical powers of the Earth.

8. *Dance of the Earth.* An exuberant dance in praise of the Earth's fertility.

PART II: THE SACRIFICE

1. *Introduction: Pagan Night.* The Sage and the girls sit motionless around the fire in front of the sacred mound. They will choose a girl to be sacrificed to ensure the earth's fertility.

2. *Mystic Circles of the Adolescents.* The girls dance the mystic circles until one stands, suddenly transfixed as she realizes that she is the Chosen One.

3. *Dance to the Glorified One.* In honor of the sacrificial victim, all dance vigorously, building into a frenzied climax.

4. *Evocation of the Ancestors.* Strong rhythmic dances invoke the blessings of the ancestors.

5. *Ritual Performance of the Ancestors.* Village elders perform a shuffling, swaying dance, to undulating and pulsating rhythmic patterns.

6. *Sacrificial Dance.* The Chosen One begins a frenzied dance and continues until she collapses and dies. The men carry her body to the foot of the sacred mound as an offering to the gods of fertility.

In the Jean Cocteau drawing, Stravinsky plays the piano section of *Le Sacre du Printemps.*
© 2002 Artists Rights Society (ARS), New York/ADAGP, Paris

As you listen to "Sacrificial Dance," many of Stravinsky's innovative techniques will become obvious; others may be more difficult to perceive upon your first hearing:

- polychords
- polytonality
- polyrhythms
- polymeters
- changing metrical patterns
- ostinato with driving rhythms

The complex form with many sections most closely resembles a rondo. Notice how the first motive keeps returning, which is the basic plan of the rondo. Repetitions of the first theme are modified. Several rhythm patterns are introduced, most as ostinatos.

Motive 1 (A)	Rhythmic Pattern 1	Motive 2 (B)	Rhythmic Pattern 1	Motive 2 (B)	Rhythmic Pattern 2	Ostinato Pattern	Motive 2 (B)
Ostinato Pattern	Transition	Motive 1 (A)	Rhythmic Pattern 3	Motive 3 (C)	Motive 1 (A)	Motive 3 (C)	Motive 1 (A)

LISTENING GUIDE

The Rite of Spring, Igor Stravinsky
"Sacrificial Dance" from *Part II: The Sacrifice*

14	0:00	MOTIVE 1	After a dissonant chord by the string section, the orchestra plays the rhythmic-melodic motive, *f;* polychords; fast tempo, unpredictable, changing meters and rhythmic patterns; ostinatos

	0:29	RHYTHM PATTERN 1	introduction to motive 2, played mainly by strings and horns, suddenly *p;* less dissonant polychords; ostinato with changing meters
	0:41	MOTIVE 2	introduced by muted trombones, *f;* imitated by muted trumpets several times, and then by horns, while strings and horns continue ostinato

	0:52	RHYTHM PATTERN 1	in lower strings and horns, *p;* then *f;* ostinato with changing meters
	1:04	MOTIVE 2	played by muted trumpet and piccolos, *f;* imitated by horns
	1:19	RHYTHM PATTERN 2	full orchestra, *ff;* ostinato with changing meters, polychords
	1:31	OSTINATO PATTERN	played by lower strings and horns, *p*

1:38	MOTIVE 2	played by muted trombones, alternating imitations with trumpets, *f*;
	OSTINATO PATTERN	while ostinato pattern 1 is played by strings and horns softly
1:47	TRANSITION SECTION	played by full orchestra, *f*; strings and flutes have fast running patterns of 5 notes to a beat, section ends with a loud chord, then short pause
1:56	MOTIVE 1	returns, similar to opening section, *f*; repeats several times, polychords, changing meters
2:24	RHYTHM PATTERN 3	polyrhythms, triplet patterns played by timpani, duple patterns played by lower strings, changing meters, loud trombone glissandos
2:33	MOTIVE 3	played by horns, then horns and strings, changing meters

Horns

2:46	MOTIVE 3	played by trumpets and strings, ostinato rhythm in duple meter, polychords, crescendo to *ff*; then short pause
3:01	MOTIVE 1	returns, similar to beginning section, *f*; changing meters, short pause
3:12	MOTIVE 3	played by brass, then overlapping imitations throughout the orchestra, mostly duple meter, ostinato
3:32	MOTIVE 1	played by low strings, *f* then *ff*; changing meters, polychords, changing ostinato patterns, then gradual crescendo to loud chord
4:29	FINAL CHORD	flute upward run to piccolo and high strings to a loud final chord emphasized by low strings and drums

CHALLENGE YOUR EXPERTISE

• Which non-European culture was the main influence on Stravinsky's use of ostinato?

LISTENING INSIGHTS

What to Listen for in Modernist and Post-Modernist Music

Contemporary classical music often uses new musical language. Be patient upon your first hearing. Once you get used to the sound, you will discover the composer's intentions. Then you can begin to form a more educated opinion about this "different" music and find a place for it among your personal values.

Summary of Terms

Ballets Russes	irregular metrical patterns	polymeters
changing metrical patterns	objectivism	polyrhythm
cubism	ostinato	polytonality
double exposure	polychords	

21

Expressionism:
Atonal Music

The term *Expressionism* is used to describe music, painting, and poetry developed in Vienna during the early decades of the twentieth century. The movement began as a rejection of *Impressionism*, which focused on the "outer" world. Expressionism, in contrast, centered on the "inner" world described in the writings of Sigmund Freud (1865–1939).

In music, Arnold Schoenberg led the Expressionistic movement. His colleagues, Anton Webern and Alban Berg, followed. Some of the painters associated with Expressionism include Pablo Picasso (1881–1973), Wassily Kandinsky (1866–1944), and Paul Klee (1879–1944).

End of Tonality?

In use since the 1600s, the major-minor tonal system of Western music had been bent and stretched by many composers, especially Wagner and Debussy. In 1908, it snapped. A young Viennese composer, Arnold Schoenberg, pushed tonality beyondits former limits. Disciples gathered, establishing a major movement still alive today: *atonality*.

Atonality

Atonal, or nontonal, music contains pitches, but melodies and harmonies are carefully constructed to avoid creating tonal centers, or home keys.

Early Atonal Experiments

Strongly influenced in his youth by Brahms, Wagner, Strauss, and Mahler, Schoenberg composed his earlier works with roots in late-nineteenth-century Viennese romanticism. New directions and experiments in music always interested him, and he often discussed his ideas with his friend Gustav Mahler.

Schoenberg concluded that because music had been gradually moving away from tonality throughout the nine-teenth century, he would take that idea to its logical destination: atonality. Experimenters such as Wagner, Strauss, Debussy, and Stravinsky had approached the threshold; Schoenberg made a quantum leap, and from 1908 on, many of his works are atonal.

ARNOLD SCHOENBERG (1874–1951)

Arnold Schoenberg (*shurn*-behrg) grew up in his native Vienna at the same time Brahms, Mahler, and Richard Strauss were working there. By age eight he was studying violin and soon began composing his own string chamber music—an interest that continued throughout his life.

Just after Schoenberg completed his schooling, his father died, leaving the family poor. Needing to support himself, young Arnold had to forsake his musical interests in order to earn a living in a Viennese bank.

Mostly self-taught as a composer, Schoenberg continued composing and performing in chamber music groups in his spare time. It was not until he took a position as music director for a Berlin cabaret that he was able to make his entire income as a professional musician. Finally, he returned to Vienna to teach and compose, interrupted by World War I, when he had to serve in the Austrian army.

Between 1918 and 1923 he formulated his twelve-tone method, which he used throughout most of his remaining compositions. In 1925, he was appointed professor of composition at the Berlin Academy of Arts.

Because he was Jewish, Schoenberg had to flee to the United States from Germany when Adolf Hitler seized power. Settling in southern California, Schoenberg attained citizenship and taught at both the University of Southern California and the University of California at Los Angeles. He died at the age of 77.

PRINCIPAL WORKS

Orchestral Music: *Verklärte Nacht* (Transfigured Night, 1917); *Pelleas und Melisande* (1903); Five Pieces for Orchestra (1909); Variations (1928); Violin Concerto (1936); Piano Concerto (1942); two chamber symphonies

Chamber Music: four string quartets, one string trio, one wind quintet, Octet (1922)

Operas: *Erwartung* (Expectation, 1909); *Die glückliche Hand* (The Fortunate Hand, 1913); *Von Heute auf Morgen* (From Today to Tomorrow, 1930); *Moses und Aron* (1932)

Choral Music: *Gurrelieder* (1911); *A Survivor from Warsaw* (1947)

Vocal Music: *The Book of the Hanging Gardens* (1909); *Pierrot lunaire* (1912); cabaret songs

Piano Music: Three Piano Pieces, Op. 11 (1909); Six Little Pieces, Op. 19 (1911); Five Piano Pieces, Op. 23 (1920); Suite (1923)

Once he had crossed over, his Viennese colleagues followed. Throughout the twentieth century, other composers saw atonality as a progressive avenue of self-expression.

Schoenberg's Twelve-Tone System

Atonal music was an inevitable development, and Schoenberg, Webern, and Berg became absorbed by it. Even Stravinsky admired the orderly procedures and intellectual nature of Schoenberg's atonal music, and he spent some time later in life composing twelve-tone music.

By 1923, Schoenberg had formulated a theoretical system for composing atonal music that would ensure both its unique status and its departure from traditional tonal music. His system is known variously as the *serial, twelve-tone,* or *dodecaphonic* method.

Dodecaphonic music

Tone-row

The twelve-tone method is highly disciplined. At its core is an ordered set, or *tone-row,* of the twelve different tones of the chromatic scale. Because Western music has only twelve different tones within an octave, each tone-row uses all of them. Only their order is different.

Looking at a model of the keyboard. You'll notice that there are only twelve tones within an octave (See Appendix B). Using tones or pitches from a higher or a lower octave does not change the *names* of the pitches or the *order* of the row—only the *register* of the pitches.

Transposed Rows   Keeping the series intact, entire rows and their treatments also can be transposed to higher and lower pitches, and each row will retain its integrity. This is true as well for traditional melodies and harmonies. Moving a melody to a different key (higher or lower) does not change our recognition of that melody or harmony.

Ensuring Atonality   In Schoenberg's method, tones of the row are rarely repeated until all have been sounded, which helps ensure atonality. With all pitches having equal importance, there can be no suggestion of a tonal center around any one pitch. Repeating pitches often tends to force a tonal center.

Atonal Harmony   Rows can provide a source of harmony as well. Taking three or four tones from any portion of the sample tone-row, we can sound them simultaneously to produce chords.

In Street, Berlin (1913), painted by Ernst Ludwig Kirchner
The Museum of Modren Art/Licensed by Scala-Art Resources, New York

Tone Row and Chords from Schoenberg's Suite for Piano, Op. 25, First Movement

E	F	G	D♭	G♭	E♭	A♭	D	B	C	A	B♭
1	2	3	4	5	6	7	8	9	10	11	12

Although the resulting chords are dissonant, usually they are compatible with the atonal nature of the row. Because it adheres to strict principles, twelve-tone music tends to be short and concise. Webern's *Symphony,* Op. 21 (1928) lasts only ten minutes, in contrast to Gustav Mahler's Third Symphony (1896), which lasts about one hour and twenty minutes.

LISTENING INSIGHTS

What to Listen For in Tone Row/Serial Music

Tone-row, or serial music sounds different from most other music. For the listener, melodies often seem fragmented and difficult to follow. Unfamiliar harmonies usually are dissonant, and it is easy for a listener to feel lost.

Schoenberg and his colleagues did not expect listeners to follow the row completely through all of its transformations. Most musicians have difficulty doing this. Instead, they felt that the tone-row provided an integral infrastructure for the work that may not always be apparent in the listening.

To get the most out of the music, you have to remain totally attentive, focusing especially on the opening section. Here is where the tone-row is revealed, usually in its basic form before it undergoes transformation. This is similar to traditional forms, such as the theme and variations or rondo, which state the theme at the beginning. Though a challenge, memorizing the tone-row, or as many of the intervals as possible, will help you recognize it through its transformations.

CHALLENGE YOUR EXPERTISE

After the premiere of which ballet did a Paris theater need repair?

LISTENING ACTIVITY

Suite for Piano (1923, Op. 25), Arnold Schoenberg
First Movement: Rasch (quick)

Large Form: Suite
Detailed Form: Highly Complex Theme and Variations
Performing Medium: Piano

Compact Disc 2, Track 19
Running Time: 0:51

Listen to the "Praeludium" from Schoenberg's *Suite for Piano,* Op. 25. The piece starts with the entire tone-row in its original form in the upper register of the piano. After only two of the row's tones are sounded, the bass register begins an imitation using a different rhythm. Following that, the row is manipulated and transformed using retrograde, inversions, retrograde-inversions, transpositions, and harmony.

Original Form of Tone Row

ALBAN BERG (1885–1935)

Alban Berg (*behrg*) was born into a financially comfortable Viennese family. Although he had no training in composition as a teenager, Berg wrote many songs. After graduating from school, he took a position in Vienna as a government accountant.

A newspaper advertisement caught Berg's attention when he was nineteen: Arnold Schoenberg was inviting composers to study with him. Berg, financially secure, responded to the ad and studied with Schoenberg for the next seven years.

During World War I, Berg spent more than three years in the Austrian army. After the war, he composed one of the twentieth century's most interesting operas, *Wozzeck* (*vo*-tseck). Mostly atonal, the work captured the torment and anxiety of the common man caught in the societal and psychological upheavals between the two World Wars.

A year after *Wozzeck,* Berg wrote his *Lyric Suite* for string quartet, using a musical language that was gentler, though still atonal. He began his next opera, *Lulu,* in 1928. The main character, Lulu, is another victim of a decaying society. After shooting her wealthy husband, she is sentenced to years of degrading experiences in prison. Once released, she becomes a prostitute, murdered at the end of the opera by Jack the Ripper.

Berg's chronic ill health restricted his composing output. At 50, when he died in Vienna, he left *Lulu* not quite finished.

PRINCIPAL WORKS

Orchestral Music: Chamber Concerto (1925); Violin Concerto (1935)

Chamber Music: String Quartet (1910); *Lyric Suite* (1926)

Operas: *Wozzeck* (1925); *Lulu* (1934)

Songs: more than seventy-five songs; *Altenberg Songs* (with orchestra, 1912)

Piano Music: Sonata (1908)

Photo by Popperfoto/Getty Images

Summary of Terms

atonal	Expressionism	tone-row
atonal harmony	major-minor tonality	transposed rows
atonal music	nontonal	twelve-tone method
atonality	serial music	twelve-tone music
dodecaphonic music	tonal center	twelve-tone row

22
Neoclassicism: Mainstream Music

Beginnings of Neoclassicism

In spite of the influence of *The Rite of Spring* (1913) on his colleagues, Stravinsky retreated from that musical language. Perhaps it was the public uproar at the ballet's premiere. Was the audience offended by the pagan subject matter? Did it object to his creative choices? Stravinsky was a working composer who had a family to support. If the audience is not ready for musical innovations, a pragmatic composer gives them something more familiar, something that communicates an idea.

As Stravinsky contemplated his next direction, Diaghilev commissioned him in 1917 to write *The Story of a Soldier (L'histoire du soldat)* for the Ballets Russes. It was during World War I. With players in the armed services, orchestras were in shambles. So Stravinsky turned to leaner, eighteenth-century techniques and wisely scored the music for a chamber ensemble of seven musicians. Taking his inspiration from the Baroque and Classical periods, he integrated the forms, idioms, and instrumental sounds of those times with his personal compositional techniques. The result was *neoclassicism*.

An Approach, Not a Style Period

Generalizing about neoclassical music is difficult, because it is neither a style nor a style period. Rather, it is a creative approach to producing new and fresh music by adopting resources from former musical style periods. Composers integrated mostly tonal, prominent melodies with twentieth-century compositional techniques.

Stravinsky began using techniques from early style periods, such as the Medieval and Baroque. His ballet *Pulcinella* (1920) was based on the music of the Baroque composer Pergolesi. With his Octet (1922), Stravinsky's shift to neoclassicism was complete. By broadening the concept of neoclassicism, composers were free to incorporate techniques from any previous style period—or several style periods—within a piece.

Neoclassicism in Russia

The same year that Stravinsky was composing *The Story of a Soldier* (1917), Prokofiev had already reached the same conclusion about neoclassicism: Audiences would be more willing to accept modern techniques as long as the musical language was familiar.

HISTORICAL PERSPECTIVE

Neoclassical Approaches

When discussing and listening to these works, it is not necessary to label them Neo-Baroque if they use Baroque-period techniques, or Neo-Renaissance if they use Renaissance styles. *Neoclassical* will do.

SERGEI PROKOFIEV (1891–1953)

Born in the Ukraine in southern Russia, Sergei Prokofiev (proh-*kohf*-yef) studied piano with his mother, who also encouraged him to compose at an early age. By age nine he had written a three-act opera. After the family moved to Moscow, his parents sent him to the Conservatory in St. Petersburg, where he studied composition with Rimsky-Korsakov.

When the turmoil of the Russian Revolution became intolerable, Prokofiev followed Diaghilev and Stravinsky to Paris. He was taken into the Russian expatriate community, which included members of the Ballets Russes. Prokofiev used Paris as his home base while traveling through post–World War I Europe and the United States.

When he decided to return to Russia in 1933, Prokofiev was greeted warmly by both the public and the government. But he soon found himself in trouble with the Stalin Regime: they accused him of writing music that was "too formalistic, too technically complicated and alien to the Soviet people." The Party Central Committee constantly pressured Prokofiev to publicly apologize for his "transgressions." Though he tried to shrug off these attacks, the stress finally affected his health. Ironically, both Joseph Stalin, his tormentor, and Prokofiev died of brain hemorrhages on the same day.

PRINCIPAL WORKS

Orchestral Music: Symphonies: No. 1 (*Classical*, 1917); No. 2 (1925); No. 3 (1928); No. 4 (1940); No. 5 (1944); No. 6 (1947); No. 7 (1952): *Peter and the Wolf* (1936); *Lieutenant Kijé Suite* (1934) from the film score; five piano concertos, two violin concertos, and a cello concerto

Chamber Music: string quartets; Flute Sonata; Violin Sonata; Cello Sonata

Piano Music: Mostly sonatas

Operas: *The Love for Three Oranges* (1921); *The Fiery Angel* (1928); *The Gambler* (1929); *War and Peace* (1944)

Ballets: *The Prodigal Son* (1929); *Romeo and Juliet* (1938); *Cinderella* (1945)

Choral Music: *Alexander Nevsky* (1939) for chorus and orchestra—from the film score

LISTENING ACTIVITY

Symphony No. 1 (Classical Symphony, 1917),
SERGEI PROKOFIEV

First Movement: Allegro
Large Form: Symphony
Detailed Form: Sonata-Allegro
Performing Medium: Chamber or Symphony Orchestra

Compact Disc 2 Tracks 20–21
Running Time: 3:37

Prokofiev composed his *Symphony No. 1 (Classical* Symphony) during the period 1916–1917 as a modern work using Classical-period compositional techniques. Scored for an orchestra similar to Haydn's, Prokofiev's four-movement symphony follows the typical late-eighteenth-century large form:

First Movement:	*Allegro* (fast, sonata form)
Second Movement:	*Larghetto* (moderately, slow rondo form)
Third Movement:	*Gavotte* (moderate dance in duple meter, song form and trio—similar to minuet and trio)
Fourth Movement:	*Allegro* (fast, sonata form)

Prokofiev's *Classical* Symphony is quite similar in style to most of Haydn's symphonies. In comparing the two composers' use of orchestral instruments, however, notice that Prokofiev utilizes the capabilities of modern, technically improved instruments; for example, violinists are required to play extremely high on their fingerboards (THEME 2). Woodwinds and brass also have parts that are considerably more demanding than those written in Haydn's day. Also, many of the melodies contain large leaps, requiring highly skilled performers.

LISTENING GUIDE

Symphony No. 1 (Classical Symphony, 1917),
SERGEI PROKOFIEV

EXPOSITION

20	0:00	THEME 1	played by the strings and woodwinds, quickly changing dynamics, *ff*; *p*, crescendo, *ff*; *p*, key of D major, duple meter; homophonic texture

| 0:11 | THEME 1 | repeats played only by the strings and in the key of C major |
| 0:19 | TRANSITION THEME | played by flute, *p;* imitated by oboe and clarinet, *p;* then by bassoon, *p* |

| 21 | 0:46 | THEME 2 | played by first violins in dominant key, *pp;* light arpeggio accompaniment played by bassoon, theme repeated several times, then *ff;* cadence to pause (exposition is not repeated) |

Development

| 1:29 | | all three themes are used throughout the development, through a series of tonal modulations |

Recapitulation

2:26	THEME 1	played by violins, *p;* in C major (not D major)
2:35	TRANSITION THEME	played by flute in the exposition original key of D major, *p;* imitated by oboes, then viola, cellos
2:56	THEME 2	played by violins, *ff;* in D major

Coda

| 3:20 | | full orchestra, *ff;* cadence to final chord in D major |

Other Russian Neoclassical Composers A group outlook on modern composition emerged from Russia. Working independently, other composers concurred with the idea of expanded neoclassicism and incorporated techniques from previous style periods, including the recent Romantic era.

In addition to Prokofiev, the composers working in this genre include *Sergei Rachmaninov (1872–1943* see biography in Chapter 17), *Dimitri Shostakovich* (see biography in this chapter), *Dmitri Kabalevsky (1904–1987)*, and *Aram Khachaturian (1903–1978)*.

Moving Back to the Mainstream

Viewed broadly, neoclassicism can be seen as an attempt to move back to mainstream music. According to mainstream composers, lack of communication with audiences runs contrary to the role of music—the tradition of Bach, Haydn, Beethoven, Schumann, and Brahms. However interesting atonal experimental music may be to the knowledgeable musician, most audiences seem to prefer tonal music. Composers need audiences who appreciate them. Without them, there is only an empty hall.

To pigeonhole the diverse lot of twentieth-century mainstream composers into rigid categories would be misleading. Despite their differences, however, they shared a common goal: to express their musical individuality in a way audiences could understand.

DIMITRI SHOSTAKOVICH (1906–1975)

Like many other composers, Dimitri Shostakovich (shos-tah-*koh*-vich) received his earliest piano training from his mother, an accomplished pianist. At age thirteen, Shostakovich entered the Conservatory in his native St. Petersburg, focusing his studies on composition. By age 19, he had completed his first symphony. Over his lifetime, he composed fifteen symphonies and a considerable legacy of various types of music.

Communist bureaucrats in control of the arts continually assailed Shostakovich's music as "too formalistic," "too self-serving," "chaotic," "coarse and primitive," and "not subservient to the Soviet State."

To continue composing, Shostakovich, like Prokofiev, often had to sign humiliating, phony apologies. Addressing his public, he promised to do better in the future. After withstanding many years of harassment by the Stalinist bureaucrats, Shostakovich died at age 69.

PRINCIPAL WORKS

Orchestral Music: fifteen symphonies (1925–1966); piano concertos, violin concertos, cello concertos; *Festival Overture* (1954); Suite from *The Age of Gold* (1929)

Chamber Music: fifteen string quartets; Piano Quintet (1940); two piano trios

Piano Music: two sonatas; twenty-four Preludes (1933); twenty-four Preludes and Fugues (1951)

Operas: *The Nose* (1930); *Katerina Izmaylova* (1963)

Ballets: *The Age of Gold* (1929)

Vaughan Williams

United Kingdom

For a country that produced many of the greatest performers, presented some of the finest concerts, and nurtured many outstanding composers from other countries, England boasted few prominent composers until the twentieth century. Since then, a notably prolific group of English composers has surfaced.

Edward Elgar (1858–1935)   Active as a performer and composer in the latter part of the nineteenth century, Elgar wrote his most popular works beginning in the 1890s and into the twentieth century: the "Serenade for Strings" (1892), *Enigma Variations* (1899), and the "Cello Concerto" (1919). Perhaps Elgar is best known for his *Pomp and Circumstance* Marches (1901–1930), widely identified with school commencement exercises.

Ralph Vaughan Williams (1872–1958)   Following his interest in English folk music, Vaughan Williams composed on *Fantasia on "Greensleeves"* (1934) and *English Folk Song Suite* (1923). His nine symhonies, especially *A Sea Symphony* (No. 1, 1910) and the popular *London Symphony* (No. 2, 1914), demonstrate his considerable talent for orchestration and the influence of his studies in Paris with Maurice Ravel. Vaughan Williams also wrote a sizable collection of choral music for the Church of England.

Gustav Holst (1874–1934)   A contemporary and close friend of Vaughan Williams, Holst also incorporated English folk songs (Suites 1 and 2 for band) in his music. The influence of Hindu mysticism is evident in his *Choral Hymns from the Rig-Veda* (1912). Brilliantly scored for orchestra, his best-known work is *The Planets* (1914–1916).

William Walton (1902–1983)   Walton composed a wide variety of works: symphonies, concertos, chamber music, ballet, and even ceremonial music for coronations (*Crown Imperial,* 1937, and *Orb and Sceptre,* 1953).

Benjamin Britten (center)

Benjamin Britten (1913–1976)   Britten was the most prolific and famous English composer of the mid-twentieth century. His outstanding works include *A Ceremony of Carols* (1942, for choir), *Spring Symphony* (1947, for vocal soloists and chorus), and *War Requiem* (1962). Britten is one of the most important contributors to twentieth-century opera, most notably with *Peter Grimes* and *Billy Budd*. His composition *The Young Person's Guide to the Orchestra* is often used to introduce newcomers to orchestral instruments. (Compact Disc 4, Tracks 23–44)

Percy Grainger (1882–1961)   Best known for his tune "In An English Country Garden," the brilliant, eccentric Grainger was born in Australia, educated in England, and lived in the United States most of his life. His early influences were little known British folk songs, which he discovered while roaming the countryside with a music pad and portable recorder.

During World War II, he was an arranger in the United States Coast Guard Band, using many of his folk song discoveries in compositions for band, for example, *Irish Tune from County Derry, Shepherd's Hey*, and *Lincolnshire Posy*.

CHALLENGE YOUR EXPERTISE

Name two composers who were forced by their government to make public apologies.

France

Erik Satie (sah-*tee*, 1866–1925)   A unique composer, Satie is famous for giving intriguing, surrealistic titles to his works: *Three Pieces in the Form of a Pear, Three Flabby Preludes for a Dog*, and *Jack in the Box*.

Satie was strongly opposed to Impressionism, which had become the popular music style in his country. His clever, antisentimental music influenced many younger French composers: Honegger, Milhaud, and Poulenc.

Arthur Honegger (ohn-ne-*gehr*, 1892–1955)   Perhaps Honegger's best-known work is the oratorio *King David*, written for amateur choruses. He wrote *Joan of Arc at the Stake* for children's chorus and large orchestra. One of his most intriguing works is *Pacific 231* (1923), a musical translation of the sounds of a speeding locomotive. The "231" in the title refers to the number and placement of wheels on the locomotive as seen from the side: *2* wheels, followed by *3* wheels, followed by *1* wheel. This configuration is well known in railroad circles.

Darius Milhaud (mee-*yoh*, 1892–1974)   Extremely prolific, Milhaud composed in almost every form—even film music. His *Suite provençale* (1937) and *Suite française* (1944) for orchestra are impressions of his native France. North and South America held a fascination for Milhaud, and he incorporated music from both continents into his pieces.

SPOTLIGHT: OUTSTANDING ARTIST-TEACHER
NADIA BOULANGER (1887–1979)

The influence of some musicians extends far beyond their personal triumphs as composers, performers, and conductors. Such distinction belongs to Nadia Boulanger (boo-lahn-*zhay*).

Few artist-teachers have earned such high esteem, not only for their knowledge of music but also for their ability to transmit their knowledge. Despite her reputation for being austere and authoritarian, Boulanger had a sincerity and warmth of spirit that opened up the universe of music to the countless young people who sought her tutelage. Aaron Copland and Leonard Bernstein were among her most notable American students.

On Nadia's 92nd birthday, Leonard Bernstein visited her in Paris. In a flash of lucidity, she recognized him, heard what he said, spoke a few words, and clung to him. He was one of the last to see her. A few weeks later, in the early hours of October 22, 1979, Nadia Boulanger died in her rue Ballu apartment.

Milhaud's ballet *La Création du Monde* (The Creation of the World, 1923) was influenced by his visit to Harlem jazz clubs in the 1920s. To avoid Nazi persecution, Milhaud left Paris in 1940 for Oakland, California, where he was a professor at Mills College until his retirement in 1971.

Francis Poulenc (poo-*lahnk,* 1899–1963)   Poulenc's songs (chansons) are among the most charming in the literature. His larger works include the *Mass in G* (1937, for chorus *a cappella*) and his opera *Dialogues des Carmelites* (Dialogues of the Carmelites, 1956).

Les Six, a group of six French composers. From left to right: Darius Milhaud, Georges Auric, Arthur Honegger, Germaine Tailleferre, Francis Polenc, and Louis Durey (not shown). Seated at the piano is the poet, artist, and novelist Jean Cocteau.

Paul Hindemith

Germany

Nationalistic aggression during the twentieth century largely displaced creative expression in both Germany and Austria. Most composers had to leave these countries; many emigrated to the United States. These were the lands that produced Bach, Handel, Mozart, Haydn, Beethoven, Schubert, Mendelssohn, Schumann, Brahms, Wagner, and Strauss. So much for war's contribution to civilization!

Paul Hindemith (*hin*-duh-mit, 1895–1963)   Hindemith stands out as Germany's most important composer and teacher in the twentieth century. Beginning his teaching career at the Berlin School of Music, from 1927 to 1937 he became the model of the artist-teacher. To escape from the Nazi regime, he came to the United States and taught at Yale University from 1940 to 1953. He then accepted a professorship at the University of Zurich.

Disturbed by the widening gap between composer and audience, Hindemith created a collection of works with a broad appeal, in contrast to pure art works. He called these compositions *Gebrauchsmusik,* or "useful music." Numerous chamber pieces fall into this category, as does his musical playlet for children, *Wir Bauen eine Stadt* (Let's Build a Town, 1930).

Hindemith used excerpts in his opera *Mathis der Maler* (Mathis the Painter, 1934) after a symphony of the same title. His outstanding ballets are *Noblissima visione* (1938) and *The Four Temperaments* (1940). Works for more unusual instruments such as a saxophone, bassoon, tuba, string bass, and harp are among his notable contributions to sonata literature.

Cyndi Lauper in a Broadway revival of the *Three Penny Opera*

CHALLENGE YOUR EXPERTISE

Which one of *Les Six* was influenced by his visits to Harlem jazz clubs? Which of his compositions shows that influence?

Kurt Weill (*vile,* 1900–1950) Close friends, Weill and Hindemith collaborated (a rare occurrence for composers) on the music for several interesting stage works. Inspired by Lindbergh's daring flight across the Atlantic is a choral piece called *Der Lindberghflug* (The Lindbergh Flight), with a text by Berthold Brecht (1898–1956).

Weill collaborated again with Brecht on the opera *The Rise and Fall of the City of Mahagonny* (1929). Written in pre-Nazi Berlin, it is a scathing commentary on twentieth-century materialism, power struggles, and sex.

The Three Penny Opera (1928) characterizes city life during the early twentieth century. One of the hit songs, "Mack the Knife," depicts modern, low-life street and cabaret people. Written in a popular chamber-opera style, *The Three Penny Opera* (1928) is based on the 1728 John Gay work *The Beggar's Opera*.

When the rise of the Nazis in Germany became intolerable in 1933, Weill and his wife Lotte Lenya fled to Paris, and then, in 1935, emigrated to the United States, where Weill composed mainly for films and Broadway shows. His last work, *Lost in the Stars* (with Maxwell Anderson, 1949), is a brilliant Broadway-style musical that comments on the Apartheid problem in South Africa from the black worker's point of view.

Carl Orff (1895–1982) Orff based his well-known dramatic cantata *Carmina burana* (1937) on a collection of thirteenth-century student songs and poems discovered in an old Bavarian monastery. With its driving rhythms and ostinati, Orff's music has been frequently used as background music in films and television.

Italy

Ottorino Respighi (reh-*spee*-ghee, 1879–1936) Writing in both neoclassical and impressionistic styles, Respighi distinguished himself by composing nationalistic symphonic poems: *Fountains of Rome, Pines of Rome,* and *Roman Festivals.*

To create a feeling of reality in portraying the countryside on the outskirts of Rome, Respighi calls for a recording of birds to be played over the loudspeaker at performances of *Pines of Rome*.

CHALLENGE YOUR EXPERTISE

What were some of the differences between The Five and *Les Six* (The Six)?

Béla Bartók (right) with violinist Rudolph Kolisch during a rehearsal of *Music for Strings, Percussion and Celesta* (1940)

Central Europe

Béla Bartók (1881–1945)   Bartók was one of the leading twentieth-century composers (see biography in Chapter 17). Collaborating and traveling with his friend Zoltán Kodály (koh-*dye,* 1882–1967), he collected and edited Hungarian folk music, which they both used extensively in their music.

When he emigrated to the United States in 1940, Bartók joined the hordes of artists escaping from Europe. Although suffering from leukemia and oppressed by financial problems, Bartók wrote his last and most popular works in the United States between intermittent hospitalizations. Finally, his problems were somewhat eased when he was invited to join a folk music research group at Columbia University.

Reflective of Hungarian peasant music, much of Bartók's music contains interesting dissonances. His most famous work, the *Concerto for Orchestra* (1943), resulted from a commission from the Boston Symphony Orchestra.

One of his last works before his death in New York in 1945 was the *Third Piano Concerto*. Gravely ill and aware of his imminent death, Bartók worked feverishly to finish the concerto so that he could leave his family less impoverished.

Ernest Bloch (*blohk,* 1880–1959)   An international musician, Bloch was influenced by his Jewish heritage. His popular work *Schelomo* (Solomon, 1915) is a plaintive rhapsody for cello and orchestra. *Baal Shem* (1923) is for violin and piano. And another popular work, *Sacred Service* (*Avodath Hakodesh*, 1930–1933), is for cantor (baritone), chorus, and orchestra.

Latin America

Heitor Villa-Lobos (vee-la-*loh*-bohsh, 1887–1959)   Villa-Lobos and Darius Milhaud met in 1915 in Brazil. Milhaud, then the French ambassador's secretary, encouraged Villa-Lobos to incorporate Brazilian folk material into his music.

Of his more than 2,000 works, his *Bachianas brasileiras* are the most widely known. In this group of nine works, Villa-Lobos blended his Brazilian heritage with the style of Johann Sebastian Bach.

Carlos Chávez (*chah*-vez, 1899–1978)   Incorporating Native American folk tunes into his music, Chavez was Mexico's most outstanding composer. *Sinfonia india, Toccata for Percussion,* and the ballet *Horsepower* are among his most important works.

CHALLENGE YOUR EXPERTISE

- Name at least two composers whose works represent more than one style.
- Which composer is associated with commencement ceremonies?
- Name two composers whose works sound like an earlier style period than when they lived.

Summary of Terms

Broadway-style   neoclassicism

23

Experimental and Technological Music

During the first half of the twentieth century, the momentum of accelerating progress swept artists toward the future. Radical changes were inevitable. Traditionalism was the past; experimentalism was the future.

Following this trend, composers have been writing works that fall into disparate categories:

- *musique concrète*
- electronic music
- computer music and mixed-media music
- aleatoric music
- chance music

Musique Concrète

French composers use the term *musique concrète* to refer to everyday sounds that they captured and manipulated with tape recorders. The techniques were startling: overdubbing, cutting and splicing, playing backward and forward, changing the speed.

Use of Tape Recordings

It was in 1942, during World War II, that the magnetic tape recorder was invented. Edgard Varèse (vah-*rehz*), a French-born musician who later emigrated to the United States, saw possibilities for using the new invention to create musical sounds. Soon, other musicians followed his lead. Lugging the clumsy portable machines, musicians headed outdoors, microphones in hand, to record the "real" (concrete) world.

For centuries, composers had tried to replicate the sounds of the world around them: Vivaldi (*The Four Seasons*), Beethoven (*Pastoral* Symphony), Mahler (Symphony No. 1), Honegger (*Pacific 231*). In *Pines of Rome*, Respighi came closest with recordings of nightingales played during live performances. Now, with the amplification ability of the tape recorder, composers could capture sounds from everywhere, no matter how puny the original source.

Music with Composer Control

By the 1950s, the composer with a tape recorder had final control over his or her music. Performers were not necessary: the composer was the performer. Pointing the microphone, the composer could choose the sound sources. Then, back in the studio, the composer could decide how to manipulate the various prerecorded sound events in order to produce the desired final tape recording.

Important *musique concrète* composers include:

John Cage
Karlheinz Stockhausen
Edgard Varèse
Otto Luening
Vladimir Ussachevsky
Iannis Xenakis

Electronic Music

Electronic music refers to sounds produced on electronic oscillators and then usually recorded and stored. At first, the term *electronic music* was used to distinguish electronically produced sounds from the manipulated sounds of *musique concrète*.

As the 1960s approached, the analog electronic music synthesizer changed recording techniques. Storing individual sounds on tape was now obsolete. Instead, both natural sounds—birds, thunder, rain—and "musical" sounds could be produced synthetically—"synthesized"—in the electronic music laboratory.

Early synthesizers had some faults. Because the music they produced was *too* precise, it sounded synthetic. Singers and instrumentalists do not perform like machines. Depending on their interpretations, live artists deliberately vary beats, tempo, pitches, and other elements of music. Realizing this, later electronic music composers used digital synthesizers to incorporate these variations into their music to "humanize" its sound.

Important electronic music composers include:

Milton Babbitt
Wendy (née Walter) Carlos
Mario Davidovsky
Charles Dodge
Philip Glass
Frederick Lesemann
Otto Luening

Karlheinz Stockhausen
Morton Subotnick
Vladimir Ussachevsky
Edgard Varèse
Charles Wuorinen
Iannis Xenakis

Computer and Mixed Media Music

Invented in 1942, the same year as the magnetic tape recorder, the computer may prove to be the most important development since the wheel. Musicians have become quite creative in exploring its technology for composing, scoring, and music education.

A composer works on a synthesizer in a computer music studio.

Common Terms Used in Computer Music

MIDI   An acronym for Musical Instrument Digital Interface, MIDI is a set of agreed-upon standards for use by keyboards, computers, and other devices. Standards make the sharing of information possible through a common "language."

MIDI

Sampling   Using a series of numbers to represent sounds of an instrument, the sound is digitally recorded and stored on disc. A composer can recall samples of a particular sound from that disc and use it in new music. Thus, the composer can access computerized information to put together an entire ensemble of mixed instruments.

Sampling

Music with Performer Control

Aleatoric Music   This music leaves many important decisions to the performer but is otherwise specific in its notation. "Alea" is the Latin word for one die in a pair of dice. "Aleator," Latin for gambler, suggests the risk and chance involved in playing this twentieth-century music.

Aleatoric Music

Chance Music   Chance music is less precise in its notation than aleatoric music. Instructions to performers are mainly general. Details (pitches, duration) happen as they will, allowing the players to create a performance that is a matter of "chance." Therefore, no two performances of the same work are identical.

Chance Music

Silence   John Cage's *4:33* (four minutes, thirty-three seconds) is typical of the playfulness of chance music. To perform this work, the player comes out on the stage, sits at the piano, starts a stopwatch, and remains there in silence, allowing the audience to fill that time with their own musical imaginations and to become aware of the sounds already present in the concert hall. Four minutes and thirty-three seconds later, the player rises and walks off the stage.

Silence

Jackson Pollock's painting
Number One (1948), using
elements of chance
Photograph © 2000 The Museum of
Modern Art, New York. 00007.68. © 2004
The Pollock-Krasner Foundation/Artists
Rights Society (ARS), New York.

In another Cage composition, *Imaginary Landscape,* his directions call for twelve radios and "random noise assemblages." Each of the twelve radios is tuned to a different station. The performance consists of constantly changing stations. Microphones placed outside the concert hall provide random noise. A pair of loudspeakers picks up the sounds onstage.

Notation and directions in chance music are rarely conventional. With specific notes and duration left to the performer, only sound events and suggestions appear. In essence, chance music is similar to improvisational theater, where actors use only a situation or character and create dialogue at their discretion. "Action" painters, such as Jackson Pollock and Salvador Dali, who drip and throw paint on the canvas and allow things to "happen," operate in a similar way.

Deck of Cards   Another interesting way to make music by chance is to use a deck of cards to select materials randomly. The technique is to translate card numbers and suits into music. For instance:

Number on card determines pitches on the 12-tone scale:

card:	ace (1)	2	3	4	5	6
pitch:	C	C-sharp	D	D-sharp	E	F

card:	7	8	9	10	Jack	Queen
pitch:	F-sharp	G	G-sharp	A	A-sharp	B

king and joker = wild cards (your choice of any pitch)
Suits on card determine duration:

clubs = eighth note or eighth rest	**spades** = quarter note or quarter rest
diamonds = half note or half rest	**hearts** = whole note or whole rest

To create a chance piece, shuffle the deck, deal the cards, and assign the results to one player. Repeat the process for the other players. Then perform the piece. This may seem simplistic, but this kind of chance music can become very complicated in its execution. Because of the random nature of each shuffle of the deck, each player will have an entirely different part.

Important composers of chance music include:

Earle Brown   Karlheinz Stockhausen
John Cage   Christian Wolff
Morton Feldman   Iannis Xenakis
Lukas Foss   LaMonte Young

Pierre Boulez in 1986

LISTENING INSIGHTS

What to Listen for in Chance and Aleatoric Music

Though serious in its philosophical position, most chance and aleatoric music has a tongue-in-cheek element, leaving room for playfulness. *Process*-oriented rather than *product*-oriented, chance music may at times sound chaotic. Most of the focus for the listener is on the unusual happenings on stage and the novel sound combinations that spontaneously develop.

Other Experimentalists

Pierre Boulez (boo-*lez*, b. 1925) Boulez favors an athematic (themeless)   **Athematic**
approach to atonal music. Using a variety of compositional techniques, his music is highly organized yet sounds very different from traditional music. In his words:

> *After the war we felt that music, like the world around us, was in a state of chaos. Our problem was to create a new musical language.*

Karlheinz Stockhausen (*shtohk*-how-zen b. 1928)   An important post–World War II German composer, Stockhausen composes in a variety of styles. Extremely complex rhythms abound in his music, along with unusually detailed instructions to the performer. Already mentioned for his work in *musique concrète,* electronic music, and chance music, Stockhausen also incorporates ideas from older styles. His popular work *Gruppen* (Groups, 1955–1957), for example, is played by three orchestras located in different areas of the concert hall—influenced by Giovanni Gabrieli's sixteenth-century polychoral style (see Chapter 9).

Karlheinz Stockhausen in 1998

Krysztof Penderecki (*kris*-**tof pen-der-***ets***-kee, b. 1933)** An eclectic composer, Penderecki combines musical elements from his native Poland with various "mainstream" and experimental techniques. Having witnessed Nazi persecution of the Jews in Poland, he composed music full of compassion for human suffering. You can hear this in his powerful *Threnody for the Victims of Hiroshima.*

Philip Glass (b. 1937) A New York-based composer, Glass has achieved popularity through his mesmerizing film music, *Koyaanisqatsi* and *Powaqqatsi.* His operas, including *Einstein on the Beach* (1975) and *1,000 Airplanes on the Roof* (1987), have won critical acclaim.

Often referred to as a *minimalist,* Glass takes bits of rhythm and pitches and repeats them over and over, while subtly changing their character. From his extensive travels, Glass has incorporated Asian, North African, and South American percussion music into his minimalist techniques.

Steve Reich (*rysh,* **b. 1936)** Also a minimalist, Reich uses ostinato to help his music evolve hypnotically, gradually—similar to a slowly changing sunset. *Musique concrète* recording techniques provide the basis for Reich's ostinati. He then moves the ostinati out of phase on other recording tracks, creating interesting polyphonic effects. His "Come Out" is an example of this technique.

CHALLENGE YOUR EXPERTISE

What might happen if the piano is not tuned before a performance of Cage's *4:33* (Four Minutes, Thirty-Three Seconds)?

What Lies Ahead?

The future is difficult to predict: Today's experiment may be tomorrow's mainstream. New approaches continue to evolve as technology advances. With world migration and new media of communication, the world as a "global community" is rapidly approaching. As cultures interact, each leaves its imprint on the others. Undoubtedly, a greater mix of ethnic and diverse cultural resources will spawn new art works.

Summary of Terms

aleatoric music
athematic
chance music
computer music
electronic music

electronic music synthesizer
MIDI (Musical Instrument Digital Interface)
minimalism
mixed-media music

musique concrète
sampling
silence

24
Classical Music in North America

Immigration

Around the turn of the twentieth century, into the port cities of New York, Boston, and Philadelphia poured the most diverse immigrant population in the history of the world. Never before had so many people come to so relatively small an area.

Russian and Polish Jews fled czarist pogroms; earlier, the Irish, Scandinavians, and Germans, and later, the Italians were forced off their farms by crop failures. Others left their homelands to avoid persecution. To all of them, North America represented "the promised land" of freedom and limitless opportunities.

The Arts in North America

The same freedom and opportunities attracted artists. America became a refuge and a home for some of the world's greatest musicians. Gustav Mahler conducted the Metropolitan Opera and the New York Philharmonic early in the twentieth century. Later, conductors such as Bruno Walter, Fritz Reiner, and Arturo Toscanini obtained major positions. Great violinists Mischa Elman and Nathan Milstein, and pianists Artur Rubinstein and Vladimir Horowitz, made their homes in the United States.

Schools of Music   To escape the Nazis and World War II, many composers found employment in America's colleges and schools of music. For example, Stravinsky taught at Harvard for a year; Arnold Schoenberg taught at both the University of Southern California and University of California, Los Angeles; Darius Milhaud taught at Mills College in California; Béla Bartók was hired as a folk-music librarian at Columbia University. Violinist Jascha Heifetz, cellist Gregon Piatigorsky, and violist William Primrose taught at the University of Southern California.

Today, many of the world's finest schools of music are in the United States and Canada, including:

Curtis Institute of Music
Indiana University School of Music
Juilliard School of Music
McGill University
New England Conservatory of Music
Northwestern University School of Music
Oberlin College Conservatory of Music
Peabody Institute
University of Illinois School of Music
University of Miami School of Music
University of Michigan School of Music
University of Rochester, Eastman School of Music
University of Southern California, Thornton School of Music
University of Toronto School of Music

Graduates of these schools now perform in the major orchestras and opera companies around the world.

Orchestras in North America   The influx of great artists from Europe helped elevate the standards of American orchestras to a world-class level. Of the great symphony orchestras in the world today, many are in the major cities of North America:

Atlanta Symphony
Baltimore Symphony
Boston Symphony
Buffalo Philharmonic
Chicago Symphony
Cleveland Orchestra
Dallas Symphony
Detroit Symphony
Houston Symphony
Indianapolis Symphony
Los Angeles Philharmonic

Minnesota Orchestra
Montreal Symphony
National Symphony (Washington, D.C.)
New Orleans Symphony
New York Philharmonic
Philadelphia Orchestra
Pittsburgh Symphony
St. Louis Symphony
San Francisco Symphony
Seattle Symphony
Toronto Symphony

American Composers

Although well-versed in European music, some distinctly American composers such as Amy Beach and Charles Ives incorporated American spirit, songs, and rhythms into their music.

AMY BEACH NÉE AMY MARCY CHENEY (1867–1944)

Although Amy Beach did not begin piano lessons until she was six, she displayed musical precocity as a toddler. At age two, she improvised alto lines against her mother's melodies. At four, she devised simple piano pieces and played hymns by ear in correct four-part harmony. After her family moved from her native New Hampshire to Boston, eight-year-old Amy gave her first public performance at a church musicale—a Chopin waltz and her own composition, "Mamma's Waltz."

With little more than a year of formal training in harmony and counterpoint, Amy taught herself composition by memorizing Bach fugues, analyzing the works of the masters, and translating orchestra treatises. She made her professional debut at age 16 at the Boston Music Hall. But her career ended in 1885 when Amy married Henry Beach, a prominent physician, who did not want his wife to be a traveling concert pianist.

For the next twenty-five years, Amy turned her attention to composing under the byline Mrs. H. H. A. Beach. Her first major work, *Mass in Eb*, was premiered by the

Handel and Haydn Society of Boston in 1892. Four years later, the Boston Symphony played her *Gaelic Symphony*, the first (performed) symphony by an American woman.

Following her husband's death in 1910, Amy traveled to Europe. There, she enjoyed success as both a performer and composer under the name Amy Beach. However, when she returned to the United States in 1914, she continued her performing career under the name Mrs. H. H. A. Beach to avoid confusing American audiences.

Amy Beach gave her last public recital in 1940, four years before her death. During her lifetime, all but three of her 150 compositions had been published. In May 1995 the last of her unpublished works, "Cabildo," a one-act chamber opera for voices and string trio, received its first professional performance at Alice Tully Hall in New York's Lincoln Center.

In 2000, the Boston Pops immortalized Amy Beach by adding her name to the granite wall of the Hatch Shell—the only woman among 86 other composers, such as Bach, Handel, Chopin, Debussy, MacDowell, and Beethoven.

PRINCIPAL WORKS

Mass in Eb ("Grand Mass," 1891); Festival Jubilee (1893); Gaelic Symphony in E, Op. 32 (1896); Sonata in A for Violin and Piano, Op. 34 (1898); Concerto for Piano and Orchestra in c# minor, Op. 45 (1899); Panama Hymn (1915); and chamber works, songs, and cantatas, including *Rose of Avontown, Chambered Nautilus,* and *Sylvania.*

CHARLES IVES (1874–1954)

Born in Danbury, Connecticut, Charles Ives was influenced by his father, who had been a bandmaster during the Civil War. The elder Ives gave Charles his first lessons in music.

Music inventiveness was part of their household as Ives's father experimented with new scales and quarter tones—the tones that fall between the traditional notes of the chromatic scale. In the 1880s, Charles experimented with *polytonality* (some years before

Stravinsky), singing in one key and accompanying himself in another.

Once accepted at Yale, Charles majored in music. But upon graduation, he realized that he would have a difficult time earning a living as a musician. So this practical Connecticut Yankee went to New York City to find a job in the business world. Charles did extremely well in business and founded one of the New York Life Insurance Company agencies.

His wealth as a businessman made it possible for him to compose as a hobby without concern for compensation. On weekends and during vacations in his country home in Connecticut, Ives composed hundreds of works.

By the time of his death in New York in 1954, only a few of his works had had public performances. His wife Harmony later uncovered dozens of works that had been gathering dust in the couple's barn, and she arranged for their performance and publication.

PRINCIPAL WORKS

Orchestral Music: four symphonies; First Orchestral Set (*Three Places in New England,* 1914); Second Orchestral Set (1915); *The Unanswered Question* (1906); *Central Park in the Dark* (1906); *Emerson Overture* (1907); *Washington's Birthday* (1909); *Robert Browning Overture* (1912); *Decoration Day* (1912); *The Fourth of July* (1913)

Chamber Music: String quartets and sonatas
Piano Music: Sonatas and studies
Choral Music: *Psalm 67* (1894); *The Celestial Country* (1899)
Organ Music: *Variations on "America"* (1891)
Songs: More than 150

Ives's Songs

You'll come to know Ives best through his songs. Mixing European art song tradition with American speech and temperament, Ives called for a unique sound. He expected full-voiced concert singers to use twangy American pronunciation.

Subjects for his songs range from a child's singing about his father ("The Greatest Man"), to a man's impression of a circus parade ("The Side Show"), to the reflections on the death of a cowhand ("Charlie Rutlage").

Ives's piano accompaniments are novel too. Behind the calm, tonal melodies of his songs, he relishes accompaniments in contrasting keys (bitonal or polytonal) and even employs atonality—although not the Schoenberg variety.

LISTENING ACTIVITY

"Charlie Rutlage" (1921), Charles Ives

from "Cowboy Songs"

Large Form: Song
Detailed Form: Song Form (loose ABA)
Performing Medium: Soprano with piano

Compact Disc 2, Track 22
Running Time: 2:55

The song "Charlie Rutlage" is pure Americana. Charlie is a California ranch hand who is accidentally killed while rounding up cattle. To enhance the mood of the story, the singer usually uses an American Western-cowboy twang, as well as song-speech—partly sung and partly spoken. To depict the accident when Charlie's horse stumbles and falls on top of him, the piano accompaniment becomes highly descriptive, employing dissonant tone clusters of sound.

© 1935 Mercury Music Corp.

LISTENING GUIDE

"Charlie Rutlage" (1921), Charles Ives

A SECTION

22   0:00   INTRODUCTION piano begins; quadruple meter; rhythmic syncopation; *mp*; Western popular music flavor; opening melody uses a pentatonic scale; major tonality; soprano entrance with American-cowboy twang; homophonic texture

Another good cowpuncher
has gone to meet his fate,
I hope he'll find a resting place,
within the golden gate,
the golden gate.

0:21   syncopated piano accompaniment continues; major tonality with growing dissonance; *mp*

Another place is vacant
on the ranch of the X I T,
'Twill be hard to find another
that's liked as well as he.

0:31   mf getting louder to forte at a cadence

The first that died was Kid White,
a man both tough and brave,

0:44   slower tempo; *p*; calmer mood

While Charlie Rutlage
makes the third to be sent to his grave,

B SECTION

1:08   faster tempo, agitated, accelerating tempo; *f*; song-speech departs from traditional sung musical line

Caused by a cowhorse falling,
while running after stock;
'Twas on the spring round up,
A place where death men mock,

1:18   faster and louder; highly agitated; tone-cluster chords

He went forward one morning
on a circle through the hills,

He was gay and full of glee
and free from earthly ills;
But when it came to finish up
the work on which he went,

1:34   a little slower, then faster and faster; louder and louder; cadencing in crashing tone-cluster chords

Nothing came back from him;
his time on earth was spent.
'Twas as he rode the round up,
an X I T turned back to the herd;
Poor Charlie shoved him in again,
his cutting horse he spurred;
Another turned; at that moment
his horse the creature spied
and turned and fell with him,

2:01   slower and softer; polychords; melody sliding up

beneath poor Charlie died,

A SECTION (RETURN)

2:19   OPENING MELODY same tempo and syncopated cowboy style as the beginning; ***p***

His relations in Texas
his face never more will see,
But I hope he'll meet his loved ones
beyond in eternity, in eternity,
I hope he'll meet his parents,
will meet them face to face,
And that they'll grasp him
by the right hand

2:46   gradually slower and softer; church hymn-like cadence chords

at the shining throne,
the shining throne,
the shining throne of grace.

LISTENING INSIGHTS

What to Listen for in the Music
of Charles Ives

Listen particularly for some of the dissonant, surrealistic sound journeys on which Ives takes you. Look for the fun in the music. Try to find the buried treasure—the hymns and popular and patriotic tunes that he has hidden everywhere. If you listen expecting traditional musical sounds, you might often feel lost. Open your mind to the possibilities and you'll be surprised.

Ives was an experimenter. Predating Stravinsky in using polychords, polytonality, polymeters, and polyrhythms, Ives felt free to follow his creative ideas without regard for what people thought. To him, creating music was a joyful process. Just for fun, Ives worked into his music some of the popular tunes of his day, church hymns, and patriotic songs. Combined with dissonant, occasionally atonal passages, the familiar tunes seem to anchor the listener to reality, while Ives moves off into uncharted regions.

Ives's favorite holiday was the Fourth of July. He wrote several works to capture the exuberance of the occasion, including "Putnam's Camp, Redding, Connecticut" from his *Three Places in New England,* and "The Fourth of July" in the third movement of his *Holidays Symphony.*

LISTENING ACTIVITY

First Orchestral Set (1914):
Three Places in New England, "Putnam's Camp,"
(Redding, Connecticut) Charles Ives

Large Form: Descriptive Orchestra Piece
Detailed Form: Sectional Modified A B A
Performing Medium: Symphony Orchestra with Extra
Wind-Band Players

Compact Disc 2 Tracks 23–26
Running Time: 6:14

As you listen to "Putnam's Camp" from *Three Places in New England,* imagine a turn-of-the-century band playing popular patriotic music on the town square. In the nearby park, children rush about in play, shouting and laughing. The American flag unfurls everywhere, making the townspeople feel festive and patriotic.

In his preface to the music, Ives supplies a written program, which is paraphrased here:

> In a Revolutionary War Memorial Park near Redding, Connecticut, a child attends a Fourth of July picnic. General Israel Putnam's soldiers spent the winter of 1778–1779 in that park. The child wanders into the woods beyond Putnam's camp ground and rests on a hillside. As the tunes of the band and the songs of the children grow fainter, the child falls asleep and dreams of the discouraged American soldiers breaking camp, marching out with fife and drum to a popular tune of their day. Suddenly, the soldiers turn back and cheer—Putnam is coming over the hills.

> Waking from his dream, the child hears the songs of the children at the picnic. He runs down to join them and listen to the band.

Three sections (A B A) reflect the events in the program:
Section One (A) sets the raucous, happy mood with a quick-step march that Ives reused from an earlier piece he wrote for band. Also featured are melody fragments, including the British army's quick-step march "The British Grenadiers," contrasted with the American army's "Yankee Doodle," and also "Battle Cry of Freedom," composed by George Frederick Root (1820–1895) during the Civil War.

Section Two (B) depicts the child's dream state. First the music gradually fades to a pause. Then a surrealistic collage of tunes begins: overlapping melodic fragments of "Yankee Doodle," "The British Grenadiers," bugle calls, church hymns, and popular tunes from Ives's day.

Section Three (A) depicts the exciting celebration when the boy awakens and rejoins his friends. Polyrhythms, polytonality, and polyphonic treatment of fragmented tunes characterize the music. A short quote from "The Star Spangled Banner" brings the piece to a resounding end.

LISTENING GUIDE

First Orchestral Set (1914):
Three Places in New England, "Putnam's Camp,"
(Redding, Connecticut) Charles Ives

SECTION ONE (A) FOURTH OF JULY CELEBRATION

23	0:00	MARCH INTRODUCTION	full orchestra; ***ff***; allegro; changing meters, syncopation; homophonic texture
	0:10	BRITISH QUICK STEP	mainly strings, musical show style; ***f***; dissonant chords

24	0:26	BRITISH GRENADIERS	fife and drum tune; quadruple meter with syncopation and polyrhythms; imitations of tune fragments; polytonal; polyphonic texture

"The British Grenadiers"

	0:52	BRITISH QUICK STEP	bugle calls played by trombones and tubas; polyrhythms, syncopation; polyphonic texture

| 1:03 | BUGLE CALLS | fragments of several tunes; polytonal |
| | BATTLE CRY OF FREEDOM | |

"The Battle Cry of Freedom"

| 1:06 | YANKEE DOODLE | |

"Yankee Doodle"

| 1:12 | POPULAR TUNE | played by strings, smoothly; *p*; constant harmony |
| 1:37 | TRANSITION | syncopation, polyrhythms; gradually slower and softer |

SECTION TWO (B) DREAM SCENE

25	2:20	BUGLE CALL	polychords and clusters; slow tempo; very soft
	2:37	OBOE TUNE	slightly faster; polyrhythms; *p*; melancholy oboe tune
	3:38	BRITISH GRENADIERS	faster; march tempo; louder
	4:13	PATRIOTIC TUNES	faster and louder; still 4 meter; polytonal

SECTION THREE (A) AWAKENING AND FOURTH OF JULY CELEBRATION

26	4:28	POPULAR TUNE	suddenly softer and calmer; 4 meter, then changing meters
	4:50	BRITISH QUICK STEP	polymedia—brass band and orchestra; overlapping tunes; polyphonic texture
	5:07	BRITISH GRENADIERS	march tempo; *f*; polyrhythms
	5:23	TRANSITION	brass; *ff*; syncopation
	5:28	BRITISH QUICK STEP	polymedia—brass band and orchestra; overlapping tunes; polyphonic texture
	5:55		fast and very loud; polyrhythms; dissonant harmony
	6:07	STAR SPANGLED BANNER	fragment in brass; then very loud, dissonant polychord

Tin Pan Alley, 26th Street, New York City, 1917.

Ives always tried to project the American spirit he acquired during his New England childhood. His music expresses it: wonderful American holidays, full of warmth and celebration and joyful din.

Polymedia   Ives enjoyed mixing media. Many of his works are surrealistic in that they juxtapose seemingly unconnected tunes and situations, much in the way events occur in a dream. His favorite experiments are combining a symphony orchestra playing in one key with a marching band playing a patriotic march, or mixing two orchestras with two conductors playing two seemingly different works on the same stage.

George Gershwin

Closing the gap between the jazz idiom and classical music, Gershwin was one of America's greatest composers. He also was among the most financially successful.

Gershwin was one of those tremendous talents—like Mozart, Mendelssohn, and Chopin—whose art seemed to pour effortlessly out of him. All of them, like supernovas, lit up the world, then suddenly died—Gershwin at age thirty-nine, Mozart at thirty-five, Mendelssohn at thirty-eight, and Chopin at thirty-nine.

Gershwin loved jazz. He played it. He expanded it. During his early years as a song plugger and improviser in the theater, he incorporated jazz elements into his music. Syncopation, ragtime, blues scales, blue notes, and bent tones abound in Gershwin's music.

GEORGE GERSHWIN (1898–1937)

George Gershwin's Russian-Jewish immigrant parents had no idea that he had musical talent when he was a child. Born in Brooklyn, New York, George seemed to be a typical street kid who excelled in sports—hockey, stickball, whatever allowed him to be physically active. But for years, without his parents knowledge, George had been taking lessons on a friend's player piano, inspired to learn music after hearing a classmate play the violin at a school assembly.

In 1910, George's mother arranged for an upright grand piano to be hoisted through the living room window of the family's Second Avenue apartment. Her intention was that the oldest son, Ira, would have lessons. No sooner was the instrument in place when George amazed his family by playing a popular song of the day. George received the lessons, to his delight and Ira's relief. Two years later, he was studying for a career as a classical pianist.

Life was economically unstable during the years leading up to World War I. Gershwin was a young teenager,

and although he loved the classics, his interest was in popular music. After working one summer as a pianist at a resort in New York's Catskill Mountains, George dropped out of high school and took a $15-a-week job as a song plugger for Remick Music Company. At 16, he added to his income by making piano rolls for player pianos. Every Saturday, George traveled to New Jersey and made six piano rolls for $35—an enormous sum for that time.

In the meantime, George was plugging his own tunes, and at age eighteen, he had his first song published, "When You Want 'Em You Can't Get 'Em—When you Got 'Em You Don't Want 'Em." That same year, another of his tunes was used in a musical revue called *The Passing Show of 1916*. Encouraged by his success, George left Remick and landed a new job as a rehearsal pianist for a show written by his idol, Jerome Kern. This was not just a job to Gershwin; it was his entry to the world of musical theater.

In 1919, Al Jolson heard Gershwin at a party playing his new song "Swanee" and asked whether he could use it in his new Broadway show. The song was a hit, selling two and a half million copies of sheet music, netting Gershwin a fortune in royalties, and making him a fixture on Broadway.

From 1920 to 1924, he composed songs for *George White's Scandals*. Then George and his brother Ira wrote a succession of hit Broadway musicals (see Chapter 26).

A great controversy arose when Paul Whiteman, a noted conductor, commissioned Gershwin to compose *Rhapsody in Blue* for performance at New York City's Aeolian Hall. Because the work is scored for piano and jazz band, concert hall managers and board members considered it unfit for a "serious" music venue. After lengthy negotiations, the management allowed the piece to have its premiere. So in 1924, with Gershwin himself the piano soloist with the Paul Whiteman Orchestra, jazz had its breakthrough into the concert hall.

George Gershwin was productive throughout his short lifetime. With Ira and famed author DuBose Heyward, George composed the first American folk opera, *Porgy and Bess* (1935). Although the work had a mixed reception from critics who did not know what to make of it, audiences worldwide loved *Porgy and Bess*, making it a staple of the contemporary repertoire.

George also wrote several more orchestral pieces, chamber music, piano music, and works for stage and film. Because of his work with movie studios, he also had a home in California. There he struck up a warm friendship with Arnold Schoenberg. Gershwin used another of his artistic talents—painting—to create a famous portrait of his friend.

In 1937, after performing his *Concerto in F* with the Los Angeles Philharmonic, George Gershwin was hospitalized with a brain tumor. He died a few months later at age 39.

PRINCIPAL WORKS

Orchestral Music: *Rhapsody in Blue* (piano concerto, 1924); *Concerto in F* (piano concerto, 1925); *An American in Paris* (tone poem, 1928); *Second Rhapsody* (piano and orchestra, 1931); *Cuban Overture* (1932)

Chamber Music: *Lullaby for String Quartet* (1919)

Piano Music: Preludes (1926)

Opera-Musical Theater: *Porgy and Bess* (1935)

Other Stage and Film Works: *Lady Be Good* (1924); *Tip Toes* (1925); *Oh, Kay* (1926); *Strike Up the Band* (1927); *Funny Face* (1927); *Rosalie* (1928); *Treasure Girl* (1928); *Show Girl* (1929); *Girl Crazy* (Hollywood Film, 1930); *Of Thee I Sing* (1931); *Pardon My English* (1933)

LISTENING ACTIVITY

Porgy and Bess, **George Gershwin**
"Bess, You Is My Woman Now"

Large Form: Opera (Musical Theater)
Detailed Form: Three-Part Song Form (Duet)
Performing Medium: Soprano, Bass-Baritone, and Orchestra

Compact Disc 3, Track 1
Running Time: 4:42

Written in 1935, two years before Gershwin's death, *Porgy and Bess* is his last important composition and perhaps his greatest work. After years of writing hit musicals, Gershwin's emphasis shifted to composing mainly serious concert music. However, he did not stray too far from his roots. Perhaps Gershwin heeded Maurice Ravel's advice about sticking with jazz and jazz-influenced concert music rather than trying to imitate European composers.

The 1925 novel and the later serious play *Porgy,* by South Carolinians DuBose Heyward and his sister Dorothy, interested Gershwin. He envisioned it as the basis for a distinctly American folk opera. George was excited about the project when he approached DuBose Heyward with his idea. His excitement was contagious. Heyward invited him to come to South Carolina with him, where the two began writing the opera.

Although a wealthy white man, Heyward had carefully and lovingly captured the speech rhythms and spirit of the African-American Gullah community in his play. He later agreed that Ira Gershwin could also write some of the lyrics. George sent for his brother, and they both soaked up African-American culture in the remote islands off the coast of South Carolina. Both Gershwins attended church services and musical gatherings, and they became familiar with the distinctive Gullah dialect, speech patterns, and musical style and performance of the islanders.

Following the brilliant overture, the curtain rises on a neighborhood called Catfish Row, and we hear the music for the opening number, a haunting song titled "Summertime." The love story begins between an unlikely couple: the crippled beggar Porgy and the flamboyant street woman Bess. In their duet in Act II, "Bess, You is My Woman Now," the lovers declare their devotion to each other.

LISTENING GUIDE

Porgy and Bess, George Gershwin
"Bess, You Is My Woman Now"

SECTION 1 (A)

1   0:00   Moderate tempo, orchestra introduction with cello solo leads into Porgy's entrance; B-flat major blues scale; complex chromatic harmonic accompaniment, syncopated rhythms

Porgy

Bess, you is my woman now,
  you is, you is
An' you mus' laugh an' sing an' dance
  for two instead of one.
Want no wrinkle on yo' brow, nohow,
because de sorrow of de past
  is all done done
Bess, my Bess!
De real happiness is jes' begun.

SECTION 1 (A)

1:19 section, main melody returns, higher key of D major.

Bess

Porgy, I's yo' woman now,

  I is, I is!

An' I ain' never goin' 'less you shares de fun

Dere's no wrinkle on my brow, no how,

SECTION 2 (B)

1:53 bridge section, faster, then slowing for return of main melody

Bess

     I   ain' go - in'   You hear me say - in', if you ain' go - in.

Bess

but I ain' goin'

You hear me sayin'

if you ain' goin'

wid you I'm stayin'

SECTION 1 (A)

2:04 main melody and tempo returns; higher key F-sharp major

Bess

Porgy, I's yo' woman now!

I's yours for ever,

2:19 transition section; imitations; softer, recitative style

Bess

Mornin' time and ev'nin' time an'

summer time an' winter time.

SECTION 1 (A)

2:45 song repeats as a duet; D major; original tempo

Porgy	**Bess**
Bess, you is my woman now an' forever,	Porgy, I's yo' woman now,
Dis life is jes' begun	I is, I is!
	An' I ain' never goin' nowhere
Bess, we two is one now an' forever	'less you shares de fun.
Oh, Bess, don' min' dose women.	Dere's no wrinkle on my brow, nohow.
You got yo' Porgy,	
You loves yo' Porgy,	

SECTION 2 (B)

3:13 faster; then slowing back to main melody

Porgy	**Bess**
I knows you means it.	I ain' goin! You hear my sayin'
I seen it in yo' eyes, Bess.	if you ain' goin' wid you I'm stayin'.

SECTION 1 (A)

3:24	original tempo; F-sharp major

Porgy	***Bess***
We'll go swingin' through de years	Porgy, I's yo' woman now!
a singin'	I's yours forever.

3:38	transition section; imitations; softer; recitative style

Porgy	***Bess***
Hmm—	Mornin' time and ev'nin' time an'
Hmm—	summer time an' winter time.
Mornin' time and ev'nin' time an'	Hmm—
summer time an' winter time.	Hmm—

3:52	coda; orchestra with jazzy clarinet, then duet

Porgy	***Bess***
My Bess,	Oh, my Porgy,
My Bess,	my man Porgy,

4:07	faster, rubato till the end cadence

Porgy	***Bess***
From dis minute I'm tellin' you	From dis minute I'm tellin' you
I take dis vow:	I take dis vow:
Oh, my Bessie,	Porgy,
We's happy now,	I's yo' woman now.
We is one now.	

LISTENING INSIGHTS

What to Listen for in Contemporary Eclectic Music

Eclecticism incorporates into a musical work materials, styles, and ideas from a variety of sources. The search for new materials was underway during the late nineteenth century, when nationalist composers gathered resources from within their own borders—folk songs and dances, indigenous instruments, and so on. Around the turn of the twentieth century, Debussy incorporated Asian scales and instruments that he had heard at the Paris World Exposition. Stravinsky, Prokofiev, and others incorporated into their neo-classical compositions materials and compositional methods from other style periods.

For American and Canadian composers exposed to the tremendous waves of im-migration from all over the globe, incorporating the cultural influences from their new citizens was inevitable. Thus, the United States and Canada became the first *world* communities. The rise of jazz and popular music developed in North America offered additional materials into the great mix of concert music.

Listening to the eclectic music of Ives, Gershwin, Copland, Bernstein, and others, you'll find a grand mixture of ideas: folk songs, folk-influenced songs, folk instru-ments, jazz and popular music melodies, harmonies, rhythms, patriotic songs, and tunes from a variety of churches—for example, the Shaker Church tune "Simple Gifts" woven into Copland's *Appalachian Spring*.

Much of the enjoyment in listening to eclectic music is in identifying the sources of the various musical resources.

Scene from *Porgy and Bess*

AARON COPLAND (1900–1990)

Like Gershwin, Aaron Copland (*cope*-land) was born in Brooklyn, New York, to recently immigrated Russian-Jewish parents. Unlike Gershwin, Copland's talent was recognized early, and he began to study music as a child. At age twenty, he went to Paris and was one of the first of many American composers to study with the famous teacher Nadia Boulanger.

Ironically, Copland had his first real exposure to jazz in Paris. Returning to the United States in 1924, Copland was determined to compose music that would be identified as "Americana" and appeal to a wide variety of audiences.

A series of commissions from Agnes de Mille (*Rodeo*) and Martha Graham (*Appalachian Spring*) launched

Copland into the ballet world, for which he produced some of the finest works of the twentieth century. Incorporating jazz and American-folk syncopations, Stravinsky's techniques, and neoclassical influences, Copland developed a highly appealing style many call American Nationalistic music.

By 1945, Copland had written the majority of his most popular compositions. He began devoting himself to conducting (mostly his own music) and teaching, spending many of his summers at the Tanglewood Music Center in Massachusetts. His most famous pupil was Leonard Bernstein.

PRINCIPAL WORKS

Orchestral Music: Symphonies: No. 1 (1928), No. 2 (1933), No. 3 (1946); *Music for the Theater* (1925); *El Salón México* (1936); *An Outdoor Overture* (1938); *Quiet City* (1940); *Lincoln Portrait* (with narrator, 1942); *Fanfare for the Common Man* (1942); Orchestral Variations (1957); *Music for a Great City* (1964); *Inscape* (1967); *Three Latin American Sketches* (1972); Piano Concerto (1926); Clarinet Concerto (1948)

Ballets: *Billy the Kid* (1938), *Rodeo* (1942), *Appalachian Spring* (1944)

Film Music: *Of Mice and Men* (1939), *Our Town* (1940), *Red Pony* (1948), *The Heiress* (1949)

Operas: *The Tender Land* (1955)

Chamber Music: Study on a Jewish Theme (1928), Violin Sonata (1943), Piano Quartet (1950), Nonet for Strings (1960), *Threnody I: Igor Stravinsky, in memoriam* (1971)

Piano Music: *Variations* (1930), Sonata (1941), Fantasy (1957), *Night Thoughts* (1972)

Songs: *Old American Songs, Twelve Poems of Emily Dickinson* (1950)

LISTENING ACTIVITY

Rodeo Ballet (1942) "Hoe Down," Aaron Copland

Large Form: Ballet Dance Scene
Detailed Form: Modified Theme and Variations
Performing Medium: Large Ballet or Symphony Orchestra

Compact Disc 3, Track 2
Running Time: 3:18

Copland composed his Old West ballet *Rodeo* in 1942. Agnes de Mille choreographed it and danced the leading role in its premiere.

Rodeo is about a cowgirl infatuated with the head wrangler and championship roper. To attract his attention, she shows off her skills as a rider. But none of the cowboys pays attention to her. However, when she appears in a feminine dress in the "Hoe Down" scene, near the end of the ballet, she has to fight off the competing cowboys. Finally, the head wrangler asks her to dance, and they join the other cowboys in a wild hoe down.

Notice how the syncopation and exciting dance rhythms capture the sound and spirit of country fiddlers.

LISTENING GUIDE

Rodeo Ballet (1942) "Hoe Down," Aaron Copland

2	0:00	FIDDLE TUNE 1	played by strings and winds; *ff*; fast tempo, duple meter; D-major tonality; homophonic texture
	0:03	FIDDLE TUNE 1— variation 1	played by trumpets, imitated by oboes and strings; *f* variation of tune 1
	0:12	FIDDLE TUNE 1	like the beginning, *ff*
	0:17	RHYTHM INTERLUDE	rhythm interlude played by strings and piano, *mf*
	0:36	FIDDLE TUNE 1	similar to beginning, played by strings and clarinet, *f*
	0:43	FIDDLE TUNE 1— variation 2	played by strings and woodwinds, *f*
	0:57	FIDDLE TUNE 1	played by strings and woodwinds, *f*
	0:59	FIDDLE TUNE 1	played by strings, imitated by woodwinds, *mf* played by full orchestra, *fff*
	1:14	FIDDLE TUNE 1	similar to beginning, *f*
	1:32	FIDDLE TUNE 2	played by trumpet, imitated by violins, then woodwinds, *f*; then *mf* sudden pause
	2:15	RHYTHM INTERLUDE	played by strings and piano; *mf—p*; rubato tempo, then slowing to held E-flat chord
	2:42	FIDDLE TUNE 1	like beginning, *f*; fast tempo again
	2:49	FIDDLE TUNE 1— variation 2	played by woodwinds, *mp*; then imitated by full orchestra, *fff*
	3:11	FIDDLE TUNE 1	played by strings and winds; *f*; crescendo to *ff* to *fff*; three quick final chords; played by full orchestra, *fff*

LEONARD BERNSTEIN (1918–1990)

A man of many talents, Leonard Bernstein successfully pursued six separate although related careers. Some associate him primarily with orchestral conducting. Others think of him as a composer for Broadway and the concert stage. Some remember him as a pianist, a teacher, a writer, and a television personality.

Lawrence, Massachusetts, was a thriving mill town in 1917 when Leonard's parents, Samuel and Jennie, settled there. Their families had been among the thousands of Russian immigrants who fled czarist oppression and anti-Semitism at the turn of the century. The following year, Leonard was born.

When Leonard was ten years old, he started his piano studies on an upright grand piano, a gift from Aunt Clara, Sam's sister. A year later, Leonard was playing Chopin and Bach. At age thirteen, he performed in two significant events: his first piano recital and his bar mitzvah. At his recital, his playing delighted the audience. His bar mitzvah was a turning point; Sam was so proud of his son that he gave him a baby grand to replace the upright.

In 1937, during his junior year as a music major at Harvard, Bernstein met celebrated conductor Dimitri Mitropoulos and lyricist-performer Adolph Green, with whom he would later collaborate on musicals. In October of that year, Bernstein made his professional debut as a pianist. In November he met Aaron Copland, who became his composition adviser and introduced him to renowned musicians, including Virgil Thomson and Nadia Boulanger.

Bernstein continued his studies with noted conductor Fritz Reiner at the Curtis Institute in Philadelphia. He spent summers at the Tanglewood summer school in Massachusetts, studying with Serge Koussevitzky, conductor of the Boston Symphony Orchestra. In 1942, he became Koussevitzky's assistant at Tanglewood, completed his first symphony (*Jeremiah*), and moved to New York. Following his appointment as assistant conductor of the New York Philharmonic, Bernstein was presented with the opportunity of a lifetime: to step in as a substitute for Bruno Walter at a Carnegie Hall concert. His conducting career soared.

Bernstein's first Broadway show, *On The Town* (1944), was an instant hit. In 1957, his most successful Broadway musical, *West Side Story,* opened and became a classic.

Concentrating on conducting, Bernstein served as permanent conductor of the New York Philharmonic from 1958 to 1968. After 1971, upon composing his theater piece *Mass,* he divided his efforts between composing and conducting, becoming a revered guest conductor for the world's most prestigious symphony orchestras.

Bernstein smoked. In fact, he smoked so much that he developed cancer. Yet he continued working until the end. In a funeral procession usually reserved for heads of state, a police escort blared sirens and blocked traffic for the motorcade of twenty limousines, carrying mourners from the Dakota, Bernstein's apartment building on Central Park West, to his burial place in Brooklyn, New York.

PRINCIPAL WORKS

Orchestral Music: Symphony No. 1 (*Jeremiah,* soprano and orchestra; 1943), Symphony No. 2 (*Age of Anxiety* for piano and orchestra, 1949); Symphony No. 3 (*Kaddish,* mixed chorus, boys' choir, soprano, speaker, and orchestra, 1963); *Chichester Psalms* (mixed chorus, boy soloist, and orchestra, 1965); *Songfest* (A Cycle of American Songs for Six Singers and Orchestra, 1977); *Slava!* (1977); *Halil* (Nocturne for Solo Flute, String Orchestra, and Percussion, 1981)

Ballets: *Fancy Free* (1944), *Facsimile* (1946), *Dybbuk* (1974)

Chamber Music: Clarinet Sonata (1942), Fanfares (1961)

Piano Music: *Seven Anniversaries* (1943), *Touches* (1980)

Stage Music: *On the Town* (1944); *Trouble in Tahiti* (1951); *Wonderful Town* (1953); *Candide* (comic operetta, 1956); *West Side Story* (1957); *Mass* (Theater Piece, 1971)

LISTENING ACTIVITY

Overture to Candide (1956), Leonard Bernstein

Large Form: Musical Theater Overture
Detailed Form: Sectional Medley of Show's Tunes
Performing Medium: Musical Theater or Large Orchestra

Compact Disc 4, Tracks 4–7
Running Time: 4:22

Though the original 1956 run on Broadway of *Candide* was short lived—only seventy-three performances—the overture has remained a concert favorite. Lillian Hellman's book and Richard Wilbur's lyrics for the original production were adapted from Voltaire's classic about mindless optimism. When the show was revised in 1974, with added lyrics by Stephen Sondheim and staging by Harold Prince, the new Broadway run was more successful.

In the musical, we accompany Candide, his frivolous fiancée Cunegonde, and his teacher Dr. Pangloss as they leave Westphalia, Germany—"The Best of All Possible Worlds"—and travel to Lisbon, Paris, Buenos Aires, and Venice. During their voyage they endure such devastations as the treachery of the Spanish Inquisition, an insurrection, a war, the rape of Cunegonde, an earthquake, the plague, and the humiliation of slavery. By the time they finally return home to Westphalia, they realize that perfection can never be attained: One must accept life's realities and try to do one's best.

Listen to Bernstein's *Overture to Candide*. The function of the overture is to set the tone, style, character, and spirit of the musical before the curtain rises. Bernstein's *Overture to Candide* is one of the most effective overtures to any musical theater work, achieving all those requirements. Although several tunes from the musical are previewed in the overture, the music focuses on the optimistic and witty tune "Glitter and Be Gay" ("If I'm not pure, at least my jewels are").

LISTENING GUIDE

Overture to Candide (1956), Leonard Bernstein

4	0:00	INTRODUCTION MUSIC	very fast, mostly duple meter; *ff*; full orchestra; tonal with some dissonant chords; homophonic texture
	0:38	BATTLE SCENE MUSIC	duple meter; march; *f*; mainly band instruments
5	1:19	OH, HAPPY WE	low woodwinds and strings; meters changing between 2 and 3; *mf*
	1:32	OH, HAPPY WE	violins and oboes added higher
	1:44	OH, HAPPY WE	full orchestra; *f*
	2:01	OH, HAPPY WE	full orchestra; *ff*
	2:12	INTRODUCTION MUSIC	duple meter; *ff*
	2:34	BATTLE SCENE MUSIC	mostly band instruments; *ff*
	2:49	OH, HAPPY WE	melody in oboes and horns; *p*
	3:00	OH, HAPPY WE	full orchestra; *ff*; section ends with silent pause
6	3:18	GLITTER AND BE GAY	woodwind melody; *pp*; then gradually getting louder and adding more instruments
	3:31	GLITTER AND BE GAY	full orchestra, horns and woodwinds imitate one beat after flutes and violins

CODA SECTION

7	3:37	GLITTER AND BE GAY	suddenly faster and softer
	3:55	GLITTER AND BE GAY	full orchestra; *ff*
	4:07	BATTLE SCENE MUSIC	full orchestra, *fff*
	4:13	OH, HAPPY WE	horns in counterplay; two final chords, first soft, last loud

Other American Composers

William Schuman (1910–92)   Raised in his native New York City, Schuman began a lively music career as a Tin Pan Alley songwriter and song plugger—à la Gershwin.

Coming late to classical music, Schuman did not hear his first symphony concert until he was twenty years old. The next day he changed his major at Columbia University to music. He continued composing and later taught at the Juilliard School of Music, serving as its president from 1945 to 1961.

An eclectic composer, Schuman purposely incorporated composition techniques similar to Copland's. With syncopation and other interesting rhythms, Schuman's music has a distinctly American flavor. His symphonies, ballet music (*Undertow*, 1940), and works for band (*Chester* Overture) are among his most popular music.

CHALLENGE YOUR EXPERTISE

- Who was the composer who supported himself during his teenage years by plugging songs and recording piano rolls?
- Whose one-act opera contains motifs derived from Creole folk tunes?

GIAN CARLO MENOTTI (B. 1911)

An Italian by birth, Gian Carlo Menotti later became a naturalized citizen of the United States. He grew up, however, in a country town on Lake Lugano on the Swiss-Italian border. Menotti's father was a prosperous businessman, and his mother was an amateur musician.

By the time he entered the Milan Conservatory of Music at age thirteen, Menotti had written two operas. In 1928, at age seventeen, he continued his musical studies at the Curtis Institute of Music in Philadelphia, where he met his lifelong friend, composer Samuel Barber.

After graduating with honors from the Curtis Institute, Menotti began receiving commissions for opera works. In 1936, his *Amelia Goes to the Ball,* a comic opera in Italian, premiered in Italy and then played at the Metropolitan Opera in New York. It was then that Menotti decided to remain in the United States to become a citizen.

From 1958 until recently, Menotti spent most of his efforts directing the Spoleto Festival of Two Worlds, located in Spoleto, Italy.

Menotti's operas have been some of the most successful of the twentieth century. He has the distinction of having composed the first opera for television, *Amahl and the Night Visitors,* commissioned by NBC. His concerns have been to make his operas realistic and accessible to North American audiences. Caring for the voice and vocal melody, Menotti has often been compared to Puccini. Though he has composed entirely in the twentieth century, Menotti's compositional techniques have been mostly traditional, conservative, and somewhat reminiscent of nineteenth-century romanticism.

PRINCIPAL WORKS

Orchestral Music: Piano Concerto in F (1945); *Sebastian,* ballet suite (1947); Concerto for Violin (1952)

Operas: *Amelia al ballo* (Amelia to the Ball, 1936); *The Old Maid and the Thief* (1939); *The Medium* (1945); *The Telephone* (1946); *The Consul* (1949); *Amahl and the Night Visitors* (1951); *The Saint of Bleecker Street* (1954); *Help, Help, the Globolinks* (1968); *The Hero* (1976); *Tamu-Tamu* (1973)

Cantatas, Madrigal Ballets: *The Unicorn, the Gorgon and the Manticore* (1956); *The Death of Bishop Brindisi* (1963); *Landscapes and Remembrances* (1976)

Chamber Music: Four Pieces for String Quartet (1936); Suite for Two Cellos and Piano (1973)

Piano Music: *Poemeti per Maria Rosa,* twelve pieces for children (1937); *Ricecare and Toccata on a Theme from The Old Maid and the Thief* (1953)

ELLEN TAAFFE ZWILICH (B. 1939)

Born in Miami, Florida, Ellen Taaffe Zwilich began to study violin at an early age. After receiving both her bachelor's and master's degrees in music from Florida State University, she studied composition with Roger Sessions and Elliot Carter at the Juilliard School of Music in New York City. Zwilich was the first woman to be awarded a doctorate in composition from Juilliard.

Commissions from the San Francisco and Indianapolis orchestras and several chamber music groups gave Zwilich opportunities to compose for a variety of performing media. Her Symphony No. 1 earned her a Pulitzer Prize in 1983.

As with other North American composers, eclecticism characterizes Zwilich's music, which draws on a wide range of diverse styles. Her twentieth-century compositional techniques blended with Romantic tonality and thematic treatment have appealed to a wide range of audiences—atypical of much of contemporary music. In fact, some of her admirers call her the champion of a "new romanticism."

PRINCIPAL WORKS

Orchestral Music: *Symposium* (1973); Chamber Symphony (1979); Symphony No. 1 (1982); Symphony No. 2 (1985); *Celebration* (tone poem, 1984); Prologue and Variations (1984); *Concerto Grosso* (1985) (after Handel); *Symbolon* (1988)

Chamber Music: Sonata for Violin and Piano (1974); String Quartet (1974); String Trio (1981); Diverti-mento (1983); Double Quartet for Strings (1984); Concerto for Trumpet and Five Players (1984)

Vocal Music: *Einsame Nacht* (Lonesome Night, song cycle, 1971); *Passages* for Soprano and Instrumental Ensemble; several other songs

LISTENING ACTIVITY

Zwilich, Concerto *Grosso 1985*
First Movement: Maestoso

Compact Disc 4, Track 36
Running Time: 2:41

Listen to the *Concerto Grosso 1985* by Ellen Taaffe Zwilich. It is scored for a chamber orchestra consisting of a small group of winds, harpsichord, and strings reminiscent of Baroque style period. The work was commissioned by the Washington Friends of Handel for the commemoration of George Frideric Handel's birth.

Zwilich patterned the *Concerto Grosso* on a violin sonata by Handel. The first movement contains several musical quotes from the original Handel work. The Handel sections are juxtaposed with contemporary polytonal arpeggios. To contrast Handel's style with Zwilich's unique contemporary style, she instructs the players to perform the Handel sections in obvious Baroque style.

The composer states that the concerto is "both inspired by Handel's sonata and, I hope, imbued with his spirit." More specifically, in neoclassical style (neo-Baroque here), she uses terraced dynamics—contrasting imitations of loud and soft sections—repeated melodic phrases, and sequences.

Interestingly, at the world premiere in 1986, the Handel violin sonata was performed preceding the Zwilich *Concerto Grosso 1985*.

LISTENING GUIDE

Zwilich, *Concerto Grosso 1985*
First Movement: Maestoso

36	0:00	HELD TONES	3 long tones on the pitch D, *f*; maestoso
	0:24	ARPEGGIO THEME	intervals based on Handel's theme, 16th note, polytonal arpeggios in flutes, oboes, violins over held D, *f*; repeated *p*
	0:41	HANDEL THEME	played by violin, harpsichord continuo in Baroque style, ornamented stately melody, *mp*; duple meter
	1:02	ARPEGGIO THEME	*f*; 16th note polytonal arpeggios played by flute and violin, imitated by various instruments
	1:22	HANDEL THEME— fragments	*p*; oboe, ornamented melody over harpsichord and basso continuo
	1:38	HANDEL THEME— fragments	violins, *f*; alternating imitations with flute and oboe, oboe fragments from the Handel theme
	1:57	HANDEL THEME— fragments	*f*; woodwinds and strings, ornamented melody in Baroque style with continuo, section ends with cadence
	2:10	ARPEGGIO THEME	woodwinds and strings together play polytonal arpeggios
	2:20	POLYCHORDS	*f*; three held polychords with harpsichord arpeggios

Neoclassical American Composers

Following Copland's goal to create music that could be accessible to the general American population, several important American composers incorporated neoclassical influences in their music.

Walter Piston (1894–1976)   A contemporary of Copland, Piston studied in France with Nadia Boulanger, as well as with Paul Dukas. He is known for his books on music theory and his teaching at Harvard (Bernstein was one of his students). Piston wrote eight symphonies, numerous concertos, and chamber music works. His ballet *The Incredible Flutist* (1938) is his most popular work.

Roger Sessions (1896–1985)   Born in Brooklyn, New York, Sessions wrote complicated, abstract music (without extramusical ideas attached) and twelve-tone music. He taught at Smith College in Massachusetts, Cleveland Institute of Music, Princeton University, University of California/Berkeley, and Juilliard School of Music.

Sessions' most successful students include Miriam Gideon, Hugo Weisgall, Vivien Fine, Donald Martino, and Ellen Taaffe Zwilich.

Samuel Barber (1910–1981)   An eclectic, neo-Romantic composer, Barber was born in Philadelphia and studied at Curtis Institute there. Some of his most popular works are his overture for *School of Scandal* (1933), String Quartet (1936), *Vanessa* (opera, 1958), "Adagio for Strings" (1936, used in the film *Platoon*), *Medea* (Ballet, 1946), and many interesting songs.

Howard Hanson (1896–1981)   From 1924 to 1964, Hanson was director of the Eastman School of Music, where he also founded and conducted the Eastman Philharmonic Orchestra. Symphony No. 1 (*Nordic,* 1923) and Symphony No. 2 (*Romantic,* 1930) are two of his popular works, along with his opera *Merry Mount* (1934).

Summary of Terms

bitonal	polymedia	polytonality
eclecticism	polymeters	quarter tones
polychords	polytonal	song plugger

Part IV
Music of Cultural Diversity

25

Jazz: The Great American Art Form

The Origins and Emergence of Jazz

Jazz has often been called "America's classical music," and indeed its influence on classical composers was clearly shown in the last chapter. But jazz has also been a key player in American popular music, bridging the gap between the two styles. In this chapter, we will briefly examine the history of this

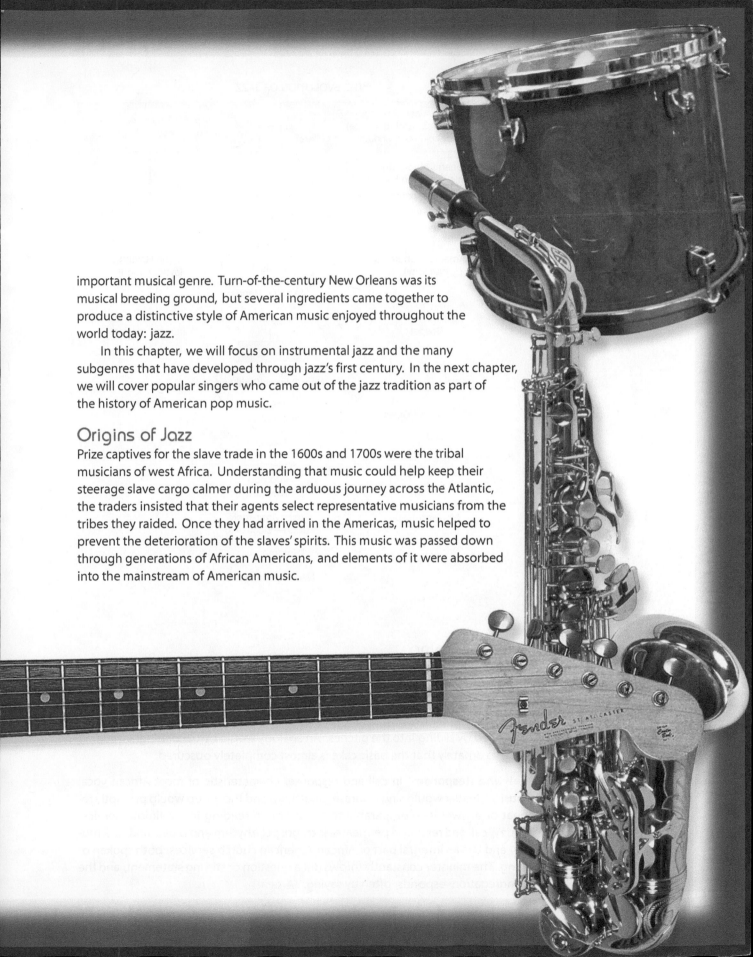

important musical genre. Turn-of-the-century New Orleans was its musical breeding ground, but several ingredients came together to produce a distinctive style of American music enjoyed throughout the world today: jazz.

In this chapter, we will focus on instrumental jazz and the many subgenres that have developed through jazz's first century. In the next chapter, we will cover popular singers who came out of the jazz tradition as part of the history of American pop music.

Origins of Jazz

Prize captives for the slave trade in the 1600s and 1700s were the tribal musicians of west Africa. Understanding that music could help keep their steerage slave cargo calmer during the arduous journey across the Atlantic, the traders insisted that their agents select representative musicians from the tribes they raided. Once they had arrived in the Americas, music helped to prevent the deterioration of the slaves' spirits. This music was passed down through generations of African Americans, and elements of it were absorbed into the mainstream of American music.

THE EVOLUTION OF JAZZ

African Singing

When you hear jazz and pop singers today, listen for the African influence, especially in the use of ornamentation. In the African singing tradition, melodies are enhanced with almost constant ornamentation surrounding the main pitches of the fundamental melody. Other pitches of the main melody are bent and approached by sliding into the pitches. An analogy would be decorating a wedding cake so ornately that the basic cake is almost completely obscured.

Call and response

Call and Response   In call and response, characteristic of most African vocal music, a leader would sing a phrase (question), and the group would promptly repeat or answer it—comparable to a responsive reading in a religious service. Today, call and response permeates jazz, gospel, rhythm and blues, and rock music, and it is an integral part of African-American church services, both spoken or sung. The minister constantly throws out a question or stirring statement, and the congregation responds, often by saying, "Amen!"

Riff   Heard throughout African singing and instrumental groups, and later in jazz, a *riff* is a short phrase repeated over and over. It fits our definition of an *ostinato*, a repeated pattern that unifies the music. Originally, riffs or ostinatos were improvised by various members of the African percussion ensemble and then imitated by the entire ensemble. Today, *riff* may refer to any repetitive passage.

Riff Ostinato

African Rhythms

African rhythms

Rhythm has often been called the "soul of Africa." Almost every African social gathering had its rhythmic accompaniment. Every tribal occasion also brought out the percussion instruments played by male members of the tribe.

Especially throughout western Africa, each percussionist had a discrete role in the ensemble. Choosing a particular instrument while still a young boy, each tribesman continued playing that instrument throughout his lifetime. Exceptional percussionists often developed into soloists, responsible for improvising new rhythmic patterns that the rest of the ensemble answered or imitated.

Syncopation   Complexities of rhythm have always been the essence of African percussion ensembles. Playing the same rhythm hour after hour at ceremonies can be boring. To maintain interest, players created variations. *Syncopation* is a variation that accents part of the beat not usually accented. Constant use of syncopation results in a *swing* or forward motion to the music.

Syncopation

When musicologists first analyzed African percussion music in the nineteenth century, they could not understand it. In contrast to European music, the musicologists heard beats accented in unusual places (syncopation). They finally concluded that "Africans don't know how to keep time."

Offbeat   The fact that African percussionists did not all play continuously on the beat also disturbed early musicologists. Later, they came to learn that African percussionists have fun trying *not* to play on the beat. Great jazz players and singers have been influenced by this relaxed, *offbeat* performing. (It's not "cool" to play on the beat—that's for Lawrence Welk.)

Offbeat

Polyrhythms   African percussion ensembles use *polyrhythms*—several overlays of conflicting rhythms that add interest to the music. Through the several World Expositions in Paris in the early 1900s, Debussy, Stravinsky, and others were so impressed with the use of polyrhythms that they incorporated them into their compositions.

Polyrhythms

Cakewalk

Cakewalk

Originating as an entertainment on Southern plantations, the *cakewalk* was a high-kicking dance. Slave couples competed for a prize, generally a cake. Those with the highest, proudest steps, often parodying the slave owner's pomposity, would "take the cake." On some plantations, the dancers moved with pails of water on their heads. The winner was the couple who could maintain the most erect posture while spilling the least amount of water.

The cakewalk's rhythms are full of syncopation. As the dance craze became widespread, concert and military bands obliged their audiences with band arrangements of the music.

United States Marine Band (1880) with its leader, John Philip Sousa (1854–1932), playing cornet (with black cape, front right)

Military bands

Military Bands

At the turn of the century, American military bands, as well as the French military bands in New Orleans, influenced the beginnings of jazz. A band played at every important occasion, especially if a parade was part of the celebration. Even a funeral procession for an important person would be headed by a band.

The funeral band

The Funeral   In New Orleans, the African-American funeral procession became a tradition. The New Orleans African-American community was a proud, distinctive society. Ultimately, their use of funeral procession bands spread into other cities—particularly to Memphis, St. Louis, and New York.

At the death of one of the community leaders, a band would assemble, usually playing secondhand instruments that had been traded in by the military bands. Performing mainly church hymns, these African-American-society marching bands headed the long, solemn parade of mourners through the streets.

Introduced to Europe by the New Orleans pianist and composer Louis Gottschalk (1829–1869), the cakewalk caught on in Europe as well. Even Debussy composed one, "Gollywog's Cakewalk," in 1908.

Blues

Blues songs became popular in the post-Civil War era among African-American performers and their audiences. These songs expressed the frustrations and obstacles—as well as the hopes and aspirations—of the newly freed population. The blues began filtering into the mainstream between 1910 and 1930 under the influence of Tin Pan Alley songwriters such as W. C. Handy ("Memphis Blues," 1912; "St. Louis Blues," 1914; and "Beale Street Blues," 1916).

Blues is characterized not only by its musical structure but also by its emotional and ironic qualities. With roots in the Mississippi Delta, the "deep blues" of artists such as Muddy Waters has a melodic structure based on the blues pentatonic: the first, fourth, and fifth tones of the scale plus altered or "accidental" thirds and sevenths. Those altered, "bent" tones that fall between major and minor tones are known as *blue notes*.

Blues Scale and Blue Notes   Contributing to jazz and other jazz-related music, the blues uses a scale containing *blue notes,* which were part of the African singing tradition. Blue notes "bend" some degrees of the traditional Western scale, usually the third, fifth, and seventh degrees.

Blues Scale and Blue Notes

Chord Pattern   Characteristic of blues is its use of predictable chord patterns. Called *blues progressions,* these patterns were derived from church hymns. The following is the basic 12-bar blues progression. Creative jazz musicians later developed more complex modifications.

Chord pattern
12-bar blues progression

12-Bar Blues Progression

To hear examples of the structure, vocal range, and controlled intensity of blues singers, listen to Bessie Smith's "Gulf Coast Blues" (1923), Robert Johnson's "Come On In My Kitchen" (1936), and Muddy Waters' "Long Distance Call" (1951).

Eddie James "Son" House, Jr. (1886 or 1902–1988)   Because of conflicting oral reports and legal documents, a question remains about Son's actual date of birth. You can hear the work of this artist on "Son House, Father of the Delta Blues: Complete 1965 Sessions" on the Legacy label.

Muddy Waters, 1981

Robert Johnson (1911–1938)   In spite of his death under mysterious circumstances at the age of 27, legendary blues guitarist Robert Johnson had lasting influence on the genre. His signature songs include "Crossroads Blues," "Me and the Devil Blues," and "Terraplane Blues."

McKinley Morganfield ("Muddy") Waters (1915–1983)   came from the Mississippi Delta and was exposed at an early age to great blues men such as Son House, Willie Brown, and Robert Johnson. Waters' first recording session in 1941–42, "The Complete Plantation Recordings," for the Library of Congress, is a CD reissue of these original recordings. In the late 1940s, he moved to Chicago and recorded primarily on the chess label, and the band he formed in 1950 helped define the Chicago sound of the blues. For ten years his following was primarily black audiences. However, at the 1960 Newport Jazz Festival Muddy Waters was "discovered" by white audiences who developed a new awareness of the blues and of the great blues artist Bessie Smith.

Bessie Smith (1894–1937)   Born in Chattanooga, Tennessee, Bessie Smith began her professional career at the age of 16, singing on the same bill as fellow blues singer Gertrude "Ma" Rainey. Known for her heavy-voiced contralto blues style, Bessie Smith became a major force in black vaudeville. By the 1920s she was a leading artist on the TOBA circuit (see Chapter 26) and at the 81 theaters in Atlanta.

Her first recording, "Down-Hearted Blues," made her the most successful black singer of her time. During her career she made almost 200 recordings, distributed in the United States and Europe, performing with important early jazz instrumentalists. Her notable recordings include "Baby Doll," "After You've Gone," "Back Water Blues," and "Nobody Knows You When You're Down and Out."

Rooted in jazz and blues, Bessie's style combined emotional intensity, an expressive attack, and blue-note inflections (stretching, bending, curving, and even hollering pitches, or notes).

New Orleans funeral procession

HISTORICAL PERSPECTIVE

Rags and Ragtime

A highly popular form of entertainment between the 1890s and 1920s, ragtime helped foster the development of jazz. African-American rhythms found their way into the highly syncopated melodies of "rags." As with jazz, military bands contributed to ragtime. While syncopation is going on in the higher parts, the lower parts play a military-band style continuous bass line (*um-pa, um-pa*) in duple meter. Also borrowed from military-band marches is the form used in most rags. In fact, most rags sound like slower marches.

Having contributed to the style and form of ragtime, band music was in turn influenced by ragtime. Seizing upon the popularity of ragtime piano music, in the 1890s, military bands added ragtime pieces to their regular fare of marches to entertain the general public—especially at outdoor concerts.

For many years during the beginning of the twentieth century, ragtime became the favorite music played in saloons and bordellos throughout much of North America.

Because syncopated rhythms and duple meter characterize both ragtime and jazz, the term *jazz* became a catchall classification for those forms. However, today we make a distinction between the two. Ragtime music, especially the works composed by Scott Joplin, was intended for classically trained pianists reading and playing notes printed on sheet music. In contrast, jazz is essentially improvised—each performance is different.

Several theories exist about the origin of the name *ragtime*. One attributed the word to African-American clog dancing, which they called *ragging*. A more popular theory is that the ragged syncopation evolved into *rag'-time* (*ragtime*), and later became *rag*.

By the time Bessie appeared in the 1929 film *St. Louis Blues,* alcoholism had coarsened her voice. Although her condition and the Depression damaged her career, Bessie continued performing into the 1930s. She died following an automobile accident.

SCOTT JOPLIN (1868–1917)

Scott Joplin was part of the generation of African-American artists born just after the Civil War. Called the "King of Ragtime," he grew up in a musical family in Texarkana, Arkansas. His father, a railroad laborer, played the violin. His mother, a domestic worker, sang and played the banjo. She persuaded one of her employers to allow young Scott to play the piano while she cleaned the house, and by the time he was an adolescent, his parents had scraped up enough money to buy him a used grand piano. Although mostly self-taught, Joplin caught the attention of a German-trained local piano teacher who gave him free lessons and introduced him to European music.

Joplin's career took off in 1895, when he began singing with quartets and accompanying minstrel troupes. Then he found work playing in saloons, bordellos, clubs, and theaters around the country. In 1899, he had his first success as a composer in Sedalia, Missouri, when he published his "Maple Leaf Rag." The piece was named after the Maple Leaf Club, a gathering place for the "best and brightest young colored people of the city."

"Maple Leaf Rag" was different from other music and made Joplin famous. By 1903, people all over the world were listening to his rags, and the royalties made him wealthy. One critic proclaimed that if American music were ever to be more than a reflection of European music, Joplin's works were the beginning.

Joplin settled in New York in 1909 and began writing operas. His second, *Treemonisha*, is a parable of racial and spiritual themes. Disappointed that every opera company rejected the work, Joplin personally produced a scaled-down version in a Harlem hall. It was 1915, and he was already suffering from syphilis. The public's negative reception to *Treemonisha* was devastating to him.

By 1917, the disease had caused paralysis, dementia, and loss of speech. Just before Joplin died, composer and pianist Eubie Blake saw him trying to perform the "Maple Leaf Rag" and said he was so far gone that he sounded like a child struggling to pick out a tune. Joplin died that year at age 48.

PRINCIPAL WORKS

Rags: "Maple Leaf Rag" (1899); "The Entertainer" (1902)—used in the film *The Sting;* "The Sycamore" (1904); "Gladiolus Rag" (1907); "Sugarcane Rag" (1908); "Wall Street Rag" (1909)

Ragtime Opera: *Treemonisha* (1911)

LISTENING ACTIVITY

"The Entertainer" (1902), Scott Joplin
A Ragtime Two-Step

Large Form: Piano Rag
Detailed Form: March Form Modified Song Form and Trio
Performing Medium: Piano

Compact Disc 4, Tracks 1–3
Running Time: 4:21

Listen to the catchy rag "The Entertainer" by the "King of Ragtime," Scott Joplin. You may remember it from the Paul Newman and Robert Redford film *The Sting* (1973), which uses the music throughout. The march form in this rag is typical of contemporaneous marches made famous by composers such as John Philip Sousa and Pat Conway.

In both marches and rags, the form contains four sections or tunes, also called *strains.* After a short introduction, section 1 is played and then repeated. This is followed by a new tune, section 2, which also is repeated. Then section 1 is played again but not repeated. The "trio" section, usually in a new key, contains two different sections, 3 and 4, each of which is repeated once. Joplin adds a brief transition between section 3 and section 4 of "The Entertainer"—a quote from section 2 that modulates the tonality back to the original key.

The following overview of the form for "The Entertainer" was used by Joplin for many of his rags:

Introduction (4 bars)	Section 1 (A) repeated (16 + 16 bars)	Section 2 (B) repeated (16 + 16 bars)	Section 1 (A) no repeats (16 bars)	*Trio* Section 3 (C) repeated (16 + 16 bars)	Transition quote from Section 2 (4 bars)	Section 4 (D) repeated (16 + 16 bars)

"The Entertainer" (1902), Scott Joplin
A RAGTIME TWO-STEP

INTRODUCTION

1 0:00 INTRODUCTION solo piano; moderate tempo in duple meter; *f;* melody in octaves major tonality; starts high, then two descending sequences to a cadence

Not fast

0:08 SECTION 1 (A) upper melody syncopated with steady bass line; homophonic texture; C-Major tonality; motive; *p;* answered *f*

0:43 SECTION 1 repeated
2 1:13 SECTION 2 (B) new tune in octaves; *f;* section is repeated with melody **one octave higher;** ends with a cadence

Repeat 8va

1:45	SECTION 2	repeated
2:17	SECTION 1	first tune returns, upper melody syncopated with steady bass line; homophonic texture; still C-Major tonality; motive, *p*; answered *f*; ends with strong cadence; this section is not repeated

TRIO

3	2:50	SECTION 3 (C)	new tune in key of F Major; *f*; answered in a lower sequence; still homophonic texture with upper melody syncopated with steady bass line

3:21	SECTION 3	repeated ending with a cadence

TRANSITION

3:52		four-bar quote from the ending of Section 2 that modulates back to the original key of C Major

3:59	SECTION 4 (D)	new tune in sequences in the original key of C Major; more softly and gently
4:29	SECTION 4	repeats, ending softly with a final cadence in C Major

Church music

Influence of European Church Music

Harmony

Harmony   Early jazz performers used the harmonies they found in the European Christian hymns. For instance, you can find the popular "When the Saints Go Marchin' In" in many turn-of-the-century Christian hymn books. This hymn and many others were used as a harmonic basis for many jazz arrangements.

When the Saints Go Marchin' In

Oh, when the saints go march-ing in,

Oh, when the saints go march-ing in,

How I want to be in that num-ber,

When the saints go march-ing in.

Bessie Smith (1928)

Creole Jazz Band (1923). Louis "Satchmo" Armstrong (cornet in the middle), Joe "King" Oliver (trombone on Armstrong's right), and Lil Hardin Armstrong (Armstrong's wife) at the piano.

Early Jazz to 1930

The Growth of Jazz

Emerging in the culturally diverse city of New Orleans, jazz rapidly spread up the Mississippi River by performers who entertained passengers on riverboats. As employment opportunities in northern factories lured the Jim-Crow-weary black population northward, jazz followed the migration to St. Louis, Kansas City, Chicago, and Detroit.

Chicago became an important center both for live entertainment and the growing market of commercial recordings. Small bands or combos became popular: Five-to-eight piece groups typically included trumpet, trombone, saxophone or clarinet, piano, string bass, drums, and occasionally guitar or banjo.

Reeling from the devastation of World War I, America in the 1920s needed a boost. Popular culture embraced the new music, and the Jazz Age spread throughout North America and parts of Europe. Hailed as the new American music, jazz reflected the renewed energy and optimism of America.

The Pioneer of Scat Singing   Louis Armstrong, hailed as a master of swing, was recognized for his perfect pitch and flawless rhythm. He developed the technique of using his voice like a musical instrument and his trumpet like a human voice. In his 1926 recording of "Heebie Jeebies," he told a story without actual words, singing in an improvisational style never heard before. A legend surrounding that recording, which Armstrong himself confirmed, is that the lyric sheet fell to the floor during the session. To continue the momentum, Armstrong improvised:

> *"Ba-ba-ba-ba heebie jeebie deh. Ay! Jeep, Dah. Boop.*
> *Dee-dah, jip bah bah, bip bip be-doo-doo-doo."*

Although his voice was considered harsh and abrasive, Armstrong's relaxed delivery and engaging warmth captured fans around the world. His vocal style

LOUIS ARMSTRONG (1901–1971)

Louis Armstrong is probably the most recognizable jazz artist prior to the Big Band Swing era of the 1930s and 1940s. In fact, most jazz historians cite Armstrong among the most influential jazz performers of the twentieth century.

Raised in New Orleans, Louis Armstrong took his trumpet and gravelly voice from the seedy dance halls and honky-tonks of Storyville to international renown. It was in a reform school known as the Colored Waif's Home for Boys that Louis received his first music instruction from the band director. Playing cornet in the band, he learned a repertoire of traditional band music, marches, and rags.

After his release in 1914, Armstrong hung around local music establishments, such as Funky Butt Hall and Mahogany Hall. Determined to become a musician, he soon met cornettist Joe "King" Oliver of the Kid Ory Band, known for its renditions of blues and ragtime. Oliver became his mentor and gave Louis a trumpet to call his own. By 1918, Armstrong was a regular in a jazz trio, and in dance and parade bands.

When Oliver left for Chicago in 1919, Armstrong replaced him in the Kid Ory Band. Later that year, he left New Orleans for a two-year stint on Mississippi River boats, refining his ability to read music and developing his ear so he could play requests from the passengers.

Armstrong's autobiography *Satchmo* tells how he got his big break when Oliver asked him to join his band in 1922. Louis honed his sense of harmony and made his first recordings with the band. Creole Jazz Band pianist Lil Hardin, who became Armstrong's wife, urged him to accept Fletcher Henderson's offer to play with his orchestra at New York's Roseland Ballroom.

Armstrong's virtuosity and improvisational skills defined Fletcher Henderson's orchestra's style and influenced generations of jazz musicians. Combining his knowledge of nineteenth century traditional sacred and secular music with twentieth-century jazz and blues, Armstrong's vision transformed everyone who heard him. His innovative use of instrumental syncopation and "scat," his liberated vocal style, encouraged other artists to take risks. His justly famous solo that opens "West End Blues" is widely cited as one of the first and greatest virtuosic solo performances in jazz.

influenced both jazz singers and popular singers from his own era through roll 'n roll, including Billie Holiday, Ella Fitzgerald, Bing Crosby, and Elvis Presley.

Representative artists of Early Jazz include:

Sidney Bechet, saxophone

Bix Beiderbecke, trumpet

Earl Hines, piano

Jelly Roll Morton, piano

Fletcher Henderson, piano and band leader

Representative Recordings for Further Listening   Jelly Roll Morton, "Black Bottom Stomp"; Sidney Bechet, "Blue Horizion"; Louis Armstrong and his Hot Seven, "West End Blues," "Struttin' with Some Barbecue."

Jazz Reaches New York City

Eventually, New York City became the center of jazz. In the 1920s, the small bands, characteristic of the early New Orleans bands were giving way to larger bands of 12 to 15 performers.

The Jazz Age was in full swing. Although Prohibition (1919–1923) banned alcohol, the night club became extremely popular. Crowds of jazz enthusiasts gathered in speakeasies to drink, dance, and watch floor shows. The era of the "big band" was developing.

Swing and the Big Bands of the 1930s and 1940s

In the early 1930s, the growth of radio and the greater affordability of mass-produced records increased the demand for jazz bands. Circuits of touring bands crisscrossed the country to play in night clubs and dance halls. The bands performed one or two nights in a city, before moving on to their next booking.

Benny Goodman with members of his big band

Big Band Arrangements

Written arrangements for big band jazz distinguished them from earlier jazz. A typical large (15-piece) swing band often consisted of:

3 or 4 trumpets

3 trombones

2 alto saxes

2 tenor saxes

1 baritone sax

piano, bass, drums and guitar

With so many instruments, it wasn't feasible for every instrumentalist to improvise at the same time as they did in the smaller combos of early jazz. But Swing-era big-band arrangements made room for improvisation by featuring one instrument soloist while the rest of the band played background parts consisting of both harmony and repetitive riffs.

Players took turns performing improvisations by passing the solos around from one player to another. Tradition called for each soloist to stand up during his improvised solo so the audience could see who was featured. The rest of the band remained seated. Audiences often stopped dancing to gather around the bandstand and get closer to the soloists.

EDWARD KENNEDY "DUKE" ELLINGTON (1899–1974)

". . . jazz has always been like the kind of man you wouldn't want your daughter to associate with."

Nicknamed "the Duke" by a boyhood friend, Edward Kennedy Ellington exuded an elegant, regal demeanor. But it was his musical brilliance that carried him to prominence in the jazz world during the 1920s. For more than forty years, Ellington remained in the artistic vanguard as a composer, pianist, and bandleader. Considered by many to be one of the greatest American composers, Duke Ellington redefined the boundaries of big band and vocal jazz with harmonic innovations.

Duke was born in Washington, D.C., and began piano lessons at the age of seven. Inspired by the ragtime pianists of the era and stride pianists such as James P. Johnson and Willie "The Lion" Smith, Ellington taught himself harmony and developed his own style. By the age of seventeen, he was performing piano professionally. However, the large jazz orchestra was to become his principal instrument.

Fats Waller encouraged Ellington to come to New York in 1923. Duke's band, The Washingtonians, established themselves by playing in speakeasies. After the death of the Cotton Club bandleader in 1927, Duke and his ensemble were offered that job. During the next two-and-a-half years, Ellington received national exposure through weekly radio broadcasts. He eventually won worldwide recognition.

After leaving the full-time Cotton Club gig, he assembled The Duke Ellington Orchestra, which appeared at the club periodically through 1938. Playing Ellington's music, the band reached a creative peak in the 1940s.

Ellington modeled some of his longer compositions, such as *Black, Brown and Beige* (1943) and *Such Sweet Thunder* (1957), on classical music forms. He composed for several films and in 1966 performed his "Sacred Music" suite, a fusion of Christian liturgy and jazz.

Duke Ellington entertained American presidents and was the country's unofficial ambassador of jazz abroad. His enduring songs include "It Don't Mean a Thing If It Ain't Got That Swing," "Sophisticated Lady," "Satin Doll," "The Mooch," "Mood Indigo," "Caravan," and "Crescendo in Blue."

Representative artists of the Swing style include:
Benny Goodman–clarinet
Edward Kennedy "Duke" Ellington–piano, composition
Harry James–trumpet
Tommy Dorsey–trombone
Glenn Miller–trombone
Artie Shaw–clarinet
Gene Krupa–drums
Roy Eldridge–trumpet
Johnny Hodges–alto sax
Art Tatum–piano
Teddy Wilson–piano
Count Basie–piano
Lester Young–tenor sax
Lionel Hampton–vibraphone

Representative Recordings for Further Listening   Fletcher Henderson, "The Stampede"; Art Tatum, "Willow Weep for Me"; Gene Krupa, "Rockin' Chair"; Count Basie "Lester Leaps In"; Benny Goodman, "Body and Soul"; Duke Ellington, "Concerto for Cutie"

Stride Piano

Stride Piano (also called "Harlem Stride") was a style of jazz piano performance made popular in the 1920s. It featured a constant beat played by the left hand against a prominent melody played by the right hand. Strong upbeats are played as single notes, octaves, or tenths, jumping to chordal downbeats in thirds and fourths. Techniques such as a walking bass or use of arpeggios added variety to the left-hand accompaniment. Although stride can be played slowly, the music is usually characterized by its fast pace. James P. Johnson, Fats Waller, and Willie "The Lion" Smith are among the most recognized exponents of stride.

Jazz After World War II

Latin Jazz of the 1940s and 1950s

Following World War II, Puerto Rico, Cuba, and other Caribbean islands were plagued by crop failures, the loss of war-related industry, and in Cuba's case, a repressive and corrupt dictatorship. To escape extreme hardship, people emigrated to the United States where jobs were more plentiful and the government more stable. For Puerto Ricans, the transition process to America was somewhat easier than for the other immigrants. Puerto Rico was a commonwealth of the United States, and its people were already American citizens. The musical *West Side Story* by Bernstein and Sondheim revolves around the issue of Puerto Rican immigration in the 1950s.

Centuries earlier, the Caribbean islands were used as holding quarters for West Africans captured against their will and brought across the Atlantic as slaves for the sugar and coffee plantations. Inspired by percussion instruments originally from West Africa, the slaves created new instruments, such as the modern timbale, claves, bongos, conga drums, maracas, and other varieties of shaken or scraped gourd instruments.

The fusion of American jazz with the highly colorful rhythmic music of the islands was quickly dubbed "Latin Jazz," and more recently, "Salsa." Large orchestras were created to fill the needs of the Caribbean islander's passion for recreational dancing. A club might employ two or even three bands for the evening to keep the music and dancing continuous.

Tito Puente, c. 1998

Representative artists and band leaders include:
Machito–singer, maracas, band leader
Perez Prado–singer-percussionist
Airto Moreira–percussionist
Tito Puente–timbales, band leader, composer, arranger

Representative Recordings for Further Listening   "Latin Jazz: La Combinación Perfecta," Smithsonian Collection. Many of the important bebop jazz artists, such as Dizzy Gillespie and Charlie Parker, joined in with the Latin jazz artists to create these recordings.

New Styles Develop

In their search for innovation and freshness in second half of the twentieth century, jazz artists experimented with many new styles: Bebop, Latin Jazz, West Coast and Cool Jazz, Free Jazz, Groove Jazz, Smooth Jazz, Contemporary Jazz, and Jazz Fusion.

Bebop (1940s and 50s)

Bebop or just "bop" grew out of swing. The term *bebop* was coined to describe the characteristic sound of the music with its fast, large pitch leaps: "be" (high pitch) and "bop" (low pitch).

After World War II, returning G.I.s got married and created the "baby boom"— a record number of children. Moving to the new housing developments in the suburbs, families were less likely to patronize urban night clubs. As Saturday-night ballroom dancing waned in popularity, the era of the "big band" was over. Juke boxes supplied the music for dancing. Venues moved to small clubs, diminishing the need for costly big bands. The remaining small instrumental jazz combos of four to six musicians performed in small clubs, often after hours, drawing a new, enthusiastic audience who came mainly to listen to the improvisational explorations of highly talented performers.

Listening, not dancing, became the focus in the 1950s. Brilliant instrumental technicians, such as Charlie Parker and Dizzy Gillespie, created fast and often frantic jazz—too complex for dancing. Bebop musicians also put aside the melodies of the easy-listening popular tunes and focused their improvisations on harmonies. With dancing no longer a factor, bebop tempos picked up speed.

Representative artists of the Bebop style include:
Charlie Parker–alto sax
Dizzy Gillespie–trumpet
Stan Getz–tenor sax
Thelonious Monk–piano
Kenny Clark–drums
Max Roach–drums

Representative Recordings for Further Listening   *The Smithsonian Collection of Classic Jazz Volume III:* Charlie Parker, "Koko," "Crazeology;" Dizzy Gillespie, "I Can't Get Started"

Cool and West Coast Jazz

In reaction to the frenetic pace of bebop performed by Charlie Parker, Dizzy Gillespie, and their disciples, a number of musicians began creating a more laid back and smoother style of jazz dubbed "cool jazz." Since many of the exponents of this style came from Los Angeles or recorded in the studios of Los Angeles, the style was also called "West Coast Cool." Trumpeter Miles Davis was one of the first bebop musicians to "cool it."

Charlie Parker, c. 1946

Representative artists of the Cool style include:

Miles Davis–trumpet
Dave Brubeck–piano
Art Pepper–alto sax
Stan Kenton–band leader
Maynard Ferguson–trumpet
Chet Baker–trumpet
Gerry Mulligan–baritone sax
George Shearing–piano
Shelly Manne–drums
Stan Getz–tenor sax
Lee Konitz–sax
Quincy Jones–trumpet, arranger, recording producer
Joe Pass–guitar

Miles Davis, c. 1989

Representative Recordings for Further Listening: Lee Konitz's album "Motion"; Stan Getz and Gerry Mulligan's album "Getz Meets Mulligan in Hi Fi';" Chet Baker's album "Baby Breeze"; Dave Brubeck's album "Time Out"; Miles Davis's album "Birth of the Cool;" Stan Kenton's "City of Glass"

Free or "Avant-Garde" Jazz   Ornette Coleman and a small group of performers began experimenting with a new type of improvisational jazz. Usually called "Free Jazz," the music shed many of the traditional elements used in most music. Philosophically, some of their inspiration for Free Jazz crossed over from twentieth-century atonal and "aleatoric" or chance music. The resulting sound created a feeling of wandering in space with little direction or return to recognizable areas.

Traditional jazz and popular music, for example, used predictable recurrent rhythm patterns of four beats. In contrast, Free Jazz performers experimented with less-used and less-predictable beat groupings of five, seven, eleven, and so on. Other characteristics are unconventional chord progressions and wandering melodic lines with no discernable key or tonal centers.

Representative artists of the Free Jazz style include:

Ornette Coleman–sax
John Coltrane–sax
John Zorn–sax, composer

John Coltrane, c. 1957

Kaoru Abe–sax (from Japan)
Ivo Perelman–sax (from Brazil)

Representative Recordings for Further Listening   Ornette Coleman's album "Dancing in your Head"; John Coltrane's album "Ascensic"; John Zorn's "Masada"; Ivo Perelman's "Seven Energies of the Universe"

Hard Bop

Developed by Horace Silver and the earlier bebop and West Coast cool jazz artists, Hard Bop returned to improvising and featured the tunes of familiar popular songs. Other influences include the gospel and soul styles of Ray Charles, Aretha Franklin, and Mahalia Jackson. Songs of this style are distinguished by an extremely fast, straight-ahead groove.

Representative artists of the Hard Bop style include:
Horace Silver–piano
Clifford Brown–trumpet
Cannonball Adderley–sax
Miles Davis–trumpet
John Coltrane–sax
Ahmad Jamal–piano
Oscar Peterson–piano
Freddie Hubbard–trumpet
Art Blakey–drums
Charlie Mingus–bass
Grover Washington–sax

Representative Recordings for Further Listening   Horace Silver's "The Hard-bop Grandpop;" Cannonball Adderly's "Work Song;" Art Blakey album "A Jazz Message;" Sonny Rollins' "Sonny Rollins and the Big Brass"; Ahmad Jamal's album "Cross Country Tour"

Jazz-Rock Fusion

This style fused or blended many diverse musical styles of jazz-rock as well as world music from the Caribbean, Africa, India, and Latin America. Its style attracted new audiences among the Woodstock generation who grew up with rock music.

Representative artists of the Jazz-Rock Fusion style include:
Chick Corea–keyboard
Herbie Hancock–piano
Keith Jarrett–piano
Cal Tjader–vibes, piano, drums
Jimi Hendrix–guitar
Chicago–band
Blood, Sweat, and Tears–band

Keith Jarrett, 1983

Representative Recordings for Further Listening   Chick Corea's "Elektric Band;" The Brecker Brothers "Return of the Brecker Brothers"

Contemporary Jazz or Smooth Jazz

Compared with earlier styles, contemporary jazz is more accessible to a wider variety of audiences. Its practitioners created a number of highly successful recordings and attracted a wider listening audience. Smoother and friendlier than previous styles, Contemporary Jazz is still popular.

Representative artists of the Contemporary Jazz style include:

Grover Washington–sax
George Benson–guitar
Don Sebesky–arranger
Dave Grusin–piano
Lee Ritenour–guitar
Chuck Mangione–trumpet

Representative Recordings for Further Listening   Dave Grusin's "The Very Best of Dave Grusin"; George Benson's "Absolute Benson"; Lee Ritenour's "The Very Best of Lee Ritenour"

The Neo-Traditionalists

From the mid-'80s, a new generation of jazz performers came forward who sought to "restore" jazz to its roots, particularly in the classic works of Armstrong, Ellington, and Charlie Parker. Led by talented trumpeter/composer Wynton Marsalis, these musicians have become leaders in contemporary jazz performance, recording, and education. Marsalis has been particularly influential, both as a performer and as head of the influential—and powerful—Jazz at Lincoln Center in New York. The neo-traditionalists have not been without their critics, however. Many feel that Marsalis has been trying to limit the development of new jazz forms, particularly jazz-rock and other contemporary fusions.

Wynton Marsalis, 1990

Summary of Terms

African rhythms	fusion	rag
bebop	fusion electronic	ragged time
blue notes	fusion/jazz-rock	ragtime
blues	gospel	rhythm and blues
blues progressions	harmony	riff
blues scale	jazz-rock	rock 'n' roll
cakewalk	military bands	slave trade
call and response	minstrelsy	soul and funk
chord pattern	offbeat	syncopation
church music	ostinato	swing
country	polyrhythms	Tin Pan Alley
funeral band	pop music	work songs

26
Popular Music

—Times, They Are A-Changin'
Bob Dylan [1964]

Composers earn a living by supplying existing markets. Bach, Mozart, and Beethoven composed repertoire for themselves, friends, or students (sonatas, concertos); accommodated the wishes and needs of their patrons (chamber pieces); produced material for public performance in large venues (operas, symphonies); and created specialized pieces to enhance church services (cantatas, oratorios).

Today's composers earn a living in today's markets. Some feed the recording industry. Broadway composers write scores for specific shows that advance the story and develop character. Film and television composers write music to establish mood and period, contribute to the ambience, intensify action or emotion, and underscore the story on the screen. Yet popular songs, film scores, and Broadway tunes may share a Pops concert program with traditional "serious" orchestral music.

Popular music does not belong to any one ethnic group, nor is it confined to a particular period of history. Archival and scholarly collections document medieval songs and a body of North American popular music, much of which originated in the British Isles in pre-Colonial days. Viennese from all walks of life once sang or hummed tunes from Mozart's eighteenth-century singspiel *The Magic Flute*. Nineteenth- and twentieth-century songwriters gave us a legacy of thousands of pieces considered to be standards.

With the emergence of the singer-songwriter, popular music began to move away from the aesthetic and focus increasingly on performers and marketing. Technology continues to stretch the possibilities. Production is in the forefront: Amplified, distorted, and synthesized sound has become the norm. Glitzy live concerts with light shows, music videos, and MTV require that music include a visual component to remain on the charts. The advent of peer-to-peer trading technology is forcing the music industry to find new ways to sustain profits.

So let's examine the genre retrospectively, recognizing that like the times, popular music is a-changin'.

The Development of Modern Popular Music

With the growth of transportation, popular entertainment became available all over the country, from the lower east side of Manhattan to the honky-tonks of the Western frontier—from the bawdy houses of the Eastern Seaboard to the show boats of the Mississippi. Like America itself, popular music evolved from cultural diversity.

After the Civil War, former slaves brought their music and dance to all parts of the United States. Endless streams of nineteenth- and twentieth-century immigrants from Eastern Europe (the Russian Pale), Western Europe (Ireland, Germany, Italy) added ingredients. Many immigrants who found work in vaudeville and the musical stage contributed their distinctive ethnic heritages, leaving an indelible fingerprint on the growing body of American popular music.

In 1914, Jerome Kern's Princess Theatre Shows became the forerunners of the modern Broadway musical (see Chapter 26) Kern and those who followed him wrote the songs that everyone knew. To name just a few, George M. Cohan, Irving Berlin, George and Ira Gershwin, Cole Porter, Rodgers and Hart, Frank Loesser, Rodgers and Hammerstein, and Lerner and Loewe mastered the art of writing show tunes that earned their place as popular music standards.

The public's appetite for popular songs helped break down barriers that had once deterred women from entering the music business. During the 1920s and 1930s, great songwriters such as composers Kay Swift and Ann Ronnell, and outstanding lyricists such as Dorothy Fields, found an outlet for their talents. Fields and Jimmy McHugh were among the renowned songwriting teams of their time. Both Kay Swift and Dorothy Fields also rose to prominence on Broadway.

Films also became a major source of great songs. When Broadway was stung by the Great Depression, Berlin, the Gershwins, Loesser, Porter, and others continued their careers in Hollywood. The outpouring of hits from the great movie musicals continued into the early 1950s.

Tin Pan Alley

From its emergence in 1892 until the 1950s, the publishers of Tin Pan Alley dominated the music industry. Their primary interest was the sales and distribution of sheet music throughout the Western world. Housed in rows of four-story brownstone buildings on New York City's West 28th Street, between Broadway and 6th Avenue, Tin Pan Alley was the commercial hub of American popular music.

The name originated during the hot summer of 1930. A journalist for the *New York Herald*, Monroe Rosenfeld, came to the area to write a story about the growing music publishing business. Windows in the brownstones were wide open to let in fresh air, and sounds spilled out into the street: the pounding of upright pianos, squealing saxophones, clattering trumpets. Rosenfeld called the block "Tin Pan Alley," and the name stuck.

Some of the greatest songwriters of all time came from Tin Pan Alley, including W. C. Handy, Irving Berlin, George and Ira Gershwin, Jerome Kern, Sammy Cahn, Sammy Fain, Harold Arlen, Arthur Schwartz, Johnny Mercer, Hoagy Carmichael, Duke Ellington, Fats Waller, Richard Rodgers, Oscar Hammerstein, and Cole Porter.

Performing Rights Organizations

By 1914 songwriters and publishers realized they needed more control of their properties. New copyright laws offered some protection but did not guarantee the collection of royalties. Thus, ASCAP (American Society of Composers, Artists, and Publishers) was founded to help collect fees for public performances and recordings. BMI (Broadcast Music, Inc.) surfaced in 1940 to monitor and log broadcast music. The activities of BMI have expanded to include nurturing new songwriters through workshops and showcases. Both ASCAP and BMI now monitor all forms of performance, broadcasting, films, and online transmission.

The Impact of Media

Starting in the 1920s, America established itself internationally as the center of popular music. Sound recordings, radio, and sound films brought the music of great songwriters to people everywhere.

The Birth of Recording

Although music written for the general public flourished from the turn of the twentieth century through the first decade, very little was recorded for public consumption. Starting in 1908, folk musicologist John Lomax (and later, his son Alan) began to record music for the Library of Congress Archive of the American Folk Song. But the early method of recording was on cylinders. Not until 1913 did the flat disc emerge.

Even if recorded music had been available, few people had access to playback equipment. Thomas Edison's wind-up phonograph and Guglielmo Marconi's crystal radio were still luxury items. A mass market for expensive wax recordings did not exist, and there were no commercial radio stations. Not until 30 years after Thomas Edison was granted a patent for a phonograph had the quality of recorded sound improved enough to spawn the early recording industry. To hear the latest songs, music lovers had to go to the theater or a department store where song-pluggers played the latest tunes on the piano to generate sheet music sales. Royalties from those sales and from public performances were the main sources of income for songwriters.

Record Companies

During the recording industry's infancy, the term "fidelity" did not apply. Capturing sound was enough of a challenge. Among the early surviving recordings (1917) is the George M. Cohan song "Over There." Today, digital remastering is making it possible to hear classic recordings dating back to the early years.

By the late 1920s, a number of record companies were electronically recording and reproducing brittle shellac phonograph records—flat discs, eight to twelve inches in diameter. Turntables played records at 78 revolutions per minute. A disc contained two songs. The A side was considered more likely to succeed, but sometimes the B side (or flip side) became the hit.

Black artists were cutting records as early as 1920 for labels like Victor, Columbia, and Blue Bird. The first black-owned company, Black Swan Records, started in 1921. Blues singer Ethel Waters, singing with Fletcher Henderson's Black Swan Band, gave the company its first hit. In 1923, Mamie Smith's recording of "Down Hearted Blues" sold more than a half million copies in a few months. By mid-century, thousands of blues and gospel records had been released, most by women vocalists.

Affordable phonograph records began to sell in the millions, exposing all genres of popular music to people around the world. By the mid-1940s, control of the music industry had completed the shift from publishers to record companies. Columbia Records' 10-inch and 12-inch, long-playing vinyl records (33-1/3 rpm), first marketed in 1948, provided multiple tracks on each side of the disc. The following year, RCA Victor introduced the smaller-diameter 45 rpm vinyl disc. Cassette tapes hit the music stores in the early 1970s, and within 10 years, compact discs began to take over. By the late '90s, Web-based "file sharing" through legal and illegal Websites posed a new challenge to record companies. The implications of this new technology are still being felt.

Films

The improvement of recording technology inevitably led to movies with sound tracks, called "talkies." Film production changed forever. In 1927, *The Jazz Singer*, starring Al Jolson, contained some songs and a few minutes of spoken dialogue. Jolson, a Russian-Jewish immigrant, had become famous for corking his face and imitating African-American minstrels singing Tin Pan Alley songs.

Although film sound was primitive for a number of years, Hollywood was steadily improving the technology. Originally, sound tracks were monophonic. Then in 1940, Walt Disney introduced stereophonic sound in the animated film *Fantasia*.

Radio and Television

With the licensing in 1920 of America's first commercial radio station, KDKA in Pittsburgh, mass-produced home radio sets became hot-selling items. Disc jockeys were hired in stations around the country. The records they played created a new market for popular music. Programs like "National Barn Dance" (1924) and "Grand Ol' Opry" (1925) sparked nationwide interest in country music. In 1923, New York's WHN offered broadcasts of pianist Fletcher Henderson and his influential big band. "Your Hit Parade," which played the Top 10 hits of the week, went on the air nationally in 1935. Starting in the 1940s, disc jockeys on local stations asked listeners to telephone in requests for their favorite songs, or dedicate them to someone.

"Your Hit Parade" expanded its loyal following after the show made the transition to television in the 1950s. The 1960s saw the debut of new dance programs, such as Dick Clark's "American Bandstand," "Dance Party," and "Soul Train." "Bandstand" became a fixture on American television for several decades.

In the early '80s, a new cable music channel was launched, MTV, showing videos to promote records that were introduced by on-air "veejays." Although MTV eventually focused on teen-oriented programming, music videos remain important in launching new acts and supporting hit records.

Popular Singing

From 1920 to the beginning of World War II, a new approach to singing, distinct from theatrical or vaudeville style, began to change American popular song. A key influence in this change was jazz music, which itself became part of popular culture beginning in the late teens-early '20s with Tin Pan Alley songs like "I Wish I Could Shimmy Like My Sister Kate." Many singers began performing with dance bands, and these bands were increasingly being called on to "jazz up" their repertoires. Meanwhile, jazz performers like Louis Armstrong (see Chapter 25) showed how the new style could be emulated by vocalists. Among the new singing stars were male "crooners" like Bing Crosby and Frank Sinatra and a group of female jazz-influenced vocalists, including Sarah Vaughan, Billie Holiday, and Ella Fitzgerald.

Ethel Waters (1896–1977)

Ethel Waters was among the most influential black singers of her era. She began her career in black vaudeville as "Sweet Mama Stringbean," shimmy dancing and singing blues. She prided herself on her excellent enunciation and eloquent delivery, even when she performed seductive songs with double-entendre lyrics. In the 1920s, she cut several hits for Black Swan Records and toured with Fletcher Henderson's Jazz All-Stars.

Ethel's supple tones, versatility, and wide singing range propelled her to stardom with such songs as "Am I Blue?" and "Memories of You." In 1933 she introduced Harold Arlen's classic "Stormy Weather" at the Cotton Club.

Ethel Waters embodied the ambitions of other black artists when she crossed over into white vaudeville ("white time") and Broadway. Ethel later broke the color barrier as the first black woman to star in a dramatic (non-musical) role on Broadway. She also won acclaim in Hollywood for her roles in *Member of the Wedding* and *Pinky*.

Ethel's signature hits include "Harlem on My Mind," "Suppertime" and "Heat Wave," from Irving Berlin's Broadway revue *As Thousands Cheer,* and "Happiness is Just a Thing Called Joe" and "Taking a Chance on Love" from the Broadway musical and film *Cabin in the Sky.*

Bing Crosby (1904–1977)

Harry Lillis Crosby was the fourth of seven children in a working-class Tacoma, Washington, family. For years, his published birth date was 1903, but the headstone, placed by his family, says 1904. The nickname "Bing" was given to him when he was seven.

Bing apparently dropped out of law school to become a professional drummer with Paul Whiteman's Rhythm Boys. He gained national attention in his 1930 film debut in *King of Jazz,* performing with the larger Whiteman Orchestra. He went on to become a vaudeville headliner, a film star, and top-selling recording artist. Crosby had regular radio shows from 1931 through the 1950s and hosted a network television show in 1964–65. His insistence on prerecording his radio shows was a significant factor in the development of magnetic recording tape. Likewise, his prerecorded television shows spurred video tape technology.

Bing was a newcomer to vaudeville when he encountered Louis Armstrong in 1926. Bing fully absorbed Armstrong's impact and would later call him "the beginning and end of music in America." From hearing

Bing Crosby, c. 1947

Armstrong, Bing perceived that "swing" could be applied in music other than jazz, adding greater dimension to any song in any setting.

During the Depression, Crosby was the most popular singer in the world. His extensive repertoire included jazz renditions of "Sweet Georgia Brown" and "Some of These Days." He collaborated with jazz greats Bix Beiderbecke and Duke Ellington. He recorded an unparalleled variety of music: ballads, hymns, nineteenth- and early-twentieth-century songs, minstrel arias, singspiel, Broadway hits, and rhythm and blues. Bing worked with Armstrong, Eddie Condon, Johnny Mercer, Woody Herman, and Rosemary Clooney. His recording of "White Christmas" is the most successful recording of all time.

Known as a crooner, Bing developed his signature style early in his career, just as the microphone was perfected. The new technology allowed him to sing more intimately, but loud enough to be heard over the band. He inspired dozens of singers, many of whom went on to influence others. But singers in the 1920s to 1940s who imitated him—Russ Colombo, Dick Haymes, Dick Todd, and Perry Como, among others—adopted aspects of his style without the jazz foundation. Few replicated his sense of rhythm.

Bing starred in a number of films, including the "Road" movies with Bob Hope and Hedy Lamarr, *Going My Way,* for which he won the 1944 Best Actor Oscar, and *High Society* in 1956, in which he teamed with Frank Sinatra, Grace Kelly, and Louis Armstrong. He called his famous duet with Sinatra ("Well, Did You Evah?") his favorite movie scene.

To the end of his career, Bing Crosby sang with expressive intimacy and impeccable timbre. His focus on the meaning of lyrics helped transform the popular song. Great lyricists such as Lorenz Hart, Cole Porter, Irving Berlin, and Yip Harburg considered him an interpreter who brought their words to life.

Frank Sinatra (1915–1998)

"Old Blue Eyes," Francis Albert Sinatra from Hoboken, New Jersey, is arguably an American icon. He began his career in the 1930s, singing in small New Jersey clubs. After a brief stint with the Harry James Orchestra, Sinatra joined Tommy Dorsey in 1940. Singing with the Dorsey organization launched Frank to stardom.

Frank Sinatra in the recording studio, c. 1950

While Bing Crosby was considered America's king of mainstream adult pop, Frank was capturing the imagination of teenagers. He expanded the audience for popular music to "bobby-soxers" who swooned at the sight of his pompadour hairstyle, two-toned jacket, big bowtie, and sex appeal. By the end of 1943, a poll in *Down Beat* magazine placed him ahead of Crosby. But contrary to prevailing myth, Sinatra and Crosby were not rivals. In fact, Frank credited Crosby as one of his early inspirations.

During the 1940s, Frank starred in movies and cut many hit records. Several years after World War II, his star began to dim. Then in 1953 he made a spectacular comeback, performing a serious role in the film *From Here to Eternity.* Shortly after that success, his singing career rebounded.

When Frank switched to Capitol in the 1950s, he worked with Nelson Riddle, Billy May, and many other highly regarded arrangers of the time. In the 1960s, Frank started his own label, Reprise Records. His position with the company earned him the nickname "Chairman of the Board."

Toward the end of the 1950s, Frank was a major headliner in Las Vegas, often performing with a group of entertainers known as the Rat Pack. But Nevada casinos and hotels were segregated, and some denied service to Sammy Davis, Jr., a member of the Rat Pack. Now a powerful figure in Las Vegas, Frank led the Rat Pack in refusing to patronize segregated properties. The release of the original *Ocean's Eleven*, starring Frank and featuring the Rat Pack, drew media attention to the segregation issue. As a result, casino and hotel owners and management relented on their policies.

Sinatra's singing career continued well into the 1990s. On his *Duets* album, he sang with stars such as U2's Bono. As he approached the age of 80, Frank had to rely on teleprompters for his lyrics, yet he remained the undisputed master of impeccable phrasing.

Throughout his later life, Frank had to deal with accusations about his affiliation with organized crime. Because of the suspicions of J. Edgar Hoover, the FBI compiled a file exceeding 2,400 pages about Sinatra. However, he publicly denied the accusations and was never charged with a crime. There was a popular notion that the character Johnny Fontane in the novel and film *The Godfather* was inspired by Frank's life and career.

Frank starred in more than twenty films, including the musicals *Anchors Aweigh* (1945), *On the Town* (1949), *Guys and Dolls* (1955), *High Society* (1956), and *Pal Joey* (1957). Among his endless hit songs are "My Way," "The Way You Look Tonight," "One For My Baby," "Night and Day," "Theme from *New York, New York*," "The Lady is a Tramp," "My Funny Valentine," "The Tender Trap," "I Get a Kick Out of You," "Stranger in the Night," "Fly Away with Me," "Love and Marriage," "Chicago," and "You Make Me Feel So Young."

After his death in 1998, Frank's funeral was held in his beloved Palm Springs, California.

Lush and Lovely: The Jazz Divas

Sarah Vaughan (1924–1990)

Repeatedly voted the top female vocalist by *Down Beat* and *Metronome* jazz magazines, Sarah Vaughan earned her nicknames "Sassy" and the "Divine One." She was able to command pitch and dynamics across three vocal octaves, and by the age of twenty was considered a legend among fellow bebop musicians. Sarah knew how to make lyrics come alive elegantly with her impressive range, emotional intensity, and effortless delivery. Many consider Vaughan a national treasure.

Vaughan began singing in the Zion Baptist Church choir at the age of seven. She was also a gifted pianist, and five years later, she had become the church organist as well soloist. Winning an amateur night competition at the Apollo Theatre in 1942 launched her professional career. Billy Eckstine, a vocalist with the Earl "Fatha" Hines Orchestra, saw her performance and recommended her to be the orchestra's second piano.

When Eckstine left Hines, he took Sarah with him to form his own group with legendary trumpeters Dizzy Gillespie and Fats Navarro,

Sarah Vaughan, c. late 1940s

saxophonists Dexter Gordon and Sonny Stitt, bassist Oscar Pettiford, and drummer Art Blakey. These musicians were among the pioneers of bebop. Vaughan developed an ear for the melodies and intricate harmonies of the bebop style. She made her debut recording with the band in 1944, and her 1945 recording of "Lover" with Gillespie and Charlie "Bird" Parker established her as a leading jazz singer.

Her marriage to trumpeter George Treadwell in 1947 began a new phase of her life. With Treadwell as her manager, Vaughan launched a prolific and artistic period of her career. She recorded almost 60 tracks for Columbia, including a collaboration with Miles Davis, and made a number of worldwide tours. Treating her voice like an instrument, she improvised rhythmic embellishments and used her contralto range to change a song's mood or direction.

From 1954 to 1959, Sarah Vaughan had a dual career, recording commercial hits for Mercury and jazz on its sister label EmArcy. Her classic recordings of "Misty" and "Tenderly" became a permanent part of her live performance sets. Among Vaughan's biggest commercial hits were "Broken Hearted Melody" and "Passing Strangers," a duet with Billy Eckstine. Some say she did her finest jazz work on EmArcy, including "Lullaby of Birdland," "Swingin' Easy," and the song that showcases her vocal style, "All of Me."

When Vaughan's contract expired, she left Mercury for Roulette. The highlight of her Roulette years is a session with the Count Basie band (without the Count), in which she displays her vocal passion and fireworks, singing "Lover Man," "I Cried For You," and "Perdido." The album *The Divine One* features songs with more intimate back-up: "You Stepped Out Of a Dream" and "Have You Met Miss Jones."

Returning to Mercury in 1963, Sarah Vaughan began an important partnership with arranger/band leader Quincy Jones for the albums *Sassy Wings the Tivoli*, *Vaughan and Voices*, and *You're Mine, You*. Her 1967 big band session in New York completed her contract. Then in the early 1970s she was back in the studio with a bigger voice, a wider range, and even stronger technique.

Sarah Vaughan continued recording and performing concerts through the 1970s, trying her hand at Latin- and African-influenced music. But smoking was taking its toll. Although her health and voice deteriorated in the 1980s, she won a Grammy for her 1982 recording of "The Man I Love" with the Los Angeles Philharmonic.

Billie Holiday (1915–1959)

The future "Lady Day" was born Eleanora Fagan Gough in Philadelphia. She adopted her stage name from film star Billie Dove. Hired as a young girl to run errands and scrub floors in a Baltimore brothel, Billie was first exposed to the music of Bessie Smith and Louis Armstrong. She later acknowledged her debt to Smith and Armstrong in helping to develop her ear and singing style.

In the early 1930s, she began night club singing in Brooklyn, New York. She moved to a small Harlem club that was popular among jazz enthusiasts. Producer-talent scout John Hammond discovered her there in 1933 and set up her three debut recording sessions with Benny Goodman. She began recording regularly with some of the finest jazz musicians of the day, often under the direction of pianist Teddy Wilson. Billie cut more than 200 sides between 1933 and 1944,

Billie Holiday, c. late 1930s

including her classic renditions of "Strange Fruit," about the lynching of blacks, and her own composition, "God Bless the Child." However, like many other performers of the day, she probably did not receive royalties from those recordings.

Although Billie had no technical training, she used her easy rhythmic delivery, unique phrasing, and emotional intensity to become an outstanding jazz singer. Appealing originally to black audiences, her style gained wider popularity in the late 1930s when she toured with Count Basie and Artie Shaw. In 1938, she became one of the first black women to be a featured singer with a major orchestra. The following year she worked at Café Society, a fashionable interracial nightclub in lower Manhattan's Greenwich Village.

Billie had some of her greatest successes with slow, melancholy songs such as "Gloomy Sunday" (1941) and "Lover Man" (1944). Part of her appeal was the poignancy of her subjects, the hint of her own wounded soul, and the trademark white gardenia in her hair.

But Billie Holiday was not kind to herself. She started using hard drugs in the early 1940s. It was her downfall, as depicted in the film adapted from her autobiography *Lady Sings the Blues*. After a highly publicized trial, Billie was jailed on drug charges in 1947. Her health and voice had been permanently affected. Despite a triumphant 1946 concert at Town hall, her role in the film *New Orleans*, club dates through the United States, and a 1954 European tour, Billie was a victim of her habit.

Ella Fitzgerald (1917–1996)

Very little has been verified about Ella's childhood, other than her early interest in dancing. As a dancer, she entered a talent contest in 1934 at the Apollo Theater, the Harlem landmark that opened doors for black performers. But when she walked out on stage, she froze. According to Ella, someone said, "Well, you're out there. Do something!" So Ella started to sing and won the contest. She followed that up by winning another contest at the Harlem Opera House. The prize was a weeklong engagement there in February 1935.

Ella Fitzgerald, 1979

Ella Fitzgerald had attracted the attention she needed, but at that time, few black bands could afford a woman vocalist. Chick Webb gave her a chance to sing with his band at a Yale University gig. The audience loved her, and Chick hired her. Audiences also noticed how young Ella was, so during her years with Webb's band, she used her youth as a gimmick. In 1938 Ella and the band recorded the nursery rhyme "A-Tisket, A-Tasket." It was Chick's only number one record, topping the Hit Parade for nearly a year. It remained one of Ella's most popular songs. Her childlike vocal quality stayed with her, even when her voice began to thicken during the later decades of her life.

By the time Ella was 20, she had become a legend not only in Harlem but in all Manhattan. Only a few black performers, such as Ethel Waters, Cab Calloway, and Duke Ellington, had reached the same level of celebrity. Ella was a mainstream star.

In a career spanning six decades, Ella made 200 albums and recorded over 2,000 songs, selling 40 million records internationally. Ella not only immortalized songs of legendary songwriters, such as Duke Ellington, Harold Arlen, and Johnny Mercer, but also the works of Broadway's greatest composers and lyricists:

Ella Sings Gershwin, The Cole Porter Songbook, The Rodgers and Hart Songbook, The Irving Berlin Songbook, the George and Ira Gershwin Songbook, The Jerome Kern Songbook, and *Ella Sings Broadway.* Those albums present Ella in her prime, singing songs as you'll never hear them again.

Through her lifetime, Ella earned worldwide recognition: *Esquire* Gold and Silver Awards in 1946 and 1947, first place in the *Down Beat* Critics' Poll for eighteen consecutive years, first place in the *Playboy* poll for thirteen years, the United States National Medal in 1987, and the French Commandeur des Arts et Lettres in 1990. She won thirteen Grammy Awards—more than any other jazz musician and more than any other woman in the history of the award. In May 2005, she became the posthumous recipient of the Ford Freedom Award, honoring an African American whose positive contributions promote lasting change.

Fans still consider Ella "The First Lady of Song." To learn more, you can visit her official website at http://www.ellafitzgerald.com.

Popular Music and World War II

Starting in 1943, disc jockeys followed American troops overseas. To boost morale, Armed Forces Radio transmitted music throughout the war zones both to the military and civilian populations. The USO established canteens for servicemen in cities across America and sponsored touring shows that brought celebrities to entertain servicemen abroad. Glenn Miller and many members of his band eventually joined the Army Air Corps. Based in London, they presented live performances and radio broadcasts to all fighting forces—on both sides of the conflict.

Wurlitzer jukebox, c. early 1940s

Back home, popular songs reflected the loneliness of separation from loved ones. Hits of the day included "Don't Get Around Much Anymore," "I'll Be Seeing You," and "I'll Walk Alone." After the GIs returned, the spending priorities of young families changed from expensive entertainment to practical automobiles, affordable housing, durable furniture, time-saving appliances, and a panoply of consumer goods. Music had to retrench. In many venues, small groups replaced the costly big bands. By the end of the 1950s, they had almost disappeared.

The Jukebox

In the 1930s, jukeboxes made the latest popular songs available for five cents a play. With money scarce during the Depression and couples separated during the war, people stayed home and danced to radio programs such as "Jukebox Saturday Night," which was also the title of a hit song of the 1940s.

The brainchild of the record industry, jukeboxes were put into restaurants, diners, pool halls, bars, bowling alleys, ice-cream parlors, and small dance halls. In teenagers' hangouts, a jukebox "satellite" was installed at every table. From there, customers could drop in their nickels and choose their favorites. The selections would queue up in the order they were requested. It became a game to see whose choice would be played next.

By 1959, the price of jukebox music had increased with inflation. People were feeding dimes and quarters into more than a half million jukeboxes across the nation. Today, authentic period jukeboxes have become prized decorator items.

Environmental Music   When researchers announced that music had a positive effect on assembly-line workers, *environmental music* was born. During World War II, factories introduced music to increase production. Today, music is everywhere—in elevators, waiting rooms, airport lounges, stores, the post office, restaurants, bowling alleys, banks, shopping malls, movie theaters, and during the interval a telephone caller waits "on hold."

Theoretically, environmental music surrounds you and helps shape your mood, whether or not you are listening to it. Sound tracks are compiled to maximize your efficiency at work, encourage you to shop leisurely, and help you relax while you're having your teeth drilled.

Music and the Music Industry
1950s to the Present: Something for Everyone

The World of Rock and Roll

Economic Impact

Now in its sixth decade of popularity, rock music has left distinct artistic and economic imprints on the pop music scene. Let's start with economics.

The music industry is big business. By the year 2000, the worldwide market had reached approximately $40 billion, thanks in large part to the symbiotic relationship between the recording industry, which provides the distribution, and talent, who supply the product.

The Rolling Stones, featuring Keith Richards (left) and Mick Jagger (right), c. 1990s

The music industry targets young people with discretionary money to buy albums. Rock dominates the market, although country is a very close second. To continue making money, the industry needs a steady stream of product—some from the idols it has created, the rest from the new talent it will tap to replace the cash-cows who dry up. Something new and someone new must always be on the horizon or in the spotlight. As a result, yesterday's stars may be tomorrow's museum pieces.

According to its ability to get "airplay" (broadcast time), an album can be a hit even if most of the songs are throwaways. One or two commercial tracks can propel sales into the millions. This success does not guarantee that a hit song will become a standard. Because the majority of today's hits tend to be identified with the original singer or group, rock stars seldom perform each other's music.

The Phenomenon of Television: MTV and VH1

With the advent of television channels dedicated to rock videos, artists found new outlets for their work. No longer is popular music merely a sound. It is dance, camera angles, costumes, make-up, attitude, and special effects. Fans do not have to wait for concerts. They can see their favorite performers with a click of the remote.

Award shows provide another promotional outlet. Golden Globes, Grammy Awards, People's Choice, American Music Awards, Country Music Awards, and shows featuring artists from almost every genre are broadcast regularly.

Les Paul and Inventions that Changed Sound

Guitarist Les Paul began recording in the 1940s after he returned from military service. Within five years he was considered one of the greatest jazz guitarists of his generation. The Les Paul Trio, with his wife Mary Ford, produced hit songs with deep, multi-layered sound, including "Tennessee Waltz," "Mockin' Bird Hill," "How High the Moon," "Vaya Con Dios," and "The World is Waiting For the Sunrise."

Les Paul was also an innovator in guitar and electronics design. After experimenting for a few years, he introduced the first solid-body electric guitar in 1952. The instrument became a driving force in popular music, encouraging new sounds of the late 1950s, powering blues rock of the late 1960s and Southern rock of the late 1970s, and contributing to the signature sounds of every genre.

In 1953, Paul perfected the multi-track recording system, which allowed lines of instrumental and vocal music to be blended together. His innovation led to sound-on-sound, over-dubbing, and reverb effects, thus advancing the art and science of studio recording.

Artistic Contributions

What is it about rock music that captures the imagination? Fans call it exciting, energetic, inclusive. Many credit the dedication and enthusiasm of the writer-performers who propagate the form. Others admire the free-form expression, both vocal and instrumental.

There is no doubt that both rock and rap have the ability to communicate—whether the lyrics are sentimental or twisted and deranged; whether they tell of unrequited love, decry the human condition, or promulgate certain political points of view.

Evidently, words are not the only elements that communicate; sometimes a prominent beat or complex rhythm interferes with the words. This is due, in part, to the technological advances that more effectively replicate, store, amplify, distort, and modify sound. Today, if a singer or instrument is off-pitch or loses the tempo during a recording session, the computer can correct it for the final mix.

Genres

Musicians have demonstrated extraordinary creativity in inventing, fusing, reinventing, cross-breeding, and naming the genres of popular music known collectively as "rock." The list includes but is not limited to rock and roll, rockabilly, surf-and-garage music, folk-rock, dance rock, cowboy-rock, heavy metal, psychedelic rock, funk, funk-rock, funk-metal, punk, punk-rock, electro-punk-rock, acid-rock, raga-rock, shock-rock, jazz-rock, digital rock, techno, hardcore, foxcore, slo-core, grindcore, industrial music, ambient music, grunge, post-grunge, alt-rock, college-rock, Brit-rock, noise-rock, post-rock, soul, neo-soul, retro-soul, rap, hip-hop, funky-neo-soul hip-hop, and more. Each genre seems to attract devotees, at least for a while.

Something for Everyone

Folk and Folk-Rock

Woody Guthrie

Surely the most influential American folk singer and writer of his generation, Woody Guthrie incorporated his personal experiences into his songs. At the age of 14, he left home to find work, with a harmonica in his pocket and a guitar slung across his back. During the late 1920s, he roamed extensively across the United States, sometimes traveling in boxcars, earning whatever he could playing in pool halls and on street corners.

In 1935 Woody settled in California. He sang regularly on radio KFVD and on stations near the Mexican border that could transmit across America and into Canada. Later, after relocating to New York, Woody sang on the national radio show "Cavalcade of America." The name Woody Guthrie became synonymous with folk music.

Woody's song "So Long (It's Been Good To Know Yuh)," included on a 1951 recording by The Weavers, hit the pop charts. His perennial favorite, the joyous "This Land is Your Land," has become an American anthem. Woody's Dust Bowl Ballads, in which he champions the rural poor, were recorded by folk musicologist Alan Lomax for the Library of Congress Archive of Folk Song.

Guthrie was the inspiration for folk singers of the 1950s and 1960s, including Pete Seeger, Tom Paxton, Phil Ochs, and Bob Dylan. After Woody's death in 1967, two concerts were staged as a tribute to him—one in Carnegie Hall (1968) and the other at the Hollywood Bowl (1970). Performers included the folk all-stars Seeger, Dylan, Judy Collins, Arlo Guthrie, Richie Havens, Ramblin' Jack Elliott, and others.

Bob Dylan, c. 2000

Woody Guthrie's autobiography, *Bound For Glory,* was made into a film, and in 1988, he was inducted into the Rock and Roll Hall of Fame.

Bob Dylan

Asked by an interviewer whether he had ever wanted to be a rock musician, Bob Dylan said, "Chuck Berry wrote rock and roll songs. I never tried [to write them]. Who wanted to be a second-rate anybody?"

Bob Dylan emerged in New York's Greenwich Village during the early 1960s. He wanted to establish his own niche and create an audience for it. Folk music allowed him to do that. Like his idol Woody Guthrie, Dylan could take his guitar and harmonica anywhere. "I knew I had to make it on something other than my looks or my voice," he said.

Dylan's debut album, released in 1962, featured reinterpretations of old folk songs as well as two originals, "Talkin' in New York" and "Song for Woody." He had found his voice—deep, moving song lyrics with unique phrasing and meter.

In 1963 his second album, *The Freewheelin' Bob Dylan,* was released. Dylan was soon hailed as the poet-spokesman of his generation. His protest tunes such as "A Hard Rain's a-Gonna Fall" and "Masters of War" raised the political awareness and social consciousness of listeners. Teachers used his lyrics to generate discussions about the grand themes of love, war, and oppression. At the July 1963 Newport Folk Festival, Dylan was heralded as the leader of the folk movement, with Joan Baez as the queen.

Bob Dylan was hot. When his album *The Times They Are a-Changin* hit the market the following year, Dylan wanna-be's—guitar-harmonica players with questionable singing voices—sprang up everywhere.

In 1965 Bob Dylan shocked his die-hard "acoustic" fans by "going electric" and venturing into folk-rock. His first half-acoustic, half-electric album, *Bringing It All Back Home,* was his first million-selling release. It featured Dylan classics "Subterranean Homesick Blues" and "Mr. Tambourine Man." The 1966 album, *Blonde on Blonde,* is considered a rock classic. Shortly after the album's release, Dylan was seriously injured in a motorcycle accident and disappeared for quite a while.

Bob Dylan won a 2001 Grammy Award for Best Contemporary Folk Album. During his long career, he has undergone personal and artistic transformations. Perhaps he made his deepest imprint with the work of his early years: "Like a Rolling Stone," "Blowin' In the Wind," and "Times They Are A-Changin.'"

Simon and Garfunkel

The five albums recorded by Paul Simon and Art Garfunkel between 1964 and 1970 made them the most commercially successful folk-rock duo of that decade. Many feel that their work, particularly their sound track for the movie *The Graduate* (1967), was as influential as Bob Dylan's and the Beatles' in symboling the attitudes of that era and expanding interest in folk and its social themes.

Their abrupt split as a duo in 1970 did not end their individual careers. Art turned to acting, then returned to music. His talent in both orchestration and arrangement led him toward performing traditional ballads, such as "When a Man Loves a Woman," "(What a) Wonderful World," "I Only Have Eyes for You," and "Crying In the Rain." Art produced several albums during the 1970s and, for a time, teamed with song writer Jimmy Webb.

Paul continued to evolve as a songwriter. He delivered a succession of appealing, upbeat tunes and earned high praise for his African-styled albums of the mid-1980s. Paul later wrote a Broadway musical titled *The Capeman*.

Together, Simon and Garfunkel won six Grammy Awards. Their final album, *Bridge Over Troubled Waters*, produced four hit singles and was declared Album of the Year. They reunited several times, including a 1981 concert in Central Park, which resulted in the release of *The Concert in Central Park* the following year. In 2003 Simon and Garfunkel received a Life Achievement Award from NARAS (National Academy of Recording Arts and Sciences).

Some of their most familiar tunes are "59th Street Bridge Song (Feelin' Groovy)," "Scarborough Fair," "Mrs. Robinson," "Bridge Over Troubled Waters," "Cecilia," "I Am a Rock," "The Sound of Silence," and "Homeward Bound."

Paul Simon's post-1970 tunes include "Me and Julio Down By the Schoolyard," "50 Ways to Leave Your Lover," "Still Crazy After All These Years," "Loves Me Like a Rock," and "Slip Slidin' Away."

The Folk Groups

Listing all the notables would be impossible. However, we'd be remiss not to acknowledge the contributions of a few groups: The Weavers, who gave Woody Guthrie his first recorded hit; the Kingston Trio, whose 1958 release of *Tom Dooley* launched the folk revival; The Byrds, whose 1965 version of "Mr. Tambourine Man" spurred the genre of folk-rock; and Peter, Paul, and Mary, who carried the folk message into the twenty-first century.

Adult Contemporary

Not every pop music writer and singer fits into the "rock" category. A large market exists among those who prefer their music to be melodic and relaxing. Dreamy ballads with orchestral back-up deserve their own category. Songs from film soundtracks and Broadway musicals, recordings by Barbra Streisand, the music of Celine Dion, recent releases by Josh Groban, and some of Elton John's songs belong here. As a side note, Elton John's "Candle in the Wind" is the best-selling song in recording history.

Rock Stars: Who Has the Staying Power?

Some say that the music industry has a notoriously short attention span. The durability of today's luminaries—Sheryl Crow, Ashanti, Christina Aguilera, and Alanis Morrisette—is unknown. A rock performer might skyrocket to stardom and then quickly disappear. Those who enjoyed an extended period of success are relaxing in the comforts of retirement.

Many of the biggest stars are dead—a few, from old age. Buddy Holly died in a plane crash. Rapper Tupac Shakur was murdered. A significant percentage of premature deaths have been due to drug or alcohol abuse; others, from sexually transmitted diseases. One might be tempted to conclude that "Sex, Drugs, and Rock and Roll" is not merely a bumper-stick slogan. In an era of materialistic greed and excess, rock may symbolize the music of excess.

Detailing the lives and careers of current stars is not useful because they may no longer be stars by the time you read this book. Instead, we offer the names of a few singers and groups, living and dead, who have left significant, lasting imprints. Some are household names.

Elvis Presley

Presley's 1977 death had no effect on his international fan base, except to reaffirm their devotion. "Elvis Lives" became a motto and a tabloid headline. Visitors to Graceland, his Memphis mansion, still produce a steady income for the Presley estate. Elvis impersonators, the subject of the film *3000 Miles to Graceland,* are tourist attractions in Las Vegas. Every January, Elvis impersonators in Japan stage a concert in honor of his birthday.

Elvis, c. 1962

Although we think of him as a rock and roll artist, Elvis never lost his country roots. When he cut his first recording in Sam Phillips' Sun Studio in Memphis, Tennessee, Elvis Presley was on the rise. After the 1956 release of "Heartbreak Hotel," he became a star. "The King" continued with a string of hits that added a new dimension to popular music, including "You Ain't Nothin' But a Hound Dog," "Blue Suede Shoes," and "Love Me Tender." During his years in the army, he entertained the troops and acted in a series of box-office successes. In 1986, he was one of the original inductees to the Rock and Roll Hall of Fame.

Elvis Presley's television appearance on "The Ed Sullivan Show" sparked unprecedented controversy. Because the singer gyrated his hips while he performed, Sullivan refused to have him shown below the waist on camera. (Imagine what Mr. Sullivan would say about today's music videos.) The young country boy exuded an irresistible sensuality to teenagers—who are today's parents and even grandparents—that made him an idol. Scores of imitators followed.

Chuck Berry

A musical icon, Chuck Berry established rock and roll as a musical form instead of a hybrid of rhythm and blues or country. His signature one-legged hop with his guitar is legendary, and his songs highlighted the correlation between rock and roll and popular culture.

Chuck Berry's understanding of the pop market enabled him to break the color barrier. At the height of his career, he was a 30-year-old black man singing to a mostly white teen-age audience. Much of his success stemmed from his ability to articulate their concerns and attitudes.

In the summer of 1955, "Maybellene" reached #5 on the Pop Charts and #1 on the R&B Charts. Berry continued with a succession of hits, including "Brown-Eyed Man," "Memphis," "Roll Over, Beethoven!" and "Johnny B. Goode," which many consider his best song.

During the 1960s, Chuck Berry's music influenced the Beatles and was recorded by the Rolling Stones. Keith Richards of the Stones called him "the epitome of rhythm and blues playing, rock and roll playing." In 1986, Chuck Berry was inducted into the Rock and Roll Hall of Fame.

The Rolling Stones

The Rolling Stones have the distinction of being the longest-running rock 'n roll act in history. In 1962, Mick Jagger, Keith Richards, boogie-woogie pianist Ian Stewart, and blues guitarist Brian Jones took the name for their group from a Muddy Waters song called "Rollin' Stone Blues." That July they made their debut at London's Marquee Club. Over the years, the group has had several changes of personnel (it now includes Charlie Watts and Ron Wood), but the Stones' performances have always maintained a high energy level.

Have they contributed anything except longevity? Absolutely. The Rolling Stones popularized a fusion of classic blues, rhythm and blues, and rock. Although it wasn't a new form, it was a fresh sound that quickly gained a following. In 1963, they cut their first single, "Come On," an obscure song by Chuck Berry. Their second single that year, "I Wanna Be Your Man" by John Lennon and Paul McCartney, reached #12 on the charts.

In contrast to the Beatles, the Stones were promoted as bad boys. They grew long hair and changed their image. "Would you let your daughter marry a Rolling Stone?" was their first major press campaign. Although the older generation scorned them, screaming teenage girls mobbed their live performances.

Incorporating other styles besides rhythm and blues, their 1980 album *Emotional Rescue* has tinges of reggae and disco. If the term "standard" can be applied to rock music, many of the Stones' hits would apply, including "(I Can't Get No) Satisfaction," "Get Off My Cloud," "Ruby Tuesday," and "Start Me Up."

The Stones' 1972 tour of the United States became the benchmark for spectacular stadium shows. Today, it takes 350 people to put on one performance. When they were inducted into the Rock and Roll Hall of Fame in 1989, guitarist Peter Townshend of The Who said, "Guys, whatever you do, don't try to grow old gracefully. It wouldn't suit you." Apparently, they took his advice seriously.

The Beatles

Throngs of hysterical teenagers greeted John, Paul, George, and Ringo when they landed in New York in February 1964 for their North American television debut on "The Ed Sullivan Show." The reception was unprecedented. Under the aegis of manager Brian Epstein, the Beatles had already become the number one (best-selling) group in England and the U.K., America, and several European countries. Their album sales were gaining momentum in Hong Kong. Something was different about the four-piece group from Liverpool—something lovable, almost irresistible about the schoolboy image of their suits, ties, and neatly trimmed haircuts—an image they would soon discard.

Perhaps no one understood the Beatles' popularity, not even the Beatles themselves. As soon as they stepped off the plane in New York, an interviewer asked them to explain the effect of their music.

"I don't know," Ringo replied, "It pleases them, I think. Well, it must 'cause they're buying it." When asked why their music excited people, Paul responded, "We don't know. Really." John followed with, "If we knew, we'd form another group and be managers."

The Beatles

The Beatles, c. 1965

The Beatles opened their Sullivan appearance with the simple, young-love number, "I Wanna Hold Your Hand." Beatle-mania ignited the record-buying public. Their fans became legion—not only for the group itself, but for each member.

When the Beatles burst onto the scene, something else was changing besides taste in popular music: social consciousness. The Beatles verbalized what many others felt about the government, the military, sexual freedom, drug use, and the absurdity of war. In a twentieth-century incarnation of Romanticism, youth protested what they considered the antics and errors of the Establishment. The Beatles sang about it, and we listened.

One of the catchphrases of the day was "Do your own thing." Even The Fab 4 took that to heart. Their eventual break-up, which many people never saw coming, seemed inevitable to them. Here are excerpts from an April 1971 *Life* magazine interview of Paul McCartney:

> *I think the troubles really began . . . when we stopped touring in 1966 . . . I felt the split coming. And John kept saying we were musically standing still . . . One night—this was the autumn of '69 . . . I thought, "That's what I miss, and they miss too—playing."*
>
> *The Beatles' way of life was like a young kid entering the big world, entering it with friends and conquering it totally. And that was fantastic. An incredible experience. So when the idea came that we should break up, I don't think any of us wanted to accept it. It was the end of a legend, even in our own minds.*

As a group, the Beatles were inducted into the Rock and Roll Hall of Fame. Later, John Lennon (1994) and Paul McCartney (1999) received individual nods. Their numerous hits include "Yesterday," "Let It Be," "Norwegian Wood," "We Can Work It Out," "You Won't See Me," "Nowhere Man," "My Sweet Lord," "Michelle," "Penny Lane," "Eleanor Rigby," and "All You Need Is Love."

Madonna

Artistically, it's difficult to place Madonna on any conventional scale. She currently ranks as the most successful singer-songwriter of all time and has proved herself to be a business pro in the tough music industry. For more than 10 years, she has run her own label, Maverick, and has full control of her music.

"The Material Girl" started her career as a dancer and released her first album, *Madonna,* in 1983. After *Like a Virgin* hit the market the following year, Madonna became an international icon. With seventeen consecutive Top 10 hit singles between 1984 and 1987, she was arguably the most influential woman in the music industry. Recently, she has released fewer albums.

Madonna, c. 2000

Like a number of other pop music stars, Madonna has expanded her career to include acting. She surprised many people with her deft handling of a leading role in *Desperately Seeking Susan.* In 1995 she lobbied for and won the title role in the film adaptation of Andrew Lloyd Webber's *Evita.* Madonna's portrayal of the power-driven wife of Argentine dictator Juan Peron won critical acclaim, and she was honored with a Golden Globe Award for Best Actress in a Musical or Comedy.

Motown

The term "Motown" is a shortened version of "Motor Town"—Detroit—where Berry Gordy established Motown Records in 1959. Berry assembled an outstanding roster of artists, and by 1964, Motown had become one of the most important and successful independent labels in the United States.

Gordy, an R&B songwriter, wanted to parlay his local success into a national audience. So he borrowed enough money to release two records (singles by Marv Johnson and Eddie Holland) on his family-owned Tamla label, which eventually came under the Motown umbrella. In 1960, he signed the Temptations. The Marvellettes gave Berry his first #1 hit, "Please Mr. Postman," the following year. Between then and 1969, the Motown label's stars included Mary Wells, the Supremes (Diana Ross), The Four Tops, Gladys Knight and the Pips, The Jackson Five, The Commodores (Lionel Ritchie), Stevie Wonder, Smokey Robinson, and Marvin Gaye.

Motown never captured the adult market, and Berry's earlier success faltered in the 1980s. Nevertheless, he remains an industry legend for his talent as a starmaker and his instincts for producing hits. MCA bought the label in 1988.

Rhythm & Blues (R&B) and Soul

Ray Charles

After losing his sight as the age of seven, Ray Charles attended the Florida State School for the Deaf and Blind where he learned to read Braille and develop his musical gift. Once he realized the connection between math and music, Ray learned to compose and arrange in his head. He wanted to become a professional musician.

The road to his success was not easy. He eventually made his way to Seattle where he worked in local clubs. Ray also met a young musician named Quincy

Ray Charles, c. 1960

Jones, whom he took under his wing, establishing a lifetime relationship. Following a trip to Los Angeles to make his first recording, Ray Charles returned to Seattle and formed a trio. In 1948, it was the first black group to have a sponsored television show in the Northwest.

In the 1950s, Ray toured with a band. Then he formed another group and played with Ruth Brown. During those years, he was a headliner at the Apollo in Harlem and had his first recorded hit, "I Got a Woman," "Georgia," and "Born to Lose" followed. He also fulfilled his dream of playing Carnegie Hall. In 1960 he made his first triumphant concert tour of Europe, and the following year assembled his own big band.

Ray Charles was successful in virtually every form of popular music. Through his efforts, R&B (formerly referred to as "race music") became respectable. He helped urge jazz into the mainstream. He added his distinctive style to country and western music. And along the way, he nurtured newcomers and was instrumental in the development of rock and roll.

In 1979 Ray Charles' rendition of "Georgia On My Mind" became the official Song of the State of Georgia, and he was inducted into the Georgia Music Hall of Fame. Ray was one of the original inductees to the Rock and Rock Hall of Fame in 1986, and an Honorary Life Chairman of the Rhythm and Blues Hall of Fame.

Among his numerous honors are the National Medal of Arts (1993), twelve Grammy Awards, the Helen Keller Personal Achievement Award (1994), an honorary Doctorate of Fine Arts from the University of South Florida, and an honorary Doctorate Degree in Performing Arts from Occidental College in Los Angeles. After a brief illness, Ray Charles died in June 2004. His life was depicted in the 2004 Hollywood film *Ray*.

Otis Redding

Many regard Otis Redding as the greatest male soul singer. Without a doubt, he was also a fine songwriter and, with the exception of James Brown, the most popular black male performer of his time.

Growing up in Georgia in the 1950s, and listening to songs by Sam Cooke and Little Richard, Redding wanted to become a singer. He cut his first record in 1960, performing in the style made famous by Little Richard. Then he found his own voice. His career took off in 1963 with the release of "These Arms of Mine." The song, the first of fifteen Otis Redding songs to make the R&B charts, hit the Top 20 that year. He crossed over into the pop charts with "I've Been Loving You Too Long" and "Try a Little Tenderness."

Aretha Franklin's recording of Redding's "Respect" made it to #1 in 1967. December 7 of that same year, he recorded his most successful song, "(Sittin' On) The Dock of the Bay." Three days later, Otis Redding died in a plane crash.

Marvin Gaye

One of the Motown's best-selling artists, Gaye first came to Detroit with the Moonglows, an East Coast doo-wop group. In 1961, he made his first record for Berry Gordy, *The Soulful Moods of Marvin Gaye*. Gaye's success soared in 1964 with his duet album with Mary Wells. One of the tunes from that recording, "My Guy," rose to #1.

Marvin Gaye aspired to become a silky crooner like Nat Cole, but his destiny was in the Top Ten. He hit paydirt when he teamed with Tammi Terrel on "You're All I Need to Get By," "Ain't No Mountain (High Enough)," and "You Ain't Livin' Till You're Lovin.'" His most formidable successes were "I Heard It Through the Grapevine" and in 1971, "What's Goin On," in which he expressed his views on Vietnam, ecology, racism, and religion.

Although his life ended violently in 1984, Marvin Gaye is remembered for the power of his music, not the tragedy of his death.

Aretha Franklin (b. 1942)

Aretha Franklin started singing in the Detroit church where her father, Reverend C. L. Franklin, served as minister. After she made her first gospel recordings at the age of 14, Motown reportedly wanted to sign her. But the renowned talent scout, John Hammond, lured her to Columbia records. Her hits for Columbia during the early 1960s included one Top Forty single, an R&B version of the Al Jolson classic "Rock-a-Bye Your Baby With a Dixie Melody." However, many have blamed Columbia for limiting her in her aspirations. While on contract there, she was presented with pop-oriented material and production that seldom allowed her to belt out with her natural gusto and develop as an R&B/soul singer.

Aretha Franklin, c. 2000

In the late 1960s and early 1970s, Franklin switched to Atlantic where she earned her title "Queen of Soul" by bringing gospel singing to pop music. During that period her career gained creative momentum. Aretha delivered her trademark intensity in recordings of such titles as "Respect," "I Never Loved a Man," "Chain of Fools," "Baby I Love You," "I Say a Little Prayer," and "The House That Jack Built." Her gospel-charged passion turned the song "Respect" into an anthem of racial and sexual pride.

Aretha Franklin's voice has retained its power through the years. She returned to her gospel roots in 1987 with the album *One Lord, One Faith, One Baptism.* Franklin continues to tour and record.

RAP: Rhyme, Rhythm, and Roots

Rap or hip-hop, which welled up from the urban ghetto, has been called the musical equivalent of urban graffiti. According to experts, the innovators were members of African-American teenage gangs in New York City's South Bronx. Rap arose to release tension and express protest—a dynamic clash and dynamic interaction of cultures.

Among the defining qualities of hip-hop are its complex rhythms and loud percussion accompaniment. The street-savvy, rhyming lyrics are disrespectful and dehumanizing. Even the names of hip-hop groups project bravura—Public Enemy, Beastie Boys, Dr. Dre. A violent message is driven home by the Murder Inc. label and album titles such as *Get Rich or Die* by rapper 50 Cent.

Queen Latifah, c. 2000

Queen Latifah, a former gangsta-rapper of the 1990s, is carving a successful film career. Latifah proved her acting talent in a series of roles and then won a featured singing role in the movie adaptation of the Broadway musical *Chicago*.

Rap crossed racial and ethnic lines with superstar white rapper Eminem, who swept the 2003 American Music Awards. In a recent interview, Eminem announced that he was not interested in rapping forever. He has already moved into record production, and he starred in the largely autobiographical film *8 Mile*.

As further evidence of rap's influence, the January 14, 2003, edition of the *Los Angeles Times* had a front-page article titled "Reading, 'Riting, and Rap." The piece stated: "Teachers are using [rap] lyrics to make literary classics relevant." One of the rap songs cited was Tupac Shakur's "Shorty Wanna Be a Thug," which pits a man's desire to live a straight life against the immorality surrounding him.

Some Classic Rock Bands

The British Invasion

The Who

Started in London by vocalist Roger Daltrey in 1961, The Who performed as The Detours until 1964 when they discovered another group by that name. The original three-piece band performed covers of pop tunes but soon moved on to loud, edgy versions of American Rhythm and Blues. Daltrey, bass guitarist John Entwistle, flamboyant drummer Keith Moon, and guitarist Pete Townshend were the core of the four-piece group. To attract fans in the band's early days, they resorted to gimmicks such as instrument smashing and flashy costumes.

The group had no more than marginal success in the United States until 1968, when Townshend devised the story that evolved into the rock opera *Tommy*.

The Who in their "mod" days, c. 1965

Intended as a last-ditch effort to save the band and provide material for their stage show, the album was only a moderate hit. But when The Who performed it on stage, *Tommy* became the highlight of their show.

Then came the Woodstock Music Festival in August 1969. The song "See Me, Feel Me" from *Tommy* was played just as the sun rose over the festival. Captured on film and shown in the movie *Woodstock,* both The Who and the rock opera became international sensations beyond their dreams. Ken Russell turned *Tommy* into a film, starring Daltrey and featuring guest stars Jack Nicholson, Eric Clapton, Elton John, Tina Turner, and Ann-Margret. It has since become a cult classic.

Some thought Keith Moon's apparent lunacy was a stunt. Whether deliberate or induced, his behavior attracted audiences and sold records. When he went off on his own, The Who replaced him with a more controlled drummer. Moon died in September 1978.

Roger Daltrey starred in a film version of John Gay's 1728 musical *The Beggar's Opera.* Pete Townshend continued writing, including another rock opera, but none of his subsequent work eclipsed or matched the success of *Tommy.* With a variety of personnel, The Who performed through the 1990s.

Pink Floyd

Pink Floyd revolutionized the way people "look" at rock music by being the first band to incorporate psychedelic light shows and photo effects into their live performances. After the group's 1966 presentation of music and lights in London's Roundhouse, the British press coined the term "underground rock." But it was their innovative music itself that boosted Pink Floyd to stardom. Coupling a powerful sound with soulful, almost-poetic lyrics, Pink Floyd created imagery that excited public imagination.

Until singer/guitarist Syd Barrett left Pink Floyd in 1968, he provided the group's early material. The remaining members—vocalist and bassist Roger Waters, keyboardist Rick Wright, drummer Nick Mason, and Barrett's replacement, David Gilmour—made Pink Floyd one of the most successful rock bands of the 1970s and early 1980s.

Dark Side of the Moon (1973) hit the top spot on the *Billboard* charts and broke all records by remaining on the Top 200 album charts for more than 740 weeks. Released in 1979, Roger Waters' epic about alienation, *The Wall,* spent over two years on the charts, inspired a film, and was the centerpiece of one of the most celebrated stage shows in rock history. But in 1983, the album *The Final Cut* ironically telegraphed the turmoil brewing in the band. Waters dominated every track; no song was cowritten by another band member. Reviewers noticed that Pink Floyd's distinguishing sound and emotion was missing.

Members of Pink Floyd, particularly Roger Waters, became ensnared in their own success. Drugs were readily available, and abuse was common. The group was dormant until 1985, and then Waters left the band. Two years later, the remaining members released *Momentary Lapse of Reason,* followed by a successful tour. Pink Floyd returned to the limelight and remained there into the mid-1990s. Three of their songs are among the Top 500 that shaped rock and roll, listed by the Rock and Roll Hall of Fame. Pink Floyd was inducted into the Rock and Roll Hall of Fame in January 1996.

Deep Purple

By 1967, the appearance of guitarist Jimi Hendrix and the psychedelic explosion blew the genre of heavy metal into the forefront. In the United Kingdom, Deep Purple was formed in February 1968 by drummer Chris Curtis, formerly of the Merseybeat group The Searchers. Originally called Roundabout, they built their popularity by recording covers of American hit songs, including "Love Potion Number Nine."

Deep Purple's first release was the progressive rock single "Hush," one of the tracks on their debut album, *Shades of Deep Purple* (June 1968). "Hush" never made it to the U. K. pop charts but rose to the Top Five the United States. Their second album *The Book of Taliesyn* (October 1968) was among the Top 20 albums in the United States.

After surviving a series of line-up changes, Deep Purple made a mid-career shift to ear-shattering heavy metal with their 1969 album *Deep Purple*. The group is considered a pioneer in that genre. *Guinness Book of World Records* bestowed Deep Purple with the distinction of "the globe's loudest band."

Deep Purple's ambitions continued to grow. They recruited singer Ian Gillian and Bassist Roger Glover from the group Episode Six. The revamped band's first album, 1970's *Concerto for Group and Orchestra,* recorded with the Royal Philharmonic Orchestra, sought to fuse rock and classical. But the album was poorly received, so guitarist Ritchie Blackmore steered the group in a different direction, which proved to be Deep Purple's most creative and commercially successful period.

As with other groups, internal creative tensions took their toll, and Deep Purple had additional personnel changes. Following a farewell trip in 1976, the group dissolved. But in 1984, the core members reunited for a new album, *Perfect Strangers,* which went platinum. *House of Blue Light* followed in 1987.

More tension arose, creating a revolving-door line-up in the late 1980s and 1990s. Despite all the upheavals, Deep Purple entered the twenty-first century alive and well.

The Moody Blues in an early publicity photo, 1968

Moody Blues

Since the release of their first full studio album, *Days of Future Past,* in October 1967, the British group Moody Blues has been a mainstay in the music industry, selling more than 55 million albums. Considered a concept album, *Days* featured the rock classics "Tuesday Afternoon" and "Knights in White Satin." Their second album (August 1968), *In Search of the Lost Chord,* included the hit singles "Ride My See-Saw" and "Voices in the Sky." Riding on that success, the Moody Blues set out on their first concert tour of the United States. Their devoted fan base continues to this day.

The Moody Blues had their period of greatest success in the early '70s, culminating in two albums in 1971, *Every Good Boy Deserves Favour* (including the hit "The Story in Your Eyes") and *Seventh Sojourn,* which held the number-one spot on the U.S. charts for five consecutive weeks, and featured the hits "I'm Just a Singer in a Rock and Roll Band" and "Isn't Life Strange?" After that, the individual members pursued solo projects, not reuniting until 1978. They had their greatest success in their reunited form in the mid-'80s, notably with 1986's major pop hit "Your Wildest Dreams." The group has continued to record and tour, sometimes performing with major symphony orchestras, such as the Night at Red Rock concert, first released as a CD in 1992 and then later as a multi-disc DVD/CD package, which was recorded with the Colorado Symphony Orchestra.

The Moody Blues has received multiple top honors both in the U.K. and the United States. The group has ensured its place in classic rock history.

Led Zeppelin

After the British group The Yardbirds broke up, members of the band reassembled as The New Yardbirds. They began performing under the name Led Zeppelin in an October 1968 concert at Surrey University. Later that month the group recorded their first album, *Led Zeppelin,* which was panned by *Rolling Stone.*

Robert Plant and Jimmy Page of Led Zeppelin
© Ross Halfin / Idols

But the group believed in themselves and embarked on a U.S. tour, starting in San Francisco. Their marketing plan was to impress the audience at Fillmore West (at the time, one of the most important rock halls) and build from there. It worked; by the time Led Zeppelin arrived in New York, their debut album was in the Top Ten and stayed there for more than a year.

Between 1969 and 1971, the group recorded *Led Zeppelin II, III,* and their best-selling and most famous, *Led Zeppelin IV* (also known as *Zoso*), which featured the most-played track in radio history, "Stairway to Heaven." Their fifth album, *Houses of the Holy* (1973), debuted at number one in both the United States and England.

Lead singer Robert Plant's automobile accident delayed the sixth album, *Presence.* It was released in 1974, the same year Led Zeppelin formed their own label, Swan Song. Their last three albums were released under that label. The future looked promising, but the death of drummer John Bonham ended the band abruptly. Jimmy Page and Robert Plant have reunited occassionally to tour and record, but the band's glory days are long past.

Led Zeppelin's innovative music combined rock, blues, and folk into a timeless sound with broad appeal. Their work has influenced many rock groups over the past three decades.

The Great American Rock Bands (1960s and 1970s)

Creedence Clearwater Revival

Although their music shared characteristics of Southern gospel-blues bayou music, the members of Creedence Clearwater came from a small town near Berkeley, California. Their sound, later referred to as "garage band rock," evolved in the late 1950s when brothers Tom and John Fogerty, Doug Clifford, and Stu Cook began playing together as Tommy Fogerty and the Blue Velvets.

Creedence Clearwater Revival, c. 1969

Coinciding with the "British Invasion" in 1964, the band auditioned for a small label, Fantasy Records, where John had been a warehouse employee. To capitalize on the British trend, an executive at Fantasy changed their name to the Golliwogs. But the seven singles the Golliwogs recorded for Fantasy went unnoticed. The last of the singles, "Porterville," was released under the new name, Creedence Clearwater Revival, probably chosen to reflect the band's interest in pollution issues.

With their debut album in 1967, John Fogerty emerged as the dominant member of Creedence Clearwater as guitarist, lead singer, songwriter, and producer. In fact, his raw-edged voice *was* the CCR sound. The rockabilly classic "Suzie Q" was their first hit.

Between 1968 and 1971 the band churned out six powerful rock albums: *Creedence Clearwater Revival, Bayou Country, Green River, Willie and the Poorboys, Cosmo's Factory,* and *Pendulum.* Eight of their singles earned gold records, and nine made the Top Ten, including "Proud Mary," Fortunate Son," and "Bad Moon Rising." "Fortunate Son" and "Who'll Stop the Rain" reflected the emotions of the anti-Vietnam War protests. The songs became anthems and were used in films that recreated the era, including *Born on the 4th of July* and *The Big Chill.* (The title song of John Fogerty's 2004 album *Déjà Vu* decries the human toll of the Iraq War.)

Despite the band's tremendous popularity, internal tensions were surfacing. Band members resented John's dominance and wanted more say in band decisions. When Tom left in February 1971 to work as a solo artist, CCR continued as a trio. But the reception to their world tour was disappointing. In October 1972, Creedence Clearwater Revival officially disbanded.

In 1993, Creedence Clearwater Revival was nominated into the Rock and Roll Hall of Fame. John Fogerty returned to active performing with the successful 1985 album *Centerfield,* and has continued to tour and record was inducted into the Songwriters Hall of Fame.

Jefferson Airplane (Later, Jefferson Starship)

California, particularly San Francisco, spawned a number of rock bands during the mid- to late-1960s. Jefferson Airplane, formed in August 1965, is regarded as the most successful of that era. Despite name changes, the group rose to popularity by playing benefits and local gigs at the Fillmore Auditorium and Carousel Ballroom, and Jefferson Airplane became one of the first rock bands to sign a major recording contract with RCA. By the end of the year, they were working on their first album.

The debut of *Jefferson Airplane Takes Off* was moderately successful. This was followed by the first two personnel changes. In October 1966 Grace Slick (born Grace Barnett Wing) joined the Airplane and brought two of the songs from her former group, The Great Society: "White Rabbit" and "Somebody To Love" were tracks on Jefferson Airplane's second album, *Surrealistic Pillow*. Both songs became Top Ten hits and have achieved status as definitive songs of the era.

Over a period of thirty-five years, the band performed more than 700 concerts in sixteen countries. In 1996, Jefferson Airplane was inducted into the Rock and Roll Hall of Fame.

Grateful Dead

Founded by Jerry Garcia in San Francisco in 1965, the Dead had a career spanning thirty years. The band's earliest roots sprouted in 1960, when Garcia met Robert

The Grateful Dead, c. 1978

Hunter, later to become the group's primary lyricist. The Grateful Dead evolved in 1964 from Mother McCree's Uptown Jug Champions, playing mainly folk and bluegrass, with Garcia on banjo and guitar, Bob Weir on guitar, and Ron "Pigpen" McKernan on keyboards.

In 1965 the band had a few name changes, included The Warlocks and The Acid Tests. By the end of that year, the name The Grateful Dead stuck. The band was living in a communal house at 710 Ashbury Street (in San Francisco's Haight-Ashbury District). Through their free concerts, the Dead was becoming one of the leaders of the growing hippie movement in San Francisco.

Although their 1966 contract with MGM Records was a disaster, ending in their being dropped, the Dead became a top draw at the Fillmore and other venues during the 1967 Summer of Love. That same year, their debut album for Warner Brothers was released, but not well received. The Grateful Dead realized that live shows were their forte, and studio work was their downfall. Although their second album, *Anthem of the Sun,* had a better reception, it wasn't until late 1969 that they had their first great "live" album, *Live Dead.* The 23-minute track "Dark Star" set the pace, with outstanding playing by Garcia and the rest of the band.

The Grateful Dead released a succession of albums in the 1970s, including *American Beauty* and *Workingman's Dead* (1970), the double album *The Grateful Dead* (1971), the triple album *Europe '72* (1972, the final album to feature "Pigpen"), *Terrapin Station* (1977), and *Shakedown Street* (1978).

By 1972 the Dead's music was getting plenty of radio airtime, and their fan base, Deadheads, spread across the country. But their 1980 album *Go To Heaven* disappointed their fans, and most of the 1980s was difficult for the band. Jerry Garcia was struggling with heroin addiction, and after the 1981 release of their live album *Dead Set,* they did not cut another album for six years. Their 1989 *Dylan and the Dead* featured songs by Bob Dylan exclusively. *Built to Last,* released the same year, received poor reviews and would be their final studio album.

The band released a couple of albums in the early 1990s, but Garcia was hospitalized in 1992 for diabetes and an enlarged heart. With his death in 1995, the Grateful Dead came to an end. To Deadheads all over the world, Jerry Garcia's passing was almost as significant as the breakup of The Beatles in 1970.

The Mamas and the Papas

Although the Mamas and the Papas—John Phillips, Denny Doherty, Cass Elliot, and Michelle Phillips—were a close-harmony singing group rather than a band, we include them in this section because of their lasting imprint both on the pop-music world and on the consciousness of their era. Their collaboration during the late 1960s as a group was relatively short, yet they came to symbolize the pop-group movement that swept Southern California.

The song "Creeque Alley" indirectly tells how the Mamas and the Papas came together. John Phillips was a member of The Journeymen when he met Michelle, who started singing with his group and became his second wife. Denny Doherty left The Halifax Three to join a group called Cass Elliot and the Big Three. The group changed its name to The Mugwumps, cut one album (eventually released in 1967), and broke up. Elliot went on to front a jazz trio, and Denny joined John and Michelle as The New Journeymen. When they moved to California, they stayed with Cass Elliot and her then-husband, Jim Hendricks. Soon, Cass officially joined the group, renamed the Mamas and the Papas. The quartet sang backup studio session vocals for Barrie McGuire before landing their own contract.

John Phillips wrote and arranged most of the material for the Mamas and the Papas. Their first album, *If You Can't Believe Your Eyes and Ears,* contains "California Dreamin'," considered the definitive West Coast vocal song. The hits kept coming: "Monday, Monday," "Dedicated to the One I Love," "Look Through your Window," "I Call Your Name," "Dream a Little Dream of Me," "Go Where You Wanna Go," 'Words of Love," "Dancin' in the Street," "Twelve-Thirty," and "Creeque Alley." John's song "San Francisco" (Be Sure to Wear Some Flowers in Your Hair) became an anthem of the flower-child era in California.

By the time the Mamas and the Papas appeared at the 1967 Monterey Pop Festival, they had reached the top, professionally and financially. But the following year, the Mamas and the Papas decided to disband.

Cass Elliot embarked on a successful solo career, recording a number of hits, making numerous television appearances, guest-hosting *The Tonight Show,* headlining in Las Vegas, performing internationally, and hosting two prime time television specials of her own. She died at the age of 33 at the top of her game. Following a performance for an adoring, sold-out audience in London's Palladium on July 29, 1974, Cass suffered a fatal heart attack. After John and Michelle divorced, Michelle began an acting career.

In 1982 John re-formed the Mamas and the Papas with founding member Denny Doherty and two new Mamas: John's daughter Mackenzie and Elaine "Spanky" McFarlane, who had sung with Spanky and Our Gang in the '60s. With various personnel changes, the group continued performing into the mid-'90s. Phillips died *in 2001.*

The Mamas and the Papas will be remembered for their timeless melodies, excellent arrangements, and sweet harmonies. In 1998, they were inducted into the Rock and Roll Hall of Fame. Cass Elliot's daughter accepted the award for her mother.

Who Else Has Been Influential?

This timeline of selected milestones may provide some answers. Certain years are intentionally omitted.

1950	Muddy Waters cuts *Rollin' Stone*—the "official" birth of rhythm and blues.
1951	Ike Turner's *Rocket 88* is released. It is considered the first rock and roll record.
1952	Gibson manufactures Les Paul's solid body guitar.
1953	Bill Haley's "Crazy Man, Crazy" is the first rock song to hit the Billboard charts.
1954	Haley's "Rock Around the Clock" is the first rock song used in a movie soundtrack.
1955	Ray Charles is credited with "inventing" soul.
1956	Wanda Jackson is "queen of rockabilly," just as Elvis-mania begins.
1957	Teen idols like Buddy Holly, Paul Anka, Fabian, and Frankie Avalon rise to popularity.
1958	Bobby Freeman's "Do You Want to Dance" starts the dance craze.
1959	The Drifters' "There Goes My Baby" introduces Latin rhythm into pop music.
1960	Everyone is doing the Twist. (Two years later, the bishop of New York forbids Catholic students to dance the Twist.)
1961	The Beach Boys launch surf music; The Shirelles release "Dedicated to the One I Love."
1963	Guitarist Eric Clapton joins the Yardbirds. A year later, the group is using guitars to produce feedback and distortion.

Woodstock rock festival in upstate New York, August 1969

1965   James Brown is credited with inventing "funk." The Righteous Brothers launch "blue-eyed soul." The Who creates a form of rebellious rock with *My Generation*.

1966   San Francisco becomes the center of "acid rock," thanks in part to Jefferson Airplane and The Grateful Dead. Frank Zappa's *Freak Out* is the first double rock and roll album. The Cream sells a million albums of improvised rock (jams).

1967   The Doors fuse rock, blues, free-form rambling, and Indian raga. Jimi Hendrix stretches the limits of the electric guitar. Pink Floyd invents space-rock.

1968   The first rock musical, *Hair,* opens on Broadway. Gram Parsons records country-rock. Van Morrison introduces abstract, free-form folk-rock.

1969   300,000 people attend the Woodstock Festival. The Who releases the concept album for the rock opera *Tommy*. Led Zeppelin plays hard-rock; King Crimson plays progressive-rock. The world's music market is now worth over $2 billion.

The 1970s were a period of fusion rather than innovation. Blending ingredients from several sources of gospel and rhythm and clues, rock musicians produced country-folk rock, alternative rock (Frank Zappa), traditional pop-rock (Bruce Springsteen, Neil Young), punk-rock, and disco-rock.

Funk, another fusion genre, was developed from gospel and Motown soul music. James Brown became known as the Godfather of Soul and the Father of Funk. Brown blended soul music with his own intensity and produced a driving, thumping form of dance music that eventually evolved into disco.

1970   British jazz-rock hits a peak. ZZ Top and the Allman Brothers introduce "Southern-rock." Smokey Robinson fuses vaudeville, classical music, and soul in *Tears of a Clown*.

1971   Andrew Lloyd Webber and Tim Rice's rock musical *Jesus Christ Superstar* opens on Broadway. The show's soundtrack is an immediate success. Alice Cooper mixes various genres and comes out with shock-rock. Marvin Gaye, Isaac Hayes, Curtis Mayfield, and Stevie Wonder cut artful soul recordings.

1974   The Grateful Dead, called the most successful band of all time, uses 25 tons of loudspeakers for their live performances.

1975   New York disc jockey Clive "Hercules" Campbell reinvents the breakbeat as "rap" and "hip-hop." The film *Tommy* is released, starring Roger Daltrey in the title role and featuring Elton John as the Pinball Wizard.

1977   The Bee Gees and the film *Saturday Night Fever* spur the disco craze.

1979   Six record companies control 70 percent of a $10 billion a year market.

The 1980s gave us techno-dance music, disco (ABBA), disco-punk, and punk-rock (Sex Pistols, Ramones). Variations of punk-rock evolved into grunge (Nirvana, Pearl Jam) and hard rock (Soundgarden). In England, psychedelic music was popular. Hip-hop emerged.

| 1980 | Sugar Hill Gang cuts "Rapper's Delight," the first hip-hop record. |
| 1983 | Michael Jackson's *Thriller* soars to #1, stays there for thirty-seven weeks, and becomes the best-selling album ever. |

During the 1990s, the popularity of hip-hop was on the rise. Gangsta rap was born in Los Angeles. There was renewed interest in melodic Britpop (U2), and in the fusion of funk, rap, and heavy-metal. In 1996 the rock musical *Rent* opened on Broadway, starring the rock musician Adam Pascal. Pascal went on to star in the film and another hit musical, *Aida*. By the end of the decade, the five "majors" controlled ninety-five percent of the world's $40 billion market.

Iceland entered the field with avant-garde rock (Sigur Rós, Björk) in the twenty-first century. Acid jazz developed from several influences, including soul, R&B, and jazz. Heavy Metal groups such as Aerosmith, Metallica, Guns N' Roses, and Marilyn Manson became more abstract and intellectual. Melodies and rhythms were no longer predictable, and lyrics were often difficult to understand. Serious-music critics held their noses.

In 2001 record sales slipped 5 percent, their first decline since the Depression. Online music downloading site, Napster, was found guilty of breaching copyright laws. Record sales continued to drop through mid-decade.

Rock and Roll Hall of Fame

The year-by-year roster of inductees into the Rock and Roll Hall of Fame is a history resource in itself. You can research the Rock and Roll Hall of Fame website at http://www.rockhall.com.

What is "Indie Rock"?

That's hard to say. Since independent rock was originally a backlash from the major label, mainstream, expensively produced rock music industry, indie calls itself "different." Distinguishing it from the mainstream is often an attempt to explain

The Rock and Roll Hall of Fame

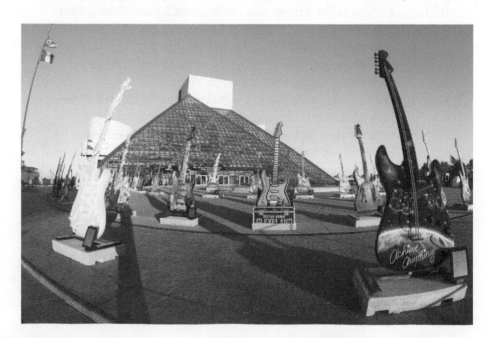

what indie rock *isn't*. Today, the trend might be a newly conceptualized, edgier version of a 1970s acoustic guitar rock classic. Tomorrow, a symphony of synthesizers might qualify. Stay tuned. To do your own research, some indie labels include Merge, Lookout, Alternative Tentacles, K Records, Thrill Jockey, and Touch and Go.

Followers of the movement claim that The Velvet Underground planted indie's roots in the 1960s when the group incorporated punk and new wave into traditional rock. Once punk became mainstream in the 1970s, post-punk bands such as Elvis Costello and Talking Heads emerged. Toward the end of the 1980s, Nirvana gained loyalists for their "alternative" rock. Once Nirvana achieved widespread airplay, the group was considered mainstream. The only historical consistency: indie rock *is* fickle.

Who's New, Who's Not

New groups and artists are constantly enter and leave the limelight. Some are discovered for the first time. Some re-emerge after a dormant career, expanding an already-loyal following. We mention a few of the lesser-known, not as advocates but to illustrate the diversity of the pop music world.

Scissor Sisters, a flamboyant nightclub group, is winning fans in the United States and the U.K. Some of their recorded music harkens back to Elton John, Pink Floyd, and Bee Gees Disco.

Kraftwerk—Ralf Hütter and Florian Schneider Esleben—began recording in Germany in the late 1960s. Calling it Robot Pop, they achieved their goal of pushing the limits of electronic music. Some refer to their recordings as sci-fi, techno-disco, or cybernetic rock.

As an 11-year-old, **Björk** made her first recording of her native Icelandic folk songs. The album also included covers of several pop standards by the Beatles. Her subsequent albums were recognized for their tireless musical invention and personal lyrics. Björk sang her Oscar-nominated song, "I've Seen It All," at the 2001 Award ceremonies.

Country Music

In the Beginning

The first settlers brought their music to the New World in the seventeenth century. Some of the songs dealt with love and love that had gone bad. Others related historical events or had supernatural themes. Eventually, the people replaced English or European folk tales with lyrics that expressed the isolation and hardships of life in the Appalachian Mountains and the Old West.

Singing was accompanied by hand-clapping and a crude, easily made violin—the "fiddle." In the mid-1800s, the banjo, brought to the South by slaves, became popular. Musicians soon organized groups of players, combining the fiddle and banjo with a mandolin, guitar, and autoharp to create the "string band." At the turn of the century, guitars became an important instrument when mass production made them more affordable. Later, country music incorporated other instruments: homemade rhythm devices such as the washboard, the accordion, the harmonica, and by the 1930s, the piano.

Jimmie Rodgers

Populist Entertainment

During the same period that minstrel troupes were traveling to cities, "medicine shows" featuring comedy, music, and dance began to criss-cross America, bringing entertainment to isolated regions of the South. Singers treated audiences to a variety of Americana: "Buffalo Gals," "Turkey in the Straw," "Jimmy Crack Corn," and, "Blue Tail Fly."

By the 1890s, string bands were touring the rural South, playing *mountain music*. In the 1920s, the style was renamed *hillbilly* and could be heard on radio "barn dance" shows. Southern musicians were now encouraged to write and perform their music professionally. Once country music caught the attention of the music industry, its popularity burgeoned. Today it boasts some of the highest-grossing albums in pop music.

Modern Country Music

Both radio and records expanded the audience. August 1, 1927, is cited as the date that changed country music history, when pioneers of the genre, The Carter Family and Jimmie Rodgers, signed contracts with Victor Records. Rodgers eventually became the first inductee (1961) into the Country Music Hall of Fame. The Original Carter Family received the honor in 1970.

In the 1930s, Bill Monroe and the team of Flatt and Scruggs were the leading exponents of *bluegrass*. The 1939 move of "Grand Ol' Opry" to Nashville was another milestone. The radio show gave wider exposure to its stars, who received national recognition. One of those stars, Roy Acuff, was later dubbed the "King of Country Music." The "Queen" was Kitty Wells.

Texas was the breeding ground for "singing cowboys" Gene Autry, Roy Rogers and Dale Evans, and the Sons of the Pioneers. They gave country music a *western sound*. Eventually, these performers moved on to Hollywood, starring in dozens of shoot-'em-up films that usually ended with a long shot of the hero riding off into the sunset, singing a song. "Happy Trails to You" was Rogers' signature song. Texas also spawned jazz-influenced *western swing*, played by groups such as Bob Wills and the Texas Playboys.

"Down-Home Eclectic"

Combining elements of early country with jazz, blues, and gospel, *Honkytonk* echoed through the music industry. The new sound first appeared toward the end of the Depression, and rose to preeminence in the 1940s with the popularity of Ernest Tubbs, Eddie Arnold, Minnie Pearl, Lefty Frizzell, and Hank Williams. Sales of Tubbs' recording "Walking the Floor Over You" topped one million. Williams hit his stride toward the end of the decade and into the early 1950s. He recorded over 100 songs, including "Your Cheatin' Heart" and the prophetic "I'll Never Get Out of This World Alive."

The 1950s gave us a fusion of hillbilly and blues called *rockabilly* and dozens of great performers, including Johnny Cash, Roy Orbison, Marty Robbins, and Charlie Rich. A rock beat was added by Jerry Lee Lewis ("Great Balls of Fire"), the Everly Brothers, and of course Elvis. By the end of the decade, the sound of country was significantly changing to the *Nashville Sound* of male singers Owen Bradley and Chet Atkins and female vocalists Tammy Wynette, Loretta Lynn, Brenda Lee, and Patsy Cline, to name a few.

Contemporary country was the genre of the 1970s. Full orchestras backed up singers, and synthesizers, studio effects, and over-dubbing enhanced recordings. Waylon Jennings and fellow "outlaw" Willie Nelson hit the charts. Kris Kristofferson parlayed his success into a film career. Singers Anne Murray and Charlie Pride nudged the country-pop crossover, and in the 1980s, capitalizing on the success of *Urban Cowboy,* singers such as Kenny Rogers and Dolly Parton continued the trend. Other performers helped to bring country music into the mainstream—Dwight Yoakam, Trisha Yearwood, and Wynonna to name a few.

In the late twentieth century, country broke into the global market by incorporating elements of rock. Today, with all areas of pop music fostering a certain "look" and "attitude," it's hard to distinguish today's platinum-record country artists Shania Twain and Faith Hill from the rock stars of their generation.

Recent Country Idols

Garth Brooks raised the bar for country music stardom. His 1989 debut album produced four Top 10 hits, and by the following year, he was headed to superstardom. With album sales of 105 million, Garth broke all previous records. "I feel country music is taking on a new role, taking on responsibility," he said, "We have to consider what we sing because more and more people are listening to country music."

Garth Brooks, c. 1995

Before Garth Brook's concerts, local papers often devoted front-page spreads and a series of articles to announce his arrival. Entertainment reporters followed him to document his every move. But Garth saw there was more to life than being a country music legend. He also had a personal life, and he decided to focus on his family. His final album was released in 2001, after he had announced his retirement.

"What do I want people to remember me by?" he said to an interviewer. "To say the man was real, that there was some of me in him."

Carrying on the black-cowboy-hat tradition, **Tim McGraw** has chalked up one hit album after another since his first release in 1992, *Welcome to the Club.* After the release of *Tim McGraw & the Dancehall Doctors,* he had his first network television special in November 2002. McGraw has also chalked up many honors and awards, starting with "Male Star of Tomorrow" in 1992 from Music City News to "Favorite Male Artist" at the 2003 American Music Awards. He has also had major hit duets with his wife, country diva, Faith Hill.

Country Music Association

Founded in 1958, the Country Music Association (CMA) was the first trade organization created to promote a specific genre of music. The CMA Awards, which predate the Grammys and American Music Awards, began television broadcasts in 1968. The Country Music Hall of Fame honors performers, promoters, leaders in music publishing and recording, broadcasters, and others in the music industry. For a list of honorees since its inception, you can access the website http://www.countrymusichalloffame.com.

Shania Twain emerged as a major country hitmaker in the early '90s, working in conjunction with producer "Mutt" Lange, who had previously produced mainstream rock acts. The two collaborated on her breakthrough second album, the

Shania Twain, 1998

enormously successful *The Woman in Me* released in 1995. The album produced several country and pop hits, including "Whose Bed Have Your Boots Been Under," "Any Man of Mine," and "(If You're Not in it for Love) I'm Out of Here." It eventually went platinum nine times, and remained on the charts for nearly 200 weeks.

Twain and Lange returned with 1997's *Come On Over.* It was a monster seller, producing many top hits, including the big ballads "You're Still the One" and "From This Moment" (both top adult contemporary hits as well as country sellers), to the spunky "That Don't Impress Me Much," "Don't Be Stupid," and "Man! I Feel Like A Woman." The album has broken all records, becoming by *Billboard's* estimation the best-selling recording by a female artist of all time, in *any* genre.

After a break to have a child in 2001, Twain returned in late 2002 with the album *Up.* In an unusual move, the CD was released in three versions; American buyers received two CDs, one mixed for the country market, the other for pop; Europeans received a unique mix of their own, plus the pop mix. The album's first single, "I'm Gonna Getcha," was an immediate #1 hit on country and pop charts. It was followed by more top hits, including "Forever and For Always" and "She's Not Just A Pretty Face." In 2004, Twain issued a *Greatest Hits* set, which—not surprisingly—entered *Billboard's* charts at #1 country and #2 in the top 200 (pop) listings.

Making and Marketing Popular Music in the Twenty-First Century

At one time, the ability to make and distribute music was exclusive to record companies and music publishers. Only professionals had the resources to acquire a stable of talent, lay down tracks, manufacture and package music media, command retail shelf space, and capture the airwaves. Today, by applying the software tools bundled into any new PC or Mac, and accessing any one of hundreds of online sites, users can not only share music but also make their own.

For example, Apple's "Garageband" allows an aspiring musician to become a recording studio, a record label, and a music marketing machine. Napster, iPod, MP3, Grokster, and other technologies have simplified the process of peer-to-peer file sharing. Record companies have not yet found a way to stop piracy without criminalizing technology. Chris Anderson, editor-in-chief of *Wired,* devotes an entire book to the shift from mass markets to niche markets.

Outlets for Promotion and Publicity

Changes occur so rapidly in pop music that print media cannot keep pace with the Internet in disseminating information. Before a publication hits the newsstands, the album du jour might have become passé. Concert promoters, radio programmers, industry executives, and dedicated downloaders now consult Internet Web magazines or webzines to stay in the know. These sites not only chronicle current trends and review new releases, they also predict what is *about to happen.*

Like the music industry itself, changes occur too quickly on the Internet to document here. Devotees can find thousands of sites posted by famous as well as unheard-of artists, passionate fan groups, obscure record labels, and aspiring webzines such as epitonic.com and dustedmagazine.com. But the sites may be gone tomorrow or replaced by new ones. Or their coverage may adjust to satisfy the traffic they generate.

Rollingstone.com, posted by the well-respected publication of the same name, is a virtual encyclopedia and remains a reliable source for the pop mainstream. Webzines such as pitchforkmedia.com have become influential as the day-to-day, week-to-week, month-to-month cultural barometers of indie rock.

27
Broadway Musical Theater

Broadway musicals embody the concept of globalism. Some shows have traveled around the world continuously since their inception. Because their themes and scores have universal appeal, musicals can be translated into various languages without sacrificing the creator's intent.

Besides love, musicals can touch on any subject: revolution, the aftereffects of war, AIDS, drug abuse, unemployment, dementia, rape, miscegenation, poverty, homelessness, cannibalism, suicide, magic and wizardry, gender issues, slavery, gambling, pogroms, prostitution, turf wars of street gangs, insanity, and man-eating plants. One often-used theme is about producing a musical. *The Producers* (2001), a musical about producing a bad musical, won eight Tony awards. *Curtains* premiered in Los Angeles in 2006.

Successful musicals are considered standard repertoire. If a show was a smash hit in Los Angeles, London, or on Broadway, you'll probably be able to see it more than once—and perhaps take your children or grandchildren. Once a show becomes part of the standard repertoire, the script might be reworked or updated, but the central theme and characters remain.

The Broadway Musical: Its Roots

European Predecessors of the Broadway Musical

Ballad opera

Ballad Opera   Starting in the first half of the eighteenth century, ballad opera differed from other opera mainly by having spoken dialogue instead of the recitative between songs. Also, much of the music was from popular tunes and folk songs of the day, to which composers set new lyrics. Most ballad operas contained simple melodies with uncomplicated harmonies, designed to appeal to middle-class audiences. Similar to Greek tragedy, plots were based on familiar material.

In England, the most popular work of the eighteenth century was John Gay's *The Beggar's Opera* (1728). Included in the repertoire of every touring company at that time, the work satirized Italian opera—especially works by Handel—the aristocracy, the British government, and its then-prime minister, Robert Walpole. Using English for its language, *The Beggar's Opera* presented an alternative to Italian, which had been the dominant opera language. With its strong book, *The Beggar's Opera* set the standard for the form and style of musical productions that followed: The book comes first.

Exactly 200 years later, the German-born composer Kurt Weill (1900–1950) wrote his popular *Dreigroschen Opera* (*The Three Penny Opera*, 1928), a modern-setting imitation of *The Beggar's Opera*.

The year 1735 marked the production of *Flora*, the first ballad opera farce staged in North America. Without scenery, costumes, or footlights, the show played in the Charleston, South Carolina, courthouse to only the handful of people who could fit into the room.

Singspiel

Mozart took inspiration from the English ballad operas and wrote his delightful *Abduction from the Harem* in 1782 for the German *singspiel*, employing the German language.

Comic opera

Comic Opera   From the French, Italian, and English repertory, comic opera resembled the French *opéra bouffe* and the German operetta. In the United States, the comic opera incorporated the English emphasis on comedy over romance.

Mozart had a special flair for comic opera. His witty and charming *Le nozze di Figaro* (*The Marriage of Figaro*, 1786), *Don Giovanni* (1787), and *Cositan Tuttle* (1790) are three of his most often performed comic operas.

Operetta

Operetta   Originating in Germany and the Austro-Hungarian Empire, the operetta incorporated every aspect of the late-nineteenth-century romanticism: love, idealism, adventure, and bravery. Wrapped in a trivial plot combined with appealing music and graceful dance, life in operettas was a delightful fantasy.

North American Roots of the Musical

African-American influences

African-American music has been a part of North American culture since the arrival of the first slave boats. Slaves preserved their customs and culture by dancing, chanting, story-telling in pantomime, and playing instruments such as the banjo and drums. Although some plantation owners objected, most did not. Still others recognized the entertainment value for their guests and organized "minstrel shows" featuring syncopated song-and-dance performances, including a "cakewalk" competition in which the highest-strutting dancers would "take the cake."

Sheet music cover for collection of songs by James Bland

Minstrelsy

As early as the 1840s, former slaves presented their unique entertainment professionally. Minstrel shows of the nineteenth century were the first musical theater that originated in America. By the 1870s, these shows had become so popular that white entertainers formed their own touring minstrel companies. Wearing gaudy costumes and blackening their faces with burnt cork, the white troupes imitated the originals.

With the performers sitting in a semicircle facing the audience, the typical show had three parts:

Part 1 featured jokes and solo songs backed by the humming of the other performers.

Part 2 was similar to vaudeville and featured whatever diverse talents the minstrel performers possessed—juggling, dancing, magic, and the like.

Part 3 was usually a parody of a play or an opera. Most often it took the form of a sentimental operetta based on idealized plantation life.

North American composers—African-American and white—viewed minstrel shows as a marketplace for their original songs. They were right. When audiences liked the songs, they would buy the sheet music. Some composers became famous: **Dan Emmett** (1815–1904), **Stephen Foster** (1826–1864), and **James A. Bland** (1854–1911). "Dixie" was the best-known minstrel song. Written originally for banjo by **Dan Emmett,** the song later acquired new lyrics and became the battle anthem of the Confederacy.

Minstrelsy

Dan Emmett

Stephen Foster

James A. Bland

STEPHEN COLLINS FOSTER (1826–1864)

Early America's most popular composer, Stephen Collins Foster, was born near Pittsburgh, Pennsylvania, on July 4, 1826, the fiftieth anniversary of the signing of the Declaration of Independence. Educated and well-to-do, Stephen's parents provided music instruction for all their children throughout their formative years. In fact, music was the primary focus in the life of Stephen's oldest sister Charlotte, an accomplished pianist, harpist, and singer. At an early age, Stephen also showed both an interest and a talent for music. His sister Henrietta taught him chords on the guitar. He learned to play both the piano and flute, and was soon able to pick out melodies on these instruments.

Stephen was educated in a succession of private schools and studied with one of Pittsburgh's finest musicians, Henry Kleber, who exposed his eager young student to the masters, particularly Mozart, Beethoven, and Weber. Trained in music conservatories in Germany, Kleber also performed as a tenor soloist and pianist. He organized and conducted a wind band and composed popular dances.

Foster joined a neighborhood minstrel group. Performing what were then called "Ethiopian songs," they created a makeshift theater out of a carriage house. Most of their songs were written and often performed by African Americans, many of whom were still slaves.

In 1845, Foster began composing Ethiopian songs for a group of men who met twice a week at his house in Pittsburgh. Calling themselves Knights of the Square Table, the group practiced Foster's multi-part harmony, accompanied by piano, guitar, flute, and violin. Foster promoted his songs to other groups and soon became one of the leading composers of minstrel songs. He was renowned for the finely crafted harmony of the chorus, which the entire minstrel troupe performed.

Foster was only eighteen when his first known ballad, "Open Thy Lattice, Love," was published. In 1849, he signed an agreement with New York music publisher Firth, Pond & Company, and at about the same time, he signed a similar contract with F. D. Benteen in Baltimore.

People were eager to buy the sheet music so they could sing and play Foster's songs at home.

Since most composers sold their songs outright, Foster's contracts set a precedent by guaranteeing him royalties of two cents for each copy of sheet music sold. Some of his songs, such as the quick-tempo "Camptown Races," became show stoppers for African-American minstrel singers.

In addition to the more than 200 works for minstrel shows, Foster was known for his "plantation songs," such as "Old Folks at Home" (1851), "Old Black Joe," and "My Old Kentucky Home" (1853). His popular ballads include "Jeanie With the Light Brown Hair" (1854) and "Come Where My Love Lies Dreaming" (1855). "Jeanie With the Light Brown Hair" was inspired by Foster's Irish background: His great-grandfather had emigrated from Londonderry, Ireland, around 1728.

During his four-year contract with E. J. Christy, Foster conducted all his work by mail. He neither met the famous Original Christy Minstrels nor watched them perform until years later. Because the printed sheet music did not mention Foster's name, some of his most enduring songs, such as "Oh! Susanna" (1848), were initially associated with E. J. Christy. When Firth and Benteen reissued the sheet music, Foster was credited for his earlier songs.

In the two years that followed (1850 and 1851), Foster published fifteen songs with Firth and fifteen songs with Benteen. His income from royalties allowed him to compose full time. As North America's most successful songwriter of his day, he himself set his earnings at more than $15,000 during his fifteen-year career—in today's terms, approximately $1 million. However, he was plagued by alcoholism, outspent his income, and was constantly in debt. By 1857, he had taken advances on future royalties and had to sell his last works outright. In 1860, he moved to New York and began churning out songs just to earn a few dollars. "Beautiful Dreamer" (1864), written in his final days, was published posthumously. Stephen Foster died in a New York charity ward at age 38.

African-American Minstrels

Perhaps the most important of the Negro writers and entertainers who joined minstrel troupes after the Civil War was **James A. Bland** (1854–1911). A well-educated man born in the North, Bland was the son of one of the first African-Americans in the United States to receive a college education. Bland started as an entertainer, but he is best remembered for the songs "Carry me Back to Old Virginny," "In the Evening by the Moonlight," and "Oh, Dem Golden Slippers." Unfortunately, all but thirty-eight of his songs have been lost.

From Minstrelsy to Vaudeville

Toward the end of the nineteenth century, traditional black-face minstrel shows declined in popularity, and many African-American entertainers moved into vaudeville. After the success of the syncopated song "All Coons Look Alike to Me" (1890, Ernest Hogan), a new term emerged: "coon songs." These racially stereo-typed songs were performed by black entertainers in white vaudeville.

Eventually, black entertainers decided to try something they called "all-Negro productions." Since African-American producers did not have access to theaters on the white vaudeville circuit, they presented some of their earliest musicals in burlesque houses. In 1896, an all-Negro show called *Oriental America* had a short Broadway run and attracted multiracial audiences. It was now clear that white theatergoers were willing to pay money to see black performers in all kinds of shows. Although Broadway did not easily open to African-American artists and producers, they slowly overcame the odds and arrived on Broadway to stay.

Will Marion Cook (1869–1944) studied at Oberlin Conservatory and became a distinguished composer, conductor, and violinist. After graduation, he pursued advanced studies in Europe and later returned to New York to study composition with Antonin Dvořák.

Will Marion Cook

In 1898, Cook composed music to lyrics by African-American poet **Paul Laurence Dunbar.** The result was a musical comedy sketch, *Clorindy, or the Origin of the Cakewalk,* which was produced at the Roof Garden of Broadway's Casino Theatre. His first hit, *In Dahomey* (1902), was the first African-American musical to play in a major Broadway theater, followed by a European tour. The extravaganza *In Abyssinia* (1906) and the musical comedy *In Bandana Land* (1907) established Cook as a major force in African-American theater.

Robert Cole (1863–1911) came to New York after his graduation from Atlanta University. He became a playwright and manager of the All-Star Company, the first African-American-owned and operated stock company, which presented his show *A Trip to Coontown* (1898), the first all-Negro musical comedy to open in New York.

Robert Cole

Cole teamed with the Johnson Brothers in 1901. They created musical shows without minstrel scenes, coon songs, or shuffling. Instead, they offered good melodies, well-orchestrated scores, and some plot continuity.

Composer **John Rosamond Johnson** (1873–1954) and his brother, poet-lyricist **James Weldon Johnson** (1871–1938) were Florida natives. Rosamond received his formal music training at the New England Conservatory of Music in Boston. After touring with the road company of *Oriental America,* he settled in New York to collaborate with his brother and Bob Cole. In 1901, they signed a

John Rosamond Johnson
James Weldon Johnson

contract with Joseph Stern and Company, the first known agreement between African-American songwriters and a Tin Pan Alley publisher.

The songs they wrote for *The Supper Club* (1902) brought them to the attention of powerful white producers Klaw and Erlanger. The Johnsons signed an exclusive three-year contract, for which they received a monthly salary, a flat fee for each production number, and royalties for each show.

After James's 1906 appointment as U.S. consul to Venezuela, Rosamond and Cole continued as a duo, writing *The Shoo-Fly Regiment* (1907) and *The Red Moon* (1909). Rosamond also composed the score for *Mr. Lode of Kole* (1909), starring renowned black vaudevillian Bert Williams.

In 1912 and 1913, Johnson was the music director of Hammerstein's Opera House in London. He returned to New York at the outbreak of World War I. In the 1920s, the Johnson brothers collaborated on two collections of Negro spirituals. Rosamond later published two collections of his popular music, *Shout Songs* (1936) and *Rolling Along in Song* (1937).

After a 10-year absence of all-black shows on Broadway, *Shuffle Along* (1921, Eubie Blake and Noble Sissle) opened at the 63rd Street Theatre. The show was an immediate success. It also made history. Not only did the show set new standards for the African-American productions that followed in the next two decades, but it also brought African-American audiences into the orchestra section of the theater—the section formerly reserved for white audiences only.

Noble Sissle (left) and Eubie Blake in 1921, at the time of their hit musical, *Shuffle Along*

Eubie Blake

Eubie (James Hubert) Blake (1883–1983) was born in Baltimore. He began to read and play music when he was six. Over the objection of Eubie's deeply religious mother, an organ salesman placed an instrument in their home. In his teens, Eubie began hanging around "bawdy houses" and learned how to play rag on the piano. At about age sixteen, he was hired as a pianist in one of the brothels and composed the first of his many rags, *The Charleston Rag,* published many years later.

Noble Sissle

Noble Sissle (1889–1975) sang in the high school glee club in his native Indianapolis. He met Eubie in 1915, and they immediately joined forces. The following year they became players in James Reese Europe's Society Orchestra. After World War I, Blake and Sissle worked as a vaudeville act, known as the Dixie Duo, performing their own compositions. They then collaborated on *Shuffle Along*.

Early Broadway Musicals

Vaudeville

Vaudeville   Vaudeville's roots go back to a fifteenth-century French village, Val-de-Vire, in Normandy. The villagers were famous for entertaining one another by composing and performing ballads and satirical songs.

Before sketches were added, the stage form of vaudeville that flourished in North America from 1878–1925 consisted of unrelated specialty acts: singers, dancers, actors, acrobats, comics, magicians, jugglers, midgets, monkeys, dogs, dancing elephants, skating bears, fire-eaters, Swiss bell ringers, xylophonists, female impersonators, and anything that was sensational and startling.

Tony Pastor

When Tony Pastor, a former minstrel showman, opened the doors of his Paterson, New Jersey, variety theater in 1865, he opened the doors to vaudeville in North America. In both his New Jersey and New York theaters, Pastor promoted family entertainment only—no smoking, no drinking, no vulgarity. E. F. Albee continued the crusade for purity, setting the moral tone for the Albee Theater in Brooklyn, the great Palace Theater in Manhattan, and the Keith circuit—a nationwide chain of vaudeville houses.

Some of America's most popular songs emerged from vaudeville. "Sidewalks of New York" (1894) by vaudevillian Charles Lawlor became the unofficial anthem of New York City. Other surviving vaudeville hits include the following:

"In the Good Old Summertime"
"The Band Played On"
"My Wild Irish Rose"
"Sweet Adeline"
"When You Were Sweet Sixteen"
"After the Ball Is Over"
"Shine on Harvest Moon"

During the early heyday of vaudeville, the popular song developed in both form and content. It matured with the influence of ragtime, blues, Tin Pan Alley, and such greats as Jerome Kern, Irving Berlin, George Gershwin, and Richard Rodgers.

Burlesque   In direct contrast to the Keith "Sunday School Circuit," as vaudeville artists called the chain, burlesque was raucous, bawdy, musical sex-and-comedy-travesty entertainment. Starting around 1868, touring companies played to audiences of men eager for naughty, grown-up amusement, though performances were fairly modest in the early years. Not until the 1920s, when striptease replaced "hootchie-cootchie" dancing, did burlesque degenerate into sexual exhibitions.

Innovative "travesty" comedy—broad parody—was burlesque's real contribution to musical theater. In fact, around 1900, it was the great vaudeville team of Joe Weber and Lew Fields who decided to try out a travesty-comedy routine in burlesque. After their successful debut, Weber and Fields left the show to open their own music hall. Critics praised their shows, commenting that the combination of lavish musical numbers and outrageous travesty offered the best "musical comedy" available.

Burlesque had begun with a tradition of satire and comedy. After World War I, when the shows replaced their hallmark comedy with vulgar sexuality, burlesque had a decline from which it could never recover. Fortunately, musical theater learned its lesson from that: Never abandon comedy.

Extravaganza and Spectacle   The embodiment of extravaganza and spectacle was New York's Hippodrome Theater (1905–1935), which occupied the entire block on Sixth Avenue between 43rd and 44th Streets. Inside, as many as 5,200 paying customers could thrill to unobstructed views of floods and fires, sensational water ballets, cavalry charges of 480 soldiers on horseback, entire baseball games, and a brilliantly costumed female chorus of 280 dancers. Six hundred performers could fit comfortably on the half-acre stage.

The Great Depression affected the economics of all theatrical forms, especially the costly extravaganza. Paying customers decreased, and public taste changed at the same time, signaling the demise of the Hippodrome.

Billy Rose

Renowned showman Billy Rose tried to revive the theater in 1935 with a spectacular production of *Jumbo* by Richard Rodgers and Lorenz Hart. The show was only a moderate success, and the era of the extravaganza was over.

Revue

The Revue   America borrowed the term *revue* from the French musical variety show that satirized Parisian high life. The new, more cohesive North American version was an energetic, nonbook show—usually built around star performers—featuring musical numbers, comedy acts, dramatic sketches, and specialty routines.

After its Broadway debut with *The Passing Show* in 1894, the revue grew in popularity. It reached its height equally in England and in North America between the two World Wars.

On Broadway, the longest-running annual revues included:

The Ziegfeld Follies	(1907–31)	25 editions
The Passing Show	(second series, 1912–24)	12 editions
George White's Scandals	(1919–31)	11 editions
Earl Carroll Vanities	(1923–32)	11 editions
The Greenwich Village Follies	(1919–28)	8 editions

Ziegfeld

Florenz Ziegfeld (1867–1932), whose shows epitomized glamour and extravagance, was the greatest exponent of the American revue. He dedicated each of his editions to the glorification of the American woman, packaging the show with a pace that built to climaxes and a spectacular finale.

Ziegfeld was a star maker. Through his casts paraded the celebrities of the era: Fanny Brice, Nora Bayes, Eva Tanguay, Marion Davies, Barbara Stanwyck,

The Ziegfeld Follies of 1918, featuring (left to right): W. C. Fields, Will Rogers, Lillian Lorraine, Eddie Cantor, and Harry Kelly

CHALLENGE YOUR EXPERTISE

- How did *Shuffle Along* make history?

Ed Wynn, Marilyn Miller, Irene Dunne, and comedians W. C. Fields, Eddie Cantor, and Will Rogers.

Over the years, Ziegfeld commissioned more than 500 songs from composers such as Jerome Kern, Victor Herbert, and Irving Berlin. Berlin is the composer most identified with the Follies and its theme song "A Pretty Girl Is Like a Melody," which he wrote for the 1919 edition.

The 1992 musical *Will Rogers' Follies* is a modern revue based on Will Rogers' career with *The Ziegfeld Follies*.

Other long-running revues introduced great American composers such as Cole Porter and Harold Rome. Between 1920 and 1924, George Gershwin wrote his first scores for *George White's Scandals*. Richard Rodgers and Lorenz Hart wrote their first complete Broadway score for *The Garrick Gaieties of 1925*. One of the songs in the score, "Manhattan," became a hit and launched their successful career collaboration.

Categories of Modern Broadway Musicals

The majority of Broadway musicals fall into the following broad classifications:

- modern operetta
- musical comedy
- musical play
- play with music
- popular opera

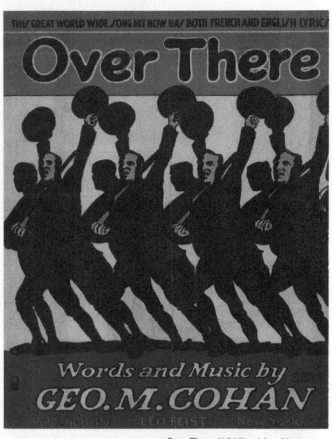

Over There (1918) with a Norman Rockwell illustration on the cover

Modern Operetta   Viennese composers Johann Strauss in *Die Fledermaus* and Franz Lehar (*lay*-har, 1870–1948) in *The Merry Widow* perfected the form. Both operettas remain in the modern repertoire. Victor Herbert, Sigmund Romberg, and Rudolf Friml refined operetta and introduced it to North American audiences.

Franz Lehar
Modern operetta

The Depression also affected operetta. Ragtime and jazz had taken the place of quaint tunes. With the emergence of Jerome Kern, George Gershwin, Cole Porter, Irving Berlin, and Richard Rodgers, the popular song had come of age. Composers were leading American musical theater into a new era.

George M. Cohan   Some of the roots of modern Broadway musical comedy are traceable to the early works of George M. Cohan (1878–1942). His "plays

Cohan

with music" were punctuated with songs created for singing actors rather than full-voiced operetta singers. And Cohan's thin plots had a hometown flavor that Americans easily related to. *Little Johnny Jones* (1904) was Cohan's first Broadway hit, giving us such songs as "Yankee Doodle Boy" and "Give My Regards to Broadway." His other popular shows included *Forty-Five Minutes from Broadway* (1906), *The Little Millionaire* (1916), and *Little Nelly Kelly* (1922). During World War I, his song "Over There," from *The Cohan Revue of 1918,* became a symbol of patriotic fervor.

SIGMUND ROMBERG (1887–1951)

The most prolific composer of popular musicals, Sigmund Romberg was born in Hungary and raised in Vienna, coming to America in 1909. Among his sixty operettas are *Maytime* and *Over the Top* (1917), *Blossom Time* (1921), *The Student Prince* (1924), *The Desert Song* (1926), *The New Moon* (1928), and *Up in Central Park* (1945).

His most enduring songs include "Deep in My Heart," "Serenade," and "Drinking Song" from *The Student Prince;* "One Alone" from *The Desert Song;* and "Lover Come Back to Me" and "Stout-Hearted Men" from *The New Moon.* From 1929 on, he wrote songs for motion pictures, including "When I Grow Too Old to Dream."

VICTOR HERBERT (1859–1924)

Victor Herbert was born in Dublin, Ireland, and emigrated to the United States in 1886. He became the first important composer of the American musical stage.

From 1893 to 1898, Herbert conducted the 22nd New York Regiment band. For the next six years, he conducted the Pittsburgh Symphony, until organizing and conducting his own orchestra in 1904.

Herbert's first success, *The Wizard and the Nile* (1895), was set in Egypt. This was followed in 1898 by *The Fortune Teller,* which premiered at the Grand Opera House in Toronto, preceding its Broadway run.

Set in Hungary, the operetta gave us "Gypsy Love Song," which has endured for many generations.

Legend has it that in 1899 and 1900, while simultaneously composing four operetta scores, Herbert, a great lover of food and drink, kept four bottles of wine chilled in a washtub of ice, sipping a different one with each score.

Among his greatest hits were *Babes in Toyland* (1903), *The Red Mill* (1906)—which had the first moving electric sign on a Broadway marquee—and *Naughty Marietta* (1910). Herbert also wrote musical scores for *The Ziegfield Follies* of 1917 and 1921–24 and composed two grand operas.

RUDOLF FRIML (1879–1972)

Considered an infant prodigy at the piano, Rudolf Friml studied in Prague with his Czech countryman Antonin Dvořák. In 1901 and 1906, Friml was accompanist for the U.S. tours of the famous Czech violinist Jan Kubelik (1880–1940). After the second tour, Friml decided to remain in the United States, becoming a naturalized citizen in 1925.

In his more than thirty operettas, Friml's formula for success was a combination of rich melody, rousing choruses, and passionate romance.

His works include *The Firefly* (1912), *You're in Love* (1917), *Rose Marie* (1924, which featured the song "Indian Love Call"), *The Vagabond King* (1925, which included "Only a Rose" and "Someday"), *The Three Musketeers* (1928), and *Bird of Paradise* (1930).

From 1930, Friml composed for movies. He wrote the famous "Donkey Serenade" for the 1937 film version of *The Firefly*.

IRVING BERLIN (1888–1989)

Irving Berlin came to New York's Lower East Side from his native Russia in 1892. Although he had no musical training, he taught himself to compose by picking out melodies on the black keys of the piano. He even worked as a singing waiter in Chinatown, performing his own songs.

Berlin's 1914 show *Watch Your Step* introduced ragtime into the theater. *As Thousands Cheer* (1933), which ranks among his finest works for the theater, includes "Heat Wave," the show-stopper he wrote for Ethel Waters, and the timeless "Easter Parade." For that song, Berlin did something that was common among musical composers of that time. He unearthed a tune he had written earlier titled "Smile and Show Your Dimple" and simply changed the lyrics.

Later, Berlin wrote two long-running Broadway hits—*Annie Get Your Gun* (1946) and *Call Me Madam* (1950)—both starring the great Ethel Merman. In 1999, *Annie Get Your Gun* was revived on Broadway.

Jerome Kern   Jerome Kern (1885–1945) brought a new attitude into musical theater: he insisted on a partnership between the story, or "book," and the music. Kern had been leading a revolution in musical theater even in his co-authored series of shows known as the Princess Theatre musicals. Staged in a 299-seat house, Kern's shows could be more intimate, a departure from the European operetta. And each show had a simple, modern, farce-oriented plot.

Princess Theatre

JEROME KERN (1885–1945)

The son of Eastern European immigrants, Jerome Kern developed a love for music from learning the Bohemian folk songs his mother sang to him. When he displayed his musical gifts at a young age, his family encouraged him. Kern studied piano, theory, and orchestration at the New York College of Music, and he continued his advanced training with private tutors in Germany. He then went to London where he met American impresario and producer Charles Frohman. Impressed with Kern's early songs, Frohman interpolated them in his West End musicals.

In 1904, Kern returned to New York and began his career on Tin Pan Alley, the center of the popular music business. Max Dreyfus, head of the music publishing firm of T. B. Harms, discovered Kern and hired him as a rehearsal pianist and song plugger. Kern used the opportunity to audition his own tunes. He finally succeeded in placing his ballad "They Didn't Believe Me" in the 1914 musical production *The Girl From Utah*—a British import despite the title.

Dissatisfied with the formulas of conventional musicals, Kern was determined to reinvent musical theater, revealing his vision in the intimate Princess Theatre Shows. These musicals were the first to break with the tradition of enormous, elaborately costumed companies performing on large stages amid ornate sets. The shows used contemporary settings, breezy stories, and small casts whose main characters were two lovers and a comedian.

It was in these early musicals that Kern began to refine the show song. The opening production was *Nobody Home* (1915). Later that year, the Princess had its first hit, *Very Good Eddie* (1915), a farce-comedy that was good enough to stand on its own without music. Working with librettists P. G. Wodehouse and Guy Bolton, Kern then turned out *Have a Heart* (1916), followed by two outstanding hits—the legendary *Oh, Boy!* (1917), and *Oh, Lady, Lady* (1918).

Kern hit his musical stride with *Sally* (1920, "Look For the Silver Lining"). Produced by Florenz Ziegfeld, the show opened at the New Amsterdam Theater and ran for a record 570 performances. Kern collaborated with Otto Harbach and Oscar Hammerstein II on *Sunny* (1925, "Who?"). He then teamed with Oscar Hammerstein II on the show that would revolutionize the Broadway musical.

The Kern–Hammerstein masterpiece, *Show Boat,* opened at the Ziegfeld Theater in December 1927. Their score contains one memorable song after another: "Ol' Man River," "Can't Help Lovin' That Man," "Make Believe," "Bill," and "Why Do I Love You?" Hammerstein's libretto was an adaptation of a successful Edna Ferber novel.

Despite these assets, Florenz Ziegfeld was certain the show would flop because of its controversial themes: interracial marriage, divorce, desertion, and alcoholism. Compounding his skepticism was the fact that for the first time, African Americans were featured in key roles interacting with Caucasians. Ziegfeld spared no expense in mounting the production. As the first distinguished, dramatic musical comedy, *Show Boat* became the benchmark for innovative productions.

Most critics welcomed the groundbreaking show, declaring that Kern and Hammerstein had created a timeless theater piece. Audiences overwhelmingly approved, although many did not know what to make of it. Through the years, *Show Boat* has grown more popular. Although racially based resistance in Toronto and New York preceded the 1995 revival, the show opened to acclaim and reaffirmed its appeal.

During the 1930s, Kern was primarily engaged in composing film musicals, but he did turn out a few moderately successful shows: *The Cat and the Fiddle* (1931), *Music in the Air* (1932), *Roberta* (1933, "Smoke Gets in Your Eyes," with Otto Harbach), and *Very Warm for May* (1939, "All the Things You Are"). In the midst of discussions about a new musical based on the life of Annie Oakley, Kern died suddenly of a brain hemorrhage in 1945. The producers, Richard Rogers and Oscar Hammerstein II, then offered the project, *Annie Get Your Gun* (1946), to Irving Berlin.

PRINCIPAL WORKS

Musicals: *Nobody Home* (1915); *Very Good Eddie* (1915); *Have a Heart* (1916); *Oh, Boy!* (1917); *Oh, Lady, Lady* (1918); *Sally* (1920); *Sunny* (1925); *Show Boat* (1927); *The Cat and the Fiddle* (1931); *Music in the Air* (1932); *Roberta* (1933); *Very Warm for May* (1939).

Film Scores: *Show Boat* (1931, 1951).

CHALLENGE YOUR EXPERTISE

• What did Tony Pastor do to change vaudeville?

HISTORICAL PERSPECTIVE

Kern's Show Boat: The New Broadway Musical

Show Boat (1927), Jerome Kern's milestone musical produced by Florenz Ziegfeld, demonstrated that dramatic literature could merge successfully with romantic song to create good theater. The *New York Times* singled out for exceptional praise the collaborative achievement of Kern's music and Oscar Hammerstein II's book and lyrics.

Daring for its time, *Show Boat* deals with delicate and controversial subjects such as love gone sour, miscegenation (racially mixed marriages), racial prejudice, alcohol and gambling addiction, and economic troubles—a major departure from the happy-go-lucky, all-is-well-with-the-world musical. Yet audiences took to the integration of music and challenging story with great enthusiasm, paving the way for later musicals such as *South Pacific, Les Misérables,* and *Miss Saigon.*

LISTENING ACTIVITY

Show Boat (1927), Jerome Kern
"Ol' Man River"

Large Form: Broadway Musical
Detailed Form: Three-part Song-form
Performing Medium: Bass Voice and Orchestra

Compact Disc 4, Tracks 8–11
Running Time: 2:17

In Act 1, the song "Ol' Man River" introduces Joe, an African-American handyman on the *Show Boat*. Originally written for the great bass Paul Robeson (1898–1976), the son of a slave, the song functions as a *leitmotif*—a recurrent theme that represents the Mississippi River and the passage of time.

In this rare recording, we hear the role of Joe as Kern and Hammerstein had conceived it for Robeson. Robeson himself felt oppressed by racial discrimination in the United States and later sought refuge in the Soviet Union for a number of years. This 1958 recording of a live Carnegie Hall concert marks Robeson's historic return to his native United States.

As a fighter for racial equality, Robeson slightly alters Hammerstein's lyrics in the recording you will hear. For example, to avoid the stereotypical dialect associated with the African American, he replaces *"dat's de ol' man"* with *"that's the ol' man."* And in the last few lines:

"I get weary
An' sick of tryin',
I'm tired of livin',
An' skeered o' dyin'"

Paul Robeson in the 1936 film version of Kern's *Show Boat*

Robeson replaces lyrics about his personal crusade for civil rights:
"But I keep laughin'
Instead of cryin'.
I must keep fightin',
Until I'm dyin'. . . ."

LISTENING GUIDE

Show Boat (1927), Jerome Kern
"Ol' Man River"

8	0:00	INTRODUCTION	piano; moderately fast; 4 meter throughout; major, mostly pentatonic scale; slowing down to cadence, emphasis on text:
	0:17	VERSE Dere's an ol' man called the Mississippi. That's the ol' man I don't like to be. What does he care If the world's got troubles? What does he care if the land ain't free?	
9	0:37	CHORUS [A] That ol' man river, That ol' man river, He mus' know sumpin' But don't say nuthin', He jes' keeps rollin', He keeps on rollin' along.	slower, steady tempo; mostly pentatonic
	1:00	CHORUS [A] He don't plant 'taters, He don't plant cotton, an' dem that plants 'em Is soon forgotten, But ol' man river, He jes' keeps rollin' along.	same music, different text
10	1:23	BRIDGE [B] You an' me, We sweat an' strain, Body all achin' an' racked wid' pain. Tote dat barge!	faster tempo; agitated; rubato; slowing to cadence

Lift dat bale!

Yo' show a little click,

An' you' lands in jail.

11   1:46   CHORUS [A]   same music as [A] with new text; cadence at end

But I keep laughin'

Instead of cryin'.

I mus' keep fightin',

Until I'm dyin'.

An' ol' man river,

He jes' keeps rollin' along!

OL' MAN RIVER
Words and Music by Jerome Kern and Oscar Hammerstein II
© Copyright 1927 by PolyGram International Publishing, Inc.
Copyright renewed.
International Copyright Secured. Used by Permission. All Rights Reserved.

Al Jolson

Al Jolson (Asa Joelson, 1886–1950), whose Lithuanian parents emigrated to the United States to escape Tsarist tyranny, rose to prominence in vaudeville as a minstrel entertainer. His father, a cantor in a Washington, D.C., synagogue, hoped his son would follow him in the profession. But young Asa, who changed his name to Al, was more interested in a show business career. He moved to New York and found work as a singing waiter until his voice cracked. Then, he and his brother Harry formed an act; Al whistled songs until his voice matured.

Al Jolson in blackface

Jolson was performing on vaudeville circuits on his own by 1905. Three years later, while performing in San Francisco, he coined the phrase that was to become the signature line of his extroverted style: "All right, all right, folks—you ain't seen nothin' yet!" Audiences loved him, and his rose quickly to stardom. Songwriter Harry Akst ("Dinah," "Baby Face," "Am I Blue?") became Jolson's lifelong associate, finding material suitable for Jolson's style.

In 1911, Jolson's success grew even larger. He not only opened at Broadway's Winter Garden but also cut his first recordings. When Jolson suggested taking the Winter Garden show on tour—sets, full cast, orchestra, and all—he accomplished something that had never been done before. The following year he had a new show at the Winter Garden.

Al customarily sang in blackface. On tour, he had to accommodate local Blue Laws by putting on Sunday shows without sets, costumes, and make-up. To maintain intimacy with the audience, he devised a platform extending from the stage apron into the first rows of seats. By 1915, Al Jolson was billed as "America's Greatest Entertainer," surpassing such contemporaries as Eddie Cantor and George Jessel. His massive appeal continued through the 1920s.

For a songwriter, having Jolson perform your song virtually guaranteed its future. In his 1918 Broadway show *Sinbad,* Jolson introduced "Rockabye Your Baby

With a Dixie Melody," "My Mammy," and a song by a young George Gershwin, "Swanee." Songs in his 1921 show *Bombo* included "April Showers," "California Here I Come," and "Toot Toot Tootsie (Goodbye)." For the rest of Jolson's career, those songs were identified with him.

Although George Jessel had starred in *The Jazz Singer* on Broadway, Warner Brothers approached Jolson for the film. It was mainly a silent movie, but the studio decided to include sound in it by interpolating some songs. The story mirrored Jolson's own life: a cantor's son defies his father's wishes and chooses a show business career. In the film, Jolson managed to incorporate his signature line before launching into "Toot Toot Tootsie." The songs and a brief scene of spoken dialogue revolutionized the motion picture industry. Al Jolson was a hot property in Hollywood. In 1928, his second sound film, *The Singing Fool*, introduced the song "Sonny Boy" (De Sylva, Brown, and Henderson). The subsequent recording became one of the first million sellers.

Although Jolson continued making films during the 1930s, the movie camera could not fully capture the excitement of his performances, and Al preferred working with live audiences. So he came back to Broadway in 1931 in the show *Wonder Bar*. But his absence from the stage as well as the Depression affected his faltering vaudeville career. He made another attempt to recapture his former glory in the 1940 show *Hold Onto Your Hats*, but it closed early when he stricken with pneumonia.

During World War II, Jolson, with Harry Akst as his accompanist, entertained troops in the United Kingdom, Europe, Africa, and Asia. The tours bolstered his career, but the endless travel affected his health. He returned home to recuperate.

The 1946 bio-film, *The Jolson Story*, revived Joison's popularity. He signed a deal with Decca Records, guest-starred on Bing Crosby's radio show, and finally was given his own radio series, which ran for four years. The 1949 film sequel, *Jolson Sings Again*, rekindled the spirit of the original and became a huge success. The following year he was negotiating with television executives for his own show.

In the meantime, Jolson and Akst entertained the troops in Korea. He returned to the States for a booking on Crosby's show, scheduled to be aired from San Francisco. But before the taping, Al Jolson suffered chest pains in his hotel room. On the night he died in October 1950, lights were dimmed on Broadway and traffic in Times Square was halted.

George Gershwin

Ira Gershwin

George and Ira Gershwin

The music of George Gershwin (1898–1937) and the lyrics of his brother Ira (1896–1983) were a remarkable collaboration. On December 1, 1924, at the Liberty Theater, the show *Lady Be Good* opened—with the first complete score by the Gershwin brothers produced on Broadway. Giving us both the title song "Lady Be Good" and "Fascinating Rhythm," the show was the jazz-age equivalent of Kern's Princess Theatre musicals of the preceding decade.

Because their first show with book writers Guy Bolton and P. G. Wodehouse had been a hit, the Gershwins again teamed up with them on *Oh, Kay!* (1926). That score contains several Gershwin classics: "Do, Do, Do," "Clap Yo' Hands," and "Someone to Watch Over Me." *Girl Crazy* (1930) gave us "Embraceable You," "I Got Rhythm," and "But Not for Me."

LISTENING INSIGHTS

What to Listen for in Broadway Musicals

Most songs in musicals contain three main elements: verse, chorus, and bridge.

Verse   Similar to the recitative in opera, the verse introduces the song (*aria* in opera) and presents the story or background. The verse was even more important in early musicals such as the *revue* or *vaudeville* because these shows contained little or no story—magicians, dancers, acrobats, and comics performed between songs. When the singer took center stage, the verse provided a vehicle to engage the audience in the song. Occasionally, when the songs were performed outside the context of the show, the verse was omitted.

Chorus [A]   The chorus is the main tune or song.

Bridge [B]   A middle, usually contrasting, section of music. The tempo, mood, and style of the bridge usually contrasts the first melody.

Typical Plans for Broadway Musical Songs are:

VERSE (optional)	CHORUS (A)	CHORUS (A)	BRIDGE (B)	CHORUS (A)

or

VERSE (optional)	CHORUS (A)	BRIDGE (B)	CHORUS (A)	BRIDGE (B)

Cowboy Curly (Gordon MacRae) singing "Oh, What a Beautiful Morning" in the opening scene from the film production of *Oklahoma*

Just as *Show Boat* had brought a new maturity to the American musical stage, *Of Thee I Sing* (1931) introduced an offbeat, adult approach to musical comedy. The show was the first musical to receive the Pulitzer Prize for Drama.

The book by George S. Kaufman and Morrie Ryskind was a send-up of American political institutions and the Establishment. To complement the story, the Gershwins explored a new style of composition, producing a score that interweaves a succession of songs, recitatives, and extended musical scenes. A distinctively native form had emerged.

COLE PORTER (1891–1964)

Composer-lyricist Cole Porter came from an affluent, socially prominent family in Peru, Indiana, and maintained an elegant lifestyle throughout his life. Serious musical training did not play a significant role during his childhood, but while at Yale, he composed football songs ("Bingo Eli Yale" and "Bulldog").

Ironically, Porter's wealth did not help his early Broadway career. After the flop of his 1916 composing debut, he realized he would have to learn his craft or remain a dilettante. So he went to France to study composition with Vincent D'Indy (dan-*dee*) at the Paris Conservatory.

By 1929, Porter resumed his career writing musicals. Whether or not the shows themselves were hits, many of the songs from those shows were to become classics. Porter distinguished himself and revealed his background with his witty, sophisticated lyrics. Instead of the everyday realities that other Depression-era lyricists dealt with, Porter's songs refer to wealth, luxury, and lavish spending.

In the autumn of 1937, both of Porter's legs were crushed in a horseback riding accident. One leg healed; the other did not and was eventually amputated. Following the accident, Porter continued to work, creating two of his biggest Broadway successes, *Leave It to Me!* (1938) and *DuBarry Was a Lady* (1939).

Between 1929 and 1955, Cole Porter wrote twelve Broadway musicals and several film scores. After his final Broadway outing—*Silk Stockings* (1955), an adaptation of the film *Ninotchka*—Porter focused his composing career on film scores and television specials.

PRINCIPAL WORKS

Fifty Million Frenchmen (1929, "You Do Something to Me"); *Wake Up and Dream* (1929, "What Is This Thing Called Love"); *The New Yorkers* (1930, "Love For Sale"); *Gay Divorcee* (1932, "Night and Day"); *Anything Goes* (1934, "Anything Goes," "I Get a Kick Out of You," "You're the Top," "All Through the Night"); *Jubilee* (1935, "Begin the Beguine" and "Just One of Those Things"); *Leave It to Me* (1938, "My Heart Belongs to Daddy"); *DuBarry Was a Lady* (1939, "Friendship" and "Do I Love You"); *Panama Hattie* (1940); *Kiss Me Kate* (1948); *Can-Can* (1953, "I Love Paris" and "It's All Right With Me"); *Silk Stockings* (1955)

Songs Written for Films: "Let's Do It" (1928); "I've Got You Under My Skin" (1936); "In the Still of the Night" (1937); and "I Concentrate on You" (1940)

RICHARD RODGERS (1902–1979)

One of the most prolific and successful Broadway musical composers, Richard Charles Rodgers was born in Hammels Station on Long Island near New York City. Studying piano from the age of six, he quickly learned to improvise and play by ear. As a teenager, he attended one Broadway show after another and was particularly impressed by the operettas of Victor Herbert and the musicals of Jerome Kern.

While studying at Columbia University in 1918, he met Lorenz Hart, and they began writing musicals together. Their first collaboration, *Fly with Me,* was written for Columbia's amateur varsity production.

Rodgers and Hart's first Broadway success was *The Garrick Gaieties* (1925), a revue-type show. Between 1926 and 1930, the team produced fourteen musicals and revues.

Called to Hollywood, Rodgers and Hart continued working together on films. After a fruitful partnership for nearly thirty musicals, their collaboration ended with the death of Lorenz Hart in 1943.

A new era began in Rodgers' life when he teamed up with the great lyricist Oscar Hammerstein II. Beginning with *Oklahoma* (1943), their eighteen-year collaboration until Hammerstein's death created a legacy of nine of Broadway's greatest and timeless musicals—including *Carousel* (1945), *South Pacific* (1949), *The King and I* (1951), and *The Sound of Music* (1959).

Even though there were earlier examples of a "book show"—*Show Boat* (1927), *Pal Joey* (Rodgers and Hart, 1940), and the Gershwins' *Of Thee I Sing* (1931)—*Oklahoma!* became the benchmark for musicals in which the songs were fully integrated dramatically and served the play. Rodgers and Hammerstein believed in the importance of music in theater—that it could reinforce emotion beyond words alone. Their songs helped move the story along, establishing mood and contributing to character development and dynamic.

After Hammerstein's death, Rodgers tried writing both the lyrics and the music. But even in his collaboration with Stephen Sondheim he was never as successful as he was when he worked with his two great collaborators, Lorenz Hart and Oscar Hammerstein II. Richard Rodgers died in New York City at age 77.

PRINCIPAL WORKS

Hit Musicals, Revues, and Films from Musicals:
The Garrick Gaieties (with Hart, 1925); *On Your Toes* (with Hart, 1936; film 1939); *Babes in Arms* (with Hart, 1937, film 1939); *Pal Joey* (with Hart and O'Hara, 1940; film 1957); *Oklahoma!* (with Hammerstein, 1943; film 1955); *Carousel* (with Hammerstein, 1945; film 1956); *South Pacific* (with Hammerstein, 1949; film 1958); *The King and I* (with Hammerstein, 1951; film 1956); *Flower Drum Song* (with Hammerstein, 1958; film 1961); *The Sound of Music* (with Hammerstein, 1959; film 1964); *Do I Hear a Waltz?* (with Laurents and Sondheim, 1965)

Original Film Scores: *Love Me Tonight* (with Hart, 1932); *State Fair* (with Hammerstein, 1945); *Words and Music* (with Hart, 1948)

Television Musicals: *Cinderella* (with Hammerstein, 1957); *Androcles and the Lion* (Rodgers and Shaw, 1967)

Television Documentary Series: *Victory at Sea* (1952); *Churchill, the Valiant Years* (1960)

STEPHEN SONDHEIM (b. 1930)

Born in New York City, Stephen Joshua Sondheim showed an early interest in Broadway musical theater. He was encouraged to pursue that interest by family friend, mentor, and neighbor Oscar Hammerstein II.

At the small, prestigious liberal arts Williams College in Massachusetts, Sondheim wrote several full-length musicals that earned him a scholarship to study for two years with the avant-garde composer Milton Babbitt.

Working with Babbitt gave Sondheim insight into contemporary sound. He mastered the inventive meters, unusual melodic intervals, and unpredictable harmonies that characterize his music.

Hammerstein passed on to Sondheim what Jerome Kern had passed on to him and Richard Rodgers: an understanding of dramatic construction. The songs in Sondheim's scores grow not only from the dramatic ideas in the story but also from the objective of giving the actor something to act—a theatrical moment. With his success, Sondheim brought another level of maturity into Broadway's musical theater.

Sondheim made his Broadway debut with incidental music to *The Girls of Summer* (1956) and as a lyricist for *West Side Story* (1957, with Leonard Bernstein). The 1962 production of *A Funny Thing Happened on the Way to the Forum*, the first for which he wrote both music and lyrics, won a Tony Award for best musical of the year. Over the years, Sondheim collaborated as lyricist with Richard Rodgers (*Do I Hear a Waltz*, 1965), and again with Bernstein in the 1974 revival of *Candide*.

PRINCIPAL WORKS

Musicals: *The Girls of Summer* (1956, incidental music); *West Side Story* (1957, lyrics, with music by Leonard Bernstein); *Gypsy* (1959, lyrics, music by Jule Styne); *A Funny Thing Happened on the Way to the Forum* (1962, lyrics and music); *Company* (1970, lyrics and music—Tony Award); *Follies* (1971, lyrics and music—Tony Award), *A Little Night Music* (1973, lyrics and music—Tony and The Standard Awards); *Pacific Overtures* (1976, lyrics and music); *Sweeney Todd* (1979, lyrics and music—Tony and The Standard Awards); *Merrily We Roll Along* (1981, lyrics and music); *Sunday in the Park with George* (1984, lyrics and music—Pulitzer Prize); *Into the Woods* (1987, lyrics and music); *Assassins* (1991, lyrics and music)

Film Music: *Stavisky* (1974); *The Seven Percent Solution* (1977); *Passion* (1994)

A Little Night Music (1973), Stephen Sondheim
"Send in the Clowns"

Large Form: Broadway Musical
Detailed Form: Three-part Song-form
Performing Medium: Soprano Voice and Orchestra

Compact Disc 4, Track 12
Running Time: 3:14

Sondheim's show was one of the big hits of Broadway's 1973 season. Mozart's serenade "Eine Kleine Nachtmusik" (A Little Night Music) provided the title for this charming work. Because of its turn-of-the-century (nineteenth to twentieth) setting, period costumes, sentimental plot, and waltz-filled score, *A Little Night Music* is usually called a modern operetta, similar to those of Franz Lehar and Johann Strauss, Jr.

The story, closely based on Ingmar Bergman's film "Smiles of a Summer Night," is set in Sweden. It is about Fredrik Egerman, a middle-aged attorney, newly remarried to a teenage girl the same age as his son. After eleven months of an unconsummated marriage, Egerman resumes an affair with his former mistress, Desirée Armfeldt—an actress whose current lover is Count Malcolm, a Swedish military officer. "Send in the Clowns" is sung in the musical by Desirée when she and Egerman meet again after years of separation.

Egerman, Desirée, Count Malcolm, and his wife meet at Desirée's mother's country estate for a brief holiday. Madame Armfeldt herself was a beautiful and notorious courtesan in her day.

By the final curtain, Egerman is relieved to learn that his wife and his eighteen-year-old son have fallen in love and have run off together. Egerman and Desirée are reunited, and the count is reconciled to being reunited with his wife.

Scene from the film version of Bernstein's *West Side Story*

LISTENING ACTIVITY

Overture to Candide (1956), Leonard Bernstein

Large Form: Broadway Musical Overture
Detailed Form: Sectional
Performing Medium: Symphony Orchestra

Compact Disc 4, Tracks 4–7
Running Time: 4:22

See Chapter 24 for background on the musical *Candide* and the Listening Guide for the Overture.

CHALLENGE YOUR EXPERTISE

• Suppose Bach, Mozart, and Brahms were alive today. Who do you think would be the most likely composer of Broadway musicals?

• Although trained as a composer, Stephen Sondheim collaborated as a lyricist with which three composers?

LISTENING ACTIVITY

Fiddler on the Roof (1964), Jerry Bock
and Sheldon Harnick
"Sunrise, Sunset"

Large Form: Broadway Musical
Detailed Form: Three-part Song-form
Performing Medium: Soprano, Baritone, Chorus, and Small Orchestra

Compact Disc 4, Track 13
Running Time: 3:05

Fiddler on the Roof, based on the story "Tevye and His Daughters" by Sholom Aleichem, is set in Anatevka, a *shtetl* (small ghetto-town) in turn-of-the-century Russia. Plagued by czarist pogroms, the townspeople live precariously—like a "fiddler on the roof."

"Sunrise, Sunset" is sung at the oldest daughter's wedding. Tevye and his wife Golde reflect on how their family has grown up and how quickly the years have gone by.

Alan Jay Lerner (1918–1986) and Frederick Loewe (1904–1988)

Alan Jay Lerner once quipped that writing lyrics was . . . "not an art but a craft, somewhere between photography and basket weaving." The son of an affluent New York City merchant, Lerner starting writing material for Hasty Pudding Club shows while

Lerner (right) and Loewe, c. 1958

he was a student at Harvard, and later a contributing writer for a number of supper club revues. Once he began working with composer Frederick Loewe, Lerner developed his superb craftsmanship and became an acclaimed lyricist-librettist.

Frederick Loewe came from a musical family. He studied composition in Vienna and had a concert career before emigrating to America with his family in 1924. Loewe began composing for theater in the 1930s but achieved nothing noteworthy until he and Lerner met accidentally. Something clicked between them, and they formed a team. Loewe's elegant, romantic style fit perfectly with Lerner's intricate, amusing, moving lyrics. They were especially successful in creating colorful settings for their musicals, such as European capitals and the early American West.

They had their first hit with *Brigadoon* (1947), a romantic fantasy set in a mythical town in Scotland. *Paint Your Wagon* (1951) takes place during the California Gold Rush. In 1956 they hit their creative peak in *My Fair Lady*, a brilliant adaptation of a George Bernard Shaw comedy set in Victorian England. Many consider it one of the finest musicals ever written.

From 1948–1951, Lerner also collaborated with composer Kurt Weill, penned the screenplay for *An American in Paris,* and worked with composer Burton Lane on the script and score for the film *Royal Wedding.* Lerner and Loewe teamed up again for the 1958 film musical *Gigi*.

Their return to Broadway with *Camelot* (1960), a musical adaptation from the Arthurian legends, was their last. Repeated complications and difficulties before its opening severely affected their health and relationship. Loewe retired. Lerner continued his career but was plagued with a series of personal and professional disappointments for the next twenty-five years.

HISTORICAL PERSPECTIVE

Rent: A Rock Opera for the '90s

After seven years of trying to transform musical theater into something more modern, **Jonathan Larson** (1960–1996) had had no luck. No one was convinced that his notions represented the direction of the future. Then in 1989, the idea for *Rent* struck him. He called it his ". . . rock opera for the '90s."

Inspired by Giacomo Puccini's opera *La Bohème,* Larson's *Rent* updates the setting from the Left Bank of Paris at the end of the nineteenth century to the East Village of Lower Manhattan at the end of the twentieth century. The characters, although exaggerated, were based on the people in his neighborhood. He also updated the life-threatening disease. Puccini's Mimi is dying from tuberculosis, a common killer of her time. In *Rent,* Mimi and her lover Roger are HIV-positive. He is a recovering addict, but she is still using drugs.

Revision followed revision, and in 1992, while riding his bicycle through the East Village, Jon passed the New York Theatre Workshop on Fourth Street. The next day, he brought the tape of the score to NYTW director James Nicola, who loved the music. Michael Greif was brought in as the director, and the four-year process of creating *Rent* had begun.

The first preview was slated for January 25, 1996. Friends noticed that Jon seemed to be exceptionally tired, despite his excitement about the opening. During a rehearsal, he collapsed and went by ambulance to the nearest hospital. The doctors diagnosed his problem as food poisoning, pumped his stomach, and sent him home. Three days later, Jon blacked out again and was diagnosed with the flu.

Despite his sore chest and fever, Jon took a taxi to watch the dress rehearsal and another taxi home. A short time later, his roommate found him on the floor of the kitchen, next to his coat. Jon had died of an aortic aneurysm—less than two weeks before his thirty-sixth birthday.

CHALLENGE YOUR EXPERTISE

- When you hear song lyrics about luxury, wealth, and extravagance, which composer-lyricist are you reminded of?

Adam Pascal (as Radames) and Heather Headley (as Aida) in Elton John's and Tim Rice's Broadway adaptation of the Verdi opera

Musicals Adapted from Other Sources

Creative teams draw on a variety of existing material for their musicals. *Annie* (1978, Charles Strouse, Martin Chamin) came from the comic strip "Little Orphan Annie." *Sunset Boulevard* (1993, Andrew Lloyd Webber, Don Black) was originally a film. *Sunday in the Park With George* (1984, Stephen Sondheim) was inspired by a Seurat painting. *Joseph and the Amazing Technicolor Dreamcoat* (Lloyd Webber, Tim Rice) came from a Bible story. *The Lion King* (1997, Elton John, Tim Rice) was an animated film. *Ragtime* (1997, Stephen Flaherty, Lynn Ahrens) is a stage adaptation of E. L. Doctorow's novel.

Musicals with Classic Themes

Aida (2000, Elton John, Tim Rice) is based on the Verdi opera set in ancient Egypt. The Broadway production opens in the Egyptian room of a modern museum where a man and a woman are viewing the exhibits, hardly aware of each other's presence. In the opening number, Princess Amneris emerges from the past and sings about events during a war between Egypt and its neighbor Nubia.

Like the opera, *Aida* tells a tale of forbidden love and political power. Radames, an Egyptian army captain, is engaged to Amneris. But he is fascinated with a strong-willed Nubian woman named Aida, who has been captured and brought to Egypt as a slave. Radames does not know that Aida is a princess. If the Egyptians were to learn who she is, her life would be in danger. Her father, the Nubian king, is also taken prisoner. His real identity is not revealed.

Radames realizes that he is in love with Aida and wants to call off his wedding. There's no hope for the lovers. For the sake of her kingdom, Aida and her father must escape. She persuades Radames to go through with the marriage so he will become powerful enough to bring peace between Egypt and Nubia. After the ceremony, he tries to stop the army from recapturing Aida. She is caught, but her father escapes. The lovers stand trial together and receive their sentence from Amneris. They are buried alive in the same tomb beneath the Egyptian desert. However, the show is not over. In the closing scene, we are transported back to the present. The man and woman in the museum finally meet.

Romeo and Juliet the Musical (music by Gerard Presgurvic, lyrics by Don Black) is set in the 1980s. Even with modernized dialogue replacing Shakespeare's passionate poetry, the book is more faithful than Bernstein's classic *West Side Story* to the original play.

Baz Luhrmann's version of the most-performed opera of all time—*La Bohème*—opened on Broadway in 2003. The new production retains the music of Giacomo Puccini and the libretto of Giuseppe Giacosa and Luigi Illica.

Composer Frank Wildhorn and lyricist Nan Knighton turned a novel into *Scarlet Pimpernel* (1998). Wildhorn wrote the score for *Jekyll and Hyde* (1990) with lyricist Leslie Bricusse. The show is based on Robert Louis Stevenson's book about the dark side of human nature.

From Hollywood to Broadway

Since its opening in 1980, *42nd Street* is among Broadway's long-running musicals. Produced by theatrical legend David Merrick, the show is an adaptation of a 1933 movie musical.

Mel Brooks, with the expert craftsmanship of Thomas Meehan, adapted his own screenplay into a gag-filled musical comedy, *The Producers* (2001, Brooks), which recreates back to burlesque and the lighthearted shows of the 1950s. Susan Stroman directed, staged, and choreographed the successful stage version, which swept the Tony Awards.

The book for *Hairspray* (2002) by Mark O'Donnell and Thomas Meehan is based on a John Waters' cult movie of the same name. Film composer Marc Shaiman wrote the music, with lyrics by Shaiman and Scott Wittman.

Thoroughly Modern Millie (2002) premiered at the La Jolla Playhouse in California before moving to Broadway. The show tells of a young girl from Kansas who comes to Manhattan during the Roaring Twenties—the height of the Jazz Age. Girls bobbed their hair and called themselves "flappers." More women were entering the workforce and trying to win control of their personal lives. Dick Scanlan and Richard Morris adapted the musical comedy book from a 1967 movie. Jeanine Tesori wrote eleven new songs for the show. Three others came from the film, and four are standards from the 1920s.

The Full Monty (2000, David Yazbek) is based on an English film. Terrence McNally's book is set in the United States and tells of six unemployed steel workers whose personal and professional lives are in crisis. When their financial problems become desperate, they resort to a one-night stand in a strip club in order to make money.

Kiss of the Spider Woman (1993, Kander and Ebb) adapted Manuel Puig's story of a revolutionary and a homosexual imprisoned in an unnamed Latin American country.

Saturday Night Fever (London, 1998; Broadway, 1999) and *Urban Cowboy* (2003) are repackaged from films starring John Travolta.

Dirty Rotten Scoundrels (2005, David Yazbek and Jeffrey Lane) was adapted from the 1988 film about two con artists on the French Riviera who try to swindle money from rich women.

The Wedding Singer (2006, Matthew Sklar, Chad Beguelin, Tim Herlihy), set in 1985, is about a wannabe rock singer who supports himself by entertaining at wedding receptions. He's the life of the party—until his fiancée jilts him. Then he falls in love with a woman who's about to marry someone else.

Musicals Using Existing Pop Music

Ma Rainey's Black Bottom, a winner of three Tonys in 1984, returned to Broadway in 2003 starring Whoopi Goldberg. Playwright August Wilson set the show in a Chicago recording studio in 1927. Instead of an original score, Wilson incorporated blues songs made famous by Ma Rainey during her singing career.

Mamma Mia! (2001) was already an international hit by the time it reached Broadway. The show weaves twenty-two hit songs by the 1970s rock group ABBA into a comedy about a single mother who operates a taverna on a mythical Greek Island. The scores includes "Dancing Queen," and the title song, "Mamma Mia."

Dance Musicals

Contact (1999), conceived by Susan Stroman and John Weidman, tells three short stories, principally through Stroman's choreography. "Swinging," using the Rodgers and Hart song "My Heart Stood Still," is set in an eighteenth-century forest clearing. "Did You Move" takes place in 1954 in an Italian restaurant in Queens, New York. A beleaguered, neglected wife fantasizes love affairs, dancing to the music of Tchaikovsky, Grieg, and Bizet. "Contact," set in the present, is the story of a suicidal man and his fascination with a woman in a yellow dress. Couples swing-dance to the music of Benny Goodman, Dion, the Beach Boys, and others.

Bring In 'Da Noise, Bring In 'Da Funk (1996) tells the history of African Americans from slavery to the present through tap dance, choreographed by Savion Glover. Daryl Waters, Zane Mark, and Ann Duquesnay composed the music, with lyrics by Reg E. Gaines.

Twyla Tharp conceived and directed the show *Movin' Out* (2003), choreographing an anthology of songs written by Billy Joel. The theater piece spans two decades—from the 1960s to the 1980s. Act I is about the agony of separation of six lifelong friends when the boys are sent to Vietnam. In Act II, the boys return as hardened veterans. The friends struggle to rebuild their lives and rekindle their friendship.

New Productions

We resist the term "revival." That implies that the show died and was brought back to life. (You wouldn't call a modern production of a Shakespearean play a "revival.") A good musical retains its appeal generation after generation and can be staged not only by professional companies but also by amateur groups. Some great hits with specialized talent demands and elaborate, expensive staging, such as *Cats, Lion King, Aida,* and *Beauty and the Beast*, require professional productions.

Savion Glover dancing, c. 2000

Oklahoma! (2002) Rodgers and Hammerstein's classic still delights audiences with Susan Stroman's choreography.

Man of La Mancha (2002, Mitch Leigh, Joe Darion) Dale Wasserman adapted Miguel Cervantes' masterpiece, *Don Quixote de La Mancha*, into a poignant, dramatic book.

Flower Drum Song (2002) Rodgers and Hammerstein's musical about immigrants in San Francisco's Chinatown has a revised book by Henry David Hwang.

Gypsy (2003) Stephen Sondheim's music and Jule Styne's lyrics bring to life the story of strip tease artist Gypsy Rose Lee and her ambitious, overbearing stage mother, Rose.

Nine (2003, Maury Yeston) The 1982 production was based on Federico Fellini's 1963 surreal film $8^1/_2$. The story concerns the mid-life crisis of a 41-year old film director and the women in his life. Yeston also wrote the score for *Titanic* (1997).

During the 2005–2006 theater season, Broadway audiences welcomed fresh productions of Stephen Sondheim's *Sweeney Todd;* one of the musical comedy classics of the 1950s, *The Pajama Game,* by Richard Adler and Jerry Ross; Michael Bennett's landmark dance musical of the 1970s, *A Chorus Line;* and a new translation by Wallace Shawn of Berthold Brecht and Kurt Weill's *The Threepenny Opera.* A new generation of off-Broadway audiences could enjoy the revue that made theater history in the 1960s and 1970s, *Jacques Brel is Alive and Well and Living in Paris.*

Other Notable Composers and Lyricists

Frank Loesser (1910–69):   Where's Charley? (1948), *Guys and Dolls* (1950), *Most Happy Fella* (1956), *How to Succeed in Business Without Really Trying* (1961, several revivals)

Jule Styne (1905–94) and Betty Comden (b. 1915) and Adolph Green (1915–2002):   *Two on the Aisle* (1951), *Peter Pan* (1954), *Bells Are Ringing* (1958), *Say Darling* (1958), *Do Re Mi* (1960), *Subways Are For Sleeping* (1961), *Fade Out— Fade In* (1964). Styne also teamed with Leo Robin for *Gentlemen Prefer Blondes* (1949), with Bob Merrill for *Funny Girl* (1961), with **Stephen Sondheim** for *Gypsy* (1958, several revivals including 2003). Comden and Green, whose 60-year collaboration ended with Adolph Green's death in October 2002, also worked with **Leonard Bernstein**: *On the Town* (1944), *Wonderful Town* (1953).

Jerry Herman (b. 1933):   *Milk and Honey* (1961), *Hello, Dolly!* (1964), *Mame* (1966), *Mack & Mabel* (1974), *La Cage aux Folles* (1983)

Richard Adler (b. 1921) and Jerry Ross (1926–1955):   *Pajama Game* (1954), *Damn Yankees* (1955)

Meredith Willson (1900–84):   *The Music Man* (1957, revival 2000), *The Unsinkable Molly Brown* (1960), *Here's Love* (1963)

John Kander (b. 1932) and Fred Ebb (b. 1932):   *Cabaret* (1966, revival 1998), *The Happy Time* (1968), *Zorba* (1968), *Chicago* (1975, revival 1997), *Woman of the Year* (1981), *Kiss of the Spider Woman* (1993), *Curtains* (2006)

Jerry Bock (b. 1928) and Sheldon Harnick (b. 1924):   *Fiorello!* (1959), *Tenderloin* (1960), *She Loves Me* (1963), *Fiddler on the Roof* (1964), *The Apple Tree* (1966)

Burton Lane (1912–97):   *Finian's Rainbow* (1947, with **E.Y. Harburg**), *On a Clear Day You Can See Forever* (1965, with Alan Jay Lerner)

Tom Jones (b. 1928) and Harvey Schmidt (b. 1929):   *The Fantasticks* (1960), *110 in the Shade* (1963), *I Do! I Do!* (1966)

Marvin Hamlisch (b. 1944):   *A Chorus Line* (1975, with Edward Kleban)

Andrew Lloyd Webber (b. 1948) and Tim Rice (b. 1944):   *Joseph and the Amazing Technicolor Dreamcoat* (1968, 1972), *Jesus Christ Superstar* (1971), *Evita* (1976), *Cats* (1981), *Starlight Express* (1984), *Phantom of the Opera* (1986, with **Charles Hart** and **Richard Stilgoe**), *Aspects of Love* (1989, with **Don Black**), *Sunset Boulevard* (1993, Black), *Bombay Dreams* (2004, Black), *The Women in White* (2005, with **David Zippel**)

Alain Boublil (b. 1941) and Claude-Michel Schönberg (b. 1944):   *Les Misérables* (Broadway 1985–2003, with Herbert Kretzmer), *Miss Saigon* (1990), *Martin Guerre* (1995)

Alan Menken (b. 1949) and Howard Ashman (1950–1991):   *Beauty and the Beast* (1994). Menken and Ashman wrote three songs for *Aladdin* (2003, in rehearsal)

Summary of Terms

African-American musicals	modern operetta	rock opera
ballad opera	musical comedy	Singspiel
bridge	musical play	Standard Award
burlesque	opéra bouffe	Tony Award
chorus	operetta	troubadours
comic opera	popular opera	vaudeville
extravaganza/spectacle	Pulitzer Prize	verse
minstrel shows	revue	

The Lion King

28
Music in the Movies

ights dim, curtains open, and the screen comes alive. The title and credits roll. As soon as the music begins—even before we watch the first scene—we know a great deal about the film. Music, or the absence of it, provides an important clue to what we are about to see: a mystery, a comedy, a love story, a horror movie, a swashbuckling adventure, a shoot-'em-up Western, or an action thriller.

Since silent film days, music and the movies have been inextricably linked. As an ingredient of the total entertainment, music adds impact, heightens action, deepens emotion, increases tension, reinforces comedy, and augments mystery. In other words, music gives life to the film medium and draws the audience into the story.

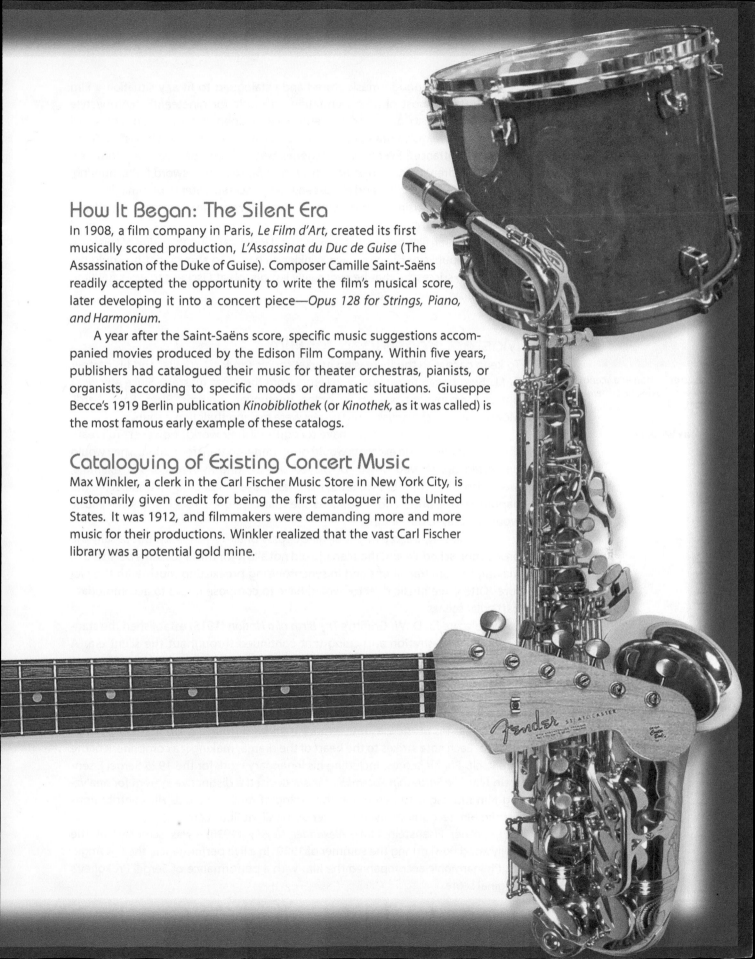

How It Began: The Silent Era

In 1908, a film company in Paris, *Le Film d'Art,* created its first musically scored production, *L'Assassinat du Duc de Guise* (The Assassination of the Duke of Guise). Composer Camille Saint-Saëns readily accepted the opportunity to write the film's musical score, later developing it into a concert piece—*Opus 128 for Strings, Piano, and Harmonium.*

A year after the Saint-Saëns score, specific music suggestions accompanied movies produced by the Edison Film Company. Within five years, publishers had catalogued their music for theater orchestras, pianists, or organists, according to specific moods or dramatic situations. Giuseppe Becce's 1919 Berlin publication *Kinobibliothek* (or *Kinothek,* as it was called) is the most famous early example of these catalogs.

Cataloguing of Existing Concert Music

Max Winkler, a clerk in the Carl Fischer Music Store in New York City, is customarily given credit for being the first cataloguer in the United States. It was 1912, and filmmakers were demanding more and more music for their productions. Winkler realized that the vast Carl Fischer library was a potential gold mine.

Buster Keaton in a scene from the silent movie *The General*

Max Winkler

Edmund Meisel

Fischer had enough music stored and catalogued to fit any situation a film maker needed, most of it concentrating on music for nineteenth-century-style melodrama: maestoso, agitato, misterioso, largo. Soon the designations changed from musical terms to dramatic elements: "villain lurks in the shadows" or "hero makes his entrance." Eventually, categories became even broader: sea storm, romance, children, chatter, parties, horror, humor, religious, sword fight, hunting, festival, orgies, forest fire, and almost anything a screenwriter might imagine.

So the enterprising Winkler wrote to the Universal Film Company. He offered to make up music cue sheets for all their films on one condition—that they would let him see each film before they released it. Understanding the value of this idea, Universal's publicity director gave Winkler a chance to show what he could do. Max was so successful that he eventually left his job at Fischer's to work full time in film music.

Masters Transcribed for Film

To keep pace with the increasing market for his services, Winkler and his partner S. M. Berg began to catalogue excerpts from the great masters. Since any work not under copyright was up for grabs, Beethoven, Brahms, Bizet, Bach, Verdi, Mozart, Grieg, Tchaikovsky, and others were making their film debuts.

The composers might not have recognized their works, however. To create the desired effect, the excerpts would often undergo transformation. They would be jazzed up, slowed down, or played out of tune as needed. For example, Mendelsson's or Wagner's wedding marches, played intact, might underscore the happiness of a bride and groom. As the marriage grew rocky, the same music would be played out of tune.

Occasionally, a score might be all-Debussy or all-Tchaikovsky, but usually the production schedule and the scenario did not allow for this. Problems persisted in making smooth transitions and in synchronizing preexisting music with the picture. Often, the music director would have to compose music to accommodate particular scenes.

The score for D. W. Griffith's *The Birth of a Nation* (1915) established the standards for orchestration and cuing that continued throughout the silent era. A joint work by Griffith and Joseph Carl Breil, a composer/orchestra leader, the score is a melange of original music interspersed with "Dixie," "The Star Spangled Banner," and quotes from Liszt, Verdi, Beethoven, Wagner, and Tchaikovsky.

Composer Edmund Meisel was responsible for another milestone in scoring silent films. His music was much more than background or an accessory to the picture. Each note strikes to the heart of the drama, making it a component of the film itself. For his scores, including his legendary work for the 1925 Sergei Eisenstein film *The Battleship Potemkin*, Meisel devised a distinctive system for analyzing film montages to determine the timing of music needed. His contributions earned him recognition as the master of the silent film score.

Another Eisenstein film—*Alexander Nevsky* (1938)—was screened at the Hollywood Bowl during the summer of 1989. In a live performance, the Los Angeles Philharmonic accompanied the film with a performance of Sergei Prokofiev's original score.

In 1981, after producer/director Francis Ford Coppola restored Abel Gance's four-hour silent masterwork *Napoleon,* Coppola arranged for special screenings in theaters that could accommodate a full orchestra. He had commissioned his father, composer Carmine Coppola, to write a new score for the movie. (Arthur Honegger composed the original.) Following the theatrical presentations with live music, Coppola used the new score as a synchronized sound track for the film.

The Role of Music in Sound Films

A beneficial side effect of silent film music was employment opportunities for instrumental players in hundreds of theaters. With the advent of sound films in 1927, however, the music track displaced live performances, and orchestra pits became empty.

From the earliest days of sound films through the summer of 1930, the most common use of music was in the musical films of the era, such as *Rio Rita, The Street Singer,* and *The Vagabond Lover.* By 1931, a few directors had incorporated music to support love scenes or to bridge silent sequences. For the most part, though, directors felt music had to be justified by the plot; for example, it had to emanate from a visible source on screen—a theater, a nightclub, a ballroom, or an organ grinder.

HISTORICAL PERSPECTIVE

From Broadway to Hollywood

The majority of films released in 1929 were musicals, almost all of which came from Broadway.

Film Music Comes of Age

During the next several years, composers skilled at writing symphonic music began to receive commissions to compose film music. Each score was unique, like a work of art in any other medium, with the best scores carrying the imprint of their composers. Music had assumed a more important function: to serve the story. A 1935 *New York Times* article characterized film music as a vital element—an accentuated background for mood and action.

Hermione Gingold and Maurice Chevalier in a scene from *Gigi*

Here are some of the composers, usually associated with concert music, who wrote original scores for films:

Malcolm Arnold	Aram Khachaturian
Leonard Bernstein	Ernesto Lecuona
Benjamin Britten	Gyorgy Ligeti
Mario Castelnuovo-Tedesco	Pietro Mascagni
Aaron Copland	Sergei Prokofiev
Rheinhold Gliere	Erik Satie
Ferde Grofe	Jan Sibelius
Hans Werner Henze	Virgil Thomson
Paul Hindemith	Ernst Toch
Gustav Holst	Edgar Varèse
Arthur Honegger	Ralph Vaughan Williams
Jacques Ibert	William Walton
Dmitri Kabalevsky	

Some films with original scores also include existing concert music pieces as recurrent themes. For example, in *Platoon* (1986), we hear not only Georges Delerue's score but also Samuel Barber's *Adagio for Strings*. Mozart's Piano Concerto No. 21 K. 467 is used as the love theme in the 1967 *Elvira Madigan*.

The Hollywood Sound

Early in the twentieth century, attitudes toward romantic music sharply changed. Orchestras and concert management organizations began to champion the works of twentieth-century composers whose musical language took a more intellectual approach than their nineteenth-century predecessors. To make room for these new compositions, music that was accessible—understandable to general audiences—was programmed less frequently. Seeking other outlets for their music, romantic-style composers turned to Hollywood.

Hollywood Sound

During the 1930s and 1940s, the lush, evocative "Hollywood Sound" enjoyed its Golden Age. The exponents of this style (such as Max Steiner, Erich Wolfgang Korngold, and Miklos Rozsa) brought to the medium an impressive music background and education. In creating the new genre, therefore, they understood the music of the past. As musicians, they stayed abreast of the latest developments in contemporary developments by studying the music of Ravel, Shostakovich, Frederick Delius (1862–1934), and Arnold Schoenberg. Despite the talent and impact of film composers, art music circles usually were condescending to movie music. Even Leonard Bernstein called it "ghastly."

The Contribution of Music to Film

In a 1949 *New York Times* article, Aaron Copland (*Of Mice and Men*, 1939; *Our Town*, 1940; *The Heiress* and *The Red Pony*, 1949) said: "Music can create a more convincing atmosphere of time and place. This atmosphere, musically speaking, is 'color.' Music creates a psychological element better than dialogue can." Copland also cited two other uses for music—as a neutral background that fills empty spots without our being aware of it, and as an intensifier that builds the drama and helps deliver the climax.

Music also builds and sustains momentum. Pay attention to how music is used in a James Bond thriller (score by John Barry) whenever Bond propels his high-tech vehicle either in pursuit or in flight from the villain. You'll find a similar technique in any action film released today.

Can you recall a film where certain music is associated with one character and then transferred to another character? *The Wizard of Oz* (1939, Oscar-winning score by Herbert Stothart) is one example. The melody we hear each time we see Miss Gulch riding her bicycle tells us that she is Dorothy's nemesis. In Oz, we hear the same melody when we see the witch ride her broom, leaving little doubt that Dorothy and her friends will eventually have to tangle with another nemesis.

Movie Music of the Golden Age

Film scores of the Golden Age—music that might be considered "schmaltzy" today—were artfully composed and executed to create and support the images we see on the screen. In addition, they were crafted to provide clues to things we could not see: what was happening *inside* a character (confusion, loneliness, fear, falling in love), what was about to happen *to* a character (discovery, betrayal, harm), what a character was like (seductive, compassionate, timid, evil), and what the character wanted (revenge, acceptance, mercy). A harp glissando expresses sentiment; blaring trumpets express heroism or victory.

LISTENING INSIGHTS

What to Listen for in Film Music

As a filmgoer, imagine the elements one might associate with a minuet played on a harpsichord, a calypso tune played on steel drums, a hillbilly song played on the banjo, and a fiery dance played on Flamenco guitar.

Because of film censorship, certain types of scenes could not be depicted from the 1930s into the 1960s. So composers suggested sex and violence by featuring certain instrumentation. Thrusting strings, saxophones, or clarinets might symbolize off-camera rape. And who can forget the driving, shrill violins that composer Bernard Herrmann used to punctuate each stab of the knife in the shower scene of Alfred Hitchcock's *Psycho*?

Imagery and Music

Film music helps imagery stay in our minds. For example, early in the classic film *Gone With the Wind* (1939, score by Max Steiner), the characters Scarlett O'Hara and her father, Gerald O'Hara, are standing under a tree on Tara, their plantation. As Mr. O'Hara imbues his daughter with his philosophy, "Land is all that matters," the films theme music swells. Then the camera pulls back, and with the music soaring, we see a silhouette of Scarlett and her father, symbolizing the prosperity of the Antebellum South. Later in the film, Scarlett returns to her plantation to find her

Clark Gable embraces Viven Leigh in *Gone with the Wind* (1939)

home and land ravaged by the Civil War. The moment we hear Steiner's theme again, we remember it, and our association between Scarlett and her deep attachment to Tara is complete. Used in imitation and repetition throughout the film, the recurrent theme keeps reminding us of the contrast between the glory of the past and the realities of the present.

Western movies present another set of images: the dusty streets of frontier towns, gunmen tumbling from second-story balconies, vast expanses of range land, crests of mountains lined with Indian warriors on ponies, circles of covered wagons, gunfights between outlaws and the posse. Even though these scenes might be considered clichés, a memorable Western movie can use these images in a unique or distinctive way. The score contributes to that uniqueness, as in the following films, all available on video: *High Noon* (1952, Dimitri Tiomkin), *The Magnificent Seven* (1960, Elmer Bernstein), *The Good, the Bad, and the Ugly* (1967, Ennio Morricone), and *Silverado* (1985, Bruce Broughton).

Some of the Great Film Composers of the Golden Age

Max Steiner

Max Steiner (1888–1971)   One of the most prolific film composers of his time, Max Steiner wrote symphonic, "wall-to-wall" scores—music that fills every moment of a film. He is known for using a "stinger chord" to punctuate the action and force the audience's attention to something specific on the screen. His outstanding scores include *King Kong* (1933), *The Informer* (1935, Academy Award), *A Star Is Born* (1937), *Gone With the Wind* (1939), *Citizen Kane* (1941), *Casablanca* (1942), *Now, Voyager* (1942, Academy Award), *Since You Went Away* (1944, Academy Award), and *Johnny Belinda* (1948).

Steiner was born in Vienna into an affluent family that boasted of its notable musicians and composers. As one story goes, it was Max's grandfather who advised Johann Strauss, Jr. to write for the theater. (Strauss later gave us such operettas as *Die Fledermaus* and *Zigeunerbaron*.)

Classically trained at the Vienna Imperial Academy, Steiner completed his music studies by the age of thirteen. Three years later, he had become an accomplished conductor. After emigrating to New York, Steiner worked with such Broadway greats as Jerome Kern, Victor Herbert, George White, Florenz Ziegfeld, and George Gershwin.

With the advent of the "talkies," Hollywood needed sound. The studios raided Broadway to supply composers, arrangers, orchestrators, copyists, music editors, and conductors to staff their expanding music departments. So Steiner went to Hollywood as an arranger-orchestrator for the 1929 musical film *Rio Rita* and became a member of the RKO music department. He composed his first complete score in 1932 for *Symphony of Six Million*—the first film to use music under dialogue.

In 1936 Steiner moved to Warner Brothers, where he remained until 1953. He then worked as a freelance composer, but as his eyesight began to fail, his productivity declined. Max Steiner completed his last film in 1965.

Erich Wolfgang Korngold

Erich Wolfgang Korngold (1897–1957)   Erich Korngold's nineteen film scores include *Anthony Adverse* (1936, Academy Award), *The Prince and the Pauper* (1937), *The*

Sea Wolf (1941), and *King's Row* (1942). He displayed his talent for music very early in life, and by age nine was called a genius by Gustav Mahler. Korngold later studied with Richard Strauss, intending to become a serious composer and conductor. He spoke of film composing as something to kill time until he could do something else.

Korngold was a master of swashbuckling melodies containing fanfares and fanfare-like music, a characteristic of his Academy Award-winning score for *The Adventures of Robin Hood* (1938)—one of seven scores he wrote for Errol Flynn movies. After completing *Robin Hood,* Korngold was preparing to return to his native Vienna to resume his concert music activities when he received word from his father to remain in the United States: Hitler had overrun Austria.

Errol Flynn in *The Adventures of Robin Hood* (1938)

Alfred Newman

David Raksin

Alfred Newman (1900–1970) Movie studios themselves were training grounds for composers. Alfred Newman, an excellent pianist, never studied composition formally. Instead, he learned to write for movies by doing it. He was born in 1900, the oldest of ten children. He was a concert pianist by age seven, and by the time he was in his twenties, Newman was working on Broadway. In 1930, Irving Berlin and George Gershwin mounted a campaign to bring him to Hollywood. Newman took the opportunity and became associated with Samuel Goldwyn for ten years.

From 1940 to 1960, Alfred Newman was the Music Director at 20th Century Fox—composing, conducting, and overseeing all musical arrangements for the studio's 26 to 54 releases a year. His influence was so great that many credit him with setting the style for film music of that period. Newman also recognized talent and was responsible for hiring noted film composers Franz Waxman, Bernard Herrmann, and David Raksin.

Alfred Newman was known for his melodic, lyrical love themes and orchestrations dominated by strings. In contrast to the wall-to-wall scores of Max Steiner, Newman's were designed to accompany the action. Among his many notable scores are *Les Misérables* (1935), *The Hunchback of Notre Dame* (1939), *How Green Was My Valley* (1941), *The Song of Bernadette* (1943, Academy Award), *Leave Her to Heaven* (1945), *Gentleman's Agreement* (1947), *Call Northside 777* (1948), *The Robe* (1953), *Love Is a Many-Splendored Thing* (1955, Academy Award), and *The Best of Everything* (1959).

In 1999, Newman Hall, a concert venue, was dedicated at the University of Southern California.

Franz Waxman (1906–1967) Born in eastern Europe, Franz Waxman showed early musical ability, and at age seventeen enrolled in the Dresden Music Academy. He soon moved on to the Berlin Music Conservatory, earning his tuition by playing piano with a jazz ensemble. In Berlin, Waxman came to the attention of conductor Bruno Walter, who encouraged him in his career.

Franz Waxman

After writing film scores for a number of German-language films, Waxman emigrated to the United States just as the Nazis were rising to power. At the beginning of his Hollywood career, he composed the score for *The Bride of Frankenstein* (1935), which not only displayed his motivic technique but also set new quality standards for the music of horror films.

Waxman wrote in various genres. His credits include *Captain's Courageous* (1937), *A Christmas Carol* (1938), *Rebecca* and *The Philadelphia Story* (1940), *Dr. Jekyll and Mr. Hyde* (1941), *Destination Tokyo* (1944), *To Have and Have Not* (1945), *Sunset Boulevard* (1950, Academy Award), *A Place in the Sun* (1951, Academy

Award), *Rear Window* (1954), *The Silver Chalice* (1955), and *Cimarron* (1960). During his later years, Waxman composed for several television series, notably *Gunsmoke, Twilight Zone,* and *Arrest and Trial.*

Hugo Friedhofer

Hugo Friedhofer (1902–1981)   A San Francisco native, Hugo Friedhofer began his Hollywood career as an orchestrator. Between 1936 and 1946, he orchestrated more than fifty scores for Max Steiner and worked on many others for Erich Korngold and Alfred Newman. His own composing career took off after he won an Oscar for *The Best Years of Our Lives* (1946). Through 1973, in addition to his many credits as co-composer or subordinate composer, Friedhofer was the principal composer for about seventy film scores, including *Body and Soul* and *The Bishop's Wife* (1947), *Joan of Arc* (1948), *Broken Arrow* (1950), *Vera Cruz* (1954), *Boy on a Dolphin, An Affair to Remember,* and *The Sun Also Rises* (1957), and *One-Eyed Jacks* (1960).

Dimitri Tiomkin

Dimitri Tiomkin (1894–1979)   Perhaps the most well-known movie composer between the early 1950s and the mid-1960s was Dimitri Tiomkin. Born in the Ukraine in 1894, he enrolled in St. Petersburg Conservatory in 1912 and studied composition with Alexander Glazunov (1865–1936). Tiomkin was working as a concert pianist by 1919, but after the October Revolution in the Soviet Union, he moved to Berlin and continued his music studies with pianist-composer Ferruccio Busoni (1866–1924). In the late 1920s, Tiomkin introduced Gershwin's *Concerto in F* to Paris audiences and included Gershwin's music in his concert tours throughout Europe.

Gary Cooper and Grace Kelly in *High Noon* (1952)

Miklos Rózsa

Tiomkin credited both Glazunov and Busoni for influencing his flair for dramatic scoring. He also developed the theory that film music could not only direct attention *to* the screen but also *from* the screen. For example, he believed that musical sounds could do what makeup could not—distract an audience from the performance of an aging actor trying to portray a young man in a love scene.

In his active film career from 1930 to 1971, Dimitri Tiomkin composed many memorable scores, including *Lost Horizon* (1937), *Duel in the Sun* (1946), *Red River* (1948), *High Noon* (1952, Academy Award), *The High and the Mighty* (1954, Academy Award), *Friendly Persuasion* (1956), *Giant* (1956), *The Old Man and the Sea* (1958, Academy Award), and *The Guns of Navarone* (1961).

Miklos Rózsa (1907–1995)   "The music of Hungary is stamped indelibly one way or another on virtually every bar I have ever put on paper," said Hungarian-born composer Miklos Rózsa. In a Hollywood career that spanned forty-five years, Rozsa composed for a variety of film genres. His music is best associated, however, with monumental biblical and historical epics—scores that convey grandeur and pageantry.

His first Oscar-winning score was for David O. Selznick's *Spellbound* (1945). It included the piano work *Spellbound Concerto.* Rozsa's numerous credits include *The Lost Weekend* (1945), *A Double Life* (1947, Academy Award), *Madame Bovary* (1949), *The Asphalt Jungle* (1950), *Quo Vadis* (1951), *Ivanhoe* (1952), *Ben-Hur* (1959, Academy Award), *King of Kings* and *El Cid* (1961), *Sodom and Gomorrah* (1962), *Eye of the Needle* (1981), and *Dead Men Don't Wear Plaid* (1982). In his later years, Rozsa taught film composition at the University of Southern California.

The Next Generation of Composers

Bernard Herrmann (1911–1975)   A student of Arnold Schoenberg, Bernard Herrmann introduced a twentieth-century sound to movie music. He was known for writing music that emphasized the mood and dramatic impact of a film, such as his score for the shadowy *Citizen Kane* (1941), the otherworldly *The Ghost and Mrs. Muir* (1948), and the original, chilling *Cape Fear* (1962). At age thirty, Herrmann won an Oscar for *All That Money Can Buy* (1941).

For eleven years, Herrmann was associated with Alfred Hitchcock, composing for such thrillers as *The Man Who Knew Too Much* (1956), *Vertigo* (1958), *North by Northwest* (1959), and *Psycho* (1960). (Danny Elfman arranged and adapted Hermann's score for the 1998 remake of *Psycho*.) Some experts have suggested that Herrmann's music was essential in creating the intensity of Hitchcock's films. Despite their long collaboration, the Herrmann-Hitchcock association ended bitterly.

In 1966, Bernard Herrmann completed the score for the futuristic *Fahrenheit 451*. He then composed in Europe for a number of years, including films for director François Truffaut. In 1976, Herrmann resurfaced in Hollywood, working with young directors on his last two films: Brian de Palma's *Obsession* and Martin Scorsese's *Taxi Driver*.

Bernard Herrmann

Anthony Perkins and Janet Leigh in *Psycho* (1960)

CHALLENGE YOUR EXPERTISE

Why did movie studios have to establish large music departments?

Elmer Bernstein (1922–2004)   With more than 200 films to his credit, Elmer Bernstein had been in the business for a decade before his initial success composing a jazz score for *The Man With the Golden Arm* (1955). Building on his new reputation, he then wrote jazz scores for *Sweet Smell of Success* (1957), *Some Came Running* (1958), and *Walk on the Wild Side* (1962). Among his great Western scores are *The Magnificent Seven* (1960, Academy Award) and *True Grit* (1969). His comedies include *Thoroughly Modern Millie* (1967, Academy Award), *Airplane* (1980), *Trading Places* (1983), and *Ghostbusters* (1984). Bernstein's more recent scores include *A Rage in Harlem* and *Rambling Rose* (1991), *The Age of Innocence* (1993), *Devil in a Blue Dress* (1995), *Hoodlum* (1996), John Grisham's *The Rainmaker* (1997), and *Twilight* (1998), *The Deep End of the Ocean* (1998), *Far From Heaven* (2002, Academy Award).

Elmer Bernstein

Jerry Goldsmith (1929–2004)   One of the most respected and prolific Hollywood composers is Jerry Goldsmith. His career began after he attended Miklos Rozsa's film composing classes at the University of Southern California in the late 1940s. Since then, the roster of his credits continues to expand in an impressive body of diverse works. His films include *Rio Conchos* (1964), *The Sand Pebbles* and *The Blue Max* (1966), *Planet of the Apes* (1968), *Patton* (1970), *Papillon* (1973), *Chinatown* (1974), *The Omen* (1976, Academy Award), *Islands in the Stream* (1977), *Coma* (1978), *Star Trek* (1979), *First Blood* (1982), *Poltergeist* (1982, Academy Award nomination), *Twilight Zone—The Movie* (1983), two more Rambo films

Jerry Goldsmith

(1985 and 1988), *Star Trek V* (1989), *Total Recall* (1990), *Forever Young* (1992), *The Ghost and the Darkness* (1996), *Air Force One, L.A. Confidential,* and *The Edge* (1997), *Deep Rising* (1998), *Star Trek Insurrection* (1998), and *The Mummy* (1999).

Quincy Jones

Quincy Jones (b. 1933)   With careers in both performing and record-producing that rival anyone in the industry, Quincy Jones burst onto the film scene with *The Pawnbroker* (1965). He followed that with *In Cold Blood* (1967), *For the Love of Ivy* (1968), *In the Heat of the Night* (1969), *They Call Me Mr. Tibbs* (1970), *The Getaway* (1972), the television series *Roots* (1977), and *The Color Purple* (1985).

Dave Grusin

Dave Grusin (b. 1934)   Dave Grusin's diverse Hollywood credits include *The Graduate* and *Divorce American Style* (1967), *Tell Them Willie Boy Is Here* (1969), *Three Days of the Condor* (1975), *Heaven Can Wait* (1978), *The Electric Horseman* and *The Champ* (1979), *Absence of Malice* and *On Golden Pond* (1981), *Reds* (1981, with Stephen Sondheim), *Tootsie* (1982), *The Little Drummer Girl* (1984), *The Milagro Beanfield War* (1988), John Grisham's *The Firm* (1993), *Selena* (1996), and *Hope Floats* (1998).

Ennio Morricone

Ennio Morricone (b. 1928)   Morricone made his mark during the 1960s as the composer for Sergio Leone's "Spaghetti Westerns," so called because they were made in Italy. These films also propelled Clint Eastwood to stardom. A notable feature of his scores is the way they contribute to the overall style of those films. Morricone's tremendous output has won him admiration by his peers and his fans. More recently, he composed scores for Leone's *Once Upon a Time in America* (1984). His many other films include *The Mission* (1986), *The Untouchables* (1987), *State of Grace* (1990), *In the Line of Fire* (1993), *Bulworth* (1998) and *Lolita* (1998). He has also scored a number of foreign films, including *Cinema Paradiso* (1988), *Tie Me Up! Tie Me Down!* (1990), *Everybody's Fine* (1990), and the three *La Cage aux Folles* films (1978, 1981, 1986).

John Barry

John Barry (b. 1933)   John Barry has enjoyed a long, prestigious career. His scores include *Born Free* (1966, Oscar for title song), *The Lion in Winter* (1968, Academy Award), *Midnight Cowboy* and the song "Everybody's Talkin' 'Bout Me" (1969), and most of the James Bond films from the early 1960s through the late 1980s, including the original James Bond theme. Barry's scores for *Out of Africa* (1985) and *Dances With Wolves* (1990) both won Academy Awards. During the past decade, he wrote music for *Indecent Proposal* (1993), *The Scarlet Letter* (1995), *Swept From the Sea* (1997), and *Mercury Rising* (1998).

Henry Mancini

Henry Mancini (1924–1994)   Of all Henry Mancini's film music, he may be best remembered for the *Pink Panther* theme (and the eight Pink Panther scores) and for his song "Moon River" from *Breakfast at Tiffany's* (1961). Both the song and film score won Oscars. The next year, he again took Best Song honors for the title song from *Days of Wine and Roses* (1962). The Mancini touch is an important adjunct in approximately ninety films, including *Experiment in Terror* (1962), *Wait Until Dark* and *Two For the Road* (1967), *Sometimes a Great Notion* (1971), and *Victor/Victoria* (1982).

Maurice Jarré

Maurice Jarré (b. 1924)   Since appearing on the film scene in the late 1950s, Maurice Jarré has composed dozens of scores, expressing himself both in the full-scale orchestral style and the electronic style. His full-scale scores include *Lawrence of Arabia* (1962, Academy Award), *Dr. Zhivago* (1965, Academy Award), *Ryan's Daughter* (1970), *The Tin Drum* (1979), *The Year of Living Dangerously* (1982),

A Passage to India (1984, Academy Award), *Mad Max: Beyond Thunderdome* (1985), *Fatal Attraction* (1987), *Ghost* (1990), and *Only the Lonely* (1991). In the electronic style, Jarré's most interesting work includes *Mosquito Coast* (1986) and *Gorillas in the Mist* (1988). His massive score for *Jacob's Ladder* (1990) blends both styles.

Lalo Schifrin (b. 1932)   During his almost-thirty-five-year Hollywood career, Lalo Schifrin has been an active conductor as well as a composer for movies and television. His films include *The President's Analyst* and *Cool Hand Luke* (1967), *Bullitt* (1968), *Dirty Harry* (1971), *Magnum Force* (1973), *The Four Musketeers* (1975), *Tank* (1983), *Sudden Impact* (1983), *The Dead Pool* (1988), *Money Talks* (1997), and *Rush Hour* (1998).

Lalo Schifrin

Music and the Magic of Animation

The Timelessness of Walt Disney

Since the earliest days of Walt Disney Productions, music has been an essential element in the creation of animated films. Walt often remarked that music helps bring animation to life. To synchronize the sound with the animation of the film *Fantasia*, he built a state-of-the-art, stereophonic sound-dubbing theater on his studio in Burbank, California.

Walt Disney

When we think of the Disney classics, we remember the wonderful songs that came from some of Walt's earliest films: "Whistle While You Work" and "Heigh-Ho" from *Snow White and the Seven Dwarfs* (1937); the Oscar-winning "When You Wish Upon a Star" from *Pinocchio* (1940); "Some Day My Prince Will Come" and the Oscar-winning "A Dream is a Wish Your Heart Makes" from *Cinderella* (1950). For the Oscar-winning film *Mary Poppins* (1964), composers Richard M. and Robert B. Sherman not only walked off with Best Song for "Chim Chim Cher-ee," but also Best Score honors.

In the 1940 classic *Fantasia*, Walt Disney added a new dimension to the partnership of music and animation. Each animated segment is a visualization of existing concert music:

Rite of Spring scene from *Fantasia*

- *Toccata and Fugue in d minor,* by Johann Sebastian Bach
- *The Nutcracker Suite,* by Peter Ilyich Tchaikovsky
- *The Sorcerer's Apprentice,* by Paul Dukas (1865–1935)
- *Rite of Spring,* by Igor Stravinsky
- *Symphony No. 6* (*Pastoral*), by Ludwig van Beethoven
- "Dance of the Hours" from *La Gioconda,* by Amilcare Ponchielli (1834–1886)
- *Night on Bald Mountain,* by Modest Mussorgsky
- *Ave Maria,* by Franz Schubert

Frank Churchill was the principal composer of *Snow White and the Seven Dwarfs* (1937), *Dumbo* (1941, Oscar), and *Bambi* (1942). **George Bruns,** who composed scores for live-action as well as animated films, was the principal composer for the studio's television series *Davy Crockett* (1955). His scores for animated films include *Sleeping Beauty* (1959), *One Hundred and One Dalmatians* (1961), *The Sword in the Stone* (1963), *JThe The Jungle Book* (1967), and *The Aristocats* (1970).

From the mid-1960s to the early 1980s, composer **Buddy Baker** contributed his sizable talent to the Disney archive. In addition to his work on live-action films, Baker wrote scores for animated films, including *The Million Dollar Duck* (1971) and *The Fox and the Hound* (1981).

Let's fast-forward to the 1980s and 1990s, when **Alan Menken** was associated with the Disney classics. Except for the Oscar-winning score by **Elton John** for *The Lion King* (1994, also Best Song, "Circle of Life"), Menken composed scores for many Disney releases: *The Little Mermaid* (1989, Oscar), *Beauty and the Beast* (1991, Oscar), *Aladdin* (1992, Oscar), *Pocahontas* (1995, Oscar for score and for Best Song "Colors of the Wind"), *The Hunchback of Notre Dame* (1995), and *Hercules* (1997).

Scene from Star Wars: *Attack of the Clones* (2002)

John Williams (b. 1932)

Born in the New York City borough of Queens, John Williams began to study piano at the age of seven, later learning trombone, trumpet, and clarinet. In 1948 his family moved to Los Angeles, where his father played in film studio orchestras. John played, arranged, and composed for his high school band. After graduation, he took courses in piano and composition at UCLA and studied privately with pianist-arranger Bobby Van Eps.

Drafted into the Air Force in 1952, Williams spent part of his tour conducting and arranging music for service bands. Following his discharge in 1954, he studied piano with the legendary Rosina Lhevine at the Julliard School of Music, working as a jazz pianist in New York nightclubs. Later he was accompanist and conductor for singer Vic Damone.

Great studio composers with whom Williams apprenticed—including Alfred Newman, Dmitri Tiomkin, and Franz Waxman—recognized his versatility and talent for orchestration. He also continued his serious music studies in Hollywood with Arthur Olaf Anderson and with the noted Italian composer Mario Castelnuovo-Tedesco.

Beginning with his first screen credit for *Because They're Young* (1960), Williams' career as a film composer gathered momentum. He soon became one of the most sought-after composers in Hollywood. During the next five years alone, he composed eight full scores. The following decade, in addition to his other film work, he scored disaster films: *Poseidon Adventure* (1972), *Earthquake* and *Towering Inferno* (1974). Williams won his first of many Academy Awards for his adaptation of the Sheldon Harnick-Jerry Bock Broadway score for *Fiddler on the Roof* (1972).

Also in 1974, a young director named Steven Spielberg asked John Williams to score his new movie *Sugarland Express,* beginning one of the greatest composer/director relationships and collaborations in motion picture history: *Jaws I* (1975, Oscar) and *Jaws II* (1979), *Close Encounters of the Third Kind* (1977), *Raiders of the Lost Ark* (1981, Oscar, and the 1984, 1989, and 2005 sequels), *E.T., the Extra Terrestrial* (1982), *Empire of the Sun* (1987), *two* Jurassic Park *films* (1993 and 1997), *Schindler's List* (1993, Oscar), *Amistad* (1997), *Saving Private Ryan* (1998), *AI* (2001).

John Williams' scores also include: *The Eiger Sanction* (1975), *Midway* and Alfred Hitchcock's last film, *Family Plot* (1976), *Star Wars* (1977, Oscar), *The Deerhunter* (1978), *Superman* (1979) and the sequels, *The Empire Strikes Back* (1980), *Born on the Fourth of July* (1989, Oscar), *JFK* (1991, Oscar), *Angela's Ashes* and *Star Wars Episode I* (1999), *The Patriot* (2000), the *Harry Potter* movies (2001, 2002, 2003), *Catch Me If You Can* and *Star Wars: Attack of the Clones* (2002), *Star Wars Episode III* and *War of the Worlds* (2005), and the two Oscar–nominated scores (2005) for *Memoirs of a Geisha* and *Munich*.

Listen to any of the powerful recurrent themes that Williams is known for. They serve as mnemonics to help us immediately associate music with a particular character, location, or dramatic situation. For example, certain music in *Jaws, Star Wars*, and *Superman* evokes immediate associations in both the original films and their sequels. Think about the ominous motive in *Jaws*. Just two repeated notes arouse fear and alert us: a shark is nearby—even if we cannot see it. When we hear the heroic *Star Wars* theme playing over the opening credits and repeated as the Jedi return, we are optimistic that ultimately the "good guys" will prevail.

Williams again evokes optimism with the heroic theme of *Superman*. As soon as we hear it and see Superman flying to the rescue, we know that this larger-than-life character has come to affirm the concept of good triumphing over evil. The "Love Theme" helps us associate the music with the relationship between the Lois Lane character and the Clark Kent-Superman character.

There is a striking similarity between the "Love Theme" and a theme from Richard Strauss's symphonic poem *Death and Transfiguration*. Even the orchestral treatment of the *Superman* score is reminiscent of late-nineteenth-century composers such as Richard Strauss and Richard Wagner.

Superman originated in 1938 as a comic-book character, and the films retain a satiric, tongue-in-cheek treatment of the hero who repeatedly saves the day against seemingly insurmountable odds. However, the romantic notion about *Superman* remains. Philosopher and poet Friedrich Nietzsche (1844–1900) promoted a doctrine that glorifies the "superman," or Übermensch, as he called him. Therefore, Williams' choice to emulate Strauss and Wagner is consistent with the nineteenth-century concept of "superman."

From 1990 to 1993, John Williams was conductor and music director of the Boston Pops. In a 1980 *Newsweek* interview, he was quoted as saying, "I know it sounds corny, but my life revolves around music."

Matching Music and Pictures

After a film is assembled, the composer and the music director discuss the score. The composer then has a relatively short time to write precisely timed music that conveys the spirit of the picture and matches the fixed image—an image already set by writers, the director, and the actors.

The Role of the Music Editor

Working with the composer, director, and film editor, the music editor makes the click track by "spotting" the picture and marking where each cue will begin and end. A hole or "click" on the film indicates a cue change, for example, when to start the "chase."

CHALLENGE YOUR EXPERTISE

Which three of the following have a similar function—recurring theme, *sostenuto*, leitmotif, *idée fixe*, coda?

If the composer wants to catch a certain action, the music editor marks the film with a *streamer*, which looks like a vertical stripe. The streamer shows tempo changes within each cue change, for example, how fast to play the "chase music." Devised by Alfred Newman, these markings are known as the Newman System.

Film scores usually are recorded in studio dubbing theaters. The conductor works to a clock. Timing is controlled by the fixed image on the screen. With the "click track" of the film projected on a screen mounted on the back wall, the conductor can watch the film while directing the orchestra.

The Stature of Movie Music Today

In the past two decades, film music has soared in popularity. Aware of the public's enjoyment of film scores, conductors are including movie themes in their concert programs. During his tenure as music director of the Boston Pops, John Williams programmed at least one piece of his music in every Pops concert. His recordings with the Boston Pops have greatly contributed to the cause of film music. Because films are among the most popular forms of entertainment, targeting the film-going audience makes sense. When people enjoy a film, they remember the music and buy the recording—such as *Titanic* (1997, score by James Horner), which not only won an Oscar but also topped the pop charts and won a Grammy for the song "My Heart Will Go On" (music and lyrics by James Horner and Will Jennings).

In a *Los Angeles Times* interview, David Raksin (*Laura*, 1944; *Forever Amber*, 1947; *The Bad and the Beautiful*, 1952) noted that film composers have become recognized for their art form, not only by the public but by the music world in general. While he was a professor at the University of Southern California, Raksin was an organizer and a panelist for the Seventh Annual New Music Festival, a forum for Hollywood composers becoming established in the industry.

LISTENING INSIGHTS

What to Listen for in Film Music

Your next trip to the movies might be an opportunity to enjoy the film at a different level. See if you can remember when the music begins and when it cuts out. When is it loud? When is it barely audible in the background? Are there extended periods without music? Which instruments are playing? Does the music tug at your heart? Does it make you smile? How does it make you feel? Do you notice the music at all?

To become fully aware of music in the movies, you need to listen. If you enjoy a score, watch the credits and notice who composed it.

CHALLENGE YOUR EXPERTISE

In filmmaking, what is the track without music called?

So Many Films—So Many Scores

Listing every composer with complete credits would be impossible. What follows is a brief sample of the many established composers who have been involved with some of the more popular or honored films:

Bruce Broughton *Young Sherlock Holmes* and *Silverado* (1985), *The Boy Who Could Fly* and *Sweet Liberty* (1986), *Betsy's Wedding* and *The Rescuers* (1990), *Honey, I Blew Up the Kids* (1992), *Homeward Bound: The Incredible Journey* (1993), *Miracle on 34th Street* (1994), *House Arrest* (1996), *Lost in Space* (1998), *One Tough Cop* (1998)

Bill Conti *Rocky* (1976, Academy Award), *Private Benjamin* (1980), *The Right Stuff* (1983, Academy Award), *The Karate Kid* (1984), *F/X* (1986), *Broadcast News* (1987), *Lean on Me* (1989), *Necessary Roughness* (1991), *Napoleon* (1996), *Thomas Crown Affair* (1999), *FX* (2001), *G* (2002)

Georges Delerue *A Man for All Seasons* (1966), *The Day of the Jackal* (1973), *Silkwood* (1983), *Agnes of God* (1985), *Platoon* (1986), *Twins* and *Beaches* (1988), *Steel Magnolias* (1989), *Joe Versus the Volcano* (1990), *Rich in Love* (1993)

Anne Dudley *The Crying Game* (1992), *Knight Moves* (1993), *The Full Monty* (1996, Academy Award for Best Comedy Score), *American History X* (1998), *The Gathering* (2002), *Tristan & Isolde* (2006)

Cliff Eidelman *Crazy People* (1990), *A Simple Twist of Fate* (1994), *Free Willy 3: The Rescue* (1997), *One True Thing* (1998), *The Lizzie McGuire Movie* (2003), *Sisterhood of the Traveling Pants* (2005)

Danny Elfman Danny Elfman, also known as Oingo Boingo, has compiled more than 120 credits as a film and television composer. After reading this abbreviated filmography, listen for his distinctive style when you see his name on opening credits. Elfman has a particular gift for quirky science fiction, comic strip characters' action films, and not-quite-horror movies. You might recall the music he scored for the *Spider Man* movies (2002 and 2004; *Spider Man 3* is scheduled for 2007 release), *Men in Black, Men in Black II, Charlotte's Web, Big Fish, Hulk, Planet of the Apes* (2001), *Spy Kids, Proof of Life, Good Will Hunting, Mission Impossible, Sleepy Hollow, The Nightmare Before Christmas, Beetlejuice,* and *Dick Tracy.*

Toby Maguire in *Spider Man 2* (2004)

Elfman wrote the score or main theme for several television series, including *Batman, The Simpsons, Dilbert,* and the recent hit *Desperate Housewives.* The themes from *Batman* and *The Simpsons* were used in the subsequent film versions. Elfman also contributed original music to the film *Chicago* (Broadway score by John Kander and Fred Ebb).

George Fenton   *Gandhi* (1982, Oscar), *Cry Freedom* (1987), *Dangerous Liaisons* (1988), *White Palace* and *Memphis Belle* (1990), *Shadowlands* (1993), *Groundhog Day* (1993), *The Madness of King George* (1994), *The Crucible* (1996), *Dangerous Beauty* (1998), *Living Out Loud, Ever After, You've Got Mail* (1998), *Anna and the King* (1999), *Sweet Home Alabama* (2002), *Bewitched* (2005)

James Horner   *Star Trek 2* (1982), *Star Trek 3* (1984), *Cocoon* (1985), *Aliens* (1986), *An American Tail* (1986), *Glory* (1989), *Field of Dreams* (1989), *Patriot Games* (1992), *Pelican Brief* (1993), *Legends of the Fall* (1994), *Braveheart* (1995), *Apollo 13* (1995), *Courage Under Fire* (1996), *The Devil's Own* (1996), *Titanic* (1997), *Deep Impact* (1998), *Perfect Storm* (2000), *A Beautiful Mind* (2001), *House of Sand and Fog* (2003), *Troy* (2004)

Mark Isham   *Quiz Show* (1994), *The Net* (1995), *Last Dance* (1996), *Blade* (1998), *October Sky* (1999), *What Women Want* (2000), *The Cooler* (2003), *Crash* (2004), *In Her Shoes* (2005)

Michael Kamen   *Brazil* (1985), three *Die Hard* films (1988, 1990, 1995), four *Lethal Weapon* films (1987, 1989, 1992, 1998), *Robin Hood: Prince of Thieves* (1991), *The Three Musketeers* (1993), *Circle of Friends* and *Don Juan DeMarco* (1994), *Mr. Holland's Opus* (1995), *Jack* (1996), *101 Dalmatians* (1996), *Event Horizon* (1997), *What Dreams May Come* (1998), *X-Men* (2000)

Randy Newman   *The Natural* (1984), *Awakenings* (1990), *Toy Story* (1995), *Michael* (1996), *James and the Giant Peach* (1996), *Cats Don't Dance* (1997), *Pleasantville* (1998), *Meet the Parents* (2000) *Seabiscuit* (2003)

Thomas Newman   Thomas Newman Youngest son of Hollywood music legend Alfred Newman, has risen to stardom in the new generation of film composers. He has written music for more than fifty films, including *The Shawshank Redemption, The Horse Whisperer, White Oleander, American Beauty, Finding Nemo, The Cinderella Man,* and *Lemony Snicket's A Series of Unfortunate Events.*

Newman's notable television scores include *Citizen Cohn* and *Angels in America.* His main theme music for the HBO series *Six Feet Under* won an Emmy Award.

Basil Poledouris   *Robocop* (1987), *The Hunt for Red October* (1990), *Quigley Down Under* (1990), *Les Misérables* (1997)

Rachel Portman   *Where Angels Fear to Tread* (1991), *Used People* (1992), *Benny and Joon* (1993), *Sirens* (1994), *Marvin's Room* (1996), *Emma* (1996), *Addicted to Love* (1996), *Beloved* (1998), *Home Fries* (1998), *Cider House Rules* (1999) *Chocolat* (2000), *Manchurian Candidate* (2004)

Graeme Revell   *The Hand That Rocks the Cradle* (1992), *The Crow* (1993), *Spawn* (1997), *The Saint* (1997), *Phoenix* (1998), *Lara Croft Tomb Raider* (2001), *Sin City* (2005), *Aeon Flux* (2006)

Richard Robbins   *Remains of the Day* (1993), *A Soldier's Daughter Never Cries* (1998)

Marc Shaiman   *When Harry Met Sally* (1989), *A Few Good Men* (1992), *Sleepless in Seattle* (1993), *The American President* (1995), *Ghosts of Mississippi* and *The First Wives Club* (1996), *In and Out* (1997), *Simon Birch* (1998), *Patch Adams* (1998), *The Kid* (2000), *Down with Love* (2003) *Rumar Has It* (2005)

Alan Silvestri   *Romancing the Stone* (1984), three *Back to the Future* films (1985, 1989, 1990), *Predator* (1987), *Who Framed Roger Rabbit?* (1988), *The Abyss* (1989), *Soapdish* (1991), *Eraser* (1996), *Contact* (1997), *Holy Man* (1998), *Practical Magic* (1998), *Stewart Little* (1, 1999; 2, 2002), *What Lies Beneath* (2000), *Lilo & Stitch* (2002) *Polar Express* (2004)

Gabriel Yared   *Camille Claudel* (1989), *The English Patient* (1996), *The Wings of the Dove* (1997), *City of Angels* (1998), *Message in a Bottle* (1999), *Cold Mountain* (2003), *Shall We Dance* (2004)

Christopher Young   Christopher Young first became known for his effective electronic music in scary thrillers such as *Hellraiser* (1987). Now he composes both orchestral and electronic music. *Tales from the Hood* and *Virtuosity* (1995), *Hard Rain* (1997), *Hush* (1998), *Urban Legend* (1998), *The Rounders* (1998), *Entrapment* (1999), *Shipping News* (2001), *Runaway Jury* (2003), *Exorcism of Emily Rose* (2005)

Hans Zimmer   *Driving Miss Daisy* (1989), *Black Rain* (1989), *Pacific Heights* (1990), *Thelma and Louise* (1991), *Backdraft* (1991), *A League of Their Own* (1992), *Cool Runnings* (1993), *Broken Arrow* (1995), *The Preacher's Wife* (1996), *As Good As it Gets* (1997), *The Thin Red Line* (1998), *Prince of Egypt* (songs by Steven Schwartz 1998), *Gladiator* (2000), *The Ring* (1, 2002; 2, 2005), *Something's Gotta Give* (2003), *Shark Tale* (2004), *Madagascar* (2005), *Da Vinci Code* (2006)

Summary of Terms

click track	sound dubbing	stinger chord
film score	sound film	streamers
motivic technique	sound track	synchronized sound track
recurrent theme	spotting	*Übermensch*

29
Contributions of
World Cultures

s new modes of transportation and electronic communication shrink the world into a "global village," as Marshall McLuhan called it, we learn about and interact with cultures different from ours.

To learn more about the music of these cultures, ethnomusi-cologists equipped with tape recorders and video cameras travel to some of the world's most remote areas to study the native music. This chapter covers only a sampling of that vast variety of folk and ethnic music.

Thus far, our focus has mainly been on music encountered in the North American and European concert halls. In the past century, an existing and distinctive wealth of folk and ethnic music from world cultures has influenced that main body of traditional Western concert music. Ethnomusicologists predict that ethnic influence will ultimately bring about even more profound changes in Western music.

Early Interactions

America's Centennial   The place is Philadelphia. The year, 1876. The event, a small-scale World Exposition to celebrate the 100th anniversary of the American Declaration of Independence. In response to invitations, music groups from distant lands perform at the event, exposing large groups of Westerners for the first time to music of diverse cultures.

Evidently the interaction was dynamic, because other major European and American cities hosted World Expositions before the turn of the century:

1878	Paris
1882	Moscow
1883	Amsterdam
1889	Paris
1893	Chicago
1897	Brussels

The late nineteenth century was a time when nationalism was taking hold, nurturing an interest in travel and world cultures. Nationalistic music became the vogue—in 1880, Tchaikovsky premiered his musical travel adventures throughout Italy with *Capriccio italien;* in 1888, Rimsky-Korsakov introduced his *Capriccio espagnole* and his Arabian-influenced *Scheherazade*.

In 1889, for the 100th anniversary of the Revolution, the French government financed the construction of the Eiffel Tower and invited a large array of ethnic music groups to perform at the World Exposition in Paris. Musicians flocked to see and hear these groups firsthand. They were impressed, and the direction of traditional Western music began to change.

Non-Western Influences in Western Art Music

You have read earlier about some of the influences of non-Western music, some inspired by the international expositions, others through less direct influence:

- Asian scales and percussion instruments were used by Puccini in his operas *Madama Butterfly* (about Japan) and *Turandot* (about China); more recently, in the hit musical *Miss Saigon* (about Vietnam and Thailand), Boublil and Schönberg abundantly use Asian scales, flutes, and percussion instruments.
- African percussion ensembles inspired Stravinsky's greater use of percussion instruments and polyrhythms.
- African music contributed significantly to American jazz.

Other Changes in Western Art Music

Scales and Tonal Material   Some composers considered traditional scales overworked. After hearing non-Western music, they began experimenting not only with Asian and African scales but also with newly devised scales and tonal systems.

Instruments   Composers have been incorporating non-Western instruments into their works for some time. What follows is a brief list of instruments you may encounter at contemporary Western music concerts:

From Africa

drums (various shapes, sizes, and
    construction material)
xylophone

wood blocks
gourds

From Islamic North Africa and Turkey

cymbals (various sizes, starting in
    the late eighteenth century)
triangle (nineteenth century)

bass drum (starting in the
    late eighteenth century)
timpani or kettledrums
    (eighteenth century)

From South and Central America

maracas
timbales
bongos

conga drum
claves
cowbell

From Asia

Korean temple blocks
Indonesian antique cymbals

Chinese gongs (tam tam,
starting in the nineteenth
century)

An African master drummer
shows a young student how to
play.

Music South of the Sahara

Encompassing more than fifty countries, Africa is home to more than 500 million
people who have developed hundreds of languages and religions and a wide
diversity of music. In spite of the diversity, there are some similar characteristics
among African musical traditions about which we can generalize.

Role of Music in African Life

Hardly a tribal or religious activity in African daily life takes place
without music. Preparations for, during, and following the hunt,
for instance, are all accompanied by prescribed musical activities, enhanced by dances, masks, and costumes. Puberty rites,
weddings, and funerals all have their customary music.

Like much non-Western music, African music has mainly
been passed orally from generation to generation. In rural areas, many African children grow up dancing and contributing
their musical talents to the tribal rituals. Everyone participates,
and as they grow older, a few become soloists and chant leaders. So integral is music in the life of each person that this interest continues even after a man or a woman leaves tribal life
to live in the city or among other cultures.

Other Instruments

African musicians use a variety of flutelike instruments, animal
horns, whistles, thumb harps, and stringed instruments in addition to instruments that have already crossed over into
Western ensembles. This wide array contributes to the rich-
ness of the overall sound.

A musician from Johannesburg,
South Africa, playing an electric
guitar that he made out of an oil
can.

The African drummers who are part of the retinue of King Oyo of the Yorbua Tribe, Nigeria, Africa

Rhythm

At the core of African music is rhythm. Melody and harmony usually are subordinate to the rhythmic drive of the music.

Polyrhythms   African music often employs multilayers of rhythms. Each percussionist may add a different rhythm, resulting in a highly complex polyrhythmic texture. Dancing adds more complexity to the performance. Each tribal dancer chooses from the various rhythms as the source of inspiration for movement.

Changing Meters and Rhythms   In the nineteenth century, after returning from Africa, one musicologist reported that "African percussionists don't seem to know how to keep time." Because he was unfamiliar with African rhythms, he failed to understand their sophistication. In fact, an important characteristic of African music is its changing rhythms and metrical groups.

Ostinato   This repetitive rhythmic pattern is at the core of African percussion ensemble music. The ostinato player helps keep a regular pattern moving forward, enabling other percussionists to improvise freely, often skirting around the steady beat.

Improvisation   African musicians strive to avoid the obvious. While some members of a percussion ensemble provide an underlying rhythmic element with a steady beat or ostinato, others are free to play "around the beat" rather than exactly "on the steady beat." After all, the beat is already there; they can feel it. Adding their own rhythmic layers is a valued form of individual expression. Focusing on one player in the group, you will hear changing, imaginative, and complex improvisations.

Vocal Music   Though usually subordinate to rhythm, African singing is still quite important. Some vocal music uses words; however, most African singing employs varieties of ostinato chants.

The pentatonic scale predominates in African music, but some pitches—microtones—differ from Western pitches. *Microtones* fall between the tones in the traditional Western chromatic scale.

Microtones

One characteristic of much of the vocal music of Africa is the use of *call and response,* discussed previously in the chapter on jazz. One member of the tribe, designated as the leader, calls out (sings) a melodic-rhythmic phrase. The rest of the singers respond, either with an exact imitation or a short, ostinato-style answer.

Call and response

African melodies are often performed using *heterophony*—singers and melodic instrumentalists all perform the same melody at the same time, each with a slightly different interpretation. Some add extra tones or ornaments to the melody, others slightly different rhythms; some players lag behind, while others perform their melody slightly ahead of the group. We find this African-style heterophony also in North American jazz.

Heterophony

Transplanted African Music

The eighteenth- and nineteenth-century slave traders transported Africans and their music to many lands, especially to the Americas. We discussed the African influence on jazz in the United States, but the music of Central and South America and the Caribbean Islands also reflects the African influence.

The exciting rhythms of *calypso* music from Trinidad developed through the singing of African slaves living on that island. Other music emerged: the *mambo* and *rumba* in Cuba, and the *bossa nova* and *conga* in Brazil. More recently, in Jamaica, *reggae* music developed from African, calypso, and rock 'n' roll rhythms.

Calypso

Mambo and rumba
Bossa nova and conga
Reggae

LISTENING ACTIVITY

If It Comes To Fighting With Guns

Ewe People of Ghana, West Africa

Compact Disc 4, Track 37
Running Time: 4:00

From the West African nation of Ghana, this traditional Ewe dance piece form is known as a *atsiagbekor.* On the recording you will hear the following instruments: five drums, one double bell (*gankoqui*), and several gourds, some with seeds, others with beads or rattles.

Music of the Romani Culture, or Gypsy Music

To understand the widespread and profound influence of Romani music, we need to trace the migration of the people we call "Gypsies." Scholars have reached consensus on the origin of the culture, both through DNA testing on modern-day

Gypsy Dancers in Spain

Gypsies and by tracing the Romani language to ancient Sanskrit and roots in Hindi, Punjabi, and related languages that are spoken in northern India.

However, the reasons for the Gypsies' migrations are not fully clear. One hypothesis is that 10,000 to 12,000 Indian musicians and entertainers were sent as a gift to the Shah of Persia in A.D. 439. The *Zot*, as they were called, later left Persia to support themselves as itinerant entertainers. The hypothesis about the second migration, about 500 years later, is that the Gypsies were a specialized group of fighting forces assembled as warriors during Muslim expansionism.

Starting from northwest India, the migrations progressed through the Persian Empire (Iran and neighboring countries), the Byzantine Empire (Turkey), the Balkans and eastern Europe, and finally into western Europe, parts of Africa, and North America. The term "Gypsies" originated in Europe, where the people mistook the wandering bands of dark-skinned people for Egyptians.

Wherever they settled, Gypsies left their mark on the culture. And because entertainment has always been an important part of Romani life, their music and dance became a permanent part of various Asian and European countries. *Takseen*, the Arabic word for improvisational playing, is characterized by the blues-like, non-rhythmic musical style of the Gypsies. Spanish flamenco music and dance is filled with Indian modalities and instruments: finger cymbals, guitar, bells, and drums. Even the hand and arm movements of flamenco dancers resemble those of Indian dancers.

In the eighteenth and nineteenth centuries, Gypsy melodies became so popular in Europe that some Romani (or Rom) musicians became touring artists.

Because of their fine musicianship, many, such as the Ungaro sect in Hungary, achieved social status and became wealthy.

Throughout the years, Jews and Gypsies not only traded and shared elements of their music but also played in each other's bands. You can hear Gypsy influences in Klezmer music and in Israeli circle dances such as the *hora*. Just listen to Jerry Bock's musical score for *Fiddler on the Roof* and you will hear Gypsy music. You will also recognize it in Franz Liszt's Hungarian Rhapsodies, in Johannes Brahms's Hungarian Dances, in Antonin Dvořák's *Slavonic Dances,* in the *Roumanian Rhapsody* by George Enescu (1881–1955), in *Hungarian Rondo* by Zoltán Kodály (1882–1967), in the operettas of Emmerich Kálmán (1882–1953), in the blues of B. B. King, and more.

Music of India

On a land area half the size of the United States reside one billion people—one-fifth of the world's population. They speak fifteen major languages, with dozens of dialects, most using different alphabets.

British, Islamic, and Asian conquerors of India have helped shape Indian music. *Ragas,* the melodic material of Indian music, have similar counterparts in Iranian and other Islamic Middle Eastern music. European instruments such as violins, clarinets, and harmoniums are used in Indian music. These instruments were adopted during the Raj, or English occupation. Indian instruments such as the *sitar,* hand cymbals, and drums, and some Indian scales can be traced to Asia.

Today, in any of the typically overcrowded cities, you will encounter many forms of music: Indian classical, folk, and popular. Recently, the predominant popular music has been *film music.* Its popularity reflects people's fascination with films and the songs that are part of those films, the majority of which are musicals.

Indian film music is a curious blend of East and West: energetic melodies, often based on Asian scales over Latin-American rhythms. Piercing, nasal-sounding singers are accompanied by instruments that may include a set of American dance-band drums, electric keyboards, guitars, violins, xylophone, celeste, bongos, and Indian sitar, *tabla* drums, or bamboo flute.

Most of the folk music still being performed in India has been handed down orally. Street folk musicians earn their livings accompanying acrobats, dancers, or street theater. Others may charm snakes by playing the *punji* (a form of gourd and reed bagpipe). Indian minstrels wander the countryside, singing traditional folk songs and accompanying themselves on a drum or a crude stringed instrument.

Indian Classical Music

Classical music in India is distinctively Indian. For more than 2,000 years, trained musicians working in the royal courts or religious temples developed the sound and traditions that survive today.

Hindustani and Karnatic Music   Since the thirteenth century, when Muslims invaded India and settled in the north, classical Indian music diverged into two closely related traditions: north Indian or Hindustani music, and south Indian

A woman performing the Odissi dance, from Khajuraho, in northern India.

Raga
(*rah*-gah)

Sitar
(sih-*tar*)

Tabla
Snake charmers
Punji
Minstrels

Ravi Shankar, c. mid-1960s

Bin
Vina

or Karnatic music. Each style uses slightly different instruments. For instance, the *bin* of the north is called the *vina* in the south. Their sizes and tones differ slightly, but at first glance, the two instruments seem identical.

Using for its melodic material *ragas,* or groupings of pitches somewhat similar to Western scales, Indian music is mainly heterophonic, with the addition of a drone. The overall sound of Indian classical music is complex and, at first, seems very different from Western music. With increased listening, however, it may eventually become more understandable.

Typical Classical Indian Musical Texture

Melody	～～～～～～～	singers (one or two)
Accompaniment and Soloists	::::::::::::::::::::	stringed instruments violin, *sitar, sarod, bin,* or *vina*
Drone	————————	*tambura* (string instrument, one or two)
Rhythm	/////////////////////////	*tabla* and other drums

Sarod

Tambura

Several Western contemporary musicians have incorporated Indian music elements into their style. After spending time in India, the Beatles included the sitar among their instruments and worked Indian-style melodies into their music.

More recently, jazz flutist Paul Horn recorded an album of improvisations that he performed in the Taj Mahal, the famous mausoleum in Agra, India. To blend Indian music with Western jazz, Horn modified his material closer to the *ragas* he heard in India.

CHALLENGE YOUR EXPERTISE

What is the origin of the word "gypsy?"

Music of Japan

Throughout history, Japan has incorporated foreign elements into its culture. Today, a wide assortment of music performances in Tokyo include:

American-style Japanese marching bands (on parade)
Japanese kabuki theater

LISTENING ACTIVITY

Netori *(Prelude)* Etenraku in Hyojo

Japan

Compact Disc 4, Track 38
Running Time: 3:00

The traditional Gagaku: *Netori* (prelude) & *Etenraku in Hyojo* is performed by singers and an orchestra of assorted instruments, most of which are heard on the recording:

Winds:
- *hichiriki*   double-reed bamboo oboe
- *kakura-bue*   six-holed bamboo flute
- *ryuteki*   seven-holed bamboo flute
- *sho*   mouth organ with seventeen reed pipes

Strings:
- *wagon*   six-stringed zither
- *gaku-so*   thirteen-stringed zither
- *biwa*   pear-shaped lute with four strings

Percussion
- *da-daiko*   large drum, played with thick sticks
- *tsuri daiko*   medium-sized suspended two-headed drum, played with two sticks
- *shoko*   small suspended gong, played with two sticks
- *kakko*   small two-headed drum, played with thin sticks

Japanese koto players

Japanese koto ensemble concert
European chorus concerts of Renaissance music
American popular and rock music
Japanese popular music (American style)
European classical music orchestra concerts

Gagaku Japanese music is traceable to the third century B.C. The *gagaku* court orchestra originated in the fifth century A.D., when eighty Korean musicians came to Japan to participate in an imperial funeral. Japanese royalty was impressed by the Korean musicians and set about developing its own court orchestras. Later, gagaku orchestras performed in the Shinto temples, where they can be heard today.

Musical traditions from other parts of Asia, especially China, entered Japanese music beginning in the seventh century A.D. Many Japanese instruments originated in China, India, Korea, and Manchuria.

From ancient times to the present, an abundance of solo and chamber music has been available for Japan's most popular instruments:

koto—a stringed lutelike instrument
kokyu—a spiked fiddle
shakuhachi—an end-blown bamboo flute
various percussion instruments

Japanese Scales

At the heart of Japanese pitch material are varieties of five-tone, *pentatonic scales,* most of which originated in China. For instance, the following scales used mainly in Japanese sacred music are identical to Chinese scales dating back to B.C. 2000.

Another extensively used pentatonic scale in modern Japanese music consists of two major third gaps:

The popular *Sakura,* or "Cherry Blossom," song uses this scale:

Sakura

Sa - ku - ra,   Sa - ku - ra,   Cher - ry   blos - soms

wave   in   the trees,   Love - ly   blos - soms   dance   in   the breeze.

Pink   and white   the   blos - soms will   fall.   Pe - tals   send - ing

scent   to—   all.   Sa - ku - ra,   Sa - ku - ra,

Smell - ing   sweet   Sa -   ku -   ra.

Theater Music

Throughout Japan's history, music usually has accompanied theatrical performances.

Nogaku   Music is an important part of the traditional *Nogaku,* or *Noh,* musical plays. Derived from Buddhism, *Noh* plays feature singers accompanied by Japanese flutes and drums.

Kabuki   Designed for the masses of common people, kabuki theater began developing its traditions in the sixteenth century. A colorful spectacle, kabuki incorporates acting, dancing, and music. Musical accompaniment is also an integral part of the Japanese puppet theater.

Music in Japanese Schools

Since the Meiji Restoration of 1868, when Emperor Mutsuhito modernized education, Western classical music replaced Japanese classical music in the schools. As further encouragement, talented Japanese musicians were sent to the music centers of Europe and America to study. These students brought back Western music and teaching methods to Japanese schools.

In the twentieth century, well-known music teachers such as Shinichi Suzuki continued teaching Western music to Japanese children. Through the Suzuki Method, thousands of Japanese youngsters learned in groups to play Vivaldi, Mozart, and other Western composers' violin and cello concertos. As a result, symphony orchestras around the world today employ many Japanese string players.

Kabuki performance with actors and musicians

Suzuki Method

The Suzuki Method is now used in a number of countries, including the United States. Using the latest methods and instruments, the Yamaha Music Education Foundation teaches Western-style music to hundreds of thousands of youngsters in Japan and the United States.

Yamaha Music Education

With this history and emphasis on Western classical music, excellent symphony orchestras and opera companies thrive throughout modern Japan. Composers such as Mozart and Beethoven are as much the favorites of Japanese audiences as they are of European and American audiences. Contemporary Japanese composers are creating new music based on European principles but reflecting the venerable and diverse Japanese cultural history.

CHALLENGE YOUR EXPERTISE

Which cultures influenced Japanese music?

LISTENING ACTIVITY

Kabuki Nagauta *Music* Ayame-Yukata,

Japan

Compact Disc 4, Track 39
Running Time: 3:30

From Japan and the popular kabuki theater, listen to the *nagauta* music "Ayame-Yukata." Since 1652, kabuki has been performed entirely by male actors. The musicians usually are seated on the stage, facing the audience and behind the actors. In this recording, we hear an assortment of instruments accompanying the male singer: *shakuhachi* (bamboo flutes), *koto* (stringed instruments), and *shamisen* (plucked fiddles).

Summary of Terms

Asian scales
bamboo flute
bin
bongos
bossa nova
call and response
calypso
changing meters
Chinese gongs (tam tam)
claves
conga
conga drum
cowbell
ethnic music
ethnomusicology
film music
gagaku
harmoniums

heterophony
Hindustani music
improvisation
Indonesian finger cymbals
kabuki
Karnatic music
kokyu
Korean temple blocks
koto
mambo
maracas
microtones
minstrels
nagauta
Nogaku
ostinato
pentatonic scale
punji

raga
reggae
rumba
Sakura
Sarod
shakuhachi
shamisen
sitar
snake charmers
Suzuki Method
tabla
tambura
timbales
vina
World Exposition
Yamaha Music Education

Finale

Audience Power in the Twenty-First Century

As an *active listener,* you are equipped with the information and skills that will serve you for a lifetime. You are ready to move on to the next level of experiencing the variety of offerings in the vast world of music. You can inspire others to join you and share the joy of discovery. You are an informed member of the audience.

Fifty years ago, your grandparents' generation passed on the legacy to your parents, who in turn, passed it on to you. The challenge, then, is maintaining continuity. How can we ensure that the work of those who came before us remains an element of our cultural future?

Milestones in Music

Changes are occurring rapidly in the world of music. Each development gives us an opportunity to reflect on earlier milestones—to look at 400 years of music in perspective and to ponder the possibilities for the future.

Seventeenth Century   Baroque-style music burst forth with great exuberance. Composers began to explore combinations of instruments with vocal soloists and ensembles. New forms included the concerto, the cantata, the oratorio, and opera. In Italy, opera houses opened to the general public. Support for the arts came from the Church, the courts, and the merchant middle class.

Eighteenth Century   String instruments were perfected. Composers wrote instrumental concertos for emerging virtuoso performers. Although much-improved orchestras were offering subscription concerts to the general public, the main support for music came from the aristocracy.

Nineteenth Century   Romanticism became dominant. Music was often associated with literature, ideas, and emotions. Predictable structure gave way to individual expression. Composers and performers attained prestige and respect, many becoming wealthy from their art. All instrument families were perfected, leading to the establishment of symphony orchestras throughout Europe. Performing arts were supported primarily by the public and the aristocracy.

Twentieth Century   The 1900s began with a rebellion against romanticism. Composers began to use new materials and sources for their music, such as atonality and irregular rhythms. Ragtime became the rage in North America, along with popular art forms such as vaudeville and musical theater. Jazz was the true American music. The popularity of rock music spread worldwide. Now a synthesizer can virtually replicate an orchestra.

What Are Today's Trends?

Some studies suggest that younger audiences demonstrate less enthusiasm than preceding generations for most "high culture" performing arts. Popular music, movies, and television are thriving, but only jazz, musical theater, opera, and ballet attract audiences of all ages.

Opera has been enjoying popularity among 18- to 24-year-olds during the past ten to fifteen years. Opera companies have been able to build on the success of musical theater, for example, the rock musical megahit *Rent* and Baz Luhrmann's Broadway staging of the opera *La Bohème*. Audiences that have grown up with an abundance of media respond to the multimedia spectacle of music, sets, dance, dramatic lighting, and theatricality that both musicals and opera provide.

Supertitles
Proscenium

Another boon to opera has been the introduction of supertitles. These English translations of the libretto projected above the proscenium make the opera accessible to the audience. Without having to memorize the entire libretto, everyone can understand the dialogue and become engaged in the story. Opera companies have discovered that an accessible production keeps an audience coming back.

A scene from Buz Luhrmann's Broadway production of *La Bohème*

Perhaps we should ask, "Will composers continue to write symphonies? If so, which orchestras will play them, and will there be audiences for the performances?"

We also should ask ourselves what we are willing to do to support art music. Will we take over the job of fund-raising? What role can an individual play in helping to ensure continuity?

Beyond Survival

Marketing Challenges

Because of seesawing state and federal funding for the arts, the responsibility for supporting music organizations falls increasingly to individuals and foundations. This means that performing arts organizations need to retain and attract audiences and donors.

Arts organizations themselves are dynamic businesses, employers, and consumers. Recognizing the extent to which these organizations enhance our lives, some communities have solicited private donations to build new concert halls and arts facilities. Others, unfortunately, face the loss of their orchestras. What might happen if government support is reduced further—or discontinued?

To foster local support, arts organizations are making greater commitments to serving their culturally diverse communities. By actively programming for people of all backgrounds, the organizations make the arts more vital, relevant, and accessible to broader audiences. If you are in those audiences, you may be able to participate in promoting our diverse cultural heritage.

Communication Is the Key

Your voice counts in encouraging governmental support. Let your elected officials know your opinions. When your representatives must decide whether to vote for or against support for the arts, they usually consider the priorities of their constituents. Your role is to communicate your views.

Performing arts organizations want to communicate with you to keep you coming back. In return, they need you to communicate with them. Although your support is implicit by your attendance of performances, *explicit* feedback through a letter or phone call often can be more effective in registering your personal opinion, your voice, and your vote. Let's explore some possibilities.

First, let the management know that you *want* to communicate; then mention *how* you'd like to go about it:

- by a questionnaire in the concert program
- by regular mail
- by telephone survey
- by fax
- by email

Stay in touch with the organization. Let management know what would interest you in future performances. Suggest ways in which the organization might make you feel included. Propose educational programs that would appeal to you and your family. Ask whether it would be possible for the conductor, a soloist, or a music educator to introduce and explain music that is different from what you're used to. Tell them whenever you enjoy a concert or a particular piece of music, to show that you are there—and that you care.

You have a lifetime of enjoyment ahead of you. Keep great music alive.

Summary of Terms

proscenium   supertitles

LISTENING ACTIVITY

Finale: Martin Bookspan, Host

Available online at www.prenhall.com/zorn

Appendix A
Basic Music Notation

To preserve composers' creative ideas, music notation developed gradually over a span of hundreds of years. Notation makes it possible for players to recreate music accurately. Here are some of the basic concepts of modern music notation.

Pitch Notation

Staff   This structure of five lines and four spaces holds printed notes, graphically indicating the relative highness and lowness of pitches.

Clefs   A clef is a symbol placed on a staff line to fix the pitch notated on that line. With that reference, performers know the pitches of the other notes on the staff. There are two main **clef** signs:

The *G clef* or *treble* (high) *clef* is an ornate symbol that circles the line around the pitch *G*.

pitch *G* →

The *F clef* or *bass* (low) *clef* contains two dots placed on either side of the "F" line to indicate the pitch *F*:

pitch *F* →

Grand Staff   Because their ranges are limited, most instruments and voices perform music using one *clef*. Keyboards, on the other hand, use a much wider range. Therefore, their parts include both *G* and *F* clefs and are displayed on a *grand staff*.

Duration or Time Notation

The shading of notes, along with stems and flags attached to them, indicates duration. Special symbols indicate the specific duration of silence or rest:

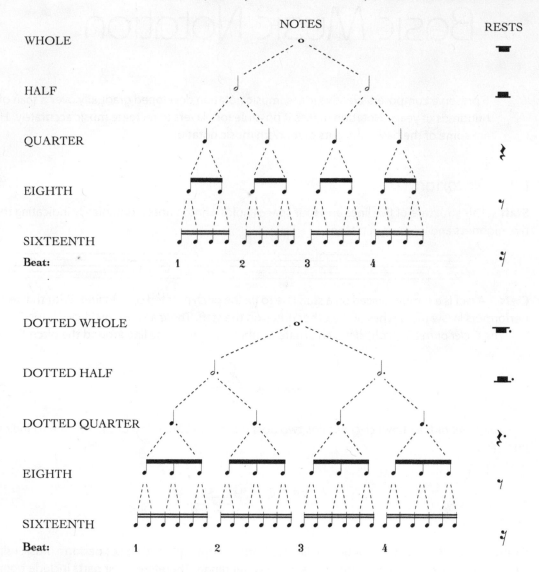

Appendix B
Common Scales in Music

Scales

A scale is notated as a series of pitches proceeding upward or downward according to a prescribed pattern. With twelve different tones in Western music, a vast variety of arrangements is possible. The most commonly used scales follow:

Chromatic Scale

This scale uses all twelve of the half tones available in Western music. Each step is a half tone.

ASCENDING

1/2 tones

DESCENDING

⌣ = whole tone   V = ¹/₂ tone   ⊔ = 1¹/₂ tones

1 (whole) tone   ¹/₂ tone   ¹/₂ tone

Sharp   The sharp # sign raises the pitch that follows it by one half tone.

Flat   The flat ♭ sign lowers the pitch that follows it by one half tone.

C Major Scale

MAJOR SCALE FORMULA						
Whole,	Whole,	Half,	Whole,	Whole,	Whole,	Half
1	1	½	1	1	1	½

C Minor Scale (Natural)

C Minor Scale (Harmonic)

C Minor Scale (Melodic)

*When descending, use natural minor.

Pentatonic

(Gapped Scale) A five-tone scale used by most early music cultures. Varying forms of *pentatonic* scales are still used in Asia, Polynesia, Africa, and by the American Indians, the Celts, and the Scots. Because of the large gap between some of the tones, this scale is also known as a *gapped scale*.

C PENTATONIC SCALE (one type only)

Whole-Tone

C WHOLE TONE

Blues Scale

Basically, this is a major scale with altered tones, called *blue notes*. The *blues scale* is used predominantly in jazz and popular music.

C BLUES SCALE

Hexatonic Blues Scale

The more commonly used blues scale is the six-note, *hexatonic* scale.

C HEXATONIC BLUES SCALE

Modes

Modes are scales used extensively in church music during the Middle Ages. More recent composers and modern folk, jazz, and rock musicians also employ some of the modes. The following are the ones most often used:

D DORIAN

E PHRYGIAN

F LYDIAN

G MIXOLYDIAN

Appendix C
Writing Reports

The Short Concert Report

1. Attach the program and ticket stub of the performance to your report.
2. Write a one-paragraph description of each work. Give your personal reaction to each piece. Describe the music as well as you can, using both your own words and the terms presented in this course.
3. Try to include:
   - performing medium (also special instruments and soloists)
   - general form (symphony, concerto, dance forms, etc.)
   - outstanding features of melody, rhythms, textures, style, and so on.

Other Directions

Do not copy from printed concert programs, music reviews, or record jackets. That is a breach of copyright. Take a pad and pen so you can jot down a few comments after movements or works. This will help you remember the music. *Only if permitted, record the performance with a small, battery-operated tape recorder. That way you can write your notes later and just enjoy the performance.

   *Most professional performances prohibit taping.

The Long Concert Report

I. General Directions
   A. Ask your instructor to recommend concerts.
   B. Select one that interests you.
   C. Type your report double-spaced. Make sure your computer printout is legible.
   D. Include a bibliography and footnotes, if necessary.
   E. Attach your program and ticket stub.

II. Pre-Concert Report
Select one major work or a group of short works scheduled on the concert.
   A. Present your research on the historical background of:
      1. the composer
      2. the composition
   B. Listen to a recording and give your general reaction to the performance and specific reaction to the music regarding the composer's use of:
      1. performing media
      2. rhythm, tempo, meter
      3. melodic materials
      4. harmony and tonality
      5. textures
      6. form

III Post-Concert Review
  A. Include background information: date, time, place, performer(s), and musical selections.
  B. Discuss your reactions to each work performed. Include both your intellectual and emotional reactions.
  C. Discuss your reactions to the quality of the performance and performer(s). Also comment on the concert ritual the performers follow.
  D. Compare the live concert performance of the major work with the recorded performance you researched.

Other Directions

Refrain from merely giving a play-by-play account of the concert; your printed program already gives that information.

Do not copy directly from sources. You may paraphrase researched sources as long as you cite these sources with footnotes and in a bibliography.

Jot down notes after movements or works to help you remember the performance. Try not to write during the live performance so that you will not distract yourself. Remember: most professional performances prohibit taping.

The Research Report

Directions

1. Choose one topic:
   - From the list of suggested research topics, choose one for your report. Or, choose an alternate topic similar to those suggested. Compare and contrast the musical selections. Use terminology you learned. Include research sources, and describe your experiences attending concerts.
2. Include biographical data on composers:
   - Explain how events in the composer's life relate to the works you have chosen to compare.
3. At the time the works were composed, what was happening in society, politics, and economics that influenced the general musical style?
   - Cite specific examples from the music you selected.
4. Include information about the performer and the recording:
   - Identify the ensemble, conductor, soloists, and any other performers mentioned on the recording.
   - Identify, if possible, the date of the recording and its production label.
5. Include a bibliography:
   - Cite all sources used to research your topic—books, articles, records, and so on.
6. Be original!
   - Do not copy directly from sources such as printed concert programs, music reviews, or record jackets. Copying word for word is a breach of copyright.
   - You may paraphrase resource material as long as you properly cite sources with footnotes and in the bibliography.

Other Directions

Avoid taking notes during the performance. To help you remember the music, jot down a few comments between movements or after the work.

Remember: Most professional concerts prohibit taping.

Suggested Research Topics

1. Compare and contrast an early and a late work by the same composer:
   - Haydn's Symphony No. 45 (*Farewell*) and Symphony No. 94 (*Surprise*)
   - Beethoven's Symphony No. 1 and Symphony No. 9 (*Choral*)
   - Beethoven's String Quartets Opus 18 and String Quartets Opus 135.
   - Verdi's operas *Rigoletto* and *Otello*
   - Puccini's operas *La Bohème* and *Turandot*
   - Mahler's Symphony No. 1 (*The Titan*) and Symphony No. 8 (*Symphony of a Thousand*)
   - Stravinsky's ballet *The Rite of Spring* and *Ebony Concerto*

2. Compare and contrast two similar works by two different composers of the same style period:
   - Bach's *Christmas* Oratorio and Handel's *Messiah* Oratorio
   - Brahms's *Academic Festival Overture* and Wagner's *Die Meistersinger von Nürnberg Overture*
   - Tchaikovsky's *Nutcracker* Ballet and Falla's Suite from *The Three Cornered Hat* Ballet
   - Gershwin's *An American in Paris* and Copland's *Appalachian Spring*
   - Rimsky-Korsakov's *Capriccio espagnole* and Tchaikovsky's *Capriccio italien*

3. Compare and contrast two similar works by two different composers from two different style periods:
   - Haydn's Symphony No. 94 (*Surprise*) and Prokofiev's Symphony No. 1 (*Classical*)
   - Vivaldi's Concerto (*Spring*) from *The Four Seasons* and Schuman's Symphony No. 1 (*Spring*)
   - Bach's *Mass in b minor* and Bernstein's *Mass*
   - Beethoven's Symphony No. 9 (*Choral*) and Stravinsky's *The Rite of Spring*

4. Other topics:
   - Discuss the differences in orchestral music in the Classical, Romantic, and twentieth-century style periods.
   - Compare the musical contributions of Felix Mendelssohn and Leonard Bernstein.
   - Trace and discuss the development of the concert tradition from the Baroque period to the present.
   - Describe and discuss the various ways in which composers and musicians from the Baroque period to the present supported themselves.
   - Describe, compare, and contrast the different ways of listening to music of the Baroque, Classical, and Romantic style periods.

Appendix D
Music Listening Checklist

Performing Medium

symphony orchestra
chamber orchestra
wind ensemble (band)
chamber music ensemble
electronic instruments

chorus (a cappella)
chorus with orchestra
solo (instrumental or vocal with orchestra)

solo (instrumental or vocal with piano)
other combinations

Rhythm—Tempo—Meter

beat prominence: strong, weak
tempo: slow, medium, fast
meter: 2, 3, other (5, 7, etc.)

subdivision: simple (2 or 4) complex (3, 5, 7, 9)
rubato (changing)
ostinato (repetitious)

basso continuo (running bass line)
silence

Melody

prominent
not prominent
smooth (long lines)
fragmented (short lines)
ornamented (trills, etc.)

plain (no ornaments)
imitation (repeated idea, in another voice or instrument)
sequences (repeated idea, same voice, new pitches

traditional scales used: major, minor
other scales used: chromatic, pentatonic, whole tone, tone-row, gapped

Harmony—Tonality

mostly consonant
mostly dissonant
major and minor chords (traditional)

polychords
quartal chords (fourths)
clusters (seconds)
major or minor tonality

polytonality
atonality

Texture

monophonic (single line)
polyphonic (many independent lines)

homophonic (sounding together, also melody with accompaniment)

mixture of textures

Form

large forms
symphony
concerto
concerto grosso

opera overture
concert overture
orchestral suite
descriptive piece

mass
oratorio
cantata
opera

chamber music (trio, quartet, quintet, sonata)

keyboard forms (sonata, fugue, nocturne, etc.)

detailed forms

strophic (A–A–A, etc.)

through-composed

free sectional

two-part (A–B, or A–A–B–B)

three-part (A–B–A)

rondo (A–B–A–C–A, etc.)

minuet and trio

theme and variations

sonata

general concept of form

developmental (repetition of ideas)

through-composed (rhapsodic, little repetition)

Appendix E
Listening Resources: Expand Your Expertise

Check out www.prenhall.com/zorn for a hyperlink to classical.com where you will find many of these selections on the "Expand Your Expertise" playlist.

Baroque Style Period

Bach:	*Cantata No. 4 Christ lag in Todesbanden* (Christ lay in the bonds of death)
	Cantata No. 80 Ein' feste Burg (A Mighty Fortress)
	Cantata No. 140 Wachet auf (Sleepers Awake)
	St. Matthew Passion
	Christmas Oratorio
	Mass in b minor
	Magnificat in D
	Brandenburg Concertos 1–6
	4 Orchestral Suites
	Well-Tempered Clavier
	Goldberg Variations
	harpsichord concertos
	violin, cello, and flute sonatas
Handel:	*Messiah* (oratorio)
	Israel in Egypt (oratorio)
	Giulio Cesare (opera)
	Music for Royal Fireworks
	Water Music
	chamber music
Monteverdi:	madrigals (for voices)
	Orfeo (opera)
D. Scarlatti	sonatas for harpsichord
A. Scarlatti	sonatas for harpsichord
Schütz:	Italian madrigals
	The Seven Words from Christ on the Cross (oratorio)
Vivaldi:	*The Four Seasons* (four concertos)
	solo concertos
	Gloria

Classical Style Period

Haydn:

Symphony No. 88 in G Major
Symphony No. 94 in G Major (*Surprise*)
Symphony No. 101 in D Major (*Clock*)
Symphony No. 104 in D Major (*London*)
Trumpet Concerto in E-Flat
String Quartet Opus 76 No. 3 in C
The Creation (oratorio)
The Seasons (oratorio)

Mozart:

Symphony No. 38 in D Major (*Prague*)
Symphony No. 40 in g minor
Symphony No. 41 in C Major (*Jupiter*)
Horn Concerto No. 2 in E-Flat Major
Horn Concerto No. 4 in E-Flat Major
Piano Concerto No. 15 in d minor
Piano Concerto No. 21 in C Major
String Quartet K. 387 in G Major
Don Giovanni (opera)
The Magic Flute (opera)
The Marriage of Figaro (opera)
Requiem Mass

Beethoven: Bridge to Romanticism

Symphonies:

No. 3 in E-Flat, Op. 55, *Eroica*
No. 5 in c minor, Op. 67
No. 6 in F, Op. 68, *Pastorale*
No. 7 in A, Op. 92
No. 9 in D, Op. 125, *Choral*

Overtures:

Egmont Overture
Leonore Overtures Nos. 1–3

Concertos:

Piano Concerto No. 3, Op. 37
Piano Concerto No. 5, Op. 73, *Emperor*
Violin Concerto, Op. 61

String Quartets:

Quartet, Op. 18, No. 2
Quartet, Op. 59, Nos. 1–3

Piano Sonatas:

No. 8, Op. 13, *Pathétique*
No. 14, Op. 27, No. 2, *Moonlight*
No. 21, Op. 53, *Waldstein*
No. 23, Op. 57, *Appassionata*

Violin Sonatas:

No. 5, Op. 24, *Spring*
No. 9, Op. 47, *Kreutzer*

Early Romantic Style Period

Berlioz:

Harold in Italy (viola and orchestra)
Symphonie fantastique
Roman Carnival Overture
Requiem

Chopin:	Piano Concertos No. 1 and No. 2
	piano music
Duparc:	songs
Faure:	songs
Grieg:	songs
Liszt:	*Les Preludes* (for orchestra)
	Faust Symphony
	Piano Concertos No. 1 and No. 2
	piano music
Mendelssohn:	Symphony No. 3, *Scottish*
	Symphony No. 4, *Italian*
	Symphony No. 5, *Reformation*
	A Midsummer Night's Dream Overture
	Hebrides Overture
	Violin Concerto
	songs
	piano Music
Schubert:	Symphony No. 8, *Unfinished*
	Symphony No. 9, *Great*
	Incidental Music to *Rosamunde*
	"Death and the Maiden" String Quartet
	"The Trout" String Quartet
	"Ave Maria" (song)
	"Die Forelle" (song) *The Trout*
	Die Schöne Mullerin (song cycle)
	Winterreise (song cycle)
Schumann, R:	Symphony No. 1, *Spring*
	Piano Concerto in a minor
	"Papillons" (piano)
	"Carnival" (piano)
	"Dichterliebe" (song cycle)

Romantic Style Period Opera

Bellini:	*I Puritani*
	La Sonnambula
	Norma
Bizet:	*Carmen*
Donizetti:	*La fille du régiment* (The Daughter of the Regiment)
Gounod:	*Faust*
Offenbach:	*Tales of Hoffman*
Puccini:	*La bohème*
	Madama Butterfly
	Tosca
	Turandot
Rossini:	*The Barber of Seville*
	William Tell

Late Romantic Style Period

Brahms:	4 Symphonies
	Piano Concerto No. 1 in d minor
	Piano Concerto No. 2 in B-flat Major
	Violin Concerto
	Tragic Overture
	A German Requiem
	Alto Rhapsody (1869)
	chamber music
	piano music
	songs
Mahler:	Symphony No. 1 (The Titan)
	Symphony No. 4
	Lieder eines fahrenden Gesellen (Songs of a Wayfarer)
	Das Lied von der Erde (The Song of the Earth)
Strauss, R:	Horn Concerto No. 1 in E-flat
	Horn Concerto No. 2 in E-flat
	Oboe Concerto
	Salome (opera)
	Der Rosenkavalier (The Cavalier of the Rose) (opera)
	Four Last Songs (with orchestra)
	songs with piano
Wagner:	See recommendations in Chapter 15

Program Music

Beethoven:	Symphony No. 6 in F *Pastoral,* Op. 68
Berlioz:	*Harold in Italy* (viola and orchestra), Op. 16
	Symphonie fantastique, Op. 14
Liszt:	Symphonic Poems: *Hamlet* and *Les préludes*
	Dante Symphony
	Faust Symphony
Mendelssohn:	*Midsummer Night's Dream Overture*
	Calm Sea and Prosperous Voyage Overture
	Hebrides (Fingal's Cave) Overture
Strauss:	*Also Sprach Zarathustra (Thus Spake Zarathustra)*
	Death and Transfiguration
	Don Juan
	Don Quixote
	Ein Heldenleben (A Hero's Life)
	Till Eulenspiegel's Merry Pranks
Tchaikovsky:	*1812 Overture*
	Francesca da Rimini
	Romeo and Juliet

Nationalism

Russia

Moussorgsky:
A Night on Bald Mountain
Pictures at an Exhibition
Boris Godunov (opera)

Rimsky-Korsakov:
Scheherazade
Capriccio espagnol

Borodin:
In the Steppes of Central Asia
Prince Igor: "Polovtsian Dances"

Tchaikovsky:
1812 Overture
Swan Lake ballet music
The Nutcracker ballet music
Piano Concerto No. 1
Violin Concerto
Symphonies 1, 2, 4, 5, 6

Rachmaninov:
Piano Concertos Nos. 1 and 2

Hungary

Bartók:
Concerto for Orchestra
Music for Strings, Percussion, and Celeste

Liszt:
Hungarian Dances

Czech Republic

Dvořák:
Carnival Overture, Op. 92
Concerto for Cello and Orchestra, Op. 104
Quartet No. 12 in F, Op. 96, *American*
Slavonic Dances
Symphony No. 9 in e minor, Op. 95 *New World*

Smetana:
The Bartered Bride opera and overture
The Moldau, symphonic poem

Scandinavia

Grieg:
Concerto in a minor for Piano and Orchestra, Op. 16
Peer Gynt Suite, No. 1 and 2, Op. 46
songs

Sibelius:
Concerto in d minor for Violin and Orchestra, Op. 47
Finlandia, Op. 26
Swan of Tuonela, Op. 22
Symphony No. 2 in D, Op. 43

United Kingdom

Elgar:
Enigma Variations, Op. 36
Pomp and Circumstance Marches (5), Op. 39

Vaughan Williams:	*Fantasia on "Greensleeves"*
	English Folk Song Suite
	London Symphony
Grainger:	*Irish Tune* from County Derry
	Lincolnshire Posy (for wind band)

Italy

| Respighi: | *Fountains of Rome* |
| | *Pines of Rome* |

Spain

Albéniz:	*Iberia*
	Suite Española
Granados:	*Spanish Dances* (12)
Falla:	*El amor brujo*
	Nights in the Gardens of Spain
	The Three-Cornered Hat

Impressionism

Debussy:	*Clair de lune* (for piano)
	Images (for orchestra)
	La Mer
	Noctures (for orchestra)
	String Quartet in g minor
	Sonata No. 1 (for cello and piano)
	Sonata No. 3 (for violin and piano)
	Syrinx (for unaccompanied flute)
Ravel:	*Alborada del gracioso*
	Bolero
	Concerto in G for Piano and Orchestra
	Daphnis et Chloé: Suite No. 2
	Pavane pour une infante défunte (orchestra)
	Scheherazade
	String Quartet in F
	La Valse

Expressionism: Atonal Music

Berg:	Concerto for Violin and Orchestra
	Lyric Suite (for string quartet)
	Quartet, Op. 3
	Sonata for Piano, Op. 1
	Three Pieces for Orchestra, Op. 6
	Wozzeck (opera)
Schoenberg:	Chamber Symphony, Op. 9
	Concerto for Violin and Orchestra, Op. 42
	Erwartung, Op. 17

	Five Pieces for Orchestra
	Gurre-Lieder
	Moses und Aron (opera)
	Pierrot Lunaire, Op. 21
	Serenade for Septet and Baritone, Op. 24
	Suite for Chamber Ensemble
	Survivor from Warsaw, Op. 46
	Variations for Orchestra, Op. 31
	Verklärte Nacht, Op. 4
	quartets
	piano music
Stravinsky:	Circus Polka
	Dumbarton Oaks Concerto
	Ebony Concerto
	The Firebird Suite
	Fireworks
	L'histoire du soldat (*The Soldier's Tale*)
	Octet for Winds
	Petrushka Suite
	Pulcinella Suite
	The Rake's Progress (opera)
	Le sacre du printemps (The Rite of Spring)
	Symphony of Psalms
Webern:	Five Movements for String Quartet, Op. 5
	Four Pieces for Violin and Piano, Op. 7
	Quartet for Violin, Clarinet, Tenor Saxophone, and Piano, Op. 22
	Symphony for Chamber Orchestra, Op. 21
	Variations for Piano Solo, Op. 27

Neoclassicism: Mainstream Music

Prokofiev:	Symphonies: No. 1 (*Classical,* 1917); No. 5 (1944); No. 7 (1952)
	Peter and the Wolf (1936)
	Lt. Kije Suite (1934) from the film score
Shostakovitch:	Symphony No. 5.
	Suite from *The Age of Gold* (1929)
	piano concertos
Vaughan Williams:	*Fantasia on "Greensleeves"* (1934)
	English Folk Song Suite (1923)
	A Sea Symphony (No. 1, 1910)
	London Symphony (No. 2, 1914)
Holst:	*The Planets* (1914–16)
Britten:	*A Ceremony of Carols* (1942, for choir)
	Spring Symphony (1947, for vocal soloists and chorus)
	War Requiem (1962)
	Peter Grimes (opera)
	Billy Budd (opera)

Elgar:	"Enigma" Variations (1899)
	Cello Concerto (1919)
	Pomp and Circumstance marches (1901–1907)
Hindemith:	*Mathis der Maler* (*Mathis the Painter,* 1934, opera and symphony)
	Noblissima visione (1938)
	sonatas for various instruments
Orff:	*Carmina Burana* (cantata)
Honegger:	*King David* (oratorio)
	Pacific 2-3-1 (1923)
Milhaud:	*Suite provençale* (1937)
	Suite française (1944), 1
	La création du monde (*The Creation of the World,* 1923)
Poulenc:	*Mass in G* (1937, for chorus a cappella)
	songs (chansons)
Weill:	*The Rise and Fall of the City of Mahagonny* (opera, 1929)
	Three Penny Opera (musical, 1928) with song "Mack the Knife"
	Lost in the Stars (musical, 1949)
Respighi:	*Fountains of Rome*
	Pines of Rome
	Roman Festivals
Bartok:	Concerto for Orchestra (1943)
Bloch:	*Schelomo (Solomon,* 1915)
	Sacred Service (*Avodath Hakodesh,* 1930–33)
Chavez:	*Simfonia India*
	Toccata for Percussion
	Horsepower (ballet)

Experimental and Technological Music
Music Concrète

The Beatles:	Mr. Kite
	Tomorrow Never Comes
Reich:	Come Out
Stockhausen:	*Gesang der Juenglinge* (speech sounds and electronic sounds)

Electronic Music

Carlos:	By Request
	Switched on Bach (CBS MS-7194)
Subotnik:	Silver Apples of the Moon

Varèse:	*Poème èlectronique*
Wuorinen:	Time's Encomium

Computer Mixed Media

Boulez:	Regions
Davidovsky:	Synchronisms No. 5
Dodge:	In Celebration
Risset:	Songs

Aleatoric Music

Eloy:	Equivalences
Stockhausen:	*Klavierstueck XI*

Chance Music

Cage:	*Atlas Eclipticalis*

Music of North America

Barber:
Overture for *School for Scandal*
String Quartet
Vanessa (opera)
"Adagio for Strings" (used in the film *Platoon*)
Medea (ballet)

Bernstein:
Symphony No. 1, *Jeremiah* (soprano and orchestra)
Symphony No. 2, *Age of Anxiety* (piano and orchestra)
Symphony No. 3, *Kaddish* (mixed chorus, boy's choir, soprano,
 speaker, and orchestra)
Chichester Psalms (mixed chorus, boy soloist, and
 orchestra)
Halil (Nocturne for Solo Flute, String Orchestra, and
 Percussion)
Fancy Free (ballet, 1944)
Candide (comic operetta, 1956)
West Side Story (musical, 1957)
Mass (Theater Piece, 1971)

Copland:
El Salón México
An Outdoor Overture
Quiet City
Lincoln Portrait (with narrator)
Clarinet Concerto
Billy the Kid (ballet, 1938)
Rodeo (ballet, 1942)
Appalachian Spring (ballet, 1944)
Fanfare for the Common Man
Violin Sonata
Old American Songs

Gershwin:	Rhapsody in Blue (piano and orchestra)
	Second Rhapsody (piano and orchestra)
	Concerto in F (piano concerto)
	An American in Paris (tone poem)
	Preludes (piano)
	Porgy and Bess (opera, 1935)
	Of Thee I Sing (musical, 1931)
Hanson:	Symphony No. 2 (Romantic)
Ives:	Second Symphony
	First Orchestral Set: *Three Places in New England*
	Second Orchestral Set
	The Unanswered Question
	Central Park in the Dark
	Washington's Birthday
	The Fourth of July
	Variations of "America" for organ
	string quartets and sonatas
	songs
Joplin:	"Maple Leaf Rag"
	"The Entertainer" (rag)—used in the film *The Sting*
Menotti:	*The Old Maid and the Thief* (opera, 1939)
	The Medium (opera, 1946)
	The Telephone (opera, 1947)
	Amahl and the Night Visitors (opera, 1951)

Broadway Musical Theater

From the vast wealth of musicals, here is a selected list. Unless noted "audio only," the show is available on video.

Richard Adler and Jerry Ross
> *Pajama Game* (1954)
> *Damn Yankees* (1955)

Leonard Bernstein
> *On the Town* (1944, with Betty Comden and Adolph Green)
> *Candide* (1956)
> *West Side Story* (1957, with Stephen Sondheim)

Jerry Bock and Sheldon Harnick
> *She Loves Me* (1963)
> *Fiddler on the Roof* (1964)

Stephen Flaherty and Lynn Ahrens
> *Ragtime* (1997) Multiple awards [audio only]

George Gershwin
> *Of Thee I Sing* (1931) [audio only]
> collections of recorded songs from various shows

Marvin Hamlisch

    A Chorus Line (1975, with Edward Kleban)

Jerry Herman

    Hello, Dolly! (1964)
    Mame (1966)
    La Cage Aux Folles (1983)

Elton John and Tim Rice

    Lion King (1997) Multiple awards [video available of the
      original animated film]
    Aida (1999)

Tom Jones and Harvey Schmidt

    The Fantasticks (1960)
    110 in the Shade (1963)
    I Do! I Do! (1966)

John Kander and Fred Ebb

    Zorba (1968)
    Cabaret (1972), Tony Award
    Chicago (1975)
    Curtains (2006)

Henry Krieger and Tom Eyen

    Dreamgirls (1982)

Burton Lane

    Finian's Rainbow (1947, with E. Y. Harburg)
    On a Clear Day You Can See Forever (1965, with Alan Jay
      Lerner)

Mitch Leigh

    Man of La Mancha (1965)

Alan Jay Lerner and Frederick Loewe

    Brigadoon (1947)
    Paint Your Wagon (1951)
    My Fair Lady (1956)
    Gigi (1958 film)
    Camelot (1960)

Frank Loesser

    Where's Charley? (1948) [audio only]
    Guys and Dolls (1950) Tony Award
    Most Happy Fella (1956) [audio only]
    How to Succeed in Business Without Really Trying (1961)

Alan Menken

    Beauty and the Beast (1994) [video available of the original
      animated film]

Cole Porter

    Kiss Me Kate (1948)
    Can-Can (1953)
    Silk Stockings (1954)

Rodgers and Hammerstein

> *Oklahoma* (1943)
> *Carousel* (1945)
> *South Pacific* (1949)
> *The King and I* (1951)
> *The Sound of Music* (1959)

Stephen Schwartz

> *Pippin* (1972) [original cast CD and DVD available]
> *Godspell* (1973) [1973 film version on video]
> *Wicked* (2003) [audio only]

Claude-Michel Schönberg and Herbert Kretzmer

> *Les Miserables* (1985) [video of a concert production]
> *Miss Saigon* (1992) [audio only]

Stephen Sondheim

> *A Funny Thing Happened on the Way to the Forum* (1962)
> *Company* (1970) [video of cast recording taping session]
> *Follies* (1971) [audio only]
> *A Little Night Music* (1973)
> *Sweeney Todd* (1979) [video of a television production]
> *Sunday in the Park with George* (1984) [video of a television production]
> *Into the Woods* (1988)

Charles Strouse

> *Bye, Bye, Birdie* (1963, with Lee Adams)
> *Applause* (1969) [audio only]
> *Annie* (1978, with Martin Charnin)

Jule Styne

> *Gentlemen Prefer Blondes* (1949, with Leo Robin)
> *Peter Pan* (1954, with Comden and Green)
> *Bells Are Ringing* (1956, with Comden and Green)
> *Gypsy* (1959, with Stephen Sondheim) [videos available of both the film and television productions]
> *Funny Girl* (1964, with Bob Merrill)

Andrew Lloyd Webber

> *Jesus Christ Superstar* (1971, with Tim Rice)
> *Evita* (1979, with Tim Rice) [video available of 1995 film version]
> *Cats* (1981) [video of television production]
> *Starlight Express* (1986) [audio only]
> *Phantom of the Opera* (1988) [audio only]
> *Sunset Boulevard* (1993) [audio only]

Kurt Weill

> *Three Penny Opera* (1928, with Berthold Brecht)
> *Mahagonny* (1930, with Brecht) [audio only]
> *Knickerbocker Holiday* (1938, with Maxwell Anderson)
> *Lady in the Dark* (1940) with Ira Gershwin [audio only]

Street Scene (1947) with Langston Hughes [audio only]
Lost in the Stars (1949) with Maxwell Anderson
   [audio only]

Meredith Willson

The Music Man (1957)
The Unsinkable Molly Brown (1960)

David Yazbek

The Full Monty (2001)
Dirty Rotten Scoundrels (2005)

Vincent Youmans

No! No! Nanette! (1925, with Otto Harbach and Irving Caesar)
   [audio only]

Appendix F
Challenge Your Expertise Answers

Chapter 3

- During the performance of a symphony, what should you do if most of the audience begins to applaud at the "wrong" time? *It's up to you whether or not to join in the applause.*
- When is a piano instead of an oboe used to "tune" the orchestra? *before a performance by a piano soloist*

Chapter 4

- What two things do a waltz and a minuet have in common? *They are both dances. They are both in three meter.*
- What term describes a melody or a section of the music that comes to a conclusion? *cadence*

Chapter 5

- In terms of creating sound, what does a violin bow have in common with a pair of drum sticks? *Both are energy sources.*
- Which instrument is the smallest of the woodwinds? *piccolo*
- What do the tuba, contrabassoon, and bass viol have in common? *They all have the lowest pitch of the section.*
- Can you think of two reasons the brass section isn't in the front of the symphony orchestra? *Violins play most of main themes. The brass section plays too loudly to be in front.*
- The term "movement" on a concert program refers to which of the following?
  1. The orchestra enters and tunes.
  2. The conductor's arms are raised.
  3. A large section of a longer work is to be played.
  4. The soloist enters.

  3. A large section of a longer work is to be played.

Chapter 7

- What group could be considered one of the first musicians' unions? *German Meistersingers*

Chapter 8

- What were three purposes of stained-glass windows? *to make the church more attractive; to depict scenes from the Bible; to use as instructional tools*

Chapter 9

- What was Antonio Vivaldi's distinctive physical feature?   *bright red hair*
- Which two Baroque-style period composers continued working after becoming blind.   *Bach, Handel*
- Why is Bach's Fugue in g minor known as the "Little"?   *to distinguish it from other fugues Bach wrote in that key*
- What two developments resulted in the concerto grosso?   *better instruments, virtuoso performers*

Chapter 11

- Which is the higher number—Mozart's age at his death or the number of symphonies he composed?   *number of symphonies (He wrote 41 symphonies before his death at age 35.)*
- How long did Beethoven study with Mozart?   *Beethoven never studied with Mozart.*
- How did archeological discoveries in 1748 promote a renewed interest in classical art and music?   *The discovery of buried ruins in Pompeii sparked a renewed interest in Greek and Roman Classical art.*
- Which Classical-period symphony ends with fewer players on stage than it begins with?   *Haydn's "Farewell" Symphony*
- Why did Haydn use Italian librettos even though his audiences spoke German?   *Italian was the traditional language for opera.*

Chapter 12

- Why did Beethoven earn more royalty income than Bach?   *Bach's music was not published commercially.*

Chapter 14

- What was Johann Maelzel's invention, and how did it affect music performance?   *Maelzel's metronome provided a standard for measuring the speed or tempo of the beat.*
- Which composer courted his loved one in a language she did not understand?   *Hector Berlioz*
- Which of the following composers could have been guests at Chopin's 30th birthday party—Mendelssohn, Schubert, Liszt, Beethoven?   *Mendelssohn, Liszt*
- Can you think of two composers who published their works under someone else's name?   *Fanny Mendelssohn, Clara Schumann.*
- How did Mendelssohn use a combination of affluence and influence in his work with other musicians?   *He raised the Gewandhaus Orchestra to a professional level by influencing the players to excel. He paid them extra from his own pocket and established a retirement fund.*

Chapter 15

- Who composed the most operas—Puccini, Rossini, or Verdi?   *Rossini*
- What is the difference between a *castrato* and a *concerto*?   *A "castrato" is a*

male soprano or alto singer. A "concerto" is an instrumental piece for one or more solo instruments.

- What are at least three ways in which Wagner exerted total control?
He wrote his own librettos; composed, orchestrated, and conducted the music; designed the sets; directed the singing.

Chapter 16

- Can you name two symphonies that do not have four movements?
Schubert's Unfinished Symphony; Beethoven's Pastoral Symphony
- How are Felix Mendelssohn's travels reflected in his works? *Scottish Symphony, Italian Symphony, Hebrides Overture*
- Which opera is associated with "tobacco and bulls"? *Carmen*
- Which opera contains elephants and pyramids? *Aida*
- What sort of records did Mahler break? *length of piece (3rd Symphony), number of players called for (8th Symphony)*
- What incentives encouraged musicians to improve their skills? *more competition; higher-paying positions; better orchestras*
- Who wrote the words for a tone poem? *No one! It is entirely an instrumental piece with no text. (However, there may be a story or program for the work that was usually written by the composer.)*

Chapter 17

- To which professional association did Nikolai Rimsky-Korsakov, Alexander Borodin, Mily Balakirev, César Cui, and Modest Moussorgsky belong? *"The Mighty Five" or "Russian Five"*
- Which popular Russian composer worked as a law clerk? *Tchaikovsky*

Chapter 18

- In addition to music, which creative art forms reflect Impressionism? *mainly painting and poetry*

Chapter 20

- Which non-European culture was the main influence in Stravinsky's use of ostinato? *African culture and its music*

Chapter 21

- After the premiere of which ballet did a Paris theatre need repair? *Igor Stravinsky's Rite of Spring*

Chapter 22

- Name two composers who were forced by their government to make public apologies. *Shostakovich and Prokofiev*
- Which one of *Les Six* was influenced by his visits to Harlem jazz clubs? *Darius Milhaud*
- Which of his compositions shows that influence? *La création du monde*

- What were some of the differences between The Five and *Les Six* (The Six)? *The Five were Russian composers—all men—who promoted purely Russian music. Les Six were French, included a woman, focused on Western music.*
- Name at least two prominent composers whose works represent more than one style period.   *Beethoven, Prokofiev*
- Which composer is associated with commencement ceremonies? *Edward Elgar*
- Name two composers whose works sound like an earlier style period than when they lived.   *Brahms, Sibelius*

Chapter 23

- What might happen if the piano is not tuned before a performance of Cage's *4:33* (Four minutes, thirty-three seconds)?   *Nothing would happen because the piano is not actually played.*

Chapter 24

- Who was the composer who supported himself during his teenage years by plugging songs and recording piano rolls?   *George Gershwin*
- Whose one-act opera contains motifs derived from Creole folk tunes? *Amy Beach*

Chapter 25

- Name several places where song pluggers worked.   *at music publishers' studios; in department stores; in theaters*
- How did the term Tin Pan Alley originate?   *The din from performers playing at the same time on New York City's 28th St. sounded like the banging of tin pans.*

Chapter 26

- How did *Shuffle Along* make history?   *The show set new standards for African-American musicals, and for the first time, African Americans were allowed to sit in the orchestra section of the theater.*
- What did Tony Pastor do to change vaudeville?   *Pastor "cleaned up" the shows and transformed vaudeville into family entertainment.*
- Suppose Bach, Mozart, and Brahms were alive today. Who do you think would be the most likely composer of Broadway musicals?   *most likely Mozart, possibly Bach*
- Although trained as a composer, Stephen Sondheim collaborated as a lyricist with which three composers?   *Leonard Bernstein, Jule Styne, and Richard Rodgers*
- When you hear song lyrics about luxury, wealth, and extravagance, which composer-lyricist are you reminded of?   *Cole Porter*

Chapter 27

- Why did movie studios have to establish large music departments?   *With the advent of "talkies," music became more important in films.*

- Which three of the following have a similar function—recurring theme, sostenuto, leitmotif, idée fixe, coda? *recurring theme, leitmotif, idée fixe*
- In film making, what is the track without music called? *"click" track*

Chapter 28

- What is the origin of the word "gypsy"? *Europeans mistook the wandering bands of dark-skinned people for Egyptians (shortened to gypsies).*
- Which cultures influenced Japanese music? *Chinese and Korean*

Appendix G
Guide to the Recordings

Composer	Title	CD/Track
Gregorian Chant	Alleluia Pascha Nostrum (excerpt)	1-1
Leonin	Alleluia Dies Sanctificatus	1-2
Palestrina	Kyrie (polyphony)	1-3
Handel	Messiah: "For Unto Us a Child Is Born"	1-4
Bach	Cantata No. 140 ("Wachet auf"): Opening Chorus	1-5
	"Alleluia"	1-6
Vivaldi	The Four Seasons Op. 8. No. 1 "Spring": 1st movement	1-7
	Bird Calls	1-8
	Storm Section	1-9
Bach	Brandenburg Concerto No. 2: 3rd Movement: Allegro assai	1-10
Bach	Fugue in G Minor ("Little")	1-11
Mozart	Variations on "Ah, Vous Dirai-Je Maman" K. 265 (excerpt)	1-12
Mozart	Horn Concerto No. 2 in E-Flat, K. 417, 3rd Movement: Theme 1: Main Theme (A)	1-13
	Theme 2 (B)	1-14
	Theme 3 (C)	1-15
	Theme 4 (D)	1-16
Beethoven	Piano Sonata No. 8 in C Minor (Pathétique) Op. 13, 3rd Movement (rondo form): Theme 1: Main Rondo Theme (A)	1-17
	Theme 2 (B)	1-18
Haydn	Symphony No. 94 in G "Surprise," 3rd Movement: Minuet (A) – Theme 1	1-19
	Trio (B) – Theme 3	1-20
	Minuet (A) – Themes 1 and 2 return	1-21
Mozart	Symphony No. 40 in G Minor K. 550, 1st Movement: Molto allegro (sonata form): Exposition (A) – Theme 1	1-22
	Theme 2	1-23
	Development (B) – Theme 1 fragments	1-24
	Recapitulation (A) – Theme 1 return	1-25
Mozart	Don Giovanni: Madamina (Opus aria: ABA form): A Section	1-26
	B Section (minuet)	1-27
Beethoven	Symphony No. 5 in C Minor: Op. 67: Exposition (A) – Theme 1	1-28
	Horn Introduction – Theme 2	1-29
	Development (B) –Theme 1 fragments	1-30
	Recapitulation – Theme 1 return	1-31
	Coda – Theme 1 modified	1-32
Berlioz	Symphonie Fantastique, 5th Movement: "Dream of a Witches Sabbath": Introduction	1-33
	Idée Fixe (Beloved Melody): Theme 1 fragment	1-34
	Dies Irae: Tolling Bells	1-35
	"Dies Irae" Part 1: Theme 2	1-36
	Witches' Round Dance: Theme 3	1-37
Schubert	The Erlkonig (art song)	2-1
Schumann	C: Scherzo, Op. 10 (excerpt)	2-2
Chopin	Fantasie Impromptu, Op. 66	2-3
Verdi	*La Traviata*, Act I: Recitative: "È strano! È strano!"	2-4
	Aria: "Aquell' amor"	2-5
	Recitative	2-6
	Aria: "Sempre libera"	2-7
Brahms	Academic Festival Overture, Op. 80: Theme 1	2-8
	Theme 3: "Stately House"	2-9
	Theme 4	2-10
	Theme 7: "Freedom Song"	2-11
	Theme 8: "Gaudeamus igitur"	2-12
Mahler	Songs of a Wayfarer: "Ging heut morgen uber Feld"	2-13
Stravinsky	The Rite of Spring: "Sacrificial Dance"	2-14
Tchaikovsky	1812 Overture, Op. 49: Theme 1 – Church Hymn	2-15
	Theme 3 – Folk Song	2-16
	Theme 6 – Lullaby	2-17
	Theme 8 – Czar's Hymn	2-18

Composer	Title	CD/Track
Schoenberg	Suite for Piano, Op. 25 "Preludium"	2-19
Prokofiev	Classical Symphony, 1st movement (sonata form): Theme 1	2-20
	Theme 2	2-21
Ives	Charlie Rutlage (song, 1921)	2-22
Ives	First Orchestral Set: Three Places in New England: "Putnam's Camp, Redding, Connecticut": Section 1: Introduction	2-23
	British Grenadiers	2-24
	Section 2: Dream Scene: Bugle Calls	2-25
	Section 3: Awakening: 4th of July Celebration	2-26
Gershwin	*Porgy and Bess* (opera): "Bess, You Is My Woman Now"	3-1
Copland	*Rodeo* (ballet): "Hoe Down"	3-2
Mendelssohn	Violin Concerto in E Minor, Op. 64 1st Movement (sonata form): Exposition: Theme 1, violin	3-3
	Theme 2: Development	3-4
	Theme fragments: Recapitulation	3-5
	Theme 1 return	3-6
Puccini	*La Bohème*, End of Act 1: Recitative: "Non sono in vena"	3-7
	Recitative: "Si sente meglio?"	3-8
	Rudolfo's Aria: "Che gelida manina"	3-9
	Mimi's Aria: "Mi chiamano Mimi"	3-10
Wagner	Overture to *Die Meistersinger*: Exposition – Mastersingers' Motive	3-11
	Love Theme	3-12
	Mastersingers' Heritage	3-13
	Prize Song	3-14
Mahler	Symphony No. 1 in D, 1st Movement: Introduction (slow): Sounds of the Forest	3-15
	Forest Melody (horns)	3-16
	Main Section (moderately fast): Main Theme – "Days of Youth"	3-17
	Development Section: Theme fragments	3-18
	Finale Section (coda): Sounds of the Forest	3-19
	Main Theme return	3-20
Debussy	Prelude to the Afternoon of a Faun: A Section – Flute chromatic melody	3-21
	B Section – Transition (clarinet)	3-22
	A Section – Flute chromatic melody	3-23
Joplin	The Entertainer: Introduction – Section 1	4-1
	Section 2	4-2
	Trio – Section 3	4-3
Bernstein	Overture to *Candide*: Introduction	4-4
	Oh, Happy We	4-5
	Glitter and Be Gay	4-6
	Coda	4-7
Kern	*Show Boat* — "Ol Man River": Introduction	4-8
	Chorus (A)	4-9
	Bridge (B)	4-10
	Chorus (A)	4-11
Sondheim	*A Little Night Music*: "Send in the Clowns"	4-12
Bock	*Fiddler on the Roof*: "Sunrise, Sunset"	4-13

Britten — The Young Person's Guide to the Orchestra, Op. 34: "Variations and Fugue on a Theme of Henry Purcell"

THEME

Purcell's Theme	4-14	Brass section	4-16	Percussion section	4-18
Woodwind section	4-15	String section	4-17	Full orchestra	4-19

VARIATIONS

Variation A – The Flute and Piccolo	4-20	Variation F – The Violas	4-25	Variation J – The Horns	4-29
Variation B – The Oboes	4-21	Variation G – The Cellos	4-26	Variation K – The Trumpets	4-30
Variation C – The Clarinets	4-22	Variation H – The Double Basses	4-27	Variation L – The Trombones	4-31
Variation D – The Bassoons	4-23	Variation I – The Harp	4-28	Variation M – Percussion	4-32
Variation E – The Violins	4-24				

FUGUE

Piccolo	4-33	Return of Theme	4-34	Coda	4-35

Composer	Title	CD/Track
Zwilich	Concerto Grosso 1985: 1st Movement	4-36
South Africa	If It Comes to Fighting with Guns – traditional	4-37
Japan	Netori (prelude) & Etenraku in Hyojo	4-38
Japan	Kabuki Naganta - Ayama-Yukata – excerpt	4-39
Bessie Smith	"Nobody Knows You When You're Down and Out"	4-40
Louis Armstrong	"Heebie Jeebies"	4-41
Bing Crosby	"White Christmas"	4-42
Charlie Parker	"Koko"	4-43
Woody Guthrie	"So Long, It's Been Good to Know You"	4-44
Larson	*Rent*: "Seasons of Love"	4-45

Glossary of Musical Terms

A cappella   Choral music without accompaniment

Accelerando   Gradual quickening of tempo

Accent   Emphasis on a particular tone

Adagio   Slow tempo

Aleatoric music   A twentieth-century method of creating music; uses vague notation to leave many musical decisions to the performer

Allegretto   Less quick than allegro; moderately fast tempo

Allegro   Lively, fast tempo

Allemande   A Baroque dance in moderate tempo and two-beat meter

Alto   A low female voice, also called contralto

Andante   Moderate, walking tempo

Andantino   Slightly faster tempo than andante

Antiphony, antiphonal   Music in which two or more groups are separated to create an echo effect and contrast

Arco   A string instrument bowing direction where the bow is used as opposed to plucking the string

Aria   An elaborate solo song with instrumental accompaniment, generally in an opera, an oratorio, or a cantata

Arpeggio   Chord tones sounded in succession rather than simultaneously

Art song   An elaborate solo song, usually composed to an existing poem, sung with accompaniment

Athematic   Music without discernible themes or melodies

Atonality   Music without tonality or key

Avant-garde   A French term used to describe radical or advanced composers or other artists

Ballad   A narrative-style folk song

Ballad opera   A type of opera, originating in the eighteenth century, which introduced spoken dialogue between songs

Ballade   (1) French trouvère poetry and songs (2) Songlike, nineteenth-century piano pieces

Bar   See *Measure*

Baritone   A male voice with a range between tenor and bass

Bass   The lowest, heaviest male voice

Basso continuo   A bass line that provides a basis for a harmonic accompaniment, most often used in Baroque music

Beat   The underlying basic rhythmic pulse

Bebop   Originating in the 1940s, a highly innovative jazz style that features small groups of instruments

Bel canto   A style of singing, particularly in Italian opera, that displays the singer's vocal agility and beautiful tone

Bin   A string instrument used in the music of northern India

Blue notes   Flatted or "bent" third, fifth, and seventh tones of a traditional major scale used in jazz and blues music

Blues   A melancholy song originating with African-American singers

Blues progression   Predictable progressions of chords in jazz and blues music, using patterns derived from church hymns

Bolero   A Spanish dance in moderate tempo with three beats per measure

Bourrée   A fast Baroque dance with two beats per measure

Bridge   (1) A musical passage between two major sections (2) The part of a stringed instrument that supports the strings

Buffo   A singer of comic roles in Italian opera

Burlesque   A raucous, bawdy, musical sex-and-comedy travesty entertainment of the late nineteenth and early twentieth centuries

Cadence   A melodic or harmonic progression that gives the effect of closing a section

Cadenza   A virtuoso passage (sometimes improvised) played by the soloist in a concerto, usually without orchestral accompaniment

Cakewalk   Originating on Southern plantations, the *cakewalk* was a high-kicking dance

Call and response   An African and African-American song style in which a leader sings phrases to which a chorus or group responds with phrases

Canon   Music in which one or more lines continue to imitate one another throughout the work

Cantata   Vocal music developed in the Baroque period for solo voice(s), instruments, and often a chorus; based either on a religious or secular text

Canzona   A short instrumental piece popular in the sixteenth and seventeenth centuries

Castrato   Castrated male soprano or alto singers, popular mainly in Italian Baroque operas

Chaconne   A work featuring variations on a progression of chords repeated throughout the work

Chamber music   Musical composition suitable for performances by two to eight players in a room or small hall

Chance music   A twentieth-century technique using general instructions to performers, allowing them to create a performance that is a matter of chance

Chorale   A hymn tune used in the German Lutheran Church

Chord   The simultaneous sounding of three or more pitches

Choreographer   The person who plans the dancers' movements

Chorus   (1) A group that sings choral music (2) A section of an opera or oratorio sung by the chorus (3) The refrain or main section of a song

Chromatic   A scale or harmonic movement of half steps

Cine music   Blend of Eastern and Western music used in popular musical films in India

Clavier   A general term indicating any keyboard instrument

Coda   The Italian word for "tail"; the section that brings the movement to a conclusion

Col legno   A special effect in string performance where the player strikes the strings with the wooden side of the bow

Coloratura   A virtuoso style of singing, usually including fast scales, arpeggios, and ornaments; often associated with a light, high soprano voice, particularly in opera

Common time   A meter that consists of four beats per measure

Concert overture   An overture not associated with an opera or a drama

Concertato   Contrasting performing groups playing together

Concertmaster   (*Konzertmeister* in German) The first chair player in the first violin section of an orchestra

Concerto   A work for solo instrument(s), usually with three movements, accompanied by an orchestra

Concerto grosso   A concerto for a small instrumental group accompanied by a small orchestra

Consonance   A group of sounds that seems pleasing or restful

Continuo   See *Basso continuo*

Contrabassoon   A large bassoon pitched an octave below the usual bassoon

Contralto   See *Alto*

Counterpoint   Two or more independent melodic lines occurring at the same time

Counter subject   The second theme in a fugue

Country   Popular music originating in the Appalachian region of the United States

Courante   A lively dance in triple meter and fast tempo

Crescendo   Gradual increase in volume

Decrescendo   Gradual decrease in volume, also called diminuendo

Development   (1) The process of developing themes (2) The section in sonata form featuring the development of themes

Dissonance A group of sounds that seems disagreeable or unpleasant

Dodecaphonic music See *Serialism*

Double stop The sounding of two different pitches simultaneously on a stringed instrument

Downbeat The accented first beat of a measure

Duet A musical work for two performers

Dynamics The various levels of intensity or loudness in music

Eclectic An incorporation of many different styles

Electronic music Sounds produced on electronic oscillators and then usually recorded and stored

English horn An alto oboe

Etude A short, instrumental composition concentrating on a particular technical aspect of performance

Exposition The opening section of fugue and sonata forms

Fantasia A short composition in free form

Finale The concluding movement of some multi-movement works and operas

Flamenco The highly rhythmic dance style of Andalusian Gypsies

Flat A sign indicating that a pitch is to be lowered by a half step

Form The structure or plan of a composition

Fortepiano See *Pianoforte*

Fugue A composition in which the main subject (theme) is presented in imitation in several parts

Fusion A blend of jazz and rock music

Gagaku Ancient Korean and Japanese court orchestras

Gamelan Javanese court music

Gavotte A dance with a moderate tempo in two-beat meter

Gesamtkunstwerk Meaning "total art work" in German; Wagner used this term for his music-dramas, over which he exerted total control of the librettos, music, orchestrations, sets, and staging

Gigue A baroque dance in compound meter with a fast tempo

Glissando A performance effect provided by rapid sliding up or down scales

Grand opera Usually serious, nineteenth-century French opera that uses elaborately costumed crowd scenes, large choruses, ballet, and lavish sets

Grave Very slowly and solemnly

Gregorian chant Monophonic church music of the Middle Ages named after Pope Gregory I; also called *plainchant*

Harmonics (1) Secondary tones that form a part of most tones (2) High-pitched tones that are produced on a string instrument by placing the finger lightly on a string

Harmony The simultaneous sounding of pitches

Harpsichord A popular keyboard instrument of the sixteenth through eighteenth centuries on which the strings are plucked when the keys are depressed

Heldentenor In German operas, a tenor who sings heroic roles

Hindustani music Music of northern India

Homophony, homophonic A texture consisting of a line of melody and accompaniment

Idée fixe Berlioz's name for the melody or theme used throughout all movements of his *Symphony fantastique*

Imitation The repetition of a melody or portion of a melody in another part

Impromptu A short piano composition that sounds improvised

Improvisation Spontaneous performance without notated music

Incidental music Music composed for performance in connection with, but not part of, a drama

Instrumentation The parts assigned to particular instruments in an ensemble

Interval The distance between two notes

Jazz A twentieth-century American musical style incorporating complex rhythms and improvisation

Kabuki Traditional Japanese theater incorporating acting, dancing, and music

Kapellmeister German term for music director

Karnatic music Music of southern India

Key   See *Tonality*

Kokyu   A Japanese spiked fiddle

Koto   A stringed, lutelike instrument of Japan

Largo   Very slow and broad tempo

Legato   Smooth, connected style of performance

Leitmotif   A motive or theme associated with a particular character or an idea, used extensively by Richard Wagner

Lento   Very slow

Libretto   The text of an opera or oratorio

Lied   (pl., Lieder) The German term for art song

Lutheran cantata   A choral work, often with instruments, for the musical portion of a Lutheran church service

Lyric opera   Nineteenth-century French opera emphasizing melody and romantic or fantasy-based stories

Ma non troppo   A performance indication meaning "but not too much," used to qualify another term, as in *allegro ma non troppo*—*"fast, but not too much"*

Madrigal   A secular work for small choir, popular in the Renaissance style period

Maestro de cappella   Italian term for music director

Major   One of the two basic scales used in Western music; see also *Minor*

Mass   The Roman Catholic Church's main service, frequently set to music (*Missa* in Latin)

Mazurka   A Polish dance in triple meter

Measure   A group of beats set off in written music by vertical lines called bar lines

Meistersinger   A member of a guild of German master musicians. The guild flourished from the fourteenth to the seventeenth centuries.

Melody   A series of consecutive pitches with a recognizable shape or tune

Meno   Means "less" in Italian

Meter   The pattern created by stressed and unstressed beats

Metronome   A device (mechanical or electrical) used to indicate the exact tempo of a composition

Mezzo-soprano   A female voice with a range between a soprano and an alto

Microtones   Pitches falling between the semitones of the Western chromatic scale

MIDI   An acronym for Musical Instrument Digital Interface; standards for use by electronic keyboards, computers, and other devices

Minimalism   Twentieth-century compositional technique using the simplest musical elements, generally repeated over and over, with subtle changes in their character

Minor   One of the two basic scales in Western music; see also *Major*

Minstrel   French poet-musician who performed throughout France during the Middle Ages

Minuet   A popular dance of the seventeenth and eighteenth centuries; uses triple meter

Minuet and trio form   A common Classical period form consisting of three parts: minuet, trio, minuet

Moderato   Moderate tempo

Modes   Scale patterns (including major and minor) derived from early church music

Monophony, monophonic   A texture consisting of a single melodic line without accompaniment

Motet   Sacred polyphonic music for voices, popular during the thirteenth through seventeenth centuries

Motive   A short melodic or rhythmic idea

Movement   A large, independent section of an instrumental composition

Music-drama   Wagner's term for his German operas

Musique concrète   Everyday sounds recorded and manipulated on the tape recorder

Mute   A device for dampening and changing the tone of an instrument

Neoclassical   A twentieth-century style that borrows compositional techniques from previous style periods

Nocturne   A short, lyrical piano piece of the Romantic period that evokes feelings associated with the night

Nogaku   Traditional Japanese musical plays

Notes   Symbols written in musical notation to indicate pitches and rhythm

Octave   An interval of eight pitches in which the first and last pitches have the same pitch name

Octet   A work for eight performers

Opera   A dramatic work, comedy or tragedy, set to music

Opera comique   Mid-nineteenth-century French opera featuring wit and satire both in the libretto and in the music

Operetta   A light opera with spoken dialogue

Opus   Literally "work"; the number indicates the order in which the composer's works were written

Oratorio   A large work for chorus, soloist, and orchestra, usually on a religious topic; performed without scenery, costumes, or action

Orchestration   The art and technique of scoring music for an orchestra or a group of instruments

Organum   Polyphonic choral church music, beginning in the ninth century

Ornament   One or more tones that embellish a melody

Ostinato   A short, persistently repeated melodic or rhythmic figure

Overture   An instrumental introduction to a larger work

Pasticcio   A cross between ballad opera and comic opera, combining a dramatic work with music by famous composers

Pentatonic scale   A scale consisting of five tones

Phrase   A relatively short melodic statement, similar to a clause or phrase in language

Piano   (1) Keyboard instrument (2) Quiet

Pianoforte   This is the complete name for the keyboard instrument usually called a *Piano*. Meaning "soft-loud" in Italian, the instrument was named *pianoforte* when it was invented in the early eighteenth century because it could play both soft and loud.

Pitch   The perceived highness or lowness of a musical sound, determined by the number of vibrations per second

Più   Means "more" in Italian

Pizzicato   A direction to string performers to pluck rather than bow the strings

Plainchant   See *Gregorian chant*

Poco   A performance direction meaning "little." For example, *poco accelerando* indicates "gradually play faster."

Polonaise   A Polish national dance, also used in piano pieces by Chopin

Polychord   Two or more triads performed simultaneously

Polymeter   Two or more contrasting meters sounded simultaneously

Polyphony, polyphonic   A texture in which two or more melodies of approximately equal importance are present at the same time

Polytonality   Several tonalities present at the same time

Prelude   (1) A short instrumental work usually played as an introduction to a larger work (2) A short, independent instrumental work

Presto   Very fast tempo

Program notes   Short descriptions or background information in the printed concert program about the music, the composer, and the performers

Programmatic music   Instrumental work descriptive of some nonmusical idea or object

Proscenium   The front area of the stage, including the curtain, apron, and arch, that is visible to the audience when the curtain is closed

Quartet   A work for four performers

Quintet   A work for five performers

Raga   Ancient melodic material used in Indian music

Ragtime   Syncopated music composed in the 1890s, usually for piano

Rallentando   Gradual slowing of tempo

Recapitulation   The section of sonata form in which the themes from the exposition are heard again

Recitative   A speechlike section found in operas, oratorios, cantatas, and other vocal works

Requiem   The funeral Mass of the Roman Catholic Church

Revue   An energetic popular entertainment show featuring musical numbers, comedy acts, dramatic sketches, and specialty routines, with no story; usually built around star performers

Rhythm   The sensation of motion in music, regulated by the duration and grouping of sounds

Rhythm and blues (R & B)   A transitional music style between swing and rock; first became popular in the African-American communities of large, Midwestern cities

Riff   Used in African and African-American music, a riff is a short phrase repeated over and over

Ritardando   Gradual slowing of the tempo

Rock'n'roll/Rock   Popular music characterized by its hard-driving beat and use of electronically amplified instruments

Rococo   The highly ornamented style in music and the other arts, prevalent in eighteenth-century European courts

Rondo   A form in which the main theme appears several times with contrasting sections between its appearances

Rubato   A performer's slight deviation from strict rhythm for expressive effect

Sampling   A series of numbers that represent sounds that have been digitally recorded and stored on computer disk

Scale   A series of pitches that proceed upward or downward according to a prescribed pattern

Scherzo   (1) A lively movement, usually in triple meter (2) A self-contained piano piece

Score   The complete notation of a work that includes a number of parts

Secular music   Nonreligious music

Sequence   The immediate repetition of a melodic idea using different pitches

Serialism   A twentieth-century method of composing, using tone-rows and all twelve tones of the chromatic scale

Sforzando   A loud, accented tone or chord

Shakuhachi   A Japanese end-blown bamboo flute

Singspiel   German eighteenth-century opera with spoken dialogue

Solo   A work in which one player or singer performs alone or is featured

Sonata   (1) A multimovement work for piano or piano and other solo instrument (2) A Baroque piece for a small instrumental ensemble

Sonata form   A large form consisting of an exposition section, followed by a development section and a recapitulation

Song cycle   A group of songs with a unifying theme

Song plugger   A pianist-singer who performed new songs to find customers for them

Songs without words   Mendelssohn's term for melodic piano pieces, written in the style of a lied or song

Soprano   The highest female voice or boy's voice

Sprechstimme   A vocal style combining speaking and singing

Staccato   A detached style of performing in detached, abrupt bursts

Stretto   A short section mainly found in the fugue where the main subject is imitated in close succession or overlapping voices

Subject   The principal melody of a fugue

Subscription concerts   A series of concerts for advance-purchase subscribers

Suite   (1) An instrumental work in several movements (2) Portions of a larger work, such as a ballet or opera, performed as a group

Supertitles   Translations of the libretto of an opera or operetta projected above the proscenium

Swing   Popular music of the 1930s and 1940s which often featured big bands

Symphonic poem   Programmatic symphony in one movement; also called a tone poem

Symphony   An extended, multimovment orchestral work

Syncopation   Accented beats not normally expected within a particular meter

Synthesizer   An electric instrument used to generate sounds

Tempo   The speed of the beats in a piece of music

Tenor   A male voice higher than a baritone or bass

Texture   The way in which the individual parts of music are layered and woven

Theme   The main melody or melodies in a piece of music

Theme and variations   Form consisting of a theme, followed by a group of variations on that theme

Timbre   Tone quality or color

Toccata   A display piece for a keyboard instrument

Tonality   A key or tonal center

Tone poem   See *Symphonic poem*

Tone-row music (twelve tone)   See *Serialism*

Tonic (key center)   The specific pitch around which a piece of music is centered

Tonic chord   A chord built on the first pitch of a major or minor scale

Transcription   An adaptation of a musical work for a different instrument, voice, or ensemble

Transposition   A piece or section of music written or performed at a pitch other than the original one

Tremolo   Rapid repetition of one pitch, or rapid alternation between two tones

Triad   A chord consisting of three pitches, usually separated by intervals of thirds

Trill   A musical ornament consisting of rapid alternations of two tones

Trio   (1) A musical work for three parts or three performers (2) The second section of a minuet and trio form

Troubadours   During the age of chivalry, singing knights of the twelfth-century court in southern France

Trouvères   Noblemen in the courts of northern France who composed and sang songs during the twelfth and thirteenth centuries

Tutti   An Italian performance term indicating that the entire ensemble plays

Twelve-tone music   See *Serialism*

Unison   Performing the same pitches or melody at the same time

Variation   A section of music in which the melody, harmony, or rhythm of a theme is repeated with some changes

Vaudeville   A variety show featuring novelty acts as well as song and dance

Verismo   Late-nineteenth-century opera that uses a realistic story, setting, and acting

Vibrato   A rapid fluctuation of pitch or pulsation of tone for expressiveness

Vina   A string instrument used in the music of southern India

Virtuoso   A highly skilled performer

Virtuoso orchestra   An orchestra consisting entirely of highly skilled (*virtuoso*) performers

Vivace   Very fast, lively tempo

Whole-tone scale   A scale in which the octave is divided into six whole steps

Wind ensemble   A wind instrument band smaller than the traditional band

Photo Credits

Prelude: Pages 2–3, Lute, photo by Geoff Dann, © Dorling Kindersley, Courtesy of the Anthony Barton Collection.

Chapter 1: Page 5, Lute, photo by Geoff Dann, © Dorling Kindersley, Courtesy of the Anthony Barton Collection. *Pages 6–7,* Lute, photo by Geoff Dann, © Dorling Kindersley, Courtesy of the Anthony Barton Collection. *Page 8,* Ellen Zwilich, photo by Ray Stanyard, courtesy of Florida State University Photo Lab. *Page 8,* Nigel Kennedy, photo by Victor Fraile, courtesy of Corbis/Reuters America LLC. *Page 8,* Concert audience, photo © Gideon Mendel/CORBIS All Rights Reserved.

Chapter 2: Pages 10–11, Lute, photo by Geoff Dann, © Dorling Kindersley, Courtesy of the Anthony Barton Collection. *Page 12,* Marilyn Horne, photo by ArenaPal/Topham, courtesy of The Image Works.

Chapter 3: Pages 14–15, Lute, photo by Geoff Dann, © Dorling Kindersley, Courtesy of the Anthony Barton Collection. *Page 16,* Chicago Youth Symphony Orchestra, photo by David Maenza, courtesy of SuperStock, Inc. *Page 16,* The Boys Choir of Harlem, photo by Michael J. Doolittle, courtesy of The Image Works. *Page 18,* Don Giovanni performance, photo by Michael Riviere, courtesy of Getty Images, Inc. *Page 19,* Rent performance, photo © Robbie Jack/CORBIS All Rights Reserved. *Page 19,* Romeo and Juliet performance, photo by Natasha-Marie Brown, courtesy of Corbis/Reuters America LLC. *Page 20,* Benaroya Symphony Hall, Seattle, photo by Chuck Pefley, courtesy of Alamy Images. *Page 22,* Opera performance, photo © Jack Vartoogian/FrontRowPhotos. *Page 24,* Music library, photo by Laimute Druskis/Pearson Education/PH College. *Page 27,* Opera audience, photo by Ryan McVay/Stone/Getty Images. *Page 28,* Seiji Ozawa, photo © Axel Zeininger/epa/CORBIS All Rights Reserved. *Page 30,* Carlo Allegri/Staff/Getty Images Entertainment/Getty Images.

Chapter 4: Page 31, French Horn, photo by Joseph Barnell, courtesy of SuperStock, Inc. *Pages 32–33,* French Horn, photo by Joseph Barnell, courtesy of SuperStock, Inc. *Pages 32–33,* Tuba, photo by Dave King, © Dorling Kindersley. *Page 36,* Cindy Blackman, photo by gkphotography, courtesy of Alamy Images. *Page 39,* Classical flutist, photo by Jeff Greenberg, courtesy of Alamy Images. *Page 40,* Cellist Yo-Yo Ma, photo by Chitose Suzuki, courtesy of AP Wide World Photos.

Chapter 5: Pages 42–43, French Horn, photo by Joseph Barnell, courtesy of SuperStock, Inc. *Pages 42–43,* Tuba, photo by Dave King, © Dorling Kindersley. *Page 44,* The Kronos String Quartet, photo by Zdenek CHRAPEK, courtesy of Lebrecht Music & Arts Photo Library. *Page 45,* Fine Arts Brass Ensemble, Lebrecht. *Page 45,* Maelström Percussion Ensemble, courtesy of Bob Accurso. *Page 46,* Orchestra rehearsal, photo by Robert E. Daemmrich, courtesy of Getty Images Inc.–Stone Allstock. *Page 48,* Woodwind section, photo by Jim Four, courtesy of Lebrecht Music & Arts Photo Library. *Page 49,* Brass section, courtesy of Steve J. Sherman. *Page 50,* Percussion section, photo by Robert Millard, courtesy of Jay D. Zorn. *Page 50,* Zubin Mehta, photo by Peter Mares/Lebrecht Music & Arts, courtesy of The Image Works. *Page 56,* Hellier' Stradivarius, courtesy of Lebrecht Music & Arts Photo Library. *Page 57,* Franz Joseph Haydn, photo © Cummer Museum of Art & Gardens, courtesy of SuperStock, Inc. *Page 62,* John Philip Sousa, courtesy of United States Marine Band. *Page 63,* Organ performer, photo © Dorothy Y Riess MD/Lebrecht. *Page 63,* Mozart at the harpsichord, photo © National Gallery Collection; By kind permission of the Trustees of the National Gallery, London/CORBIS All Rights Reserved. *Page 65,* Fortepiano, photo by Royal Academy of Music, courtesy of Lebrecht Music & Arts Photo Library. *Page 65,* Computer music studio, photo by Dan Nelken, courtesy of Dan Nelken Studio Inc.

Chapter 6: Page 69, Piano, photo © Judith Miller/Dorling Kindersley/Sloans & Kenyon. *Pages 70–71,* Hurdy Gurdy, photo by C Squared Studios, courtesy of Getty Images, Inc.–Photodisc. *Pages 70–71,* Violin, photo by Royal Academy of Music, courtesy of Lebrecht Music & Arts Photo Library. *Pages 70–71,* Medieval Harp, photo by Geoff Dann, © Dorling Kindersley, Courtesy of the Anthony Barton Collection. *Page 72,* Porgy and Bess performance, photo by ArenaPal/Topham, courtesy of Alamy Images.

Chapter 7: Pages 74–75, Hurdy Gurdy, photo by C Squared Studios, courtesy of Getty Images, Inc.–Photodisc. *Pages 74–75,* Violin, photo by Royal Academy of Music, courtesy of Lebrecht Music & Arts Photo Library. *Pages 74–75,* Medieval Harp, photo by Geoff Dann, © Dorling Kindersley, Courtesy of the Anthony Barton Collection. *Page 76,* Spanish Gothic cathedral, photo by J. Mariani, courtesy of eStock Photography LLC. *Page 79,* Notre Dame (exterior), courtesy of Corbis Royalty Free. *Page 80,* Lute Player and Harpist, courtesy of Courtesy of the Library of Congress. *Page 80,* Dancing in the Middle Ages, courtesy of The Granger Collection. *Page 80,* Michal Adamczyk/Fotolia. *Page 81,* Statue of David, photo by Buonarroti, Michelangelo (1475–1564), courtesy of Galleria dell' Accademia, Florence, Italy/The Bridgeman Art Library. *Page 82,* Leonardo da Vinci sketch, courtesy of Images Inc. *Page 83,* Prophet Jeremiah by Michelangelo, Sistine Ceiling, photo by Scala, courtesy of Art Resource, N.Y. *Page 84,* Palestrina title page, courtesy of Art Resource/Bildarchiv Preussischer Kulturbesitz. *Page 85,* Orlando di Lasso, photo by Lebrecht Music & Arts, courtesy of Lebrecht Music & Arts Photo Library. *Page 86,* William Byrd, photo by Abigail Lebrecht, courtesy of Lebrecht Music & Arts Photo Library.

Chapter 8: Pages 88–89, Hurdy Gurdy, photo by C Squared Studios, courtesy of Getty Images, Inc.–Photodisc. *Pages 88–89,* Violin, photo by Royal Academy of Music, courtesy of Lebrecht Music & Arts Photo Library. *Pages 88–89,* Medieval Harp, photo by Geoff Dann, © Dorling Kindersley, Courtesy of the Anthony Barton Collection. *Page 90,* Portrait of Martin Luther, courtesy of SuperStock, Inc. *Page 90,* Basilica of St. Peter's, photo by Murat Ayranci, courtesy of SuperStock, Inc. *Page 91,* Gothic Duomo in Montova, Italy, photo by Max Osini, courtesy of Piero Scaruffi.

Chapter 9: Pages 92–93, Hurdy Gurdy, photo by C Squared Studios, courtesy of Getty Images, Inc.–Photodisc. *Pages 92–93,* Violin, photo by Royal Academy of Music, courtesy of Lebrecht Music & Arts Photo Library. *Pages 92–93,* Medieval Harp, photo by Geoff Dann, © Dorling Kindersley, Courtesy of the Anthony Barton Collection. *Page 94,* Basilica of St. Mark (exterior), photo © William Manning/CORBIS All Rights Reserved. *Page 94,* Basilica of St. Mark (interior), photo © John Heseltine/CORBIS All Rights Reserved. *Page 96,* Claudio Monteverdi, courtesy of The Granger Collection. *Page 98,* Heinrich Schütz, courtesy of Corbis/Bettmann. *Page 99,* George Frideric Handel, courtesy of German Information Center. *Page 100,* English Baroque Soloists, courtesy of Monteverdi Choir & Orchestra Ltd. *Page 104,* Luthern cantata, courtesy of Art Resource/The New York Public Library. *Page 105,* Johann Sebastian Bach, courtesy of German Information Center. *Page 110,* Antonio Vivaldi, courtesy of Art Resource/Bildarchiv Preussischer Kulturbesitz. *Page 114,* Bach at the keyboard with his family, courtesy of Stock Montage, Inc./Historical Pictures Collection.

Chapter 10: Pages 118–119, Hurdy Gurdy, photo by C Squared Studios, courtesy of Getty Images, Inc.–Photodisc. *Pages 118–119,* Violin, photo by Royal Academy of Music, courtesy of Lebrecht Music & Arts Photo Library. *Pages 118–119,* Medieval Harp, photo by Geoff Dann, © Dorling Kindersley, Courtesy of the Anthony Barton Collection. *Page 120,* Dancing the Minuet, courtesy of Corbis/Bettmann. *Page 121,* Ruins at Pompeii, Italy, photo © Mimmo Jodice/CORBIS All Rights Reserved. *Page 122,* 18th century mansion, photo © NTPL/Mike Williams, courtesy of The Image Works.

Chapter 11: Pages 124–125, Hurdy Gurdy, photo by C Squared Studios, courtesy of Getty Images, Inc.–Photodisc. *Pages 124–125,* Violin, photo by Royal Academy of Music, courtesy of Lebrecht Music & Arts Photo Library. *Pages 124–125,* Medieval Harp, photo by Geoff Dann, © Dorling Kindersley, Courtesy of the Anthony Barton Collection. *Page 126,* Young Beethoven, courtesy of Corbis/Bettmann. *Page 126,* Wolfgang Amadeus Mozart, courtesy of Museo Civico, Bologna, Italy/The Bridgeman Art Library. *Page 128,* Joseph Haydn, photo by Vienna Society for the Friends of Music, Austria, courtesy of SuperStock, Inc. *Page 129,* Esterházy Palace, photo © Vittoriano Rastelli/CORBIS All Rights Reserved. *Page 131,* Painting, Baroque, 18th Century. Della Croce, Johann Nepomuk (18th), "The Mozart Family" (1780–1781). Oil on canvas. 140 x 186 cm. Mozart House, Salzburg,

Austria. Erich Lessing/Art Resource. *Page 133,* Mozart's apartment, Martin Siepmann/imageBROKER/Alamy. *Page 138,* Schönbrunn Palace in Vienna, courtesy of Jay D. Zorn. *Page 142, Don Giovanni* performance, photo © Robbie Jack/CORBIS All Rights Reserved.

Chapter 12: Pages 146–147, Tuba, photo by Dave King, © Dorling Kindersley. *Pages 146–147,* Piano, © Judith Miller/Dorling Kindersley/Sloans & Kenyon. *Pages 146–147,* Oboe, photo by Philip Dowell, © Dorling Kindersley. *Pages 146–147,* Classical Guitar, photo © Dorling Kindersley. *Page 148,* Ludwig van Beethoven. *Page 150,* Ludwig van Beethoven's Broadwood piano, photo by Visual Arts Library–London, courtesy of Alamy Images. *Page 152,* Streicher Piano Factory.

Chapter 13: Pages 158–159, Tuba, photo by Dave King, © Dorling Kindersley. *Pages 158–159,* Piano, © Judith Miller/Dorling Kindersley/Sloans & Kenyon. *Pages 158–159,* Oboe, photo by Philip Dowell, © Dorling Kindersley. *Pages 158–159,* Classical Guitar, photo © Dorling Kindersley. *Page 160,* Delacroix's "Liberty Leading the People", photo by Erich Lessing, courtesy of Art Resource, N.Y.

Chapter 14: Pages 164–165, Tuba, photo by Dave King, © Dorling Kindersley. *Pages 164–165,* Piano, © Judith Miller/Dorling Kindersley/Sloans & Kenyon. *Pages 164–165,* Oboe, photo by Philip Dowell, © Dorling Kindersley. *Pages 164–165,* Classical Guitar, photo © Dorling Kindersley. *Page 166,* Hector Berlioz, photo by Lebrecht Music & Arts, courtesy of Lebrecht Music & Arts Photo Library. *Page 167,* Hector Berlioz at 29, courtesy of Art Resource, N.Y. *Page 167,* Portrait of Harriet Smithson (1800–54) (oil on canvas), French School, (19th century)/Private Collection, Lauros/Giraudon/The Bridgeman Art Library International. *Page 172,* GL Archive/Alamy. *Page 173,* Franz Schubert playing the piano with Johann Michael Vogl singing, photo by Lebrecht Music & Arts, courtesy of Lebrecht Music & Arts Photo Library. *Page 176,* Robert Schumann, photo by Lebrecht Music & Arts, courtesy of Lebrecht Music & Arts Photo Library. *Page 177,* Clara and Robert Schumann, courtesy of Getty Images Inc. – Stone Allstock. *Page 177,* Pictorial Press Ltd/Alamy. *Page 180,* North Wind Picture Archives/Alamy. *Page 182,* North Wind Picture Archives/Alamy. *Page 183,* Felix Mendelssohn, photo by Eichhorn Albert (1811–1851), courtesy of Private Collection/The Bridgeman Art Library International. *Page 184,* Fanny Mendelssohn, photo by Abigail Lebrecht, courtesy of Lebrecht Music & Arts Photo Library.

Chapter 15: Pages 188–189, Tuba, photo by Dave King, © Dorling Kindersley. *Pages 188–189,* Piano, © Judith Miller/Dorling Kindersley/Sloans & Kenyon. *Pages 188–189,* Oboe, photo by Philip Dowell, © Dorling Kindersley. *Pages 188–189,* Classical Guitar, photo © Dorling Kindersley. *Page 191, Falstaff* performance, courtesy of Jack Vartoogian. *Page 192,* Gaetano Donizetti, photo by Lebrecht Music & Arts, courtesy of Lebrecht Music & Arts Photo Library. *Page 192,* Vincenzo Bellini, photo by Italian School, (19th century), courtesy of Museo Civico, Bologna, Italy/The Bridgeman Art Library International. *Page 193,* Gioacchino Rossini, courtesy of SuperStock, Inc. *Page 193,* Giuseppe Verdi, photo © Giraudon/Art Resource, N.Y.. *Page 197,* Giacomo Puccini, photo by Lebrecht Music & Arts, courtesy of Lebrecht Music & Arts Photo Library. *Page 198, La Bohème,* courtesy of Jay D. Zorn. *Page 199,* Jacques Offenbach, photo by Lebrecht Music & Arts, courtesy of Lebrecht Music & Arts Photo Library. *Page 201,* Pictorial Press Ltd/Alamy. *Page 202, Carmen* performance, photo © Robbie Jack/CORBIS All Rights Reserved. *Page 203,* Carl Maria von Weber, photo by Lebrecht Music & Arts, courtesy of The Image Works. *Page 203,* Richard Wagner, photo by Lebrecht Music & Arts, courtesy of Lebrecht Music & Arts Photo Library.

Chapter 16: Pages 208–209, Tuba, photo by Dave King, © Dorling Kindersley. *Pages 208–209,* Piano, © Judith Miller/Dorling Kindersley/Sloans & Kenyon. *Pages 208–209,* Oboe, photo by Philip Dowell, © Dorling Kindersley. *Pages 208–209,* Classical Guitar, photo © Dorling Kindersley. *Page 211,* Johannes Brahms, photo by Lebrecht Music & Arts, courtesy of Lebrecht Music & Arts Photo Library. *Page 216,* Gustav Mahler, photo by Lebrecht Music & Arts, courtesy of Lebrecht Music & Arts Photo Library. *Page 223,* Richard Strauss, photo by Lebrecht Music & Arts, courtesy of Lebrecht Music & Arts Photo Library.

Chapter 17: Pages 226–227, Tuba, photo by Dave King, © Dorling Kindersley. *Pages 226–227,* Piano, © Judith Miller/Dorling Kindersley/Sloans & Kenyon. *Pages 226–227,* Oboe, photo by Philip Dowell, © Dorling Kindersley. *Pages 226–227,* Classical Guitar, photo © Dorling Kindersley. *Page 228, The Nutcracker Suite* performance, photo by Martha Swope, courtesy of Getty Images/Time Life Pictures. *Page 229,* Modest Mussorgsky, photo by Lebrecht

Music & Arts, courtesy of Lebrecht Music & Arts Photo Library. *Page 230,* Postcard of Piotr Ilyich Tchaikovsky (1840–93) (colour litho), Serov, H. (19th century)/ Private Collection, Archives Charmet/The Bridgeman Art Library International. *Page 230, Kremlin Square,* photo © Mark Sykes/Alamy. *Page 231, 1812 Overture* performance, photo © Joseph Sohm/CORBIS All Rights Reserved. *Page 234,* Nikolai Rimsky–Korsakov, photo by Lebrecht Music & Arts, courtesy of Lebrecht Music & Arts Photo Library. *Page 235,* Sergei Rachmaninov, courtesy of SuperStock, Inc. *Page 236,* Béla Bartók, photo by Archivo Iconografico, S.A., courtesy of Corbis/Bettmann. *Page 237,* Jean Sibelius, courtesy of Corbis/ Bettmann.

Chapter 18: Pages 238–239, Tuba, photo by Dave King, © Dorling Kindersley. *Pages 238–239,* Piano, © Judith Miller/Dorling Kindersley/Sloans & Kenyon. *Pages 238–239,* Oboe, photo by Philip Dowell, © Dorling Kindersley. *Pages 238–239,* Classical Guitar, photo © Dorling Kindersley. *Page 240,* Haystacks at Sunset, Frosty Weather, 1891, Monet, Claude (1840–1926)/ Private Collection/The Bridgeman Art Library International. *Page 241,* Claude Debussy, photo by Jacques–Emile Blanche, courtesy of Lebrecht Music & Arts Photo Library. *Page 242,* Painting of Cathedral of Rouen, photo by Hervé Lewandowski, © Réunion des Musées Nationaux/Art Resource. *Page 242,* Photograph of Cathedral of Rouen, photo by Ian Dagnall, courtesy of Alamy Images. *Page 243,* Eiffel Tower, Paris, photo by V.C.L., courtesy of Getty Images, Inc.–Taxi. *Page 246,* Maurice Ravel, photo © Giraudon/Art Resource, courtesy of Art Resource, N.Y.

Chapter 19: Pages 248–249, Yamaha DX7 Synthesizer, photo by Dave King, © Dorling Kindersley. *Pages 248–249,* Early Record Player, photo by Clive Streeter, © Dorling Kindersley. *Pages 248–249,* Apple iPod, courtesy of Dorling Kindersley Media Library. *Page 250,* Pablo Picasso (1881–1973), "Guernica," 1937. Oil on canvas, 350 x 782 cm. Museo Nacional Centro de Arte Reina Sofia, Madrid, Spain. © 2004 Estate of Pablo Picasso/Artists Rights Society (ARS), New York. John Bigelow Taylor/Art Resource, NY. *Page 250,* Picasso and Stravinsky in a sketch by Jean Cocteau. The Spanish artist designed the decors for Pulcinella (1920)/© 2002 Artists Rights Society (ARS), New York/ADAGP, Paris/Estate of Pablo Picasso. *Page 251,* Georgia O'Keeffe, American, 1887–1986, "Ram's Head, White Hollyhock–Hills," 1935. Oil on canvas, 30 x 36 in. (76.2 x 91.5 cm.) Brooklyn Museum of Art, Bequest of Edith and Milton Lowenthal, 1992.11.28. © 2000 The Georgia O'Keeffe Foundation/Artists Rights Society (ARS), New York.

Chapter 20: Pages 256–257, Yamaha DX7 Synthesizer, photo by Dave King, © Dorling Kindersley. *Pages 256–257,* Early Record Player, photo by Clive Streeter, © Dorling Kindersley. *Pages 256–257,* Apple iPod, courtesy of Dorling Kindersley Media Library. *Page 258,* Igor Stravinsky, photo by Fondation Theodore Strawinsky, courtesy of Lebrecht Music & Arts Photo Library. *Page 259, The Three Musicians,* photo by Picasso, Pablo (1881–1973), courtesy of Museum of Modern Art, New York, USA/The Bridgeman Art Library. *Page 260,* Lebrecht Music & Arts, courtesy of Lebrecht Music & Arts Photo Library. *Page 262, The Rite of Spring,* photo by Laurie Lewis, courtesy of Lebrecht Music & Arts Photo Library. *Page 264,* Stravinsky plays the piano.

Chapter 21: Pages 266–267, Yamaha DX7 Synthesizer, photo by Dave King, © Dorling Kindersley. *Pages 266–267,* Early Record Player, photo by Clive Streeter, © Dorling Kindersley. *Pages 266–267,* Apple iPod, courtesy of Dorling Kindersley Media Library. *Page 268,* Arnold Schoenberg, photo © Arnold Schoenberg Institute/Lebrecht. *Page 269,* Ernst Ludwig Kirchner, "Street, Berlin", 1913. Oil on Canvas. 47 1/2" x 37 7/8" (120.6 x 91.1 cm). The Museum of Modern Art/Licensed by Scala–Art Resource, NY. *Page 271,* Popperfoto/Getty Images.

Chapter 22: Pages 272–273, Yamaha DX7 Synthesizer, photo by Dave King, © Dorling Kindersley. *Pages 272–273,* Early Record Player, photo by Clive Streeter, © Dorling Kindersley. *Pages 272–273,* Apple iPod, courtesy of Dorling Kindersley Media Library. *Page 274,* Sergei Prokofiev, courtesy of The Bridgeman Art Library International. *Page 277,* Dimitri Shostakovich, courtesy of Lebrecht Music & Arts Photo Library. *Page 278,* Vaughn Williams, photo by Dudley Styles, courtesy of Royal College of Music. *Page 278,* Benjamin Britten, photo by Kurt Hutton, courtesy of Getty Images Inc.–Stone Allstock. *Page 279,* Nadia Boulanger, photo by UPI, courtesy of Corbis/Bettmann. *Page 280,* Les Six, courtesy of Corbis/Bettmann. *Page 280,* Paul Hindemith, courtesy of Culver Pictures, Inc. *Page 281,* Cyndi Lauper, photo by Joan Marcus Photography. *Page 282,* Béla Bartók, courtesy of Corbis/Bettmann.

Chapter 23: Pages 284–285, Yamaha DX7 Synthesizer, photo by Dave King, © Dorling Kindersley. Pages 284–285, Early Record Player, photo by Clive Streeter, © Dorling Kindersley. Pages 284–285, Apple iPod, courtesy of Dorling Kindersley Media Library. Page 287, Composer working on a synthesizer, photo by Dan Nelken, courtesy of Dan Nelken Studio Inc. Page 288, Jackson Pollock "One (Number 31, 1950)" 1950. Oil and enamel on unprimed canvas, 8 ft. 10 in. x 17 ft. 5 5/8 in. (269.5 x 530.8 cm). The Museum of Modern Art/Licensed by Scala–Art Resource, NY. Sidney and Harriet Janis Collection Fund (by exchange). Photograph © 2000 The Museum of Modern Art, New York. 00007.68. © 2004 The Pollock–Krasner Foundation/Artists Rights Society (ARS), New York. Page 289, Pierre Boulez, photo © Neal Preston/CORBIS All Rights Reserved. Page 290, Karlheinz Stockhausen, photo © Roland Scheidemann/dpa/CORBIS All Rights Reserved.

Chapter 24: Pages 292–293, Yamaha DX7 Synthesizer, photo by Dave King, © Dorling Kindersley. Pages 292–293, Early Record Player, photo by Clive Streeter, © Dorling Kindersley. Pages 292–293, Apple iPod, courtesy of Dorling Kindersley Media Library. Page 295, Amy Beach Née Amy Marcy Cheney Beach, courtesy of Milne Special Collections and Archives, University of New Hampshire Library. Page 295, Charles Ives, courtesy of National Archives and Records Administration, Still Picture Branch. Page 302, Tin Pan Alley, courtesy of Getty Images Inc. – Hulton Archive Photos. Page 302, George Gershwin, photo © Bettmann/CORBIS All Rights Reserved. Page 306, Porgy and Bess performance, photo © Jacques M. Chenet/CORBIS All Rights Reserved. Page 307, Aaron Copland, photo © Bettmann/CORBIS All Rights Reserved. Page 309, Leonard Bernstein, photo by Erich Auerbach, courtesy of Getty Images, Inc. Page 311, Gian Carlo Menotti, photo by ArenaPal/Clive Barda/Topham, courtesy of The Image Works. Page 312, Ellen Taaffe Zwilich, photo by Ray Stanyard/Florida State University.

Chapter 25: Page 315, Alto Sax by Selmer classical music, entertainment, photo by Chris Stock, courtesy of Lebrecht Music & Arts Photo Library. Pages 316–317, Electric guitar, photo by Garth Blore, © Dorling Kindersley. Pages 316–317, Alto Sax, photo by Chris Stock, courtesy of Lebrecht Music & Arts Photo Library. Page 320, US Marine Band, courtesy of U. S. Army Photograph. Page 322, Muddy Waters, photo © Derick A. Thomas; Dat's Jazz/CORBIS All Rights Reserved. Page 322, New Orleans funeral, photo by Chris Graythen, courtesy of Getty Images, Inc. Page 323, Scott Joplin, courtesy of Art Resource/The New York Public Library for the Performing Arts. Page 327, Bessie Smith, courtesy of Corbis/Bettmann. Page 327, Creole Jazz Band, courtesy of Culver Pictures, Inc. Page 328, Louis Armstrong, Pictorial Press Ltd/Alamy. Page 329, Benny Goodman, courtesy of Corbis/Bettmann. Page 330, Duke Ellington, Pictorial Press Ltd/Alamy. Page 332, Tito Puente, photo by Mike Albans, courtesy of AP Wide World Photos. Page 333, Charlie Parker, photo © Underwood & Underwood/CORBIS All Rights Reserved. Page 333, Miles Davis, photo © Lynn Goldsmith / CORBIS All Rights Reserved. Page 334, John Coltrane, Michael Ochs Archives/Stringer/Getty Images. Page 334, Keith Jarrett, photo © Deborah Feingold/CORBIS All Rights Reserved. Page 335, Wynton Marsalis, photo © Lynn Goldsmith/CORBIS All Rights Reserved.

Chapter 26: Pages 336–337, Electric guitar, photo by Garth Blore, © Dorling Kindersley. Pages 336–337, Alto Sax, photo by Chris Stock, courtesy of Lebrecht Music & Arts Photo Library. Page 341, Bing Crosby, photo © Bettmann/CORBIS All Rights Reserved. Page 342, Frank Sinatra, courtesy of Getty Images Inc.–Hulton Archive Photos. Page 343, Sarah Vaughn, courtesy of Frank Driggs Collection. Page 344, Billie Holiday, courtesy of Getty Images Inc.–Hulton Archive Photos. Page 345, Ella Fitzgerald, photo © Neal Preston/CORBIS All Rights Reserved. Page 346, Early juke box, Pictorial Press Ltd/Alamy. Page 347, The Rolling Stones, photo by Dave Hogan, courtesy of Getty Images, Inc. Page 350, Bob Dylan, photo by Luciano Viti, courtesy of Retna Ltd. Page 352, Elvis Presley, photo © Doc Pele/Stills/RetnaUK. Page 354, The Beatles, photo © CAT'S/ CORBIS All Rights Reserved. Page 355, Madonna, photo by Camera Press/Mark Shenley, courtesy of Retna Ltd. Page 356, Ray Charles, photo by David Redfern/Redferns, courtesy of Retna Ltd. Page 357, Queen Latifah, photo by Robb D. Cohen, courtesy of Retna Ltd. Page 357, Aretha Franklin, photo by Frank Micelotta, courtesy of Getty Images, Inc. Page 358, British Band The Who British band members of The Who, lead singer

Roger Daltrey, drummer Keith Moon, bass player John Entwistle and guitarist Pete Townshend, photo by Tony Frank/Sygma, courtesy of Corbis/Sygma. Page 360, The Moody Blues, photo by Hulton–Deutsch Collection, © Bettmann/CORBIS All Rights Reserved. Page 361, Jimmy Page and Robert Plant, photo by Ross Halfin, courtesy of Idols Licensing & Publicity Ltd. Page 362, Creedence Clearwater Revival, photo by Evening Standard, courtesy of Getty Images, Inc. Page 364, The Grateful Dead, photo by Henry Grossman/Time Life Pictures, courtesy of Getty Images, Inc. Page 366, Woodstock, photo by Bill Eppridge/Time Life Pictures, courtesy of Getty Images, Inc. Page 368, Rock and Roll Hall of Fame, photo by Paul Spinelli, courtesy of Getty Images, Inc. Page 369, Jimmie Rodgers. Page 371, Garth Brooks, photo by Pool Photo, courtesy of Getty Images, Inc. Page 372, Shania Twain, photo © Neal Preston/CORBIS All Rights Reserved.

Chapter 27: Pages 374–375, Electric guitar, photo by Garth Blore, © Dorling Kindersley. Pages 374–375, Alto Sax, photo by Chris Stock, courtesy of Lebrecht Music & Arts Photo Library. Page 377, Cover for James Bland songs, courtesy of Courtesy of the Library of Congress. Page 378, Stephen Collins Foster, 1826–1864. Watercolor by Walter L. White, cf from Ambrotype, Foster Hall Collection, Center for American Music, University of Pittsburgh. Source ID#120. Page 380, Noble Sissle and Eubie Blake, courtesy of The Maryland Historical Society, Baltimore, MD. Page 382, The Ziegfeld Follies, courtesy of Culver Pictures, Inc. Page 383, Over There magazine cover, courtesy of William Perkins Library Rare Book Collection, Duke University. Page 384, Sigmund Romberg, © Bettmann/CORBIS All Rights Reserved. Page 384, Victor Herbert, photo by Lebrecht Music & Arts, courtesy of Lebrecht Music & Arts Photo Library. Page 385, Rudolf Friml, © Bettmann/CORBIS All Rights Reserved. Page 385, Irving Berlin, photo © John Springer Collection/CORBIS All Rights Reserved. Page 386, Jerome Kern, courtesy of Corbis/Bettmann. Page 387, Pictorial Press Ltd/Alamy. Page 389, Al Jolson, photo by Hulton Archive, courtesy of Getty Images, Inc. Page 391, Oklahoma! (1955) Directed by Fred Zinnemann, shown from left: Shirley Jones, Gordon MacRae, courtesy of Photofest. Page 391, Cole Porter, courtesy of Corbis/Bettmann. Page 392, Richard Rodgers, © Bettmann/CORBIS All Rights Reserved. Page 393, Stephen Sondheim, photo by Henry Grossman/Time & Life Pictures, courtesy of Getty Images, Inc. Page 394, West Side Story performance, courtesy of Culver Pictures, Inc. Page 396, Alan Jay Lerner and Frederick Loewe, photo © John Springer Collection/CORBIS All Rights Reserved. Page 397, Verdi performance, photo by Hyperion Theatricals/Joan Marcus, courtesy of Photofest. Page 399, Savion Glover, photo by Peter Kramer, courtesy of Getty Images, Inc. Page 401, Lion King performance, courtesy of Joan Marcus Photography.

Chapter 28: Pages 402–403, Electric guitar, photo by Garth Blore, © Dorling Kindersley. Pages 402–403, Alto Sax, photo by Chris Stock, courtesy of Lebrecht Music & Arts Photo Library. Page 404, The General performance, courtesy of Culver Pictures, Inc. Page 405, Gigi performance, photo by Springer, courtesy of Corbis/Bettmann. Page 407, Pictorial Press Ltd/Alamy. Page 409, AF archive/Alamy. Page 410, AF archive/Alamy. Page 411, cineclassico/Alamy. Page 413, Rite of Spring scene from Fantasia © Disney. Page 414, Photos 12/Alamy. Page 417, AF archive/Alamy.

Chapter 29: Pages 420–421, Electric guitar, photo by Garth Blore, © Dorling Kindersley. Pages 420–421, Alto Sax, photo by Chris Stock, courtesy of Lebrecht Music & Arts Photo Library. Page 423, Abouri Tribe playing the Tam–Tam Drum, photo by M and E. Bernheim, courtesy of Woodfin Camp & Associates. Page 423, Oil can electric guitar, photo by Jason Laure Photography. Page 424, Yorubi Tribe drummers, photo by M & E Bernheim, courtesy of Woodfin Camp & Associates. Page 426, Gypsy dancers, Peter M. Wilson/Alamy. Page 427, Indian Odissi dance, photo © Lindsay Hebberd/Corbis All Rights Reserved. Page 427, Ravi Shankar, photo by David Farrell, courtesy of Lebrecht Music & Arts Photo Library. Page 429, Japanese koto players, photo by ArenaPal/Topham, courtesy of The Image Works. Page 431, Kabuki performance, photo by Mike Yamashita, courtesy of Woodfin Camp & Associates.

Finale: Page 436, La Boheme performance, photo by Sue Adler/Agence France Presse/Getty Images.

Index